TRAVELER'S GUIDE TO

ALASKAN CAMPING

Explore Alaska And The Yukon With RV Or Tent

Third Edition

Mike and Terri Church

ROLLING HOMES PRESS

Published by
Rolling Homes Press
161 Rainbow Dr., #6157
Livingston, TX 77399-1061
www.rollinghomes.com

Printed in the United States of America
First Printing 2005

Publisher's Cataloging in Publication

Church, Mike.
Traveler's guide to Alaskan camping : explore Alaska and the Yukon
    with RV or tent / Mike and Terri Church–Third Edition
    p.cm.
    Includes index.
    Library of Congress Control Number: 2005900491
    ISBN 0-9749471-1-3

    1. Alaska–Guidebooks. 2. Camping–Alaska–Guidebooks. 3. Recreational Living–Alaska–Guidebooks. 4. Camping Sites, Facilities, etc.–Alaska–Guidebooks. I. Church, Terri. II. Title. III. Alaskan Camping

F902.3C.48 2005   2005 900491
917.9804/52–dc21

*This book is dedicated
to the memory of our grandparents,*

MURIEL AND CARL JOHNSON

Muriel and Carl lived most of their lives in Fairbanks, Alaska. They fished, hunted, dug clams, and picked wild berries every year and enjoyed Alaska to its fullest. Our love of Alaska, the outdoors, and camping came from them.

Other Books by Mike and Terri Church
and
Rolling Homes Press

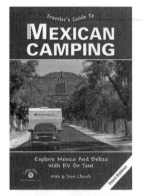

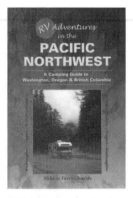

Traveler's Guide To
Mexican Camping

Traveler's Guide To
Camping Mexico's Baja

RV Adventures in the
Pacific Northwest

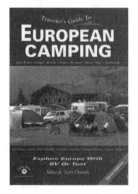

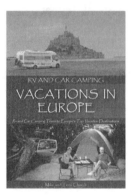

Traveler's Guide To
European Camping

RV and Car Camping
Vacations in Europe

A brief summary of the above books is provided on pages 446 and 447

www.rollinghomes.com

When traveling by RV the most complete and up-to-date information on RV parks is always important. To provide our readers with the most current and accurate information available we maintain a Website which lists all known updates and changes to information listed in our books. Just go to our Website at www.rollinghomes.com and click on the *Book Updates Online* button to review the most current information.

Warning, Disclosure, and Communication With The Authors and Publishers

Half the fun of travel is the unexpected, and self-guided camping travel can produce much in the way of unexpected pleasures, and also complications and problems. This book is designed to increase the pleasures of Alaskan camping and reduce the number of unexpected problems you may encounter. You can help ensure a smooth trip by doing additional advance research, planning ahead, and exercising caution when appropriate. There can be no guarantee that your trip will be trouble free.

Although the authors and publisher have done their best to ensure that the information presented in this book was correct at the time of publication they do not assume and hereby disclaim any liability to any party for any loss or damage caused by errors, omissions, or any other cause.

In a book like this it is inevitable that there will be omissions or mistakes, especially as things do change over time. If you find inaccuracies we would like to hear about them so that they can be corrected in future editions. We would also like to hear about your enjoyable experiences. If you come upon an outstanding campground or destination please let us know, those kinds of things may also find their way to future versions of the guide or to our Internet site. You can reach us by mail at:

Rolling Homes Press
161 Rainbow Dr., #6157
Livingston, TX 77399-1061

You can also communicate with us by sending an Email through our Website at:

www.rollinghomes.com

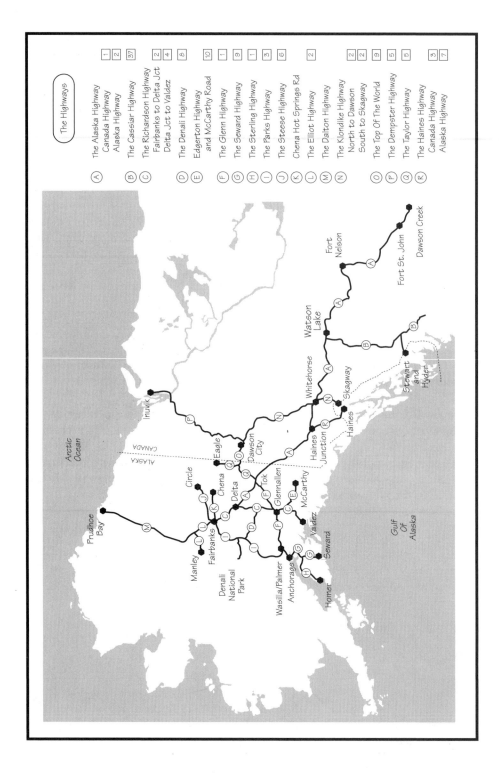

The Highways

(A) The Alaska Highway [1]
     Canada Highway [2]
     Alaska Highway [37]

(B) The Cassiar Highway [2]

(C) The Richardson Highway
     Fairbanks to Delta Jct [2]
     Delta Jct to Valdez [4]

(D) The Denali Highway [8]

(E) Edgerton Highway
     and McCarthy Road [10]

(F) The Glenn Highway [1]

(G) The Seward Highway [9]

(H) The Sterling Highway [1]

(I) The Parks Highway [3]

(J) The Steese Highway [6]

(K) Chena Hot Springs Rd [2]

(L) The Elliot Highway [2]

(M) The Dalton Highway [2]

(N) The Klondike Highway
     North to Dawson [2]
     South to Skagway [2]

(O) The Top Of The World [9]

(P) The Dempster Highway [5]

(Q) The Taylor Highway [5]

(R) The Haines Highway
     Canada Highway [3]
     Alaska Highway [7]

TABLE OF CONTENTS

INTRODUCTION

For most people Alaska is the dream camping destination. No wonder! There is just no other destination with the same combination of accessibility, scenery, wildlife, outdoor activities, history, facilities, and support. Any camping trip to Alaska, whether in an RV or on foot, along the road system or a remote river, for sightseeing or for fishing, is bound to be the trip of a lifetime.

We've been traveling extensively in an RV for several years now. We've camped around the U.S., Europe, and Mexico. There are lots of places to go and lots to see, but it seems that each year finds us back in Alaska.

We do have a few more Alaska connections than most people. One of us, Mike, was born and raised in Fairbanks. His family arrived there in 1906, fresh from Dawson City and the gold rush there–his grandmother was one of the few children born in Dawson City during the gold rush. There's an Alcan connection too–his mother first came to Alaska in 1947 over the highway, a year before it officially opened to civilian traffic. He's lived in Fairbanks, Anchorage, Cooper Landing, Kenai, Homer, Nenana, Tok, and even Denali Park. Terri arrived in Alaska the day after she graduated from college and lived and worked in Fairbanks, Kenai, and Anchorage for over ten years. We're full-timer RV travelers now, but the state continues to draw us back.

Mike was introduced to camping by his grandparents, both true sourdoughs. His earliest camping experiences were travels along the Richardson between Fairbanks and Anchorage in the fifties, the campground most nights was a gravel pit and dinner was a grayling from a nearby stream. Very few summers since then have gone by without at least one camping vacation somewhere in the state.

Traveler's Guide to Alaskan Camping is one of six guidebooks we have written. The others are very similar in some ways to this one. They are *Traveler's Guide to European Camping, RV and Car Camping Vacations in Europe, Traveler's Guide to Mexican Camping, Traveler's Guide to Camping Mexico's Baja* and *RV Adventures in the Pacific Northwest*. The six volumes are the key to a world of travel fun! We hope you will join us.

A L A S K A

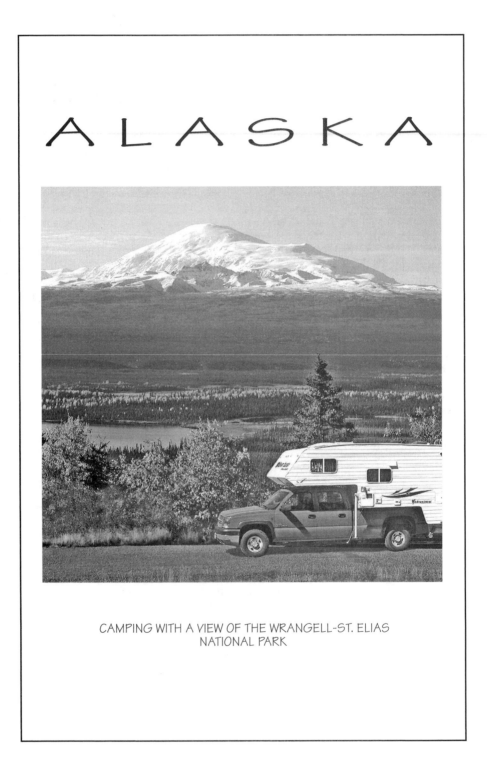

CAMPING WITH A VIEW OF THE WRANGELL-ST. ELIAS
NATIONAL PARK

Chapter 1

Why Camp Alaska?

Each year tens of thousands of people head out to camp in Alaska. Some are RVers who drive their rigs up the Alaska Highway. Some are Alaska residents who have waited through the long winter for breakup and summer days of fishing, hiking, floating rivers and enjoying the great outdoors. Others are nature lovers and adventure campers from around the world drawn to some of the most spectacular wilderness anywhere.

There are probably as many reasons to camp Alaska as there are people who do it, but here are a few.

The Attractions

The State of Alaska holds so much wilderness that it is difficult to even grasp its immensity. There are 587,878 square miles in Alaska and about 630,000 residents. That works out to 1 square mile for each person. That's a lot of country with few people, especially when you realize that most of the people are in the cities. As you drive Alaska's highways you'll often cover miles and miles without sighting another person. Leave the road system and you're really alone. The pure solitude is sometimes almost overwhelming, but it's an experience to be treasured in today's world.

Scenery-wise Alaska is unbeatable. Southeast Alaska has deep blue fjords surrounded by steep mountains and glaciers. The Interior's tree-covered hills march into the distance bathed by the light of the midnight sun. Icy Mt. McKinley looms above you as it rises to 20,320 feet from its nearly-sea level base. Beauty is everywhere you look.

Want to see wildlife? Alaska has big animals like grizzly bears, caribou, and moose and small ones like beavers and porcupines. Along the coast you can spot whales and sea otters. Each spring millions of birds migrate to Alaska for your viewing pleasure, over 300 species are present. Most appreciated by novice birdwatchers seem to be bald eagles, which are actually common in some areas, or perhaps the puffins that can easily be seen from the tour boats that visit nesting islands from Seward and Homer.

Outdoor sports enthusiasts go crazy in Alaska. The fishing is world class and much of it can be accessed from the road system. Ocean kayakers can explore Southeast Alaska, Prince William Sound, Kodiak Island, and the fjords of the Kenai Peninsula. If you prefer rivers you should be aware that Alaska is home to over twenty designated National Wild and Scenic Rivers, and most are truly wild and scenic. There is an extensive system of hiking trails on the Kenai Peninsula and there are many other trails north of Fairbanks and in Southeast Alaska. You can also hike where there are nothing but animal trails in places like Gates of the Arctic National Park and Lake Clark National Park.

Speaking of national parks–Alaska has nine of them plus two historical national parks. And that's just the beginning. There are national parks, national monuments, national preserves, national forests, and wildlife refuges. And the State of Alaska has its own huge state parks. Almost all of this land is easily accessible to outdoors enthusiasts although they may have to hitch a ride on a boat or airplane to get there.

The wilderness isn't the only attraction in Alaska. There's history too. Gold has played an important part in the history of the state; you can hike the Chilkoot Trail, float the Yukon, or visit famous gold-mining areas like Dawson City, Nome, Circle, or the Fortymile Country.

The Alcan Highway was one of the greatest engineering and construction projects of its time, a drive along it is the best way to appreciate the accomplishment. All along the highway you'll find museums and historical markers. It would be fun even if there weren't hundreds of fishing steams, lots of opportunities to spot wildlife, and gobs of beautiful scenery.

There's another huge engineering project in Alaska that has been in the news over the last 25 years–the Trans-Alaska Oil Pipeline. The arguments over oil in Alaska are still hot. During your visit you can see for yourself if the oil facilities on the North Slope seem to be scaring the caribou, whether the 800-mile pipeline is really an eyesore, and walk the previously oil-soaked beaches of Prince William Sound to assess the visible damage.

The truth is that there is enough to do and see in Alaska to bring you back each year for many years. The few things we've described above are just the beginning, you need to come and see for yourself.

Why Camp?

It is hard to understand how anyone would visit Alaska and not camp. Along the highways and in the wilderness there is no better way to appreciate the country. If you spend your time riding a tour bus and staying in hotels you'll soon find yourself wondering what all the excitement is about. After all, most people really don't come to Alaska for the restaurants, hotels, and souvenir shops. An important part of the Alaska experience has always been the freedom to do your own thing, and a guided tour doesn't really give you that.

Camping doesn't really mean roughing it. Modern RVs provide a lot of comfort. Screens on the windows mean that you aren't at the mercy of mosquitoes while you cook, eat, relax and sleep. Furnaces and comfortable beds mean you'll sleep well and wake to a warm rig. Sophisticated plumbing systems mean you can take a hot shower every day. Uncrowded roads make driving an RV a snap, and there's no better wildlife-viewing platform than the high seats of an RV. If you don't have your own RV or if you don't want to drive it up the Alaska Highway you can easily rent an RV in Alaska and spend a week or two exploring the state.

You don't really even need an RV to enjoy the camping along Alaska's road system. It's easy to pack a tent, sleeping bags, and camping equipment into the trunk of a car and hit the road. Most of the state is plenty warm enough for you to be comfortable during June, July, and August. Just make sure you have a good tent that is rain and bug proof, and sleeping bags that will keep you warm down to 40° F or so if you run into an unusually cold night.

If you want to visit the country away from the road system camping is really your only viable alternative. Oh sure, you could stay in one of those $4,000 per week fishing lodges, but how much fun could that be? Most of the state is accessible using either aircraft or boats, and the only real costs for a camper are equipment, food and transportation. There is one additional alternative, the state and federal government own many small cabins scattered around the state, and they rent them out for a very reasonable fee. They're nothing fancy, really just a high-class form of camping, so we don't feel guilty about covering them in this book about camping. See Chapter 14 - *Camping Away From the Road System* for more information.

The Alaska Grand Tour

One of the best ways to show you what Alaska has to offer is to outline an itinerary for an RV trip to Alaska. This is the Full Monty, the mother of all road trips, a drive to Alaska on the Alaska Highway. It is a full tour of most of the roads of Alaska and much of the Yukon, and a return by Alaska State Ferry through Southeast Alaska.

Set aside as much time as possible for this tour, we wouldn't even attempt it in less than two months. Below we lay it out in 50 days, but you'll add some days for relaxing or choose some interesting side trips. Timing is essential, you want to do this between May 15 and September 15. Just one of the suggested week-long side trip additions would make this a two-month trip.

If you have only a week or two for a vacation in Alaska there is no problem. Just fly into Anchorage, rent a car or RV, and head for the Kenai Peninsula or Denali National Park. Rental vehicles are also available in other towns including Fairbanks and Whitehorse. See Chapter 2 for information about RV rental outfits.

You also don't need much time to visit off-the-road destinations in Alaska. Visiting most of them involves only doing your research by mail or on the Web, flying a commercial carrier to a departure city or town, and then using a charter airplane or boat to get into the bush. All of this can be easily arranged by telephone and you can probably be camping on your first day in Alaska. See Chapter 14 for more information.

You will notice that much of the time in the itinerary below is actually spent getting to and returning from Alaska. We allow a full two weeks just for getting to the beginning of the Alaska Highway and returning home from Prince Rupert. This isn't unreasonable, take a good look at a map.

The itinerary below can be modified, a couple of ideas suggest themselves. Many visitors do not venture south to Anchorage and the Kenai Peninsula. They limit the Alaska portion of their visit to Fairbanks, Denali Park, and perhaps Valdez. This would cut about a week off our itinerary. We wouldn't do it, but you can.

Another possible change is to drive both ways and not use the ferry system for your return. If you return on the Cassiar Highway you won't have to drive the same highway both ways and will see some new country.

A word of warning here. It will be necessary to plan ahead and make reservations for the Alaska State Ferry portion of this trip long before you leave home. See Chapter 13 for more information about the ferries. It might also be worthwhile to make camping and bus reservations at Denali Park before leaving home, see Chapter 9 for information about this.

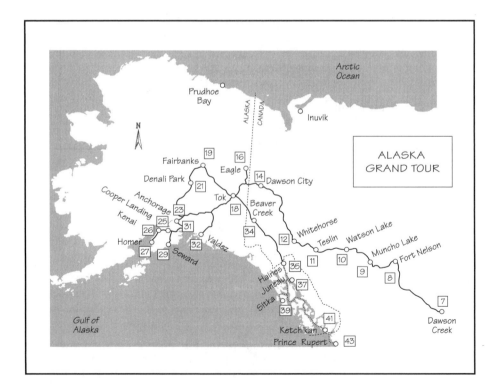

WHERE IT ALL BEGINS - MILE "O" OF THE ALASKA HIGHWAY

As you read through the itinerary you can refer to the Table of Contents in the front of this book and the Index at the back to find more detailed information about routes, destinations, activities, and campgrounds.

Days 1 to 7 - Getting to Dawson Creek - You're on your own getting to Dawson Creek. For some folks from the southern U.S. it will probably take more than a week. Figure three days from Seattle (817 miles or 1,318 km) if you've come up the west coast and three days from Great Falls in northern Montana (875 miles or 1,411 km) if you come from east of the Rockies. You'll probably wish you had more time for both of these routes, there are lots of interesting stops and side trips. In Dawson Creek stock up on groceries and make sure your rig is in tip-top condition.

Day 8 - Dawson Creek to Fort Nelson - 283 miles (456 km), 6 hours - The road is excellent between Dawson Creek and Fort Nelson, good fast paved two-lane road. Be sure to start watching for wildlife, there are both bears and moose in the area. You have a choice between three excellent RV parks in Fort Nelson. We like to stay at one of the two that are near the center of town. Take a look at the museum and attend the show at the Phoenix Theater.

Day 9 - Fort Nelson to Muncho Lake - 153 miles (247 km), 4 hours - Between Fort Nelson and Muncho Lake the highway climbs into the mountains. The road is fine, you just won't be able to make great time because it climbs and descends and has more curves and hills than the road farther south. At Muncho Lake do a little fishing for lake trout or just enjoy the beautiful lake and mountains. In the evening make the short hike to the nearby mineral lick to see if any stone sheep are there.

Day 10 - Muncho Lake to Watson Lake - 177 miles (285 km), 6 hours - Get an early start for the best chance to see animals along the road. Stop at Liard Hot Springs for a dip and stay to fix a nice relaxed lunch. It's only another 136 miles to Watson Lake. In Watson Lake visit the Signpost Forest and the visitor center's Alcan exhibit, you might also attend a show at the new Northern Lights Centre. If this seem like a lot of activities for one day just remember that the days are long this far north.

Day 11 - Watson Lake to Teslin - 163 miles (263 km), 4 hours - This is a short day's drive, but get an early start anyway. Spend some time in Teslin, shop at the Nisutlin Trading Post and visit the George Johnson Museum. Then drive on another 8 miles to Mukluk Annie's Salmon Bake. Dry camp for free along the lakeshore and enjoy the salmon bake in the evening. Top things off by joining your fellow campers for a houseboat ride on Teslin Lake.

Day 12 and 13 - Teslin to Whitehorse - 100 miles (161 km), 2 hours - Another short day's drive will bring you to Whitehorse. You have many campgrounds to choose from and you might as well spend two days here in the capital of the Yukon Territory. There's lots to see and do. See the sternwheeler *Klondike* and cruise through Miles Canyon. Don't forget to stock up on groceries here, you won't be seeing big stores again for a while.

Day 14 and 15 - Whitehorse to Dawson City - 327 miles (527 km), 7 hours - The road to Dawson City is excellent so you can easily drive through in one day if you get an early start. Don't forget to stop at the overlook for the view of Five Finger Rapids. With the long days this far north you'll probably have lots of energy left when you get to Dawson, so make an evening of it and see the Gaslight Follies at the Palace Grand Theater. That should put you in the proper mood to spend the following day exploring Dawson and the creeks. In the evening of your second day in Dawson you can visit Diamond Tooth Gertie's gambling hall.

If you have an extra week you can use it here. Drive the Dempster Highway up across the Arctic Circle to Inuvik. Driving out and back on this 456 mile (735 km) gravel road will let you visit some of the most remote country you've ever seen.

Day 16 and 17 - Dawson City to Eagle - 144 miles (232 km), 5 hours - This trip over the Top of the World Highway and then up to Eagle on the Taylor Highway is your first real taste of gravel unless you drove the Dempster. It also finally brings you to Alaska! The Taylor portion of the route is a small road so take it easy. Enjoy the wilderness. Spend a day relaxing in little laid-back Eagle and take the historic tour, it's one of Alaska's most enjoyable.

Day 18 - Eagle to Tok - 173 miles (279 km), 6 hours - You'll return to the Alaska Highway today after a morning on the gravel. Tok has the highest per capita number of RV spaces in the state, it's the first Alaskan town most Alaska Highway travelers reach. The most important thing to do here is visit the Tok Visitor Centers.

Day 19 and 20 - Tok to Fairbanks - 206 miles (332 km), 5 hours - Today you'll follow the Tanana River downstream to Alaska's second-largest city. We've allotted two days for Fairbanks, it probably won't be enough. Don't miss everyone's Fairbanks favorite–a cruise on the riverboat *Discovery*. Visit the gold fields near Fox

PANNING FOR GOLD AT BONANZA CREEK NEAR DAWSON CITY

or Ester where you'll find the Malemute Saloon. In a quieter vein, the University Museum is one of the best in the state.

Here's another place you can easily add a week to your trip, or even two weeks. Several roads lead north from Fairbanks including the Dalton Highway to the North Slope and Prudhoe Bay. The Steese, Chena Hot Springs, and Elliott Highways are all worth a look-see, this is also excellent hiking and canoeing country.

Day 21 and 22 - Fairbanks to Denali Park - 121 miles (195 km), 2.5 hours - If you've made reservations you can camp in the park. Otherwise you'll probably be perfectly happy in one of the many campsites outside the park entrance. The thing you must do here is take a shuttle-bus trip into the park at least as far as Eielson Visitor's Center. Denali Park is probably the best place you will ever visit for observing grizzly bears up close. Cross your fingers for a clear day to see the mountain.

Day 23 and 24 - Denali Park to Anchorage - 237 miles (382 km), 5 hours - Today's trip is a cruiser, down through Broad Pass and across the Mat-Su Valley on Alaska's best roads. You'll actually have some four-lane freeway going into Anchorage. Anchorage is the best place in the state to get any maintenance problems fixed and stock up on supplies. During your layover check the sporting-goods stores to see which spots are hot on the Kenai Peninsula and pick up some fishing tackle.

Anchorage is one of the most livable cities anywhere. This is your chance to visit a good restaurant and explore the town. Wander around Town Square and 4th Avenue, all decked out with flowers, and perhaps catch a performance in the Alaska Center

for the Performing Arts or tour the new Alaska Native Heritage Center. Treat yourself
to a night out at an outstanding restaurant and a visit to Mr. Whitekeys' *Whale Fat
Follies* at the Fly By Night Club.

Day 25 - Anchorage to Cooper Landing - 101 miles (163 km), 3 hours - Drive
down scenic Turnagain Arm and make sure you stop at Portage Glacier. In Cooper
Landing, if you've timed it right, you can "combat fish" at the mouth of the Russian
River and fill your icebox with red salmon. If not just enjoy some of Alaska's best
scenery. Hikers will find what may be the finest trails in the state leading into the
mountains nearby. There's also an excellent float trip down the Upper Kenai.

Day 26 - Cooper Landing to Kenai - 57 miles (92 km), 1.5 hours - Avoid
the Soldotna fishing crowds and stay in Kenai. Visit the historic Russian church and
perhaps see some beluga whales chasing salmon below the bluff. Ask at your campground or the information center about clam tides, you might have arrived at the
perfect time for a clamming expedition.

Day 27 and 28 - Kenai to Homer - 97 miles (156 km), 2.5 hours - Today's
drive brings you to another scenic highlight, Homer. You can camp in town or out on
the bustling spit. Either way consider a halibut fishing trip or a bird-watching cruise
out to Gull Island and Halibut Cove or Seldovia.

Day 29 and 30 - Homer to Seward - 173 miles (279 km), 4 hours - A day of
backtracking and a chance to see the things you missed on the way down to Homer.
Perhaps a visit to Ninilchik or a pause to wet a line in one of the many world-famous

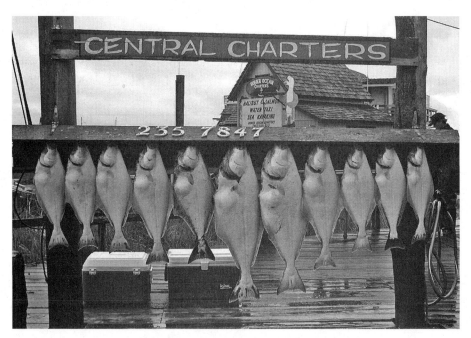

CATCH FROM A HOMER HALIBUT CHARTER

fishing rivers along the route. In Seward the silver salmon may be running or you might take a cruise into the Kenai Fjords National Park to see whales, sea otters, puffins, and glaciers.

Day 31- Seward to Anchorage - 126 miles (203 km), 3 hours - Back to Anchorage to stock up and prepare for the drive south.

Here's something to consider. The Alaska State Ferry runs from Seward to Valdez most Thursday mornings. There are even more frequent trips between Whittier and Valdez, some through Cordova. You can save yourself two days and about 430 miles of driving by taking this ferry. It will cost more than making the road trip but it's a lot easier and just as scenic.

Day 32 and 33 - Anchorage to Valdez - 304 miles (490 km), 7 hours - A long day of driving through beautiful country will bring you to Valdez. See the huge oil tankers, fish for salmon or take a scenic cruise across Prince William Sound to Columbia Glacier.

Day 34 - Valdez to Beaver Creek - 399 miles (644 km), 9 hours - Another very long day of driving. To shorten it a bit you could stay at any of the campgrounds between Tok and Beaver Creek. On the other hand, like a horse heading home you may want to spend a long day on the road.

Day 35 and 36 - Beaver Creek to Haines - 336 mile (542 km), 8 hours - You drive south along Kluane Lake, through Haines Junction, and then across the Chilkat Pass to tidewater at the head of the Inside Passage. This is the last day on the road for a week, you'll let the ferry captain do the driving as far as Prince Rupert. During your layover day in Haines take the water taxi up the Lynn Canal to Skagway and spend the day touring this gold rush town.

Day 37 and 38 - Ferry to Juneau, 4.5 hours - Use your time in Juneau to explore Alaska's capital. If you have the time consider a cruise to Glacier Bay National Park or Tracy Arm or a helicopter flight to the top of the nearby ice field.

Day 39 and 40 - Ferry to Sitka, 9 hours - You've seen Alaska's present capital, now wander around the former capital of Russian America. Don't miss the Sheldon Jackson Museum.

Day 41 and 42 - Ferry to Ketchikan, 19 hours cruising time plus possible time in port in Petersburg and Wrangell - Consider booking a stateroom for this segment of your ferry trip. Ketchikan is Alaska's totem pole center. You also might take a cruise or sightseeing flight to Misty Fjords National Monument, your last chance to visit really pristine wilderness before leaving the state.

Day 43 - Ferry to Prince Rupert, 6 hours - You'll save yourself a bundle by leaving Alaska through Prince Rupert rather than riding the ferry all the way to Bellingham.

Day 44 to 50 - Drive home - From Prince Rupert to Seattle is 1,035 miles, Prince Rupert to Great Falls is 1,235 miles. Both routes are paved all the way.

Once you reach home you can start planning next year's trip.

Chapter 2

Details, Details, Details

Animals (Wildlife)

For most visitors to Alaska the wildlife is a huge attraction. During even a road trip to the state you are likely to see grizzly bears, black bears, moose, caribou, stone and Dall sheep, mountain goats, and perhaps even a musk ox. In addition to these large mammals Alaska has some of the best bird-watching opportunities anywhere, over 350 species are present. Marine mammals including whales, sea otters, and seals are common in many saltwater areas easily accessible on short sightseeing cruises. You can even watch fish at the many salmon-spawning viewing sites.

Be sure to bring along a set of binoculars and perhaps a spotting scope. These are particularly useful for birders but will also help you spot and enjoy watching larger animals.

You can see more wildlife while driving if you: 1. Watch closely and don't drive too fast; 2. Plan to be on the road in the early morning and late evening when animals are most active; 3. Get away from the road system by hiking or using air or water transportation.

As you drive along make sure to keep an eye on the brush line along the road. During the spring (May, June) and during berry season (July and August) there are often bears feeding in the wide cleared open areas next to the highways. RVers have an advantage over those driving passenger cars since they have an elevated seating position. Stop often to check likely habitats. Moose are often browsing in the water near the shores of lakes along the road. Bears are sometimes seen on gravel bars along rivers. It is often possible to see bears, sheep and goats on grassy mountainsides with a pair of binoculars. If you aren't proactive in your wildlife watching you'll only see the few animals that cross directly in front of your vehicle.

You'll see more animals if you schedule your driving in the early morning and late evening. That's when animals are most active. With the long daylight hours during June and July it would actually be possible to see wildlife during the entire night, but a nighttime driving schedule would probably be going a little overboard. Perhaps early starts and late stops with an afternoon nap thrown in makes more sense.

There are some outstanding places to see wildlife in the state and on the routes north, here are a few. In both **Stone Mountain Park** and **Muncho Lake Park** along the Alaska Highway both stone sheep and caribou are often spotted. Just outside Hyder, Alaska near the Cassiar Highway is **Fish Creek** where you can see both brown and black bears as well as bald eagles during the August salmon runs. **Haines, Alaska** is world famous for its congregation of bald eagles during the late fall along the Chilkat River but it's also a good place to see grizzlies along the short Chilkoot River outside town. On a bus ride into **Denali Park** it would be unusual not to see several grizzlies as well as assorted caribou, sheep, and smaller animals. A boat tour from Seward into the **Kenai Fjords National Park** or from Juneau into **Glacier Bay** in Southeast Alaska will probably net you a whale spotting or two, not to mention sea otters, puffins, sea lions, dolphins, and perhaps seals. Even as you just drive the highways, you're bound to see a moose or two and even the occasional bear.

There's another side to the wildlife in the North. Some of it presents a certain amount

WATCH FOR BISON ALONG THE ROAD NEAR LIARD HOT SPRINGS

of danger, particularly large animals like bears and moose. Bears are attracted by food so proper food and garbage handling procedures are important when camping. Tent campers will want to keep food in vehicles or suspended from trees. In the tundra country where this isn't possible make sure to cache your food far from your tent or use bear-proof containers. Garbage containers in campgrounds are now often bear proof, if they aren't you should consider the location of garbage containers when choosing your campsite.

Many people consider the presence of grizzlies an indicator of true wilderness. They are widespread in Alaska and quite common in many places. Grizzlies can be extremely dangerous since they are big, fast, and sometimes aggressive. On the other hand, fishermen often share streams with grizzlies and hikers in some places often find themselves with bears as visitors in camp. You'll find pamphlets about the proper way to handle yourself in bear country at many information offices. Thousands of people spend time in the northern wilderness with no problems, you just have to take care and do things properly. See Chapter 14 for a more thorough discussion of bear safety.

Border Crossings

It is very possible that your Alaska camping trip will involve several border crossings. These are generally uneventful but there are a few things you should bear in mind.

No visa or passport is required for U.S. or Canadian citizens crossing either way across Canadian or U.S. borders but proof of citizenship must be carried. This means a passport, certified birth certificate, or voters registration card, along with a photo I.D. like your drivers license. A drivers license alone is not enough. If you have children along it is very important to have certified copies of their birth certificates and permission letters from parents if they are not yours.

For your vehicle you'll want the following: registration, up-to-date license tags, and proof of insurance. Make sure you have your vehicle registration with you and if you are not the legal owner a signed statement that it is OK to take it out of the country. You can get a Canadian Nonresident Interprovince Motor Vehicle Liability Insurance Card from your insurance company. It is likely that you will not have to show any of these documents but having them on hand is definitely nice if you are asked for them.

Guns are always a problem going into Canada. Rifles and shotguns are sometimes allowed, pistols never are. Border agents are allowed some discretion so it is important that you show the proper image and attitude if you want to cross the border with a weapon. Self defense is definitely not considered a proper reason to carry a weapon in Canada. We've been turned back at the border when en route to Alaska during hunting season, and we're definitely clean-cut and non-threatening. Never fib about weapons, vehicles are often searched at the border and penalties are steep. If you are allowed to bring a firearm in there is a form to fill out and a $50 Canadian fee. The best policy is to forget about taking a gun through Canada.

Many people like to carry pepper spray for defense against bears. This often presents a problem at the Canadian border. Spays designed for defense against people definitely aren't allowed. With bear spray, as with guns, the border agent has quite a bit of discretion so be polite.

Dogs, cats, or small animals need a recent rabies vaccination and a certificate stating so from a veterinarian. Your veterinarian will probably know about this.

Make sure your automobile insurance is good in Canada (or the U.S. if you are Canadian). Check into the deductible for your windows since you may get a ding or two during your trip.

Both Canada and the U.S. have regulations about importing certain things (like souvenirs) made of restricted animal parts like ivory and hides. Unfortunately the regulations are not the same so some things purchased in Canada can't come into the U.S. and vice versa. Check this if possible before purchase.

Finally, when crossing into Canada you must theoretically have enough money on hand to get where you are going and back out of Canada. There are no hard and fast rules. We've never had problems carrying bank cards that allow us to get cash along the way. You probably won't even be asked unless you look to the customs officer like you might not have enough cash to get by.

For more information about border crossings you can use these addresses and phone numbers: Canadian Customs & Revenue Agency, Pacific Region, Main Floor, 333 Dunsmuir St., Vancouver, BC , V6B 5R4; (204) 983-2500 or (506) 636-5064 or United States Customs, PO Box 7407, Washington, D.C. 20044; 202 566-8195. The Seattle number is (206) 553-4676. Also see links on our website, www.rollinghomes. com.

Budget

Each person has his or her own idea of an acceptable standard of living so there is no one budget for every person. On the other hand, if you are camping you are not at the mercy of the local tourist economy like a traveler staying in hotels. In Alaska, you'll save a lot of money by camping. Here are some guidelines that should help.

The Canadian dollar has appreciated against the U.S. Dollar in recent years. This has driven prices up for U.S. travelers and in this book has pushed many Canadian campgrounds into a higher price category. Still, Canadian campgrounds are generally a bargain even if gas and food prices are not. A Canadian dollar converted to about $.89 U.S in 2004.

In general, transportation is a big part of the price of things along the highways and in Alaska. Fuel, groceries, and services get more expensive as you get farther into the bush. This applies along the Alaska Highway too. Expect prices on remote sections of the roads to be much higher than in Dawson Creek or Whitehorse. Fill your tanks and buy your groceries in the larger towns. See also the *Fuel Cost* section in this chapter.

Alaskan prices are much more reasonable in larger towns than in years past. Much of the gasoline is refined in the state and prices are comparable to the Lower 48 in the big cities. Groceries too are reasonable. Although most are shipped from the Lower 48 there is lots of competition in the big cities like Anchorage, Fairbanks, Kenai and Juneau. In other places prices are higher, transportation and lack of competition become more important.

Campfires

A campfire is a big part of a cheerful and enjoyable campsite. Fortunately, you'll have lots of opportunities to have a campfire while camping in the North. Virtually all governmental campgrounds in both Alaska and Canada have firepits or rings. Many privately operated campgrounds outside towns have them too. We've included information about whether a campground has firepits in the individual campground descriptions.

A very nice feature of the government campgrounds in both the Yukon and British Columbia is free firewood. It is usually dry but seldom split, bring along an axe. In Alaska free firewood is no longer provided. Many campgrounds, however, have it for sale.

Wilderness campers will find that the forested areas of southcentral and central Alaska have lots of dry downed wood, the best is usually in the form of dead spruce. Campfires are perfectly acceptable in these areas if extreme care is taken not to start a wild fire. Stoves still work best for cooking. Make sure your fire is on mineral, not vegetable soil. Gravel bars in rivers are the best place for fires, they are generally scoured clean by the high water each spring.

In Southeast Alaska there may be plenty of wood but it is often too wet to burn. In the far west and north there are often no trees so firewood is scarce. Campers in these areas will have to rely on portable stoves.

Campgrounds

Throughout the areas covered in this book you will have a choice: government or privately-operated campgrounds. In general you can expect government campgrounds to have more scenic locations with more land per camper. They also almost always provide picnic tables and firepits. On the other hand, toilets are almost always outhouses (pit toilets) and there are never hookups or showers.

In Alaska you will find that government campgrounds are run by either the State of Alaska, the United States Forest Service (USFS), the United States Fish and Wildlife Service (USF&W), the National Parks Service (NPS), or one of the local governments. Information about all of the Alaskan governmental campgrounds run by all of these organizations and their related public lands are available from four Alaska Public Lands Information Centers located in Anchorage (Anchorage APLIC, 605 W. 4th Ave., Suite 105, Anchorage, AK 99501; 907 271-2737) , Fairbanks (Fairbanks APLIC, 250 N. Cushman St., Suite 1A, Fairbanks, AK 99701; 907 456-0527), Tok (Tok APLIC, 1314 Alaska Hwy (PO Box 359), Tok, AK 99780; 907 883-5666), and Ketchikan (Southeast APLIC, 50 Main St., Ketchikan, AK 99901; 907 228-6220). While similar, there are some differences between these government campgrounds. Note that the *Campground Index* at the back of the book identifies the campground type.

State of Alaska campgrounds are scattered throughout the state virtually wherever there are highways. They usually charge a fee, most commonly between $5 and $15 per night, per party. Many of their campgrounds are now run by independent contractors as the state tries to improve services and cut costs. A few campgrounds have been virtually abandoned, a process the state calls "passive management". This usually happens in somewhat remote locations where contractors are not willing to take over management. You can still camp at these places for free but don't expect picnic tables or useable outhouses. Clean up after yourself and pack out your trash.

The United States Forest Service (USFS) operates the second highest number of campgrounds in Alaska. These are in Chugach National Forest on the Kenai Peninsula near Anchorage and in the Tongass National Forest in Southeast Alaska. They vary in quality, a few have been upgraded recently with large sites, paved roads, and handicapped facilities – Russian River near Cooper Landing and Williwaw near Portage Glacier are two of the upgraded ones. Some also accept reservations including Williwaw, Ptarmigan Creek, Trail River, Cooper Creek, and Russian River. Call (877) 444-6777 for reservations or visit www.reserveusa.com on the Internet. Daily camping fees are usually about $10 and there is usually a 14 day limit. Wilderness tent camping outside the developed campground areas is also allowed in these forests.

The National Park Service (NPS) has more parkland in Alaska than in all of the rest of the country, but they have very few developed campgrounds. The only ones connected to the road system are those in Denali National Park, one tent-camping area at the Exit Glacier near Seward, and one near Skagway at the foot of the Chilkoot Trail. There are also walk-in tent campgrounds in Glacier Bay National Park & Preserve and Katmai National Park & Preserve. The National Park Service also manages the Klondike Gold Rush National Park which has campgrounds along the Chilkoot Trail and the Sitka National Historical Park which has no camping at all. Wilderness camping is allowed throughout the national parks, monuments, preserves and national wild rivers throughout the state with some restrictions.

The Bureau of Land Management manages campgrounds on federal lands not controlled by other agencies. In Alaska these include campgrounds along the Dalton Highway Pipeline Corridor and those along National Wild Rivers like the Gulkana and the Fortymile. BLM campgrounds are often small with limited facilities but in recent years many have been upgraded and have large sites, handicaped-accessible vault toilets, and even dump stations.

The U.S. Fish and Wildlife Service (USF&W) manages 16 national wildlife refuges with 77 million acres in Alaska. In Alaska their nicest campgrounds are in the Kenai National Wildlife Refuge.

The Yukon Territory maintains many campgrounds along roads throughout the territory. They are usually fairly large and located near water. The usual facilities include outhouses, picnic tables, firepits and free firewood. There are also often picnic shelters and children's playgrounds. A few years ago a new payment system was put into effect that required you to buy vouchers elsewhere before visiting these campgrounds. This system has been modified to allow payment at the campgrounds, you no longer must have the vouchers. Most Yukon campgrounds cost $12 Canadian. These territorial campgrounds usually have a 14-day limit.

British Columbia Provincial Campgrounds are located along the roads throughout the Province. They usually provide about the same amenities as the campgrounds in the Yukon Territory although many are upgraded with paved roads and parking pads. You pay at the campground in British Columbia.

There are many excellent commercial campgrounds in Alaska. Most have electricity, sewer, and water hookups as well as modern restrooms with flush toilets and hot showers. When you are visiting one of the urban areas in the North, private campgrounds are usually much more conveniently located than government ones.

Private campgrounds in both Canada and Alaska are in competition primarily with the government which has free land and can impose hard-to-meet and expensive restrictions upon private owners. Among these are dump station requirements, charges for signage, and just plain taxes. We suggest that you give the private campground operator a break whenever possible. Here's an example. Don't dump your holding tanks at a rural campground when you could just as conveniently do so later in the day at a campground or dump station hooked up to a municipal sewage system. Holding tank discharge is difficult and expensive for a remote campground to handle, many campgrounds must pay to have their dump station contents pumped out and hauled away.

Camping Reservations

We generally do not bother with reservations for a campground in the evening. On the other hand, we're generally happy with almost any campsite at the end of a long day and we usually travel in a small rig. If you want the best campsites (like along the water) or if you are planning to visit one of the most popular destinations during a busy part of the season (like when the salmon are running) you can call ahead to make a reservation. In the campground section we make a note when campground reservations are a good idea. You will also find campground telephone numbers and addresses there. As you travel along you'll quickly realize whether you need reservations or not, it just depends upon how many people are traveling at the same time you are.

Camping Vehicles and Tents

You can camp in Alaska, the Yukon, and British Columbia in any kind of rig, or without one if you like.

If you are planning to camp in the back country away from the roads you will be tent camping. You can also comfortably tent camp from the trunk of a car or when bicycling. A tent with a floor and good bug screens is essential. Have some kind of waterproof fly for rainy periods, they can last for many days. A plastic sheet with poles and guy ropes is very useful around the campsite during long rainy periods. A dark-colored tent is nice to block out the light during those summer periods when it never really gets dark. You may be surprised at how hard it is to sleep in the daylight. Consider bringing some kind of blindfold for sleeping. A large water container is useful in campgrounds. Bring an axe if you plan to burn wood, that in the campgrounds is often not split. If you are tough it is possible to tent camp all year, but the best months are June, July, and August.

Pickup campers and vans are very popular with Alaska residents. They let you use all of the campgrounds and also find good free camping spots. Their small size and maneuverability is a big plus when you get a little off the beaten track. An additional thing to keep in mind - charges on the ferries are based upon length.

Motorhomes, trailers, and fifth-wheels have to be the most comfortable camping vehicles. If you are driving the highway just to visit don't buy a special rig for Alaska camping since virtually anything will work as long as it is durable and in good condition. Most major roads are paved and high mountain passes are actually uncommon. If you want to travel the few long gravel highways you probably won't want to be pulling a trailer since flying gravel can be hard on them. If you have a trailer or fifth-wheel consider bringing along a tent for use while exploring the gravel roads like the Dalton Highway, Dempster Highway, or the roads north of Fairbanks. Any kind of rig provides big advantages in bug protection and extends the comfortable season for camping.

Caravans

RV caravan tours to Alaska are very popular. They generally start in the U.S. or perhaps Dawson Creek and spend many weeks driving up the Alaska Highway or the Cassiar, exploring the state, and then returning by either road or ferry. There are lots of variations.

A typical caravan tour is composed of about 20 rigs. The price paid generally includes a knowledgeable caravan leader in his own RV, a tail-gunner or caboose RV with an experienced mechanic, campground fees, many meals and tours at stops along the way, and lots of camaraderie. Many people love RV tours because someone else does all the planning, there is security in numbers, and a good caravan can be a very memorable experience. They aren't for everyone, however.

Remember that there will be a lot of costs in addition to those covered by the fee paid to the caravan company including fuel, insurance, maintenance, ferry charges, and groceries. We hear a lot of good things about caravans, but also many complaints. Common problems include caravans that do not spend enough time at interesting places, delays due to mechanical problems with other rigs in the caravan, and poor caravan leaders who do not really know the territory. A badly run caravan can be a disaster.

We've given the names, addresses and phone numbers below of some of the leading caravan companies. Give them a call or write a letter to get information about the tours they will be offering for the coming year. Once you have received the information do not hesitate to call back and ask questions. Ask for the names and phone numbers of people who have recently taken tours with the same caravan leader scheduled to be in charge of the tour you are considering. Call these references and find out what they liked and what they didn't like. They are likely to have some strong feelings about these things.

Adventure Caravans, 125 Promise Lane, Livingston, TX 77351-0855; 800 872-7897 and 936 327-3428.

Alaskan Discovery RV Tours; 645 G Street, Anchorage, AK 99501; 800 842-7764.

Fantasy RV Tours, Inc., 103 West Tomachi Avenue, Suite C, Gunnison, CO 81230; 800 952-8496.

Tracks to Adventure, 2811 Jackson Ave., El Paso, TX 79930; 800 351-6053.

Cash and Credit Cards

There are really only two currency problems that you are likely to run into during a trip to Alaska. The first is that cash and perhaps credit cards are the preferred tender in the cities and along highways. Cash machines are easy to find in larger towns but not available in all of the small ones. Credit cards (Master Card and Visa) are almost always accepted for gas and in restaurants. You should probably keep a cash stash (say $200) available for emergencies. Out of state checks are unlikely to be accepted anywhere.

The second challenge is Canadian currency, and it isn't really much of a challenge. Don't convert on a transaction-by-transaction basis, it will cost you a lot. Instead, stop at a bank or cash machine when you reach a sizeable town after crossing the border to get a Canadian cash fund. Cash machines will accept your U.S. card and they give a good exchange rate. Check with your bank card issuer before leaving home to make sure it will work in Canada, sometimes special PIN numbers (personal identification numbers) are needed for international use.

CB Radio

A CB radio can be useful for emergencies and for communication between rigs if you are traveling as part of a group. No standard frequency is used for communications in Alaska but channel 9 and 11 are used for emergencies. If those don't work try 14 and 19. Channel 19 is the frequency used by truckers on the Dalton Highway.

Children

One of the nice things about an Alaska outdoors trip is that the summer visitors season coincides with the summer school recess. An outdoors vacation is perfect for children of all ages and present opportunities for all types of activities.

One thing to keep in mind is that distances can be long and the driving sometimes a little boring. Remember, the Alaska Highway was originally described as miles and miles of miles and miles. The scenery is sometimes spectacular but there will also be many driving hours to fill with activities.

Clothing

For RV campers it is important to bring warm clothing like sweaters, jackets, and long underwear so that you are comfortable outdoors on cloudy days and in the evening. Otherwise you will spend little time outside and miss the pleasures of the evening campfire or stroll. A really heavy coat probably isn't necessary, instead have things you can layer to suit your activities and the temperature. You don't want to spend all of your time indoors while visiting this premier wilderness area. There are also some more specific things you should bring along.

Don't forget your bathing suit for Liard Hot Springs, and others. Also some lakes.

People commonly swim at Big Lake in the Mat-Su and at Harding and Birch Lakes near Fairbanks. Shorts can be useful when the temperatures rise over 70° F and the mosquitoes are temporarily somewhere else.

Rain gear is a necessity. Southcentral and Southeast sometimes have long periods of rainy weather and you'll have to get out in it if you want to be active.

Bring hiking boots. Also consider rubber break-up boots or some kind of waterproof hiking boots for hiking in wet areas. Trails in much of Alaska are very wet. Fishermen will want hip boots or waders.

Hikers and bikers have special requirements. See Chapter 14 for more about this.

Distances

As you plan your camping trip to Alaska and as you drive the highways you have to remember that the distances can make for some long driving days. It is difficult to cover over 300 miles in a reasonable day of driving. We've included a mileage chart nearby so that you can find the mileage information you need in one place.

Driving and Road Conditions

Most of your driving in northern Canada and Alaska will be on two-lane roads. For safety's sake you should leave your headlights on at all times to enhance the visibility of your rig to traffic approaching from the other direction. In the Yukon this is the law. Experiments have shown that the use of headlights on two-lane roads does reduce the accident rate substantially, on dusty gravel roads it's even more important.

In both Alaska and Canada the use of seatbelts is mandatory. Radar detectors are illegal in the Yukon Territory.

Frost heaves are a unique road hazard in Alaska and the Yukon. They are caused by both permafrost and the constant freezing and thawing of water in the gravel underlying the pavement. After being bounced off the ceiling by the first couple you hit you'll learn to keep a sharp lookout for them. We've seen them so bad that we had to unhook our tow car and drive it separately to save the hitch.

You can find road condition reports on the internet (see links from www.rolling-homes.com) and also get them by telephone: Alaska (while in the state) 511 or 800 478-7675, Yukon Territory 867 456-7623 or toll free (while in the Yukon) 877 456-7623, British Columbia 250 774-7447.

Dump Stations

There are plenty of dump stations to fill your needs while visiting the North Country but in remote areas they are not as common as you might sometimes wish. In Canada you'll find them marked as sani-dumps. It is important to plan ahead so you don't find yourself with a full holding tank miles from the nearest place to empty it.

In general, remember to always empty your tanks when you are in a town. More heavily populated areas have sewage treatment plants and can deal with sewage more easily than can operators in remote areas who either depend upon cesspools and drainage fields or pay high charges for pumping services.

DISTANCE TABLE

Miles

The diagonal of the chart lists the following locations (in order): Anchorage, Cantwell, Chena Hot Springs, Circle, Dawson City, Deadhorse, Delta Junction, Denali Park, Eagle, Fairbanks, Fort Nelson, Fort St. John, Glennallen, Haines, Haines Junction, Homer, Hyder, Prince Rupert, Seattle, Skagway, Stewart, Tok, Valdez, Watson Lake, Whitehorse.

Distances above the diagonal are in **Miles**; distances below the diagonal are in **Kilometers**.

From \ To	Anchorage	Cantwell	Chena Hot Springs	Circle	Dawson City	Deadhorse	Delta Junction	Denali Park	Eagle	Fairbanks	Fort Nelson	Fort St. John	Glennallen	Haines	Haines Junction	Homer	Hyder	Prince Rupert	Seattle	Skagway	Stewart	Tok	Valdez	Watson Lake	Whitehorse
Anchorage	—	2160	419	520	515	1610	340	237	501	358	1327	1657	189	775	625	226	996	1605	847	2435	126	832	147	1387	328
Cantwell	2160	—	2099	214	555	1222	219	500	379	1205	2206	1755	957	1375	998	207	1810	1058	1122	85	1143	207	85	1752	285
Chena Hot Springs	675	2099	—	3379	454	1549	1650	159	260	295	1390	1609	219	500	379	595	1175	939	283	47	1343	151	1562	1083	1319
Circle	837	214	3379	—	555	1222	1650	159	260	295	514	144	440	541	162	393	1488	1366	281	98	121	500	379	1205	1441
Dawson City	829	3574	345	3574	—	2238	475	828	232	635	1782	2135	195	158	76	456	1512	1892	774	2396	261	98	261	2038	2201
Deadhorse	2592	894	2494	2657	256	—	610	995	995	1336	868	489	1694	1950	753	874	1369	1605	803	1412	738	1142	990	980	1222
Delta Junction	547	731	419	256	419	828	—	353	452	805	610	368	384	1386	1232	648	505	1474	710	1453	484	1694	1100	864	1689
Denali Park	382	2494	256	419	828	995	353	—	1083	379	1205	1441	249	308	356	774	555	405	566	463	727	625	1336	868	625
Eagle	807	2657	293	293	232	995	452	1083	—	379	1441	1205	249	1134	1370	236	854	702	958	958	460	503	584	874	1369
Fairbanks	576	256	295	3476	635	1336	805	379	379	—	1826	2206	1755	937	998	1051	810	940	1006	1407	500	727	460	503	584
Fort Nelson	2136	3476	1390	514	1782	868	610	1205	1441	1826	—	380	1826	937	668	1293	1624	1823	1188	1839	1612	245	356	308	727
Fort St. John	2668	708	1609	144	2135	489	368	1441	1205	2206	380	—	2206	1755	957	1051	810	1510	2880	2500	2204	2584	1592	1212	1083
Glennallen	304	98	219	440	195	1694	384	249	249	1755	1826	2206	—	610	1744	1940	2124	2320	380	496	401	1826	2206	957	1205
Haines	1248	2038	500	541	158	1950	1386	308	1134	937	937	1755	610	—	1370	236	582	152	851	1222	1625	1967	1360	1578	1594
Haines Junction	1006	2418	379	162	76	753	1232	356	1370	998	668	957	1744	1370	—	957	937	696	668	1293	1624	1823	1188	1839	3159
Homer	364	2581	595	393	456	874	648	774	236	1051	1293	1051	1940	236	957	—	245	957	1130	2500	2204	2584	1592	1212	1191
Hyder	1604	499	1175	1488	1512	1369	505	555	854	810	1624	810	2124	582	937	245	—	85	1625	1752	285	1810	1058	1122	217
Prince Rupert	2584	1150	939	1366	1892	1605	1474	405	702	940	1823	1510	2320	152	696	957	85	—	1222	1831	173	1122	866	989	1199
Seattle	1364	908	283	281	774	803	710	566	958	1006	1188	2880	380	851	668	1130	1625	1222	—	1625	1930	1972	2802	2561	1819
Skagway	3920	1038	47	98	2396	1412	1453	463	958	1407	1839	2500	496	1222	1293	2500	1752	1831	1625	—	94	979	766	1534	1023
Stewart	203	507	1343	121	261	738	484	727	460	500	1612	2204	401	1625	1624	2204	285	173	1930	94	—	654	758	475	1059
Tok	1340	2486	151	500	98	1142	1694	625	503	727	245	2584	1826	1967	1823	2584	1810	1122	1972	979	654	—	504	451	1313
Valdez	237	2648	1562	379	261	990	1100	1336	584	460	356	1592	2206	1360	1188	1592	1058	866	2802	766	758	504	—	1144	404
Watson Lake	2233	869	1083	1205	2038	980	1453	868	874	503	308	1212	957	1578	1839	1212	1122	989	2561	1534	475	451	1144	—	254
Whitehorse	528	3175	1319	1441	2201	1222	1689	625	1369	584	727	1083	1205	1594	3159	1191	217	1199	1819	1023	1059	1313	404	254	—

Kilometers

Few government campgrounds have dump stations. Private campgrounds allow visitors to dump, usually for a fee. This is a reasonable charge, in remote areas operators often have to pay high pump-out fees on a per gallon basis. If you aren't staying in the campground you should help pay the fee.

Many gas stations also have dump stations and some communities provide them too. At the end of each of the campground chapters in this book is a listing of dump stations not located in campgrounds.

Fishing

Everyone knows that Alaska offers a wide selection of fishing opportunities. Along the Alaska Highway and throughout the Interior rivers, streams, and lakes have grayling, lake trout, and even salmon. Southcentral Alaska offers many river fishing hot spots, especially along the Parks Highway near Wasilla and on the Kenai Peninsula in the Soldotna area. Both Seward and Valdez are known for their saltwater salmon fishing and Homer is a big halibut charter center. Every Southeast destination mentioned in this book offers at least saltwater fishing possibilities.

The best fishing tends not to be right along the highways, especially if you are not fishing for salmon. A fly-out fishing trip should be a part of any fisherman's trip to Alaska. A time-honored technique for catching fish along streams crossing the highways is to walk some distance up or downstream from the road to reach less easily accessed waters. On the other hand, I can remember many occasions when I've hooked a fish on the first cast into a pool directly under the highway bridge.

Fishermen from outside Alaska will find that trout and salmon fishing may require a new assortment of tackle. Local knowledge is essential and tackle is available almost everywhere since fishing is such a popular recreational pursuit. The best prices, however, are in the larger cities. It would be worth your time to pick up one of the readily available Alaska fishing guidebooks before leaving home to make sure you bring the right poles, reels, and more expensive equipment. See the *Travel Library* section of this chapter for some suggestions. You can buy terminal tackle once you reach the

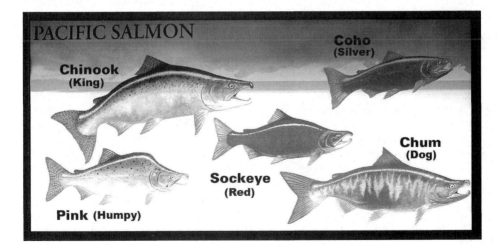

area where you plan to fish. A small boat or canoe can be very useful, particularly if you enjoy lake fishing.

British Columbia, the Yukon, and Alaska all require resident and non-resident fishing licenses. Additional licenses are required in some parks, for example, there is a Canadian National Park license required for fishing in Kluane National Park. Licenses can usually be issued by tackle stores, a good excuse to go in and ask questions. Regulation booklets are readily available for all areas where licenses are sold and at Tourist Information offices. For general information about Alaska sportfishing write to Alaska Department of Fish & Game, PO Box 25526, Juneau, AK 99802. See our website, www.rollinghomes.com, for links for buying Alaska licenses and links to Alaska fishing information.

Free Camping

Many RVers love to find a free campsite. The thrill of spending the night parked without paying anyone a fee is hard to deny. If you love to free camp and successfully find good parking spots in the Lower 48 there is no doubt you'll love Alaska. Many Alaska campers never use a formal campground.

On the other hand, we prefer formal campgrounds for many reasons. They are safer because there are usually many fellow campers around. You never have to get up in the middle of the night to answer a trooper's knock and be told to move on. Garbage is usually properly handled so that it won't attract bears. Alaska's campgrounds don't cost much, particularly the government ones, and they are often in a much more attractive and scenic location than any free pull-off. Campgrounds also provide picnic tables, toilets, firewood, firepits, and sometimes showers.

It is probably a fact of life that if you spend a night camping outside a campground you are breaking some kind of law. It may be a trespass law, it may be a vagrancy law, it may be something else. That doesn't necessarily mean that anyone will care. We often see people camping on city streets, in parking lots, or on pull-offs along the road. The key is to be low profile, don't make a pest of yourself, and don't obstruct traffic.

In general, the farther you are from civilization the easier it is to find free camping spots. In the less populated areas of the state no one is likely to care if you pull off the road at a good looking spot next to a river or on an abandoned section of road. Just make sure not to park in places where there are no-parking signs, don't block access, and avoid private property.

There are a couple of unusual free camping possibilities in the cities of Anchorage and Kenai. For several years the Seward Highway Wal-Mart in Anchorage has allowed self-contained RVers to park overnight in their huge parking lot. The new Wal-Mart in Whitehorse is doing the same thing. In Kenai the Fred Meyer store actually encourages RVers to park in their lot, they have even installed dump stations. The situation at these stores could change at any time due to political pressure from RV park owners or a change of heart of store management.

Fuel Cost

Both gasoline and diesel are readily available throughout Alaska and the Yukon but prices vary widely and change often. You'll find that we have included relative gas and diesel price graphs near the beginning of many chapters. These graphs show gas prices relative to those in Anchorage that we observed during July and August 2004. This was a period of extremely high gas prices in both the U.S. and Canada. We have shown prices as a percent of prices in Anchorage, Alaska at the same time. The price in Anchorage during that period averaged $1.98 for gas, $1.93 for diesel. Alaska gas and diesel prices tend to be slightly lower than those in the Lower 48.

The graphs should be of interest because they show the effect of transportation costs. In general, large cities with good transportation services have better prices. If you have a large rig it makes sense to take a look and plan your fill-ups accordingly.

How Much Time is Required for a Visit to Alaska

The time you'll need for an Alaska trip depends upon your starting point, of course. For an Alaska resident a weekend is plenty of time for a visit to a salmon stream or hiking trail. For an RVer from the Lower 48 much more time is required. Remember, it is quite a journey from most places to Dawson Creek which is just the beginning of the Alaska Highway. Dawson Creek is 817 miles north of Seattle, Washington and 875 miles north of Great Falls, Montana.

If you are planning to drive the Alaska Highway and want to see at least part of the state give yourself at least three weeks from the time you reach Dawson Creek. It takes most people about a week to drive the highway to Anchorage or Fairbanks. After driving that far you deserve to have some time to explore and relax. Most caravan companies allow at least 5 weeks for their guided trips and they don't visit all areas of the state. Our itinerary in Chapter 1 requires a good two months if you don't want to exhaust yourself. Three months would be better.

The quickest and most relaxing way for a non-resident to visit Alaska is to rent an RV in one of the major towns. Take a look at the *Motorhome and RV Rentals* section in this chapter for more information. With a rental you can have an enjoyable trip even if you only have a week available for your visit.

Information by Mail, Phone or the Internet - Prepare for Your Trip

It is always a good idea to know as much as you can about a destination before you go. Knowing what to expect makes planning easier and increases your appreciation of the new places you see and the things there are to do.

There is a great deal of information available about Alaska, the Yukon, and British Columbia. Computer users should visit our website, www.rollinghomes.com, for links to many sources of information about Alaska, the Yukon, and British Columbia. Most websites include address if you prefer to have some printed materials mailed to you. Finally, the *Travel Library* section of this chapter and our Website contain information about an excellent selection of books about many aspects of visiting Alaska and the Yukon.

Here are some places to write for general information about the state and the roads north:

Alaska Division of Tourism, PO Box 110801, Juneau, Alaska 99811; 907 465-2017.

Alaska Public Lands Information Center, 605 W. 4th Ave., Suite 105, Anchorage, AK 99501; 907 271-2737.

Alaska Travel Industry Association, Dept. 9408, 2600 Cordova Street, Suite 201, Anchorage, AK 99503-2745.

Alaska Wilderness Recreation and Tourism Association, 2207 Spenard Rd., Suite 201, Anchorage, AK 99503; 907 258-3171.

Northern British Columbia Tourism Association 850 River Road, Prince George, B.C., Canada; 800 663-8843.

Northern Rockies Alaska Highway Tourism Association; 888 785-2544.

Tourism Yukon, Government of the Yukon, Box 2703, Whitehorse, Y.T. Y1A 2C6, Canada; 800 661-0494.

Insects and Other Pests (like bears)

Alaska and the Yukon are famous for their mosquitoes. They also both are home to two other northland pests–white sox and no-see-ums. On the positive side, there are no poisonous snakes. Bears, both blacks and browns, often fall into the pest category, particularly around campgrounds, dumps, and fishing streams. Even the shy and slow-witted moose can sometimes be a problem.

Mosquitoes, white sox and no-see-ums are not present in all locations and at all times. Many variables including the amount of standing water, the severity of the winter, the time of the season, and the strength of the breeze make a big difference. When you pick a campsite it pays to stay away from puddles and swampy areas and pick a site with at least the possibility of a breeze.

Mosquitoes are present throughout the summer. They appear as soon as the weather begins to get warm in May and last until the hard freezes in September. They are at their worst in the early season just after breakup. Scientists say that only the females will attack you, but it seems to us that they must all be females. It actually takes a mosquito about a minute to poke into you, inject the saliva that keeps your blood from being too thick to suck, and begin drawing blood. It is the saliva that causes the mosquito prick to itch afterwards.

White sox are also known as black flies in other places, the ones in Alaska have white on their legs. They are present from midsummer until freezing. Their bite is actually worse than that of a mosquito.

No-see-ums are very small and travel in swarms. They tend to land and then crawl under your clothing. Any breeze at all will keep them down, and you can probably outrun them at even a walking pace since they are slow fliers. Their bite is every bit as bad as a white sox and they are present during about the same period.

If you use the proper techniques these flying pests can be dealt with and you can enjoy the outdoors. When they are present you should wear clothing that covers your arms and legs. Some people think that dark colored clothing attracts them.

Anti-insect products containing DEET (diethyl-meta-toluamide) or citronella work best. There is some question about DEET's safety, it is pretty powerful stuff. Be aware that DEET is a solvent and will soften and damage things like plastic fishing lines and plastic watches. Citronella isn't as effective but does not have these problems. We use DEET. Some folks also swear by Skin-So-Soft, an Avon skin cream which wasn't even designed to repel insects but has a cult following.

Another essential product to have along is an anti-itch product, often these are combined with an antiseptic. Once you receive the inevitable bite an anti-itch cream will help you forget about it and reduce the scratching and swelling that results.

It is very important to have good insect screens on your rig and on your tent. You must have some retreat to get away from the bugs when they are really bad, and they will occasionally be very bad. Tent campers should have a head net. They may look funny but when you need them they are priceless and allow you to lead an almost normal life while setting up camp, preparing food, or even while hiking.

Bears can be a problem in camp, particularly if you don't take the proper precautions. They are attracted by food so there are two rules that you should always follow. Do not feed them and keep a very clean camp. All food items must be inside a rig or hung out of reach away from the tent and campsite. Cook away from your tent, never cook in your tent. Make sure your tent is clean if you have done so in the past. Dispose of trash well away from the tent and campsite. Camp away from trash barrels. In the wilderness watch for bear trails, especially along streams and beaches and do not set up your tent near them. Dogs seem to attract bears so it is best not to have one along in bear country. For much more about bear safety see *Chapter 14 – Camping Away From the Road System* in this book.

Moose can be dangerous. They seem slow-moving and stolid but they are huge, can cover ground quickly, and when riled sometimes protect themselves by trying to stomp their foe. Don't get too close when taking pictures and be careful around mothers and calves. They often stomp dogs and bears, they can do the same to you. Dogs and moose don't mix well, dogs often harass moose and cause real problems, don't let your dog run loose.

Internet Sites

Every day there are more and more internet sites devoted to Alaska, the Yukon, and B.C. They are a great way to familiarize yourself with the North Country before leaving home. Rather than trying to list them all here we have set up our own Website: **www.rollinghomes.com**. On it you will find links to other Websites with a lot of good information.

We have another use for our Website. As a small publisher we can only afford to update our travel guides on a three to five year cycle. In order to keep the books more current we publish updated information on the Web. Our site has pages for each of our books with updates referenced by page number. We gather information for these updates ourselves and also depend upon information sent in by our readers and others. This information is only posted on the Website until we issue a new edition, once the new edition comes out we remove the page and post updates only for the new book.

Laundry

Finding a place to do your laundry won't be a problem in Alaska and the Yukon. Almost all privately-owned RV parks have coin-operated clothes washing equipment. If you are camping in government campgrounds you will be able to find a public laundromat with little problem. Even the smallest communities usually have a laundromat since many locals don't have running water or electricity. Laundromats also often have shower facilities, this is good to know if you frequent government campgrounds or free camp.

Mail

Alaska, the Yukon, and British Columbia all have excellent mail service. Outlying areas have slightly slower service than you may be accustomed to, add a couple of days for towns along the highways. Even outlying villages off the road system often have frequent airmail service since aircraft are their only link to the outside world.

In the U.S. just have your mail sent to General Delivery of a town you expect to visit. Some of the important zip codes are as follows: Anchorage 99510, Fairbanks 99701, Juneau 99801, Ketchikan 99901, Kenai 99611, Homer 99603, Seward 99664, Valdez 99686, Tok 99780, Denali National Park 99755.

Motorhome and RV Rentals

If you don't have your own rig for an Alaska trip you can always rent one. This is an extremely popular way to visit Alaska. Here are some of the rental outfits. Note that some are located in Alaska while others are in British Columbia, Alberta, or the Yukon Territory. Reserve your rental RV as early as possible, many companies are fully booked by the time the camping season arrives. Often there is an early booking discount. The rental company listing below is only a starting point. All of these companies will send you an information pack if you request information. When you receive the packages take a look at the following items to compare them.

   - Types of rigs including age
   - Rates
   - Mileage charges
   - Required deposits
   - Insurance coverage and related extra charges
   - Pick up and drop off procedures, times, and locations
   - Availability of one-way rentals
   - Extra charges for housekeeping and linen packages
   - Limitations on where you can take the rig, and extra charges for gravel roads
   - Pets allowed?

ABC Motorhome & Car Rentals, 3875 Old International Airport Rd., Anchorage, AK 99502; (800) 421-7456, (907) 279-2000, Fax (907) 243-6363, Website: www. abcmotorhome.com.

Adventures in Alaska RV Rentals, 1145 Shypoke Dr., Fairbanks, AK 99709; (907) 458-7368, Website: www.adventuresAkRV.com.

Alaska Dream RV Rental, PO Box 92972, Anchorage, AK 99509; (907) 278-7368, (888) 357-7368, Website: www.alaskadreamrv.com.

Alaska Highway Cruises, 9085 Glacier Highway, Suite 301, Juneau, AK 99801; (800) 323-5757, Website: www.alaskarv.com.

 Alaska Motorhome Rentals, 9085 Glacier Hwy, Suite 301, Juneau, AK 99801; (800) 254-9929, Fax (425) 882-2479, Website: www.alaskarv.com.

Alaska Panorama, 712 West Potter Drive, Anchorage, AK 99518; (907) 562-1401, (800) 478-1401, Fax (907) 561-8762, Website: www.alaskapanorama.com.

Alaska Vacation Motorhome Rentals, 1120 E. Huffman #587, Anchorage, AK 99515; (800) 648-1448, Website: www.alaskavacationmotorhomerentals.com.

Alaskan Superior RV Services, Inc., 801 E. 82nd Ave, Unit 3A, Anchorage, AK 99518; (800) 764-4625, (907) 561-7723, Fax (907) 561-2093, Website: www.goal-aska.com.

Alexander's RV, PO Box 221805, Anchorage, AK 99502; (888) 660-5115, (907) 563-5115, Fax (907) 563-5154, Website: www.alaska-rv.com.

Alldrive Canada Inc., 1908 - 10th Avenue S.W., Calgary, Alberta T3C 0J8, Canada; (403) 245-2935, (888) 736-8787, Fax (403) 245-2959, Website: www.alldrive.com.

Canadream Campers, 110 Copper Rd., Whitehorse, Y.T. Y1A 2Z6, Canada; (867) 668-3610, Fax (867) 668-3795, Website: www.canadream.com.

Candan RV Rentals, 20257 Langley Bypass, Langley, B.C. V3A 6K9, Canada; (604) 530-3645, Fax (604) 530-1696, Website: www.candan.com.

Clippership Motorhome Rentals, Inc., 5401 Old Seward Highway, Anchorage, AK 99518; (800) 421-3456 or (907) 562-7051, Fax (907) 562-7053, Website: www. clippershiprv.com.

Fraserway RV Rentals, 9039 Quartz Road, Whitehorse, Yukon, Y1A 4Z5; (800) 661-2441 or (867) 668-3438, Fax (867) 68-3449, Website: www.fraserwayrvrentals. com.

Go North Alaska Adventure Travel Center, PO Box 60147, Fairbanks, AK 99706, (907) 479-7272, (866) 236-7272, Fax (907) 474-1041, Website: www.gonorthalaska. com.

Go West Motorhome Rentals, 1577 Lloyd Avenue, North Vancouver, B.C. V7P 3K8, Canada; (604) 987-5288, (800) 661-8813, Website www.go-west.com.

Great Alaskan Holidays, 3901 W. International Airport Road, Anchorage, AK 99502; (888) 225-2752, (907) 248-7777, Website: www.greatalaskanholidays.com.

Murphy's RV Inc., PO Box 92307, Anchorage, AK 99509; (800) 582-5123, (907) 562-0601, Fax (907) 562-0680, Website: www.alaskaone.com/murphyrv.

Recreation Rentals of Alaska, (907) 336-4423, Fax (907) 336-4423, Website: www. rentalaskarvs.com.

Sweet Retreat Motorhome Rentals, 6820 Arctic Blvd., Anchorage, AK 99518; (800) 759-4861, (907) 344-9155, Fax (907) 344-8279, Website: www.sweetretreat. com.

Some rental outfits have an extra charge for gravel roads or restrict driving on them. Check on this if you plan to explore them. Dropping the rig off at another location tends to be very expensive.

Northern Lights and the Midnight Sun

One of the reasons that Alaska has a special ambiance is the far northern location. The midnight sun and the northern lights are manifestations of this.

During June and July the days are very long. Baseball games are played at midnight, people are full of energy and work and play until all hours of the night. Most Alaskans love this, for them it helps make up for the long, dark winter. You'll probably like it too, but many people have trouble sleeping in broad daylight. Either take along something to cover your eyes when you are sleeping or cover the windows of your rig with something to keep out the light, many people use aluminum foil. Tenters may find that a dark-colored tent helps.

The longest day of the year is June 20 or 21. It is known as the summer solstice. On that day a person standing on the Arctic Circle would be able to see the sun all night long if the terrain were perfectly flat. As a practical matter, people from Fairbanks go to the summits north of town where they have some altitude and are guaranteed the sun for their summer solstice celebration even though they really aren't as far north as the Arctic Circle.

One reason to plan a late trip to Alaska is the northern lights. You won't be able to see them unless it is dark at night, and for campers that means September.

There's a great exhibit on northern lights at the University of Alaska museum in Fairbanks. There's also a new theater devoted to shows about the northern lights in Watson Lake, Y.T. Either of them provides a good introduction.

To see the northern lights you'll need a clear dark night. They do not appear every night but if you keep an eye open you'll eventually have a good sighting. They'll be toward the north and are usually best after midnight. The best area for northern light observations along the road system is the band stretching from Fairbanks to Fort Nelson.

Photography

Wildlife, scenery, and outdoor sports, all make great photography subjects. If you're traveling by RV bring your gear. If you have to carry it in a backpack you'll have to pack lighter, but don't forget a camera.

Definitely bring along a telephoto. Also fast film so that you can take advantage of it. A tripod is very useful for telephoto photography. You'll also want a medium length lens that can be hand held since wildlife often won't stick around while you set up your tripod. For dark blue skies use a polarizing filter.

Propane

You'll have no problem finding propane throughout the North Country. All larger towns have several sources and virtually every smaller town also has some place where you can fill up. Just ask at the campground for advice. Plan ahead so that you don't run out while far from civilization.

Public Transportation

There's a variety of public transportation in the North. Many of the larger towns have bus systems that work great for getting around while staying at a campground on the outskirts of town. A limited number of busses ply the highways. State ferries connect the towns of southeast Alaska and also run to Kodiak, Cordova and out the Aleutian Chain. And in the bush you might find that public transportation will take the form of a small airplane.

The cities of Anchorage, Fairbanks, Whitehorse, Juneau and Ketchikan all have public bus systems. Many of the city campgrounds are on or near a bus route.

While intercity busses are infrequent in Alaska and the Yukon it is possible for travelers without their own wheels to get around. In places where there is enough demand service is available, although often in the form of vans able to carry only a few passengers. Bus service offerings tend to change frequently, just as airline service offerings do. Check with information centers for more details about available bus transportation.

Small vans provide service along several routes. Probably the most interesting are runs from Anchorage and Fairbanks to Denali National Park, from Fairbanks up the Dalton Highway, and from Glennallen to McCarthy. You will be able to find information about these and other van operations locally.

The Alaska Railroad offers some interesting transportation options. The railroad is very tourist-friendly, they have excellent schedules for sightseeing and also can arrange tours at the destinations. Trains run between Anchorage and Fairbanks with stops in Talkeetna and at Denali National Park. They also run to Seward and to Whittier from Anchorage. Contact the railroad at PO Box 107500, Anchorage, AK 99510: (800) 544-0552, (907) 265-2494, Website at www.alaska.net/~akrr/. They have a good brochure outlining their services.

Air transportation in Alaska is widespread and easy to find. Airlines flying modern jets provide scheduled service between larger cities. From the larger cities smaller operators flying light aircraft provide both scheduled and charter flights to any village with a safe airstrip and to a huge selection of lakes and rivers large enough for a float-equipped airplane. If you are bound for a remote campsite it is generally more economical to fly a scheduled operator to a hub town or village near your eventual destination and then charter a small aircraft for a short flight. More information about access to remote locations is included in Chapter 14 of this book.

Telephones

The good news is that phones in Alaska and Canada use much the same system that is used in the Lower 48. You can direct dial in and out of Canada and Alaska using the normal area code and seven-digit number format. It is not necessary to use an international country code when calling Canada from the U.S. or the U.S. from Canada. The area code for all of Alaska is 907, for all of the Yukon it has recently been changed to 867, and for all of British Columbia except the Vancouver area it is 250.

Telephone rates are more expensive than those in the Lower 48. Sometimes, especially in remote areas you will notice an echo or delay because telephone signals are bounced off a satellite.

We have found that some U.S. calling cards will not work in Canada. Before entering Canada you should call your service provider and make sure your card will work in Canada, and particularly in remote areas of the Yukon along the highway. Otherwise you may find yourself out of touch with home.

Time Zones

All of Alaska except the very western islands of the Aleutian Chain are in one time zone and use Alaska Time. This is one hour earlier than Pacific time as used on the West Coast of the U.S. and Canada. The Yukon is on Pacific Time also. British Columbia has two time zones, Pacific time is used in most areas but the far eastern area of the Province including the part of the Alaska Highway from Dawson Creek north to Fort Nelson is on Mountain Time. Alaska, the Yukon, and British Columbia all observe daylight saving time.

Tourist Information Offices

Tourist information is very easy to find throughout Alaska, the Yukon, and British Columbia. Any town of even moderate size seems to have a tourist office, we've tried to give their locations and phone numbers in the city descriptions included in the campground chapters of this book. The U.S. government and the Alaska government also have information offices in various locations, usually related to government-owned lands like national forests and state and national parks. You'll find addresses and phone numbers throughout the book. To easily find them go to the index and look for entries under the following headings: Visitor Information, local; Alaska Public Lands Information Center; BLM addresses; NPS addresses; State of Alaska addresses; USF&W Service addresses; and USFS addresses. As a practical matter, if you can't figure out the governmental agency that can answer your question it is best to call one of the Alaska Public Lands Information Centers, if they can't answer your question they can direct you to the proper agency.

Travel Library

One of the best things about traveling in your own vehicle is that you have plenty of room for a library. Your appreciation of the country will be much improved by a little background reading and the availability of a few reference books as you travel.

The Milepost (Morris Communications Corporation; Augusta, GA; 2004, ISBN 1892154145) is the bible of Alaska highway travel with a new edition issued each year. It contains a wealth of information about services, history, sights, and just about everything else. It also has mile-by-mile logs of all of the routes to and in Alaska. The one drawback to the Milepost is that almost all commercial facilities mentioned are advertisers who write their own descriptions. Enough said.

Off-highway campers have their own Milepost, *The Alaska Wilderness Guide* by the Milepost editors (Morris Communications Corporation; Augusta, GA; 2001; ISBN 1892154099).

Probably the best history of the Klondike gold rush readily available is *The Klondike Fever: The Life and Death of the Last Great Gold Rush* by Pierre Berton (Carroll & Graf, New York, N.Y.; 1985; ISBN 0881841390). First published in 1958 this book continues in print today, which is a real testimony to it's quality. The author grew up in Dawson City.

As you sit beside your campfire in the evening you'll probably find you have lots of light for reading. Make sure to have a copy of the **poems of Robert Service** on hand. His ballads of the gold rush days have a special resonance when you visit the far North and they are widely available in bookstores in the Yukon and Alaska.

In a place like Alaska, especially away from the roads, you'll need maps. A good place to start is DeLorme Mapping's *Alaska Atlas & Gazetteer* (ISBN 0899332897) which has 1:300,000 and 1:1,400,000 scale topographic maps covering the entire state. Later you'll want to get maps that show more detail for hiking or when you get away from the highway.

There are two excellent guides to hiking in Alaska. The classic is *55 Ways to the Wilderness in Southcentral Alaska* by Helen Nienhueser and John Wolf (The Mountaineers; Seattle, Washington; 2002; ISBN 0898867916). *Hiking Alaska* by Dean Littlepage (Falcon Press Publishing Co., Inc.; Helena, Montana; 1997; ISBN 1560445513) is a new favorite and covers the entire state.

A good guide to floatable Alaska rivers is *The Alaska River Guide: Canoeing, Kayaking, and Rafting in the Last Frontier* by Karen Jettmar (Alaska Northwest Books; Seattle, Washington; 1998; ISBN 0882404970).

Fishermen will need a guide showing techniques and other information about Alaskan fishing. Readily available is *The Highway Angler* by Gunnar Pedersen (Fishing Alaska Publications; Anchorage, Alaska; 2003; ISBN 0962155144).

The ultimate guide to Alaska's government lands is the encyclopedic *Wild Alaska: The Complete Guide to Parks, Preserves, Wildlife Refuges, and Other Public Lands, Second Edition* by Nancy Lange Simmerman and Tricia Brown (The Mountaineers; Seattle, Washington; 1999; ISBN 0898865832).

If you are interested in spending some time in the wilderness cabins offered by the various government agencies in Alaska you can't go wrong with the new *How to Rent a Public Cabin In Southcentral Alaska* by Andromeda Romano-Lax (Wilderness Press; Berkeley, California; 1999; ISBN 0899972276).

You'll find links for purchasing many of these books and others on our Website, **www.rollinghomes.com.**

Units of Measurement

Alaska uses the same measurement systems as the Lower 48–miles, gallons, and degrees Fahrenheit. Canada does not, there you have to deal with kilometers, liters, and degrees Celsius.

Here are a few conversion factors and tricks to help you cope.

One kilometer is about .62 miles. For converting miles to kilometers divide the number of miles by .62. For converting kilometers to miles multiply the kilometers by .62. Since kilometers are shorter than miles the number of kilometers after converting will always be more than the number of miles, if they aren't you divided when you should have multiplied or multiplied when you should have divided.

For liquid measurement it is usually enough to know that a liter is about the same as a quart. When you need more accuracy, like when you are trying to make some sense out of your miles per gallon calculations, there are 3.79 liters in a U.S. gallon.

Here are a few useful conversion factors:

> 1 km = .62 mile
> 1 mile = 1.61 km
> 1 meter = 3.28 feet
> 1 foot = .3 meters
> 1 liter = .26 U.S. gallon
> 1 U.S. gallon = 3.79 liters
> 1 kilogram = 2.21 pounds
> 1 pound = .45 kilograms
> Convert from °F to °C by subtracting 32 and multiplying by 5/9
> Convert from °C to °F by multiplying by 1.8 and adding 32

Vehicle Preparation and Breakdowns

Vehicle preparation for the trip north runs the gamut. Some people do nothing more than change the oil. Others definitely go overboard. We tend to take the middle road. It is important to have a rig that will not go haywire on you and force you to make expensive repairs (not to mention incur an expensive tow bill) in an isolated location.

Make sure that your tires are in very good shape and that you have a spare. Consider carrying two spares if you plan to spend a lot of time on gravel roads like the Dalton Highway (Prudhoe Bay Haul Road) or the Dempster. Make sure that you have a good jack and tire wrench that will work on your rig, some new motorhomes do not come with either. Even if you don't want to change a tire on one of the huge rigs yourself you should at least have the tools to let someone help you and a spare tire of each size used by your rig or rigs. Big rigs sometimes don't have the space for a mounted spare, consider bringing along a much lighter and easier-to-pack unmounted one. It's a lot easier to get that tire mounted than to wait for a week while the tire you need it shipped in.

Do a complete systems check before you leave home. If you have a nagging problem with something in your vehicle, say a balky refrigerator or a leak of some kind make sure to fix it before heading north. It is bound to get worse during a long trip and repairs are definitely not cheaper up north.

Bring jumper cables and small tool kit. Spares are usually not necessary but if you know of some filter or essential part that is particularly difficult to find you might want to bring an extra along so that you are not faced with a long delay in a remote location. If a part isn't essential you can sometimes get your rig to a place where parts are available, we once drove over 500 miles in second gear to reach Whitehorse when an electronic part in our motorhome's transmission went south near Muncho Lake.

Emergency road service insurance is very worthwhile even if it is only for the peace of mind. Towing charges can be very high, especially in remote areas. Make sure your plan will cover you in northern Canada and Alaska and on remote roads.

Gravel roads are probably the hazard requiring the most vehicle preparation. Fortunately, you're really likely to run into few of them if you keep to the main highways. The Alaska Highway is paved for the entire distance although there are likely to be some unpaved sections where upgrades and road repairs are underway. The Cassiar Highway now has under 100 miles of unpaved road. The only other gravel most people are likely to encounter is the Klondike Loop between Dawson City and Tok. More aggressive travelers will see gravel if they drive the Taylor Highway north to Eagle, the Denali Highway between the Tangle Lakes and the Parks Highway, the Nabesna Road, the McCarthy road to McCarthy, the Dalton Highway to Prudhoe Bay, the Dempster Highway from Dawson City to Inuvik, and the roads north of Fairbanks to Circle and Manley Hot Springs. Read on if you plan to travel these roads.

The way you drive on gravel directly affects the damage you will receive from flying rocks. Most damage from rocks is done by you when you run in to a flying rock thrown into the air by someone else. Your forward speed makes all the difference. You'll find that if you slow to about 35 mph (55 kph) when a car passes you in either direction you will reduce rock damage by about 90%. That's our estimate, but it's close. Be particularly alert when on freshly finished seal coat before it is swept. Speeds tend to be high on these very smooth sections of highway, but there's lots of loose gravel so windshields are often damaged.

There are a few things that can easily be done to cope with dust on gravel roads. You may already know the spots where dust leaks into your RV. Consider using duct tape to seal leaky storage compartments and doors while underway. It also helps to have a positive air pressure inside your vehicle, turn on your dash heater or air conditioner fan and close your windows to do this.

Even if you drive carefully you may expect at least a little rock damage. The large front windshields of RVs are particularly vulnerable. They are virtually impossible to protect so drive carefully and make sure you have insurance. We make sure that we get small dings repaired when we reach Anchorage or Fairbanks so cracks won't spread. Forward facing windows on trailers, campers and motorhomes (not wind-shields) can be protected with cardboard and tape. The cardboard covering may also help you sleep in the midnight sun.

Rocks can also hit your headlights. You can buy inexpensive protectors in auto shops that will save your headlights. Radiators also sometimes get hit by rocks, you can protect them with metal screening. This has always seemed like overkill to us but many people do it. We've had no radiator problems due to leaving ours unprotected. Diesel pushers should consider screening for radiators, they seem to be much more vulnerable than rigs with front-mounted radiators.

Plumbing and dump fixtures on RVs are often made of plastic and hang down where flying rocks from the tires will easily hit and break them. Consider carrying extras or building rock deflectors. We find that wrapping them with fiberglass insulation and duct tape is effective and easy, but not very pretty. Don't forget the copper pipes and valves of your propane system. They can be covered with insulation or a rubber hose that has been split for installation and then taped.

Vehicles that are being towed are particularly vulnerable to rocks thrown up by the towing vehicle. Use cardboard or plywood shields on the front of trailers and fifth-wheels. Fit your tow vehicle with good mud flaps and cover the nose of a towed car with something to protect it from flying rocks. Don't worry about how it looks, you'll save it from a lot of damage. If you don't want to do this consider unhooking and driving the car separately when you reach a stretch of gravel.

Gravel sections of the Alaska Highway are often treated with chemicals to keep the dust down. You should wash your RV after traversing these areas because the chemicals are corrosive, many campgrounds provide washing facilities. Don't forget the underside of the vehicle.

In "the old days" travelers on the Alaska Highway seemed to often get leaks in their gas tanks from flying rocks. This isn't likely today since there are so few miles of gravel. A quick fix used then was to rub the outside of the puncture with a bar of soap, it often worked until you could reach a repair shop.

Water

It is easy to fall into the trap of thinking that drinking water in a place as huge and unspoiled as Alaska must be safe. This is not exactly the case, you must be just as careful about your drinking water in the North as you would be in the Lower 48.

Giardia (causes beaver fever) and other contaminants are wide-spread in Alaska, even in places far from the nearest settlement. Use a filter or water treatment on all surface water. This is likely to be a problem only if you are camping away from the road system since good pure water is available at almost all private campgrounds and many government ones. We have noted, however, that Yukon Government campgrounds often post a notice that their water must be purified. You should do so if posted.

Campgrounds may have good water but getting the water into your rig at a government campground may be difficult. Many have hand pumps or faucets that can not be used with a hose. Your only solution may be to pump water into a container and then fill your vehicle's water tank using a funnel. If you plan to camp solely at government campgrounds you will probably want to add a bucket and funnel to your equipment list. For more about water treatment see Chapter 14.

When to Camp - The Season and Weather

This book is primarily aimed at the summer camper. Most camping facilities are open from break-up in the middle of May until freeze-up sometime in September or early October. Many government campgrounds close in September but many others stay open until the snow flies. Actually, most of the RVing traffic from warmer climes disappears during the first part of September and only local hunters are in the campgrounds until snow and cold force them to close.

June, July, and August are the most popular camping months, the high season. There are few mosquitoes in May but things haven't really dried out from break-up in many areas. The end of the month is often OK. The ice in many lakes does not go out until mid-May. Things start to turn green in June and in many areas this month has the least rain. July is the warmest month, the Fairbanks area can see 90° F, Anchorage residents are happy with 70°. August sees the days start to grown shorter and the temperature fall just a little. September is the fall, trees quickly turn yellow and "termination dust"–snow– begins to appear on the hills. By the end of the month in the Interior the leaves are gone and the hard freezes have started.

Southcentral - The best weather in the Anchorage area including the Susitna Valley and the Kenai Peninsula is June–July and August have a little more rain. Expect 50° to 70° F in Anchorage, slightly warmer on the Kenai Peninsula and in the Mat-Su Valley. The Anchorage bowl can sock in for long periods, if it does just head for the Kenai or the Interior.

Interior - The weather is pretty good in the Interior during all three high-season months. Fairbanks often has temperatures in the 70° to 80° F range. There's more rain in the summer than snow in the winter but the Interior is fairly dry. Expect a few rainy periods but many days of clear or partly-clear weather with perhaps a rain shower or two. September is our favorite month in the Interior. Temperatures start to fall but aren't bad if you have a heated RV for getting up in the morning, campgrounds are virtually empty, the northern lights are out at night, and the trees are beautiful.

Southeast - Expect rain in Southeast. If you get lucky and have a few days of sunshine consider yourself blessed. The scenery is spectacular when the sun shines. Temperatures in southeast are mild, say 45° to 60° F during most of the summer. Rainfall patterns are important. June is the driest month with rainfall increasing through the summer until October, which is the wettest month. Also note that rainfall is heaviest in the south and lightest in the north.

Chapter 3

How To Use The Destination Chapters

Chapters 4 through 14 of this book contain information about the many camping destinations available to you in Alaska and along the Alaska and Cassiar Highways. Chapters 4 through 13 covering campgrounds along the highways, are all similarly arranged. Each covers the campgrounds along a major highway route. Chapter 14 on *Camping Away from the Road System* follows a different self-explanatory format, this chapter does not apply to it.

Introductory Road Map

Each of the campground chapters begins with a road map. The map shows a lot of information that will allow you to use it as an index to find campgrounds as you travel. The map shows the route covered in the chapter and also the most important towns. Many towns along the route have their own maps which are placed later in the chapter and show in-town campground locations. Dotted lines outline areas outside towns that have their own campground location maps. These two types of maps together cover all areas along the road system. An index on the initial map page shows the names of all route and town descriptions in the chapter and the page number where each starts.

Introductory Text

Each chapter starts with an **Introduction** giving important information about the route or routes covered in the chapter. Usually there is something of the history of the route and the area, a description of the lay of the land, and a summary of the highlights. These might be important towns, unusual geographical or physical features, or outstanding destinations of one kind or another.

In Alaska outdoor activities are a primary attraction. We have discovered, however, that it is very easy to miss an area's outdoor attractions if you don't have a handy guide. For this reason we've included information about four different kinds of outdoor activities that we think will be popular with our readers: Fishing; Boating Rafting, Canoeing, and Kayaking; Hiking and Mountain Biking; and Wildlife Viewing. Our intention is not to try to replace the many individual guides that are published about each of these activities, we just want you to be aware of each area's attractions. If you are interested you can look farther for more detailed information. We've included references in many places to help you do just that. Some of the books listed in Chapter 2 will also be helpful.

In this section you'll find that we have included gas and diesel price charts. These charts show fuel prices we observed during July and August 2004. We have shown prices as a percent of prices in Anchorage Alaska at the same time. The charts aren't there to tell you exactly how much fuel will costs, they're to help you predict the places that may have the lowest prices. These charts should help you plan your fill-ups.

Route and Town Descriptions

Following the introductory material in each chapter is the **Routes, Towns, and Campgrounds** section. In addition to the campground overview maps described below this section has a few paragraphs of text describing each route or town. We've described the local attractions and also included information about the location and phone number of the visitor center in each town if there happens to be one.

Our descriptions of the destinations and routes in this book are intended to give you an idea of what the city or region has to offer. They are by no means complete, you will undoubtedly need additional guides during your visit. Local visitor centers in Alaska and along the roads north are essential stops, they have lots of interesting materials and usually are staffed by knowledgeable locals.

We have given population and altitude information for each major town. These are our estimates. Population figures are constantly changing and sometimes they reflect artificial political boundaries, we've just tried to give you some idea ahead of time of what you can expect by giving you our best estimate based upon many different sources. The altitudes are also estimates, some are based upon the local airport altitude which may be somewhat different than the altitude of the central business district, we've tried to correct for this.

We've also included many mileage figures. Mileages are the best way to fix locations along the roads in the north but they are often not 100% accurate for several reasons. Most northern roads have mileposts placed along them and these mileposts are used to determine location. It would be prohibitively expensive to change them all each time a road is straightened and shortened. You will find that many older establishments along the Alaska Highway list addresses based upon historical mileposts that are twenty or more miles different than today's mileposts, which are really kilometer posts. Another problem is that many of the mileposts are missing for one reason or another.

If you examine guidebooks to rural Alaska and the roads north you will see that each has slightly different mileage numbers as each tries in its own way to cope with the problems. We've done the same and no doubt you will find some of our figures that do not quite agree with your own odometer. This may be because we usually round to the nearest mile or kilometer. None of this should cause you any big problems, the north is pretty empty and if you are close to a destination you will usually have no problem finding it.

As everyone knows the U.S. uses miles and Canada uses kilometers. We've tried to use miles when we are writing about Alaska and kilometers when we are writing about Canada. When we give distances (not Mileposts or Kilometerposts) we usually give both miles and kilometers. Some users of this book will have odometers marked in miles and some will have them marked in kilometers.

Campground Overview Maps

Each important city or town and each region between the towns has its own campground overview maps. These maps are designed to do two things: they quickly show you the lay of the land and the campgrounds that are available, and if you examine them more carefully they will help you drive right to the campground you have decided to use.

There are two different types of campground overview maps. The first is a city map. Each city map is associated with a written description of the city and a listing of the campgrounds in that city. The second type is an area map. These usually show the road between two cities and each is associated with a description of that road and also a listing of the campgrounds on that road. Campgrounds are not shown on two different maps. In some cases a campground that might be shown along the road between towns is instead shown on a town map. This happens when we think the campground is a good place to stay for a visit to the town even though it might be located a short distance down the road.

While the maps are for the most part self-explanatory here is a key.

Campground Descriptions

Each campground section begins with address and telephone number. While it is not generally necessary to obtain campground reservations in Alaska you may want to do so for some very popular campgrounds. This is particularly true in areas where people congregate to wait for ferries or where weekend crowds from nearby cities are likely to plug the campgrounds.

One thing you will not find in our campground descriptions is a rating with some kind of system of stars, checks, or tree icons. Hopefully we've included enough information in our campground descriptions to let you make your own analysis.

We've included limited information about campground prices. The price you pay depends upon the type of rig you drive, the number in your party, your use of hookups, and sometimes even the time of year.

Generally you can expect that tent campers will pay the least. Throughout the north the prices charged by commercial campgrounds for both tenters and dry sites are heavily influenced by the prices charged in the many government campgrounds. Usually the commercial price is a dollar or two more than local government campgrounds because commercial campgrounds generally have additional amenities like showers and dump stations.

RV charges depend more upon the hookups used than the size of the rig. Expect dry sites to cost a few dollars more than a space in a government campground, electricity will add a few dollars, and a sewer hookup a few more.

There is one more important factor. In remote locations hookups and dump station use can be more expensive than in a city. Electricity is sometimes generated on site, this can be a costly proposition. Dump stations in remote areas are often septic systems, sometimes everything you dump must be pumped out by the operator and trucked away. This also is an expensive operation. We always try to dump our tanks in a town with a city sewer system, it's better for the environment and it saves everyone a lot of trouble and money.

We've grouped the campground fees into the following categories in our campground descriptions:

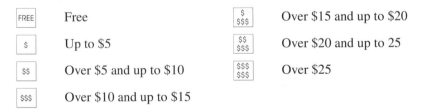

FREE	Free		$ / $$$	Over $15 and up to $20
$	Up to $5		$$ / $$$	Over $20 and up to 25
$$	Over $5 and up to $10		$$$ / $$$	Over $25
$$$	Over $10 and up to $15			

These prices are in U.S. dollars. They are summer prices for an RV with 2 people using full hookups if available. In government campgrounds the prices are for an RV. Note that in most government campgrounds there is only one price.

You'll find that this book has a much larger campground description than most guidebooks. We've tried to include more information so you can make a more informed decision about which one you want to pick for your stay.

Campground icons can be useful for a quick overview of campground facilities or if you are quickly looking for a particular feature. The following is a key to the symbols used in this book.

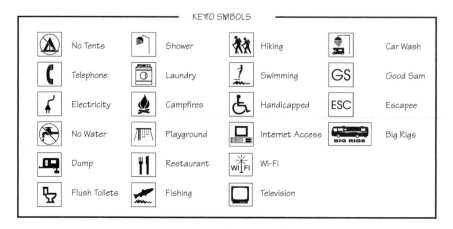

Most of the campgrounds in this book accept both RVs and tents. If the campground is for tents only we say so in the text. If an RV campground does not accept tents or we feel that it is not suitable for tents we show the no tents symbol.

A few campgrounds listed provide no drinking water and we use a no water symbol for them. If water is provided, even if it is posted as non-potable, we do not use the symbol. Most water provided at campgrounds is fine, we don't purify water from pumps or taps unless it is posted as non-potable.

We show the dump station symbol only if there is a dump station. If sewer drains are available we say so in the text. Note that in the far north drains can be a real maintenance problem due to very cold winter temperatures and permafrost, many campgrounds do not have them.

We show a toilet symbol if a campground has flush toilets. If there are no toilets of any kind we say so in the text. The rest of the campgrounds listed have what we've identified as outhouses, pit toilets, or more modern and less smelly vault toilets.

We show a campfire symbol if there are fire pits or if a central campfire area is provided. Many commercial campgrounds do not allow campfires at the individual spaces but do have a central campfire area. Almost all government campgrounds have firepits or grills.

We show a restaurant symbol if there is one at the campground or if one is within easy walking distance.

We show a fishing symbol if fishing is possible within easy walking distance.

We show a hiking symbol is there are hiking trails near the campground. This could mean there is a short nature trail or it could mean that a long cross-country trail starts nearby. Generally we try to say which it is.

The swimming symbol is used if any swimming is available. Since few campgrounds have swimming pools (usually just the few hot springs) this probably means lake swimming. The lakes in Alaska are usually only warm enough for swimming in July and early August, and even then only if you're young or very tough.

We use the handicapped facilities symbol if a campground advertises that it has handicapped facilities or if we identified them when we visited. Provisions provided for the handicapped vary considerably. We advise that you check with the camp-ground operator directly before your visit to determine exactly what the situation is and whether you should reserve a particular space.

More and more campground have modem outlets or computers for email access. Our symbol for internet access means the campground offers one or the other.

We have included a Wi-Fi symbol if wireless internet is available. Usually there is an extra charge for this.

The television symbol means that television connections are available at some sites. This may be satellite or cable.

The vehicle wash symbol means that there is an area for washing rigs. This may be a pressure system or just a hose.

Many campgrounds give a Good Sam discount. We note them if they advertise that they do. The discount is 10%.

A few campgrounds give an Escapee discount to members of the Escapee RV Club. We note them if they are listed in the Escapee Discount Directory. The discount is usually 15% if the camping fee is over $10.

Our big rig symbol is included if the campground is suitable for rigs to 40 feet. Often we expand upon this in the text.

GPS (Global Positioning System) Coordinates

You will note that for some of the campgrounds we have provided a GPS Location. GPS is a new navigation tool that uses signals from satellites. For less than $150 you can now buy a hand-held receiver that will give you your latitude, longitude, and ap-proximate altitude anywhere in the world. You can also enter the coordinates we have given for the campgrounds in this book into the receiver and it will tell you exactly where the campground lies in relation to your position. If our maps and descriptions just don't lead you to the campground you can fall back on the GPS information.

If you don't have a GPS receiver already you certainly don't need to go out and buy one to use this book. On the other hand, if you do have one bring it along. We expect that GPS will actually be installed in many vehicles during the next few years so we thought we'd get a jump on things. If you are finding that our readings are not entirely accurate you should check to see which Map Datum your machine is set to use. The coordinates in this book are based upon the World Geodetic System 1984 (WGS 84) datum.

Finally, if you are going to go on a hike from the campground and use the GPS as a tool to help you return **do not use** our readings. Take your own reading before leav-ing the campground to ensure accuracy.

Dump Stations

At the end of each chapter we have included a listing of dump stations that are not located in campgrounds. Some of the information comes from information provided from government organizations and from lists obtained from gasoline distributors.

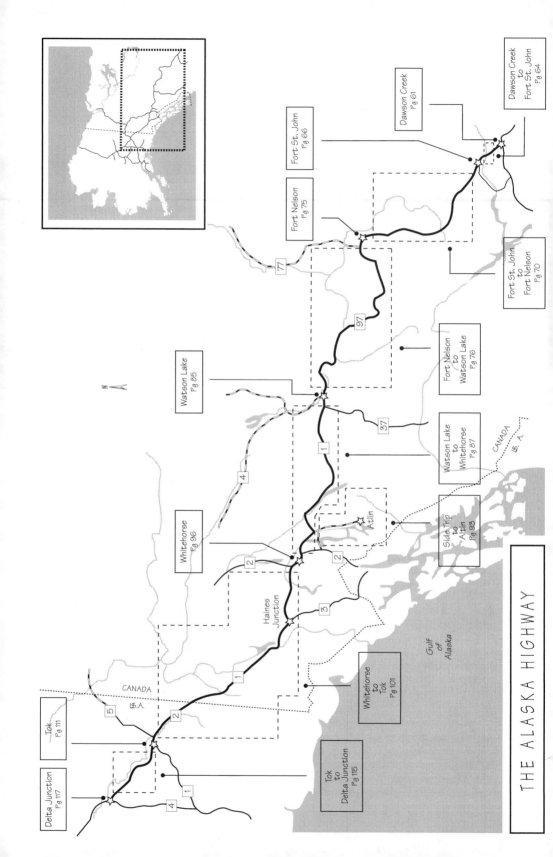

THE ALASKA HIGHWAY

Dawson Creek to Fort St. John Pg 64

Dawson Creek Pg 61

Fort St. John Pg 66

Fort Nelson Pg 75

Fort St. John to Fort Nelson Pg 70

Fort Nelson to Watson Lake Pg 76

Watson Lake Pg 85

Watson Lake to Whitehorse Pg 87

Side Trip to Atlin Pg 93

Whitehorse Pg 96

Whitehorse to Tok Pg 101

Tok Pg 111

Tok to Delta Junction Pg 115

Delta Junction Pg 117

Atlin

Haines Junction

CANADA
U.S.A.

Gulf of Alaska

N

Chapter 4

The Alaska Highway

INTRODUCTION

For many years the Alaska Highway (the Alcan) has held a special place in the hearts of adventurous highway travelers. This major highway was constructed through almost unexplored wilderness during World War II. It opened a huge and fascination territory—Alaska, the Yukon, and Northern British Columbia—to anyone who could climb into a vehicle and drive north.

The Alaska Highway begins at Dawson Creek in British Columbia. Just getting to Dawson Creek is an adventure. From Seattle the driving distance to Dawson Creek is 815 miles, from Great Falls, Montana it is 867 miles. Information about the routes to Dawson Creek could fill several guidebooks, unfortunately there is not room for it here. For the most part you can be confident that the roads leading north to Dawson Creek are paved and services easy to find.

We'll start our coverage at Dawson Creek. Some folks may decide to follow one of the other routes north: the Cassiar Highway (Chapter 5 in this book) or the ferry routes through the Inside Passage (Chapter 13 in this book).

Highlights

The Alcan (Alaska-Canada Highway), now called the **Alaska Highway**, is itself an interesting destination. Construction of the highway from Dawson Creek to Tok, Alaska was undertaken during World War II to provide a supply route to Alaska in case the Japanese gained control of water routes. Construction was begun in 1942 with little prior exploration of some remote portions of the route chosen. Planned routings were only approximations and construction techniques to deal with permafrost and swampy terrain had not been developed. U.S. Army constructions crews punched a narrow, rough, and almost impassible road through the mountains and tundra from Dawson Creek to Delta, Alaska in eight months. Since that time crews have been continuously upgrading the road. Anyone planning to drive the Alaska Highway should read one of the many books that have been written about the project. We recommend one in the *Travel Library* section in Chapter 2.

As you travel along the highway you will find many information boards commemorating events during road construction. You'll also see many Historic Signposts with original Alcan mileages on them. They are of little use today for navigation since road mileage has changed, but they designate important spots along the road. There are also several museums covering the highway construction along the route, including ones in Dawson Creek, Fort Nelson, Watson Lake, and Whitehorse.

There are seven small towns along the Alaska Highway. These are **Dawson Creek**, **Fort St. John/Taylor**, **Fort Nelson**, **Watson Lake**, **Whitehorse**, **Tok**, and **Delta Junction**. These towns are the best place to buy provisions and get repair work done if you need it. They also have interesting histories, museums, and good campgrounds. Each is covered in more detail later in this chapter.

You'll find miles and miles of virtually empty country along the highway but the section of road through the Rocky Mountains between Fort Nelson and Watson Lake stands out. There are two British Columbia Provincial Parks along this segment of road: **Stone Mountain Provincial Park** and **Muncho Lake Provincial Park**. Both have campgrounds and offer opportunities to view wildlife including caribou and stone sheep.

At Km 765 of the highway, about 213 km (132 miles) south of Watson Lake is **Liard Hot Springs**. Liard has two pools where you can soak in the hot spring water (no sulfur) with changing rooms and benches in the natural pools. The lower pool is particularly nice with a pebbled bottom and benches in the water. There's also a provincial campground and several commercial campgrounds nearby. Seems like everyone traveling the highway stops here for at least a quick dip.

As you travel along the highway keep an eye peeled for wildlife. Moose are likely to burst from the underbrush and cross in front of you. If one does, watch out. There's likely to be a calf or two following along behind. Bears are often spotted feeding in the cleared areas along the road. This isn't a zoo so animals aren't guaranteed, but if you keep your eyes open you will see them.

The Road and Fuel

The Alaska Highway stretches 1,300 miles from Dawson Creek in British Columbia to Delta Junction in Alaska. Along the way it crosses the Rocky Mountains and passes through the province of British Columbia the Yukon Territory and the state of Alaska. The road is without a doubt one of the most interesting in North America. It is also very long.

FUEL PRICE COMPARISON - RECORDED AUGUST 2004

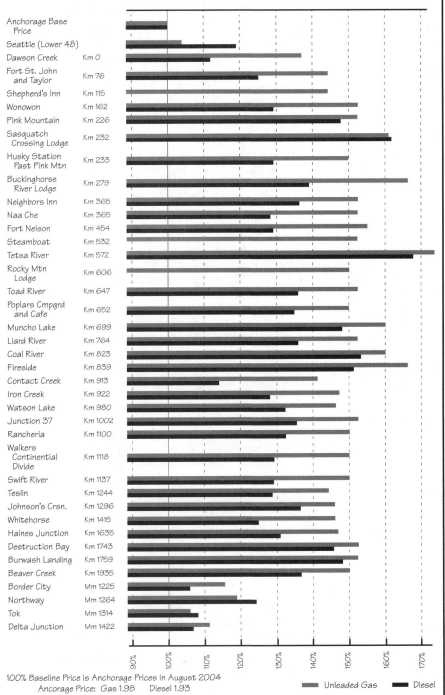

Anchorage Base Price		
Seattle (Lower 48)		
Dawson Creek	Km 0	
Fort St. John and Taylor	Km 76	
Shepherd's Inn	Km 115	
Wonowon	Km 162	
Pink Mountain	Km 226	
Sasquatch Crossing Lodge	Km 232	
Husky Station Past Pink Mtn	Km 233	
Buckinghorse River Lodge	Km 279	
Neighbors Inn	Km 365	
Naa Che	Km 365	
Fort Nelson	Km 454	
Steamboat	Km 532	
Tetsa River	Km 572	
Rocky Mtn Lodge	Km 606	
Toad River	Km 647	
Poplars Cmpgrd and Cafe	Km 652	
Muncho Lake	Km 699	
Liard River	Km 764	
Coal River	Km 823	
Fireside	Km 839	
Contact Creek	Km 913	
Iron Creek	Km 922	
Watson Lake	Km 980	
Junction 37	Km 1002	
Rancheria	Km 1100	
Walkers Continential Divide	Km 1118	
Swift River	Km 1137	
Teslin	Km 1244	
Johnson's Crsn.	Km 1296	
Whitehorse	Km 1415	
Haines Junction	Km 1635	
Destruction Bay	Km 1743	
Burwash Landing	Km 1759	
Beaver Creek	Km 1935	
Border City	Mm 1225	
Northway	Mm 1264	
Tok	Mm 1314	
Delta Junction	Mm 1422	

100% Baseline Price is Anchorage Prices in August 2004
Ancorage Price: Gas 1.98   Diesel 1.93

Unleaded Gas   Diesel

The entire length of the Alaska Highway is now paved. This doesn't mean you won't find stretches of gravel, however. The road is constantly being upgraded and repaired and you are bound to run into patches of dirt and gravel. All road work has to be done during the summer when temperatures are above freezing so road work follows the same pattern each year. As early as possible in the spring (May) sections of road are torn up and work commences. By fall the road has to be ready for winter so by late August and September many of the places that were bad in the early summer have been finished or temporarily surfaced. We think that early September is the best time for campers to travel the highway.

Mileage markings along the highway can be confusing. The road was originally marked in miles. It was longer then, between Dawson Creek and the Alaska border the road was originally 1,971 kilometers (1,222 miles) long, now it is about 53 kilometers (33 miles) shorter. Many establishments along the road still use their original milepost locations as an address (they're usually called Historic Miles) and there are occasional historic milepost monuments along the road for tourism purposes.

Today the entire Canadian portion of the road has been re-posted with kilometer markers. In both British Columbia and the Yukon the kilometer posts are located on the right side of the road going north. In British Columbia there's one every 5 kilometers, in the Yukon they're usually every two kilometers. Only recently were the Yukon mileposts brought into agreement with those in B.C. so you'll find some confusion in older guides. In Champagne near Haines Junction the system falls apart a little, extensive recent roadwork from there to the Alaska border means that many kilometer posts are missing and none have been upgraded to agree with those farther south in the Yukon and British Columbia. We use actual kilometer post readings to designate locations of Canadian campgrounds in this chapter. Sometimes the Historic Mile figure is also given because it's the mailing address used by many establishments.

At the Alaska border things change. Alaska uses miles, of course. They also use the original Alcan mileage as a starting point at the border. Although the border is now about 1,189 miles from Dawson Creek mileposts at the Alaska border start at 1,222. We use mile markings that conform to those you will find along the road. In a few cases they may be slightly different than the actual driving distance since there has also been some straightening of the road in Alaska and mileposts are not always updated.

As a practical matter you'll find that all of this makes little difference. When you are on the road it is easy to find things you are watching for, a few kilometers or miles one way or another will make less difference than you might think.

 ### Fishing

One of the joys of traveling on the Alaska Highway is the many opportunities to wet a line at the many rivers and streams that cross the highway. Often fishing isn't great near the road but a little hike will change your luck.

Remember, along this highway you are in British Columbia, the Yukon Territory, and Alaska. Each has its own licensing requirements and regulations. Also, in Canada the fishing is good in several of the parks you pass through, and they have their own requirements. See the Fishing section of Chapter 2 in this book for more information.

Between Dawson Creek and Fort Nelson try the **Peace River** (Km 55) for grayling and Dollies; **Charlie Lake** (Km 81) for walleye, and perch; the **Sikanni Chief River** (Km 256) for grayling, northern pike, and Dollies; the **Buckinghorse River** (Km 279) for grayling; **Beaver Creek** (Km 328); and the **Prophet River** (Km 349) for Dollies and grayling.

From Fort Nelson to Watson Lake try the **Tetsa River** (Km 551) for grayling and Dollies; **Summit Lake** (Km 598) for lake trout, rainbows, and grayling; **115 Creek** and **MacDonald Creek** (Km 615) for grayling and Dollies; **MacDonald River** (Km 628) for grayling and Dollies; **Racing River** (Km 641) for Dollies and grayling; **Toad River** (Km 672) for grayling and Dollies; **Muncho Lake** (Km 701) for lake trout, rainbows, Dollies, and grayling; the **Trout River** (Km 733) for grayling; the **Liard River** (Km 763) for northern pike, grayling and Dollies; **Iron Creek Lake** (Km 922) for stocked rainbows; **Hyland River** (Km 937) for lake trout, grayling and Dollies; and finally, **Watson Lake** for lake trout and grayling.

From Watson Lake to Whitehorse are the **Upper Liard River** (Km 991) for grayling and Dollies; the **Rancheria River** (Km 1,063) for grayling and Dollies; the **Swift River** (Km 1,137) for grayling; **Morley Lake and River** (Km 1,204) for lake trout, northern pike, and grayling; **Teslin Lake** (Km 1,244) for lake trout, grayling and northern pike; the **Teslin River at Johnson's Crossing** (Km 1,296) for lake trout, northern pike, and grayling; **Squanga Lake** (Km 1,316) for northern pike, grayling, whitefish, and lake trout and nearby Salmo Lake is stocked with rainbows; **Marsh Lake** (Km 1,370) for lake trout, northern pike, and grayling; and **Wolf Creek** (Km 1,408) for grayling. Several lakes near Whitehorse are stocked with rainbows including the Hidden Lakes and Chadden Lake.

Between Whitehorse and Tok try Pine Lake (Km 1,628) for lake trout, grayling and pike; huge **Kluane Lake** (from Km 1,693 to Km 1,780) for lake trout, grayling, and northern pike; **Edith Creek** (Km 1,844) for grayling; **Pickhandle Lake** (Km 1,865) for lake trout, grayling, and Dollies; **Deadman Lake** (Mile 1,249) for northern pike; and **Moose Creek and the Chisana River** on the Northway Road (from Mile 1,264) for northern pike.

 ### Hiking and Mountain Biking

We think that the best hiking along the Alaska Highway is in Canada's **Kluane National Park** near Haines Junction. The Kluane National Park Visitor's Center (PO Box 5495, Haines Junction, Y.T., YOB 1L0; (867) 634-2345) is in Haines Junction and has maps and information as well as hiking guidebooks. There's also a visitor's center farther north at Sheep Mountain (Km 1,707) at the south end of Kluane Lake. You must sign in and out at a visitor center or by phone when hiking at Kluane so the rangers know who is out in the park. Some good trails are the 85-km **Cottonwood Trail** from the Kathleen Lake Campground (See Chapter 12 - *Skagway and Haines*) back to the road at Dezadeash Lodge near Dezadeash Lake; the 15-km **Auriol Loop Trail** from 6 km south of Haines Junction on the Haines Highway (Km 239); the 24-km **Alsek Pass Trail** from near the Bear Creek Lodge at Km 1,646 of the Alaska Highway, and the **Slim River Trails** near Kluane Lake that start near the Sheep Mountain Visitor Center at Km 1,707 of the Alaska

Highway. Many of these trails are mining trails or roads leading to old remote mining sites.

Wildlife Viewing

As you head north from Dawson Creek on the highway you should begin to get into the habit of actively watching for wildlife. Most of the north is not a zoo or park with large numbers of animals waiting near the roadside for you to happen by and see them. On the other hand, there are many more animals than most people see, it is quite easy to drive right by and miss them.

You may have a chance to try your spotting skills early in the trip. If it is July watch the bushes in the cleared area back to the tree line along the road. Between Fort St. John and Fort Nelson there are often bears, sometimes grizzlies, feeding there. Most people don't notice them.

In **Stone Mountain Provincial Park** near Summit Lake at Km 597 caribou and stone sheep are often present.

Near **Muncho Lake** at about Km 727 there are often stone sheep on the road, there is a mineral lick nearby. If you follow the short trail to the lick your chance of spotting animals is even better.

In Kluane National Park at Km 1,707 at the south end of Kluane Lake Dall sheep are often visible on **Sheep Mountain**. There's a visitor center there with a viewing scope. The sheep are in the area in the spring and fall.

THE ORIGINAL MILE "0" SIGN AT THE START OF THE ALASKA HIGHWAY

THE ALASKA HIGHWAY

THE ROUTES, TOWNS AND CAMPGROUNDS

DAWSON CREEK
Population 13,000, Elevation 2,200 feet

Dawson Creek is the kick-off point for a drive up the Alaska Highway. Don't confuse this town with Dawson City, the gold rush town located on the Yukon River north of Whitehorse. Dawson Creek is well equipped to provide groceries and vehicle supplies. This might be a good place to have any vehicle modifications done in preparation for gravel farther north, see *Vehicle Preparation* in Chapter 2. Don't be deceived by the small population figure above, Dawson Creek really serves as an important services town in the agricultural Peace River Block with a population of over 50,000 people.

You'll want to visit the **Dawson Creek Visitor Information Centre** (900 Alaska Avenue, Dawson Creek, B.C., V1G 4T6; 250 782-9595) for information about sights and campgrounds north along the highway. It is located near the intersection of Highway 49 and Highway 2 near the center of town. They can also give you information about road conditions farther north. It is in a complex called the NAR (Northern Alberta Railway) Park which also houses the **Dawson Creek Station Museum** which concentrates on the agricultural history of the area and the Alcan. They have an excellent film of the building of the Alaska Highway, a good introduction. In the same

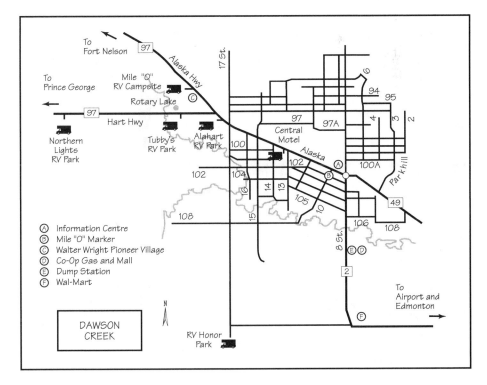

complex is the **Dawson Creek Art Gallery**. In the parking lot is the Mile Zero Cairn, claimed to be the true Mile 0 of the Alaska Highway. You're probably more familiar with the second Mile 0 Marker in town, it's a short two-block stroll away. You want to take a photo of each before mounting your expedition north.

If you have a little more time in Dawson Creek you might want to visit the **Walter Wright Pioneer Village** at the **Mile 0 Rotary Park**, there are historic buildings from before the highway was constructed. The park is located near the intersection of the Hart and Alaska Highways.

Dawson Creek hosts the Fall Fair Exhibition and Pro Rodeo about the middle of August.

There are six campgrounds in Dawson Creek and many more north as far as Fort St. John. Dawson Creek's shopping malls are located off Highway 2, the road that leaves Dawson City to the south toward Grand Prairie and Edmonton.

Dawson Creek Campgrounds

MILE O RV CAMPSITE (CITY OF DAWSON CREEK)

Address: 900 Alaska Avenue (PO Box 2383),
                 Dawson Creek, B. C. V1G 4T9
Telephone: (250) 782-2590   **Fax:**   (250) 782-1479
Email: mile0campground@aol.com
Website: www.citydirect.ca/mile0

GPS Location: N 55° 46' 12.1", W 120° 15' 39.5"

We think that this may be the nicest campground in Dawson Creek. Since it's a city-owned campground its attractiveness at any given time depends greatly upon the quality of the management, the folks managing it for the last decade or so have been doing a good job. It's also the least expensive of the larger campgrounds in town.

This is a large grassy park-like campground with scattered shade trees. Camping spaces are widely separated off wide drives and have picnic tables. Most of the 72 sites are back-ins but 5 are pull-thrus. Many sites will accommodate rigs to 45 feet. Vehicle sites have either water and electricity (30 or 20 amp) or are dry, there is a dump station. The combination restroom, laundromat, and kitchen shelter building is well maintained and there are free hot showers. A picnic shelter makes things more comfortable for tenters and there is an outdoor swimming pool (really a cement pond called Rotary Lake) nearby as well as the Walter Wright Pioneer Village outdoor museum.

The campground is on the west side of the Alaska Highway just north of its junction with Highway 97 from Prince George.

NORTHERN LIGHTS RV PARK

Address: Box 2476, Dawson Creek, B. C. V1G 4T9
Telephone: (250) 782-9433 or (888) 414-9433
Email: nlrv@pris.bc.ca
Website: http://www.pris.bc.ca/rvpark

GPS Location: N 55° 45' 58.9", W 120° 17' 27.0"

If you are approaching Dawson Creek from the direction of Prince George this is the first RV park you'll see. It's hard to see from the road but this is a good facility with views over Dawson Creek to the east. It's also the place to stay if you want to have any work done to protect your rig or tow car from gravel hazards on the road.

There are about 70 sites, a large proportion of them are large pull-thrus with room for rigs to 45 feet and slide-outs. Most are full hookup sites with 30-amp service and TV hookups. Sites have picnic tables and grass strips separate them. There are some firepits and also a tenting area. Restrooms have free hot showers, there is a laundromat, and also a dump station and free RV-wash area. Headlight protectors, bug screens, and rock guards are available if you want to gird up for the Alaska Highway, window rock chip repairs are available if you're on the way south.

The campground is located on the south side of Highway 97S from Prince George about 2.4 km (1.5 miles) west of its intersection with the Alaska Highway, Highway 97N.

🚐 TUBBY'S RV PARK

Address: 1913-96 Ave., Dawson Creek, B.C. V1G 1M2
**Telephone
and Fax:**   (250) 782-2584

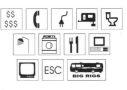

GPS Location: N 55° 45' 59.9", W 120° 15' 37.1"

Many caravans stop here and Tubby's is very easy to spot from the highway. They have a 3-bay RV wash out front.

The campground has at least 100 campsites although some of these are separated from the others and used for permanently located mobile homes. The camping area is a large gravel lot with a little grass, a grassy tent-camping area lines the western edge. There are a variety of hookup options including full-hookups (20 and 30amp). Pull-thrus are available and some sites will take rigs to 45 feet. There are some firepits, the campground has free hot showers and a laundromat, also a dump station.

Tubby's is one of the three campgrounds clustered around the junction of the Alaska Highway (Hwy. 97N) and the Hart Highway (97S). It is .5 km (.3 miles) west of the junction on the south side of the Hart Highway.

🚐 ALAHART RV PARK

Address: 1725 Alaska Avenue,
                  Dawson Creek, B.C. V1G 1P5
Telephone: (250) 782-4702   **Fax:** (250) 782-7302
Email: alahart@pris.ca
Website: www.alahartrvpark.com

GPS Location: N 55° 45' 56.6", W 120° 15' 09.3"

Alahart RV Park is the most centrally located of the major Dawson Creek RV parks, the closest to the central business area. This campground is open all year long, they keep several spaces cleared of snow and have heated restrooms and showers in the motel for winter use.

The Alahart has some 50 back-in spaces arranged around a circular drive on a gently sloping grassy lot. These sites can accommodate rigs to 40 feet but spacing is tight if the campground is full although slide-outs are not a problem. Grass separates the spaces and small trees have been planted. Forty sites have electric, sewer, and water hookups, the remaining ten have electricity and water. Cable TV is also available. A restroom building with hot showers is in the center of the campground and there are dump and water fill stations and a laundromat.

From the intersection of Highway 97 from Prince George with the Alaska Highway head south toward central Dawson Creek. The campground is on the right almost immediately. You might miss it because it sits behind a small restaurant called Rockwells Pub next to the motel.

CENTRAL MOTEL

Address: 1301 Alaska Avenue, Dawson Creek, B.C. V1G 1ZA
Telephone: (250) 782-825

GPS Location: N 55° 45' 42.8", W 120° 14' 17.0"

The Central is an older small hotel not far from the center of Dawson Creek. It has eight to ten full-hookup sites behind the motel buildings at the side of the property. These are back-in sites with parking on grass but with a gravel drive. There are no restrooms available to RV guests so only self-contained rigs are suitable for this campground.

To find the Central drive southeast on Alaska Avenue from the junction of Highway 97 from Prince George with the Alaska Highway at the north side of Dawson Creek. The motel is on the right in 1.1 km (.7 mile).

RV HONOR PARK

GPS Location: N 55° 44' 09.5", W 120° 15' 02.2"

This is a new camping area just outside town. Proceeds are used to help support a local women's shelter.

This campground is a large flat gravel area with no trees. There are about six large pull-thru sites with 30-amp electricity supplied by long cables laying on the ground. No water or sewer drains are available. There is lots more space for parking without hookups. The only other amenities are picnic tables. The campground has no restroom facilities so it is only suitable for self-contained rigs.

To most easily reach the park drive southeast on Alaska Avenue from the junction of Highway 97 from Prince George with the Alaska Highway and the north end of Dawson Creek. After just .2 km (.1 mile) turn right onto 17th Street. Follow 17th for about 3.2 km (2 miles) and just after crossing Adams Road you'll see the camping area on your right.

FROM DAWSON CREEK TO TAYLOR AND FORT ST. JOHN
76 Kilometers (47 Miles)

When the US Army arrived in Dawson Creek to begin building the Alcan there was already a small road north to Fort St. John. Unfortunately there were several rivers along the road with no bridges so the first order of business was to hurry up and get supplies north to Fort St. John before the ice melted.

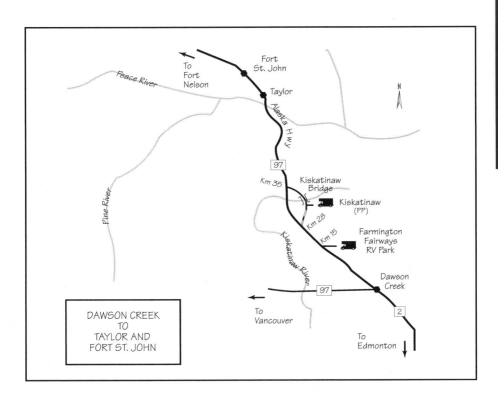

DAWSON CREEK
TO
TAYLOR AND
FORT ST. JOHN

Today the road is excellent and the bridges are all in so the hour-long drive north is uneventful. You might want to take a short side trip at Km 34.5 to visit the old curved wooden Kiskatinaw Bridge. This is the only original timber bridge remaining along the Alaska Highway. The access road is part of the original highway and is no longer on the main route.

Dawson Creek to Taylor and Fort St. John Campgrounds

FARMINGTON FAIRWAYS RV PARK

Address:	Historic Mile 10 Alaska Highway (PO Box 32), Farmington, B.C. V0C 1N0
Telephone:	(250) 843-7774
Fax:	(250) 843-7778
Email:	jenmcdowell@shaw.ca
Website:	www.farmingtonfairways.com

GPS Location: N 55° 51' 29.9", W 120° 23' 45.9"

Here's a one-of-a-kind stop along the Alaska Highway, a combination campground and golf course. The course is 9 holes, and there is also a driving range and a licensed clubhouse. RVers staying at the campground get a greens-fee discount.

There are actually two campgrounds here. One is a 26-site RV campground that has large pull-thru sites with electrical and water hookups. Sites are large and located in an open area near the clubhouse. There is also a camping area with no hookups set in a wooded area nearby. This camping area has 28 sites, some large enough for big rigs, and has picnic tables and firepits. Facilities include a portable-type building housing restrooms with free showers and a laundromat. There is also a dump station.

The Farmington Fairways in located near Km 15 of the Alaska Highway on the east side of the highway.

⚏ KISKATINAW PROVINCIAL PARK CAMPGROUND

Location: 5.3 Kilometer on Old Alaska Highway
loop which leaves the Alaska Highway near Km 35

GPS Location: N 55° 57' 29.4", W 120° 33' 42.5"

The Kiskatinaw River Bridge is a popular sightseeing stop for visitors traveling the Alaska Highway. This is the only original wood bridge still in use and is interesting because it curves as it crosses high above the river. The campground is right next to the bridge.

This government campground offers 28 back-in sites on a rather narrow access loop. The sites are well-separated in poplar and spruce trees and some are right along the river. Some sites are large enough for rigs to about 35 feet. All have picnic tables and firepits, there are outhouses and a water pump.

To reach the campground you must drive 5.3 km (3.2 miles) along a paved section of the old Alcan which leaves the new road near Km 34.5. You'll reach and pass over the bridge just before the campground entrance. There is also access to the bridge and campground from Km 28 at the other end of the loop of old road, but the northern access road is in better condition.

TAYLOR AND FORT ST. JOHN
Population Taylor 1,500, Fort St. John 18,000, Elevation 2,300 feet

You'll drive through the town of Taylor about 21 km (13 miles) south of Fort St. John and just north of the Peace River bridge at Km 55. This is a nicely laid out town with several huge industrial complexes including a gas processing plant and a pulp mill.

Fort St. John was originally a fur trading post known as Rocky Mountain Fort, settled in 1794. It's the oldest non-First Nation town in British Columbia. Today gas and oil are the biggest industries. The largest oil and gas field in British Columbia is nearby.

The **Fort St. John-North Peace Museum** at Centennial Park covers the town's history as a fur trading center as well as the construction of the Alaska Highway. It is located near the easy to spot oil derrick to the north of the highway as it passes south of town. The **Visitor Info Center** (9923-96th Ave., Fort St. John, B.C. V1J 1K9; 250 785-3033) is also located here.

The drive to the **W.A.C. Bennett Dam** is a popular side trip from Fort St. John. Drive north on the Alaska Highway to Km 140 and then on Highway 29 west through Hudson's Hope to the dam. The total distance one-way is 99 km (61 miles). This huge earth-filled dam provides 40% of British Columbia's electricity and forms Williston Lake, pilots who have flown the "trench" will be familiar with the long, skinny lake,

British Columbia's largest. Tours of the power station are available. Another dam nearby, the **Peace Canyon Dam**, has self-guided tours. The town of **Hudson's Hope** is an old fur trading center and has a museum with exhibits related to the dinosaur fossils found in the area.

Fort St. John is just as good a place to stock up for your trip up the highway as Dawson Creek. The Totem Mall is on the right as you enter town from the south and there is a city dump station near Km 72 on the right as you drive north.

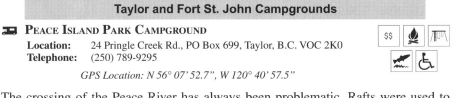

Taylor and Fort St. John Campgrounds

PEACE ISLAND PARK CAMPGROUND

Location:	24 Pringle Creek Rd., PO Box 699, Taylor, B.C. VOC 2K0
Telephone:	(250) 789-9295

$$ *GPS Location: N 56° 07' 52.7", W 120° 40' 57.5"* $$

The crossing of the Peace River has always been problematic. Rafts were used to move road-building equipment after an ice bridge went out during the spring thaw of 1942. Several timber bridges were built and washed out before a suspension bridge was finished in 1943, but this bridge collapsed in 1957. The current bridge looks pretty solid but you might keep an eye on it from this campground.

The campground sits on an island in the middle of the river and is reached by a causeway from the south. The park has large playing fields and picnic areas but also

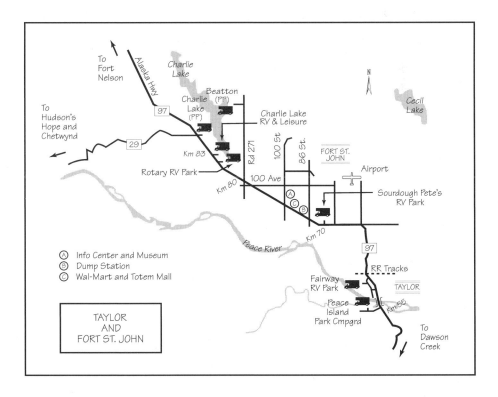

campsites. There are 35 formal campsites plus tent sites. The camping sites have picnic tables and firepits and there are outhouses and free firewood.

To reach the campground drive west along the river on Pringle Creek Road from the south end of the Peace River bridge near Km 55 of the Alaska Highway. After leaving the highway the campground entrance is at .6 km (.4 miles), turn right and follow the driveway through the trees and across the causeway to the park.

FAIRWAY RV PARK

Address:	10034 100th Street, PO Box 429,
	Taylor, B.C. V0C 2K0
Telephone:	(250) 789-3794
Fax:	(250) 789-3722

GPS Location: N 56° 09' 26.3", W 120° 41' 13.5"

The little town of Taylor on the north bank of the Peace River is neat and attractive. Unfortunately the town has a natural gas processing plant and there is sometimes a faint smell of rotten eggs. The Fairway is one of the nicest urban campgrounds along the highway.

There are 16 back-in or pull-thru spaces with parking on gravel surrounded by nicely clipped grass. Big rigs can usually arrange to drive directly into their spaces without backing. All sites are full hookup with 30-amp electricity. The restrooms are beautiful with individual tiled rooms and coin-operated hot showers. There is also a laundry area.

Coming from the south zero your odometer at the north end of the Peace River Bridge. At 1.8 km (1.1 miles) turn left onto a parallel access road just before an Esso station and follow the access road north for another .3 km (.2 miles) to the campground. From the north turn right onto the parallel access road just after crossing the railroad tracks and you will come to the campground in about .2 km (.1 mile).

SOURDOUGH PETE'S RV PARK

Address:	7704 Alaska Rd (S1 C25 RR1),
	Fort St. John, B.C. V1J 4M6
Telephone:	(250) 785-9255 or (800) 227-8388
Fax:	(250) 785-9287
Email:	rfurman@pris.bc.ca

GPS Location: N 56° 13' 26.0", W 120° 48' 15.8"

Sourdough Pete's is one of the newer campgrounds on the Alaska Highway. All of the RV sites are large pull-thrus, a sure sign of a newer park.

The 80 sites all have electrical hookups and water, about half are full-hookups with 30-amp electricity. There are also some tent spaces. Sites are suitable for rigs to 45 feet. The restrooms have hot showers (small fee) and there is a laundromat and small store. At the back of the park is a gazebo with a campfire area. There is also a dump station.

The campground is located at Km 70 of the Alaska Highway (Historic Mile 44) about 3 km (2 miles) south of Ft. St. John. Watch for the big blue derrick with the park sign on top.

BEATTON PROVINCIAL PARK CAMPGROUND

Location: East side of Charlie Lake

GPS Location: N 56° 19' 59.8", W 120° 57' 04.4"

Beatton is not right next to the highway, you must drive around the south side of Charlie Lake to reach this campground which is located on the east shore of the lake. In addition to swimming, boating and fishing in the lake this park has miles of cross-country ski trails that double as good hiking trails in the summer.

The campground has 37 paved back-in sites off paved access roads. Like other B.C. Provincial parks this one offers picnic tables and firepits at each site, outhouses, and a water pump. Camping sites are set in trees and some are along the lake, they're suitable for rigs to 30 feet. There is also a nearby boat-launching ramp.

The paved road to the park (Beaton-Montney Rd 271) leaves the Alaska Highway near Km 80. Head north for 7.7 km (4.8 miles), then turn left and drive another mile to the park entrance on the left.

ROTARY RV PARK

Address: PO Box 6306, Ft. St. John, B.C. V1J 4H8
Telephone: (250) 785-1700
Email: office@rvparkcanada.com
Website: www.rvparkcanada.com

GPS Location: N 56° 16' 35.8", W 120° 57' 18.1"

With a tall chain-link fence surrounding it this has got to be the most secure campground on the Alaska Highway. It has spacious grassy areas between sites and good facilities and is a popular campground, particularly for larger rigs. There is a nearby boat ramp for fishermen interested in the walleye that Charlie Lake is known for and limited groceries as well as a restaurant are available in the vicinity.

The Rotary RV Park has 40 serviced sites. Some are pull-thrus and there is lots of room to maneuver and park rigs to 40 feet. Each has a picnic table and firepit. There are also tent sites. Restrooms are spic-and-span and have hot showers (small fee). There is also a laundromat and a dump station. A pay phone with modem outlet provides internet access.

To reach the campground just turn east off the highway near Km 82. You can see the campground from the highway.

CHARLIE LAKE RV AND LEISURE

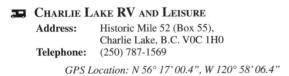

Address: Historic Mile 52 (Box 55),
Charlie Lake, B.C. V0C 1H0
Telephone: (250) 787-1569

GPS Location: N 56° 17' 00.4", W 120° 58' 06.4"

Camping at this campground feels a lot like pitching the tent in the back yard of your house when you were a kid, you'll feel right at home. The campground is near but not on the shore of Charlie Lake. There are 37 sites. Most are back-in RV spaces with full hookups but there are 6 nice tent sites and a few pull-thrus and also some sites with only electricity. A few sites will take rigs to 40 feet but maneuvering room is tight. Small trees provide decent separation. Sites have picnic tables and firepits.

The restrooms have hot showers (small fee) and there is a laundry area. Canoes are available for rent.

The campground is located east of the Alaska Highway near Km 83.

CHARLIE LAKE PROVINCIAL PARK CAMPGROUND

Location: West shore of Charlie Lake near Km 83 of the Alaska Highway

GPS Location: N 56° 18' 21.3", W 121° 00' 14.0"

This large Provincial campground is convenient to the highway and very nice, it has paved access roads and large back-in sites. There are 58 of them, set in a grove of trees. Many of the sites have room for large rigs and there is plenty of maneuvering room. Each has a picnic table and firepit, there are outhouses and a picnic/kitchen shelter and children's playground. A 2-kilometer (1.2-mile) trail leads to the lake and there is even a dump station.

FROM FORT ST. JOHN TO FORT NELSON
381 Kilometers (236 Miles)

The section of the Alaska Highway between Fort St. John and Fort Nelson is in excellent condition. The road skirts the eastern edge of the Rocky Mountains as if waiting for the chance to leave the plains and climb toward the west. When the troops arrived to build the Alaska Highway in 1942 there was only a winter road between

A BLACK BEAR FEEDING ALONG THE SHOULDER OF THE HIGHWAY

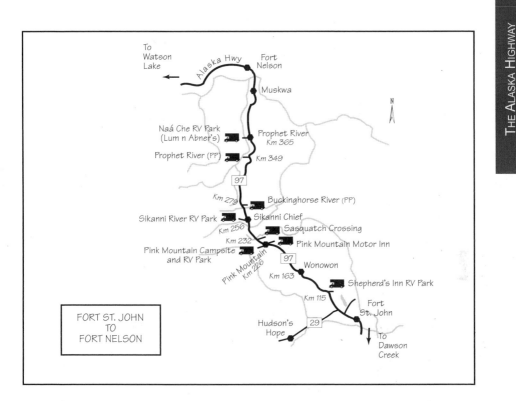

Fort St. John and Fort Nelson and it was not deemed suitable for an upgrade to an all-weather road. Instead the road was moved westward into the foothills of the Rockies where the terrain was better drained and the road easier to build.

During the mid-summer berry season keep an eye on the brush line along the highway. We've spotted many bears, both blacks and browns, along this section of highway feeding on the berries.

Just 9 kilometers (6 miles) north of Fort St. John near Km 81 (Mile 51) is Charlie Lake. There are two provincial park campgrounds here and two private ones. The lake is famous for its walleye fishing. We've included these Charlie Lake campgrounds under the Fort St. John heading above since they are so close.

North of Charlie Lake you'll find miles of empty highway with the occasional tiny settlement. These include Wonowon at Km 163 (Historic Mile 101, get it?), Pink Mountain at Km 226, Sikanni Chief at Km 256 and Prophet River at Km 365. Most of these settlements have little more than a roadhouse and perhaps a campground.

Recently the region from Fort St. John to Fort Nelson has been a beehive of natural gas exploration. Several of the campgrounds have been converted to crew quarters using Atco-type portable units or perhaps just RVs. The campgrounds we list continue to cater primarily to RV travelers. You may spot a few additional places in this section that we do not list where you could spend the night but the traveler's campgrounds provide a more pleasant experience.

Fort St. John to Fort Nelson Campgrounds

SHEPHERD'S INN RV PARK

Address:	Historic Mile 72 Alaska Highway (PO Box 6425), Fort St. John, B.C. V1J 4H8
Telephone:	(250) 827-3676 **Fax** (250) 827-3135
Email:	shepherd@ocol.com

GPS Location: N 56° 31' 27.1", W 121° 14' 00.0"

The Shepherd's Inn is a restaurant, motel, and gas station with five pull-thru full-service RV sites located in a large well-mowed grassy field. One of the hotel rooms is usually available for showers and restrooms for campers. The facility is located at Km 115 of the Alaska Highway. It's closed on Sundays.

PINK MOUNTAIN MOTOR INN

Address:	Historic Mile 143 Alaska Highway, Pink Mountain, B.C. V0C 2B0
Telephone:	(250) 772-3234
Fax:	(250) 774-1071

GPS Location: N 57° 02' 28.3", W 122° 30' 31.6"

The Pink Mountain Motor Inn is a motel, restaurant, gas station, laundromat, and campground. The campground has 16 back-in sites with electric hookups set in spruce trees. Another 10 pull-thru sites are out front in the motel parking lot. Water is available and there's a dump station. Electricity here is produced by generator. Sites in the woods have picnic tables and there is a restroom building with coin-op showers. While the motel has seen better days the campground behind is usually in pretty good condition. We suggest you take a look at both this place and the one across the highway before settling in.

The campground is on the east side of the road near Km 226.

PINK MOUNTAIN CAMPSITE AND RV PARK

Address:	Historic Mile 143 (Box 73), Pink Mountain, B.C. V0C 2B0
Telephone and Fax:	(250) 772-5133

GPS Location: N 57° 02' 23.9", W 122° 30' 34.0"

Behind a log building housing a post office, very small grocery and liquor store, and gift shop with gas out front you'll find a variety of campsites set in spruce trees. Some have full hookups and some are pull-thrus, there are also some very good tent sites. This campground also has a dump station and laundromat.

Look for the campground on the west side of the Alaska Highway near Km 226 across from the Pink Mountain Motor Inn.

SASQUATCH CROSSING

Address:	Box 573, Fort Nelson, B.C. V0C 2R0
Telephone:	(250) 772-3220

GPS Location: N 57° 04' 35.5", W 122° 34' 41.0"

Formerly called the Sportsman Inn, this is a motel and restaurant with a line of 11 large back-in sites along the south side that stretch back from the highway. These are large full-hookup sites (15 and 30-amp outlets), some have permanently-located rigs in them. There are no restrooms or showers available for the campers but if you are self-contained this could be a decent place to spend the night. There is a dump station.

The campground is on the east side of the highway near Km 232 (Historic Mile 147).

⛟ SIKANNI RIVER RV PARK

Address:	Historic Mile 162 (Box 4), Pink Mountain, B.C. V0C 2B0
Telephone and Fax:	(250) 772-5400

GPS Location: N 57° 14' 17.4", W 122° 41' 37.9"

Coming from north or south watch carefully as you approach the Sikanni River because you won't see the campground until you're almost past as you highball down the hill and cross the river.

This campground has about 35 sites along the edges of a large gravel area near the river. Some have full hookups (20-amp electricity) and pull-thrus, there are also tent sites. Sites have picnic tables and fire rings and some will take rigs to 40 feet. There are hot showers, flush toilets, and a laundromat, as well as a dump station. Power here is produced by a generator but it is hardly noticeable and the setting is very scenic.

Sikanni River RV Park is located on the north shore of the Sikanni River near Km 256 (Historic Mile 162) of the Alaska Highway.

⛟ BUCKINGHORSE RIVER PROVINCIAL PARK CAMPGROUND

Location:	Near Km 279 of the Alaska Highway

GPS Location: N 57° 22' 59.0", W 122° 50' 44.4"

The Buckinghorse River campground has 33 back-in spaces next to the Buckinghorse River. They are not separated, this is really more of a parking lot than a campground. Sites are long enough for rigs to about 30 feet. The camp sites are some distance from the highway and are along a creek that has some grayling so this is a good place to overnight. A nice feature is the Buckinghorse River Lodge across the highway which has a cafe, showers, and phone. They also manage this campground. Sites have picnic tables and firepits and there are outhouses and a hand-operated water pump.

⛟ PROPHET RIVER PROVINCIAL PARK

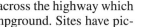

Location:	Near Km 349 of the Alaska Highway
Telephone:	(250) 263-4265

GPS Location: N 57° 58' 16.4", W 122° 46' 31.2"

This provincial park campground is now managed by a private contractor. There are large back-in and pull-thru sites suitable for large rigs with slideouts. Most sites have picnic tables and firepits. Facilities include outhouses, a hand-operated water pump, and a small store at the entrance. Future plans include showers, laundry and sani-dump. The Prophet river is nearby and you can follow a trail down to take a look or maybe wet a line.

Watch for a side road and good sign on the west side of the highway near Km 349.

NAÁ CHE RV PARK (LUM N ABNER'S)

Address:	General Delivery, Historic Mile 233, Alaska Highway, Prophet River, B.C. V0C 2V0
Telephone:	(250) 773-6366
Fax:	(250) 773-6322

GPS Location: 58° 05' 45.4", W 122° 42' 46.0"

Lum n Abner's has been a roadhouse and campground for many years dating back to 1947. It was recently purchased by the local First Nation band and big changes are underway.

Facilities on both sides of the road are under the same ownership. On the east there's a gas station and garage with many fairly run down RV spaces out front, it's called Neighbors Inn. On the other side is the old Lum n Abners, now also called the Naá Che RV Park. Behind it a new RV park has been installed. There are about 34 sites, 12 have 30-amp electricity and sewer with several suitable for big rigs. There were no restrooms when we visited in 2004 but they are planned for 2005. The old lodge building remains and is used as a restaurant.

The campground is located near Km 365 (Historic Mile 233).

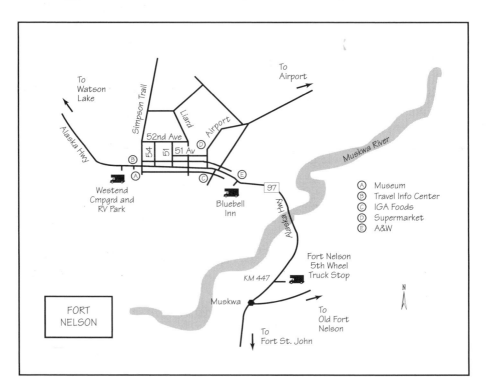

FORT NELSON
Population 5,500, Elevation 1,400 feet

Little Fort Nelson has become something of an economic center in recent years. Before the construction of the Alaska Highway the population of this fur town was fewer than 500 people. Today the town is a rail head and has wood processing plants, a natural gas processing plant, and serves as trade center for the McConachie Creek agricultural subdivision. It's also home to the northern-most traffic light in B.C.

Fort Nelson visitors usually take in the **Fort Nelson Heritage Museum** which has displays about local history, wildlife, and the construction of the Alaska Highway. Across the street from the museum is the **Travel Info Center** (Bag Service 399, Fort Nelson, B.C. V0C 1R0; 250 774-6400 or 250 774-2541). An interesting offering in Fort Nelson is the **Fort Nelson Welcomes Visitors Program** where local residents give presentations explaining their lifestyle. It's held at the Phoenix Theater, ask about it at the visitor's center.

There are two supermarkets in town for groceries and three good-sized campgrounds.

Fort Nelson Campgrounds

FORT NELSON 5TH WHEEL TRUCK STOP

Address:	RR #1 Historic Mile 293 Alaska Hwy.,
	Ft. Nelson, B.C. V0C 1R0
Telephone:	(250) 774-7071

GPS Location: N 58° 44' 36.5", W 122° 40' 40.0"

One of three good RV parks in Ft. Nelson, the 5th Wheel is the most southerly of the three, you'll see it as you approach town on the Alaska Highway from the south.

This is a large service station with a restaurant, a grocery store, and an RV park in the rear. They have about 60 large fully-serviced sites with 30-amp electricity in a large field behind the station. Many of them are long pull-thrus, separated by grassy strips with small trees and with a picnic table at each site. There's lots of room to maneuver, caravans with big rigs often stay here. The restrooms are clean and warm, they're located in the main building along with the restaurant and store. Showers are free. There's also a dump station.

Watch for this campground near Km 447 of the Alaska Highway, about 8 km (5 miles) south of Ft. Nelson.

BLUEBELL INN

Address:	4203 50th Ave S (Box 931), Fort Nelson,
	B.C. V0C 1R0,
Telephone:	(250) 774-6961 or (800) 663-5267
Fax:	(250) 774-6983
Email:	bluebellinn@northwestel.net

GPS Location: N 58° 48' 08.1", W 122° 40' 48.0"

This is a brand-new campground located behind a modern motel in the center of Fort Nelson. There are about 42 campsites, both back-in and pull-thru. These are large

THE ALASKA HIGHWAY

sites on gravel with full hookups including 30-amp power. They have picnic tables and there is one fire pit. A restroom building in the middle of the camping area offers flush toilets and hot showers and out front there's a laundromat, a convenience store and gas pumps. There's internet access in the campground office.

The Blue Bell Inn is on the south side of the highway in central Fort Nelson, it's across from the A&W.

WESTEND CAMPGROUND AND RV PARK

Address:	Box 398, Ft. Nelson, B.C. V0C 1R0
Telephone:	(250) 774-2340
Fax:	(250) 774-2840
Email:	westend@fnbc.net

GPS Location: N 58° 48' 16.3", W 122° 43' 13.9"

Located in the western outskirts of Ft. Nelson this campground is right next door to the museum and across the street from the town's recreation center.

The Westend has an almost bewildering array of sites. There are long pull-thrus, starburst back-ins, and others, some 160 in all. Most have picnic tables and firepits with free firewood provided. All serviced sites now have 30-amp power and TV hookups. Recreational facilities include a mini-golf course and a playground. Showers are available for a small fee and there is also a laundromat, a pressure RV wash, and a dump station.

As you enter Ft. Nelson on the Alaska Highway from the west watch for the Westend on the right.

FROM FORT NELSON TO WATSON LAKE
532 Kilometers (330 Miles)

The miles from Fort Nelson to Watson Lake are some of the most scenic along the Alaska Highway. The road climbs through the Rocky Mountains and reaches the highest point of the highway near **Summit Lake** at Km 597–4,250 feet. The road is paved but narrow in some places and drivers shouldn't expect to make the same kind of speeds that were possible in the Dawson Creek to Fort Nelson section.

When army crews started cutting the Alaska Highway west from Fort Nelson toward Watson Lake the route through the mountains had not been surveyed. In fact, the route had not even been scouted on foot. There was some concern that there might not even be a suitable route through the mountains. Some quick work including getting help from local trappers was necessary. One of the toughest challenges on this part of the highway was building the section of road along Muncho Lake near Km 725.

There are three Provincial Parks between Fort Nelson and the Yukon border. The first of these (heading north) is **Stone Mountain Provincial Park** near Km 597. You cross the highest pass along the whole highway here right next to a cute little campground along Summit Lake. There are several hiking trails in the vicinity and you stand a good chance of seeing stone sheep or caribou here.

You'll pass through **Muncho Lake Provincial Park** from Km 655 to Km 737 of

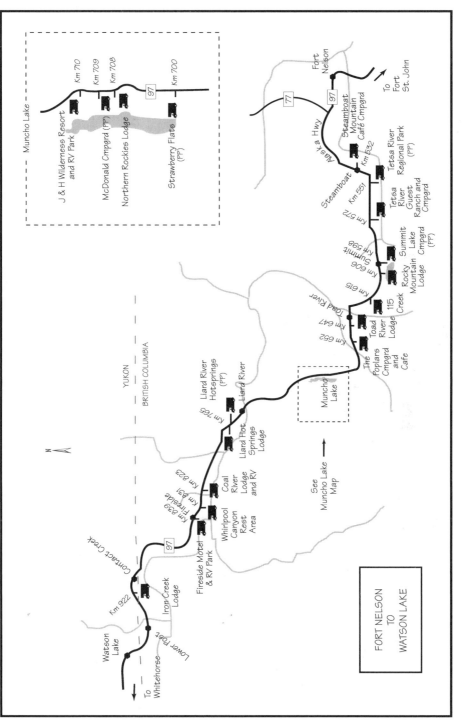

FORT NELSON
TO
WATSON LAKE

the Highway. The road runs along the shore of this long, deep lake for about 11 kilometers (7 miles). There are two provincial campgrounds and several commercial
campgrounds. The lake has huge lake trout and boat tours are available. Watch for
stone sheep along the highway just north of the lake, they are attracted by mineral
licks in the area and are often on the road. There's a short trail to the mineral licks at
Km 727 to view the mineral seeps and perhaps see sheep or caribou.

Liard River Hot Springs Provincial Park is near Km 765. There is a provincial
campground with a commercial campgrounds nearby. The two hot pools at the
springs have temperatures to 110° F. Almost everyone stops here for a dip. There is
a half-mile boardwalk to the pools.

After Liard Hot Springs the road gets better and you can cruise into Watson Lake at a
good clip. A point of interest is **Contact Creek** at Km 909 (Historic Mile 588) where
crews working west from Fort Nelson and east from Whitehorse hooked up when
building the Alaska Highway.

The highway crosses into the Yukon Territory at Km 906. It crosses and re-crosses
the border 7 times before reaching Watson Lake.

Fort Nelson to Watson Lake Campgrounds

STEAMBOAT MOUNTAIN CAFÉ CAMPGROUND
> **Address:**   Historic Mile 351 Alaska Highway (Box 1240),
>   Fort Nelson, B.C. V0C 1R0
> **Telephone:**   (250) 774-3388

GPS Location: N 58° 40' 33.3", W 123° 42' 39.4"

This is a small restaurant with some campsites out back that have a view that won't
quit. Long a popular place to stop and have a picnic or a meal, now there are five
pull-thru RV sites out back with full hookups (15-amp power, generated on site).
There are also more sites along the bluff with great views but no hookups. Tents are
welcome too. Restrooms are limited to those in the restaurant and an outhouse and
there is no shower.

Watch for the campground on the south side of the highway near Km 532 as the road
climbs steeply up the eastern slope of Steamboat Mountain.

TETSA RIVER REGIONAL PARK
> **Location:**   At the end of a 2 km (1.2 mile) road leaving
>   the Alaska Hwy. near Km 551

GPS Location: N 58° 39' 14.7", W 123° 56' 25.3"

This is a quiet provincial campground located far enough from the highway for peace
and quiet but close enough for convenience. Grayling fishing in the river here is
good.

There are 25 large back-in sites, many overlooking the river. This is a wooded campground with separated sites having the normal picnic table and firepit. Big rigs will
find the sites suitable if they exercise care. There's also a tent-camping area. There
are outhouses and free firewood.

The road into the campground leaves the highway near Km 551. Follow the gravel road a distance of about 2 km (1.2 miles).

Tetsa River Guest Ranch and Campground

Address:	Historic Mile 375 Alaska Highway (Box 238), Fort Nelson, B.C. V0C 1R0
Telephone:	(250) 774-1005

GPS Location: N 58° 39' 08.4", W 124° 14' 08.1"

Tetsa River Outfitters specializes in horse-oriented activities such as trail rides, but they also offer some camping opportunities. RVers will find about seven or eight locations where they can hook up to electricity (15 amp, generator on site) and water and there is a dump station. Much more room is available for dry camping and there is an area in the trees for tents and small rigs. Showers are available, gas is sold, and there are even some rooms for rent.

The operation is located on the south side of the highway near Km 572.

Summit Lake Provincial Campground

Location:	Near Km 598 of the Alaska Hwy.

GPS Location: N 58° 39' 04.3", W 124° 39' 03.4"

This campground is located in high alpine country in Stone Mountain Provincial Park. Its site is at the east end of Summit Lake very near the highway. This pass is the highest point of the Alaska Highway, 1,295 meters (4,250 feet). You'll probably think that it seems much higher. Several excellent hiking trails leave the road from the vicinity of the campground and caribou are often present nearby.

There are 28 sites that are separated but since there are no trees here they are not really very private. Road noise is a problem and the weather can be harsh since the altitude is high and this is a pass. Sites have picnic tables and firepits and the campground has outhouses, some sites will take big rigs and slideouts present no problem. There's also a boat launch but fishing in the lake and on MacDonald Creek running by the campground is poor due to the cold water.

Rocky Mountain Lodge

Address:	Historic Mile 397 Alaska Highway, B.C.
Telephone and Fax:	(250) 774-7001
Email:	alcan397@hotmail.com

GPS Location: N 58° 39' 43.3", W 124° 46' 21.1"

This lodge offers free overnight parking if you fill up. There's also a dump station. It's located near Km 606.

115 Creek Former Provincial Campground

Location:	Near Km 615 of the Alaska Highway

GPS Location: N 58° 43' 02.6", W 124° 54' 48.0"

This is nothing more than a wayside along the highway. At one time it was actually a campground but the outhouses, tables, and firepits have all been removed. All that remains are the cement slabs where the tables once were and a dumpster. Still, it is a popular place for RVs to spend the night, people apparently became attached to the place back when it really was a campground. There is room for about 10 rigs to parallel park here. You can fish in 115 Creek and MacDonald Creek and caribou and moose are often seen in the vicinity. A large beaver dam is located on the river behind the campground.

The wayside is completely unmarked, it is just east of 115 Creek bridge on the south side of the highway.

TOAD RIVER LODGE

Address:	Historic Mile 422 Alaska Highway
	(Box 7780), Toad River, B.C. V0C 2X0
Telephone:	(250) 232-5401
Fax:	(250) 232-5215
Email:	toadriverlodge@lincsat.com
Website:	www.toadriverlodge.com

GPS Location: N 58° 50' 48.6", W 125° 13' 54.2"

The camping facilities at Toad River Lodge are much improved over the last few years. This is now one of the nicer places to stay between Fort Nelson and Watson Lake. In the café take a look at the ceiling, it is covered by one of the largest hat collections anywhere.

There are 25 RV spaces, four are long pull-thrus with 30-amp outlets, water, and TV. Others are back-in sites, some with full hookups, some with electricity (15-amp outlets) and water, and some with no hookups at all. Some sites will take rigs to 40 feet. The ones at the back of the property overlook Reflection Lake. Power is generated on-site but noise is minimal, there are free showers, a laundromat, a dump station, a café, and a gas station.

The lodge is located near Km 647 of the Alaska Highway.

THE POPLARS CAMPGROUND AND CAFE

Address:	Box 30, Toad River, B.C. V0C 2X0
Telephone:	(250) 232-5465

GPS Location: N 58° 51' 05.5", W 125° 18' 38.8"

Not far down the road from Toad River is another great campground. The Poplars is a pleasant RV campground located in magnificent mountain country. There are 45 pull-thru sites, some are big full-hookup sites with 30-amp power suitable for rigs to 40 feet. Sites have picnic tables and fire rings. Restrooms have hot showers and there is also a café.

The Poplars is located near Km **652** (Historic Mile 426) of the Alaska Highway.

STRAWBERRY FLATS CAMPGROUND - MUNCHO LAKE PROVINCIAL PARK

Location:	Km 700 of the Alaska Highway

GPS Location: N 58° 56' 50.5", W 125° 46' 10.7"

This is a nice provincial campground on the shore of Muncho Lake. The 15 sites are separated and many are on the lakeshore. All have picnic tables and firepits and many are suitable for large rigs. There are outhouses, free firewood, and a dock. Given a choice between this provincial campground and the one just down the road we'd stay here because it is generally quieter and less used.

NORTHERN ROCKIES LODGE

Address:	Box 8, Muncho Lake, B.C. V0C 1Z0
Telephone:	(250) 776-3481 or (800) 663-5269
Fax:	(250) 776-3482
Email:	liardair@northern-rockies-lodge.com
Website:	www.northern-rockies-lodge.com

GPS Location: N 59° 00' 31.8", W 125° 46' 19.3"

You can't miss this beautiful log lodge on the shores of Muncho Lake even if you aren't looking out for it. In addition to the hotel they sell gas, have a restaurant and bakery, and also operate an active bush-flying operation off the lake out front.

There are also some 30 RV camping sites here. Four are fairly large back-in sites along the lake shore (for rigs to 35 feet) with 20-amp electric and water hookups. The remaining sites are farther back but still near the lake and also have hookups, some full hookups. The lodge also offers flush toilets and showers, a laundromat, and a dump station. A new shower and restroom building is being built just for the RV park.

The lodge is located at Km 708 (Historic Mile 462) of the Alaska Highway.

MCDONALD CAMPGROUND - MUNCHO LAKE PROVINCIAL PARK

Location:	Near Km 709 of the Alaska Highway

GPS Location: N 59° 01' 11.6", W 125° 46' 21.0"

This lakeside campground has 15 back-in separated spaces located along the lake. Some are suitable for large rigs. They have picnic tables and firepits. The campground also has outhouses, free firewood, a hand operated water pump, and a boat ramp.

J&H WILDERNESS RESORT & RV PARK

Address:	Historic Mile 463 Alaska Highway (PO Box 38), Muncho Lake, B.C. V0C 1Z0
Telephone:	(250) 776-3453
Fax:	(250) 776-3454

GPS Location: N 59° 01' 45.5", W 125° 46' 45.5"

This is the caravan capital of Muncho Lake, during July you can occasionally catch four different Caravans in this campground at one time. Like the other commercial lakeside campground here it has a dock and the caravan companies often arrange a boat tour of the lake.

The J&H has about 70 sites of various kinds arranged on a terraced lot sloping down to Muncho Lake. Some are large pull-thrus and there are a variety of hookup options including full, partial and dry sites. Some sites will take rigs to 45 feet. Power is generated on-site and outlets are 15 and 20 amp. Sites have picnic tables and fires are allowed in designated areas. Restrooms have flush toilets and hot showers and the campground also offers gas, a deli, a small grocery store and a dump station.

The resort is located near Km 710 (Historic Mile 463) of the Alaska Highway.

LIARD RIVER HOT SPRINGS PROVINCIAL PARK

Location: Near Km 765 of the Alaska Highway
Res.:   (800) 689-9025

GPS Location: N 59° 25' 32.8", W 126° 06' 10.0"

Almost everyone traveling the highway stops at Laird Hot Springs for a soak, even if only for a short time. The outdoor pools are just the right temperature and a great place to meet other travelers. In addition to the campground there is a large parking lot next to the quarter-mile boardwalk out to the springs and another across the highway.

The Provincial campground is located right next to the springs. There are 53 well-separated back-in sites, each has a picnic table and firepit. Some sites will take rigs to 40 feet. There are outhouses, a hand water pump, and free firewood. While there are no showers you can always take a dip in the springs which have lots of water flow and only a slight sulfur smell. This is a very popular campground, arrive early in the day or make reservations if you plan to stay here during late June, July, and early August. There is also an overflow area across the highway, just a gravel lot with no services. The fee for overnighting in the overflow area is $10 Canadian.

LIARD HOTSPRINGS LODGE

Address: Historic Mile 497 Alaska Highway, Liard River,
                 B.C. V1G 4J8
**Telephone
and Fax:**   (250) 776-7349
Email: lhotspringsl@hotmail.com

GPS Location: N 59° 25' 31.2", W 126° 06' 22.2"

If you are looking for a campground with hookups in the Liard Hot Springs area this is your only choice, and it's not a bad one. In fact, hookups here cost little more than sites without hookups at the springs and the location is not far away. And the lodge usually doesn't fill up as fast as the provincial park does.

There are about 36 RV sites located in a clearing a short distance behind the gas pumps and garage. Seventeen have electric hookups and are pull-thrus, some suitable for rigs to 40 feet. Grass separates the sites. Some picnic tables are available and many sites have firepits. There is also a tent camping area in trees nearby. Power is generated on-site. There is a dump and water fill station as well as a cafe, a small grocery store, gas sales, and guest rooms.

Liard Hotsprings Lodge is located near Km 765 of the Alaska Highway, about .2 km (.1 mile) from the hot springs parking lot.

COAL RIVER LODGE AND RV

Address: Historic Mile 533, Alaska Highway, B.C.
Telephone: (250) 776-7306
Email: drogers@pris.bc.ca

GPS Location: N 59° 39' 28.3", W 126° 57' 10.0"

This roadhouse-style campground has fuel, a cafe, lodging and a campground. There are 12 sites suitable for rigs to 40 feet with electricity (20-amp outlets) and water in a gravel lot next to the other facilities. These are side-by-side pull-thrus with rails

A FAVORITE STOP ALONG THE HIGHWAY IS LIARD HOT SPINGS

between the sites. Restrooms have flush toilets and hot showers and there is a laundromat. The Coal River Lodge is at Km 823 of the Alaska Highway.

WHIRLPOOL CANYON REST AREA

Location: Near Km 831 of the Alaska Highway

GPS Location: N 59° 37' 28.2", W 127° 05' 05.9"

This small rest area is a popular boondocking spot. It has about 8 sites, a couple are large enough for big rigs. However, if there are big rigs already here you'll probably have to back out as maneuvering room is limited. There are no amenities other than a dumpster. One small site is very scenic and overlooks the Mountain Portage Rapids of the Liard River. The road into the campsite is usually unmarked, it is on the south side of the highway and is only about 200 meters long so you can walk in and look around before committing yourself.

FIRESIDE MOTEL AND RV PARK

Address: Historic Mile 543 Alaska Highway,
Fireside, B.C. V0C 1P0
Telephone: (250) 776-7302

GPS Location: N 59° 40' 26.4", W 127° 09' 10.6"

Fireside is a community along the highway with two "Fireside" related stories. During the construction of the highway the name Fireside came from the fireplace here that was popular with highway workers. Years later, in 1982, the lodge here was destroyed by a raging forest fire.

The current rebuilt Fireside is a motel with 12 full-service (30 amp) RV sites. Only full-hookup sites are available. It also has a good restaurant and fuel pumps.

The campground is located at Km 839 of the Alaska Highway on the south side of the road.

▣ IRON CREEK LODGE

Address: Historic Mile 596 Alaska Hwy. (Box 854), Watson Lake, Y.T. Y0A 1C0

Telephone and Fax: (867) 536-2266

GPS Location: N 60° 00' 10.7", W 127° 55' 23.1"

This roadhouse-style facility offers a lake stocked with fish and recently expanded its camping offerings. Note that the Iron Creek Lodge is in the Yukon Territory, the road briefly dodges north of the border before retreating south into BC again.

There are about 50 large pull-thru and back-in sites in a large gravel lot near the lake and out of sight of the highway. These sites have 20-amp outlets and water and there is a dump station. There are also tent sites. The lodge has restrooms with flush toilets and coin-op showers. Other lodge facilities include gas sales, a motel, a small store, and a cafe. Power is generated on-site.

The lodge is located near Km 922 of the Alaska Highway.

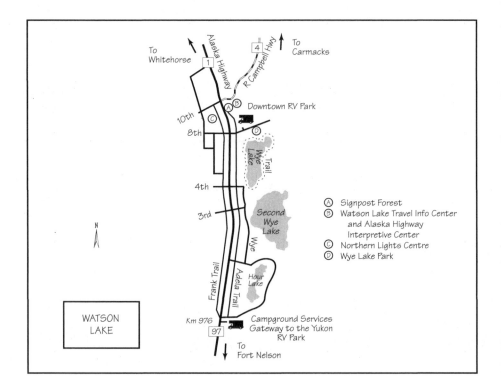

WATSON LAKE
Population 1,750, Elevation 2,250 feet

Watson Lake serves as the trade center for the southeastern Yukon. The little town is located near the junction of the Cassiar Highway and the Alaska Highway. It also is at the junction of the gravel-surfaced Campbell Highway running northwest to meet the Klondike Loop at Carmacks. For travelers on the Alaska Highway Watson is often an overnight stop between Fort Nelson and Whitehorse. Either of these towns is a one-day drive away although driving from Fort Nelson to Watson Lake in one day makes for a long day of driving, especially if you stop at Liard Hot Springs.

Probably the most famous sight in Watson Lake is the **Signpost Forest**. Started by a highway worker during the construction of the Alaska Highway the original signpost has grown to a true forest with over 10,000 signs. You can put one up yourself if you wish. Right next to the signpost forest is the **Watson Lake Travel Info Center** (867 536-7469) and **Alaska Highway Interpretive Center**. The latter is full of information about the building of the highway. Watson Lake also has a new attraction, the **Northern Lights Centre**. This is a planetarium featuring northern lights shows. If you feel like stretching your legs after a long day on the road you might want to follow the nature trail around **Wye Lake**. It's a good trail with boardwalks to let you get closer to the birds.

Watson Lake has two decent campgrounds in or near town. To the west is a gov-

DEEP IN THE SIGNPOST FOREST

ernment campground and two commercial ones near the junction with the Cassiar Highway. These last three are included in the next section. There are also small supermarkets and vehicle repair facilities. For major repairs, however, we recommend waiting for Whitehorse if at all possible.

Watson Lake Campgrounds

🚐 CAMPGROUND SERVICES, GATEWAY TO THE YUKON RV PARK

Address: Box 826, Watson Lake, Y.T. Y0A 1C0
Telephone: (867) 536-7448   **Fax:** (867) 536-7971
Email: watsonlakecampground@hotmail.com

GPS Location: N 60° 03' 00.6", W 128° 39' 17.3"

This is the largest of the Watson Lake RV parks. It is the first RV park you'll come to in Watson Lake if you are approaching on the Alaska Highway from the south. You'll have to drive if you want to visit central Watson Lake, probably the only important disadvantage to this campground. If you want to walk in the distance is nearly 3 km (2 miles).

There are about 140 camping sites in this large campground. Many are pull-thrus with electricity, sewer, and water. Many others sites, both pull-thrus and back-ins, offer 15 and 30-amp outlets and water or are dry. Some sites will take rigs to 45 feet. The campground has many trees and a layout that is a little hard to figure out, it is pleasantly unorganized. When you check in you'll be led to your site or given a map so this isn't a problem. There are quite a few amenities: flush toilets and coin-op showers, laundromat, vehicle wash, a real grocery store, a children's playground, hiking trails, a meeting pavilion, and gas, diesel and propane sales.

If you're approaching Watson Lake from the south on the Alaska Highway watch for the campground on the right near Km 976 (Historic Mile 632).

🚐 DOWNTOWN RV PARK

Address: Box 300, Watson Lake, Y.T. Y0A 1C0
Telephone: (867) 536-2646
Email: selliott@yknet.yk.ca

GPS Location: N 60° 03' 48.4", W 128° 42' 22.8"

For convenient access to central Watson Lake there's no beating the Downtown RV Park. The lack of ambiance here–the park is basically a big gravel lot–is mitigated by Wye Lake which is located just across the road and is encircled by a walking and nature trail. You can easily walk from the campground to buy groceries or visit Watson Lake's biggest attractions: the Signpost Forest and Northern Lights Centre.

The Downtown has about 70 full-hookup sites (20 and 30 amps). Most are back-ins but about 20 are pull-thrus. Many sites will take rigs to 45 feet. There are clean restrooms with flush toilets and hot showers and a very popular large area with hoses to wash down your rig with no fee. There is also a laundromat.

The campground is well-signed in the middle of Watson Lake. It sits about a block north of the highway.

FROM WATSON LAKE TO WHITEHORSE
455 Kilometers (282 Miles)

The Alaska Highway between Watson Lake and Whitehorse is an excellent paved two-lane road with long flat straight stretches, particularly near Whitehorse.

The road actually crosses the continental divide as it gently climbs up through the Rancheria Valley and then descends along the Swift River. It then follows the shores of two large lakes through the upper Yukon basin: Teslin Lake and Marsh Lake.

At Km 1,002, about 21 kilometers (13 miles) west of Watson Lake is the junction with Highway 37, the **Cassiar Highway**. The Cassiar is an alternate route for many people traveling to Alaska and is covered in Chapter 5 in this book.

At Km 1,120 the highway crosses the **continental divide**. The waters to the east drain into the Arctic Ocean, those to the west into the Yukon.

The small town of **Teslin** at Km 1,244 is the only community of any size along the highway between Watson Lake and Whitehorse. Teslin has a large RV park, restaurants, and service stations. There's also a store in the village of Teslin just off the highway. Teslin has a population of about 500 and has one of the largest First Nation populations in the Yukon. The town has an interesting museum, the **George Johnston Museum**, which is well worth a stop. There's also a new attraction, the **Tlingit Heritage Center**.

There are several more campgrounds, both government and commercial, along the shore of **Teslin Lake**. This huge lake has excellent fishing for lake trout and near inlets and near the outlet you will find grayling and pike.

At Km 1,341 is **Jake's Corner**. From here Yukon Highway 8 (the Tagish Road) leads 55 kilometers (34 miles) west to a junction with the Skagway-Whitehorse road (Klondike Highway 2) at Carcross. Just 2 kilometers (1 mile) down the Tagish Road is another junction, this one with Yukon Highway 7 to Atlin. Both the Tagish Road and Atlin are covered as a side trip below.

Watson Lake to Whitehorse Campgrounds

WATSON LAKE CAMPGROUND (YUKON GOVERNMENT)
Location: Near Km 984 of the Alaska Highway

GPS Location: N 60° 05' 23.5", W 128° 49' 13.5"

If you are heading north this is probably the first Yukon government campground you will have a chance to visit, and it's a good one.

There are about 55 sites off two circular drives. Some are large pull-thrus. All sites are well separated with lots of big trees and natural vegetation, they have picnic tables and firepits. Free firewood is provided and there are outhouses. None of the campsites are actually next to the lake but there is a day-use area with a boat launch at the lake. Trails connect the lake with the campground.

To reach the campground you head north on a gravel road from near Km 984 of the

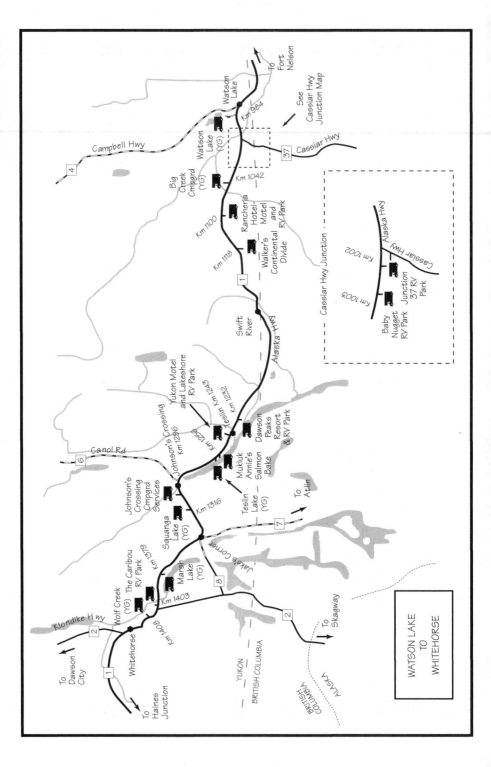

Alaska Highway. This is about 4 km (2.5 miles) west of central Watson Lake. At 2.1 km (1.3 miles) the road bends right and at 6.1 km (3.8 miles) reaches the campground.

JUNCTION 37 RV PARK

Address:	Historic Mile 649 Alaska Highway, Watson Lake, Y.T.
Telephone:	(867) 536-2794 **Fax:** (867) 536-7902

GPS Location: N 60° 01' 27.8", W 129° 03' 40.7"

Travelers coming north on the Cassiar Highway meet those traveling the Alaska Highway at a junction near Km 1,002 of the Alaska Highway, about 21 kilometers (13 miles) west of Watson Lake. On the corner is a large establishment with two service stations, repair shop, cafe, motel, small grocery store, souvenir shop and an RV park.

There are about 70 camping sites located on gravel behind the other facilities. Twenty-six sites have full hookups (20 and 30 amp), some are pull-thrus and there is lots of room for big rigs. There are quite a few trees separating sites and some have picnic tables and a few have fire rings. Hot showers are available as is a laundromat. There's also a free dump station.

BABY NUGGET RV PARK

Address:	Historic Mile 650 Alaska Highway (Box 850), Watson Lake, Y.T. Y0A 1C0
Telephone:	(867) 536-2307
Email:	rv@nuggetcity.com
Website:	www.nuggetcity.com

GPS Location: N 60° 01' 39.9", W 129° 04' 56.8"

The Baby Nugget is a large new RV park, an unusual occurrence along the Alaska Highway. It has been built with big rigs in mind, there are acres of maneuvering room. The whole operation here is known as Nugget City, It includes The Northern Beaver Post Gift Shop, Northern Beaver Post Cottages, Wolf It Down Restaurant, and Baby Nugget RV Park.

There are about 100 RV sites, most of them are very large pull-thrus with 15, 30 or 50-amp outlets. Some have water and fewer sewer. Restrooms are nice and have good showers and a laundromat. There's also a dump station and a vehicle washing facility.

The campground is on the Alaska highway .5 mile west of its junction with the Cassiar Highway. It is 22 km (14 miles) west of Watson Lake, near Km 1,002.

BIG CREEK CAMPGROUND (YUKON GOVERNMENT)

Location:	Km 1042 of the Alaska Highway

This is a pleasant campground next to Big Creek with most of the 15 sites arranged around an open gravel parking area. Any size rig is OK here. Sites have picnic tables and fire pits. There's also a water pump, handicapped accessible pit toilets, free firewood, and a cooking shelter.

THE ALASKA HIGHWAY

RANCHERIA HOTEL-MOTEL AND RV PARK

Address:	Historic Milepost 710 Alaska Highway, YT, Y0A 1A0
Telephone:	(867) 851-6456
Fax:	(867) 851-6316
Email:	bevart@pocketmail.com

GPS Location: N 60° 05' 16.8", W 130° 36' 12.6"

At first glance this appears to be one of the ubiquitous roadhouse-style operations with campgrounds that are little more than an afterthought. There are the usual gas pumps, cafe, cocktail lounge, and motel. However, in the trees to the west is an unusually nice little campground.

Rancheria has about 50 camping sites. Some sites are large pull-thrus. Twenty sites have electric hookups (some 30 amp) and there is a dump and water fill station. Big rigs can use this campground if they maneuver carefully. This campground is laid out like a government campground with trees and natural vegetation separating sites and one of the sites overlooks the river. The restrooms have hot showers.

Rancheria is located near Km 1,100 of the Alaska Highway.

WALKER'S CONTINENTAL DIVIDE

Address:	Historic Mile 721 Alaska Highway (General Delivery), Swift River, Y.T. Y0A 1C0
Telephone:	(867) 851-6451

GPS Location: N 60° 04' 40.9", W 130° 54' 42.4"

Walker's is a roadhouse-style campground that has been much improved in recent years. In addition to the 6 older back-in sites with electricity (10 amp) and water there are 20 new sites behind the roadhouse. Ten are huge pull-thrus with 30-amp outlets (but 10-amp breakers) and water hookups. There's also a dump station, a laundry, and hot showers. Electricity is generated on-site. Walker's also offers gas and has a café, a bakery, and a pub. They are located at Km 1,118 of the Alaska Highway.

DAWSON PEAKS RESORT & RV PARK

Address:	Box 80, Teslin, Y.T. Y0A 1B0
Telephone and Fax:	(867) 390-2244
Email:	info@dawsonpeaks.ca
Website:	www.dawsonpeaks,ca

GPS Location: N 60° 06' 36.8", W 132° 33' 10.4"

Dawson Peaks Resort stands out as one of the better places to stay along this section of the Alaska Highway. They have a very good restaurant, a gift shop, and a pleasant RV park.

The campground has 28 sites, 15 of them with 20-amp power. Several are pull-thrus but maneuvering room can be tight, drivers of really big rigs should walk in and take a look. The sites are separated and situated above the lake. Picnic tables and fire rings are at each site and firewood is provided. A small road leads down to a boat ramp. There is a dump station and hot showers are available.

Watch for the Dawson Peaks near Km 1,232 (Historic Mile 797) of the Alaska Highway.

🚐 YUKON MOTEL AND LAKESHORE RV PARK

Address:	Box 187, Teslin, Y.T. Y0A 1B0
Telephone:	(867) 390-2575
Fax:	(867) 390-2003
Email:	yukonmotel@yknet.yk.ca
Website:	www.yukonmotel.com

GPS Location: N 60° 10' 03.5", W 132° 42' 30.6"

The Yukon Motel in Teslin is a large modern facility with a motel, a very popular restaurant, cocktail lounge, gas station, and wildlife museum. It sits near the bridge on Nisutlin Bay.

Below the restaurant in a large open flat area near the water is a large RV park. There are about 70 sites. Many are pull-thrus and are suitable for rigs to 40 feet. There are some full-hookup sites but most offer electricity (20 or 30 amp) and water, there are also a few dry sites. Satellite TV connections are available. Restrooms have flush toilets and hot showers and there is a laundromat, a dump station, and a vehicle wash.

The campground is located near Km 1,243 (Historic Mile 804) of the Alaska Highway in the small town of Teslin.

🚐 MUKLUK ANNIE'S SALMON BAKE

Address:	Historic Mile 812 Alaska Highway (Box 101), Teslin, Y.T. Y0A 1B0
Telephone:	(867) 390-2600

GPS Location: N 60° 13' 23.3", W 132° 53' 44.2"

Mukluk Annie's is one of the most popular campgrounds along the highway, almost a required stop. This is a restaurant that specializes in salmon. It has a large associated camping area which has free no-hookup sites for those who eat in the restaurant. Since the restaurant prices are reasonable and the food good this is an excellent deal.

The campground has about 26 sites with electricity (15 amp) and water hookups. These sites are not free. There are an additional 100 or so free dry vehicle and tent sites. Many sites will take rigs to 40 feet. The campground is set in trees overlooking Teslin Lake. A dump and water fill are included with the free sites, showers cost $3 but are free to those in the utility sites.

Mukluk Annie's is located on the shore of Teslin Lake near Km 1,256 of the Alaska Highway.

🚐 TESLIN LAKE CAMPGROUND (YUKON GOVERNMENT)

Location:	Near Km 1258 of the Alaska Highway

GPS Location: N 60° 13' 56.5", W 132° 54' 38.4"

This is a government campground set in trees overlooking Teslin Lake. There are 27 spaces, six are long parallel-types that are good for big rigs. Of course there are picnic tables, firepits, vault toilets, a picnic shelter, a water well and free firewood. There's also a playground. Fishing in the lake is good for lake trout.

JOHNSON'S CROSSING CAMPGROUND
SERVICES

Address:	Historic Mile 836, Alaska Highway,
	Johnson's Crossing, Y.T. Y1A 9Z0
Telephone:	(867) 390-2607

GPS Location: N 60° 28' 58.8", W 133° 18' 26.4"

Although Johnson's Crossing is a roadhouse it is an attractive historic one with a pretty good campground. The old roadhouse building houses a souvenir shop and small grocery store as well as a bakery and restaurant. It sits on the shore of the Teslin River near Teslin Lake and offers good grayling fishing in the river and lake fishing for lake trout nearby.

The campground is set in trees with separated sites. There are about 35 sites, many of them are pull-thrus suitable for rigs to 40 feet. Full hookup (30 amp), partial hookup, dry, and tent sites are available. Fire rings and picnic tables are provided and there is also a dump station. A wash house has flush toilets and hot showers.

The roadhouse is located near Km 1,296 of the Alaska Highway.

 SQUANGA LAKE CAMPGROUND (YUKON GOVERNMENT)

| Location: | Near Km 1,316 of the Alaska Highway |

GPS Location: N 60° 26' 49.8", W 133° 36' 08.7"

This small government campground has 16 spaces, one is a pull-thru. Some larger sites in this campground are suitable for big rigs. None are on the lake. If you're towing and want to check the campground out there is a loop so you can turn around. The campground has picnic tables, firepits, free firewood, outhouses, a picnic shelter, a water pump, and a boat launch. You can fish here for pike, grayling, and rainbows.

 MARSH LAKE CAMPGROUND
(YUKON GOVERNMENT)

| Location: | Near Km 1,379 of the Alaska Highway |

GPS Location: N 60° 33' 32.8", W 134° 26' 47.2"

This large government campground has 41 separated sites off a loop road. Nine are pull-thrus and 4 are tent sites. Many sites are suitable for large rigs. There are picnic tables, firepits, outhouses, free firewood, a picnic shelter, and a playground.

 THE CARIBOU RV PARK

Address:	Box 10346, Whitehorse, Y.T. Y1A 7A1
Telephone	
and Fax:	(867) 668-2961
Email:	northof60@polarcom.com
Website:	www.sourdough.yk.ca

GPS Location: N 60° 35' 52.5", W 134° 51' 09.2"

The Caribou is located south of Whitehorse but near enough that you can easily drive in to see the sights. The campground has a wilderness feeling although it's conveniently located next to the highway. It's our favorite place to stay near Whitehorse. This is a very nice campground, run by the owners and friendly, you can tell they appreciate your business.

There are 27 large sites with 30-amp electricity and water hookups. Most are pull-thrus. There are also dry and tent sites, many in trees. If you've always wanted to sleep in a teepee this is the place. Restrooms with hot showers are very nice, they're individual rooms with toilet, sink and shower. There is also a laundry. The campground has a dump station, a few grocery items, a dishwashing station for tent campers and a vehicle washing station for RVers. There's also a restaurant next to the campground that specializes in German and Swiss dishes but also has North American favorites.

The entrance road for the Caribou is located near Km 1,403 (Historic Mile 904) of the Alaska Highway. That's 16 km (10 miles) south of the southern access road into Whitehorse.

WOLF CREEK CAMPGROUND (YUKON GOVERNMENT)

Location: Near Km 1,408 of the Alaska Highway

GPS Location: N 60° 36' 26.7", W 134° 56' 37.8"

Wolf Creek Campground has 37 vehicle sites and additional tent sites arranged off a circular drive in a treed valley not far from Whitehorse. Several of the sites are pull-thrus and many sites will take large rigs. Wolf Creek runs right through the middle of the campground. There are picnic tables, firepits, free firewood, a playground, water pumps, picnic shelters, and outhouses.

Side Trip to Tagish Road and Atlin

At Km 1,296 of the Alaska Highway another road, Yukon Highway 8 (the Tagish Road), leads 55 kilometers (34 miles) west to a junction with the Skagway-Whitehorse highway (Klondike Highway 2) at Carcross. Just 2 kilometers (1 mile) down the Tagish Road is another junction, this one with Yukon Highway 7 to Atlin.

If you are bound for Skagway Highway 8 provides a shortcut. While this road has been only paved for about half of it's length in the past, during our last visit it appeared that much of the gravel portion was being prepared for paving. There are two campgrounds along this road, they are listed below.

The road south to Atlin follows the shore of Little Atlin Lake and then Atlin Lake. It's very scenic and a road suitable for any rig. The first 64 km (40 miles) are decent gravel, then there is a 28 km (17 mile) section of paved road leading in to town.

The town of **Atlin** is a destination in itself, in fact Atlin has been promoted as a tourist destination since at least 1917. In those days visitors would arrive on boats. The route was from Carcross across Tagish Lake and up Taku Arm, by railroad on a 3.2 km (2 mile) line from Taku Landing to Scotia Bay, and then across Atlin Lake. The **MV Tarahne**, which you will see pulled up on the shore in Atlin, was used for this run.

The population of Atlin is about 400 people. This was originally a gold rush town. The first rush was in 1899 and gold was mined here using dredges for many years after that. To get oriented you'll want to visit the **Tourist Information Center** at the **Atlin Historical Museum** at the corner of Third Street and Trainor Avenue (PO Box 365, Atlin, B.C., V0W 1A0; 250 651-7522). Other attractions in town include the **Globe Theatre** and the **MV Tarahne**. You can drive out Discovery Road about a mile to the **Pioneer Cemetery** near the airport, the mining ghost town of **Discovery** is at Km 8.7 on Discovery Road. There is a public **gold-panning area** on Spruce Creek Road. To get there drive out Discovery Road for 5.8 km (3.6 miles) and turn right onto Spruce Creek road, the panning area is 1.4 km (.9 mile) down this road. It is possible to drive out Discovery Road to the dam on **Surprise Lake**, a distance of 19 km (12 miles) from town. Finally, Warm Bay Road runs south for 26.7 km (16.6 miles) past Pine Creek Campground and provides access to several small recreation sites including **Warm Spring** at Km 23.3 (Mile 14.5). Warm Bay Road cuts off Discovery road to the south just a short distance outside town.

Atlin has a campground in town with hookups and another not far out of town, both are listed below. There are also other smaller places with very limited facilities on the small outlying roads that are suitable for smaller rigs. There is a primitive dump station about 4 km (2.5 miles) out of town on Discovery Road.

▄ TAGISH CAMPGROUND (YUKON GOVERNMENT)

Location: Km 20.4 of Hwy. 8 (The Tagish Road)

GPS Location: N 60° 19' 01.5", W 134° 15' 20.9"

The Tagish Campground has 28 sites, there are a variety of back-in and pull-thru sites, some are suitable for large rigs. Sites have picnic tables and firepits and there are outhouses. This campground is located near the Six Mile River channel between Marsh Lake and Tagish Lake, there is a boat ramp.

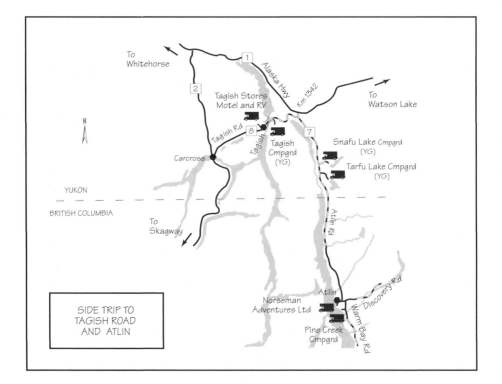

THE ALASKA HIGHWAY

The campground is located on the south side of the highway some 20.4 km (12.7 miles) from Jake's Corner at Km 1,394 of the Alaska Highway. It is just east of the Tagish River Bridge.

TAGISH STORES MOTEL AND RV

Address:	211 Main Street (PO Box 31165), Whitehorse, Y.T. Y1A 5P7
Location:	Km 22 on Hwy. 8
Telephone:	(867) 399-3344
Email:	tagishstores@excite.com

GPS Location: N 60° 18' 28.8", W 134° 16' 21.3"

This little campground is located in trees behind a small store and café set back off the highway. There are nine sites that are suitable for carefully driven large rigs, they have 15 and 30-amp power and a sani-dump and water fill station are available. Modern restrooms have flush toilets and hot showers. The operation also offers motel rooms.

The campground is located on the north side of the Tagish Road at Km 22 in the settlement of Tagish. This is 22 km (14 miles) from Jake's Corner at Km 1,394 of the Alaska Highway, just a short distance west of the Tagish River Bridge

SNAFU LAKE CAMPGROUND (YUKON GOVERNMENT)

Location:	Km 26.2 of the Atlin Road

GPS Location: N 60° 08' 03.7", W 133° 48' 32.4"

This campground has 4 sites next to Snafu Lake. Sites have picnic tables and firepits and there are outhouses and a boat ramp. Firewood is provided. Due to the access road, small sites, and limited maneuvering room this campground is only suitable for motorhomes to about 30 feet or small trailers. Access is via a 1.3 km (.7 mile) dirt road from Km 26.2 of the Atlin Road.

TARFU LAKE CAMPGROUND (YUKON GOVERNMENT)

Location:	Km 32.5 of the Atlin Road

GPS Location: N 60° 03' 48.7", W 133° 45' 15.7"

This campground has 8 sometimes poorly defined sites arranged in pines and aspens near Tarfu Lake. Due to the access road and uneven sites it is probably only suitable for rigs to about 30 feet. There are picnic tables at some sites and fire pits. Outhouses are provided as is firewood. The campground is on a hillside above Tarfu lake and has a boat ramp. The access road is narrow and rough, it leads 3.7 km (2.3 miles) east from Km 32.4 of the Atlin Road.

NORSEMAN ADVENTURES LTD.

Address:	Box 184, Atlin B.C. V0W 1A0
Telephone:	(250) 651-7535 or (604) 823-2259 (Winter)
Email:	vig@uniserve.com

GPS Location: N 59° 34' 09.6", W 133° 42' 13.9"

Norseman Adventures has a campground, marina, and houseboat rental operation in Atlin. The campground has a beautiful situation on the lakeshore, there are 20 sites with electricity (either 15 or 30 amp) and water hookups. Some sites have picnic tables and all are suitable for any size rig. The only restrooms are outhouses so there are no showers. Although the campground does not have a dump station there is one outside town.

When you arrive in Atlin just make your way down to First Street near the lake and then follow it south until it curves to the right, you'll see the campground on the lakeshore.

▣ PINE CREEK CAMPGROUND
Location: Km 2.2 Warm Bay Road

$	♦

GPS Location: N 59° 33' 38.1", W 133° 39' 59.4"

The Pine Creek Campground is a community campground in a forest setting with about 20 sites. Each has a picnic table and fire drum or ring, restrooms are outhouses. It is suitable for rigs to about 30 feet.

To reach the campground drive out Discovery Road for about 6 km (.4 miles) and turn right on Warm Bay Road. You'll see the campground on your right 2.2 km (1.4 mile) from the turn.

WHITEHORSE
Population 23,000, Elevation 2,300 feet

Whitehorse is the capital of the Yukon Territory and by far the largest town with about 60% of the territory's population. This is the best place along the Alaska Highway for vehicle repairs, banking, grocery shopping, and acting like a tourist.

Whitehorse was founded during the Klondike gold rush. The section of river upriver from town, Miles Canyon and the White Horse Rapids, was so dangerous that two rail trams were built around it to portage the boats and goods of the prospectors floating down to Dawson City. This was also the head of navigation of the Yukon, a natural place for a town. Large steamboats could go no farther although other steamboats plied the waters of the lakes upstream. Very soon the railroad from Skagway tied Whitehorse to the sea and cemented Whitehorse's position as the supply center for the Yukon. For a long time, though, Dawson City remained the capital of the territory, only in 1953 was the government moved to Whitehorse.

The large **Tourism Yukon Visitor Reception Centre** is located on 2nd Avenue (Box 2703, Whitehorse, Y.T., Y1A 2C6; 867 667-5340). The town is well supplied with interesting things to see and do. Those aimed specifically at the tourist trade include the excellent **Frantic Follies Vaudeville Revue** at the Westmark Hotel, the **MV Schwatka** tour of Miles Canyon, the **Yukon Botanical Gardens**, and the **SS Klondike** restored riverboat. Tickets and transportation to most of these are available at RV parks. You might also find the town's museums to be interesting. The **MacBride Museum** is located downtown and has gold rush-era exhibits. The **Yukon Transportation Museum** at the airport covers the full range of transportation in the Yukon. Finally, **Beringia**, also near the airport, has displays covering the ice age era when this particular area was ice free and home to woolly mammoths. After all those museums you might find a visit to the Yukon's only brewery to be inviting, the **Yukon Brewing Company** offers tours and samples at 11 a.m. and 4 p.m.

THE SS KLONDIKE IN WHITEHORSE

An interesting hike is the one to Canyon City. Drive to Km 1,416 of the Alaska Highway and follow the Miles Canyon Road .5 km (.3 Mile) to a Y and then turn right to a parking lot. A trail leads to a suspension bridge across **Miles Canyon**. Turn right on the far side of the river and in another 1.7 km (1.1 mile) you'll come to the site of the gold rush town of **Canyon City**. Boats coming down river offloaded here and trams carried passengers and goods downstream past the rapids. Not much remains except the site and the former tram grades. If you enjoy walking you'll find that the hike above covers only part of a well developed trail system along both sides of the river upstream of central Whitehorse, the **fish ladder** on the right bank is accessible from this trail and the float planes on **Schwatka Lake** are also interesting.

Whitehorse has two **golf courses** that are open to the public: Meadow Lakes Golf and Country Club (867 668-4653) with 9 holes and Mountainview Public Golf Course with 18 holes (867 633-6020).

There is enough to see and do in Whitehorse to justify several days of visiting. Whitehorse is also something of a crossroads so you may find yourself here more than once. From Whitehorse the Klondike Highway leads south to Skagway and the Klondike Loop leads northward to Dawson City. The Alaska Highway and this book lead west toward Haines Junction and Alaska.

Whitehorse Campgrounds

See also Caribou RV Park, page 92; and Wolf Creek YT Campground, page 93.

THE ALASKA HIGHWAY

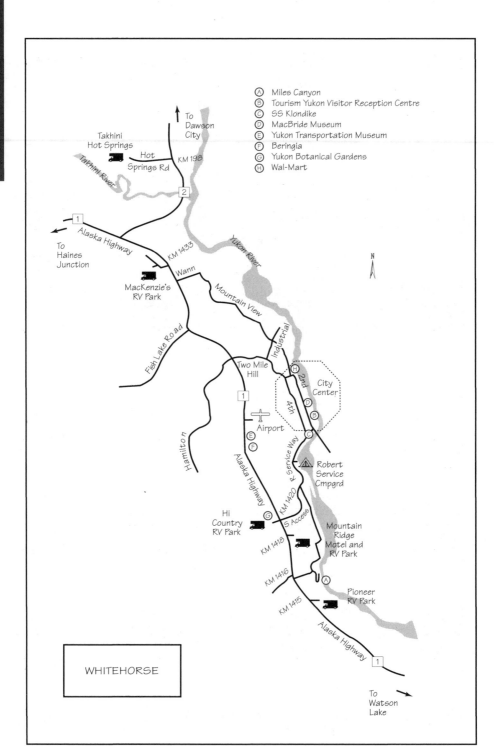

Ⓐ Miles Canyon
Ⓑ Tourism Yukon Visitor Reception Centre
Ⓒ SS Klondike
Ⓓ MacBride Museum
Ⓔ Yukon Transportation Museum
Ⓕ Beringia
Ⓖ Yukon Botanical Gardens
Ⓗ Wal-Mart

To Dawson City

Takhini Hot Springs

Hot Springs Rd

KM 198

Takhini River

2

1

Alaska Highway

To Haines Junction

KM 1433

Wann

MacKenzie's RV Park

Mountain View

Yukon River

Fish Lake Road

Industrial

Two Mile Hill

City Center

N

1

Airport

2nd

4th

R Service Way

Hamilton

Alaska Highway

Robert Service Cmpgrd

Hi Country RV Park

S Access

KM 1420

Mountain Ridge Motel and RV Park

KM 1418

KM 1416

KM 1415

Pioneer RV Park

Alaska Highway

1

WHITEHORSE

To Watson Lake

PIONEER RV PARK

Address:	91091 Alaska Highway, Whitehorse, Y.T. Y1A 5V9
Telephone:	(867) 668-5944 **Fax:** (867) 668-5947
Email:	info@pioneer-rv-park.com
Website:	www.pioneer-rv-park.com

GPS Location: N 60° 38' 58.5", W 135° 01' 14.3"

The Pioneer is a very large and popular RV park located some four miles from downtown Whitehorse. There are about 150 sites with something to please almost everyone. Sites include full and partial hookups (30-amp outlets), pull-thrus, back-ins in the trees, and dry or tent sites. TV hookups are available and there is a dump station. Other amenities include showers; laundromat; small grocery store; a recreation hall; breakfast service; gas, diesel and propane sales; a gift shop; and a RV wash facility. You can get tickets here for most of the tours and attractions in Whitehorse and bus service into town is available.

The campground is located near Km 1,415 of the Alaska Highway. This is 4.5 km (2.8 miles) south of the highway's junction with the southern entrance road to downtown Whitehorse, about 6.5 km (4 miles) from downtown Whitehorse.

MOUNTAIN RIDGE MOTEL AND RV PARK

Address:	PO Box 5211, Whitehorse, Y.T. Y1A 4Z1
Telephone:	(867) 667-4202
Email:	mountain@Yukon.net

GPS Location: N 60° 40' 28.8", W 135° 03' 09.1"

The small Mountain Ridge Motel has 12 pull-thru sites with full hookups in the parking lot. Three have 30-amp service and the remainder have 20 amp. There are two restrooms with showers and a laundromat accessible to those camping in the sites. The Mountain Ridge Motel is located near Km 1,418 of the Alaska Highway. This is 1.1 km (.7 mile) south of the South Access Road junction.

HI COUNTRY RV PARK

Address:	91374 Alaska Highway, Whitehorse, Y.T. Y1A 6E4
Telephone:	(867) 667-7445 or (877) 458-3806
Fax:	(867) 668-6342
Email:	hicountryrv@polarcom.com

GPS Location: N 60° 41' 00.1", W 135° 03' 36.9"

This is a good Whitehorse campground. It is close enough to town for convenience and has campsites with trees and decent facilities.

The Hi-Country has about 130 sites. Some are in open areas without trees and others have some trees separating sites. There are a variety of sites. Large pull-thrus with full hookups including TV are available as well as water and electric back-ins and dry sites in trees. Some sites will take rigs to 45 feet. There are some picnic tables and fire rings. They have good restroom facilities with hot showers, a laundromat, a convenience/tourist shop, vehicle washing facilities, and a dump station. Firewood can be purchased. Bus transportation in to town is available.

The Hi Country is located just off the Alaska Highway with the access road near Km 1,420. This is right across from the southern access road to Whitehorse.

ROBERT SERVICE CAMPGROUND

Address: Box 5418, Whitehorse, Y.T. Y1A 5H4
Telephone: (403) 668-3721

GPS Location: N 60° 42' 04.0", W 135° 02' 50.0"

Whitehorse has a tent-only campground located within easy walking distance of downtown. The Robert Service Campground has 60 tent sites set in the woods near the river. Sites have picnic tables and firepits. There are flush toilets and hot showers, a small kiosk-style restaurant, free firewood, and a picnic shelter.

To reach the campground from downtown walk or drive south along the river. You'll end up on what is called the South Access Road and soon see the campground sign on the left.

MacKENZIE'S RV PARK

Address: 18 Azure Road, Whitehorse, Y.T. Y1A 6E1
Telephone: (867) 633-2337
Fax: (867) 667-6797
Email: tdmacken@yknet.yk.ca

GPS Location: N 60° 46' 43.2", W 135° 09' 49.8"

MacKenzie's is one of the nicest of the Whitehorse RV parks. It is some distance from town, about 10 km (6 miles). This isn't much of a problem if you have a vehicle since Whitehorse does a good job of providing parking in town. This campground remains open all year (only electric hookups are available in winter) so it is a good overnight stop you can count on when heading south late in September or October.

MacKenzie's has about 100 sites. Near the main services buildings and the entrance is a large open gravel area with 80 full hookup sites, many are pull-thrus. These sites will take rigs to 45 feet. Behind these is a treed area with mostly dry back-in no-hookup sites. All sites have picnic tables. There are flush toilets, free showers (for 2 guests per night), dump stations, coin-op laundromat, cable TV, groceries, video rentals, and coin-op pressure vehicle wash.

The campground is located west of Whitehorse just off the Alaska Highway. Turn south onto Azure Road at Km 1,433, you'll see the campground to your left. It is well signed. This location is about 5 km (3 miles) toward Whitehorse from the intersection of the Alaska Highway and Highway 2 to Dawson City.

TAKHINI HOT SPRINGS

Address: PO Box 20404, Whitehorse, Y.T. Y1A 7A2
Telephone: (867) 633-2706
Fax: (867) 668-2689
Email: hotsprings@yknet.yk.ca
Website: www.takhinihotsprings.yk.ca

GPS Location: N 60° 52' 43.1", W 135° 21' 27.9"

For something different near Whitehorse you might try the city's favorite swimming hole: Takhini Hot Springs. They have a shallow but nice swimming pool that is kept comfortably hot, but not steaming, about 100° F.

The hot springs has a 96-site campground. There are 15 sites with 15-amp outlets, the remainder are dry. Most sites are set in a grove of pine and aspen and have decent separation with firepits and picnic tables. This area has some outhouses. There is also an open area suitable for big rigs with no hookups. There are flush toilets and showers at the pool as well as a laundromat, and a snack bar. There's also a dump station and a water fill point. Horse trail rides are offered. Bathing facilities are limited to the pool and showers in the dressing room which have an additional fee, but the hot water feels great and there's no smelly sulfur in it.

To find the campground follow the paved access highway from Km 198 of the North Klondike Highway for 9.2 kilometers (5.7 miles).

FROM WHITEHORSE TO TOK
639 Kilometers (396 Miles)

The Alaska Highway from Whitehorse to Tok is paved, but much of it is narrow. This is where you will meet the nemesis of road maintenance in the north, the frost heave. Frost heaves are the result of building roads across permafrost, and they are virtually impossible for road builders to conquer. These unpredictable dips and mounds mean that you must often hold your speed down, especially if you are driving a large rig or pulling a trailer. The road gets better each year but it pays to stay alert.

This section is where using the kilometer posts gets complicated. At the far side of Champagne, 92 km (57 miles) west of Whitehorse, kilometer posts jump from 1518 to 1574, meaning that the northern mileposts are off by 55 kilometers. Some time in the next few years as highway work between this point and the Alaska border is completed the kilometer posts will be corrected, but until then we'll use the old kilometer posts because they're the ones that are there.

Because this is a slower section of highway you might consider covering it in two days rather than one. We like to overnight at one of the campgrounds near beautiful Kluane Lake.

Almost immediately after leaving Whitehorse you will come to the junction with Highway 2 north to Dawson City. This road, known as the Klondike Loop, is covered in Chapter 11 of this book.

Continuing west the next important settlement is **Haines Junction** at Km 1,635.3. Watch yourself in Haines Junction, if you aren't alert you'll end up on the road to Haines rather than the Alaska Highway to Tok. The 245 kilometer (152 mile) long Haines Highway is covered in Chapter 12 of this book. Haines Junction serves as the jump-off point for expeditions into Kluane National Park. This small town of about 800 has the **Kluane National Park Visitors Center** (PO Box 5495, Haines Junction, Y.T., YOB 1L0; (867) 634-2345), as well as stores, restaurants, gas stations, and RV parks.

From Haines Junction the highway gradually climbs over 3,280 foot **Bear Creek Summit** and then descends to skirt the west side of emerald green **Kluane Lake**. Near the southwest shore of the lake at Km 1,707 is Kluane Park's **Sheep Mountain** visitor center where Dall sheep are often seen in the spring and fall.

Kluane Lake is the largest lake in the Yukon and there are two communities—Burwash Landing and Destruction Bay—and several campgrounds along its length. The lake's unusual color is caused by glacial silt suspended in the water and reflecting the sky.

After Kluane Lake the road deteriorates somewhat because of swampy ground and permafrost. Construction has been underway here for several years and you may run into sections of gravel. On the other hand, there are also some sections of brand-new beautiful highway.

At Km 1,935 is the little town of Beaver Creek. This is the site of the Canadian border station and also of several hotels and a good RV park.

You reach the **Alaska border** at Km 1,967 (Historic Mile 1221.8). At the top of the hill is the U.S. border station and customs. There is usually little or no delay.

At this point distance markers change again. Now you're back in the U.S. and the markers are mileposts again. They start at the border at 1221.8 and continue to count up until reaching Delta Junction, the end of the Alaska Highway.

With recent improvements to the Alaska Highway on the Canadian side you may not notice much difference in the road on the Alaska side. Not many years ago crossing the border brought pure bliss, smooth pavement after more than 1,200 miles of gravel. From the border you can reach the first Alaska town of any size, Tok, in a little over an hour and a half, the distance is 92 miles (148 km).

Whitehorse to Tok Campgrounds

OTTER FALLS CUTOFF

Address:	Box 5450, Haines Jct., Y.T. Y0B 1L0
Telephone:	(867) 634-2812
Fax:	(867) 634-2133
Email:	bbeecher@yknet.ca

GPS Location: N 60° 51' 16.1", W 137° 02' 02.6"

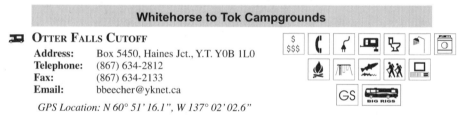

The Otter Falls Cutoff is a combination motel, gas station, grocery store, wildlife museum, and RV park along a section of the highway that doesn't have many other establishments of any kind, including campgrounds. It's a good place to stay if you want to take a side trip to see Otter Falls, 28.6 km (17.4 miles) up Aishihik Road. The road isn't suitable for large RVs and the falls only have water when there is a release from Aishihik Power Plant. There's a schedule posted at the cutoff or you can take a guided tour from the campground.

There are about 50 sites, they offer water and electric hookups and suitable for large rigs, in an open gravel and grass lot next to the store. Additional dry sites are located under trees nearby and on the opposite side of the store and gas pumps. Some sites have firepits and picnic tables. Showers are available and there is a playground. There is also a dump station. A birdwatching trail has recently been added and there is fishing nearby.

The Otter Falls Cutoff is at the junction with Aishihik Road at Km 1,602 of the Alaska Highway. This is 121 Km (75 miles) west of Whitehorse and 33 kilometers (20 miles) east of the Haines Junction.

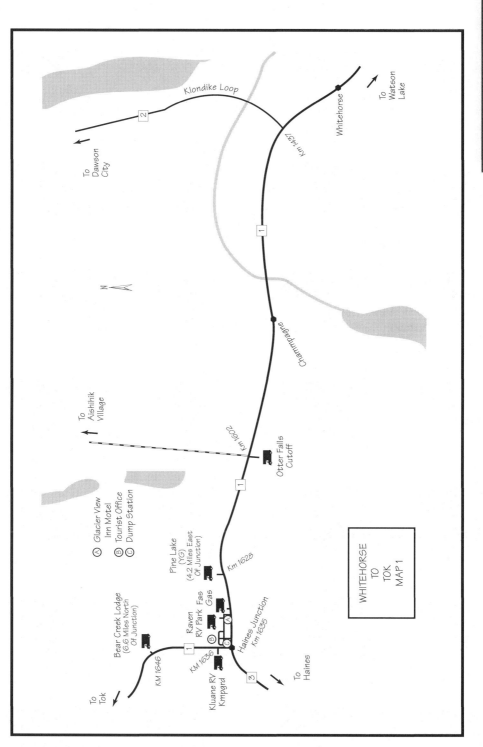

THE ALASKA HIGHWAY

To Watson Lake

Whitehorse

Km 1457

Klondike Loop

2

To Dawson City

1

N

Champagne

Km 1602

Otter Falls Cutoff

1

To Aishihik Village

Ⓐ Glacier View Inn Motel
Ⓑ Tourist Office
Ⓒ Dump Station

Pine Lake (YG) (4.2 Miles East Of Junction)

Km 1628

Bear Creek Lodge (6.6 Miles North Of Junction)

Raven RV Park

Fas Gas

Haines Junction Km 1635

KM 1646

1

KM 1636

Kluane RV Kmpgrd

3

To Haines

To Tok

WHITEHORSE TO TOK MAP 1

PINE LAKE CAMPGROUND (YUKON GOVERNMENT)

Location: Km 1,628 of the Alaska Highway

GPS Location: N 60° 47' 56.9", W 137° 29' 18.0"

This government campground is located just outside Haines Junction, gateway to the Kluane National Park. There are 42 sites here, 6 are pull-thrus, and there is plenty of room for big rigs in most of the sites. All sites have picnic tables and firepits and are well-separated with spruce trees and other natural vegetation. There are outhouses, a covered kitchen and picnic area, drinking water, a boat launch, and swimming in Pine Lake for the hardy.

FAS GAS

Address: PO Box 5345, Haines Junction, Y.T. Y0B 1L0
Telephone: (867) 634-2505
Fax: (867) 634-3834
Email: vandoug@yt.sympatico.ca

GPS Location: N 60° 45' 39.9", W 137° 31' 03.8"

About the first thing you see when you approach Haines Junction from the Whitehorse direction is a Fas Gas station on the north side of the road. They have 23 RV spaces with electricity (30-amp outlets) and water hookups in an open area next to the station. Nine are pull-thrus and sites have room for big rigs. There is also a sani-dump. The price of an overnight stay includes a water fill-up and a holding tank dump. Recently restrooms with showers have been added.

RAVEN RV PARK

Location: Behind the Glacier View Inn Motel
Telephone: (867) 634-2500

GPS Location: N 60° 45' 25.3", W 137° 30' 57.3"

This tiny RV park with 6 pull-thru full-hookup spaces is easy to miss. As you approach from the Whitehorse direction watch for the Glacier View Inn Motel and Chevron station. Turn on the road just east of the inn and you'll see the Raven RV Park just ahead. It has flush toilets and hot showers in a small building near the sites but these are sometimes not available, they were closed last time we visited. Instructions for an unattended check-in are posted if no one is around. The campground is not associated with the Glacier View Inn.

KLUANE RV KAMPGROUND

Address: Box 5496, Haines Junction, Y.T. Y0B 1L0
Telephone: (867) 634-2709 or (866) 634-6789
Fax: (867) 634-2735
Email: kluanerv@yknet.yk.ca

GPS Location: N 60° 45' 09.5", W 137° 31' 16.0"

This is the largest full-service RV park in Haines Junction. There are about 100 spaces, most are pull-thrus and there is lots of room for maneuvering since the campground is a large open gravel field. Full hookup, partial hookup, and dry sites are available, as are tent sites. There are some picnic tables but not at most sites. The Kluane has restrooms and showers (individual rooms) in the main building as well as a small store and laundromat. Cable TV is available and there is also a dump station, a vehicle wash, and a service station with gas, diesel, and propane. A good 5 km (3 mile) hiking trail leads from the campground.

The campground is located at Km 1,636 of the Alaska Highway, about 1.1 km (.7 mile) west of the junction.

▣ BEAR CREEK LODGE

Address:	Historic Mile 1022 Alaska Hwy., Y.T. Y1A 3V4
Telephone:	(867) 634-2301
Fax:	(867) 634-2302

GPS Location: N 60° 47' 47.7", W 137° 40' 31.6"

Bear Creek Lodge (formerly the Mackintosh Lodge) is a roadhouse-type highway stop offering rooms, gas, and a restaurant as well as the RV park. There are 8 pull-thru spaces with full hookups (20-amp outlets) on a gravel area behind the motel building. Quite a few additional rigs can park with electricity or no utilities. There are also tent sites in a nearby area of trees. Showers are available in the motel building as are flush toilets. There is also a dump station. The Alsek Pass Trail starts across the road, this would be a good place to camp if you want to hike it.

The Bear Creek is at Km 1,646 (Historic Milepost 1,022) of the Alaska Highway, about 11 km (7 miles) north of the Haines Junction.

▣ COTTONWOOD RV PARK AND CAMPGROUND

Address:	Historic Mile 1067 Alaska Highway, Destruction Bay, Y.T.
Res.:	(867) 634-2739 **Fax:** (867) 634-2429

GPS Location: N 61° 05' 16.4", W 138° 32' 05.9"

The Cottonwood is one of our favorite stops along the Alaska Highway. It is a beautiful campground in a beautiful location.

The campground must have at least 70 camping sites of various types scattered along the shore of Kluane Lake. The small trees and shrubs that occur naturally in the· area separate the sites, much like in a government campground. About 30 sites have electricity and 20 of these also have water hookups. The electric-only sites are on the waterfront while many of the water and electric sites are pull-thrus. Sites have firepits and picnic tables. The restroom building has flush toilets and free hot showers. Power here is produced by a generator but the noise is almost impossible to hear from the camping sites and the generator operates 24 hours. There's a small grocery and gift store, Gopher Golf (mini golf), a rental hot tub, a laundromat, and dump and water fill stations.

The campground is located at Km 1,717 of the Alaska Highway, about 26 km (16 miles) south of Destruction Bay and on the shore of Kluane Lake.

▣ CONGDON CREEK CAMPGROUND (YUKON GOVERNMENT)

Location:	Near Km 1,725 of the Alaska Highway

GPS Location: N 61° 09' 07.7", W 138° 33' 02.5"

Congdon Creek is a large government campground adjoining Kluane Lake. There

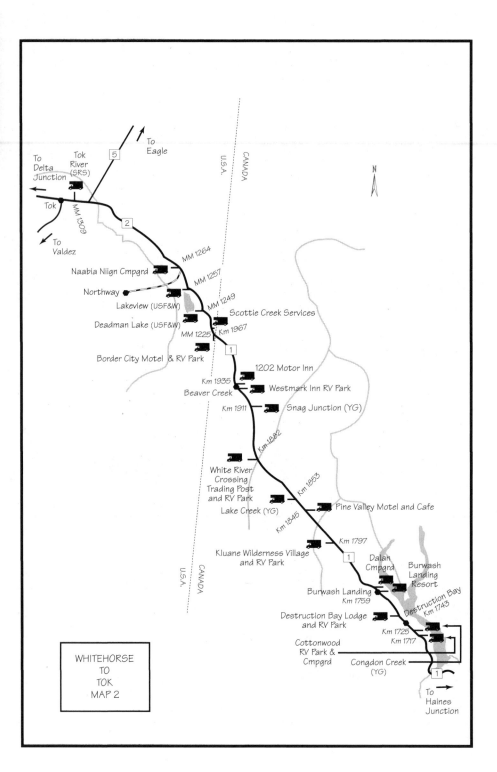

To Eagle

Tok River (SRS)

To Delta Junction

5

Tok

To Valdez

MM 1309

2

MM 1264

MM 1257

Naabia Niign Cmpgrd

Northway

Lakeview (USF&W)

MM 1249

Deadman Lake (USF&W)

Scottie Creek Services

Km 1967

MM 1225

Border City Motel & RV Park

1

1202 Motor Inn

Km 1935

Beaver Creek   Westmark Inn RV Park

Km 1911   Snag Junction (YG)

Km 1882

White River Crossing Trading Post and RV Park

Km 1853

Lake Creek (YG)   Pine Valley Motel and Cafe

Km 1845

Kluane Wilderness Village and RV Park

Km 1797

1

Dalan Cmpgrd

Burwash Landing Resort

Burwash Landing

Km 1759

Destruction Bay

Destruction Bay Lodge and RV Park

Km 1743

Km 1725

Km 1717

Cottonwood RV Park & Cmpgrd

Congdon Creek (YG)

To Haines Junction

1

N

U.S.A.   CANADA

U.S.A.   CANADA

WHITEHORSE
TO
TOK
MAP 2

THE ALASKA HIGHWAY

are some 81 spaces here, about 26 are pull-thrus. They are well separated and set in spruce and alder, many are along the lakeshore. All have firepits and picnic tables. Sites here are mostly large, it's a good campground for today's large rigs. In fact, RVs are preferred during some periods, occasionally the campground is closed to tenters due to the presence of bears. The campground also offers outhouses, free firewood, kitchen shelters, hand-operated water pump, playground and a boat launch.

DESTRUCTION BAY LODGE AND RV PARK

Address:	Historic Mile 1,083 Alaska Highway,
	Destruction Bay, Y.T. Y0B 1H0
Telephone:	(867) 841-5332

GPS Location: N 61° 15' 12.4", W 138° 48' 30.0"

The camping slots at this facility occupy a large gravel lot beside and behind the gas station, restaurant, and gift shop. There are 40 pull-thru sites with water and electric (30-amp) hookups. Many of these are pull-thrus suitable for rigs to 45 feet. There is also space for dry camping. Restrooms are inside the restaurant building and are individual rooms with toilet and free shower. There is also a laundromat and a dump station. Rig washing is allowed at your site.

Destruction Bay Lodge is near Km 1,743 of the Alaska Highway.

BURWASH LANDING RESORT

Address:	Historic Mile 1,093 Alaska Highway,
	Burwash Landing, Y.T. Y1A 3V4
Telephone:	(403) 841-4441
Fax:	(403) 841-4040

GPS Location: N 61° 21' 27.7", W 138° 59' 50.6"

This old-time resort on the shore of Kluane Lake has 10 back-in (or pull-in) sites with electricity (20 amp) and water hookups situated along the water next to a restaurant/bar/lodge. The site is an open gravel area and visitors to the lodge park in pretty much the same lot. Since this is just a gravel lot any size rig will fit although larger rigs will be a bit of a parking obstacle. There's also a nice grass covered tent camping area away from the parking lot making this one of the best tent-camping campgrounds in the area. There are picnic tables in the tent-camping area and one along the lakeshore near the back-in RV sites. Showers are available in the lodge for an extra fee and the restaurant is popular with locals and travelers. There's also a dump station.

To reach the camping area turn in at the sign near a gas station near Km 1,759 Drive down to the lake, a distance of about .5 km (.3 miles).

DALAN CAMPGROUND

Address:	Box 20, Burwash Landing, Y.T. Y0B 1V0
Telephone:	(867) 841-5501
Email:	kluanefn@yt.simpatico.ca
Website:	www.kfnyukon.com

GPS Location: N 61° 21' 56.2", W 138° 59' 57.8"

Although now run by the Kluane First Nation this campground appears to have been a Yukon Government campground at one time. The entry road is mostly unpaved, it's about 1.2 km long. There are 24 separated sites, three are large pull-thrus. Several sites are near the lake shore. There are picnic tables, firepits, free firewood, a water pump, outhouses, and even a dump station. The 1 km (.6 mile) access road leaves the Alaska Highway near Kilometer 1,760.

KLUANE WILDERNESS VILLAGE AND RV PARK

Address: Historic Mile 1118 Alaska Highway, Y.T. Y0B 1H0
Telephone: (867) 841-4141

GPS Location: N 61° 34' 56.2", W 139° 22' 49.5"

This large roadhouse-style operation offers lots of pull-thru sites. There are about 55 of these side-by-side sites, mostly with full hookups. Site are suitable for rigs to 45 feet. There are also some sites with only electricity and water and many dry sites. Power is generated on-site. Showers are free to campers and quite nice. There is also a dump station, laundromat, small grocery store, restaurant, saloon, motel and gas station. This campground is open all year. The Kluane Wilderness Village is located near Km 1,797 of the Alaska Highway.

PINE VALLEY MOTEL AND CAFE

Address: Historic Mile 1,147 Alaska Highway (Box 4832), Whitehorse, Y.T. Y1A 4N6
Telephone and Fax: (867) 862-7407

GPS Location: N 61° 48' 23.3", W 140° 02' 47.1"

This roadhouse-style campground has decent campsites with trees separating the sites and a small creek alongside. There are 41 sites, 11 are pull-thrus with electricity and water hookups. There are also dry sites, picnic tables, and hot showers. Maneuvering room for really big rigs is a tight, the campground is best for rigs to 35 feet. There's also a cafe, and gas. The Pine Valley is near Km 1,845 of the Alaska Highway.

LAKE CREEK CAMPGROUND (YUKON GOVERNMENT)

Location: Near Km 1,853 of the Alaska Highway

GPS Location: N 61° 51' 21.8", W 140° 09' 06.6"

This small 27-site government campground has large separated sites suitable for large rigs, thirteen are pull-thrus and several border the creek. There are picnic tables, firepits, free firewood, outhouses, a kitchen shelter, and a hand water pump.

WHITE RIVER CROSSING TRADING POST AND RV PARK

Address: Historic Mile 1169 Alaska Highway, Yukon
Telephone: (867) 862-7408 **Fax:** (867) 862-7601

GPS Location: N 61° 59' 07.0", W 140° 32' 16.1"

The White River Crossing Trading Post and RV Park offers gasoline and a large RV and tent camping area nearby. Sites are set in a grassy area to the left of the old lodge buildings, some trees provide shade. There are about 12 pull-thru sites with full hookups and 30-amp power as well as many more just offering electricity or no hookups. Some sites will take rigs to 45 feet. Picnic tables and firepits are provided, there is a dump station, and also hot showers. The campground offers a salmon and buffalo barbeque, if you attend you get free overnight no-hookup parking.

The campground is located at Km 1882 of the Alaska Highway.

⛺ SNAG JUNCTION CAMPGROUND (YUKON GOVERNMENT)
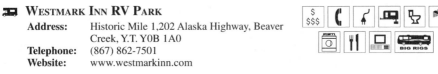
Location: Near Km 1,911 of the Alaska Highway

GPS Location: N 62° 14' 21.1", W 140° 41' 10.4"

Snag Junction is a small government campground with 15 separated back-in and parallel-parking sites. Some are near a small lake and all have picnic tables and firepits. A few will take large rigs and there is a circular drive if you want to pull in and take a look without unhooking. There are outhouses, free firewood, and a kitchen shelter.

⛺ WESTMARK INN RV PARK
Address: Historic Mile 1,202 Alaska Highway, Beaver
                 Creek, Y.T. Y0B 1A0
Telephone: (867) 862-7501
Website: www.westmarkinn.com

GPS Location: N 62° 22' 56.7", W 140° 52' 30.1"

This big newer campground stands out along this section of the Alaska Highway. It is associated with the Westmark Inn next door, an overnight stop for cruise ship passengers traveling by bus between Haines and Fairbanks. They even offer entertainment, the hotel puts on a musical in its dinner theater.

There are 67 sites here with electric (30 and 50 amp) and water hookups. Over half of them are large pull-thrus. Each site has a small tree but it will be a long time before they offer much shade. Sites also have picnic tables and barbecues. There are hot showers and flush toilets in the washrooms, there's also a laundromat, a mini-mart, gas sales, and two dump stations.

Watch for the campground just north of the Westmark Inn in Beaver Creek.

⛺ 1202 MOTOR INN

Address: Mile 1202 Alaska Highway, Beaver
                 Creek, Y.T. Y0B 1A0
Telephone: (867) 862-7600
Fax: (867) 862-7601
Website: www.1202motorinn.com

GPS Location: N 62° 23' 13.5", W 140° 52' 24.0"

The 1202 seems to be the most popular stop in Beaver Creek, their restaurant, gift shop, and gas station are always busy. They also offer a basic campground.

There are about 20 electric-only sites and another 10 smaller sites without hookups. A string of back-ins stretches along the left side of the main building and there are many pull-thru sites at the rear suitable for large rigs. There is also a water fill area and a dump station.

The campground is located in the town of Beaver Creek at Mile 1202 of the Alaska Highway, km 1935.

BORDER CITY MOTEL & RV PARK

Address: Mile 1,225 Alaska Highway, Alaska
Telephone: (907) 774-2205
Email: BorderCityLodge@worldnet.att.net

GPS Location: N 62° 39' 51.3", W 141° 03' 28.8"

Border City is the first stop north of the Alaska border. If you've been pushing all day to reach Alaska this isn't a bad place to stop at the end of the day and celebrate.

This is a large roadhouse with gas station, motel, and gift shop. In a large field to the south are 22 large pull-thru sites with 30-amp outlets and water. There are also some smaller back-in sites behind the roadhouse. Power is generated on-site. There are flush toilets and hot showers, and a dump station.

The lodge is located at Mile 1,225 of the Alaska Highway, 3.7 miles (6 km) north of the U.S. Customs station.

SCOTTIE CREEK SERVICES

Address: Mile 1,226 Alaska Highway, Alaska
Telephone: (907) 774-2009

GPS Location: N 62° 40' 12.5", W 141° 03' 39.7"

This gas station on a hillside overlooking the highway and the Border City Lodge offers no-frills sites with full hookups. The sites are on a series of flats above and behind the station with large-rig access possible. Showers are available as are a washing machine and dump station.

DEADMAN LAKE CAMPGROUND (USF&W)

Location: Near Mile 1,249 of the Alaska Highway

GPS Location: N 62° 53' 19.7", W 141° 32' 28.7"

This is a small campground and the entrance is very easy to miss. The roads and spaces have recently been improved, with care it is suitable for rigs to 35 feet. A circular drive lets you turn around if you drive in for a look. There are 15 separated sites set in black spruce along Deadman Lake. Sites have picnic tables and firepits and there are outhouses. There's a boat ramp and dock and the lake is good for pike, there's also a nature trail. This is prime mosquito country. Leave the highway at about Mile 1,249 and follow the gravel and dirt road for 1.1 miles (1.8 km) to the campground.

LAKEVIEW CAMPGROUND (USF&W)

Location: Near Mile 1,257 of the Alaska Highway

GPS Location: N 62° 57' 52.3", W 141° 38' 26.9"

Another very small public campground, this one on Yarger Lake. There are 11 sites and little maneuvering room but there is a tight circular drive. A 30-foot rig is about the max for this campground. Sites have picnic tables and firepits, and there is an outhouse. None of these sites is directly on the Lake. The entrance road here is about .3 miles (.5 km) long.

Ｖ Naabia Niign Campground

Address:	PO Box 476, Northway, AK 99764	
Telephone		
and Fax:	(907) 778-2297	
Website:	www.birchbaskets.com	

GPS Location: N 63° 00' 36.4", W 141° 48' 06.5"

Naabia Niign Campground has 20 back-in sites set in trees behind and below a gas station, laundromat, mini-mart, and gift shop. Six sites have full hookups (20 and 30 amp). Sites have picnic tables and firepits. Flush toilets and showers are located up in the laundromat. There is also a dump station.

The campground is located at Mile 1,264 of the Alaska Highway.

Ｖ Tok River State Recreation Site

Location:	Near Mile 1,309 of the Alaska Highway

GPS Location: N 63° 19' 31.9", W 142° 49' 54.4"

This state campground now been modernized and is now quite nice. There are 27 vehicle site and 8 tents sites off a circular drive. Five sites are pull-thrus and are suitable for larger rigs. Most sites are separated by vegetation. There are picnic tables and firepits, as well as outhouses and a boat ramp. This campground sometimes has a host and firewood is on sale.

TOK
Population 1,400, Elevation 1,650 feet

Tok is your first Alaska town, and probably the last you'll see on the way home too. You'll find that Tok is a very RV friendly town. With 7 RV parks and a population of only 1,400 the population would almost double if the parks were full. You'll find pretty much all services available here with RV parks, restaurants, stores, and repair facilities.

The **Tok Mainstreet Alaska Visitor Center** (907 883-5775) is located in a large log building in the northeast quadrant of the intersection of the Alaska Highway and the Tok Cutoff. This is an important stop, you can pick up a ton of information about the whole state. Nearby, just to the east, is the **APLIC** or **Alaska Public Lands Information Center** (PO Box 359, Tok, AK 99780; 907 883-5666). It concentrates on public lands (parks, etc.) and you can also try to make Alaska State Ferry Reservations, although you probably should have done that long before you left home.

The **APLIC** is one of four in the state, the others are in Fairbanks, Anchorage, and Ketchikan. There is so much federal and state land in Alaska that the governing organizations–eight different ones including the National Parks Service, the Bureau of Land Management, the U.S. Fish and Wildlife Service, and the State of Alaska–have set these information centers up in an attempt to make it easy for people to find all the information they need in one place. The information centers are a good place to start, but often it is necessary actually go to the governing organization for all the information you need. This center caters more to highway travelers than the others and may not be the best place to look for information about off-highway camping possibilities. See Chapter 14 - *Camping Away From the Road System* for more information.

There aren't a lot of tourist attractions in Tok, but one you might enjoy is called **Mukluk Land**. Covering nine acres it's a collection of interesting stuff. Call it exhibits or call it junk, there's something for everyone. In addition to the exhibits there are also things to do like gold panning and mini golf. Mukluk Land it on the south side of the road leading toward Fairbanks, it's 2.8 miles (4.5 km) from the junction with the Glenn Cutoff to Anchorage.

In Tok you must make an important decision. Will you continue up the Alaska Highway to Fairbanks or will you turn south toward Valdez and Anchorage? An amazingly large number of people head for Fairbanks and never see the southern part of the state. Don't be one of them. See it all. You've come a long way.

Tok Campgrounds

TOK GATEWAY SALMON BAKE

Address:	PO Box 482, Tok, AK 99780
Telephone:	(907) 883-5555
Fax:	(907) 883-5023
Email:	edyoung@aptalaska.net

GPS Location: N 63° 20' 03.3", W 142° 57' 16.0"

The first campground you'll see in Tok is hidden behind a salmon bake restaurant on

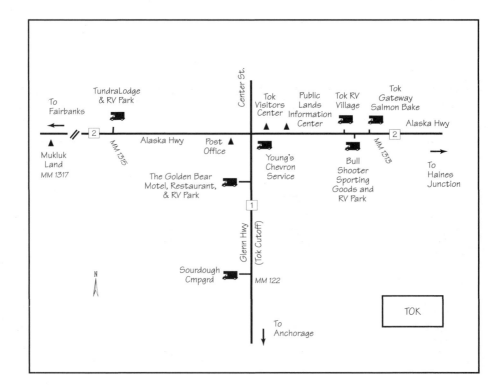

THE ALASKA HIGHWAY

your right as you enter town from the direction of the border. There are 39 pull-thru or back-in sites set in a grove of spruce trees. Some are full-hookup, others are partial or tent sites. A modern restroom building has hot showers and flush toilets and there is a dump station. The restaurant out front is pretty good too.

The Gateway is on the north side of the Alaska Highway near Mile 1,313. It is 1 mile (1.6 km) east of the intersection of the Tok Cutoff and the Alaska Highway, the first campground you reach when approaching Tok from Canada.

 BULL SHOOTER SPORTING GOODS AND RV PARK

Address:	PO Box 553, Tok, AK 99780
Telephone:	(907) 883-5625
Email:	thebull@aptalaska.net
Website:	www.aptalaska.net/~the bull/index.htm

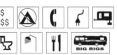

GPS Location: N 63° 20' 01.4", W 142° 57' 45.3"

The Bull Shooter is a nicely groomed and conveniently located campground tucked behind a sporting goods store. There are about 25 sites, most are pull-thrus with grass separating them. There are full service sites with 30-amp power, sites with just water and electricity, and dry sites. Maneuvering room for big rigs is more than adequate. The washrooms have flush toilets and free showers and there is a dump station. There's also a good restaurant across the highway.

Watch for the Bull Shooter on the south side of the Alaska Highway .9 miles (1.5 km) east of the intersection with the Tok Cutoff.

 TOK RV VILLAGE

Address:	Mile 1313.2 Alaska Hwy. (PO Box 739), Tok, AK 99780
Telephone:	(907) 883-5877 or (800) 478-5878
Fax:	(907) 883-5878
Email:	tokrv@aptalaska.net

GPS Location: N 63° 20' 05.6", W 142° 57' 55.8"

The Tok RV Village is without a doubt the most popular place to stay in town. It's a large campground and has modern facilities. Most caravans stay here.

The campground has about 160 sites. There are all types of sites including lots of pull-thrus. Fifty-amp power is available at some sites and some sites will take rigs to 45 feet. Some but not all sites have fire pits, some have television hookups. This campground has scattered spruce trees but is mostly open. The campground offers free showers to overnighters, a laundromat, and a gift shop which also has a few RV supplies. There is a dump and water-fill station. Wi-fi is available and there is a modem outlet.

The campground is located at Mile 1,313 of the Alaska Highway, about .8 miles (1.3 km) east of the intersection with the Tok Cutoff.

 YOUNG'S CHEVRON SERVICE

Address:	PO Box 167, Tok, AK 99780
Telephone:	(907) 883-2821

GPS Location: N 63° 20' 06.7", W 142° 59' 06.9"

This Chevron station offers one of the best deals for RVs in Tok. They have about 10 large back-in sites in back of the station with picnic tables and firepits but no hook-ups. If you fill up at the station you can stay for free. They also have a dump station, a vehicle washing station, and limited groceries and fast-food items in their store. They also have Young's Café next door.

The station is on the south side of the highway just east of the junction of the Glenn and Alaska highways, it's across from the visitor centers.

▄ THE GOLDEN BEAR MOTEL, RESTAURANT, AND RV PARK

Address:	PO Box 500, Tok, AK 99780
Telephone:	(907) 883-2561 or (866) 883-2561
Fax:	(907) 883-5950
Email:	gldnbear@aptalaska.net
Website:	http://www.tokalaska.com/901

GPS Location: N 63° 19' 52.1", W 142° 59' 30.1"

The Golden Bear has about 45 sites in an older campground that has not been modernized for today's larger rigs. Many sites are pull-thrus but access is cramped. Full-hookup, water and electric, and dry sites are offered. Power is 20 amp. There are also tent sites. The campground sits in a grove of spruce trees and sites have picnic tables. Flush toilets and hot showers are included in the price of your site. This campground also offers a laundromat, dump station, and a restaurant.

The campground is located just south of the intersection of the Tok Cutoff and the Alaska Highway on the west side of the highway.

▄ SOURDOUGH CAMPGROUND

Address:	Box 47, Tok, Alaska 99780
Telephone:	(907) 883-5543, (800) 789-5543
Email:	sourdoughcamp@aol.com
Website:	www.sourdoughcampground.com

GPS Location: N 63° 18' 41.2", W 143° 00' 15.4"

This is one of the original campgrounds in Tok, in fact we believe it was the first one. The Sourdough is a little farther from the center of town than the other Tok campgrounds and is on the road to Anchorage so many Fairbanks-bound travelers never even see it until they return home after a visit to Southcentral. That's too bad since this is the most interesting of the Tok campgrounds. The owners here make a big effort to entertain and introduce new visitors to the state. They have a sourdough pancake breakfast as well as a dinner often featuring entertainment by local artists and a pancake toss (don't ask, you'll have to see it). This is one campground where you'll know you're appreciated.

The Sourdough is medium-sized campground with about 75 camping sites in a fairly dense patch of spruce. Parking pads are gravel and have picnic tables. Both 20 and 30-amp outlets are offered, and sites are available with various combinations of electrical, water, and sewer hookups as well as without any services at all. Fifty-amp power is planned for the near future. Some pull-thrus are available, also a tent-camping area. There is a gift shop, a laundromat, and a coin-operated high-pressure vehicle wash. Hot showers are free. There is a dump station.

To reach the campground take the Tok Cutoff toward Anchorage from central Tok, the campground is about 1.5 mile (2.4 km) from the intersection on the right at Mile 122.8.

TUNDRA LODGE AND RV PARK

Address: PO Box 760, Tok, Alaska 99780
Telephone: (907) 883-7875   **Fax:** (907) 883-7876
Email: tundrarv@aptalaska.net

GPS Location: N 63° 20' 19.8", W 143° 01' 02.2"

The Tundra is a good RV park that probably suffers a little for business because it is on the far side of Tok and folks coming in to town from the east just don't see it in time. It has a very pleasant and spacious camping area with good facilities, and an excellent price compared with the places to the east.

This is a large park. There are some 80 sites here: pull-thrus, full-hookups, partial hookups, and dry. Twenty, 30, and 50-amp electricity is available. All are in a nice setting with many trees, they also have picnic tables and firepits with wood. Showers are free and there is a laundromat, a vehicle wash, a dump station, and even a cocktail lounge and meeting room.

The campground is located at Mile 1,315 of the Alaska Highway, about .8 miles (1.3 km) west of the junction with the Tok Cutoff.

FROM TOK TO DELTA JUNCTION
108 Miles (174 Kilometers)

From Tok the Alaska Highway follows the wide Tanana Valley northwest to Delta Junction. The road is excellent, the entire trip takes less than two hours. At Delta Junction the Alaska Highway ends. The Richardson Highway runs north 98 miles (158 km) to Fairbanks and south 266 miles (429 km) to Valdez.

Campgrounds Tok to Delta Junction

MOON LAKE STATE RECREATION SITE

Location: Mile 1,332 Alaska Highway

GPS Location: N 63° 22' 33.0", W 143° 32' 39.3"

This campground is located alongside Moon Lake, a pretty little swimming lake just off the highway. There are 17 back-in sites near the water with picnic tables, firepits, and outhouses. They are suitable for rigs to about 30 feet. Water is from a hand pump, there's a boat launch, and firewood can be purchased. Locals park their float airplanes along the shore so you can get a good look (but don't touch), there is a swimming beach here too. The short access road leads north from the Alaska Highway just east of Mile 1,332, about 18 miles (29 km) west of Tok.

DOT LAKE LODGE

Address: PO Box 2255, Dot Lake, Alaska 99737
Telephone: (907) 882-2691

GPS Location: N 63° 39' 40.7", W 144° 03' 57.9"

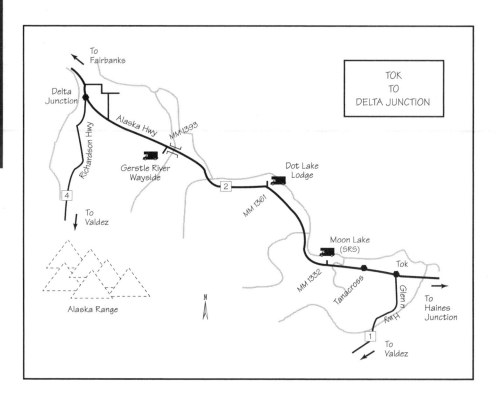

When you drive by you might not spot the RV sites at this roadhouse-style operation. From the road you can see that it has pretty much everything else–service station (gas, diesel, propane), a café, groceries, and a car wash area.

There are four back-in RV sites suitable for rigs to about 35 feet, they have 20-amp outlets and sewer drains. There is also a large tent and boondocking area in back along the shore of marshy little Dot Lake. It's quiet and pleasant back there and there is plenty of room for larger rigs. A small building has modern coin-op showers and a laundromat. Firewood is available.

You'll see the Dot Lake Lodge on the south side of the highway near Mile 1,361

GERSTLE RIVER WAYSIDE

FREE

Location: Alaska Highway at Mile 1,393,
                  about 29 miles east of Delta Junction

GPS Location: N 63° 49' 09.2", W 144° 55' 43.2"

This wayside has a large circular drive that is back off the highway. In the center are picnic tables and firepits. Outhouses are provided.

Watch for the entrance road just west of the Gerstle River at Mile 1,393 of the Alaska Highway, about 29 miles (47 km) east of Delta Junction.

DELTA JUNCTION
Population 850, Elevation 1,200 feet

Delta Junction started as a construction camp on the old Richardson Highway before the Alaska Highway was built. The surrounding country has become an important agricultural area.

Delta is known for the **bison** that were transported into the area in the 1920s. There are now over 400 of them and they roam pretty much where they want to. You may be fortunate enough to see some, a popular place to try is the overlook at Mile 241 of the Richardson Highway about 25 miles south of town. On our last visit a large herd of them blocked us as they crossed the highway about five miles east of Delta on the Alaska Highway, no doubt headed for some local farmer's grain field. Watch out for them along the road, a collision with a bison will do your rig no good.

The Delta Junction Visitor Center (PO Box 987, Delta Junction, AK 99737; 877 895-5068 or 907 895-5068) is located at the Y where the Alaska Highway meets the Richardson. Just to the south is the **Sullivan Roadhouse Museum** (907 895-5068). This roadhouse was recently moved to its present location from an army gunnery range.

Rika's Roadhouse, 9 miles north toward Fairbanks, was constructed at a ferry crossing of the Tanana River. This, like the Sullivan Roadhouse, was one of the original Richardson Highway roadhouses and is today a state park. A walk around the

BISON HERD CROSSING THE HIGHWAY NEAR DELTA JUNCTION

THE ALASKA HIGHWAY

grounds is rewarding, there's a restaurant and a gift shop. You can even camp in the parking area.

Delta Junction has a several campgrounds in the vicinity and makes a good overnight stop. Some are actually on the Richardson Highway but are included here because they are close enough to Delta to be considered when spending the night here.

Delta Junction Campgrounds

BERGSTAD'S TRAVEL TRAILER AND RV PARK

Address: Mile 1421 Alaska Highway (PO Box 273),
Delta Junction, Alaska 99737
Telephone: (907) 895-4856

GPS Location: N 64° 01' 46.0", W 145° 42' 00.9"

Bergstad's has a line of full-hookup sites in a large grassy field next to the highway. We find that few people stop here, it's often hard to find someone around to check in and pay. There are either 50 pull-thru sites or 100 back-ins, it depends upon the number of folks staying in the campground. There is also lots of room for rigs not needing hookups and for tenters in a wooded area. There are restrooms with hot showers and a laundromat as well as a dump station.

Bergstad's is the first of the Delta RV parks you reach if you are approaching on the Alaska Highway from the east. It is on the north side of the road at Mile 1,421, one mile (1.6 km) from the intersection of the Alaska and the Richardson Highway.

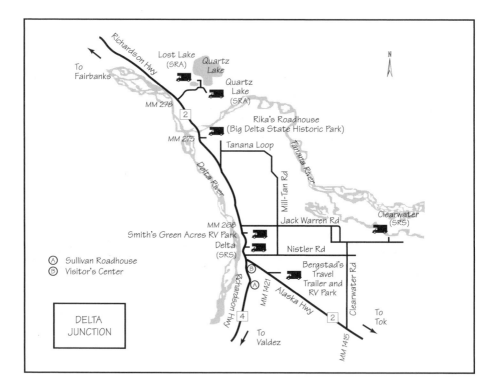

DELTA STATE RECREATION SITE

    Location: Delta Junction, Alaska

GPS Location: N 64° 03' 11.9", W 145° 44' 11.2"

This is a pleasant and convenient state campground. It is located right next to the Delta airport, a real plus for us aviation lovers. If you happen to be flying the Alaska Highway this is a convenient camping spot.

There are 24 spaces, maximum rig size here would be about 30 feet. The campground is set in a grove of trees but there is still plenty of light. There are picnic tables and firepits and wood bundles can be purchased. A water tap is provided and there are outhouses.

The campground is located along the east side of the Richardson Highway in Delta about 1.1 miles (1.8 km) north of the intersection of the Alaska Highway and Richardson Highways.

SMITH'S GREEN ACRES RV PARK

Address:	2428 Richardson Highway (PO Box 1129), Delta Junction, AK 99737
Telephone:	(907) 895-4369 or (800) 895-4369
Fax	(907) 895-4110
Email:	garvpark@wildak.net
Website:	www.greenacresrvpark.com

GPS Location: N 64° 03' 55.0", W 145° 44' 28.1"

This is an excellent campground, one of our regular stops. If you are headed north on the Alaska Highway and still have some driving left in you when you reach Tok you might consider pushing on another easy 100 miles or so to Delta.

Smith's Green Acres has about 80 sites of all types: pull-thrus, full utilities (20, 30 and 50-amp electric), electric and water, dry, and even tent sites. They cover a large field with a few trees and some grass. There are also a few permanents near the rear of the campground. The services building houses restrooms with free hot showers and a laundromat. There is also a dump station and water fill station.

Watch for this campground on the east side of the road about 1.5 miles (2.4 km) north of the junction of the Richardson and the Alaska Highway. The Richardson mileage is 268.

CLEARWATER STATE RECREATION SITE

    Location: East of Delta Junction on Clearwater Rd.

GPS Location: N 64° 03' 08.7", W 145° 25' 58.4"

This campground is located on what is known locally as the Delta Clearwater (to distinguish it from another nearby river which is also known as the Clearwater). It is a very clear river offering good grayling fishing. The campground is a popular access point for river boaters, there is a boat ramp.

There are 15 sites, two of them are large pull-thrus. They have picnic tables and firepits and decent separation and surrounding vegetation with trees. There are outhouses and a hand-operated water pump. Firewood can be purchased.

There are two ways to access this campground. The first is the paved Clearwater Road from the Alaska Highway at mile 1,415, about 7 miles (11.3 km) east of the Alaska Highway-Richardson junction in Delta. Follow signs about 8.5 miles (13.7 km) to the campground. The second is the Jack Warren Road, also paved, which leaves the Richardson near Mile 268, about 2 miles (3.2 km) north of the Alaska Highway-Richardson junction in Delta. Follow signs about 11 miles (17.7 km) to the campground on this road.

RIKA'S ROADHOUSE
(BIG DELTA STATE HISTORIC PARK)

Location: Mile 275 Richardson Highway

GPS Location: N 64° 09' 16.7", W 145° 50' 32.3"

You should stop and take a look at Rika's Roadhouse even if you don't want to camp here. This restored roadhouse was one of the originals along the old Valdez to Fairbanks trail. A ferry crossed the very dangerous Tanana River at this point. There is a self-guided tour, a museum, a restaurant, and also a gift shop. The Trans-Alaska oil pipeline crosses the Tanana just down the road.

The camping area is really just the parking lot for the park. There are at least twenty large back-in sites. A few sites have picnic tables and firepits and there are nearby vault toilets. There is also a dump and water-fill station nearby.

The roadhouse is located near Mile 275 of the Richardson just south of the bridge over the Tanana. A short road leads back to the roadhouse from the highway.

QUARTZ LAKE CAMPGROUND
(QUARTZ LAKE STATE RECREATION AREA)

Location: Mile 278 of the Richardson Highway

GPS Location: N 64° 11' 51.5", W 145° 49' 33.7"

This is a nice little campground on a popular area lake. Quartz lake gets warm enough for swimming and is also a popular fishing lake.

There are two camping areas here. The large lakeshore parking lot can be used for camping, rigs to 45 feet are fine. It has a few picnic tables, firepits, and outhouses. On the hillside above this lot is a more normal state campground with 16 back in spaces separated by trees and natural vegetation. Some are long enough for medium-sized rigs. These sites have picnic tables, firepits, and there are vault toilets. There's a campground host and firewood is sold.

The campground is located about 2.7 miles (4.4 km) from the Richardson Highway on a paved road. The access road leaves the highway at about Mile 278, about 11 miles (17.7 km) north of Delta Junction. You'll drive across the pipeline which dives underground to pass under the campground access road, this is a good place to get a picture of it.

LOST LAKE CAMPGROUND
(QUARTZ LAKE STATE RECREATION AREA)

Location: Mile 278 of the Richardson Highway,

GPS Location: N 64° 11' 45.0", W 145° 50' 25.3"

Near the Quartz Lake Campground is another much smaller one, the Lost Lake Campground. Trails lead between the two.

This campground has 11 medium to short sites. They are normal state campground back-in type sites with picnic tables and firepits. Separation is good. There are out-houses and a hand-operated water pump. One site is right along the lake.

You come to this campground before reaching the Quartz Lake Campground. Follow the access road from Mile 278 of the Richardson Highway about 11 miles (17.7 km) north of Delta Junction. The Lost Lake Campground is at mile 2.3 (3.7 km) of the paved access road.

ALASKA HIGHWAY DUMP STATIONS

Dump stations (called sani-dumps in Canada) are sometimes hard to find in the north. Even when you do find one you will probably have to pay to use it because handling sewage in an area with few sewer systems can be expensive. Plan ahead by dumping when you can, preferably when in a larger town that has a sewer system. Many of the campgrounds listed in this book have dump stations, you can usually pay to use them even if you aren't staying at the campground. Many service stations also have dump stations, particularly if they have an associated camping area.

Here are some additional sites, some of this information is taken from government publications and has not been confirmed:

In **Dawson Creek** there's a dump station near Coop Gas and the Safeway on 8th.

In **Ft. St. John** there is a city dump station near Km 72 (Mile 45) on the right at 86th Street as you drive north.

In **Fort Nelson** there is a dump station at the Esso on the north side of the highway on the corner of Airport Road, the road that leads to the big supermarket.

Watson Lake has a city dump station at Wye Lake Park across from Downtown RV Park. Also easily accessible is a free dump station at Junction 37 Services, the service station at the junction of the Cassiar and Alaska Highways.

In **Atlin** you can dump at the city dump outside town.

In **Whitehorse** try Yukon Tire Centre, Trails North Esso, 2nd Avenue Chevron, or Shell Service.

In **Haines Junction** try the Fas Gas at the east entrance to town and also Haines Junction Shell which is on the corner where the highway to Haines cuts off to the south.

In **Destruction Bay** try the sewage lagoon at the south side of town.

In **Tok** Young's Chevron at Mile 1314.1 of the Alaska Highway has an easily acces-sible dump station.

In **Delta Junction** there is an easily accessible state-operated dump station behind Rika's Roadhouse.

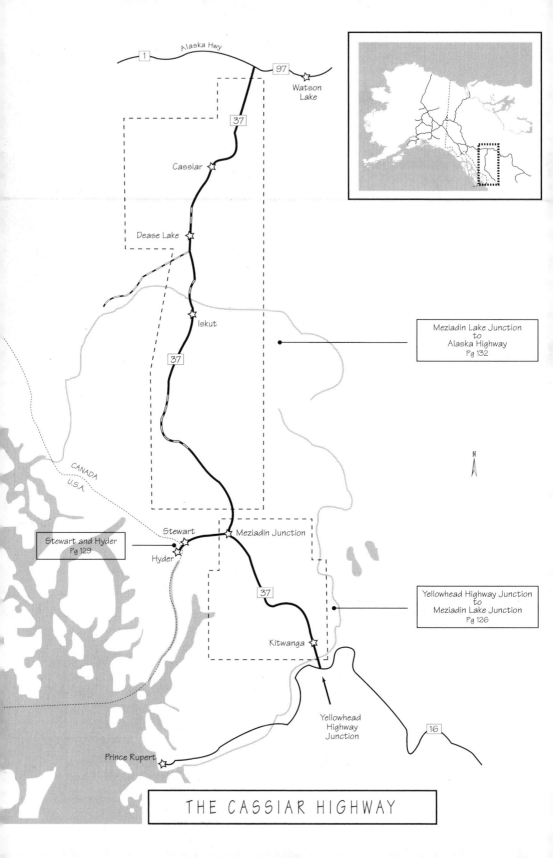

1 Alaska Hwy
97
Watson Lake

37

Cassiar

Dease Lake

Iskut

37

Meziadin Lake Junction
to
Alaska Highway
Pg 132

CANADA
U.S.A.

N

Stewart
Meziadin Junction

Stewart and Hyder
Pg 129

Hyder

37

Yellowhead Highway Junction
to
Meziadin Lake Junction
Pg 126

Kitwanga

16

Yellowhead
Highway
Junction

Prince Rupert

THE CASSIAR HIGHWAY

Chapter 5

The Cassiar Highway

INTRODUCTION

The Cassiar follows a route north much closer to the coast than the Alcan or Alaska Highway. Actually the Cassiar route was one of those considered during World War II when plans were being made to build the Alcan. At that time there was fear that the Cassiar route was too close to the coast and therefore might be in danger from the Japanese. Because the Cassiar Highway wasn't completed until 1972 it is the newest route to Alaska and therefore something of an adventure. Short portions of the road remain unpaved and fuel and supply stops can be a little far apart. On the other hand, wildlife is sometimes more plentiful than on the Alaska Highway and the scenery is great!

Highlights

The area around the junction of the Yellowhead Highway (Hwy. 16) and the Cassiar Highway (Hwy. 37) has a number of interesting First Nation (American Indian) attractions. The reconstructed village of 'Ksan is adjacent to the first campground listed below, 'Ksan Campsite and Trailer Park. See the directions to that campground to find the village. At the southern end of the Cassiar is the village of Gitwangak which is home to a fine collection of totem poles. The town of Gitanyow about 21km (13 miles) to the north also has a large group of totem poles. Near Kitwanga, off a circle road 4.3 km (2.7 miles) north of the Cassiar-Yellowhead junction is **Kitwanga Fort National Historic Site (Battle Hill)**, a First Nation for-

A VIEW OF BEAR GLACIER ON THE ROAD TO STEWART AND HYDER

tified village site. It's just beyond the Kitwanga Centennial Park Campground, see instructions for how to find that campground below.

One hundred fifty-seven kilometers (97 miles) north of the beginning of the Cassiar a paved road runs west for 62 scenic kilometers (38 miles) to the coastal towns of **Stewart, British Columbia** and **Hyder, Alaska**. There's a drive-up glacier en route (the **Bear Glacier**) and when you reach the coast you'll find two entirely different kinds of towns: orderly Canadian Stewart and the tiny Alaskan bush town of Hyder. Even better, just outside Hyder when the fish are running is one of the better places to see bears in all of Alaska. The road to Stewart and Hyder is excellent, don't miss this side trip.

The Road and Fuel

The Cassiar Highway runs 724 kilometers (449 miles) north through the wilderness from the Yellowhead Highway (Hwy. 16) near the small town of Kitwanga to join the Alaska Highway near Watson Lake in the Yukon Territory. It is a good alternate route to the Alaska Highway. From Prince George the distance to the Alaska border is 124 miles shorter via the Cassiar than via the Alaska Highway from Dawson Creek. If you do choose to drive the Cassiar to Alaska you will still drive much of the Alaska Highway, the two roads join near Watson Lake.

The Cassiar is now paved most of the way but there are several unpaved stretches north of the cutoff to Stewart and Hyder. Work continues and each year the length of the gravel is less. When we drove the route in August 2004 the total gravel was

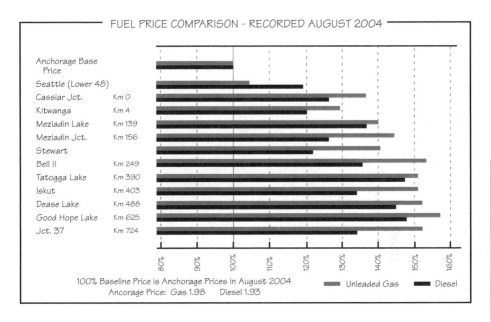

FUEL PRICE COMPARISON - RECORDED AUGUST 2004

		Unleaded Gas	Diesel
Anchorage Base Price			
Seattle (Lower 48)			
Cassiar Jct.	Km 0		
Kitwanga	Km 4		
Meziadin Lake	Km 139		
Meziadin Jct.	Km 156		
Stewart			
Bell II	Km 249		
Tatogga Lake	Km 390		
Iskut	Km 403		
Dease Lake	Km 488		
Good Hope Lake	Km 625		
Jct. 37	Km 724		

100% Baseline Price is Anchorage Prices in August 2004
Ancorage Price: Gas 1.98   Diesel 1.93

81.1 kilometers (50.3 miles). Much of this was construction, not permanent gravel, the longest section of gravel was 26.5 kilometers (16.4 miles). The condition of these gravel stretches varies, when we drove the road it was pretty good with vehicle speeds of about 45 mph possible most of the time although there were areas where road improvement work was underway and it was necessary to follow pilot cars. They were soon behind us, however, and the uncrowded and scenic nature of the route more than compensates for the hour or two of gravel. Many truckers now use the Cassiar rather than the longer and sometimes slower Alaska Highway so it is clear that the Cassiar is a viable alternate to the southern portion of the Alaska highway.

The Cassiar remains less traveled than the Alaska Highway and has fewer service stops. You should be well prepared when traveling and plan ahead, don't run out of gas or forget to bring a spare tire.

Distance and location markings along the Cassiar are in kilometers. Posts are placed every 5 kilometers. The kilometer posts are not necessarily accurate, they have not always been corrected for mileage changes due to road straightening. Campground locations in this book are based upon the kilometer posts. They start at the junction with the Yellowhead Highway in the south and increase heading north.

Fishing

The Cassiar Highway passes over or along many rivers, lakes and streams. Many of them offer excellent fishing. Take the time to stop and give a few a try. Several of the campgrounds listed in this section are on lakes with fishing possibilities. See the individual campground listings for more information. As always, don't hesitate to ask the locals for fishing tips. Most of this route is within British Columbia and fishing licenses are required.

Wildlife Viewing

One of the best reasons to visit Hyder is to see the bears. When the salmon are running from the middle of July until early September there are a lot of them around, both blacks and grizzlies. The best place to see them is at **Fish Creek**, a 5 km (3 mile) drive on a good gravel road on the far side of Hyder. A new viewing platform was constructed in 2001 at Fish Creek making observation much easier and safer.

The northern section of the Cassiar also offers wildlife-viewing possibilities. We've often seen stone sheep near the road near Km 618, and if you are traveling in the early spring you may see woodland caribou along the section of road between Dease Lake and the Alaska Highway. All along the highway watch the ditches and cleared areas out to the tree line, black bears are common and grizzlies not uncommon during berry season.

THE ROUTES, TOWNS, AND CAMPGROUNDS

FROM YELLOWHEAD HIGHWAY JUNCTION TO THE MEZIADIN LAKE JUNCTION
157 Kilometers (97 Miles)

The Cassiar Highway leaves the Yellowhead Highway some 481 kilometers (298 miles) west of Prince George and 243 kilometers (151 miles) east of Prince Rupert. It immediately crosses the Skeena River Bridge and in just .2 miles (.3 km) a road goes east to Gitwangak which is home to a fine collection of totem poles. If you find these interesting there's another group at Gitanyow along a short road from the highway about 21 km (13 miles) to the north.

Two miles north of Gitwangak you'll come to Kitwanga. This is the home of the **Kitwanga Fort National Historic Site (Battle Hill)** and has a modern RV park and a very small village campground.

From Kitwanga the road runs north through gently rolling scenic country with a few lakes to big Meziadin Lake and its provincial campground at Km 155. The cutoff going west to Stewart and Hyder is at Km 157.

Yellowhead Highway Junction to the Meziadin Lake Junction Campgrounds

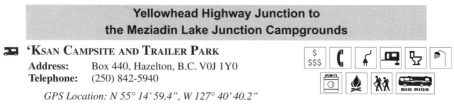

'KSAN CAMPSITE AND TRAILER PARK

    Address: Box 440, Hazelton, B.C. V0J 1Y0
    Telephone: (250) 842-5940

    GPS Location: N 55° 14' 59.4", W 127° 40' 40.2"

While not really on the Cassiar Highway, this campground is located near the southern end. It sits next to the river near historic Old Hazleton, also right next to the 'Ksan Historical Village and Museum which has totem poles and traditional First Nation cedar houses. With these two attractions so close-by, and such a nice campground, it makes a good place to spend the night before heading north on the Cassiar.

The campground has 30 large pull-thru sites with 30-amp outlets, water, and sewer arranged in a large grassy field broken up by grass-covered mounds, very attractive. Picnic tables are provided. There are also many tent and no-hookup sites, some in a loop with individual sites separated by natural vegetation. There is a restroom building with hot showers, a dump station, and a telephone. Firewood is provided.

To reach the campground leave the east-west Hwy. 16 near Km 284, there is a visitor center with sani-dump on the corner. Go north on the paved road, you'll cross an impressive suspension bridge at one mile (1.6 km), pass through a populated area, continue straight where the main road makes a 90-degree right at 3.7 miles (6 km) and at 4.6 miles (7.4 km) you'll see the campground entrance on your left, this is also the entrance to the historical village. Old Hazelton is straight ahead less than a mile.

CASSIAR RV PARK

Address:	PO Box 301, Kitwanga, B.C. V0J 2A0
Telephone and Fax:	(250) 849-5799
Email:	cassiarrv@navigata.net

GPS Location: N 55° 06' 52.4", W 128° 02' 00.6"

This RV park is the first of a thin line of campgrounds along the Cassiar. It has some of the nicest facilities and is especially popular with folks returning from the north. To them pulling in here feels like arriving back in civilization.

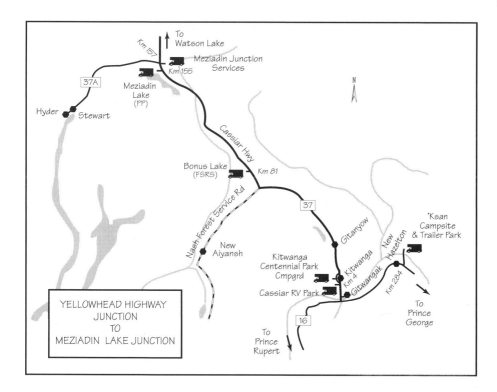

The campground has parking in three separate areas. There are 25 full-hookup spaces with 30-amp outlets in an area near the office and restrooms, some are pull-thrus. Overlooking the office on a small hill to the right are 7 double pull-thrus making up 14 sites with 20-amp outlets and water. Another large area beyond the office has another 16 or so sites, some with 20-amp outlets. Many sites are large enough for any size rig and access is easy. There is well-clipped grass throughout the campground and also some tent sites. Restroom, shower, and laundry facilities are first-rate. There's a dump station and a high-pressure vehicle wash. Campfires are allowed in a few designated areas. There's also a trail from the RV park to a salmon-counting station on the Kitwanga River. The distance is less than a mile.

From the Cassiar Highway at Km 4 drive .6 kilometer (.4 miles) west on Barcalow Rd. The campground is on the left.

🚐 KITWANGA CENTENNIAL PARK CAMPGROUND

Location: Across from the Tempo gas station on Kitwanga Valley Rd.

GPS Location: N 55° 06' 44.2", W 128° 01' 25.7"

This is a simple village-run campground in Kitwanga. There are 11 small back-in sites in a grove of trees with no utilities. Outhouses are provided as well as tables, fire pits, and firewood. We found the campground in good condition on our last visit. It is suitable for rigs to about 25 feet. Stays are limited to three days.

Easiest access is from Km 4.2 of the Cassiar. Follow Kitwanga Valley Road left for .6 kilometer (.4 mile) to the Tempo service station, the campground is across the street. Campground maintenance contributions are accepted at the service station.

🚐 BONUS LAKE RECREATION AREA

Location: Near Km 81 of the Cassiar Highway

GPS Location: N 55° 36' 33.2", W 128° 37' 11.3"

This is a small forest service recreation site with three picnic tables, fire rings, an outhouse, and a dock located on little Bonus Lake. It is just off the highway, a convenient and inexpensive place to spend the night. Access to the sites is down a short but fairly steep ramp so it is not suitable for rigs over about 25 feet.

🚐 MEZIADIN LAKE PROVINCIAL PARK (B.C. GOVERNMENT)

Location: Km 155 of the Cassiar Highway

GPS Location: N 56° 05' 23.0", W 129° 18' 14.2"

Meziadin Lake campground is located on the shores of huge Meziadin Lake near the junction where the Stewart/Hyder road meets the Cassiar. The lake has good Dolly Varden and rainbow trout fishing and the campground has a boat ramp. Bears are common at this campground so don't leave food outside your rig and dispose of garbage properly.

There are now 62 spaces at Meziadin Lake with many along the lake. The remaining sites are above and behind the lakefront ones, most of these have views. Most sites will take very big rigs. Facilities include the boat ramp, picnic tables, outhouses and a well for drinking water.

The campground is located west of Highway 37 near Km 155.

MEZIADIN JUNCTION SERVICES

Location: Junction of Hwy. 37 and Hwy. 37A
Telephone: (250) 636-9240

GPS Location: N 56° 05' 59.0", W 129° 18' 22.0"

This roadhouse-style operation offers gas, repairs, a restaurant, and RV spaces. The RV sites are very basic and in poor repair. There are 8 very long back-in sites with 20-amp electrical outlets (30-amp breakers), some also have water and there is a sani-dump. There is additional parking room for boondocking.

The campground is located at Km 156 of the Cassiar. It is at the junction with the 65-kilometer (40-mile) road to Stewart and Hyder on the coast.

STEWART AND HYDER
Population Stewart 500, Hyder 100, Elevation sea level

The 65 kilometer (40-mile) road that descends from the Cassiar Highway down to Stewart and Hyder on the coast is one of the most scenic in British Columbia. The entire distance is paved and grades are no problem for even the largest rigs. At about Kilometer 24 (Mile 15) is an overlook with excellent views of the **Bear Glacier** just across the valley. Near the coast the highway threads its way through Stewart, laid

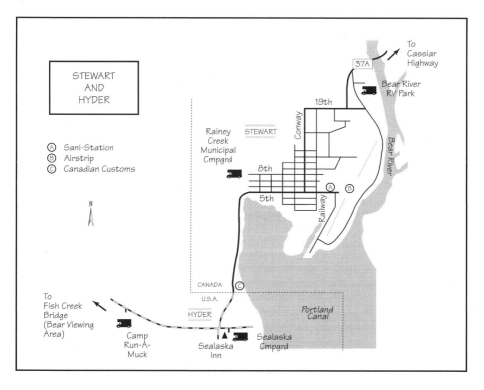

out in an organized grid pattern, and then follows the shore of the **Portland Canal**, a 90-mile-long fjord, a mile or so to the border and little Hyder. There is no U.S. border post or inspection going into Hyder but there is a Canadian post when you return to Stewart.

Much larger Stewart with its paved streets is the best place for purchasing supplies and has a gas station and decent-sized grocery store. There is also a town dump station. Funky Hyder is more interesting with gravel streets, several bars and souvenir stores and an excellent bear-viewing area from the middle of July to early September during the chum (dog salmon) and pink salmon run on **Fish Creek** about 3 miles (5 km) outside town.

If you have a smaller rig or a tow car consider making the drive to the **Salmon Glacier** overlook, out beyond the Fish Creek bear-viewing area. The overlook is 23 miles (37 km) on gravel from Hyder but the view of the glacier is spectacular. Check at the information center in Stewart for an excellent pamphlet that describes the route.

Stewart and Hyder Campgrounds

▣ RAINEY CREEK MUNICIPAL CAMPGROUND

Address:	PO Box 306, Stewart, B.C. V0T 1W0
Telephone:	(250) 636-2537 **Fax:** (250) 636-2668
Email:	stewhydcofc@hotmail.com
Website:	www.stewart-hyder.com

GPS Location: N 55° 56' 19.0", W 129° 59' 53.2"

This is the most popular campground in Stewart/Hyder. It is conveniently located in town, you can easily stroll downtown. The many campers staying in this campground each summer are a big boost to the local economy. The office people are excellent sources of information about the area.

The campground has about 90 RV sites and an additional area for tent camping. Sixty-five of the RV sites offer electricity, some 20 amp and some 30 amp. Sites in this campground aren't overly spacious, some will take large rigs to 40 feet but exercise caution. Picnic tables and fire pits are provided. One water fill station services the campground, there is a dump station but when we visited it was not in service. Campers were using a station provided by the city several blocks away on Fifth Ave. Restrooms are in a cement block building and are well-maintained and clean. The showers are coin-operated. Stewart's downtown area is within walking distance and there are tennis courts, a hiking trail, and a playground adjoining the campground.

As you enter downtown Stewart watch for 8th. Turn right and follow this street to where it ends against the mountain. That's where the campground entrance is located.

▣ BEAR RIVER RV PARK

Address:	PO Box 665, Stewart, B.C. V0T 1W0
Telephone:	(250) 636-9205
Email:	brtc@stewartbc.com
Website:	www.stewartbc.com/rvpark

GPS Location: N 55° 57' 08.8", W 129° 58' 41.2"

This is an established RV park with quite a few permanently-located units. It also has some 30 back-in sites spread around the park available for travelers. Sites have 30-amp outlets, water, and sewer and TV hookups, as well as picnic tables. They'll take rigs to 45 feet. Restrooms with hot showers are located in an ATCO-type building, fires are allowed in a few designated places.

The campground is located near the entrance to Stewart from the east. Coming in to town from the east you'll cross a bridge over the river and just beyond is a left turn signed for the campground.

SEALASKA CAMPGROUND

Address:	999 Premier Avenue (PO Box 33), Hyder, AK 99923
Telephone:	(250) 636-2486 or (888) 393-1199

GPS Location: N 55° 54' 40.3", W 130° 01' 14.3"

This campground is the place to stay in Hyder if you don't need hookups.

After crossing the border into Hyder you will come to a T in the road. Just half a block or so to the left is the Sealaska Inn. You can check in to the campground in the bar. Just to the left of the hotel is the camping area. Parking is on grass and there's good maneuvering and parking room for large rigs. There are no hookups but picnic tables and fire pits are provided. A building with laundromat, showers, and flush toilets sits out front.

A GRIZZLY BEAR AT FISH CREEK NEAR HYDER

A FREE CAMPING SPOT AT SALMON GLACIER

CAMP RUN-A-MUCK

Address:	PO Box 150, Hyder, Alaska 99923
Telephone:	(888) 393-1199 or (250) 636-9006
Email:	camprunamuck@usa.net

GPS Location: N 55° 55' 13.3", W 130° 01' 51.3"

For hookups in Hyder there is one choice. This is Camp Run-a-Muck. The name of the campground overstates the case, actually this is a pretty well-run place.

Campsites for larger rigs are in a large gravel area along the road north out of town toward Fish Creek and Salmon Glacier. There are about 60 sites, many pull-thrus, with 30-amp outlets and water. Some sites will take rigs to 45 feet. Some also have sewer. Picnic tables and fire pits are provided. Smaller sites are located back in the trees, many of these also have electricity and water. There is a dump station as well as a building with restrooms, coin-op showers, and a laundromat.

When you enter Hyder you'll drive past the few gift shops and bars on the main road and come to a T. Turn right and drive about a half-mile. The campground is on the left, you can't possible miss it.

FROM THE MEZIADIN LAKE JUNCTION TO THE ALASKA HIGHWAY
567 Kilometers (352 Miles)

After leaving the Meziadin Junction you reach the section of the Cassiar where there is some gravel. This road can be fine and allow speeds of 40 MPH and up, or it can have potholes and washboards that mean speeds down to 25 MPH if you want to keep the cabinets on the walls. Fortunately the gravel sections only total about 50 miles and end just north of Dease Lake, about 200 miles to the north.

There are really only a few small population centers along this section. One is little Iskut (population about 300) at Km 405 and the other Dease Lake at Km 487. Both have small grocery stores. Iskut sits between the **Spatsizi Wilderness Provincial Park** to the east of the highway and **Mount Edziza Provincial Park** to the west, both are becoming popular wilderness destinations and along the highway are a string of lakes that are excellent for fishing and canoeing.

The community of Dease Lake marks the junction with a cutoff to **Telegraph Creek** on the Stikine River. The original route into the Cassiar area was along this road from Telegraph Creek, the Stikine is a navigable river and was traveled by large sternwheelers almost to Telegraph Creek from the mouth near Wrangell, Alaska. Now the 70 mile-long gravel road is used to go the other way, it is suitable for small to medium rigs only and is a bit of an expedition. If you want to drive this road check first in Dease Lake for information about road conditions. Telegraph Creek has a population of about 300.

Meziadin Lake Junction to the Alaska Highway Campgrounds

🚐 **BELL II LODGE**

Location:	Km 249 Hwy. 37N
Telephone:	(604) 881-8530 or (877) 617-2288
Email:	info@bell2lodge.com
Website:	www.bell2lodge.com

GPS Location: N 56° 44' 35.5", W 129° 47' 36.4"

The Bell II is a very modern roadhouse and lodge. In the winter it is used for heliskiing but in the summer it relies on highway traffic and has a nice RV park.

There are 12 large pull-thru sites, nine have full hookups (15 amp). There are also five back-in camping sites with no services suitable for smaller rigs or tent campers. Restrooms are new and have showers, there is a sani-dump. The hotel also has a restaurant and gas sales.

The location of the lodge at Km 249 is about 93 km (58 miles) north of the junction with the road out to Stewart and Hyder.

🚐 **WILLOW RIDGE RESORT**

Address:	Km 353 Hwy. 37N (PO Box 99),
	Iskut, B.C. V0J 1K0

GPS Location: N 57° 26' 22.8", W 130° 13' 02.1"

This little campground sits on a ridge well above the highway. There are about 20 sites, 6 are long pull-thrus with 30-amp electrical, sewer, and water hookups. Power is produced by a on-site generator. The others are a mix of pull-thrus and back-in sites. Sites are set in trees and are decently separated. Showers are available and there is a laundromat and small store.

Watch for the entrance road leading to the east from Km 353 of the Cassiar . The decent road leads a short distance to the top of the ridge and the resort.

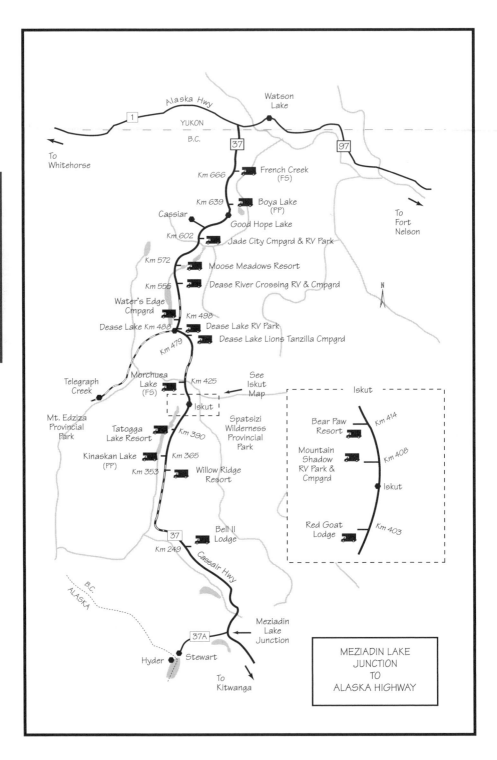

KINASKAN LAKE PROVINCIAL PARK (B.C. GOVERNMENT)
Location: Km 365 of the Cassiar Highway

GPS Location: N 57° 31' 47.9", W 130° 11' 02.5"

Kinaskan Lake is a beautiful lakeside campground with much more separation between sites and privacy than is found at the next lakeside park to the south - Meziadin Lake. Rainbow trout fishing in the large lake is an attraction here (during late summer) as is the Mowdade Trail to volcanic Mt. Edziza Park to the west. Some visitors even swim in the lake. We find that RV caravans often stop here.

The campground has 50 spaces, many of them quite large, and also many along the lake. All have the customary picnic table and firepit. The campground has outhouses, a water pump, free firewood, and a boat launching ramp.

TATOGGA LAKE RESORT
Address: Box 59, Iskut, B.C. V0J 1K0
Telephone: (250) 234-3526

GPS Location: N 57° 42' 39.9", W 129° 59' 31.0"

Despite the name this establishment seems less like a resort than a traditional roadhouse. The log restaurant building is tastefully decorated with moose antlers. They also sell gas. Hiking, fishing, and canoeing excursions are available, including fly-in trips. Behind the buildings located along the highway is a large field with campsites that slopes down toward (but not all the way to) Tatogga Lake.

The campground itself has about 30 sites, most of them offer 20-amp electricity and water hookups. Some will take rigs to 45 feet but take a look before driving in to make sure you have adequate maneuvering room and that the ground is firm. Hot showers are available and there is a dump station.

The resort is located on the west side of the Cassiar Highway near Km 390.

RED GOAT LODGE
Address: Box 101, Iskut, B.C. V0J 1K0
Telephone: (250) 234-3261 or (888) RED-GOAT
Email: redgoatlodge@aol.com

GPS Location: N 57° 48' 55.2", W 129° 57' 40.7"

The Red Goat Lodge is a bed and breakfast and hostel with a campground next to the lake out front. Canoes are available for rent, guided canoe tours and shuttles can be arranged, and fishing on Eddontenajon Lake out front is decent in July and August.

The campground at the lodge has about 26 sites, several are along the lake. Many have electricity and water hookups, at least three are large pull-thrus. Access for larger rigs is tight here, leave your big rig on the highway and walk down to take a look if you are thinking of stopping. There is a dump station and showers and a laundromat are available.

Watch for the sign and driveway on the west side of the Cassiar Highway near Km 403 about 3 kilometers (2 miles) south of Iskut.

⊞ MOUNTAIN SHADOW RV PARK AND CAMPGROUND

Address: Box 3, Iskut, B.C. V0J 1K0
Telephone: Summer (250) 234-3333, Winter (415) 897-4445
Email: mtshadowbc@aol.com

GPS Location: N 57° 51' 41.4", W 130° 01' 04.1"

When we're looking for a campground in this section of the Cassiar we head for the Mountain Shadow RV Park. It's a meticulously laid out and maintained facility with both large pull-thru sites and secluded back-ins. Views to the west are spectacular and a short path takes you to a small lake which offers rainbow trout fishing and bird watching.

The campground has two different camping areas. For large rigs to 45 feet there are 10 pull-thrus with lots of room and water and electricity (20 or 30-amp) hook-ups. In the same area are another 10 large back-ins with water and electricity. Smaller rigs and tent campers will appreciated the 11 back-in spaces in trees, three with electrical hook-ups. There are fire pits in this area. All sites have picnic tables. Showers (no extra charge) are available, there are flush toilets, and there is a dump station.

A wide and well-maintained entrance road leads down a gentle slope to the campground from near Km 408 of the Cassiar Highway. Watch for the sign on the west side of the highway.

⊞ BEAR PAW RESORT

Address: PO Box 69, Iskut, B.C. V0J 1K0
Telephone: (250) 234-3005

GPS Location: N 57° 54' 13.9", W 130° 03' 15.6"

The Bear Paw seems to us to be a sort of Euro-style dude ranch. The clientele seems to be mostly European and the main ranch is much like a Swiss chalet. Guests here are offered guided wilderness tours and scenic horseback riding among other upscale offerings.

The camping area is on the right as you come down the driveway from the highway. It's obviously designed for smaller rigs and tents, the back-in government campground-style separated sites and limited maneuvering room are only suitable for rigs to about 25 feet. There are no hookups but there are picnic tables and fire pits and firewood is provided. There are also two rental tepees. Hot showers are available and family-style meals are served in the chalet. There's also a hot tub.

The Bear Paw is on the west side of the highway at about Km 414.

⊞ MORCHUEA LAKE FOREST SERVICE CAMPSITE

Location: Near Km 425 of the Cassiar Highway

GPS Location: N 57° 59' 07.4", W 130° 03' 47.8"

This is a small forest service recreation site with a few picnic tables, fire rings, an outhouse, and a boat ramp. It is near the highway and is suitable for rigs to 30 feet.

⊞ DEASE LAKE LIONS TANZILLA CAMPGROUND

Location: Km 479 of the Cassiar Highway

GPS Location: N 58° 22' 08.2", W 129° 54' 46.9"

This little campground is a gem, it is a government-style place but operated by the local Lions Club. And it cost less than the Provincial campgrounds. It sits on the bank of the Tanzilla River just east of the highway.

There are 16 back-in sites with tables and fire pits. These are individual separated sites, parking is on gravel under pine trees. The campground is suitable for rigs to about 30 feet. Firewood is available for an extra charge.

🚐 DEASE LAKE RV PARK

Address: PO Box 129, Dease Lake, B.C. V0C 1L0
Telephone: (250) 771-4666
Email: deaselakerv@home.com

GPS Location: N 58° 25' 57.6", W 129° 59' 08.6"

Large RV owners will appreciate this campground. Although it is little more than a large gravel lot filled with RV sites there is lots of room and the surface is solid and well drained.

There are about 22 large pull-thru sites suitable for rigs to 45 feet. All have electricity (30 amp) and water and half also have sewer hookups. There are also a number of large back-in sites, also with power and water hookups. The new tiled bathrooms have flush toilets and showers and a new RV pressure wash is being installed. There is also a dump station.

The campground is located on the East side of the Cassiar near the Telegraph Creek Road junction in the community of Dease Lake near Km 488.

THE ROAD WINDS THROUGH THE MOUNTAINS ON THE CASSIAR

THE CASSIAR HIGHWAY

WATER'S EDGE CAMPGROUND

Location: Km 498 of the Cassiar Highway

GPS Location: N 58° 31' 10.6", W 130° 01' 42.9"

This is a new private campground that is much like a provincial forest service campground. It has no hookups but the back-in sites along the shore of Dease Lake are good for RVs to 30 feet and tents. They have picnic tables, pits, and an outhouse.

The campground is on the west side of the highway near Km 498. There's a wide quarter-mile-long gravel road down to the lake shore and the sites are off a loop if you wish to take a look without unhooking a tow vehicle. There's also a boat ramp.

DEASE RIVER CROSSING RV & CAMPGROUND

Location: Km 555, Highway 37,
Dease Lake, B.C. V0C 1L0

GPS Location: N 58° 56' 46.1", W 129° 51' 53.3"

This is a new campground located next to the highway on the shore of a wide area of the Dease River. It is very scenic, a great location.

There are about 20 well-separated sites in an open area, some on the lakefront, and many are suitable for large rigs. Picnic tables and fire pits are provided. The campground has no hookups but water is available and there are hot showers, flush toilets, and a sani-dump. Rental cabins and rental canoes are also available.

MOOSE MEADOWS RESORT

Address: PO Box 299, Dease Lake, B.C. V0C 1L0

GPS Location: N 59° 04' 17.1", W 129° 43' 20.7"

Moose Meadows is a rustic resort with friendly management in a beautiful location on the shore of Cotton Lake. Canoes are available for exploring and fishing. If you feel like going on a longer expedition shuttle service is available for Dease River floats of up to 180 miles.

The facilities at Moose Meadows are more appropriate to tent campers and self-contained rigs than to RVers looking for hookup sites. There are several very nice parking spots on the shore of the lake and others nearby. Some are fine for large rigs and there's plenty of maneuvering room. There is a dump station but no electricity is available. The campground has only outhouses but does have showers. There's also a boat launch, a wood-fired sauna, and an RV wash area.

Moose Meadows is located just off the highway near Km 572. This is about 50 miles north of the Telegraph Creek junction in Dease Lake.

JADE CITY CAMPGROUND AND RV PARK

Address: PO Box A8, Jade City, Cassiar, B.C. V0C 1E0
Website: www.jadecitybccanada.com

GPS Location: N 59° 14' 57.4", W 129° 39' 00.7"

Jade City is a popular stop although there's little here except a gas station and a jade and jewelry store. The store offers a good selection of jade carvings and jewelry and a nice little free campground next door. It will remind you of a government campground, the amenities are similar. It has about 30 back-in spaces in a grove of pines. Sites are suitable for rigs to about 35 feet. There are no hookups but there are outhouses, a sani-dump, and water is available. The price is right.

Jade City is on the east side of the Cassiar Highway near Km 602.

BOYA LAKE PROVINCIAL PARK (B.C. GOVERNMENT)
    Location: Km 639 of the Cassiar Highway
        GPS Location: N 59° 22' 07.2", W 129° 06' 23.4"

The farthest north provincial park campground along the Cassiar is on the shores of crystal clear Boya Lake. On a clear day this lake is a beautiful bright blue, great for photos. Unfortunately the fishing is very poor in the lake. The nearby Dease River does have grayling.

The campground has about 45 sites. Some are along the lake, a few are pull-thrus, and some are tent sites. Some sites will take rigs over 45 feet long. All sites have picnic tables and firepits, there are outhouses, free firewood, water pumps, a dock, and a boat ramp. Some sites will suit large rigs. There's a hiking trail along the lake shore and to the river.

The 2.4-kilometer (1.5-mile) entrance road heads east from near Km 639 of the Cassiar Highway. This is about 93 kilometers (57 miles) south of the junction of the Cassiar and the Alaska Highway. Campsites are on loops so you can drive in and check for empty sites even if you are towing.

FRENCH CREEK FOREST SERVICE CAMPSITE
    Location: Near Km 666 of the Cassiar Highway
        GPS Location: N 59° 35' 38.1", W 129° 13' 11.2"

This is a small forest service recreation site with a few picnic tables, fire rings, and an outhouse. It's located along French Creek. While it is near the highway it is only suitable for rigs to about 24 feet and you must exercise care so that brush along the narrow access road does not scratch the sides of your rig.

The campground is on the east side of the highway near Km 666.5.

CASSIAR HIGHWAY DUMP STATIONS

Before you start north you might want to take advantage of the free sani-dump at the Infocentre in the **Hazeltons** at Km 284 of Highway 16. It's some 42 kilometers (26 miles) east of the junction of Highway 16 and the Cassiar Highway. The Infocentre is on the corner where Highway 62 goes north to Old Hazelton .

Most of the dump stations along the Cassiar (called sani-dumps in Canada) are in private campgrounds. We've noted those campgrounds offering dump stations by a symbol, expect to pay a fee if you aren't staying at the campground, and sometimes if you are.

There is one important exception. The town of **Stewart** has an inexpensive city-operated dump station with excellent access. See the Stewart map in this book on page 129 for the location.

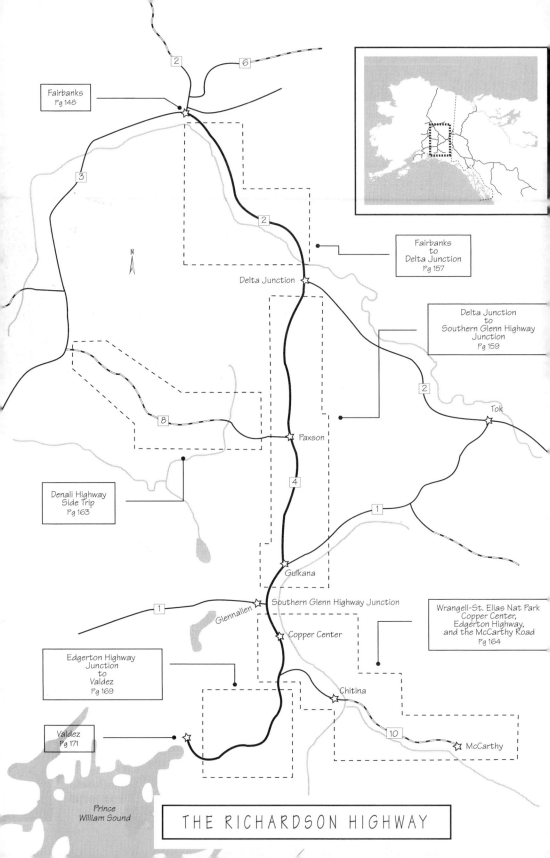

Fairbanks
Pg 148

Fairbanks
to
Delta Junction
Pg 157

Delta Junction

Delta Junction
to
Southern Glenn Highway
Junction
Pg 159

Paxson

Tok

Denali Highway
Side Trip
Pg 163

Gulkana

Southern Glenn Highway Junction

Glennallen

Copper Center

Wrangell-St. Elias Nat Park
Copper Center,
Edgerton Highway,
and the McCarthy Road
Pg 164

Edgerton Highway
Junction
to
Valdez
Pg 169

Chitina

Valdez
Pg 171

McCarthy

Prince
William Sound

THE RICHARDSON HIGHWAY

Chapter 6

The Richardson Highway

INTRODUCTION

The Richardson is Alaska's oldest major highway. It runs from tidewater at Valdez to Fairbanks in the interior. The Richardson is also one of the state's most scenic highways with natural scenery including distant mountain peaks, wide interior valleys, overhanging glaciers, and mountain passes.

In this guide we'll cover the Richardson from north to south. This may seem strange at first. After all, the highway mileposts go from south to north. We think most people will first drive most of this road from north to south so that's the way we laid things out.

You are likely to travel only segments of the Richardson. If you've driven the Alaska Highway from the south you'll probably join it at Delta Junction near Mile 266 and drive north to Fairbanks. Alternately, you may drive the Richardson for only a few miles between the two segments of the Glenn Highway on your way to Anchorage. If you decide to visit Valdez you'll drive quite a bit of the Richardson, including some of its most scenic sections.

 Highlights

The cities at each end of the Richardson, **Fairbanks** and **Valdez**, are two of the most popular destinations in the state. They're very different, of course, but most people want to see them both.

The **Trans-Alaska Oil Pipeline** has been a top Alaska news story for many years. You'll have lots of chances to see it while driving the Richardson since the pipeline parallels the highway for most of its length. There will be times when you can't see the pipeline from the highway but it is usually not far away. There are viewing areas and displays at Mile 215, Mile 88, and Mile 65. You'll probably also spot Pump Station 9 at Mile 258, Pump Station 10 at Mile 219, and Pump Station 12 at Mile 65.

The Richardson began as a gold rush trail to Eagle, Alaska even before Fairbanks was founded. Very soon, however, most people traveling along it were following a new left fork toward Fairbanks. In 1910 the road was upgraded to allow the use of automobiles. Roadhouses were built along the road at approximately 10 mile (16 km) intervals (one day's travel before automobiles) by private individuals. Most roadhouses disappeared but a few remain. **Rika's Roadhouse** at Mile 275 just north of Delta Junction is now a state park and makes an interesting stop. Another that is still standing and operating is the **Copper Center Lodge**, in Copper Center just off the main highway near Mile 101. In Delta the **Sullivan Roadhouse** is an excellent little museum. This roadhouse was recently moved to its present location from an army gunnery range.

The Richardson will give you several opportunities to take a good look at glaciers. The best of the bunch is the **Worthington Glacier** at Mile 30 just north of Thompson Pass. Paved handicapped-accessible paths lead to an overlook near the glacier.

As Denali National Park gets more and more crowded the National Park Service would like us to visit Alaska's other national park with road access. This is the **Wrangell-St. Elias National Park**. Unfortunately, opportunities for access to Wrangell-St. Elias National Park are limited. There are two driving routes, the Nabesna Road (from Mile 60 of the Tok Cutoff - See Chapter 7 - *The Glenn Highway*) and the Edgerton Highway and McCarthy Road (from Mile 83 of the Richardson), but both are rough and not really suitable for larger RVs. We cover the Edgerton Highway and McCarthy Road in more detail later in the chapter.

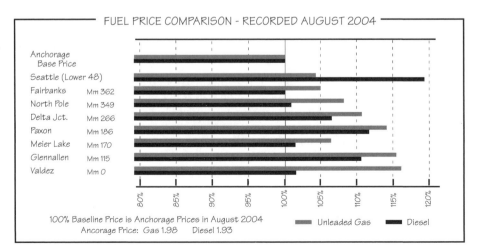

The Road And Fuel

The Richardson Highway was once the major route into the interior of the state. Until the Alaska Railroad from Seward to Fairbanks was finished in 1923 the choice was between the Richardson Highway and river boat down the Yukon. Much later, in 1971, the Parks Highway opened. Today most Anchorage to Fairbanks traffic follows the Parks so the Richardson is not really heavily traveled.

All of the Richardson is paved. Most is pretty good road but not up to the same standards as the much newer Parks Highway. There are some sections of road that have permafrost problems. Most of the wear and tear of the pipeline construction years along this route has been repaired.

The Richardson Highway, from Fairbanks to Valdez, is 368 miles (594 km) long. Mile markers along the highway count up from just outside Valdez to Fairbanks. We'll travel in the opposite direction in this chapter, from Fairbanks to Valdez.

Fishing

In Alaska timing is an important part of catching fish, particularly salmon. You can't catch fish if they aren't there. Salmon arrive in runs and may be entirely absent the rest of the time. For timing purposes there are two regions traversed by the Richardson Highway: the Tanana Valley and Prince William Sound/Copper Valley. In general the Tanana Valley salmon arrive later because they have farther to travel from the ocean. In the Tanana Valley July is the king month, in the Copper Valley they show up in the middle of June while in salt water it's early June. Copper Valley reds are present from late June to the end of August, Copper Valley silvers are present from the middle of August until the middle of September. In Valdez expect pinks in July and August with a July peak and silvers just a little later with an August peak.

Many of the good fishing locations near Fairbanks are actually north of town. See Chapter 10 - *North of Fairbanks* for information about them.

From Fairbanks to Paxson most of the fishing along the Richardson Highway is lake fishing. A small boat is a big help. Try the **Chena Lakes** (Mile 347) for rainbows and silvers, **Lost Lake** (off a side road at Mile 306) for rainbows, **Birch Lake** (Mile 306) for rainbows, **Quartz Lake** (Mile 278) for rainbows, **Fielding Lake** (Mile 200) for lake trout and grayling, and **Summit Lake** (Mile 195) for grayling and lake trout.

At Paxson (Mile 185) the Denali Highway heads west toward Denali Park and the Parks Highway. Along the Denali try fishing **Ten Mile Lake** (Mile 10) for lake trout and grayling, **Denali-Clearwater Creek** (Mile 18) for grayling, the **Tangle Lakes** (at about Mile 21) for grayling and lake trout, **Clearwater Creek** (Mile 56) for grayling, and **Brushkana Creek** (Mile 104) for grayling.

Back on the Richardson Highway and heading south from Paxson try **Paxson Lake** (Mile 175) for grayling and lake trout; **Dick Lake** (Mile 173) for grayling; **Meiers Lake** (Mile 170) for grayling; **Gillespie Lake** (Mile 168) for grayling; **Sourdough Creek** (Mile 147) for grayling in the creek and also access to the Gulkana River; **trails to the Gulkana River** (Mile 141, 136, and 129) for kings, reds, rainbows, and grayling; **Bear Creek** (Mile 127) for grayling; the **Gulkana River mouth** (Mile 123 with a 1.5 mile trail to mouth) for kings, reds, grayling, and rainbows; the **Klutina River** at Copper Center for kings, reds, grayling and Dollies; the **Squirrel Creek gravel pit** (Mile 80) for grayling and rainbows; the **Little Tonsina River** (Mile 65) for Dollies; **Worthington Lake** (Mile 28) for rainbows; **Blueberry Lake** (Mile 24) for rainbows and grayling; and **Robe River** (Mile 5) for Dollies and reds using flies.

At Mile 83 the Edgerton Highway leads east to Chitina, the Copper River, the McCarthy Road, and eventually, McCarthy. The Copper River near Chitina is the scene of one of Alaska's most interesting fisheries, the salmon dip-net fishery. It is open only to Alaska residents and special permits are required. Big nets with handles over 20 feet long are used to catch fish in water that is just too silt-laden to be fished using other methods. It's fun to just watch. Other fishing possibilities along the road are **Liberty Falls** (Mile 25) for grayling, **Second Lake** (Mile 36) for rainbows and grayling, **First Lake** (Mile 37) for rainbows and grayling, **Chitina Lake** (Mile 39) for grayling, the **Copper River** (Mile 1 McCarthy Road) for red salmon and king salmon, **Strelna Creek** (Mile 15, McCarthy Road) for Dollies, **Lou's Lake** (Mile 26, McCarthy Road) for silvers and grayling, and **Long Lake** (Mile 45, McCarthy Road) for grayling, lake trout, silvers, and Dollies.

Valdez is the top sport fishing destination on Prince William Sound. This is a great place to join a charter operator for a day of salmon fishing. Valdez also has some of the best and easiest beach fishing for pinks and silvers in Alaska at **Allison Point** near the **Solomon Gulch Hatchery** on Dayville Road. There are three different fish-

THE PINKS ARE JUMPING IN VALDEZ

ing derbies with prizes in Valdez. Dates vary slightly from year to year but the Halibut Derby runs all summer, the Pink Salmon Derby is in July, and the Silver Salmon Derby is in August. Check out the rules before you go fishing, you must follow them to win.

A large proportion of the campgrounds along the Richardson are in locations that offer fishing possibilities. This is a little surprising since most people don't think of this area of Alaska as being a top fishing destination.

Boating, Rafting, Canoeing, and Kayaking

When Fairbanks residents head out for a day of swimming, water skiing, and fun on the water they generally end up at **Harding Lake** (Mile 321, Richardson Highway) or **Birch Lake** (Mile 306, Richardson Highway). The **Chena Lakes Recreation Area** (Mile 347, Richardson Highway) is dedicated to non-powered boats and aquatic sports. North of Fairbanks there are several possibilities for river float and canoe trips, see Chapter 10 - *North of Fairbanks*, for information.

Between Delta Junction and the Gakona Junction there are two popular floatable rivers–the north-flowing **Delta River** and the south-flowing **Gulkana River**. Both are designated Wild and Scenic Rivers and are administered by the BLM (Glennallen District Office, PO Box 147, Glennallen, AK 99588; 907 822-3217). A Delta River trip starts by crossing the Tangle Lakes from a put-in at the Tangle Lakes Campground at Mile 21 of the Denali Highway. From the lakes the float is mainly Class II with a portage around a falls. The first take-out is at Mile 212 of the Richardson Highway. This trip is suitable for canoes, kayaks, and rafts. The **Gulkana River** has several different forks and possible routes, but the most popular float is from Paxson Lake (Mile 175, Richardson Highway) to take-outs at Sourdough Campground (Mile 148, Richardson Highway), Poplar Grove (Mile 137, Richardson Highway with 1-mile trail) or the Richardson Highway Bridge (Mile 127, Richardson Highway). You can also put in at Sourdough to avoid the worst stretches of white water. Water is mostly Class II and a portage is required around Canyon Rapids. The Gulkana is a well-known fishing stream offering excellent red and king fishing during their respective runs. Rafts, kayaks, and canoes (only for good canoeists) are suitable. Both of these rivers have long stretches that are remote from road access and can be dangerous. If you plan to float them prepare yourself with adequate research and make sure you have the proper experience and equipment.

Several large lakes along this stretch of road are also popular with boaters. They are **Fielding Lake** (Mile 200), **Summit Lake** (Mile 195), and **Paxson Lake** (Mile 175).

Visitors to the Wrangell-St. Elias National Park will find that commercial operators offer whitewater rafting on rivers in the park including the **Chitina River**, the **Kennicott River**, and the **Nizina River**. Some of these rivers can be pretty challenging and entrance and exit points are often not obvious or easy to reach. Commercially guided tours are the best way to float them.

Valdez sits on the shore of the Valdez Arm which leads out into **Prince William Sound**. These waters are some of the best in the world for ocean kayaking. Possible routes are unlimited and range from a day trip on the Arm to something much longer, say a 150 mile (242 km) crossing to Whittier. Several state marine parks with tent campsites are within a day's paddle of Valdez. Use of a charter vessel to drop you far out in the sound can save many days of paddling if you want to explore some of the more remote reaches of the sound.

Hiking and Mountain Biking

Most good hikes in the Fairbanks area are north of town. See Chapter 10 - *North of Fairbanks* for information about them. One exception is Creamers Field, formally known as **Creamer's Field Migratory Waterfowl Refuge**. The refuge is located on the northern outskirts of Fairbanks along College Road. There is a 2 mile (3 km) guided nature trail with observation platforms. The best months for observing waterfowl are April, May, and August.

The entire **Denali Highway** has become a popular mountain bike route. One hundred and fourteen miles (184 km) of gravel are hard going on a touring bike, but mountain bikes have no problems and traffic is minimal. There are also some high-country hiking routes from the highway. This is a popular hunting area and there are many off-road vehicle trails, many are not very good for hiking because the wheeled vehicles tend to tear up the tundra leaving a muddy mess. Some of the best hikes are away from the trails. The **Landmark Lake** hike from Mile 25 follows an old dirt road 2.4 miles (.4 km) to Landmark Gap Lake, you can catch grayling in the lake and hike the surrounding hills. The route in is suitable for hiking or mountain bikes. From Mile 37 just west of **Maclaren Summit** (4,086 ft.) you can hike north on an old vehicle trail through a region of small lakes and big views. Go as far as you want across the open tundra, the first part of the trail is fine for mountain bikes. Mountain bikers will also like the 12 mile (19 km) **Maclaren River Road** heading north for 12 miles (19 km) from Mile 43 to the Maclaren Glacier.

There are several decent trails in the Wrangell-St. Elias National Park accessible from the Edgerton Highway and the McCarthy Road. Two trails lead from the Nugget Creek Road near Mile 13.5 of the McCarthy Road. **Dixie Pass** is an 11 mile (18 km) strenuous back-packing trip that takes at least three days. Much of the route is not on well-defined trail, you must have good maps and route instructions before attempting it. The **Nugget Creek Trail** is easier to follow since it follows an old mining road. The 15 mile (24 km) trail is also suitable for mountain bikes and leads to an old mining works and an unmaintained park cabin overlooking the Kuskulana Glacier.

At the end of the McCarthy Road there's a parking lot where you can camp in your RV or tent, from there you must either walk or catch a shuttle the 1 mile (1.6 km) to McCarthy and 5 miles (8 km) to Kennicott. A mountain bike comes in very handy here for transportation since you must cross a foot bridge to reach the towns from the parking lot. From Kennicott there are at least three trails for strenuous day hikes or easy overnighters: **Bonanza Mine Trail**, **Jumbo Mine Trail**, and **Root Glacier Trail**. Portions of these trails can be done on mountain bikes.

Mountain bikers might want to try the **Bernard Creek Trail** at Mile 79 of the Richardson. The BLM recommends this 15 mile (24 km) road east to Kimball Pass and it looks good on the map. There's another similar road called the **Klutina Lake Trail** from about Mile 101 of the Copper Center Bypass section of the Richardson that goes east for 25 miles (40 km) up the Klutina River to Klutina Lake.

In Valdez the most popular hike is probably the **Solomon Gulch Trail**. The trail starts across from the Solomon Gulch Fish Hatchery on Dayville Road. The 1.3 mile (2.1 km) trail climbs steeply to the Solomon Creek power plant dam and offers great views of the town of Valdez across Port Valdez.

Wildlife Viewing

Bird lovers will love the **Creamer's Field Migratory Waterfowl Refuge.** It is located just north of Fairbanks, there are nature trails and a visitor's center with displays and volunteers to answer questions and lead hikes. Spring and fall are the best times to visit because the area is full of migrating waterfowl. The visitor center telephone number is (907) 452-5162.

Almost **anywhere along the Richardson** you are likely to suddenly spot a moose, maybe when you least expect them. Keep your eyes peeled. Isolated caribou are also often spotted on portions of the road passing through the Alaska Range. Also watch along streams for signs of beaver.

Bison were introduced into the Delta Junction area in 1928. They did well, today there are over 400 of them and there is an annual hunt to keep the numbers in check. The huge animals can be a problem, they love the grain that is grown by the farmers around Delta Junction and no fence seems to keep them out of the fields. The **Delta Junction State Bison Range** has been set aside for them but they tend to go where they want. In early summer you can often see them on the flats near the Delta River

BIRD LOVERS WILL ENJOY A VISIT TO CREAMER'S FIELD

from viewpoints between Mile 265 and Mile 241. A pair of binoculars will help you spot them.

The **Denali Highway** is an excellent place to spot animals, perhaps because the country is so open and the traffic so sparse. The Nelchina Caribou herd is present during the fall. Caribou and grizzly bears tend to stick to the wide-open areas, watch for moose and black bears where there are trees. It pays to stop occasionally and examine the open country with a pair of binoculars.

Wrangell-St. Elias National Park is accessible from the Richardson Highway by following the Edgerton Highway east to McCarthy. There's lots of game in this largest of U.S. national parks including Dall sheep, mountain goats, brown and black bear, moose, caribou, and even bison. Viewing the animals, however, isn't quite as easy as in Denali Park. There's no long road through the park with vistas in all directions as there is at Denali. Watch for animals along the McCarthy access road, you're likely to see a moose or two. To really see animals in this park, however, you need to get out and hike away from the roads or take a sightseeing flight.

In Valdez make sure to stop at the **Crooked Creek salmon spawning area** which is just outside town along the highway. From Valdez you can access the waterways of **Prince William Sound** on charter boats, cruise boats, ferries, or even with a kayak. The sound is home to Steller sea lions, seals, sea otters, orcas, gray and humpback whales, eagles, and a virtually unlimited number of marine birds, shorebirds, raptors, and ducks.

THE ROUTES, TOWNS, AND CAMPGROUNDS

FAIRBANKS
Population 33,000, Elevation 440 feet

Fairbanks may be only Alaska's second largest town but there is no doubt that the interior city is a more popular destination among Alaska Highway RVers than much larger Anchorage. This may be because Fairbanks appreciates its RVing visitors. There are lots of things to do in the area and many good RV parks. Fairbanks serves as a gateway to both the Denali Park area (121 miles (195 km) south on the Parks Highway) and the roads extending to the north, one as far as Prudhoe Bay (see Chapter 10 of this book). For RV travelers from the south Fairbanks may also be more popular than Anchorage because its summer weather is much nicer. There's a lot less rain in the interior and evenings never really get dark because of the midnight sun.

Fairbanks is the older of the two largest Alaska cities. The town was founded in 1901 and soon became a supply center for nearby gold fields. Gold continues to be mined in the area. Today Fairbanks is still a supply center, but now the area served includes most of Interior Alaska and the North Slope. The population of 33,000 shown above is only for the city, if you add in the surrounding area (the borough), the population is over 80,000 people.

You'll have no problem finding out about the available attractions in Fairbanks and the whole northern part of the state. The **Fairbanks Visitors Information Center** sits on the banks of the Chena River downtown near the corner of First and Cushman (550 First Avenue; 907 456-5774 or 800 327-5774). The **Alaska Public Lands Information Center** is nearby (250 N. Cushman Street, Fairbanks, AK 99701; 907 456-0527). All of the major commercial RV parks in town can set you up with commercial tour operators or give you suggestions for exploring on your own.

Pioneer Park, the town's historical theme park, makes a good afternoon's destination that can easily stretch into the evening. On the grounds you'll find several museums, the sternwheel riverboat Nenana, historical displays, souvenir shops, and a salmon-bake restaurant.

After seeing the riverboat at Pioneer Park you'll probably want to take a ride on one. The most popular attraction in Fairbanks has got to be the **Riverboat Discovery**. This sternwheeler makes twice daily trips down the Chena to the Tanana and is usually packed with visitors enjoying an extremely well-done trip including a stop at Old Chena Indian Village.

On the campus of the University of Alaska you'll find one of the most interesting museums in the state. The **University of Alaska Museum of the North** has displays about gold mining, natural history, the Alaska Highway, mastodons and dinosaurs, the northern lights, and lots more. You don't want to miss it! The museum is being greatly expanded, doubling in size, the new wing should be open in 2005. Nearby you'll find the University's **Georgeson Botanical Gardens**, these experimental gardens are a great place to see big vegetables and beautiful flowers.

THE RIVERBOAT DISCOVERY HAS TO BE ONE OF FAIRBANK'S TOP ATTRACTIONS

THE RICHARDSON HIGHWAY

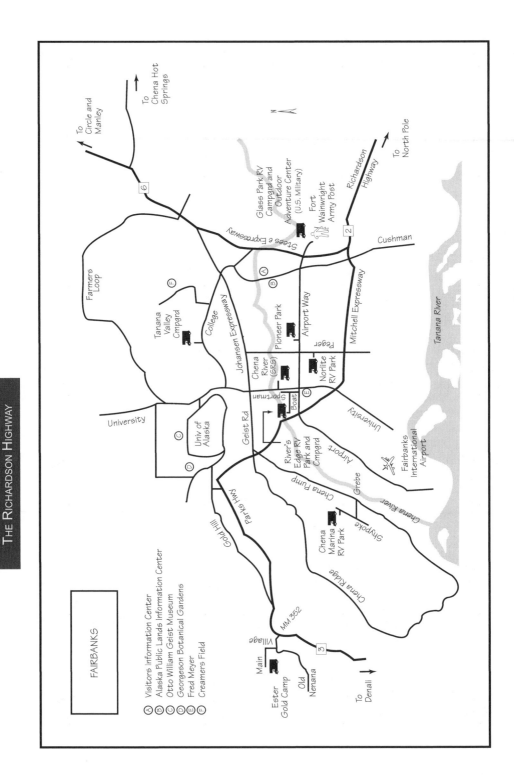

FAIRBANKS

Ⓐ Visitors Information Center
Ⓑ Alaska Public Lands Information Center
Ⓒ Otto William Geist Museum
Ⓓ Georgeson Botanical Gardens
Ⓔ Fred Meyer
Ⓕ Creamers Field

A big part of the history of Fairbanks and Alaska is gold mining. Near Fairbanks are two areas that have been extensively mined using huge floating dredges that left rows and rows of gravel "tailing piles". Both have exhibits that are well worth visiting. North of town out the Steese Highway is the Goldstream area around the little town of Fox. There you'll find both **Dredge No. 8** and the **El Dorado Gold Mine**. Both are commercial operations with hefty entrance fees and both are well worth the money. West of Fairbanks along the Parks Highway is another region of tailing piles along Ester Creek. Here you'll find the **Ester Gold Camp**, another commercial operation best known for its Malamute Saloon but also offering a restaurant and RV camping.

Fairbanks has 3 golf courses: Chena Bend (907 353-6223) has 18 holes and is located on Fort Wainwright but is open to the civilian public, Fairbanks Golf and Country Club (907 479-6555) has nine holes and the North Star Golf Club (907 457-4653) has 18 holes All are open to the public.

There are several interesting celebrations and events during the summer in Fairbanks. **Golden Days** during the middle of July is when the city celebrates its past with a parade and other events lasting five days. The **Tanana Valley State Fair** is held during the first half of August.

To send general delivery mail to Fairbanks you should use the 99701 zip code. This takes it to the only post office in town that handles general delivery mail, the one downtown that backs onto Barnette between Third and Fourth not far from the Public Lands and Log Cabin information centers.

Fairbanks Campgrounds

🚐 **CHENA MARINA RV PARK**

Address:	1145 Shypoke Dr., Fairbanks, AK 99709
Telephone:	(907) 479-4653
Fax:	(907) 479-0575
Email:	chenarv@mosquitonet.com
Website:	www.chenarvpark.com

GPS Location: N 64° 49' 02.1", W 147° 54' 43.4"

For aviation enthusiasts this is the best Fairbanks campground. The Chena Marina Campground is on the shore of the Chena Marina floatplane pond. Most good-weather days see a lot of takeoffs and landings. A bonus, the staff here seems to be the friendliest in town.

The campground has about 70 sites, many are large pull-thrus. The majority of the sites have 30-amp electricity, water, and cable-TV hookups although there are also a few full hook-up slots with sewer. The sites are very large with lots of grass separating them, there are picnic tables. Restrooms are individual rooms with toilet, sink and shower. There is a laundromat and comfortable indoor and outdoor lounge areas provide a place for trip planning and to watch TV and use the provided modem outlet. Wi-fi has recently been installed and some site have instant-on telephone service. The campground has a dump station and water fill station. There is also a vehicle wash station. Campground staff is more than willing to help you arrange local tours and excursions. Fishing for northern pike in the float-plane pond is allowed. Reservations are recommended.

To get to the campground follow the Chena Pump Road for 2.8 miles (4.5 km) from its intersection with the Parks Highway near the University. Turn right on Grebe Drive, then right again on Shypoke Dr. The campground will soon appear on your left.

CHENA RIVER STATE RECREATION SITE

Location: On the banks of the Chena River
              off University Ave.

GPS Location: N 64° 50' 22.2", W 147° 48' 38.3"

This is a state campground right in the middle of Fairbanks, it has a convenient location and is very popular. Two large supermarkets are within easy walking distance. This campground is now privately managed and electrical hookups have been added.

There are 56 back-in sites well separated with trees and natural vegetation, some with room for rigs to 40 feet. Eleven have 30-amp electrical hookups and water. There are also 5 tent sites. All have picnic tables and firepits. There are flush toilets but not showers. The campground also has a boat launch and a dump station. There is a 5 day camping limit during the June 10 to August 10 high season.

You will find the campground on the east side of University Avenue just south of the bridge over the Chena River.

RIVER'S EDGE RV PARK & CAMPGROUND

Address: 4140 Boat St., Fairbanks, AK 99709
Telephone: (907) 474-0286 or (800) 770-3343
Email: info@riversedge.net
Website: www.riversedge.net

GPS Location: N 64° 50' 22.1", W 147° 50' 04.3"

One of the nicer and more popular campgrounds in Fairbanks is the Rivers Edge. It sits on the south bank of the Chena River, has lots of grass and trees and specializes in arranging tours.

The campground has about 190 sites. There are a variety of types, full and partial hookups (30 amp), pull-thrus with lots of room for big rigs, dry sites for vehicles and also tent sites. All have picnic tables. The restrooms offer flush toilets and free hot showers, there is a coin-op laundromat and a gift shop. A special phone room as lots of modem hookups. There is also a vehicle wash station and dump and water-fill stations. Reservations are recommended.

The campground is located just off Airport Way, one of Fairbanks' main arterials. Turn onto Sportsman's Way across from the Fred Meyer store, immediately turn left on Boat Street, and then watch for the campground on the right.

NORLITE RV PARK

Address: 1660 Peger Road, Fairbanks, AK 99709
Telephone: (907) 474-0206
Email: reservations@norlite.com
Website: www.norlite.com

GPS Location: N 64° 50' 01.6", W 147° 46' 47.9"

This is one of the older Fairbanks campgrounds. It has recently become smaller as some sites have turned into residential lots.

The campground has a variety of sites. Some are set in trees, others are open pull-thrus. Both full and partial hook-up, as well as no-hookup sites are available. Electricity is either 20 or 30 amp and there is a dump station. The campground also has full restrooms with hot showers and a laundry.

The campground is located just a tenth of a mile south of Airport Road, turn at the corner on the west side of Pioneer Park.

🚐 PIONEER PARK

Location: Just off Airport Way at Peger Road

GPS Location: N 64° 50' 15.2", W 147° 46' 27.4"

The Pioneer Park city-run theme park offers dry camping in its huge parking lot. Lots of people take them up on it. There are no hookups but there is a water-fill station. There is also a city dump station very nearby where Moore Rd. (just east of Pioneer Park) meets 2nd Ave. Either chemical toilets are provided or you are allowed to use the restrooms inside the park which are open until midnight. Sometimes there is even a host at this camping area. Check in at the main gate entry booth, the attendant will tell you where to find the bathrooms. There's a four day limit for campers here. During the busy part of the summer there is a salmon bake located at the park.

Pioneer Park is centrally located just off Airport Way near the Peger Road intersection.

🚐 TANANA VALLEY CAMPGROUND

Address: 1800 College Rd., Fairbanks, AK 99709
Telephone: (907) 456-7956
Email: tvcg@tananavalleyfair.org
Website: www.tananavalleyfair.org/campground

GPS Location: N 64° 51' 52.7", W 147° 45' 33.6"

The Tanana Valley Fair is a popular area attraction during the first or second week of August. Don't try to stay in this campground that week, the place is probably a madhouse. At other times, however, the campground makes a convenient and pleasant base.

There are about 50 camping sites with picnic tables and firepits. They are set in a grove of trees and have pretty good separation. Rigs to 40 feet can park in some spaces but maneuvering room is limited. Fifteen of the sites have 30-amp power. There are also some tent sites reserved for hikers and bikers. The campground has flush toilets, free hot showers, a dump station, and a coin-op laundry. In past years there has been a conscientious and helpful host at this campground and firewood for sale. There's also a small kiosk-type café. There is convenient bus service along College Road to downtown and the university. The Creamer's Field Bird Sanctuary is also close by.

The campground is located at the Tanana Valley Fairgrounds on College Road. From the Parks Highway take the Geist Road exit and head east to University Ave., a distance of 1.5 miles (2.4 km). Turn left and drive north for .4 miles (.6 km) to College

Road, turn right on College Rd. and drive .3 miles (.5 km). You will see the campground on your left.

▄▄ ESTER GOLD CAMP

Address:	PO Box 109, Ester, Alaska 99725
Telephone:	(907) 479-2500 or (800) 676-6925
Fax:	(907) 474-1780
Email:	akvisit@gci.net
Website:	www.akvisit.com

GPS Location: N 64° 50' 46.5", W 148° 01' 11.2"

The Ester Gold Camp (officially listed on the National Register of Historic Places as Ester Camp Historic District) is the restored town of Ester City. This gold camp had its heyday in the early 1900's, it has been restored and offers gold rush-style entertainment in the Malamute Saloon, a restaurant, a hotel, a gift shop, and most importantly, a small RV park.

There are 16 back-in sites on a gravel lot and three tent sites nearby, none of the sites has hookups. Restrooms and free showers are located in the bunkhouse. There are picnic tables but no firepits. There is a dump station and potable water is available.

Ester Gold Camp is located just off the Parks Highway at Mile 352, about 6 miles (10 km) from Fairbanks. Follow the signs west for a half-mile (.8 km) to the camp.

▄▄ GLASS PARK RV CAMPGROUND AND OUTDOOR ADVENTURE CENTER – U.S. MILITARY

Location:	Fort Wainwright

There is a military campground on Fort Wainwright. It is only open to active military personnel, National Guard personnel, reservists, retired military, and Department of Defense employees. Reservations can be obtained at Outdoor Recreation Branch, Director, P.O. Box 35436, Fort Wainwright, AK 99703-0436 (907 353-6349). The campground has 48 RV spaces, most have electric and water hookups and there is a dump station. There are also 50 tent sites. Showers are available.

North Pole and Badger Road Campgrounds

▄▄ RIVERVIEW RV PARK

Address:	1316 Badger Road, Fairbanks, AK 99705
Telephone:	(907) 488-6281 or (888) 488-6392
Fax:	(907) 488-0555
Email:	dfickes@mosquitonet.com
Website:	www.alaskaone.com/riverview

GPS Location: N 64° 49' 56.6", W 147° 31' 02.8"

The Riverview is a large and well-maintained campground with a quiet location along the Chena River several miles outside Fairbanks.

The campground has about 160 spaces, many are large pull-thrus. Full utility hook-ups are offered including 30 and 50-amp electric and cable TV. Spaces are separated by grass and some trees. Picnic tables are provided. Individual shower rooms provide privacy. The campground sits behind a gas station and convenience store with the same ownership and also has a part-time restaurant, the Riverside Cookout, next

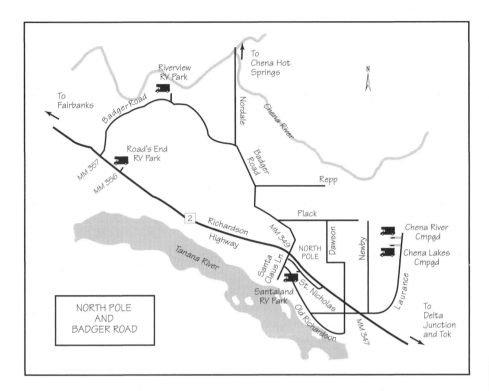

to the river. Other features include a small 3-hole pitch-and-putt golf course and a vehicle wash.

The Riverview is located on Badger Road. The best access route is from the Richardson Highway near Mile 357. Follow Badger Road for 2.7 miles (4.4 km), you'll see the campground on the left.

ROAD'S END RV PARK

Address: 1463 Wescott Lane, North Pole, AK 99705
Telephone: (907) 488-0295

GPS Location: N 64° 48' 07.9", W 147° 33' 07.7"

This is a fairly small RV park located right on the Richardson between North Pole and Fairbanks. The Road's End accepts long-term rigs, but it also has some good spaces for travelers.

The campground has about 50 full-hookup and closely-packed back-in spaces. Interior roads are gravel and parking is on grass. Showers are included in the daily rate. There is a laundromat and also a dump station.

Watch for the Road's End on the north side of the Richardson at about Mile 356. This is about 6 miles (10 km) from Fairbanks.

THE RICHARDSON HIGHWAY

SANTALAND RV PARK

Address:	125 St. Nicholas Drive, North Pole, AK 99705
Telephone:	(907) 488-9123 or (888) 488-9123
Email:	info@SantalandRV.com
Website:	www.SantalandRV.com

GPS Location: N 64° 45' 13.0", W 147° 20' 22.6"

Everyone knows that Santa lives at the North Pole, this campground is right next to the Santa Claus House, in fact it's owned and operated by the same people. The RV park is decorated to match with red and green picnic tables and a big Santa Claus statue out front. Children staying here like being able to walk over to see Santa's reindeer in a pen next door and there are walking trails across the stream out back.

The campground is one of the largest and most popular in the Fairbanks area with about 85 RV spaces and also a tent-camping area. There are full and partial hookup sites, also pull-thrus with plenty of room for the largest rigs. Electricity is 30 or 50 amp and there are television hookups too. Sites have picnic tables and are separated by grass. The large building at the front of the park houses the office, a gift shop, the laundromat, and individual bathrooms with sink, shower, and toilet. Any of the many local excursions and tours can be booked here and the very popular Santa Claus House (with its gift shop) is right next door.

The campground is located in North Pole, a Fairbanks suburb. Take the Santa Claus Lane exit from the Richardson Highway near Mile 349, then head south. Just before the Pizza Hut turn left on St. Nicholas Drive, the campground is on the right just after Santa Claus House some .6 mile (1 km) from the freeway exit. If you were coming from out of town you probably saw the huge Santa as you passed on the freeway before taking the exit.

CHENA LAKES RECREATION AREA

Location:	19 miles (31 km) from Fairbanks off the Richardson Highway
Telephone:	(907) 488-1655
Email:	parksrec@co.fairbanks.ak.us

GPS Location: N 64° 45' 14.4", W 147° 13' 07.3"

One of the big disasters in modern Alaskan history was the almost complete flooding of Fairbanks by the Chena River in 1967. To prevent this from happening again a major flood-control project was undertaken. Huge dikes were built to divert flood water, and some of the gravel came from what is now the Chena River Lakes Recreation Area. Built by the Corps of Engineers and managed by the North Star Borough this is one of the best camping areas in the Fairbanks region and certainly one of the best deals.

There are actually two campgrounds in the Recreation area. One is the Lake Park with 45 sites and the other is the River Park with 35 sites. Most sites are large back-ins although there are also some pull-thrus. There are also additional tent sites including some on a small island in Chena Lake. Both camping areas offer large back-in and pull-thru wilderness-type sites with good separation by trees and natural vegetation. Sites have picnic tables and firepits. There are outhouses and hand-operated water pumps. The recreation area also has a dump and water-fill station as well as boat ramps, covered picnic areas and swimming beaches. There are also extensive paved bike trails and a fish-counting operation which monitors salmon ascending the river.

Follow Laurance Road from its intersection with the Richardson Highway at Mile 347 for 2.6 miles (4.2 km) to the recreation area entrance gate.

FROM FAIRBANKS TO DELTA JUNCTION
98 Miles (158 Kilometers)

Between Fairbanks and Delta Junction the Richardson follows the north bank of the Tanana River. Much of the time the river is not visible from the highway. The Tanana is a very dangerous, muddy, fast-moving river that carries tons of mud and silt. Where it does adjoin the road it is often a problem because it threatens to wash out the highway as it unpredictably tries to change course.

For the first 25 miles (40 km) or so the Richardson is a new four-lane divided highway. You'll cruise past Fairbanks's southern suburb, North Pole, at Mile 349, about 14 miles (23 km) from Fairbanks. Most people stop in North Pole to visit **Santa Claus House** where you can pick up a toy or Christmas ornament and arrange to have Santa send a letter to someone back home. Twenty-five miles (40 km) from Fairbanks you'll see the long runway at Eielson Air Force Base on your left, watch for a long line of KC-135 tankers, F-16s, and the occasional flight of A-10 Thunderbolts.

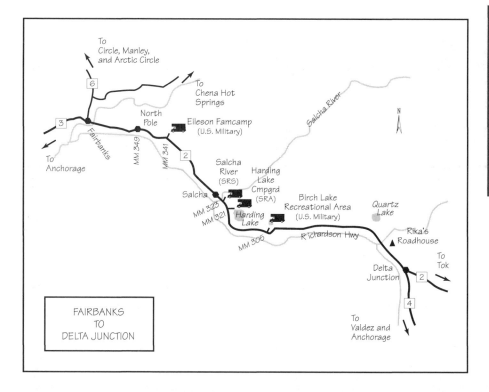

THE RICHARDSON HIGHWAY

At Eielson the road narrows down to two lanes and stays that way all the way to Valdez. For most of the distance to Delta Junction you'll have low bluffs on your left and the river on your right. At Mile 275 the road crosses the Tanana. The Trans-Alaska Oil Pipeline crosses at this same spot, you can't miss it.

Just south of the river crossing, at Mile 275 is the entrance road to the **Big Delta State Historical Site and Rika's Roadhouse**. This is one of the few remaining roadhouses along the Richardson and a good place to stop and stretch your legs. Delta Junction is just 9 miles (15 km) farther south.

Delta is where the Alaska Highway from the Lower 48 officially ends, so see Chapter 4 - *The Alaska Highway* for information about Delta Junction and its campgrounds.

Fairbanks to Delta Junction Campgrounds

🚐 EIELSON FAMCAMP – U.S. MILITARY
Location: Eielson Air Force Base

This is a campground on Eielson Air Force Base. It is only open to active military personnel, National Guard personnel, reservists, retired military, and Department of Defense employees. Reservations can be obtained at Eielson Famcamp, 354 SVS/SVRO, 3112 Broadway Avenue, Unit 6B, Eielson AFB, AK 99702-1885 (907 377-1232). The campground has 41 RV spaces with electric and water hookups and 10 tent sites. A laundry, dump site and showers are also available.

🚐 SALCHA RIVER STATE RECREATION SITE
Location: 41 miles (66 km) south of Fairbanks on the Richardson Highway

GPS Location: N 64° 28' 04.2", W 146° 55' 25.6"

Designed primarily to be a boat-launching area for the clear-running Salcha River, this recreation site also allows camping. There is a huge parking lot with about 60 sites where camping is allowed and also 3 designated campsites along its borders. The recreation site has a few of the customary picnic tables and firepits, there are vault toilets and a hand-operated water pump. The boat ramp can be a busy place, particularly on weekends. Stays here are limited to 15 days.

The access road for this area is at Mile 323 of the Richardson Highway, just southeast of the bridge over the Salcha.

🚐 HARDING LAKE CAMPGROUND
Location: 44 miles (71 km) from Fairbanks off the Richardson Highway

GPS Location: N 64° 26' 15.1", W 146° 52' 46.8"

Harding Lake is one of the few large lakes near Fairbanks, it is surrounded by cabins owned by local residents. The Harding Lake State Recreation Area gives the rest of us access to the lake. The recreation area offers a large beach with swimming, picnicking, sports fields and hiking trails as well as camping. Weekends can be crowded because Fairbanks is so close.

This campground has about 90 back-in sites and additional tent sites. These are wilderness sites with surrounding natural vegetation and trees, however, they are not as well separated as the sites in most State of Alaska campgrounds. Some are large enough for rigs to about 35 feet. They are situated back from the lake and have no views. Sites have picnic tables, firepits and dish-water drains. The campground has vault toilets. Other facilities include a dump station, a water-fill station, and a boat ramp. Stays here are limited to 15 days.

The paved access road to the campground leaves the Richardson Highway at Mile 321. It will lead you about .6 mile (1 km) to the campground.

🚐 BIRCH LAKE RECREATION AREA – U.S. MILITARY
Location: Mile 305 Richardson Highway

There is a military campground on Birch Lake, about 55 miles (89 km) outside Fairbanks. It is only open to active military personnel, National Guard personnel, reservists, retired military, and Department of Defense employees. Reservations can be obtained at 354 SVS/SVRO, 3112 Broadway Street, U-6, Eielson AFB, AK 99702-1875 (907 488-6161). In addition to cabins the area has 34 RV spaces with electric hookups and 14 tent spaces. Water is available and there are restrooms and showers.

FROM DELTA JUNCTION TO THE SOUTHERN GLENN HIGHWAY JUNCTION
151 Miles (244 Kilometers)

Driving south from Delta Junction you'll pass through **Fort Greeley**, probably with-

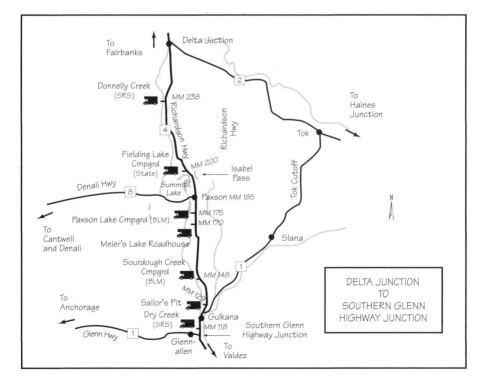

out even noticing. The fort was closed in 2001 but reactivated as a national missile defense site in 2002.

At Mile 244 there is a pull-off and overlook that in good weather offers views of three Alaska Range peaks to the southwest. These are **Mount Deborah** (12,339 ft.), **Mount Hess** (11,940 ft.), and **Mount Hayes** (13,832 ft.). This viewpoint is also a popular place to glass for the **Delta bison herd**.

The Richardson soon begins climbing through the Alaska Range to **Isabel Pass**. This 3,284 foot crossing is very gradual, you'll hardly know when you reach the top at Summit Lake at Mile 198. Before reaching the summit watch for pipeline Pump Station Number 10 at Mile 219. Also watch for the **Gulkana Glacier** at Mile 197. The summit is where the watersheds of the Yukon River and the Copper River meet.

From Summit Lake the road gradually descends to the Paxson Junction with the Denali Highway at Mile 185. The Denali Highway is discussed in a following section in this chapter.

Another important junction, this time the North Junction with the Glenn Highway (also called the Tok Cutoff), is at Mile 128. For 13 miles (21 km) the Glenn and the Richardson are the same highway, then at Mile 115 is the South Junction where the Glenn heads west through Glennallen to Anchorage.

Delta Junction to the Southern Glenn Highway Junction Campgrounds

DONNELLY CREEK STATE RECREATION SITE
    Location: Near Mile 238 of the Richardson Highway

GPS Location: N 63° 40' 26.5", W 145° 53' 02.6"

Donnelly Creek campground is one of the older ones operated by the state and doesn't get a lot of visitors except during hunting season. Still, this small campground makes a good place to spend the night along a section of road that doesn't have many places to stay.

There are now 11 back-in sites arranged around a loop road, one site has been filled with a host's cabin. Spaces are well separated in willows and white spruce but are small, rig size is limited to about 30 feet in these formal sites. All have firepits and picnic tables. The campground has outhouses and a hand operated water pump. There's also a large area for overflow camping and for folks with big rigs. Stays here are limited to 15 days.

Watch for the campground near Mile 238 of the Richardson Highway on the west side of the road.

FIELDING LAKE STATE CAMPGROUND
    Location: Near Mile 200 of the Richardson Highway

GPS Location: N 63° 11' 40.7", W 145° 38' 58.6"

Fielding Lake campground sits near the shore of a lake offering good lake trout and grayling fishing. There are a few private cabins in and near the campground vicinity. This lake is situated above the tree line in Isabel Pass so the surroundings are a little barren and unprotected from the weather. However, the views in this region can be spectacular.

There are about 15 sites here, not all of them well defined. Many are side-by-side sharing small parking areas. All are along a stream that runs into the lake. Any size rig will find maneuvering and parking room. Firepits, picnic tables, and outhouses are available. There is also a boat ramp. Stays here are limited to 15 days.

To reach the campground follow the gravel road which leaves the Richardson Highway near Mile 200 for 1.6 miles (2.6 km). The condition of this entrance road varies but even large rigs should always be able to negotiate it.

⊞ Paxson Lake BLM Campground

Location: Near Mile 175 of the Richardson Highway

GPS Location: N 62° 53' 05.1", W 145° 29' 09.8"

This large campground is popular with RVers because it offers nice large spaces, some are even pull-thrus. There is also a dump station. Paxson Lake is quite large and offers lake trout, grayling, and even red salmon fishing. Many people float the Gulkana River from here to the Sourdough Campground mentioned below.

The campground has 39 vehicle spaces, 9 of these are pull-thrus. Some will take rigs to 40 feet. There is also a tent-camping area. Spaces are well separated with many spruce trees. They have firepits and picnic tables but are not located along the lake shore. This campground has outhouses, water, and a dump station. There is also a boat ramp. The time limit for this campground is fourteen days.

From Mile 175 of the Richardson Highway follow a wide gravel access road west for 1.6 miles (2.6 km) to the campground.

⊞ Meier's Lake Roadhouse

Address: Mile 170 Richardson Highway
                  (HC72, Box 7190), Delta Junction, AK 99737
Telephone: (907) 822-3151

GPS Location: N 62° 49' 01.2", W 145° 29' 47.6"

This roadhouse operation occupies a site along an empty stretch of highway near a lake known for its grayling fishing. If you don't need hookups it's hard to beat this deal.

There are some 20 very large pull-thru RV sites located behind the roadhouse. They have informal firepits and some have old wire spools that serve as tables. There's a dump station and hot showers as well as a grocery store, gas, a restaurant, a lounge, and boat rentals. Camping at the sites is free.

The roadhouse is on the west side of the highway at Mile 170.

⊞ Sourdough Creek BLM Campground

Location: Near Mile 148 of the Richardson Highway

GPS Location: N 62° 31' 39.0", W 145° 30' 57.2"

This large campground is located along the Gulkana River and is a take-out point for people floating from Paxson Lake and a put-in point for people planning to float the lower river. A large area is set aside for parking rigs belonging to boaters. Fishing in the Gulkana and Sourdough Creek for grayling, rainbows and king salmon is quite good.

THE RICHARDSON HIGHWAY

The campground itself has 43 sites. These are large sites suitable for big rigs, some are pull-thrus. The sites are separated by natural vegetation including black spruce and have picnic tables and firepits. There are outhouses, a nature trail, a boat launch area, and a covered picnic area.

🚐 SAILOR'S PIT

Location: Mile 129 Richardson Highway

GPS Location: N 62° 17' 59.2", W 145° 21' 47.8"

This is a popular access point for fishing the Gulkana River. It's run by Ahtna, Inc., the local native corporation. Parking here has been in a large gravel pit but roads have been built and RV camping slots are being constructed in the trees between the pit and the river.

Access is via a good gravel road suitable for any vehicle that leaves the Richardson near Mile 129 and leads down the hill to the west and the Gulkana River.

🚐 DRY CREEK STATE RECREATION SITE

Location: Mile 118 of the Richardson Hwy.

GPS Location: N 62° 09' 07.8", W 145° 28' 30.4"

Dry Creek campground is conveniently located just north of the junction of the Glenn and Richardson Highways at Glennallen. It's managed by a private contractor.

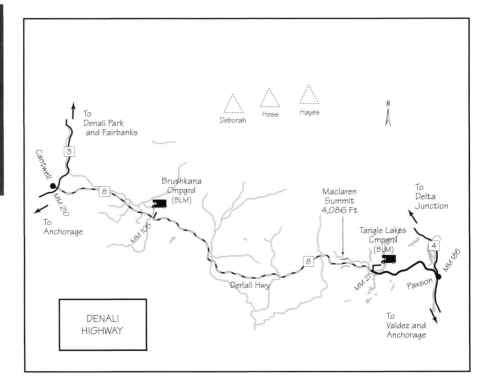

There are about 60 well-separated vehicle sites at this campground. Most are back-ins but one area has a number of pull-thrus with room for rigs to 40 feet. There are also some walk-in tent sites. All sites have picnic tables and firepits. There are outhouses and a hand-operated water pump.

The campground is located just west of the highway across from the Gulkana Airport, it is near Mile 118 of the Richardson Highway. This is three miles (5 km) north of the junction with the Glenn Highway at Glennallen.

Denali Highway Side Trip

The Denali Highway runs from Paxson at Mile 185 on the Richardson Highway to the Parks Highway at Mile 210. This is a distance of 135 miles (218 km), only the eastern-most 21 miles (34 km) are paved. Before the Parks Highway was finished the Denali Highway served as an access route to Denali National Park, today the road is little-used and traversed mostly by outdoors-oriented travelers. In the fall it is a popular hunting area but all summer the road is used almost exclusively by wildlife watchers, fishermen, hikers, canoeists, and scenery lovers. It really doesn't serve as a preferred route to anywhere else.

There are two formal BLM campgrounds along the highway but there are many more places where an RVer can just pull over and spend the night. The route covered is mostly high plateau dotted with lakes, fishing in many of them is good and it's not hard to see wildlife if you take the time to search with your binoculars. Maclaren Summit at Mile 35 is the second-highest highway pass in the state (4,086 ft.), second only to Atigun Pass on the Dalton Highway.

TANGLE LAKES CAMPGROUND (BLM)

Location: Mile 21 Denali Highway

GPS Location: N 63° 02' 59.4", W 146° 00' 25.9"

The Tangle Lakes Campground is located in high country with little in the way of trees. In good weather the vistas are wonderful. The campground is often used as a starting point for floats of the Delta River which is a designated a National Wild and Scenic River.

The campground has about 28 sites. They are separated by small bushes and are really not well defined, they're spread over a large area. Some, in effect, are pull-thrus or parallel parking spots suitable for big rigs. Some sites overlook the lake. The campground has a hand pump for water, outhouses, and a boat ramp.

The campground is located on the north side of the Denali Highway near the end of the pavement at Mile 21.

BRUSHKANA CAMPGROUND (BLM)

Location: Mile 105 Denali Highway

GPS Location: N 63° 17' 29.6", W 148° 03' 29.3"

The Brushkana Campground has about18 back-in camping sites as well as an overflow area suitable for RVs. Sites have picnic tables and firepits, there are outhouses. Fish for grayling in Brushkana Creek.

WRANGELL-ST. ELIAS NATIONAL PARK, COPPER CENTER, EDGERTON HIGHWAY AND THE McCARTHY ROAD

32 Miles (52 Kilometers) on the Richardson from the Glennallen Junction to the Edgerton Junction

Not far south of the Glenn Highway junction is an old town, **Copper Center**, which was founded in 1896 as a government agricultural experimental station. The main road now bypasses Copper Center, if you want to drive through town take a left at the junction at Mile 106 for the Old Richardson Highway. Near Mile 100 (off the Old Richardson loop) are the two entrances to an inner loop road which runs through old Copper Center. Off this road is the old **Copper Center Lodge**, one of the original roadhouses along the Richardson and still in operation. Copper Center now has a population of about 500 and has several interesting stops including the lodge, the **George Ashby Memorial Museum**, the log **Chapel on the Hill**, and a couple of king and red salmon fishing-oriented camping areas along the Klutina River which runs into the Copper River here.

Just north of the Copper Center loop entrance road is another entrance road, at Mile 106.6. This one to the brand new **Wrangell-St. Elias National Park Visitor's Center** (PO Box 439, Copper Center, AK 99573; 907 822-5234). The visitor center is not in the park, it's in Copper Center so that it is more accessible to the public, and because you need to stop and get information before heading for the park. The ranger

THE KENNICOTT COPPER MINE

THE RICHARDSON HIGHWAY

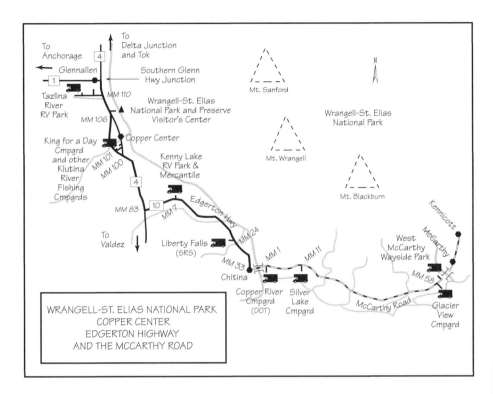

here can fill you in on the park which has very limited road access. The two access roads are the Nabesna Road off the Tok Cutoff (see Chapter 7 - *The Glenn Highway*) and the Edgerton Highway at Mile 83 of the Richardson (see below).

The Copper Center loop rejoins the Richardson Highway at Mile 100. Soon there's another junction, this one with the **Edgerton Highway** at Mile 83. The Edgerton provides access to McCarthy and the Wrangell-St. Elias National Park. Think of the road as having two sections. The first is the Edgerton Highway. It is a 35 mile (56.5 km) paved highway running through Kenny Lake and Chitina and then crossing the Copper River on a good modern bridge. At Chitina the paving ends and at the Copper River the McCarthy Road begins. The **McCarthy Road** is an unpaved 58 mile (94 km) narrow dirt and gravel road following an old railway roadbed. Occasionally spikes from the old railroad have been known to work loose and puncture tires. The road is not suitable for large RVs but pickup campers, vans, and RVs to 30 feet are fine. A van service runs from Glennallen to McCarthy and is an excellent way to get to McCarthy if you don't want to drive, check at the park visitor's center in Copper Center for information. There are several small commercial campgrounds and camping areas along the McCarthy Road and near its end.

At the end of the McCarthy road is a parking lot and from the parking lot there is now a walking bridge across the Kennicott River to McCarthy and Kennicott. Shuttle vans pick people up on the far side of the river. The distance to McCarthy is about a mile (1.6 km), Kennicott is about 5 miles (8 km) distant.

McCarthy, with a population of about 25, is the service center for this area. You'll find lodging, a restaurant or two, and guide services in McCarthy.

Kennicott is the reason for the development in this area. From 1910 to 1930 this was the location of a huge copper mine. Ore was transported to tidewater at Cordova along the railroad that formed the base for the road you probably traveled to get here. Red-painted buildings remain and are being restored (they're off limits) and there is a lodge. Hiking trails lead up the adjoining Kennicott Glacier and up the mountainside above the structures.

Wrangell-St. Elias National Park, Copper Center, Edgerton Highway and the McCarthy Road Campgrounds

TAZLINA RIVER RV PARK

| **Address:** | PO Box 277, Glennallen, AK 99588 |
| **Telephone:** | (907) 822-3546 |

GPS Location: N 62° 03' 02.1", W 145° 26' 01.1"

This small RV park is co-located with a mobile home park. It is a little incongruous considering its location in the middle of the Alaska wilderness, but this campground is one of the best places to overnight in the area.

There's a small unattended sign-in booth across the road from about 12 RV sites, mostly back-ins but with a couple of pull-thrus. They have electricity (20-amp outlets) and water hookups. The campground has hot showers (included in the nightly fee), a laundromat, and a dump station.

The entrance to the subdivision and the RV park is at Mile 110.5 of the Richardson Highway, about 4.5 miles (7.3 km) south of the intersection of the Glenn and the Richardson Highways in Glennallen. The entrance road goes west from the highway, take the second right for the campground. The huge empty lot to the south was one of the pipe storage yards when the oil pipeline was being built.

KING FOR A DAY CAMPGROUND AND OTHER KLUTINA RIVER FISHING CAMPGROUNDS

Address:	PO Box 372, Copper Center, AK 99573
Location:	Along the Klutina River near Mile 101 of the Richardson Highway
Telephone:	(907) 822-3092
Email:	king4day@alaska.net

GPS Location: N 61° 57' 08.2", W 145° 19' 06.4"

There are at least three of these campgrounds. They are used by fishermen fishing the Klutina River, well known for its runs of king and red salmon. These places are located between the old and new Richardson Highway routes, a short distance, along the banks of the river. The campgrounds are known as King For a Day Campground, Grove's Klutina River King Salmon Charters and Fish Camp, and Klutina Salmon Charters. Keep in mind that the single-minded object of pretty much everyone in these campgrounds is to catch fish, there's not a lot of concern about the amenities. When the fish are running they're crowded, when there are no fish they're likely to be closed.

King for a Day Campground has the nicest facilities. It has about 50 sites suitable for RVs, some next to the river, some with electrical hookups. There are even a few full-hookup sites at this campground and room enough for big rigs. There is a dump station and water fill as well as recreation room, hot showers, laundry, and fishing charters. The location and contact information in the title block above is for this campground. It is located next to the new Richardson Highway near Mile 101, fourteen miles (23 km) south of the southern junction of the Richardson with the Glenn.

Nearby, next to the river on the old highway, are Groves Klutina River King Salmon Charters (907 822-5822) and Klutina Salmon Charters Campground (907 822-3991). These places are much more basic with a few electrical hookups. Water fills and dump stations are available as are basic bathroom facilities including showers. Room for big rigs is scarce and access can be difficult, walk in to check them out before taking in a big rig. You can reach these campgrounds by driving the Copper Center Bypass or by taking a short good gravel road between the Bypass and the Richardson that runs from the entrance of King for a Day Campground toward the east.

KENNY LAKE RV PARK AND MERCANTILE

Address: HC 60, Box 230, Copper Center, Alaska 99573
Telephone: (907) 822-3313
Email: knnylake@alaska.net
Website: www.kennylake.com

GPS Location: N 61° 44' 09.2", W 144° 57' 09.2"

Kenny Lake Mercantile is located on the Edgerton Highway between Chitina and the Richardson Highway. It is a well-run fairly new roadhouse-style facility with restaurant, laundromat, hotel, groceries and campground. This is a good place to base your rig when catching the shuttle or driving a tow car into McCarthy.

There are 20 camping spaces. Ten are back-in sites with electrical hookups (20 amp) in the cleared yard near the store and laundromat/shower building. There is lots of room for rigs to 45 feet. Ten others are large pull-thru camping sites with no utility hookups set in trees in a secluded area nearby. The restrooms and coin-op showers share a building with the laundromat and cafe. There's also a grocery store and a gift shop in separate buildings as well as gas and diesel pumps. Both a dump station and water-fill station are provided.

This campground is on the north side of the Edgerton Highway some 7.2 miles (11.6 km) from its junction with the Richardson Highway.

LIBERTY FALLS STATE RECREATION SITE

Location: Mile 24 of the Edgerton Hwy.

GPS Location: N 61° 37' 20.0", W 144° 32' 42.6"

This very small campground is probably most suitable for tent campers. It sits in a small canyon next to the highway with a creek running through. Little Liberty Falls forms the centerpiece of the campground.

There are about seven tent camping sites, some with platforms located on a sloping hillside. For vehicles there are 3 back-in sites in trees. Although two sites will take big rigs the access roads are narrow and sites not level, we don't recommend this campground for rigs over 30 feet. There are picnic tables, firepits, outhouses and a water pump which was out of service when we visited. Stays here are limited to 4 days.

Watch for the campground on the south side of the Edgerton Highway near Mile 24. There are two entrances with the access road looping through the campground.

➡ DEPARTMENT OF TRANSPORTATION COPPER RIVER CAMPGROUND

Location: East end of Copper River Bridge on the Edgerton Hwy.

GPS Location: N 61° 31' 42.8", W 144° 24' 16.7"

This small camping area on the banks of the Copper River is extremely popular when the salmon are running, any other time you're likely to be on your own.

There are about 12 sites with picnic tables and firepits located in a grove of cotton-woods. This campground has few amenities but does offer outhouses. There is plenty of room for big rigs.

To find the campground follow the Edgerton Highway to Chitina, through town, and across the Copper River Bridge. The camping area is on the south side of the highway just after the bridge near what would be Mile 35 of the Edgerton except that this part of the highway is called the McCarthy Road.

➡ SILVER LAKE CAMPGROUND

Address: Mile 11, (PO Box 28), Chitina, AK 99566
Website: www.angelfire.com/journal2/amerivoice/silverlake/

GPS Location: N 61° 31' 01.4", W 144° 10' 28.1"

Located just nine miles (14.5 km) beyond the Copper River Bridge, Silver Lake is stocked with rainbow trout. There is a private campground on the shores of the lake. About 25 tightly packed sites are arranged around a circular driveway and below next to the lake. Services are basic but this campground offers convenient access to the lake. We wouldn't take anything over 25 feet into this place although the owner says rigs to 30 feet stay here. Motorboats, canoes, and rowboats are available for rent and there is a boat-launch ramp. The owner also provides towing and tire repair services.

➡ GLACIER VIEW CAMPGROUND

Location: One-half mile (.9 km) from the end of the McCarthy Road
Telephone: (907) 554-4490
Email: cepton@msn.com
Website: www.glacierviewcampground.com

GPS Location: N 61° 26' 07.1", W 142° 57' 33.1"

Just a half-mile (.9 km) from the end of the McCarthy Road is a camping area that is far better than the parking lot at the end. This campground has 20 back-in sites separated by natural vegetation. They are located on a loop road and well separated, most have picnic tables and fire rings. The slots are suitable for rigs to about 25 feet, about the largest rig you'd want to drive to McCarthy. The campground also has outhouses, hot showers, and a simple restaurant. Bikes are rented to make the trip to McCarthy and Kennicott and tires are repaired. Best of all, camping here costs less than at the parking lot at the end of the road.

🚐 WEST McCARTHY WAYSIDE PARK

Location: At Mile 58 (the end) of the McCarthy Road next to the
footbridge, 93 Miles from the Richardson Highway Junction

GPS Location: N 61° 26' 03.6", W 142° 56' 36.9"

When you reach the end of the road to McCarthy you can't drive into town. Instead you must park and walk across a footbridge. The land where you park is privately owned, in the summer of 2004 the charge was $10 per day to park and $20 to camp for the night. Facilities are minimal, there are outhouses and a public telephone. There's a small kiosk with information about the shuttles and also a few supplies.

FROM THE EDGERTON HIGHWAY JUNCTION TO VALDEZ
83 Miles (143 Kilometers)

From the Edgerton Highway junction the Richardson continues south through the Copper River Valley.

At Mile 29 a short side road leads to a parking lot and overlook for the **Worthington Glacier**, an easy place to get very close to a glacier.

The road crosses **Thompson Pass** at Mile 26. Thompson is only 2,678 feet high but seems higher. The huge snowfall here means that the vegetation is truly alpine. After the pass the road descends steeply and then passes through scenic **Keystone Canyon** to end, according to the mileposts, four miles (6 km) short of Valdez. This is because the entire town of Valdez was moved to a new site after the 1964 Good Friday earth-

NO NEED TO STOP AT THE OVERLOOK FOR A GREAT VIEW OF WORTHINGTON GLACIER

THE RICHARDSON HIGHWAY

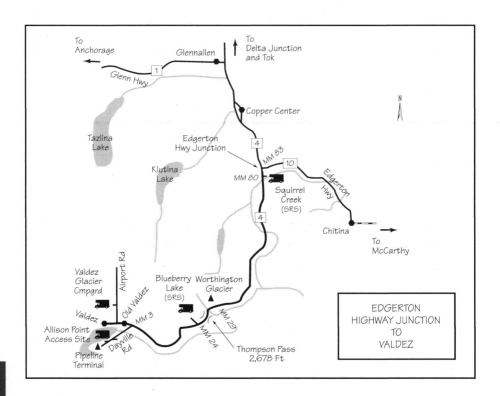

quake. Continue straight ahead to the new town site.

Edgerton Highway Junction to Valdez Campgrounds

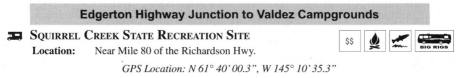

SQUIRREL CREEK STATE RECREATION SITE
Location: Near Mile 80 of the Richardson Hwy.

GPS Location: N 61° 40' 00.3", W 145° 10' 35.3"

A small campground with nice sites and offering some fishing for grayling where Squirrel Creek empties into the Tonsina River. There are also fish in the gravel pit next to the campground.

There are about 25 sites of various types, some are around a gravel lot and others are individual separated sites. Many will take large rigs. Take a look on foot before driving into any blind entrances if you have a large rig, you might have to back out. The area has cottonwood trees and some sites are along Squirrel Creek. They all have firepits and picnic tables, there are outhouses and a hand-operated water pump.

The campground is situated just east of the Richardson Highway near Mile 80.

BLUEBERRY LAKE STATE RECREATION SITE
Location: Near Mile 24 of the Richardson Highway

GPS Location: N 61° 07' 15.3", W 145° 41' 53.6"

This is a small campground, fairly close to Valdez, with a spectacular location. It sits below the summit of Thompson pass, surrounded by mountains and meadows. Little Blueberry Lake adjoins the campground. Bears are frequently seen nearby.

There are 13 numbered vehicle sites, four picnic shelters, and a few tent-camping sites. Stunted alders are the primary local vegetation. Firepits, picnic tables, out-houses, and a water pump are available.

Watch for the .8 mile (1.3 km) access road near Mile 24 of the Richardson Highway.

ALLISON POINT ACCESS SITE (CITY OF VALDEZ)
    Location: Near the Alyeska Terminal across from Valdez
    Telephone: (907) 835-2282

GPS Location: N 61° 04' 58.0", W 146° 19' 43.4"

This campground's reason for being is salmon fishing. Either pink or silver salmon can be caught from the shore during their respective runs. There is a salmon hatchery nearby, that's why there are so many fish here. The contractor (Capt. Jims) who runs this camping area also runs the Valdez Glacier Campground below.

Seventy back-in parking lot spaces line the road for about a half-mile. Some, on the ocean side of the road, are pretty nice sites with excellent views across the fiord to Valdez. There is no separation between adjoining parking slots. Outhouses are provided and drinking water is hauled to the campground. There is also a host.

The camping area is located along the access road to the oil-tank farm across the bay from Valdez. To get there follow Dayville Road from Mile 3 of the Richardson Highway. The campground lines the road from Mile 3.6 to Mile 4 of the Dayville Road.

VALDEZ GLACIER CAMPGROUND (CITY OF VALDEZ)
    Location: 2.3 miles (3.7 km) on Valdez Airport Rd.
    Telephone: (907) 835-2282

GPS Location: N 61° 08' 18.6", W 146° 12' 17.4"

This very large government campground is run by a contractor for the city of Valdez. It offers the services you would expect in a government campground, the price is reasonable and Valdez is only a short drive away.

There are 101 camping spaces arranged off paved access roads. About 14 sites are pull-thrus, the rest are back-ins. A few sites will handle rigs to 45 feet. Each space has a picnic table and firepit, toilets are outhouse-type and there is a water pump. Tent camping sites are available. Most of the vegetation is cottonwood or alder and spaces are well separated. There is a fifteen day limit on stays in this park.

The campground is located past the airport on the paved Airport Road that leaves the Richardson Highway at Mile 3.4. You'll pass the airport at .8 mile (1.3 km) and find the campground at 2.3 miles (3.7 km).

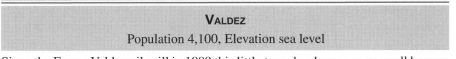

VALDEZ
Population 4,100, Elevation sea level

Since the Exxon Valdez oil spill in 1989 this little town has become very well known.

THE RICHARDSON HIGHWAY

Most people even know how to pronounce it now (Val-DEEZ). Before the pipeline the town may have been best known for its tremendous winter snowfall which sometimes exceeds 40 feet.

The oil spill wasn't the first disaster to strike Valdez. In 1964 the town was virtually destroyed during the Good Friday Earthquake. The present town is brand new, not much is left of old Valdez which was four miles (6.5 km) to the east.

The top summer attraction in Valdez seems to be the fish. Three fishing derbies run throughout the summer: the Halibut Derby for most of the summer, the Pink Salmon Derby at the end of June and most of July, and the Silver Salmon Derby in August. You can easily charter a boat, use your own, or fish from the beach. Fishermen practically fill Valdez's many campgrounds during the summer.

The **Valdez Visitor Center** is at 200 Fairbanks Drive (Box 1603, Valdez 99686; 800 770-5954 or 907 835-4636) at the center of town near the Municipal Building and Library. You'll see that the new version of Valdez built after the earthquake doesn't have a traditional downtown area, things are pretty spread out for such a small town.

Valdez is a port for the **Alaska Marine Highway**. From here you can catch a ferry to Cordova, Whittier, or Seward. That's one way got get out on Prince William Sound but a better way is one of the many cruise boats that work out of Valdez. The most popular destination is no doubt the **Columbia Glacier**.

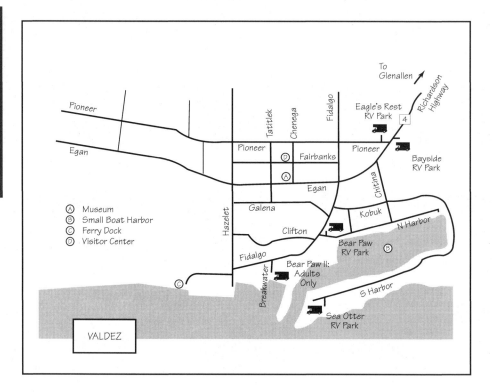

The **Valdez oil terminal** is located across the Port Valdez from the town. You can easily see the huge oil storage tanks and usually a loading tanker from the Valdez waterfront.

Valdez also has a **museum** (217 Eagan Drive). It has displays on the history of the area and on the oil pipeline.

Valdez is a small town but very busy during the summer. Tourism, fishing, and pipeline activities are all happening at the same time. There are lots of camping slots in Valdez and also, for such a small town, an adequate service infrastructure including a couple of medium-sized supermarkets.

Valdez Campgrounds

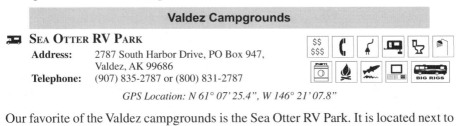

SEA OTTER RV PARK

Address:	2787 South Harbor Drive, PO Box 947, Valdez, AK 99686
Telephone:	(907) 835-2787 or (800) 831-2787

GPS Location: N 61° 07' 25.4", W 146° 21' 07.8"

Our favorite of the Valdez campgrounds is the Sea Otter RV Park. It is located next to the ocean on the peninsula that forms the ocean side of the small boat harbor.

The Sea Otter has 200 or more sites set on a large flat gravel area (there is some landscaping) next to the water. Fifty of the sites are waterfront, campfires are allowed at only these sites. Most sites have electricity and water hookups and are wide back-ins but a few are available with full hookups and there are a few pull-thrus. Restrooms are private rooms with showers, there is a laundromat, and the campground has a dump station. Reservations are recommended.

As you arrive in Valdez on the Richardson you'll pass the Eagles Rest and Bayside RV Parks. Watch for Chitina Ave. Turn left here and follow the road until you see a sign to the left for the Sea Otter and Kobuk. Turn left and follow the road as it curves around the small boat harbor. The campground is on the left at .8 miles (1.3 km) near the road end.

EAGLE'S REST RV PARK

Address:	139 E. Pioneer (PO Box 610), Valdez, AK 99686
Telephone:	(907) 835-2373 or (800) 553-7275
Fax:	(907) 835-5267
Email:	rvpark@alaska.net
Website:	www.eaglesrestrv.com

GPS Location: N 61° 07' 52.8", W 146° 20' 43.8"

Valdez's largest RV park is also probably its best promoted. You'll undoubtedly run into pamphlets and cards singing its praises long before you reach Valdez. It is also likely to be the first place you see when you reach town. That's OK because this is a friendly and well-run campground.

The Eagle's Rest has over 200 vehicle spaces and also a grassy area for tents. The vehicle area is a large gravel lot with little landscaping, much like practically every other campground in Valdez. Full hookup (30 and 50-amp power), partial, and dry sites are available. The central office building has restrooms with hot showers, two

THE RICHARDSON HIGHWAY

laundromats, and a fish cleaning area. There's also a Tesoro gas station right in the campground. This is the farthest campground from the waterfront, but still within easy walking distance.

As you enter Valdez on the Richardson Highway watch for the Eagle's Rest on the right.

BAYSIDE RV PARK

Address:	230 E. Egan Drive (PO Box 466), Valdez, AK 99686
Telephone:	(907) 835-4425 or (888) 835-4425
Email:	bayside1@alaska.net

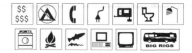

GPS Location: N 61° 07' 49.5", W 146° 20' 37.7"

The Bayside is the newest RV park in Valdez. This is not a waterfront campground but it is within walking distance of the boat harbor. The personable owner actively manages this campground and is very willing to offer fishing tips, he wants you to be successful.

Like most Valdez campgrounds this is a large gravel lot with lots of room to maneuver. The campground has over 100 vehicle spaces. Ninety-four are full-service sites and 70 are pull-thrus. Most sites have 30-amp power but a few offer 50 amp. There are also TV hookups. Nice restrooms have hot showers and there is a dump station.

You can't miss the Bayside. As you arrive in Valdez on the Richardson Highway you'll see the campground on your left as you enter town.

BEAR PAW RV PARK

Address:	101 North Harbor Dr. (PO Box 93), Valdez, AK 99686
Telephone:	(907) 835-2530
Email:	bpawcamp@alaska.net
Website:	http://alaska.net/~pbpawcamp/

GPS Location: N 61° 07' 37.0", W 146° 20' 59.8"

The Bear Paw is conveniently located just across the road from the small boat harbor. If you are in Valdez to take advantage of the available fishing charters this is a good base.

The campground is a large fenced gravel lot, but not quite as huge as a couple of the other campgrounds in town. It was the first of the big RV parks in Valdez. There are a variety of site types, some are pull-thrus. Electricity is 30 amp and there are full hookup, electric only, and dry sites are available. Some site have cable TV and there's also a dump station. The campground has restrooms with hot showers in private rooms and is convenient to a laundromat, restaurants, charter boat operators and central Valdez. The same owners also operate an adult park and a tent camping area nearby. The tent camping area is in a small grove of alders behind the adult park and has tent platforms and picnic tables. Reservations are recommended.

The easiest way to find the campground is to follow the Richardson into town until you see Fidalgo. Turn left on Fidalgo and drive .1 mile (.2 km) to the corner with N. Harbor Dr. The Bear Paw is on the corner on the left.

BEAR PAW II: ADULTS ONLY

Address: PO Box 93, Valdez, AK 99686
Telephone: (907) 835-2530

GPS Location: N 61° 07' 28.8", W 146° 21' 19.2"

The Bear Paw Adult Camper Park is nicely located right on the water at the entrance to the Valdez small boat harbor. While not quite as convenient as the other Bear Paw campground the scenic location easily compensates.

There are about 30 back-in spaces in this park. They have 30-amp electricity, sewer, water and TV hookups. There are picnic tables and a dump station.

To find this campground follow the Richardson into town until you see Fidalgo. Turn left here and drive .1 mile (.2 km) to the corner with N. Harbor Dr. The Bear Paw is on the left, you check in here. Then continue toward the water on Fidalgo for another .2 miles (.3 km) until you see a small street (Breakwater) going left. Turn here and you'll soon come to a dead end at the water with the campground to your left.

RICHARDSON HIGHWAY DUMP STATIONS

Travelers in Alaska should try to use dump stations in larger cities, on the Richardson that means Fairbanks and Valdez. Many of the campgrounds in this chapter have dump stations or sewer hookups. There is generally a fee, particularly if you are not staying at the campground, which is only fair. The section of road between Delta Junction and Glennallen has few places to dump, note that the Paxson Lake BLM Campground near Mile 175 has a dump station.

In **Fairbanks** there is a municipal dump station near Pioneer Park at the intersection of Moore Road and 2nd Avenue. Among the many gas stations with dump stations available to customers are the Holiday station at 2300 South Cushman Street, the Holiday station at 4105 Geist Road, Mike's University Chevron at 3245 College Road, Alaska Chevron at 333 Illinois Street, Airport Way Texaco at Airport and Lathrop, South Cushman Texaco on South Cushman, Sourdough Fuel at Van Horn Rd. and Lathrop, Sourdough Fuel off the Johansen Expressway, and the Parks Highway Truck Stop (Tesoro) at Mile 352.5 of the Parks Highway near Ester.

In **North Pole** there is a dump station at the Tesoro station at 3392 Badger Road. This is just north of the main North Pole exit, on the opposite side of the highway from the McDonalds and the Safeway store. There is also one at the nearby Sourdough Fuel station.

See Chapter 4 - *The Alaska Highway* for Delta Junction dump stations.

See Chapter 7 - *The Glenn Highway* for Glennallen dump stations.

In **Valdez** most campgrounds have dump stations but also try the Tesoro Station at the corner of Meals and Egan.

THE RICHARDSON HIGHWAY

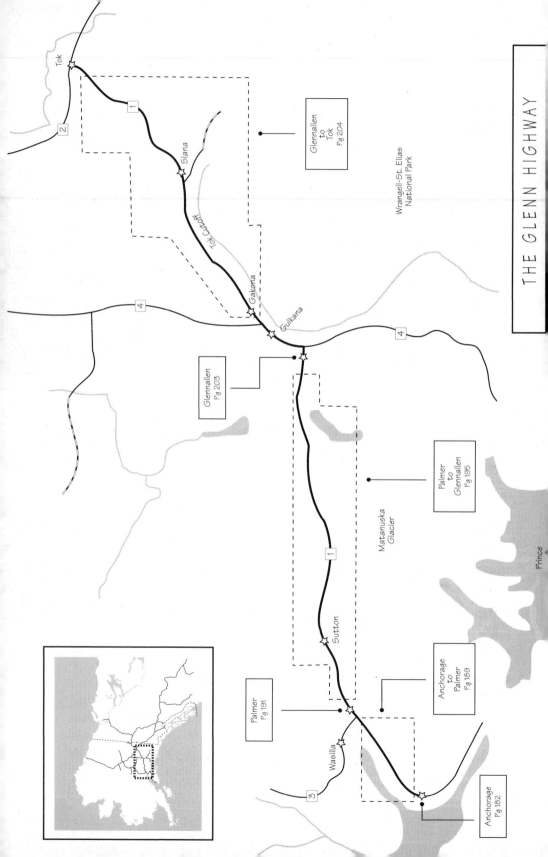

THE GLENN HIGHWAY

Tok

Slana

Tok Cutoff

Gakona

Gulkana

Wrangell-St. Elias
National Park

Glennallen
to
Tok
Pg 204

Glennallen
Pg 203

Palmer
to
Glennallen
Pg 195

Matanuska
Glacier

Sutton

Palmer
Pg 191

Anchorage
to
Palmer
Pg 189

Wasilla

Anchorage
Pg 182

Prince

Chapter 7

The Glenn Highway

INTRODUCTION

The Glenn Highway runs northeast 189 miles (305 km) from Anchorage on the shores of Cook Inlet to meet with the Richardson Highway near Glennallen. It then follows the Richardson north just 14 miles (23 km). Leaving the Richardson again at Gakona Junction the Glenn becomes the Tok Cutoff and crosses the northern Copper River country, threads through Mentasta Pass, and meets the Alaska Highway at Tok, a distance of 125 miles (202 km). The entire Glenn Highway from Anchorage to Tok is 328 miles (529 km) long.

If you are starting your trip in Anchorage, the Glenn to the Gakona Junction is the first part of one of two possible routes to Fairbanks. If you have driven up the Alaska Highway, the Glenn is your quickest route from Tok to Anchorage and the Kenai Peninsula.

Highlights

The Glenn highway starts in **Anchorage**, the state's largest town and commercial center. Visitors from outside the state shouldn't skip a visit to Anchorage, your trip to Alaska isn't complete until you've seen this city that is so different from the rest of the state.

The **Matanuska Valley** is Alaska's most successful agricultural area. In recent years it has also become something of an Anchorage suburb. This large area north of Knik Arm is usually known as the Mat-Su Valley because it combines the valleys of two rivers, the Matanuska River in the east and the Susitna River in the west. The Glenn Highway travels through the Matanuska Valley while the Parks Highway (see Chapter 9 - *The Parks Highway*) cuts off to head up the Susitna Valley.

As the Glenn climbs out of the Matanuska Valley you'll have a chance to see some very scenic country. A highlight is the **Matanuska Glacier** descending out of the Chugach Mountains to the south and visible from scenic viewpoints near the highway.

Once you reach the Glennallen area and turn north you'll have some great views of the mountains of the **Wrangell-St. Elias National Park** to the southeast. You'll find more about this park in Chapter 6 - *The Richardson Highway*.

The Road and Fuel

The Glenn Highway was only a rough trail until World War II. Then it was improved to connect the military bases in Anchorage with the Alcan. Until the Parks Highway was completed in 1971 the Glenn was Anchorage's only connecting road to the rest of the state and the Lower 48.

From Anchorage to Tok is a distance of 328 miles (529 km), a long drive but possible in a long day. The entire highway is paved but it is all two-lane road except for a short segment near Anchorage. Many sections, particularly on the Tok Cutoff, have permafrost problems and larger rigs are forced to drive slowly to stay in one piece.

Mileposts on the Glenn Highway run from south to north, but there are three segments of them. From Anchorage to the junction with the Richardson Highway near Glennallen they run from 1 to 189. Then there is a short section of the Richardson Highway with mileposts indicating the distance from Valdez. Back on the Tok Cutoff mileposts start at the south end at 1 and run up to 125 at Tok.

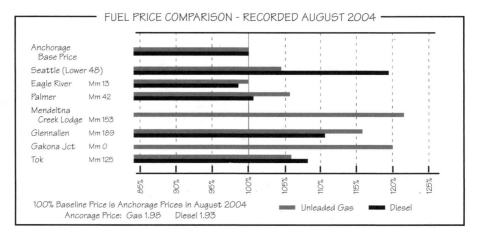

Fishing

Ship Creek, almost in downtown Anchorage, is the second most popular fishing site in the state with only the Russian River receiving more angler/days of fishing pressure. The best campground for fishing here is Ship Creek Landing RV Park which is within walking distance.

Many lakes in the Matanuska Valley are stocked with rainbow trout. See Chapter 9 - *Parks Highway* for more information about other fishing lakes in the Matanuska Valley, but also consider spending the night at one of the four campgrounds near the Kepler-Bradley Lakes State Recreation Area. You'll find stocked rainbow trout in the lakes.

Lake Louise is a large lake reached by gravel road from the Glenn Highway at Mile 160 and offers campers with their own boats the opportunity to catch large lake trout and grayling. The State's Lake Louise Recreation Area with the Lake Louise and Army Point Campgrounds is right on the lake.

As you drive up the Glenn Highway you may want to wet a line in one or another of the many small streams and lakes along the road. Here are a few to try: Moose Creek (Mile 55), Granite Creek (Mile 62), Kings River (Mile 66), Chickaloon River (Mile 78), Long Lake (Mile 85), Mendeltna Creek (Mile 153), Gergie Lake and Arizona Lake (Mile 155), Mae West Lake (by 1-mile trail from Mile 169), Tolsona Lake (Mile 170), Tolsona Creek (Mile 173), Moose Creek (Mile 186), the Gulkana River (access trail at Mile 123 of the Richardson), the Gakona River (Mile 1 of the Tok Cutoff), Tulsona Creek (Mile 15 to 18 Tok Cutoff), Sinona Creek (Mile 35 Tok Cutoff), Chistochina River (Mile 35 of the Tok Cutoff) Ahtell Creek (Mile 61 Tok Cutoff), Carlson Creek and Lake (Mile 68 Tok Cutoff, trail 2.5 miles up creek to lake), Mable Creek (Mile 76 Tok Cutoff), and Mentasta Lake (Mile 81.5 on the old Slana-Tok bypass). In the low country expect Dollies and rainbows, in higher country you are more likely to find grayling.

Boating, Rafting, Canoeing, and Kayaking

Anchorage is a waterfront city but don't expect to see many small boats on the Inlet out front. Cook Inlet is notoriously dangerous with a tidal range of near 30 feet, extremely cold muddy water, and frequent strong winds from nearby passes. Much farther south, off the Kenai Peninsula and in Kachemak Bay many people do use small boats on the Inlet but even there extreme caution is the rule.

The glacial **Eagle River** near Anchorage is a convenient and popular canoe, kayak and rafting river just outside Anchorage. Commercial rafting companies run the river. Access is from near the Eagle River Visitor Center and there are several take-out points. The first portion of the float is Class I, but Class II and Class III rapids near Eagle River require caution. Check with Chugach State Park personnel for more information. The Eagle River Campground sits on the river and is used as a take-out point by rafters, but note that it is just below the Class III Campground Rapids. After the campground the river passes under the Glenn Highway, do not continue past this point because the river becomes very dangerous.

The **Knik River** near Palmer is a braided river running from Knik Glacier for about 26 miles (42 km) to Knik Arm. This is a Class I - II glacial river with access to the upper river off the Knik River Road. The operators of the Mt. View RV Park run jet boat tours up the river. There are also commercial rafting tours of the Knik River.

Commercial raft tour companies run raft excursions on the glacial **Matanuska River** from Chickaloon which is near Mile 76 of the highway.

Lake Louise is a very large lake in the Copper Valley region west of Glennallen. It connects to Susitna Lake and Tyone Lake. Fishing and water sports are both popular on the lake, you can stay at the Lake Louise Recreation Area campgrounds on the lakeshore.

Hiking and Mountain Biking

Anchorage has one of the best systems of bike paths in the country, there are 121 miles (195 km) of paved trails. Don't miss the chance to explore them on foot or on a bike. The best is the **Tony Knowles Coastal Trail** which runs along the shore of Cook Inlet from Westchester Lagoon past the airport and connects with miles of cross-country ski trails in Kincaid Park. This trail has been designated a National Recreation Trail. Other trails connect at Westchester Lagoon and lead downtown or east to the university and Russian Jack Park. In fact, bike trails lead out along the Glenn Highway past Eagle River.

Chugach State Park just outside Anchorage has some of the best hiking and mountain bike trails in the state. The mountainous terrain means mostly dry trails and great views over Anchorage and Cook Inlet. There are access points to the trails in Anchorage's Upper Hillside area as well as from Eklutna Lake and the Eagle River Visitor Center. An excellent place to camp while taking advantage of the park is the Eklutna Lake Campground. See Chapter 14 - *Camping Away From The Road System* for more information about Chugach State Park.

Wildlife Viewing

The city of **Anchorage** offers an amazing variety of wildlife viewing opportunities. Hikers on the bike trails, particularly the Tony Knowles Coastal Trail, will see a variety of birds. Chances of meeting a moose are pretty high, there are thought to be about 1,000 of them living in Anchorage, as well as about 50 black bears and another 10 or so browns. Bird lovers will also want to visit Potter Marsh, see Chapter 8 - *The Kenai Peninsula* for more information. During the summer it is often possible to see white beluga whales chasing salmon and hooligan from the Resolution Park viewing platform overlooking Cook Inlet at the corner of 3rd and L Street.

To get warmed up (especially if you have kids along) visit the **Alaska Zoo** for guaranteed sightings of Alaska wildlife. Head out the Seward Highway and take the O'Malley off ramp. Turn toward the mountains and watch for the entrance on the left side of the road.

Chugach State Park's **Eagle River Visitor Center** has wildlife displays, videos about local wildlife, and you can often see Dall sheep on the mountainsides. There's also a nature trail. Along more remote trails in **Chugach State Park** you may see both brown and black bears, moose, goats, bald eagles, and sharp-shinned hawks. You reach the visitor center by exiting the Glenn Highway at Mile 13 and then following the paved Eagle River Road for just over 12 miles (19 km). For more about Chugach State Park see Chapter 14 - *Camping Away From the Road System*.

A MOOSE OBEYS THE TRAFFIC SIGNS IN ANCHORAGE

Just a little farther from Anchorage the **Eklutna Lake Valley** and surrounding hill-sides, also inside Chugach State Park, is a good place to see Dall sheep, moose, and perhaps even mountain goats if you are willing to hike the trails leading into the mountains from the campground.

The **Palmer Hay Flats** are a good place to watch ducks and moose. Take the Rabbit Slough access road at Mile 35 of the Glenn Highway.

In the Matanuska Valley there is another quite unusual animal viewing stop. The **Musk Ox Farm** (Mile 50.1 Glenn Highway; 907 745-4151) has a herd of 35 do-mestic musk oxen. They're being raised for their hair (called qiviut and harvested by combing the animals) and as a tourist attraction. There is a visitor's center and op-portunities for photographing the oxen. Fairbanks also has a musk ox farm but your only chance of seeing a musk ox from the road in Alaska is on the Dalton Highway, a much longer drive.

As you travel up the Glenn Highway stop to search for Dall sheep on the mountain-side at **Sheep Mountain**. It's on the north side of the road from about Mile 106 to Mile 113. You may also recognize that this extremely scenic stretch of road is used as a location for many cover photos on publications about driving or RVing in Alaska.

As you cross the high open country between Mile 115 and Glennallen keep you eyes peeled for caribou, this is part of the range of the **Nelchina herd**.

THE GLENN HIGHWAY

THE ROUTES, TOWNS, AND CAMPGROUNDS

ANCHORAGE
Population 275,000, Elevation near sea level

Anchorage is by far the largest town in Alaska, almost half of the state's population lives here. Many visitors to the state avoid Anchorage because they see no reason to spend time in a place that is much like any medium-sized western city in the Lower 48.

The fact is that Anchorage has its own charm. It sits on a point of land bounded on two sides by water and on the third by the Chugach Mountains. The city/borough (they're one entity) covers 1,955 square miles, about the same area as the state of Delaware. This largest city in Alaska is really not far from the surrounding wilderness, the huge Chugach State Park overlooks the city from the east and offers hiking trails, wildlife, and mountains to 8,000 feet.

Anchorage's weather, due to the city's location along the ocean and near several mountain passes, tends to be much cooler and cloudier than the weather in the Interior around Fairbanks. 70° F is a heat wave in this part of the state. The dry summer month is June. July and August get quite a bit of rain.

Even though Anchorage is the largest town in the state you will find driving to be very easy. Locals complain, but the morning and evening rush hours are really quite short and roads are plentiful and wide. The large stores in the suburban area outside downtown Anchorage have huge parking lots and lots of room to maneuver. The large grocery chains are Carr's and Safeway (both actually now owned by Safeway), you'll also find Wal-Mart, Fred Meyer, Costco, Borders, and Barnes & Noble. The city has a bus system called the People Mover (Ride Line information number is 907 343-6543) and most city RV parks are on the routes. The downtown Transit Center is at 6th and G Street. There's a special lot for RV parking downtown. It's north of the Holiday Inn on Third Ave. between A and C Streets.

Anchorage's central downtown area along 4th Avenue seems to have been almost totally dedicated to summer tourism. On the corner of 4th and F Street is the **Log Cabin Visitor's Information Center** (524 W. 4th Ave., Anchorage, AK 99501; 907 274-3531). This little sod-roofed cabin looks like a prospector's shack decked out with flower baskets, you can find information at the center about almost anything to do with Anchorage. A walking tour route starts at the information center, you can get a map inside. Across the street and on the next block is the **Alaska Public Lands Information Center** (605 West Fourth Avenue, Suite 105, Anchorage, AK 99501; 907 271-2737) one of four similar centers with exhibits and information about public land and parks (both national and state owned) all around the state. The others are in Tok, Fairbanks, and Ketchikan. Near these two Anchorage information centers you will find many small shops and a mall complete with a Nordstrom's and a Penny's.

An important downtown site is the **Anchorage Museum of History and Art** (121 West 7th Ave.; 907 343-4326). It has excellent historical, cultural and art exhibits. Another good museum is the **Heritage Library Museum** located in the Wells Fargo

FLOAT PLANES AT LAKE HOOD

Bank Building at the corner of Northern Lights and C Street (907 248-5325). It has displays of Alaska paintings and native artifacts.

The Anchorage International Airport is a busy place, but even busier (in terms of landings and takeoffs) and more interesting during the summer is the nearby **Lake Hood Seaplane Base**. With over 800 takeoffs or landings in a peak summer day it is the busiest water airfield in the world and a great place to find a bush pilot to fly you out into the real Alaska. It can be fun to find a quiet place to park along the lakeshore and watch the constant coming and going of small aircraft, particularly on Friday evening or Sunday afternoon on a good-weather summer weekend. On the south shore of the lake you'll find the **Alaska Aviation Heritage Museum** (4721 Aircraft Dr; 907 248-5325).

A relatively new addition to the Anchorage scene is the **Alaska Native Heritage Center** (800 315-6608), a 26-acre first-class facility with exhibits and programs about native culture throughout the state.

Anchorage is known for its **bicycle and walking paths**. They run through many wooded areas of town as well as along the shore of Cook Inlet from downtown to well past the airport. Get out and stretch your legs, walkers often see a moose or two along the trail.

Those interested in catching a salmon have an opportunity to do so right in Anchorage. **Ship Creek** has good runs of king and silver salmon and is within a mile of the central downtown area. The king run is in June, the silver run is in late August and

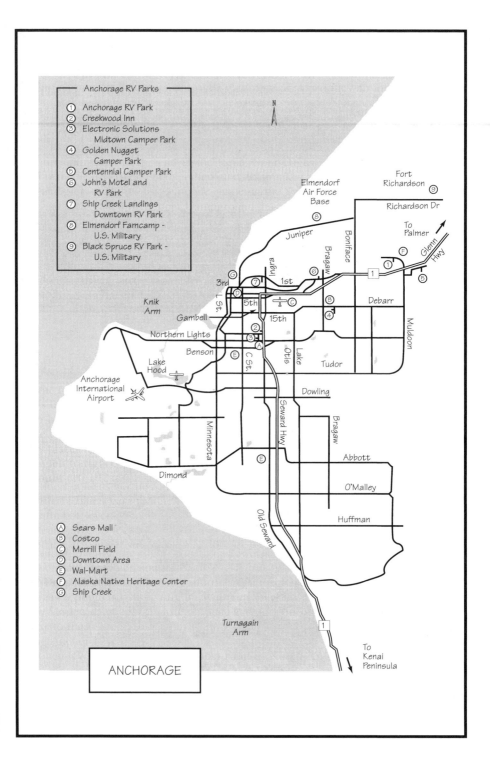

Anchorage RV Parks

1. Anchorage RV Park
2. Creekwood Inn
3. Electronic Solutions Midtown Camper Park
4. Golden Nugget Camper Park
5. Centennial Camper Park
6. John's Motel and RV Park
7. Ship Creek Landings Downtown RV Park
8. Elmendorf Famcamp - U.S. Military
9. Black Spruce RV Park - U.S. Military

A. Sears Mall
B. Costco
C. Merrill Field
D. Downtown Area
E. Wal-Mart
F. Alaska Native Heritage Center
G. Ship Creek

ANCHORAGE

THE GLENN HIGHWAY

early September. There's a king salmon derby in June, a silver salmon derby in August. Even-numbered years (like 2004 or 2006) also bring a run of pink salmon. This is shoulder-to-shoulder combat fishing at it's best (or worse) but can be amazingly productive. At least drive down and take a look.

Anchorage has five golf courses. The Anchorage Golf Course (3651 O'Malley Road; 907 522-3363) has 18 holes. Tanglewood Lakes Golf Club (11701 Brayton Drive: 907 345-4600) also has 18 holes. Russian Jack Springs Park (907 343-6992) is a 9-hole course with Astroturf greens. Two military courses are open to civilians: Eagle Glen Golf Course (907 552-2773) is an 18-hole Air Force course and Moose Run Golf Course (907 428-0056) is an 36-hole Army course.

If you are planning to fly to Alaska and rent an RV Anchorage is your best choice for a base. See Chapter 2 for a listing of RV rental companies. Almost all direct flights into Alaska (except those into Southeast) stop first in Anchorage. From here you can hit the road and head south for the scenery and fishing of the Kenai Peninsula or North to Denali Park or the Copper River Valley. RVers who have driven a rig up the highway will find that Anchorage has the most complete and reasonably-priced collection of service facilities available anywhere in Alaska or the Yukon.

Anchorage Campgrounds

🚐 **ANCHORAGE RV PARK**

Address:	1200 North Muldoon Road, Anchorage, AK 99506
Telephone:	(907) 338-7275 or (800) 400-7275
Email:	info@anchrvpark.com
Website:	www.anchrvpark.com

GPS Location: N 61° 13' 51.1", W 149° 44' 30.1"

This newest RV park in Anchorage is also the nicest. Located near the Glenn Highway entrance to the city the large campground has quiet, well-spaced sites, and brand-new facilities.

There are almost 200 spaces, all with full hook-ups including 20, 30, or 50-amp service. Some of the sites are pull-thrus, all are gravel-surfaced and surrounded by native ground cover. Picnic tables are provided. You'll probably notice that a lot more land was used to build this campground than most comparable commercial operations. There are television hookup sites and also sites with instant-on telephone outlets for overnight use. Restrooms are spacious and clean and the hot showers are free. The campground also offers a coin-operated laundry, a small store, and a dump station. The nearby Muldoon area of Anchorage offers good shopping for necessities, the downtown area is a 10-minute drive from the campground and city bus service (Routes 3 and 4) is available. A bike trail runs near the campground and connects to the extensive Anchorage system as well as running out along the Glenn Highway past Eagle River.

From the Glenn Highway northeast of central Anchorage take the Muldoon Road exit. Head north, the road soon curves to the left and you will see the campground on the left.

CREEKWOOD INN

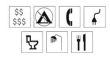

Address: 2150 Gambell Street, Anchorage, AK 99503
Telephone: (907) 258-6006 or (800) 478-6008
Fax: (907) 279-8972
Email: info@creekwoodinn-alaska.com
Website: www.creekwoodinn-alaska.com

GPS Location: N 61° 12' 03.6", W 149° 52' 06.3"

The Creekwood, formerly the Hillside, has a convenient central location near Anchorage's Sullivan Arena and next to the Chester Creek bike trails. These trails will lead you down Chester Creek to Cook Inlet and then either downtown or along the Inlet past the airport. They're one of Anchorage's nicest features. The Hillside is one of the few Alaska campgrounds open year-round, as a result it has quite a few older permanently-located units.

All of the 65 or so slots in this campground are back-in. Most have full hookups with 30-amp outlets and cable TV although a few electric-only spaces are available. There is a central services building with bathrooms, showers and laundry for the RV park. The motel office can book excursions and tours. Rigs over 35 feet long will find this campground a tight fit, sites are very tightly spaced. Reservations are recommended.

The campground is most easily reached by driving south on Gambell Street from just east of the downtown area. Gambell is the street that becomes the Seward Highway farther south. Gambell crosses 15th and descends into the Chester Creek Valley, you will see the Sullivan Arena on your right. As the road begins to ascend you will see the Creekwood Inn on your right. From the south you'll have to go north to 15th and return toward the south to enter the park.

ELECTRONIC SOLUTIONS MIDTOWN CAMPER PARK

Address: 545 E. Northern Lights Blvd., Anchorage, AK 99503
Telephone: (907) 277-2407

GPS Location: N 61° 11' 45.6", W 149° 52' 23.1"

It's hard to beat the Midtown for convenience, just right for short visits to the big city.

The Midtown is nothing if not simple. There are about 40 back-in spaces in a gravel lot on Fairbanks Street just off Northern Lights Blvd. The large Sears Mall and Carr's supermarket are just across Northern Lights. Most sites have full hookups with 15-amp service, a few have 30 amp. Sites are best for rigs to 35 feet. There is a decently maintained restroom building with free hot showers. We have found the location to be quiet although there is no formal security. The owners live relatively close and manage the park out of their electronics store out front.

As you head west on Northern Lights from its intersection with the Seward Highway watch for Fairbanks Street on the right. The campground will be on your left just after the turn.

THE GLENN HIGHWAY

GOLDEN NUGGET CAMPER PARK

Address:	4100 DeBarr Road, Anchorage, AK 99508
Telephone:	(907) 333-5311 or (800) 449-2012
Email:	gnugget@alaska.net
Website:	www.alaskan.com/camperpark

GPS Location: N 61° 12' 31.5", W 149° 48' 00.4"

The Golden Nugget is a huge RV park. Some folks think the campground's location across the street from the Costco store is its best feature, but it is also conveniently close to the 9-hole golf course (Astroturf greens) at Russian Jack Park and the city's bike-trail system. The campground also has good city bus service to downtown.

The campground has 215 RV sites, most are full hook-ups. Some sites are pull-thrus, many have room for large rigs. There are picnic tables at the sites and also a tent area. The restrooms are well-maintained and clean with free showers and there is also a laundry, a playground, a picnic area, and a modem hookup available in the office.

The campground is located near the corner of Bragaw and DeBarr. One possible access route would be to take the Muldoon Road exit from the Glenn Highway. Travel south on Muldoon Road to DeBarr, then west on DeBarr. You will cross the Boniface Parkway and then climb and descend a small hill, just after descending the hill you will see a Costco store ahead on your right, the campground is on your left. Turn left on Hoyt Street and then right into the campground.

CENTENNIAL CAMPER PARK
(MUNICIPALITY OF ANCHORAGE)

Address:	8300 Glenn Highway (Box 196650), Anchorage, AK 99519
Telephone:	(907) 343-6986
Email:	brossardddl@ci.anchorage.ak.us

GPS Location: N 61° 13' 41.7", W 149° 43' 20.7"

Centennial Park is a Municipality of Anchorage campground. Government campgrounds tend to offer more space and Centennial Park is no exception. While most sites are not overly large they are well-separated and there are lots of trees. This is also the least expensive formal campground in town.

The campground offers about 90 spaces for vehicle campers and also large grassy areas for tenters. There are no hook-ups. A few sites are very large, the rest are medium-sized back-ins, some will accommodate larger rigs. Restrooms are very basic but do offer hot coin-operated showers. There is also a dump station. Campfires are allowed in this campground. City bus service is available. The bike trail to Eagle River is just across the Glenn Highway. There is a seven day limit at this campground.

To reach Centennial Park head south on Muldoon Road from the Glenn Highway interchange. Almost immediately turn left onto Boundary Ave., the first turn south of the highway. From there it is easy to follow signs for about a half-mile to the campground.

THE GLENN HIGHWAY

☕ JOHN'S MOTEL AND RV PARK

Address:	3543 Mountain View Drive, Anchorage, AK 99508
Telephone:	(907) 277-4332 or (800) 478-4332
Fax:	(907) 272-0739
Email:	leonuf@aol.com
Website:	johnsmotel.com

GPS Location: N 61° 13' 27.9", W 149° 48' 48.6"

This older RV park and motel in Anchorage's Mountain View district is easy to find and conveniently located. This is an adult-only campground. Good city bus service is available.

The campground has about 45 back-in sites, most with full hookups including 30-amp service and cable TV. Parking is on concrete wheel pads with gravel or grass surrounding them. There are restrooms with free showers, a laundry, a gift shop, and a dump station. Groceries and RV supplies are available nearby as are restaurants. The staff in the motel office will help you arrange tours or excursions. John's is open year-round.

To reach the campground turn north from the Glenn Highway on Bragaw. Drive .2 miles (.3 km) to the first stop light (Mountain View Drive) and turn left. The campground will be on your right in another .1 mile (.2 km).

☕ SHIP CREEK LANDINGS DOWNTOWN RV PARK

Address:	150 N. Ingra Street, Anchorage, AK 99501
Telephone:	(907) 277-0877 or (888) 778-7700,
Fax:	(907) 277-3808
Email:	alaskarv@aol.com
Website:	www.alaskarv.com

GPS Location: N 61° 13' 19.4", W 149° 52' 16.1"

Ship Creek Landing is the closest RV park to downtown. Visitors interested in the central tourist area will love the fact that they can walk there in about ten minutes. The downside is that the campground is near the railroad yards so there's quite a bit of related whistle noise here.

This campground is relatively new. There are about 150 campsites, most are large back-in spaces with full hookups and 30-amp power although there are a handful of pull-thrus. An area is also provided for tent camping. The campground itself is a large gravel area below a bluff which blocks much of the southern sun. There is lots of room for big rigs, picnic tables are provided. The restrooms are in reasonably good condition with hot showers and there is a laundry.

If you are arriving on the Glenn Highway from the north zero your odometer as you pass the Muldoon Road freeway interchange at the entrance to town. Continue for 4.5 miles (7.2 km) to Ingra Street (the sixth stoplight the last time we were in town). Turn right on Ingra and go three blocks to the stop sign at the bottom of the hill. Turn left and you will see the campground entrance on your left.

☕ ELMENDORF FAMCAMP – US MILITARY

Location:	Elmendorf Air Force Base

THE GLENN HIGHWAY

There is a military campground on Elmendorf Air Force Base. It is only open to active military personnel, National Guard personnel, reservists, retired military, and Department of Defense employees. No reservations are accepted. The contact address is SVS, RE: Elmendorf FAMCAMP, 3 SVS/SVRO, Bldg. 7301, 13th Street, Elmendorf AFB, AK 99506-5000; (907) 552-2023. The campground has 62 RV sites with electricity and water hookups and 10 tent sites. Laundry, dump, and showers are available.

BLACK SPRUCE RV PARK – US MILITARY
Location: Fort Richardson

There is a military campground on Fort Richardson. It is only open to active military personnel, National Guard personnel, reservists, retired military, and Department of Defense employees. No reservations are accepted. The contact address is Outdoor Rec. Center, Bldg. 794, Davis Hwy. between 2nd and 5th Streets, Fort Richardson, AK 99505-6600; (907) 384-1476. The campground has 39 full-hookup RV sites and 5 sites with electricity and water hookups. There are also 7 no-hookup sites at Upper Otter Lake Campground. Both showers and a dump site are available.

FROM ANCHORAGE TO PALMER
42 Miles (68 Kilometers)

From Anchorage a four-lane divided highway runs north through a region of rolling hills between the Chugach Mountains and Knik Arm. The Anchorage suburb of **Eagle River** is at Mile 13, it has a population of about 18,000. Eagle River has supermarkets and restaurants. The paved Eagle River Road runs back into the Chugach Mountains for 13 miles (21 km) to the **Chugach State Park Nature Center**. Trails lead from the center into the park.

At about Mile 26 the road becomes two-lane and at Mile 31 the highway crosses the Knik River and enters the Matanuska Valley. At a junction at Mile 35 the Parks Highway cuts off to the west. Follow this road to Denali Park and for the shortest route to Fairbanks. See Chapter 9 - The *Parks Highway* for information about the route.

A few miles after the Parks Highway junction the road reaches Palmer at Mile 42.

Anchorage to Palmer Campgrounds

EAGLE RIVER CAMPGROUND (CHUGACH STATE PARK)
Location: Near Mile 12 Glenn Highway
GPS Location: N 61° 18' 22.7", W 149° 34' 17.0"

This large state campground is said to be one of the most popular in Alaska. This is understandable considering its location near the largest city in the state. Still, it doesn't seem to be hard to find a site if you arrive reasonably early in the day and avoid weekends. The campground is situated along the Eagle River near the Glenn Highway.

This large campground has 57 spaces including eight walk-in tent sites. RV sites are back-ins, most are roomy enough for large rigs. There's also an overflow area. All in-

THE GLENN HIGHWAY

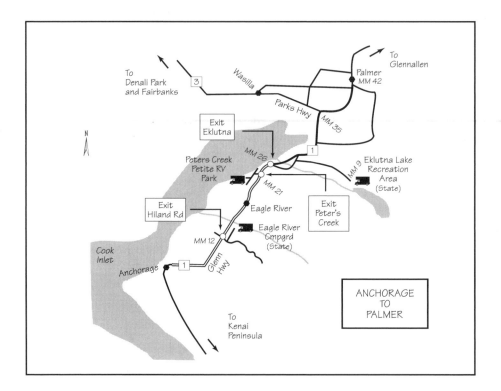

terior roads and parking pads are paved and sites have picnic tables and firepits. The camping sites are well-separated and there are lots of trees and natural area. Most toilets are vault toilets. There are also indoor flush toilets available at one building but no showers. There is a large dump station facility and water is available at the station for rig fill-ups. The campground is run by a private contractor, it has a 4-day limit and there is usually a host who sells firewood.

Take the Hiland Road Exit from the Glenn Highway near the 12 mile marker. The campground access road entrance is right at this interchange. The road runs north along the east side of the highway for about 1.4 miles (2.3 km) to the campground.

▄▆ EKLUTNA LAKE RECREATION AREA (CHUGACH STATE PARK)

Location:	Mile 9 Eklutna Lake Road

GPS Location: N 61° 24' 40.3", W 149°08' 58.9"

This very nice state campground near Anchorage is located high in the Chugach mountains. It's a wilderness campground easily accessed by big rigs. The campground sits next to Eklutna Lake, source of drinking water and hydroelectric power for Anchorage. There are several good hiking and biking trails from the campground leading into the surrounding Chugach State Park.

Eklutna Lake Campground has been upgraded to modern standards. Roads and sites are paved and many sites will take larger rigs. There are 40 back-in sites, 1 pull-thru, and 8 tent sites in the normal campground area. An additional 15 back-in sites are in an overflow area. Sites have picnic tables and fire pits. Restrooms are modern vault toilets and there are scattered faucets for water. There is also a walk-in boat launching area (for canoes and kayaks). The campground has a 15-day limit.

Access to the campground is via the Eklutna Road which leaves the old Glenn Highway just east of the Eklutna exit from the 26 mile (42 km) point of the new Glenn Highway in Eagle River. The paved access road is nine miles (15 km) long, the last seven miles (11 km) are narrow but easily passable in any rig.

PETERS CREEK PETITE RV PARK

    Address: 20940 Bill Stephens Dr., Chugiak, AK 99567-5676
    Telephone: (907) 688-2487

        GPS Location: N 61° 24' 35.2", W 149° 26' 52.1"

This small campground is conveniently located near the Glenn Highway with easy frequent bus connections into Anchorage. There are about 20 spaces, 16 have full hook-ups with 20 or 30-amp outlets. The campground is best for self-contained rigs, the only restroom facility is a port-a-potty.

To reach the campground take the South Peters Creek exit from the Glenn Highway near the 21 mile (34 km) point. The campground is on the west side of the freeway, Almost immediately as you head west the road T's, turn left at the T and drive about a tenth of a mile, the campground will be on your right.

PALMER
Population 4,500, Elevation 250 feet

Palmer was founded in 1916 as a stop on the newly constructed Alaska Railroad and served as the supply center and rail head for the surrounding area. In 1934 the Matanuska Valley around Palmer was the destination for 202 families from depressed areas in the Lower 48, the U.S. government moved them to the Matanuska Valley to take advantage of the area's obvious agricultural potential. Today's Palmer is surrounded by both farms and residential areas that stretch westward through the valley to Wasilla on the Parks Highway.

The **Mat-Su Visitor's Center** (HC01, Box 6166J21, Palmer, Alaska 99645; 907 746-5000) is actually located just off the Parks Highway at about Mile 36. This is very near the junction of the Glenn and Parks Highways. Palmer also has its own visitor's center, the **Palmer Visitors Center** (Palmer Chamber of Commerce, PO Box 45, Palmer, Alaska 99645; 907 745-2880) in town near the railroad tracks at South Valley Way and East Fireweed. It has a gift shop and a small museum describing the valley's agricultural history. Across the street is the **Palmer Farmers and Crafts Market** where you can buy local vegetables. You'll also find them at several roadside stands along major roads in the valley. If you are in the area during the week before Labor Day (the last week in August) be sure to visit the **Alaska State Fair** and take a look at some of the really big prize-winning vegetables that result from the long summer daylight hours.

THE GLENN HIGHWAY

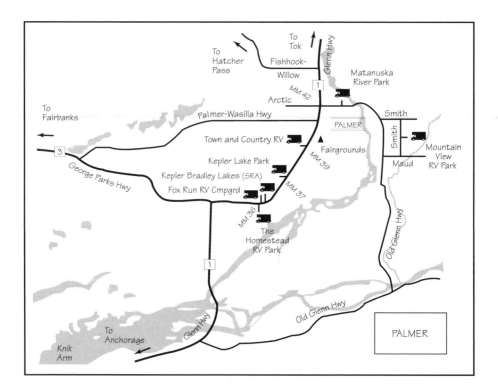

Golfers will be glad to hear that Palmer has a course. The 18-hole **Palmer Golf Course** (907 745-4653) is located behind the State Fairgrounds on Inner Springer Road which leaves the Glenn Highway at about Mile 40 and is open from 6 a.m. to 11 p.m.

A very interesting side trip from the Palmer area is **Hatcher Pass**. There's more about Hatcher Pass and the Independence Mine in Chapter 9 - *The Parks Highway*, but one of the best access routes is Fishhook Road which heads west from the Glenn Highway at Mile 49.5 near Palmer.

Palmer Campgrounds

MOUNTAIN VIEW RV PARK

Address:	PO Box 2521, Palmer, AK 99645
Telephone:	(907) 745-5747 or (800) 264-4582
Fax:	(907) 745-1700

GPS Location: N 61° 35' 41.4", W 149° 01' 30.8"

This large and friendly park in the quiet countryside east of Palmer offers an unusual attraction, airboat tours up the nearby Knik River.

The campground has about 106 spaces, most are large pull-thrus with 30-amp electricity, water, and sewer. The entire campground is a large open field, perhaps not as attractive as a treed area but a popular feature here since it means fewer mosquitoes and lots of sunshine. There's also lots of room for big rigs. A designated tent-camping area is provided. Another popular feature at this campground is the many individual bathrooms, each with toilet, sink and shower. There is also a coin-operated laundry and a community firepit with wood supplied by the campground.

To drive to the campground follow Arctic Street east from its junction with the Glenn Highway just outside Palmer near Mile 42. This takes you along the route of the Old Glenn Highway, it used to swing much closer to the mountains than the current routing across the hay flats to Anchorage. Follow the highway east for 2.8 miles (4.5 km), then turn left onto Smith Road, drive .6 miles (1 km), and turn right. You'll see the campground on your left in .3 mile (.5 km).

MATANUSKA RIVER PARK (MATANUSKA-SUSITNA BOROUGH)

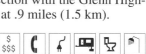

Location: Mile 17 Old Glenn Highway

GPS Location: N 61° 36' 30.7", W 149° 05' 25.3"

This is a nice campground operated by the local borough. The 101-acre park is more than a campground, there are hiking trails along the Matanuska River, playing fields, and a picnic area.

There are two camping areas. One is an open grassy area with back-in slots for about 40 rigs. A few of these sites will take rigs to 40 feet if the ground is dry. The RV sites have 30-amp outlets. The other area has about 45 back-in slots along winding roads through a forested area with picnic tables and fire-pits, a traditional government-type Alaska campground with no hookups. Less traditional are the flush toilets and coin-operated hot showers at this campground. Water is available and there is a dump station.

Follow Arctic (Old Glenn Highway) east from its intersection with the Glenn Highway near Palmer, the campground entrance is on the left at .9 miles (1.5 km).

TOWN AND COUNTRY RV

Address: Mile 39.5 Glenn Highway, Palmer, AK 99654
Telephone: (907) 746-6642

GPS Location: N 61° 34' 15.6", W 149° 09' 05.3"

This is a newer campground located just south of Palmer on the Glenn Highway. It has about 30 large pull-thru sites with electricity and water, 21 of them offer sewer. Some sites have cable TV and there is also a dump station. Grass separates the sites. A central building houses restrooms with showers and a laundry.

The campground is located near Mile 39 of the Glenn Highway near the state fairgrounds. You can easily spot the campground from the highway, it's on the west side.

KEPLER LAKE PARK

Address: HC02 Box 7810, Palmer, AK 99645
Telephone: (907) 745-0429

GPS Location: N 61° 33' 06.6", W 149° 11' 57.6"

The campground has a variety of sites. There are five back-in RV sites for RVs along the highway above the office buildings suitable for rigs to about 35 feet. These have full hookups. Along the lake near the office are about 10 more sites that are most suitable for tent campers or small RVs. Across the bridge in front of the office and up a narrow road on a ridge are another 20 larger sites in trees, they seem to be suitable for rigs to about 25 feet. Restrooms here are port-a-potties and outhouses. Pedal boats and other small watercraft are available for rent when an attendant is present.

Kepler Lake Park is located just off the Glenn Highway near Mile 37.

KEPLER BRADLEY LAKES STATE RECREATION SITE

Location: Mile 36 of the Glenn Highway

GPS Location: N 61° 33' 06.2", W 149° 13' 36.1"

The Kepler Bradley Lakes have long been a popular fishing destination. Recently the parking area has been opened to RV camping and there are a few tent sites. This is a large gravel lot suitable for any sized rig. There are vault toilets, hiking trails, and, of course, the lakes.

The entrance to the Kepler Bradley Lakes SRA is off the Glenn Highway near Mile 36. This is just north of the entrance to the Fox Run Campground.

FOX RUN RV CAMPGROUND

Address: PO Box 4174, Palmer, AK 99645
Telephone: (907) 745-6120
Email: foxrun@alaska.net
Website: www.foxrun.freeservers.com

GPS Location: N 61° 33' 06.6", W 149° 13' 43.9"

This campground is situated next to Matanuska Lake, part of the Kepler-Bradley lake complex. Much of this area is part of a state recreation area with stocked lakes and hiking trails.

The campground has 34 sites, 22 are full-hookup, most with 30-amp outlets but some with 50 amp. Many are pull-thrus with plenty of room for big rigs. There are also 7 sites with water and electric and 5 dry sites as well as a tent-camping area. Showers and laundry machines are available.

The campground is located at Mile 36 of the Glenn Highway, right across the road from The Homestead RV Park.

THE HOMESTEAD RV PARK

Address: Glenn Highway Mile 36 (PO Box 4215), Palmer, AK 99645
Telephone: (907) 745-6005 or (800) 478-3570
Email: homesteadrvpark@att.net
Website: www.homesteadrvpark.com

GPS Location: N 61° 33' 06.4", W 149° 13' 59.6"

This popular campground has an extremely convenient location, a sunny setting, and decent restrooms.

The campground has 68 sites sitting on a birch-covered bluff overlooking the Knik Valley and mountains to the east. Five good sites in their own separate area are provided for tent campers. Most of the remaining sites are large pull-thrus, they have 30-amp electric and water hook-ups. The campground has a dump station at the entrance. Restrooms are in a modern but sod-roofed log building and offer hot showers, there is also a coin-operated laundry. Fishing is possible in the lakes across the highway. The people in the office can help you with local tours and excursions.

The campground is easy to find since it is right next to the Glenn Highway near Mile 36. This is about .9 miles (1.4 km) north of the intersection of the Parks and Glenn Highways.

FROM PALMER TO GLENNALLEN
147 Miles (237 Kilometers)

After Palmer the highway begins to wind its way through a mountain pass and climb toward the Copper River Valley. At Mile 101 is the Matanuska Glacier State Recreation Site which has a viewing area overlooking the **Matanuska Glacier**. For a closer look at the glacier you can drive in to the private Glacier Park, which allows RV and tent camping. For many miles along the highway there are spectacular views to the south of the Chugach Range. The mountains to the north are the Talkeetna Mountains.

After climbing out of the Matanuska Valley the road runs through **Tahneta Pass** and across 3,322-foot **Eureka Summit**, then through a high plateau region with hundreds of little lakes and scattered black spruce trees. Many of the lakes have good

MATANUSKA GLACIER FROM THE OVERLOOK AREA

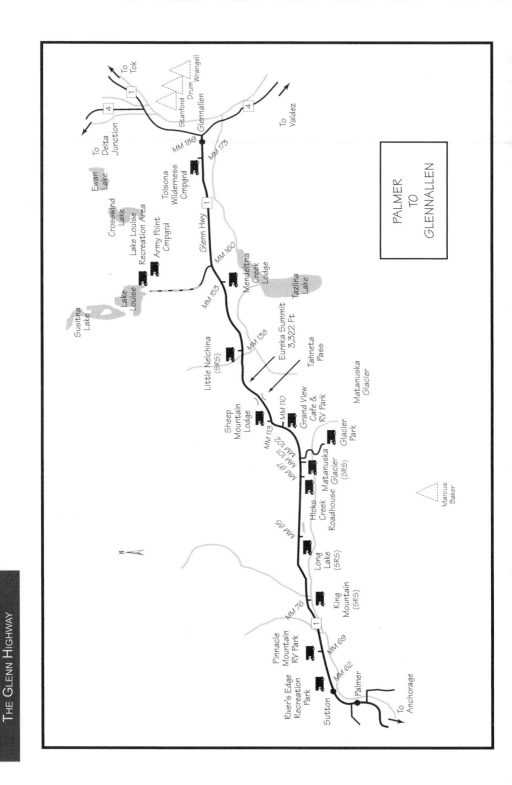

PALMER
TO
GLENNALLEN

fishing but they're difficult to access. There is a gravel road that runs north for 17 miles (27 km) from Mile 160 to **Lake Louise** which has excellent fishing and two state campgrounds.

Once you pass the Lake Louise junction you'll start to see the Wrangell Mountains ahead. From left to right the peaks are **Mount Sanford** (16,237 feet), **Mount Drum** (12,010 feet), and **Mount Wrangell** (14,163 feet). All of them are in the Wrangell-St. Elias National park. See Chapter 6 - *The Richardson Highway* for more about this park. The road reaches Glennallen at Mile 187.

Palmer to Glennallen Campgrounds

RIVER'S EDGE RECREATION PARK

    Address: PO Box 364, Sutton, AK 99674
    Telephone: (907) 746-2267 or (907) 745-6245

    GPS Location: N 61° 42' 42.4", W 148° 50' 56.5"

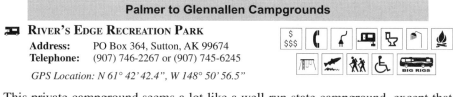

This private campground seems a lot like a well-run state campground, except that there are some electrical hookups and restrooms with flush toilets and hot showers. Unfortunately, the location next to Granite Creek doesn't mean that you can camp right on the water, there is a large gravel dike separating the campground from the creek. Overall, though, this is a very pleasant little campground.

There are 27 sites, over half have 20 or 30-amp electrical outlets, most are scattered back-ins but there are several pull-thrus. Some sites will take rigs to 40 feet. Many sites have picnic tables and firepits and there is a dump and water fill station. The new and modern restroom building is accessible to handicapped campers and there is an extra fee for showers. You can fish in Granite Creek and there is a bicycle path along the highway to the little town of Sutton.

The campground is located on the Glenn Highway near Mile 62, some 20 miles (32 km) from Palmer.

PINNACLE MOUNTAIN RV PARK

    Address: Mile 69.7 Glenn Highway, Sutton, AK 99674
    Telephone: (907) 746-6531

    GPS Location: N 61° 44' 39.6", W 148° 39' 34.7"

This is a new campground located along the Glenn Highway near Sutton. In addition to the campground the lodge offers groceries and a laundry. A restaurant is also planned.

There are 42 campsites. Twelve are large pull-thrus on gravel and grass next to the lodge building. These sites have 30-amp electrical and water hookups. Other campsites are in the trees behind, some are pull-thrus with electricity, others are smaller sites without services. Some sites have picnic tables, there are restrooms with hot showers and a dump station.

The campground is located right on the Glenn Highway at Mile 69.7.

KING MOUNTAIN STATE RECREATION SITE

    Location: Mile 76 Glenn Highway

    GPS Location: N 61° 46' 30.1", W 148° 29' 44.2"

THE GLENN HIGHWAY

The best of the state campgrounds for smaller rigs along this section of the Glenn Highway is undoubtedly King Mountain. There are some 24 smallish back-in sites suitable for rigs to about 30 feet in a wooded setting next to the milky Matanuska River. Sites have picnic tables and firepits and there are outhouses and a water pump. This campground also has a boat launch and a kitchen/picnic shelter. There is a 7-day stay limit at this campground.

🚐 LONG LAKE STATE RECREATION SITE

Location: Mile 85 Glenn Highway

GPS Location: N 61° 48' 14.0", W 148° 14' 13.0"

Long Lake is very scenic, especially if your are descending from the high country near Glennallen. There's the sheltered little lake surrounded by trees, fishermen in small boats dot the surface. Camping possibilities here are limited. This appears to be one of those state campgrounds that is being "passively managed". In other words, it's not being maintained. The gravel lot has room for a rig or two and there are a few very small sites back in the woods. The picnic tables and fire pits that used to be here are now gone. There is still an outhouse and the price is right. There's a small boat ramp and you can catch grayling in the lake.

🚐 HICKS CREEK ROADHOUSE

Address: HC 3 Box 8410, Palmer, AK 99645
Telephone: (907) 745-8213
Email: hickscreek@hotmail.com

GPS Location: N 61° 47' 33.4", W 147° 56' 02.8"

THE VEIW FROM THE GRAND VIEW RV PARK

Back behind this little roadhouse-style operation is a pleasant little camping area. There are about 15 campsites set in cottonwood trees behind the roadhouse. Four of them are pull-thrus with electrical hookups (really more like long extension cords). Some sites have picnic tables and some have firepits. Maneuvering room is limited so walk in and take a look, we think maximum rig size is about 35 feet. The laundry building also houses some decent coin-op showers. The lodge is located on the south side of the Glenn Highway near Mile 97.

MATANUSKA GLACIER STATE RECREATION SITE
Location: Mile 101 of the Glenn Highway

GPS Location: N 61° 48' 00.6", W 147° 48' 54.6"

This recreation site gets lots of visitors because it offers a viewpoint with good views of the Matanuska Glacier. Many tour busses and passing motorists make the stop.

There are also 9 vehicle camping sites for rigs to about 26 feet. The sites are well separated and have picnic tables and firepits. Camping is also allowed in the overlook parking lot, this area will take any size rig and the price is lower. The campground has modern vault toilets and a water pump.

Watch for the recreation site on the south side of the Glenn Highway near Mile 101.

GLACIER PARK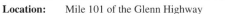
Address: HC03 Box 8449, Palmer, AK 99645
Telephone: (907) 745-2534 or (888) 253-4480
Email: blueice@gci.net
Website: www.matanuskaglacier.com

GPS Location: N 61° 47' 35.2", W 147° 47' 50.3"

Glacier Park is a unique private operation. They have an impressive road that descends from the highway to the flat bench near the Matanuska Glacier. You leave the highway near Mile 102 and descend to a gatehouse area at about .8 miles (1.3 km). Here you'll find a small restaurant and gift shop. To pass on to the glacier overlook you must pay a fee of $10.00 per person plus $10 per vehicle. The overlook is at 3.1 miles (5 km) and is popular for picnics. From the parking area it is usually possible to walk to the rapidly retreating glacier.

Camping facilities at Glacier Park are limited. At the overlook it is possible to dry camp in the parking area if you have a self-contained rig. There are picnic tables and an outhouse but this is an exposed location with often blustery weather. Near the gatehouse complex there is an 8-space tent camping area suitable for tents or small rigs with picnic tables, firepits, and an outhouse.

GRAND VIEW CAFÉ & RV PARK
Address: HC03 Box 8484, Palmer, AK 99645,
                   Palmer, AK 99654
Telephone: (907) 746-4480
Website: www.grandviewrv.com

GPS Location: N 61° 47' 54.5", W 147° 36' 32.3"

This campground has a spectacular location next to the highway in a high mountain pass. You can often spot Dall sheep from the campsites.

THE GLENN HIGHWAY

The campground has 19 large pull-thru sites situated on a big gravel bench next to the highway. They are all either full hookup or water and electric sites, some with 30-amp power and some with 50 amp. There are showers, a dump station, a laundry and a café. The campground is located near Mile 110 of the Glenn Highway and is easy to spot from the road.

SHEEP MOUNTAIN LODGE

Address: HC 03 Box 8490, Palmer, AK 99645
Telephone: (907) 745-5121 or (877) 645-5121
Email: sheepmtl@alaska.net
Website: www.sheepmountain.com

GPS Location: N 61° 48' 43.5", W 147° 29' 54.5"

The real reason for stopping here is the restaurant, it is excellent. There are also nice rental cabins. Camping is limited to parking in the lot in front of the lodge near the highway. Electrical hookups for four rigs are available. Tents are not accommodated. You can pay a little extra for a hot shower in the immaculate restrooms or to soak in the hot tub.

The lodge is located on the north side of the highway near Mile 113.5 of the Glenn Highway.

LITTLE NELCHINA STATE RECREATION SITE

Location: Mile 138 of the Glenn Highway

GPS Location: N 61° 59' 27.0", W 146° 56' 47.7"

This little state recreation site is tucked into a small canyon near the highway. It's "passively managed" by the State, but still in pretty good shape. Access is via a short stretch of the old highway that was abandoned during road-straightening construction.

There are 8 sites in this camping area. Several of them are along the creek in spruce and cottonwoods. Most are fairly small and are back-ins or tent sites. There are outhouses and a raft launching area. The picnic tables have disappeared and there is no drinking water, but this isn't a bad place to stop for the night if you have a rig up to about 25 feet long. You can hike upriver to some fossil beds.

The campground isn't right on the main road. Instead, it's off an old section of the highway that has been bypassed by the new highway. There's no sign, you turn onto the old section of road, which is still paved, near Mile 138 and drive about a hundred yards to the camping area entrance.

MENDELTNA CREEK LODGE

Address: HC1 Box 2560, Glennallen, AK 99588
Telephone: (907) 822-3346

GPS Location: N 62° 02' 54.7", W 146° 32' 19.0"

Formerly called the K.R.O.A., this is a full service campground seemingly situated in the middle of nowhere. There are at about 80 camping spaces in a large gravel lot behind the restaurant and cabins out front. Trees break up the large expanse of the campground. Many sites are pull-thrus and have either full or electric (20 amp) and water hookups, there is also a dump station. Some sites are along the Little Mendeltna, a small stream running along the side of the campground. There are picnic tables and some sites have circles of rocks forming fire rings. The laundry/shower building has flush toilets and hot showers.

The campground is located on the south side of the Glenn Highway near Mile 153. This is about 30 miles (48 km) from Glennallen and near the half-way point if you are driving between either Tok or Valdez and Anchorage.

🚐 LAKE LOUISE STATE RECREATION AREA
LAKE LOUISE AND ARMY POINT CAMPGROUNDS

| Location: | Mile 16 Lake Louise Road, |
| | Leaves Glenn Highway at Mile 160 |

GPS Location: N 62° 16' 54.0", W 146° 32' 33.9"

Lake Louise is a huge lake that is very popular year-round, which is surprising considering its remote location. In the summer fishing, especially for lake trout, is popular. In late summer the water is warm enough for swimming (you've got to be tough) and water sports. During the fall this is a popular hunting area and in the winter this can be great snow machining and ice fishing country.

There are two modern state campgrounds located right next to each other on the southwest shore of the lake with 68 camping spaces. They really make up one large campground. Most of the sites here are back-ins in large gravel parking areas but a few are separated sites. The trees in the area are very small dwarf species or shrubs so don't expect a lot of privacy even if you get one of the separated spaces. There are

A GREAT VIEW OF THE WRANGELL-ST ELIAS PARK APPROACIHING GLENNALLEN

picnic tables and firepits. Other offerings are outhouses, water pumps, a boat launching area, and a nice little beach with a walking trail between the two campgrounds. There is a 15-day limit here.

To reach the campgrounds you must follow Lake Louise Road north from near Mile 160 of the Glenn Highway. The campgrounds are at Mile 16. This road is paved for the first four miles (6.5 km), then turns to gravel.

TOLSONA WILDERNESS CAMPGROUND

Address:	PO Box 23, Glennallen, AK 99588
Telephone:	(907) 822-3865
Email:	twcg@alaska.net
Website:	www.tolsona.com

GPS Location: N 62° 06' 48.7", W 145° 58' 27.8"

Probably the best spot to stop for the evening or a week along the whole Glenn Highway is the Tolsona Wilderness Campground. This is a commercial campground with the advantages and ambiance of a government campground. It is also located almost a mile from the highway so road noise is entirely absent. If you are looking for an interesting hike ask how to reach the nearby Tolsona mud volcanoes.

Tolsona is a large campground, there are some 90 sites. Most are back-ins but there are also a few pull-thrus. About 40 of the sites have electricity (20 or 30 amps) and water hookups. The remainder are dry. Many sites are on the banks of Tolsona Creek

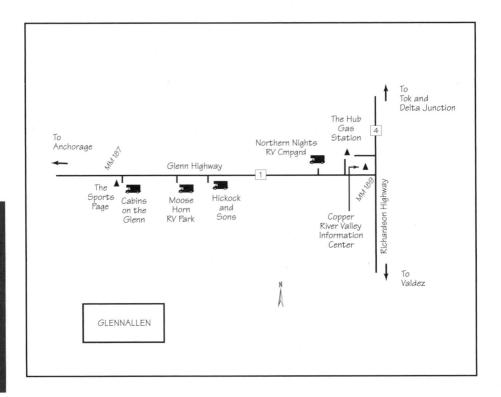

which runs right through the campground, and which has grayling. Some sites will take big rigs and some are pull-thrus. Campsites are well-separated and the campground is wooded with white spruce. Each site has a picnic table and firepit. There are restrooms with flush toilets and inexpensive coin-op showers, a laundry, a dump station and water fill site, and even playing fields.

The .8 mile (1.3 km) long gravel access road leaves the Glenn Highway near Mile 173. This is about 13 miles (21 km) west of Glennallen.

GLENNALLEN
Population 500, Elevation 1,450 feet

Glennallen occupies a strategic position just west of the south junction of the Richardson and Glenn highways. It serves as the supply center for the huge but sparsely populated Copper River Valley and has lots of government offices including the Bureau of Land Management, State Troopers, and Fish and Game. You'll find that the services are strung along the highway and include RV parks, grocery stores, restaurants, and gas stations. The **Copper River Valley Information Center** is a sod-roofed log cabin located right at the junction of the Glenn and Richardson Highways.

Glennallen Campgrounds

CABINS ON THE GLENN

Address:	Mile 187 Glenn Hwy., Glennallen, AK 99588
Telephone:	(907) 822-5833
Email:	sportspg@alaska.net

GPS Location: N 62° 06' 28.3", W 145° 32' 18.1"

This is the newest campground in Glennallen. In addition to the campground they have several rental cabins. The campground has 21 sites for RVs. Ten are large pull-thrus with full hookups (20 and 30 amps). There is one back-in site with full hookups as well as 10 more sites with water and electricity. Bathrooms and showers were in the rear of The Sports Page sporting goods store that sits in front of the campground.

Cabins on the Glenn sits behind a sporting goods store called "The Sports Page". It is near Mile 187 of the Glenn highway, 2 miles (3.2 km) west of the Southern Glenn junction.

MOOSE HORN RV PARK

Address:	Mile 187.7 Glenn Hwy., Glennallen, AK 99588
Telephone:	907 822-3953

GPS Location: N 62° 06' 26.6", W 145° 31' 23.6"

If you happen to reach Glennallen late in the day and need a place to stop for the evening with full hookups you might try this small campground. There are 12 back-in spaces with 30-amp outlets, sewer and water in an open gravel field. There's also a dump station. The campground is located on the south side of the Glenn Highway in Glennallen some 1.5 miles (2.4 km) west of the junction with the Richardson Highway.

THE GLENN HIGHWAY

⊐ HICKOCK AND SONS

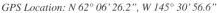

Telephone: (907) 822-3437

GPS Location: N 62° 06' 26.2", W 145° 30' 56.6"

Self-contained campers who like to keep things simple will like this place. The campground has 10 pull-thru sites. There are 20-amp electric and water hookups, most have sewer and there is also a dump station. All are set on a gravel lot behind a small office building and next to the large car wash building. Watch for the campground on the south side of the highway in Glennallen about 1.3 miles (2.1 km) west of the Glenn's junction with the Richardson Highway.

⊐ NORTHERN NIGHTS RV CAMPGROUND

Address: Mile 188.7 Glenn Hwy. (PO Box 528),
Glennallen, AK 99588
Telephone: (907) 822-3199
Email: nnites@yahoo.com
Website: www.alaska-rv-campground-glennallen-northernnights.net

GPS Location: N 62° 06' 28.3", W 145° 29' 10.6"

This campground is actively managed by it's owners and offers a good combination of features for travelers. Several of the campgrounds in Glennallen seem virtually abandoned, this is one of the exceptions.

The campground has 26 sites set in a spruce grove. The gravel sites are well separated for a commercial campground and many are pull-thrus. There are 30-amp electrical and water hookups and a dump station and also RV sites with no hookups. Nice tent sites with parking pads and tent platforms are located in the rear of the campground. All sites have fire rings and tables. A computer is available for email and there was even a Wi-Fi connection last time we visited.

The campground is located on the north side of the Glenn Highway in Glennallen .3 miles (.5 km) west of the intersection of the Glenn and Richardson Highways.

FROM GLENNALLEN TO TOK
139 Miles (224 Kilometers)

From Glennallen the Glenn and Richardson are the same road for 14 miles (23 km) northward to the Gakona junction. From there a section of road runs northeast to Tok, it is commonly called the Tok Cutoff.

For many miles the Tok Cutoff runs along high ground overlooking the Copper River. At higher points there are great views toward the southeast and the Wrangell-St. Elias National Park and Mt. Drum (12,010 feet) and Mt. Sanford (16,237 feet). Much of this road is on permafrost and the frost heaves can be terrible.

At Mile 60 there is a junction with the **Nabesna Road**. This gravel road runs 45 miles (73 km) into the Wrangell-St. Elias National Park and Preserve to the former gold-mining town of Nabesna. There's a ranger station for the park about a quarter-mile in. They can fill you in on road conditions and camping possibilities. There are no formal government campgrounds but there are lots of places to park your rig and boondock. The road is paved for just 4 miles (6.5 km), it is decent gravel to Mile 28,

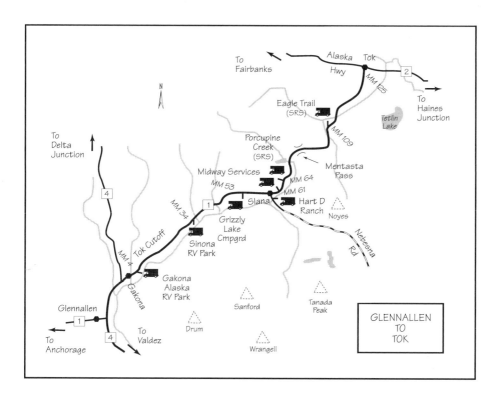

then it deteriorates further with some sometimes dicey stream fords. There are no park facilities along the road but the scenery is spectacular. There are several good fishing lakes and also some hiking possibilities. The park service seems to be trying to interest visitors in this part of the park, you will probably be able to get some good information from the ranger at the station.

After passing the Nabesna Road the highway runs through **Mentasta Pass** and crosses the 2,234-foot summit to pass through the Alaska Range from the Copper River drainage into the Tanana and Yukon drainage. The road reaches Tok junction at Mile 125 where it joins the Alaska Highway some 93 miles (150 km) from the Alaska border. See Chapter 4 - *The Alaska Highway* for information about Tok.

Glennallen to Tok Campgrounds

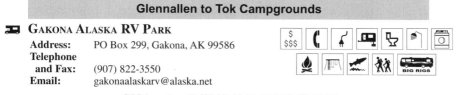

GAKONA ALASKA RV PARK

Address: PO Box 299, Gakona, AK 99586
Telephone and Fax: (907) 822-3550
Email: gakonaalaskarv@alaska.net

GPS Location: N 62° 18' 31.3", W 145° 13' 58.1"

This campground has about 50 large sites sitting on a large open gravel area next to the Copper River. Some spaces are pull-thrus and some back-ins, all have lots of room for maneuvering. Full service (20, 30 and 50 amp), water and electric, electric only, and dry sites are available. An older restroom building has flush toilets and hot

THE GLENN HIGHWAY

showers and there is a laundry and dump station. Other attractions include a playground, some picnic tables, and firepits.

The entrance road to the campground is on the Tok Cutoff some 4.2 miles (6.8 km) northeast of the junction of the Richardson and the Tok Cutoff (Gakona Junction).

SINONA RV PARK

Address: SR 224 Mile 34.4 Tok Cutoff, Chistochina, AK 99586
Telephone: (907) 822-3886

GPS Location: N 62° 35' 07.6", W 144° 39' 07.0"

The small Sinona RV Park has about 15 sites, many are pull-thrus. Sites have 20-amp electric, sewer, and water hookups. The gravel sites are separated by grass strips and there are some trees scattered around the camping area. There are also tent sites. Restrooms have flush toilets and hot showers and firewood is available. The campground is located near the highway at Mile 34.4 of the Tok Cutoff.

GRIZZLY LAKE CAMPGROUND

Address: PO Box 340, Gakona, AK 99586
Telephone: (907) 822-5214

GPS Location: N 62° 42' 52.5", W 144° 11' 59.6"

This small bed and breakfast occupies a scenic site near the Tok Cutoff on a small lake with great views toward the Wrangell-St Elias Park to the east. They have parking with no hookups for RVs and tent sites. They also offer showers. If you are interested in stopping here and have a large rig you should probably walk the short distance down from the highway to check maneuvering room. Watch for the sign and entrance road on the east side of the highway near Mile 53 of the Tok Cutoff.

HART D RANCH

Address: .5 Mile Nabesna Road, Slana, AK 99586
**Telephone
and Fax:**   (907) 822-3973
Website: www.hartd.com

GPS Location: N 62° 42' 27.9", W 143° 58' 08.3"

The campground has about 40 sites, some are pull-thrus with electricity, water, and sewer hookups. They are nicely arranged and separated by vegetation and trees. Maneuvering room is a little tight but big rigs can use this campground if they are careful. A generator is used to provide power. You'll probably quickly become accustomed to the slow putt-putt, many rural Alaskans do. There is a dump station and restrooms are available with hot showers.

To reach the campground follow the Nabesna Road east from near Mile 60 of the Tok Cutoff. At .5 miles (.9 km) turn left into the post office parking lot and continue on through to the campground. If no one is at the campground office (a residence) try going next door to the post office, the owner often is running it too.

MIDWAY SERVICES

Location: Mile 61 Tok Cutoff, Slana, AK 99586
Telephone: (907) 822-5877

GPS Location: N 62° 43' 07.0", W 143° 57' 39.9"

This is a roadhouse style operation with a grocery store. There is room for about three rigs to park in the area in front of the store with electrical outlets and there is an area for tents too along Ahtel Creek. There is no charge for tent camping. Inside the building are restrooms, hot showers, a laundry, internet access, and a grocery store.

PORCUPINE CREEK STATE RECREATION SITE
Location: Near Mile 64 of the Tok Cutoff

GPS Location: N 62° 43' 39.9", W 143° 52' 16.2"

This small state campground has 12 back-in sites arranged around an open cleared driveway area. Each site has a picnic table and firepit. These are large sites suitable for big rigs. There are outhouses and a water pump. The time limit here is 15 days.

EAGLE TRAIL STATE RECREATION SITE
Location: Near Mile 109 of the Tok Cutoff

Eagle Trail is a large and pleasant state campground. It celebrates the Eagle Trail, built from Valdez to Eagle (and including a telegraph line) to improve communications with the gold fields. A short trail nearby follows portions of the Eagle Trail.

The campground has about 35 sites including 5 for tenters. They are arranged in 5 wheel-like groups with back-in sites for RVs to about 35 feet. There is good separation between sites and they are set in a wooded area. All have picnic tables and firepits. There are pit toilets and a water pump. The campground has a 15 day limit.

GLENN HIGHWAY DUMP STATIONS

Many of the campgrounds in this chapter have either dump stations or sewer hookups. In most cases use of the dump stations is either restricted to people staying at the campground or requires payment of a fee. Try to empty your holding tanks in one of the larger cities where proper sewer treatment is guaranteed and isn't a financial burden to the campground owner.

In **Anchorage** many gas stations have dump stations available to customers. Here are some of them: Holiday at 1500 East 5th Ave. on the north side of Merrill Field; Holiday in the northeast quadrant of the intersection of DeBarr and Boniface (5501 DeBarr); Chevron at 6th and Ingra (832 East 6th Ave); Tesoro in the Fred Meyer parking lot in the southeast quadrant of the intersection of the Seward Highway and Northern Lights (2811 Seward Highway); Chevron in the northwest quadrant of the intersection of Spenard and Minnesota (3608 Minnesota).

In **Eagle River** try the Tesoro on the east side of the highway at 12139 Old Glenn Highway and also the Williams Express across the street.

In **Palmer** go to Palmer Chevron, 439 West Evergreen. The station here is often difficult to access due to congestion. Better is the dump station .8 miles (1.3 km) east at the Matanuska River Park.

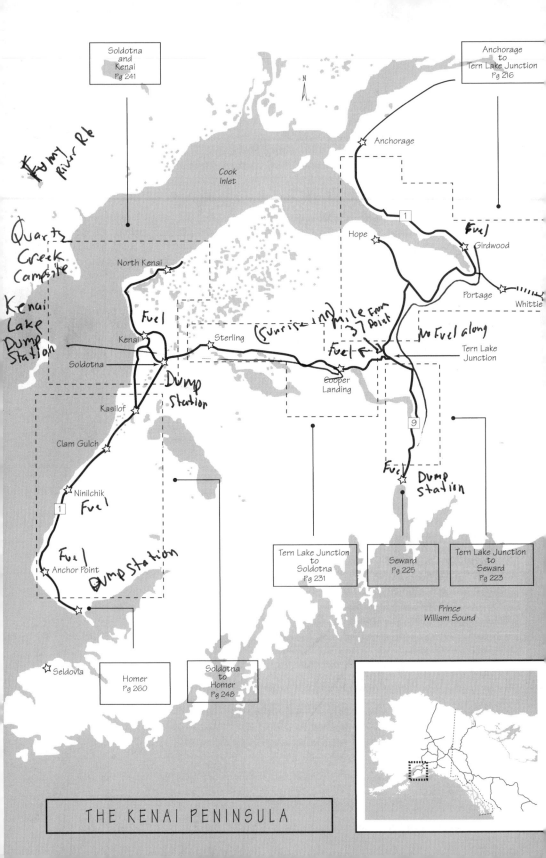

THE KENAI PENINSULA

Chapter 8

The Kenai Peninsula

INTRODUCTION

The one region in Alaska with the most to offer campers has got to be the Kenai Peninsula. This huge wilderness playground, almost an island, has something for everyone.

The Kenai is the most popular place in the state for campers from Anchorage. The state's largest city is home to the state's largest group of campers, and on weekends during the summer they head south every Friday night and usually return on Sunday evening. That means that there are many camping sites on the Kenai. With a little planning you can easily arrange to enjoy the Kenai during the week when it isn't very crowded, on weekends you can be comfortably parked in a beautiful campsite and watch the weekenders arrive with a cocktail (or fishing pole) in your hand.

 The busiest time of the season is late June and July when both king and red salmon are running in the lower Kenai and the rivers south toward Homer. During that period don't forget than many campgrounds, including almost all commercial campgrounds and many Forest Service campgrounds, take reservations. See the individual campground listings for more information.

Highlights

Three major population centers are located on the Kenai Peninsula, these are **Seward**, **Kenai-Soldotna**, and **Homer**. Each of them has many campgrounds and is covered in more detail below.

The **Seward Highway** is a designated National Forest Scenic Byway. Attractions along the way like **Turnagain Arm**, the **Alyeska Ski Area**, **Portage Glacier**, **Turnagain Pass**, **Kenai Lake**, and the **Exit Glacier** are excellent reasons to make this drive.

Much of the Peninsula is federal or state land. While there you can visit **Chugach National Forest**, **Kenai Fjords National Park**, the **Kenai National Wildlife Refuge**, and the **Kachemak Bay State Park**. If you like the outdoors you'll love the Kenai Peninsula. It's one of the best places in Alaska to find beautiful scenery, fishing, hiking, canoeing, kayaking, and just about anything you want to do in the outdoors.

The Road and Fuel

Two highways combine to give access to the Kenai Peninsula. From Anchorage the only route to the south is the **Seward Highway**. The Seward Highway is very scenic and has been designated a National Forest Scenic Byway. This two-lane paved road hugs the cliffs along Turnagain Arm until reaching Girdwood, then circles around the end of Turnagain to climb into the mountains onto the Kenai Peninsula proper. Ninety-two miles (148 km) from Anchorage the peninsula's second highway, the Sterling Highway, branches off to the west. The Seward Highway continues south, eventually ending at Seward on the south coast. By law headlights are required to be on at all times along this road.

The **Sterling Highway** leads west from its junction with the Seward Highway. After some 11 miles (18 km) it leaves the mountains and crosses the flatlands until reaching Soldotna near the west coast of the Kenai. The highway then follows the coast

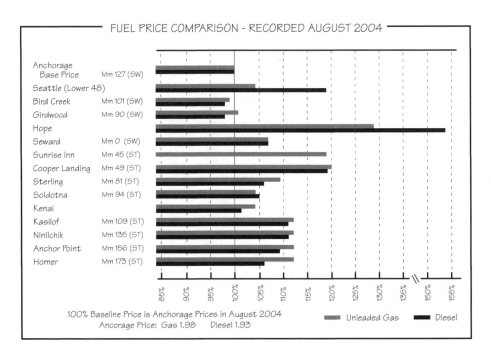

FUEL PRICE COMPARISON - RECORDED AUGUST 2004

Anchorage Base Price	Mm 127 (SW)
Seattle (Lower 48)	
Bird Creek	Mm 101 (SW)
Girdwood	Mm 90 (SW)
Hope	
Seward	Mm 0 (SW)
Sunrise Inn	Mm 45 (ST)
Cooper Landing	Mm 49 (ST)
Sterling	Mm 81 (ST)
Soldotna	Mm 94 (ST)
Kenai	
Kasilof	Mm 109 (ST)
Ninilchik	Mm 135 (ST)
Anchor Point	Mm 156 (ST)
Homer	Mm 173 (ST)

100% Baseline Price is Anchorage Prices in August 2004
Ancorage Price: Gas 1.98   Diesel 1.93

Unleaded Gas   Diesel

south to Homer, ending at the point of the Homer Spit.

From Anchorage to Seward along the Seward Highway is a distance of 127 miles (205 km). Mileposts along the Seward Highway start in Seward and run north to Anchorage. Several important side roads lead off from the Seward Highway including the Alyeska Highway (Mile 90), the Portage Valley Highway (Mile 79), and the Hope Highway (Mile 57). From Mile 90 at Girdwood to Mile 7 about 6 miles from Seward there is no gas available on the Seward Highway so be prepared. If you find yourself running low you can turn west on the Sterling Highway at Mile 37 and drive 8 miles to buy gas at the Sunrise Inn.

The Sterling Highway from Tern Lake Junction to Homer is 143 miles (231 km) long. Mileposts along this highway are confusing because they start in Seward which is not even on the highway. Tern Lake Junction, the highway's starting point, is at Mile 37. Mileposts count up from there. Important side roads off the Sterling Highway include the Skilak Lake Loop (Mile 58 and Mile 75) and the Kenai Spur Road (Mile 94).

The highway designation system used on these two roads is also confusing because the names and numbers do not designate the same stretches of roads. Highway 1 includes the Seward Highway from Anchorage to Tern Lake Junction and then the Sterling Highway to Homer. The Seward Highway from Tern Lake Junction to Seward is known as Highway 9.

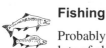 ### Fishing

Probably the most popular attraction on the Kenai is the fishing. You have lots of choices: king salmon on the world famous Kenai River and other streams, halibut out of Homer or Deep Creek, silver salmon in Seward, red salmon at the Russian River, trout from dozens of lakes and streams. The truth is that there are excellent fishing opportunities on the Kenai during the entire summer. The fish are almost everywhere so we'll only mention the highlights.

The possibilities for catching salmon start almost as soon as you start down the Seward Highway from Anchorage. **Indian Creek** (Mile 103) and **Bird Creek** (Mile 101) have heavy runs of pink salmon in July and August. Remember, Cook Inlet pinks only run in large numbers during even numbered-years like 2004 and 2006. The **Twentymile River** (Mile 81) and the **Placer River** (Mile 78) have an interesting dip net fishery for hooligan in May. It's as much fun to watch as it is to fish.

Seward is best-known for its silver salmon. You can catch them from the beach or from boats during August. The Seward Silver Salmon derby is held during the second week of August. Seward also offers fishing for kings, pinks, halibut, and sea-run Dollies.

When heading down the Sterling Highway from the intersection at Tern Lake the fishing action is dominated by the **Kenai River** all the way to Soldotna/Kenai. There are fish, especially trout and Dollies, in other places, notable Quartz Creek and the lakes of the Kenai Mountains and the Kenai Moose Range, but most people are after big salmon in the Kenai.

The first stop is the **Russian River**. This tributary of the Kenai is fished in two places, the Russian itself and the Kenai where the Russian flows in. The area of the Kenai just below the mouth of the Russian receives extremely heavy fishing pressure. During late June and again in late July fishermen are elbow to elbow flipping flies to red salmon on both side of the river. They wouldn't be there if their chances of catching fish weren't extremely good. Access to the far side of the Kenai away from the road is by ferry from Mile 55 of the Sterling Highway. Silver fishing in the Russian is good in August, so is Dolly and catch-and-release rainbow fishing. Fishing regulations for the Russian can be complicated and different from those for the surrounding area so check them out.

The **Upper Kenai**, from the outlet of Kenai Lake to Skilak Lake, is a beautiful emerald-colored stream 17 miles (27 km) in length. The Sterling Highway runs along it between Mile 48 and Mile 57, then the river turns away from the road and enters a canyon. You can fish from the bank or from a raft or drift boat to reach otherwise inaccessible waters. Fish for reds in late June and late July into August. Silvers appear in August and September and again in October and November. The area is closed to king fishing. This is also a good place to fish for rainbows and Dollies, especially in

THE KENAI RIVER IS KNOWN FOR REALLY BIG FISH

the fall. Again, the regulations should be checked carefully when fishing this water.

The **Lower Kenai** is the king fishery. It runs 50 miles (81 km) from the Skilak Lake outlet to salt water near Kenai. The Sterling Highway does not run along this river very much, but there is access all along its length using side roads. A lot of the fishing is from boats, this is big water. There are two runs of kings, one in June and the other starting in mid July. There are also two runs each of reds and silver salmon, and there are also Dollies and rainbows. For best results on the lower Kenai hire a guide, they have the knowledge and the boats. No fisherman should visit Alaska and not spend at least a day on a guided Kenai king fishing expedition.

From Soldotna the Sterling highway heads south, and along the way it passes over a string of extremely productive rivers flowing west into Cook Inlet. These include the **Kasilof River and Crooked Creek** (Mile 109), the **Ninilchik River** (Mile 135), **Deep Creek** (Mile 137), and the **Anchor River** (Mile 157). All have large state campgrounds near the river and offer fishing for kings and silvers.

There is also a substantial salt water fishery in **Cook Inlet from Ninilchik to Anchor Point**. Along the shore fishermen find kings, pinks, silvers, and even halibut. Charter operators from **Deep Creek** in larger boats offer excellent halibut fishing, they fish some of the same waters as charter boats out of Homer.

Homer is at the end of the road. Most fishermen come to Homer for the halibut. They fish from charter boats and often limit out with two halibut in the ten to thirty pound range. Occasionally a halibut as large as 400 pounds (that's right!) is caught. Homer also has its "fishing hole" near the end of the Spit which is designed just to give tourists a better-than-fighting chance to catch a king or silver. This is a terminal fishery with no place to spawn. Hatchery king and silver fingerlings are released here and come back as adults just to be caught.

Have you ever gone clamming? Digging for razor clams along Cook Inlet beaches is like claming nowhere else. During the lowest tides (you can't reach them any other time) it is easy to get your limit, and the limit is 60 clams. You can easily equip yourself for clamming in Soldotna or Kenai, you only need a fishing license, a clam shovel, boots and a bucket. Head for either Clam Gulch or Ninilchik. Once you're on the beach just watch someone who's finding clams, it's easy if you use the right technique. You'll also need a few tips on cleaning those clams. Check around your campground, during the clam tides you'll probably have no trouble finding an expert. A word to the wise, limit your enthusiasm when you're digging, cleaning clams can take longer than digging them and it's not nearly as much fun.

It's important to check fishing regulations carefully because they can be complicated and they do change. The State of Alaska puts out some great little regulation booklets and they're easy to get at sporting goods stores and tourist information locations. Another good source of information is the Alaska Department of Fish and Game (ADF&G) website: www.sf.adg.state.ak.us/statewide/sf_home.cfm.

Boating, Rafting, Canoeing, and Kayaking

The Kenai has an excellent canoe trail system. The Kenai National Wildlife Refuge's **Swanson River Canoe Route** is a week-long trail passing through lakes and along the Swanson River. Another trail in the moose range, the **Swan Lake Route**, is similar. See Chapter 14 - *Camping Away From the Road System*.

A popular rafting trip is a float of the **Upper Kenai**. The section from the Kenai Lake outlet to Jean Creek is primarily a fishing trip but there are sections of Class III water. From Jean Creek to Skilak Lake is Class III water in the Kenai Canyon. Neither section is a place for inexperienced rafters. Your best bet is to float with a commercial operator. They can be found in Anchorage and Cooper Landing. Canoeists also like to float the **Lower Kenai** between Skilak Lake and Jim's landing, the take-out there allows them to avoid rapids below the landing.

Ocean kayakers will find three exceptional areas accessible on the Kenai Peninsula. The first is world-famous **Prince William Sound**. While not really on the Kenai Peninsula we'll mention it here since access is possible via the new road to Portage near Mile 80 of the Seward Highway. Resurrection Bay near Seward has excellent kayaking waters, since the **Kenai Fjords** are a long paddle away try catching a lift with a excursion or charter boat operator. Finally, **Kachemak Bay** has miles of relatively protected shoreline across from Homer. All of these areas are further described in Chapter 14 - *Camping Away From the Road System*.

Hiking and Mountain Biking

The Kenai Peninsula has the best selection of good hiking trails in all of Alaska. Probably the best known is the **Resurrection Pass Trail** that runs from Hope to Cooper Landing and then on to Seward. Hiking the whole thing would take over a week. This is a popular mountain bike trail but be careful. Grizzly bears are often on the trail and it is possible to get very close on a bike before you see the bear or the bear sees you, that's a recipe for trouble. Other trails lead to lakes, ridges, and glaciers. Several hiking guidebooks describe hikes in this area, check our Chapter 2 - *Details, Details, Details* for our suggestions. Here are a few of our favorite hikes.

The **Primrose Trail** from Primrose Campground on Kenai Lake and the **Lost Lake Trail** from Lost Lake Subdivision near Mile 5 of the Seward Highway both go to the same place, a big alpine lake called Lost Lake. The one-way distance from either is 7 miles, you can also make a traverse out of this hike. This trail is open to bikes.

Johnson Pass is usually hiked as a traverse. This is a historic trail that was originally part of a pack route from Seward to Sunrise and Hope. It is also part of the historic Iditarod Trail. This 23-mile trail is a popular mountain bike route. Trailheads are near Mile 32 and Mile 64 of the Seward Highway.

Across Kachemak Bay from Homer is **Kachemak Bay State Park**. It has lots of hiking trails, see Chapter 14 - *Camping Away From the Road System* for more information.

Wildlife Viewing

Almost as soon as you leave Anchorage heading south you'll come to one of the most-visited bird-watching sites in the state–**Potter Marsh**. Near Mile 117 of the Seward Highway is a quarter-mile boardwalk leading into the marsh. Best viewing is in April and May but all summer long you might spot a variety of ducks, Canada geese, bald eagles, grebes, loons, yellowlegs, and Arctic terns. There's also a salmon spawning area.

Just a little farther south, near Beluga Point (Mile 110) or Windy Corner (Mile 106) along **Turnagain Arm** Dall sheep often come all the way down to the road to pose for pictures. Also keep an eye open for bald eagles along the shoreline and beluga whales offshore when the hooligan or salmon are running, particularly near Bird Creek.

Kenai Fjords National Park, accessible in excursion boats from Seward, is one of the best places in the state to see seabirds and marine mammals. On a typical day trip you might spot whales (humpback, minke, or gray), orcas, Steller sea lions, harbor seals, sea otters, and Dall porpoises. Some trips visit the Chiswell Islands to see colonies of puffins, murres, and kittiwakes. You might even sight mountain goats or bears from the boat. This is also a good place to get away from the crowds, see Chapter 14 - *Camping Away from the Road System*.

The **Kenai Mountains** may seem almost civilized since they are laced with hiking trails, but stay alert. Hikers shouldn't be surprised to see grizzly bears in the high country, not to mention even more common black bears. Valleys often have moose and beaver. A desire to see some wildlife is an excellent reason to get out and do some hiking.

Near the north shore of Kenai Lake at Mile 46 of the Sterling Highway there's a parking area just for viewing sheep and goats with binoculars and spotting scopes. Directly north of the site is **Near Mountain** where Dall sheep are often visible. Across Kenai Lake is **Cecil Rhode Mountain** which sometimes has mountain goats. Also watch for bears a little farther down the mountains.

At the mouth of the Kenai River near the town of Kenai are the **Kenai River Flats**. In April the flats are covered with snow geese migrating to Siberia. There's also a small herd of caribou that uses the flats as a calving area in May. Later in the year birders can see a variety of water birds and ducks as well as several bald eagles. Best viewing is from the Kenai River Access Road. Another attraction here is the beluga whales and harbor seals attracted by hooligan and salmon runs, they may be best seen from the Kenai bluff.

The **Kenai National Wildlife Refuge** used to be known as the Kenai National Moose Range. That should give you some idea of what you should be watching for. It's a huge (2,000,000 acres) flatland covering almost all of the western Kenai Peninsula. You've got to keep your eyes open, the moose in most areas are hunted in the fall so they may be wary. Still, there are so many of them that you're sure to spot some. When heading into the refuge stop at the visitor contact station at Mile 58 of the Sterling Highway for a map and information. The Kenai National Wildlife Refuge Headquarters (USF&W) is near Soldotna on Ski Hill Road (off the Sterling Highway at Mile 98) and has wildlife displays and information (PO Box 2139, Soldotna, AK 99669; (907) 262-7021). They also administer the Swanson River and Swan Lake Canoe Trails.

Kachemak Bay near Homer also has an excellent place to watch seabirds. **Gull Is-**

land is a short excursion boat or kayak ride away, it is home to some 12,000 seabirds, much like the Chiswell Islands. Kayakers and other visitors to the south side of the bay often see sea otters, harbor seals, and Dall porpoises.

Homer is also an excellent place to book a charter flight to **the west side of Cook Inlet** to see grizzly bears. It's probably the best location in the state to see concentrations of bears during the salmon season when they congregate near the coast in large numbers to catch fish. This isn't a cheap trip, but it's worth the money.

THE ROUTES, TOWNS, AND CAMPGROUNDS

From Anchorage to Tern Lake Junction
90 Miles (145 Kilometers)

The real start of the Seward Highway begins near central Anchorage at the corner of Gambell Street and 5th and 6th Avenues (the Glenn Highway). Gambell (the Seward Highway) heads south, stopping at many stoplights, and then turns into a four-lane expressway until meeting Turnagain Arm near **Potter Flats** at Mile 117. This is where you leave Anchorage's suburbs and abruptly find yourself in what would be considered wilderness in most places.

The highway now runs between cliffs and the rocky edge of muddy **Turnagain Arm**. In recent years this has become a popular if somewhat dangerous wind-surfing area. Stay off the mud flats, they can be like quicksand and the tides come in very rapidly. You're also likely to see climbers on the rocks along the road. Another frequent sight is Dall sheep on the rocks just above the road or even on the road itself. When the tide is in watch the waves on the right, there are often Beluga whales very near the highway. If you see a lot of cars pulled off the road they have probably spotted the whales.

At Mile 90, twenty-five miles (40 km) from Potter Flats is the cutoff to **Girdwood** and the Alyeska Ski Resort. Girdwood is a popular weekend get-away for Anchorage residents and explains the excellent road from Anchorage to this point. Summer visitors will find some hiking possibilities and can ride a tram up onto the ski slope for a great view.

At Mile 79 the Seward Highway reaches the Portage Valley Highway. **Portage Glacier**, at Mile 5.5, is one of Alaska's most-visited tourist sites. The **Begich, Boggs Visitor Center** (907 783-2326) has a viewing area, displays, a film, and naturalists. You can also take a boat ride to get a closer view of the glacier which has retreated to the point that good views are not available from the visitor's center. Along the access road you can see small hanging glaciers above the road and also stop and watch spawning salmon at a viewpoint at Williwaw Creek near Mile 4. There are two good USFS campgrounds along this road.

A new addition to the Portage Valley Highway runs beyond what is now the turnoff to the Begich Boggs Visitor Center. This is a new road to **Whittier**. Beyond the turnoff it runs through a small tunnel and then reaches a toll booth and parking area. This road shares a 2.2-mile single-lane tunnel with a train. Traffic runs one way and

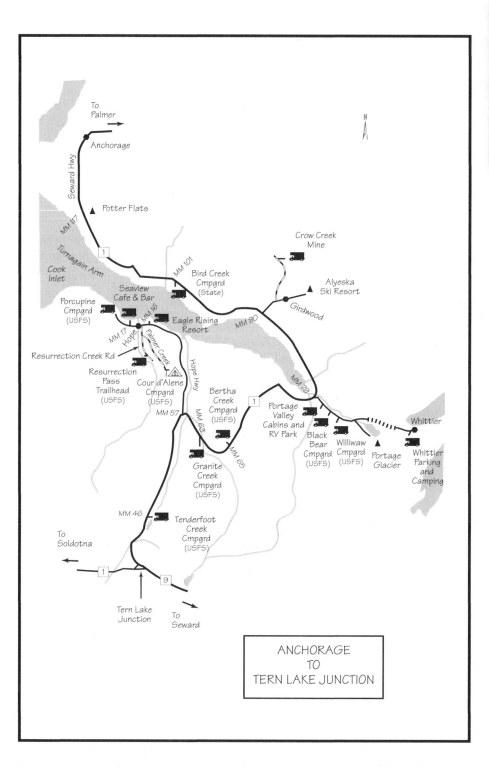

ANCHORAGE
TO
TERN LAKE JUNCTION

is usually allowed through at one-hour intervals unless train traffic interrupts. Any size RV can drive through, the toll is $12 for a passenger vehicle, most RVs pay $35. The toll is only collected eastbound. Check the web site that is linked to our web site at www.rollinghomes.com for more information.

Whittier is a small town located at the head of the Passage Canal, a fjord that connects with Prince William Sound. The Alaska state ferries run from Whittier to the Prince William Sound ports of Valdez and Cordova. The town of Whittier was built by the government during World War II and has little to offer other than access to Prince William Sound. Cruise companies offer tours from Whittier of the sound. There is now an RV park in Whittier.

After passing Portage the Seward Highway begins climbing into the mountains at Mile 75. This long hill has always been a problem area for trucks and RVers because they are forced to slow by the long climb. New passing lanes are making the road much safer. Before long the highway approaches the tree line at not much over 1,000 feet, you can glass for bears on the slopes on both sides.

At a junction at Mile 57 the Hope Highway descends north for 18 miles (29 km) along Sixmile Creek to Turnagain Arm and the old gold-mining town of **Hope**. The virtual ghost town sits at the mouth of Resurrection Creek. There's good pink salmon fishing during August and upstream you'll find gold panning possibilities and the trailhead for the Resurrection Pass Trail. Hope has an interesting little museum, the **Hope and Sunrise Historical and Mining Museum**.

After passing the Hope Highway junction the road continues through mountains past Upper and Lower Summit Lakes and Jerome Lake to the Tern Lake Junction with the Sterling Highway.

Anchorage to Tern Lake Junction Campgrounds

BIRD CREEK CAMPGROUND (CHUGACH STATE PARK)

$$						

Location: Mile 101 Seward Highway

GPS Location: N 60° 58' 19.7", W 149° 27' 36.1"

Bird Creek is the closest government wilderness campground to Anchorage. It is also conveniently located near Bird Creek, a popular and relatively good fishing spot for pink salmon in late July and August. Coastal views of the cliffs and tide flats along Turnagain Arm are spectacular. Bald eagles and Dall sheep are often seen nearby and a paved bike trail runs right next to the campground.

The small campground has 28 vehicle sites south of the highway. Several are long enough for rigs to about 35 feet. There are also tent sites. The campground has well water, outhouses, a telephone, and picnic tables. There is sometimes a host. Interior roads are gravel, so are camping pads. There is a paved lot across the road providing 16 overflow camping spaces for RVs to 40 feet. It sits well above the highway and provides excellent views south across Turnagain Arm to the Kenai Peninsula. Stays here are limited to 7 days.

To find Bird Creek Campground just drive south from Anchorage on the Seward

Highway. The campground is on the right about 16 miles (26 km) after the highway meets Turnagain Arm just outside Anchorage. The campground is near Mile 101.

CROW CREEK MINE

Address:	PO Box 113, Girdwood, AK 99587
Telephone:	(907) 278-8060 (Off-site)
Website:	www.crowcreekgoldmine.com

GPS Location: N 61° 00' 00.4", W 149° 04' 58.2"

If you are looking for an interesting campsite not far from Anchorage and are willing to do without hookups you will enjoy the Crow Creek Mine. Crow Creek was a working placer mine, it is now a National Historic Site, and offers displays and buildings from early days and the chance to pan for gold. Gold mining here was no joke, Crow Creek was the most productive placer stream in southcentral Alaska with over 40,000 ounces produced since 1896.

The mine has a small camping area next to the gravel parking lot with fire rings and picnic tables. RVs can park overnight in the parking lot. There are no hook-ups but chemical toilets are available and drinking water can be purchased at the gift shop.

The Crow Creek Mine is located near Girdwood, home of Alyeska, Alaska's largest ski area. Girdwood is about 42 miles (68 km) southeast of Anchorage off the Seward Highway. Take the Girdwood cutoff near Mile 90 and drive into the valley for 1.9 miles (2.6 km) to the Crow Creek Road which goes left. Follow this gravel road for 3.1 miles (5 km), turn right at the mine entrance road, and you will reach the parking lot in another .4 miles (.6 km).

PORTAGE VALLEY CABINS AND RV PARK

Location:	Mile 1.7 of the Portage Valley Road
Telephone:	(907) 783-3111
Website:	www.PortageValleyCabins.com

GPS Location: N 60° 48' 12.8", W 148° 55' 59.1"

This is a private RV park, the only one in the Portage Valley. If you like electrical hookups you might like this campground better than the Forest Service campgrounds farther up the valley.

There are 12 back-in sites suitable for large rigs. These sites have 20-amp electrical hookups. There's also lots of room for tent camping and parking without hookups. The campground has showers available, restrooms are a port-a-potty.

BLACK BEAR CAMPGROUND (USFS)

| Location: | Mile 3.7 of Portage Valley Highway |

GPS Location: N 60° 47' 21.2", W 148° 53' 21.4"

Black Bear Campground is a small U.S. Forest Service campground located conveniently near Portage Glacier. It has not been upgraded with paving and large sites like the nearby Williwaw Campground so there are often sites available here when Williwaw is full.

Black Bear is a wooded campground with 12 sites, two are pull-thrus. This campground is best for tents and rigs to about 25 feet although a few sites will take rigs to

THE KENAI PENINSULA

30 feet. There is a water pump, bear-proof food lockers, picnic tables, firepits, and outhouses. Maximum stay at the campground is 14 days.

To find Black Bear take the Portage Valley Highway near Mile 79 of the Seward Highway (48 miles (77 km) from Anchorage). Drive toward the glacier for 3.7 miles (6 km), the campground is on the right.

WILLIWAW CAMPGROUND (USFS)

Location:	Mile 4.1 of Portage Valley Highway
Res.:	(877) 444-6777
Website	
For Res.:	www.reserveusa.com

GPS Location: N 60° 47' 11.2", W 148° 52' 37.4"

This government campground near Portage Glacier has been upgraded with wide paved roads and large paved sites. It sits below overhanging Middle Glacier and is right next to the Williwaw Creek salmon viewing area.

There are 60 sites in the campground. Many are pull-thrus and most are large enough for large rigs. Sites have picnic tables and firepits. There is a hand-operated water pump and outhouses. The campground has a host and amphitheater for campfire programs and reservations can be made. There's also a nature trail. Maximum stay at the campground is 14 days.

You can find Williwaw on the Portage Valley Highway which leaves the Seward Highway at Mile 79 (48 miles (77 km) from Anchorage). The campground is 4.1 miles (6.6 km) from the junction.

WHITTIER PARKING AND CAMPING

| Location: | Whittier, Alaska |

GPS Location: N 60° 46' 16.8", W 148° 41' 16.9"

Whittier has a large gravel camping area set above and behind the busy port area. There's lots of room, most sites are not lined out so you can park where you wish. Port-a-potties are provided.

To reach the campground watch for the signs to the parking lot on your right just after passing the cruise ship docks. They'll take you to a large parking lot, this isn't the campground. Either pass though the parking lot or around it's left side to the camping area up the valley behind.

BERTHA CREEK CAMPGROUND (USFS)

| Location: | Near Mile 65 of the Seward Highway |

GPS Location: N 60° 45' 04.4", W 149° 15' 14.8"

This is a small government campground in high country near the highway. There are 12 sites, a few will take larger rigs to about 35 feet but maneuvering room is tight so 30 feet is probably the maximum size rig that should use this campground. Roads are gravel and so are the sites. Picnic tables, firepits, and bear-proof storage containers are provided. There is a hand-pump water well and outhouses. Maximum stay at this campground is 14 days.

THE KENAI PENINSULA

Bertha Creek Campground is located on the west side of the road near Mile 65 of the Seward Highway about 62 miles (100 km) from Anchorage.

GRANITE CREEK CAMPGROUND (USFS)

Location:	Near Mile 63 of the Seward Highway
Res.:	(877) 444-6777
Website	
For Res.:	www.reserveusa.com

GPS Location: N 60° 43' 29.0", W 149° 17' 39.2"

Granite Creek Campground is a 19-site campground located in a spruce and cotton-wood forest next to a rushing glacial stream. The roads in the campground are gravel and so are the sites. Many are located next to the creek. All are back-in sites, they have picnic tables and firepits. Narrow roads and lack of maneuvering room limit rig size here to about 30 feet. The campground has a hand-operated water pump and outhouses. This campground sometimes has a host and firewood is available. You can make reservations at this campground, see the telephone number and website above. Maximum stay is 14 days.

The access road to the campground leaves the Seward Highway near Mile 63. Drive south on the access road for .8 miles to reach the campground.

EAGLE RISING RESORT

Address:	Mile 15.5 Hope Highway (Box 50),
	Hope, AK 99605-0090
Telephone:	(907) 782-3222 or 888-31-eagle
Email:	eaglerising@alaska.net
Website:	www.eaglerisingresort.com

GPS Location: N 60° 55' 10.1", W 149° 37' 13.2"

Formerly called Henry's One Stop, this campground is located about a mile from the historic Hope town site and is an important gathering place for Hope area residents since it has one of the few public telephones and grocery stores.

There are 12 camping sites located next to the store. All have 20-amp electrical out-lets and water, all but one have sewer hook-ups also. A few are pull-thrus. There is also a dump station. Maneuvering room is restricted in this campground but a few sites will take carefully driven large rigs to 40 feet. Eagle Rising has a small grocery store with movie rentals, offers showers, and has a public telephone. Reservations are recommended.

The campground is located near Mile 16 of the Hope Highway on the north side of the road. Just past Eagle Rising Resort the Resurrection Creek Road goes left provid-ing access to the Resurrection Trail.

SEAVIEW CAFÉ AND BAR

Address:	PO Box 110, Hope, AK 99605
Telephone:	(907) 782-3300
Fax:	(907) 782-3344
Email:	seaviewinhope@hotmail.com

GPS Location: N 60° 55' 15.8", W 149° 38' 39.5"

For a convenient place to stay when you visit the old gold-mining town of Hope

you'll probably want to stay at the Seaview. It is located right at the edge of town, you can take a walking tour right from your campsite.

The Seaview has 21 sites, 15 have 20-amp outlets and water is available. The campground is located on the shore of Turnagain Arm next to the mouth of Resurrection Creek. There are pot-a-potties and a bar and a café. The campground is located right next to the mouth of Resurrection Creek so fishing for pink salmon is extremely handy.

To reach Hope and the Seaview follow the Hope Highway for 17 miles (27 km) from its intersection near Mile 57 of the Seward Highway. The campground is well-signed from the edge of town.

⊞ PORCUPINE CAMPGROUND (USFS)

Location:	Mile 18 of the Hope Highway, the end of the road	
Res.:	(877) 444-6777	
Website		
For Res.:	www.reserveusa.com	

GPS Location: N 60° 55' 42.9", W 149° 39' 34.4"

The Porcupine Campground makes a great destination for a weekend trip from Anchorage. There are hiking trails along Turnagain Arm and to other nearby locations. Both Hope and the Resurrection Creek mining area are nearby.

This state campground has 24 sites, most are back-in but there are a couple of pull-thrus. This is one of the USFS upgraded campgrounds, however, sites and access roads are tight. A couple of the sites will take rigs up to 35 feet but the campground is best for rigs to 30 feet. Interior roads are paved as are parking pads. Each site has a picnic table and fire ring and they are well-separated with natural vegetation and trees. The campground has vault toilets and a hand-pump for water. Reservations are possible, see the information above. Maximum stay at the campground is 14 days.

You reach the campground by following the Hope Highway all the way to the end, a distance of eighteen miles (29 km) from the junction with the Seward Highway near Mile 57.

⊞ RESURRECTION PASS TRAILHEAD (USFS)

Location:	Near the end of Resurrection Creek Road

GPS Location: N 60° 52' 10.2", W 149° 37' 48.1"

This is an almost undeveloped campsite that is very popular with gold panners searching for gold in the creek. From May 15 to July 15 you can be sure that this campground will be full of prospectors. The rest of the year it is almost empty.

There is room for about 10 parties to camp under cottonwood trees next to Resurrection Creek. There are no real designated sites but repeated use has resulted in established sites, most have fire rings but no tables. There are outhouses.

A hundred yards or so down the creek is the parking area for the very popular Resurrection Trail. There are also outhouses here and many people overnight in this parking area, particularly if they are getting ready to head out on the trail of if they are waiting for a party of hikers.

The Resurrection Creek Road leaves the Hope Highway at Mile 16. This is 1.8 miles (2.9 km) from where the Hope Highway ends at the Porcupine Campground. Drive south on the Resurrection Creek Road following signs for the Resurrection Trail. The only Y is at .7 miles (1.1 km) where the Palmer Creek Road goes left, you want to go right. The Resurrection Pass Trailhead Campground is 4.3 miles (6.9 km) from the Hope Highway junction.

COEUR D' ALENE CAMPGROUND (USFS)

Location: Mile 7.7 Palmer Creek Road

FREE

GPS Location: N 60° 50' 58.9", W 149° 32' 05.8"

This is a little tent-only campground located far up the narrow gravel Palmer Creek Road. There are about 8 tent sites with picnic tables and firepits located fairly close together. The campground has an outhouse. This is a popular area for hiking and mountain bikes.

To reach the campground follow the Palmer Creek Road as it leaves the Hope Highway at Mile 16. In just .7 miles (1.1 km) the road forks, the Resurrection Pass Road goes right and the Palmer Creek Road left. Continue on the Palmer Creek road and in another 7 miles (11.3 km) you'll reach the campground. Maximum stat here is 14 days.

TENDERFOOT CREEK CAMPGROUND (USFS)

Location:	Near Mile 46 of the Seward Highway
Res:	(877) 444-6777
Website	
For Res.:	www.reserveusa.com

$$

GPS Location: N 60° 38' 13.0", W 149° 29' 49.0"

This is a very nice campground on the shore of Summit Lake. It sits across the valley from the highway so there is little road noise, a nice feature. Nearby Summit Lake Lodge has a restaurant. Reservations are possible, see the information above.

There are 27 separated sites, 7 are pull-thrus. Each site has a picnic table and fire ring and there are outhouses and a boat ramp. Some sites are right next to the beach. A few of the pull-thrus will take rigs to 35 feet but the narrow access road and limited maneuvering room should limit rigs using this campground to 30 feet. There is sometimes a host. Maximum stay here is 14 days.

The .5 mile (.8 km) gravel entrance road leaves the Seward Highway near Mile 46, just north of the Summit Lake Lodge.

FROM TERN LAKE JUNCTION TO SEWARD
35 Miles (56 Kilometers)

From Tern Lake the two-lane paved Seward Highway continues toward Seward. At Mile 29 it passes through a small town called **Moose Pass** and then passes the south end of Kenai Lake at Mile 17. Several good USFS campgrounds are located along this stretch of road. Very soon the outskirts of Seward begin to appear.

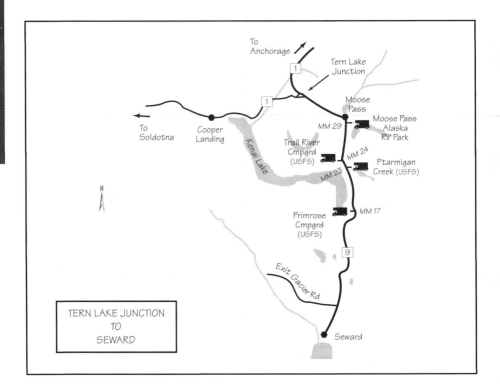

Tern Lake Junction to Seward Campgrounds

MOOSE PASS ALASKA RV PARK

Location:	Near Mile 29 of the Seward Highway
Telephone:	(907) 288-3184
Email:	info@moosepassrvpark.com
Website:	www.moosepassrvpark.com

GPS Location: N 60° 29' 07.3", W 149° 22' 13.6"

This small commercial RV park has about 30 sites on gravel with small trees separating sites. Many sites have 30-amp electrical hookups. The campground has no showers and the only restrooms are outhouses. A restaurant is nearby. The campground entrance is on the east side of the highway in Moose Pass, near Mile 29 of the Seward Highway.

TRAIL RIVER CAMPGROUND (USFS)

Location:	Near Mile 24 of the Seward Highway
Res.:	(877) 444-6777
Website	
For Res.:	www.reserveusa.com

GPS Location: N 60° 25' 05.8", W 149° 22' 17.9"

The Trail River Campground is located along the Lower Trail River and Kenai Lake. Fishing is good for Dolly Varden and rainbows. Reservations are possible, see the information above.

There are about 60 separated campsites arranged off loops. Some of these are good-sized sites suitable for rigs to 35 feet, there are even some pull-thrus. A few sites are along the lake. Each site has a picnic table and firepit, there are vault toilets and hand-operated water pumps. This campground also has some large group campsites available and there is a host. Maximum stay here is 14 days.

The 1.2 mile (1.9 km) long entrance road leaves the Seward Highway near Mile 24.

⛟ PTARMIGAN CREEK (USFS)

Location:	Near Mile 23 of the Seward Highway
Res.:	(877) 444-6777
Website	
For Res.:	www.reserveusa.com

GPS Location: N 60° 24' 19.5", W 149° 21' 54.9"

This is another USFS campground that takes reservations. A 3.5 mile long hiking trail to Ptarmigan Lake starts at the campground. Most sites will take rigs to 25 feet, two pull-thrus will take 40-footers. There are a total of 16 sites. They are separated and have picnic tables and firepits. Toilets are outhouse type. A fish-viewing platform is great for watching spawning salmon in Ptarmigan Creek. Maximum stay here is 14 days. The campground entrance is on the east side of the Seward Highway near Mile 23.

⛟ PRIMROSE LANDING CAMPGROUND (USFS)

| Location: | Near Mile 17 of the Seward Highway |

GPS Location: N 60° 20' 25.9", W 149° 22' 04.8"

Primrose is a small campground located near the southern shore of Kenai Lake. A hiking trail leading to Lost Lake starts from the campground.

There are 10 formal sites here, they are separated back-ins and are large enough for rigs to 30 feet. Each has its picnic table and firepit. There is also an overflow area, a flat gravel lot next to the lake. This is good for larger rigs. There are vault toilets in both campground areas and a boat launch. Maximum stay here is 14 days.

A one-mile access road leaves the Seward Highway near Mile 17 and runs past some private homes to the campground. The first short section is paved, then it turns to gravel.

SEWARD
Population 3,500, Elevation near sea level

Seward was founded in 1903 as an ice-free port which could be the southern end of an Alaska railroad. Private attempts to build one didn't go well until the U.S. government took over in 1915. Construction of a line through newly settled Anchorage to Fairbanks was finished in 1923.

In 1980 the ice fields and coastline to the west of Seward were designated as the **Kenai Fjords National Park**. Gradually the park has attracted more and more visitors. The usual access is on excursion boats making day trips from Seward. Visitors see whales, sea otters, mountain goats, puffins, and other marine birds and animals.

The only road access to the park is the Exit Glacier Road which leaves the Seward Highway at Mile 4. The 9-mile road leads to a parking lot, small tent campground, and trails to the glacier. More challenging trails also lead to a view of the Harding Ice Field. The **Kenai Fjords National Park** (PO Box 1727, Seward, Alaska 99664; 907 224-3175) has a visitor center near the boat harbor on Fourth Avenue. They have slide shows and can answer questions and supply information about the park.

Seward's latest attraction, and it's an impressive one, is the **Alaska SeaLife Center** (800 224-2525). This marine laboratory and aquarium was partially funded by the Exxon Valdez Oil Spill Settlement fund, it opened in 1998. It's a large facility with first-class displays of Alaska marine mammals, fish, and birds, well worth a visit.

Seward has two Visitor Information Centers. One is at Mile 2 of the Seward Highway as you enter town. The other is in a railroad car at 3rd and Jefferson downtown. For information contact: PO Box 749, Seward, Alaska 99664; (907) 224-8051.

Seward is also well known for its fishing. A very popular and productive **silver salmon derby** is held in the middle of August. Charter operators are easy to find or you can use your own boat for fishing for salmon, rockfish, and halibut.

There are a couple of good hiking trails in the Seward area. The **Mt. Marathon Trail** is the scene of a race on the 4th of July. It goes to the top of 3,022 foot Mt. Marathon and back. For something flatter try the Caine's Head Trails leading south along the coast to **Caine's Head State Recreation Area**.

FISHERMEN ON RESURRECTION BAY IN SEWARD

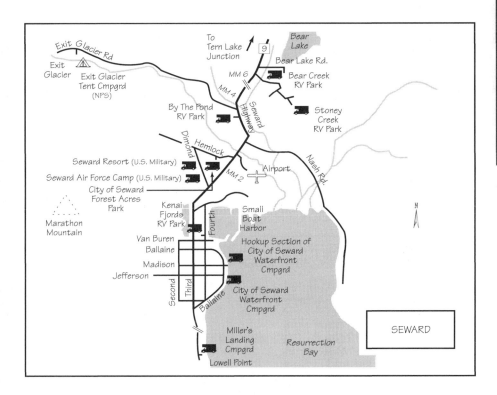

Seward is a great place to be on the **4th of July**. The Mt. Marathon race is the center-piece of a great traditional celebration. RVers from all over make special plans to be in Seward on the Fourth.

Seward Campgrounds

 **EXIT GLACIER TENT CAMPGROUND (NPS)**

Location: Mile 8.2 of the Exit Glacier Road

GPS Location: N 60° 11' 29.1", W 149° 37' 10.0"

This is a nice tent campground located just outside the entrance gate for the Exit Glacier parking lot. The design is unique and may be a look into the future of government tent campgrounds in Alaska.

There are 12 widely-spaced walk-in tent sites set between a parking area and the river. Sites have no picnic tables or fire areas. Near the parking area is a covered food preparation area with picnic tables and a food storage area. To reduce bear problems no food is allowed at the campsites, all food preparation and storage is at the food preparation pavilion. The campground also has handicapped accessible vault toilets and a hand-operated water pump.

To find the campground take the Exit Glacier Road which goes west from the Seward Highway near Mile 4, the campground will be on your left at Mile 8.2.

⊒ BEAR CREEK RV PARK

Address:	Box 2209, Seward, AK 99664
Telephone:	(907) 224-5725 or (877) 924-5725
Email:	bearcreekrvpk@seward.net
Website:	bearcreekrv.com

GPS Location: N 60° 11'04.1", W 149° 22'21.6"

Like the Stoney Creek RV Park below, this campground is a full-service place located outside of town. It's an older park but well-managed. There's a state-operated fish weir nearby that can be quite interesting when the salmon are running.

This commercial campground has about 100 sites. There are a variety of site types including full, partial and no-hookup sites. A few spaces are pull-thrus. These are full-hookup sites with 30-amp power and also TV. There are some picnic tables. The campground has flush toilets, hot showers, a small grocery, a game room, propane sales, a dump station, and modem outlet. They can help you make arrangements for the various tours and boat excursions from Seward and during June through August they have a courtesy van for getting in to town.

The campground is located at Mile .3 of the Bear Lake Road. This road leaves the Seward Highway at Mile 6.6 and goes east.

⊒ STONEY CREEK RV PARK

Address:	13760 Leslie Place, Seward, AK 99664
Telephone:	(907) 224-6465 or (877) 437-6366
Email:	info@stoneycreekrvpark.com
Website:	www.stoneycreekrvpark.com

GPS Location: N 60° 10'51.0", W 149° 22'42.1"

The Stoney Creek RV Park is the newest full-service campground in Seward and arguably has the nicest facilities. The downside is that the location is somewhat remote. It's not near the downtown area.

The campground has about 80 spaces. These are big sites suitable for large modern rigs. They are set in a large gravel lot, there is a patch of clipped grass and a picnic table at each site. About half the sites are pull-thrus. Full-hookup spaces are available with 50-amp power to some and cable TV. The central facilities building has hot showers and a coin-operated laundry and there is a dump station. There's also a free courtesy van for travel into Seward.

To find the campground take Stoney Creek Avenue east from Mile 6.3 of the Seward Highway north of Seward. Pass over the railroad tracks and at .2 mile (.3 km) turn right on Bruno. Follow Bruno .2 mile (.3 km) as it turns left, crosses the creek and then turns right. Turn left on Winterset (also called Trail) and then in another .2 mile (.3 km) turn left on Leslie Place. The campground is .1 mile (.2 km) down Leslie on the right.

⊒ BY THE POND RV PARK

Address:	Mile 3 (PO Box 25), Seward, AK 99664
Telephone:	(907) 224-2401

GPS Location: N 60° 08'44.1", W 149° 25'01.3"

This small RV park is also away from central Seward but closer than the two listed above. It's next to the highway but the sites are back behind the namesake pond.

The campground has no hookups. There are about 25 designated camping sites set in a grove of spruce trees. There is also a large flat gravel lot behind them suitable for any size rig. Designated sites have picnic tables and fire rings, there are port-a-potties and no showers.

The campground is easy to find. It's on the west side of the Seward Highway north of Seward at about Mile 3.

🚐 CITY OF SEWARD
     WATERFRONT CAMPGROUND

Location: On waterfront south of small boat harbor

GPS Location: N 60° 06' 24.4", W 149° 26' 07.4"

Most of the thousands of RVers who visit Seward during the year dry camp in the huge gravel lots along the waterfront. Along hundreds of yards of waterfront you can park with the nose of your rig just feet from the water looking out on a spectacular view. Much of the area has no utility hookups, however see the two following entries. There are also two grassy areas for tent campers. Flush toilets and coin-op showers are available at two locations. The best is a new city restroom facility located near the intersection of Ballaine Blvd. and Madison Street. This is about the middle of the very spread-out camping area. Older restrooms and showers are also available in the harbormaster's building near the boat harbor. There are payment kiosks with instructions for registration and payment posted at most entrances to the camping area. There's also a new dump station (free) near the intersection of A St. and Ballaine Boulevard.

🚐 HOOKUP SECTION OF CITY OF SEWARD
     WATERFRONT CAMPGROUND

Location: On the waterfront near intersection of Madison St. and Ballaine Blvd.

GPS Location: N 60° 06' 24.4", W 149° 26' 07.4"

This camping area is part of the Seward Waterfront Campground but operates almost as a separate area. There are now almost 100 back-in or pull-in sites suitable for any size rig. They have 30-amp electrical outlets and water. Many are along the waterfront. The restroom building with coin-op showers is adjacent and there is usually a host. Reservations are not taken.

To find the camping area just drive south on Third Avenue which is the continuation of the Seward Highway as you enter town. You'll pass Monroe St, turn left at the next corner which is Madison St., the camping area is four blocks ahead.

🚐 KENAI FJORDS RV PARK

Location: Corner of 4th and Van Buren Street

GPS Location: N 60° 06' 51.9", W 149° 26' 27.6"

This gravel lot appears at first to be part of the huge city dry camping area. If you look closer you will see that there are 38 closely-spaced back-in slots arranged around the border of a gravel lot. All have 30-amp electric outlets and some have water. There are no restroom or shower facilities but facilities are available nearby. A self-registration board is located at the entrance to the lot.

The campground is located at the corner of 4th and Van Buren Street just south of the small boat harbor and across the street off Fourth Avenue.

⛺ City of Seward Forest Acres Park

Location: Mile 2.3 of the Seward Highway
                  on Hemlock Ave.

GPS Location: N 60° 08' 04.3", W 149° 25' 53.0"

This city campground is located along the highway coming in to Seward. It's easy to miss because the sites are back in the trees. If you are looking for a quiet location away from the waterfront you might like this campground.

There are about 40 back-in sites scattered around the park. Most are well separated. There are no hookups although water is available at a faucet. Some sites have picnic tables and firepits and there is sometimes a host. There are also restrooms without showers, a playground, and tennis courts. Maneuvering room for big rigs is limited although they will fit in a few sites in unmarked open areas.

Coming in to Seward watch for airport road on your left. In another .3 miles (.5 km) Hemlock Avenue goes right, turn here and then make the first left into the campground. Hemlock Avenue is at about Mile 2.3 of the Seward Highway.

⛺ Miller's Landing Campground

Address: Box 81, Seward, AK 99664
Telephone: (907) 224-5739 or (866) 541-5739
Fax: (907) 224-9197
Email: millerslanding@alaska.com
Website: www.millerslandingak.com

GPS Location: N 60° 04' 15.1", W 149° 26' 10.4"

For something different in the Seward area try Miller's Landing. This beachfront campground looks at first like it is constructed of driftwood collected by a beachcomber, but they have electric hookups, hot showers, and offer lots of recreational options. You can rent kayaks or small outboard skiffs, ride a water taxi to a remote cove, hike to nearby Cain's Head State Park or Tonsina Creek, or just beach comb and fish right out front. Best of all, when the fish are running the location is far from the madness of central Seward.

The campground has over 30 sites. There is a line of 15 sites overlooking the beach with 30-amp electrical hookups, also a few more electrical hookups back from the water. Many of these sites aren't quiet level. The remaining smaller sites are in trees back from the water, a few in this area also offer electricity. Water is available but there is no dump station. Flush toilets and hot showers are provided. There is a small store for fishing tackle and you can get lots of advice about things to do and see in the area. Fishing charters run out of the campground, boats and motors as well as sea kayaks are available for rent and guided sea kayak tours (and lessons) are available.

To reach Millers drive right through Seward and find the small gravel road that continues to follow the shoreline below the cliffs to the south. This is Lowell Point Road.

The campground is 2.2 miles (3.5 km) from the end of the pavement. Big rigs should have no problem if they take it easy.

MILITARY CAMPGROUNDS

Seward has two military campgrounds. They are only open to active military personnel, National Guard personnel, reservists, retired military, and Department of Defense employees. Both take reservations and have many facilities in addition to the campground areas. The first is **Seward Air Force Camp** (PO Box 915, Seward, AK 99664-5000; (907) 552-1110). It has 35 RV/Trailer spaces with electricity and water hookups and 47 tent/camper spaces without hookups. There is a dump station and restrooms with showers. The second is **Seward Resort** (PO Box 329, Seward, AK 99664-5000; (907) 384-1110. It has 40 RV/Trailer spaces with electric hookups and 10 tent spaces with showers and a dump station. Both are located just north of Seward, watch for signs as you arrive in town.

FROM TERN LAKE JUNCTION TO SOLDOTNA AND KENAI
58 Miles (94 Kilometers)

From its junction with the Seward Highway at Mile 37 the Sterling Highway starts west through scenic mountainous country. At Mile 45 it reaches the north edge of Kenai Lake and follows the lakeshore to the lake's outlet, the Kenai River.

The **Kenai River** is world famous for its king salmon. The current record for a Kenai king is 97 pounds. The river flows 17 miles (27 km) from Kenai Lake to Skilak Lake.

THE RUSSIAN RIVER FERRY

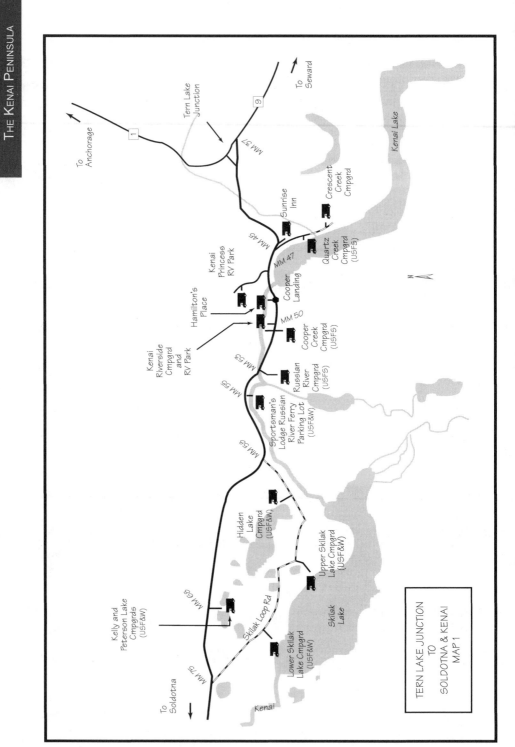

This part of the river is known as the upper Kenai. The lower Kenai flows from Skilak Lake 50 miles (81 km) to Cook Inlet at Kenai. The river is a playground, it offers fishing for king, red, silver and pink salmon as well as opportunities for both white and flat-water boating.

The Sterling Highway follows the upper Kenai through the **Cooper Landing** area to a junction with the gravel Skilak Lake Road at Mile 58. This section of the Sterling Highway is lined with campgrounds and has probably the most heavily-fished location in the entire state, the Kenai River just below the **Russian River** mouth at Mile 55 of the highway. Even if you don't fish you'll enjoy watching the action during the red salmon runs.

The highway now enters the **Kenai National Wildlife Refuge**. The Skilak Loop Road is a 19 mile (31 km) gravel road that leaves the Sterling Highway at Mile 58 and rejoins it at Mile 75. This road gives access to campgrounds and boat ramps on Skilak Lake at two points and also to a very nice campground on Hidden Lake.

After the Sterling Highway passes the junction with the Skilak Lake Road it crosses the flat Kenai National Wildlife Refuge and reaches little Sterling at Mile 81. Sterling has a few stores and services, it is located where the Moose River enters the Kenai, another popular fishing spot. Near Sterling, at Mile 83, the 29 mile (47 km) Swanson River Road leads north to the Swanson River and Swan Lake Canoe Routes. See Chapter 14 for more about these routes.

After Sterling the highway begins to pass through the outskirts of Soldotna which it reaches at Mile 94.

Tern Lake Junction to Soldotna and Kenai Campgrounds

SUNRISE INN

Address:	PO Box 835, Cooper Landing, AK 99572
Telephone:	(907) 595-1222
Email:	sunrise@arctic.net
Website:	www.alaskasunriseinn.com

GPS Location: N 60° 29' 07.2", W 149° 43' 57.2"

This roadhouse-style facility has the traditional gas pumps, restaurant, lounge, gift shop, and motel rooms. It also has a nicely wooded camping area out back. This is a small campground with separated spaces with picnic tables. Some have electrical hookups. Maneuvering room is limited so we don't recommend it for rigs over 35 feet. Flush toilets are available. The Sunrise Lodge is located near Mile 45 of the Sterling Highway, about 7 miles (11.3 km) from the junction with the Seward Highway.

QUARTZ CREEK CAMPGROUND (USFS)

Location:	Mile .3 of Quartz Creek Road
Res.:	(877) 444-6777
Website	
For Res.:	www.reserveusa.com

GPS Location: N 60° 28' 43.8", W 149° 43' 41.5"

Quartz is one of the prettiest government campgrounds in Alaska, particularly if you manage to snag one of the few lakefront sites. Altogether there are 45 spacious vehicle sites off two loops and also a tent area next to the lake. Sites are separated and both the parking pads and access roads are paved. There are a few pull-thrus but most sites are back-ins, all sites have picnic tables and firepits. Water is available from faucets. An unusual feature here is flush toilets, there are no showers. Also, there's a dump station on the access road. The campground has a boat ramp. Exercise caution boating on Kenai Lake, the wind comes up quickly. Reservations can be made at this campground, see the phone number listed above. Maximum stay here is 14 days.

Turn south on the Quartz Creek Road near Mile 45 of the Sterling Highway. This is right next to the Sunrise Inn. Drive .3 miles (.5 km) on the paved road to the first entrance road. An entrance to the second loop road is another three-tenths mile farther along.

CRESCENT CREEK CAMPGROUND (USFS)

Location:	Mile 2.9 of the Quartz Creek Road
Res.:	(877) 444-6777
Website	
For Res.:	www.reserveusa.com

GPS Location: N 60° 29' 50.2", W 149° 40' 46.5"

This small government campground is a good base if you plan to hike the good six-mile-long trail up to Crescent Lake or if you want to fish Quartz Creek. There are nine separated sites set in trees. Each site has a picnic table and firepit. Site size and available maneuvering room limit rig size in this campground to about 35 feet. There are outhouses and a hand operated water pump. Reservations can be made at this campground, see the phone number listed above. Maximum stay here is 14 days.

To reach the campground drive 2.9 miles (4.7 km) down the gravel Quartz Creek Road, the campground entrance is on the left.

KENAI PRINCESS RV PARK

Address:	PO Box 676, Cooper Landing, AK 99572
Telephone:	(907) 595-1425
Website:	www.princesslodges.com

GPS Location: N 60° 29' 29.2", W 149° 51' 03.4"

Princess Cruises (of Love Boat fame) has several hotels scattered around Alaska where cruise boat passengers stay during the land portion of their Alaska visit. One of these is hidden on a back road in Cooper Landing. This one is different from all the others, it has an RV park. If you stay here you can recover from a hard day of fishing by relaxing in one of their hot tubs or in the hotel lounge.

There are 28 large back-in RV spaces. They are separated by grassy areas and have full hookups with 30-amp power. There are restrooms with flush toilets and hot showers as well as a small convenience store, a laundromat, and a dump station. People staying at the RV park are welcome to use the hotel's facilities including restaurant, bar, hot tubs, and exercise room. Reservations are recommended.

To reach the campground turn north at Mile 47.7 of the Sterling Highway just east of the Kenai River bridge at the outlet of Kenai Lake. Follow paved Bean Creek Road for 2 miles (3.2 km) to the hotel and campground.

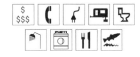

🚐 HAMILTON'S PLACE

Address:	Box 569, Cooper Landing, AK 99572
Telephone:	(907) 595-1260
Email:	hamiltonsplace@starband.net
Website:	www.hamiltonsplace.com

GPS Location: N 60° 29' 23.9", W 149° 49' 34.8"

Hamilton's Place has been in the same location for many years, a handy place to stop in Cooper Landing during the drive between Kenai and Anchorage. Hamilton's is a gas station, restaurant, bar, grocery store, liquor store, tackle shop, and RV park.

There are about 20 back-in sites overlooking the river located behind the buildings along the road. Eight have full hookups, the rest power and water only. There is room for rigs to about 32 feet. Restrooms have hot showers.

The campground is located at Mile 48.5 of the Sterling Highway, .5 miles west of the Kenai River bridge in the community of Cooper Landing.

🚐 KENAI RIVERSIDE CAMPGROUND AND RV PARK

Address:	PO Box 774, Cooper Landing, AK 99572
Telephone:	(907) 595-1406 or (888) KEN-AIRV
Email:	info@kenairiversidecampground.com
Website:	www.kenairiversidecampground.com

GPS Location: N 60° 29' 11.0", W 149° 51' 42.7"

If you are looking for a place with hookups that is convenient to the Upper Kenai and Russian River fishery you'll like the Kenai Riverside. Some folks check in for a month at time.

There are about 25 sites. Some are dry and some have electricity (20 and 30 amps) and water connections. Many are large pull-thus suitable for any size rig. There are additional tent sites. Flush toilets and hot showers are available and there is a dump station. You can fish from the bank at the campground or arrange a guided float trip.

The campground is located between the river and the road near Mile 50 of the Sterling Highway.

🚐 COOPER CREEK CAMPGROUND (USFS)

Location:	On both sides of the Sterling Highway near Mile 51
Res.:	(877) 444-6777
Website	
For Res.:	www.reserveusa.com

GPS Location: N 60° 29' 02.2", W 149° 52' 55.7"

This little Forest Service campground is one of the oldest in the neighborhood and still popular since it's located in one of the most beautiful areas of the state. You can reserve a site here. There are 27 back-in sites and two tent-only sites. Seven are near the Kenai River on the north side of the highway and the rest occupy a circular drive on the other side of the road along little Cooper Creek. Several of the sites will take rigs to about 35 feet but maneuvering room is tight. Each site has a picnic table and firepit, there is a water pump, and there are outhouses on both sides of the road. Maximum stay here is 14 days. It's located at Mile 50.7 of the Sterling Highway.

RUSSIAN RIVER CAMPGROUND (USFS)

Location:	Entrance at Mile 53 Sterling Highway
Res.:	(877) 444-6777
Website	
For Res.:	www.reserveusa.com

GPS Location: N 60° 28' 55.0", W 149° 56' 35.3"

The huge Russian River campground is one of the most popular in the state, particularly when the red salmon are running in the Russian River. During the red salmon runs, from June 15 to August 20, you are limited to a three-day stay here, reservations are available. The very popular Russian Lakes hiking trail starts from this campground and there is a fee for parking for hikers.

Eighty-three separated sites are arranged off a number of circular drives. All access roads and parking pads are paved and sites are large, a few are pull-thrus. Many are suitable for rigs to 40 feet and over. They all have picnic tables and firepits. There are outhouses and some flush toilets, also a dump station.

The entrance road for the campground leaves the Sterling Highway near Mile 53. Almost immediately you'll come to the manned entrance kiosk where your fee will be collected and a site assigned.

SPORTSMAN'S LODGE RUSSIAN RIVER FERRY PARKING LOT (USF&W)

Location:	Near Mile 55 of the Sterling Highway

GPS Location: N 60° 29' 07.4", W 150° 00' 21.5"

The most crowded and perhaps the most productive sports fishery in the state of Alaska is located on the Kenai River downstream from the outlet of the Russian River. There is a cable ferry located here so fishermen can work both sides of the Kenai. The parking lot at the ferry is a popular dry-camping area. Fishing goes on 24 hours a day although the gate is closed from 9 p.m. to 8 a.m. This is a show not to be missed.

There is probably room for about 60 rigs to park in back-in side-by-side spaces. There are also a few tent-camping sites. There are outhouses and fish-cleaning tables but no other amenities. The camping fee is collected at a kiosk on the entrance road when the fish are running. There's also a two-day time limit here. There is an additional fee for the pedestrian ferry.

KELLY AND PETERSEN LAKE CAMPGROUNDS (USF&W)

Location:	Near Mile 68 of the Sterling Highway

GPS Location: N 60° 31' 47.4", W 150° 23' 08.8"

Near Mile 68 of the Sterling Highway a small road leads a mile south to two little lakes: Kelly and Petersen. Both have room for a few campers in open gravel lots next to the lakes, any size rig is fine. There are a few picnic tables and firepits as well as vault toilets, hand water pumps, and launching ramps. Stays here are limited to 14 days. Both lakes have rainbow trout. The Seven Lakes Trail starts at Kelly Lake and connects with Skilak Road at Engineer Lake, a distance of 4.5 miles (7.3 km).

▄ HIDDEN LAKE CAMPGROUND (USF&W)

Location: 4 Miles from the Eastern junction of
            Skilak Lake Loop Road and the Sterling Highway

GPS Location: N 60° 27' 52.9", W 150° 12' 04.4"

This large, modern, and nicely laid out government campground is well worth nego-
tiating four miles of gravel to reach. It adjoins Hidden Lake which has decent fishing
for lake trout and rainbows in the early summer. You'll need a boat, however. Hidden
Lake is much smaller than nearby Skilak Lake and much safer.

There are 45 large well-separated sites arranged off paved loop roads. Sites have
large picnic tables and firepits and some are suitable for rigs to 40 feet. Three of them
are pull-thrus and nice paved handicapped sites are available. There are outhouses
and a dump station. Down by the lake are a boat launch ramp and a few camping
spaces as well as an amphitheater where campfire programs are sometimes offered.
The campground also has a large overflow parking area. Stays here are limited to 7
days.

The gravel Skilak Loop Road leaves the Sterling Highway at Mile 58 (eastern junction) and at Mile 75 (western junction). The campground entrance road is 4 miles
(6.5 km) from the eastern junction and 15 miles (24 km) from the western junction.

▄ UPPER SKILAK LAKE CAMPGROUND (USF&W)

Location: 9 Miles from the Eastern junction of
            Skilak Lake Loop Road and the Sterling Highway

GPS Location: N 60° 26' 24.0", W 150° 19' 15.9"

The Upper Skilak Lake campground has a boat launch that is used as a take-out by
boats and rafts that float the Upper Kenai River from Cooper Landing. Boating on
Skilak Lake is considered very dangerous because winds come up suddenly. This
is another first class government campground with paved access roads and parking
pads as well as some lakefront campsites.

There are 15 separated vehicle sites and 10 walk-in tent sites at this campground.
Sites have the normal picnic tables and firepits. The sites here are small, some will
take rigs to 30 feet. There are very nice vault toilets (with skylights) and a water
pump as well as a covered picnic area and a boat ramp and large boat trailer parking
area. There is no dump station at this campground but there is one located nearby in
the middle of nowhere along the Skilak Loop Road 12 miles from the east junction
and 8 miles from the west junction. Stays here are limited to 7 days.

To reach the campground follow a gravel access road for 2 miles (3.2 km) from a
point on the Skilak Loop Road that is 9 miles (14.5 km) from the east junction and
11 miles (18 km) from the west junction.

▄ LOWER SKILAK LAKE CAMPGROUND (USF&W)   FREE

Location: 6 Miles from the western junction of
            Skilak Lake Loop Road and the Sterling Highway

GPS Location: N 60° 28' 44.9", W 150° 27' 08.9"

Lower Skilak Lake Campground has a boat ramp that provides easy access to the
Middle Kenai River, the Kenai leaves Skilak Lake about 2 miles from the camp-

THE KENAI PENINSULA

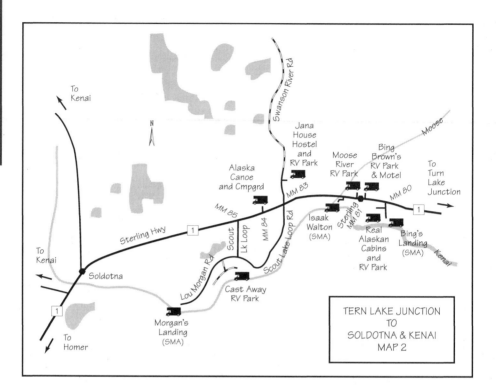

ground. This campground has not been upgraded like the Upper Skilak Campground, it's not nearly as upscale. Exercise extreme caution when boating on Skilak Lake, winds come up very suddenly and this is a big lake.

The small campground has 7 separated sites. They are suitable for rigs to about 30 feet. They have picnic tables and firepits, there are handicapped outhouses and a water pump. There are also five tent sites along the lake. Stays here are limited to 14 days.

A 1-mile gravel access road leaves the Skilak Lake Loop Road 6 miles (10 km) from the western junction with the Sterling Highway and 14 miles (23 km) from the eastern junction.

BING'S LANDING CAMPGROUND
– KENAI RIVER SMA

$$ | 🔥 | 🎣 | 🥾 | ♿ | 🚌 BIG RIGS

Location: Near Mile 80 of the Sterling Highway

GPS Location: N 60° 31' 14.1", W 150° 42' 14.8"

Bing's Landing is primarily used by fishermen accessing the middle Kenai River. There is an important boat launching area here, and also a campground.

In the modern campground here there are 36 long back-in sites with picnic tables and firepits. These sites are nicely separated and there are handicapped-access vault toilets. There's also a covered picnic area and a hand-operated water pump. This campground has a seven day limit from May through September.

The access road to Bing's is at Mile 80 of the Sterling Highway.

REAL ALASKAN CABINS AND RV PARK

Address:	Box 69, Sterling, Alaska 99772
Telephone:	(907) 262-6077
Email:	realalaskan@worldnet.att.net
Website:	www.realalaskan.com

GPS Location: N 60° 31' 26.0", W 150° 42' 33.8"

This small private campground is nicely designed with trees separating sites and room for larger rigs. It is located near the highway just east of Sterling on the access road to Bing's Landing.

The campground has 33 sites with 30-amp electricity and water. Four are pull-thrus, the others are long back-ins. Some sites will take rigs to 40 feet. Access roads and parking pads are gravel separated by trees, natural vegetation and grass; there are even some flowers. There are flush toilets and showers available.

To reach the campground just take the road south toward Bing's Landing near Mile 80 of the Sterling Highway, the campground entrance is on the right just a tenth of a mile from the highway.

BING BROWN'S RV PARK AND MOTEL

Address:	PO Box 1039, Sterling, AK 99672
Telephone:	(907) 262-4780
Website:	www.bingbrowns.com

GPS Location: N 60° 31' 37.5", W 150° 43' 37.2"

This campground is located behind a motel in the small town of Sterling. There are about 15 full-hookup sites and about 10 with only electricity as well as a grassy area for no hookup camping or tenting. Sites will take big rigs and there is plenty of maneuvering room. Picnic tables are provided. Restrooms offer flush toilets and coin-op showers, there is a dump station as well as a laundromat, a small store with fishing tackle, and a liquor store

Bing Brown's is on the north side of the highway near Mile 81 in the town of Sterling.

MOOSE RIVER RV PARK

Location:	Mile 81.5 Sterling Highway, Sterling, Alaska
Telephone:	(907) 260-7829
Email:	merkes@stayalaska.com
Website:	www.stayalaska.com

GPS Location: N 60° 32' 06.5", W 150° 44' 31.8"

This is a new campground located in the town of Sterling. It has 30 sites, some are pull-thrus. Sites have full hookups and some will take rigs to 45 feet. Each site has a picnic table and there is a central campfire area. Restrooms with showers are in the main building which is also an expresso café, there's also a modem outlet, a computer for internet access, and Wi-Fi.

The campground is easy to find. It's in Sterling on the north side of the highway just east of a Tesoro station at Mile 81.5.

IZAAK WALTON CAMPGROUND – KENAI RIVER SMA

Location: Near Mile 82 of the Sterling Highway, in Sterling

GPS Location: N 60° 32' 09.4", W 150° 45' 17.3"

As the name suggests this is a campground primarily used by fishermen. It is located at the point where the Moose River enters the Kenai in Sterling and is a popular place to fish from the bank for salmon using flies.

The campground has some 31 sites, seven of these are tent sites. Most are short separated sites off a paved but narrow circular access road. This is not a good campground for large rigs, a few sites will take rigs to 30 feet but 25 feet is more comfortable. Picnic tables are provided as well as outhouses and a water pump. There is also a boat launch. The campground has a seven day limit.

This campground is located at the confluence of the Kenai and Moose Rivers in Sterling near Mile 82 of the Sterling Highway.

JANA HOUSE HOSTEL AND RV PARK

Address: 38670 Swanson River Rd (PO Box 287),
                 Sterling, AK 99672
Telephone: (907) 260-4151   **Fax:**   (907) 562-9982
Email: janamae@alaska.com

GPS Location: N 60° 32' 29.0", W 150° 47' 36.6"

Jana House is a huge building that serves as a hostel. It is located just outside Sterling on the Swanson River Road just a half-mile or so from the Sterling Highway.

Behind the hostel building are ten very large full-hookup RV sites with 60-amp outlets. The sites are situated on a large gravel lot so there's plenty of room. Picnic tables are provided. RVers can use the bathrooms and showers inside the main building.

To reach the campground drive north from Mile 83 of the Sterling Highway (just west of Sterling) on the Swanson River Road. After .4 mile (.6 km) you'll see the large hostel building on your right.

ALASKA CANOE AND CAMPGROUND

Address: 35292 Sterling Hwy., Sterling, AK 99672
Telephone: (907) 262-2331
Email: alaskacanoe@yahoo.com
Website: www.alaskacanoetrips.com

GPS Location: N 60° 32' 14.0", W 150° 48' 12.1"

Just outside Sterling there's a small campground that specializes in information and rental canoes for the various canoe routes in the area. They also rent mountain bikes.

There are 25 sites located behind the main building. Some are full hookup with 20 or 30-amp power. There are also tent sites. RV sites are not really long, we'd say that folks with rigs over 30 feet should take a look before entering, there's plenty of room out front to park and do so. There are restrooms with flush toilets and hot showers.

The campground is located on the north side of the Sterling Highway near Mile 84 which is just west of Sterling.

 **MORGAN'S LANDING CAMPGROUND**
    – KENAI RIVER SMA

Location: Scout Loop Road from Mile 85 of the Sterling Highway

GPS Location: N 60° 30' 02.1", W 150° 51' 53.4"

This fairly large state campground is another popular access point for the middle Kenai River. The Alaska State Parks headquarters for the district is also located here.

There are 41 sites with tables and firepits. Many are pull-thrus suitable for rigs of any size. The campground has vault toilets, a water faucet, and a host. There's also an overflow area where you can camp for a night while waiting for a standard campsite to open up. Stays here are limited to 7 days.

Best access to the campground is from Mile 85 of the Sterling Highway. Follow the Scout Lake Loop Road for 1.6 miles (2.6 km), then turn right on Lou Morgan Road. The campground will appear in another 2.5 miles (4.2 km).

 **CAST AWAY RV PARK**
    Address: PO Box 189, Sterling, AK 99672
    Telephone: (907) 262-7219 or (800) 478-6446

    GPS Location: N 60° 30' 29.6", W 150° 51' 17.4"

Just off the road out to Morgan's Landing you'll find a nice riverfront RV Park. There's lots of space in this park but not many sites, the emphasis is on lots of room and great fishing.

There are ten very large back-in sites. These are large sites suitable for any size rig spaced very far apart around the edges of a large lawn area. Sites have 30-amp power and there's a dump station and water fill station. A large chalet-style building overlooks the campground and river, inside are restrooms with nice separate rooms containing toilets, showers, and sinks. There's also a laundry room and espresso bar. The Castaway also has separate rental rooms and cabins as well as bank fishing in the Kenai River. If you want to stay here, particularly during the fishing season, you had better call ahead and make a reservation.

To reach the campground leave the Sterling Highway near Mile 85 and drive south on Scout Lake Loop Road for 1.6 miles (2.6 km) to Lou Morgan Road. Turn right and drive .8 miles (1.3 km) and you'll see the gravel Martins Road on the left. Follow it for .5 mile (.8 km) to a T, turn left and you'll soon reach the Castaway.

SOLDOTNA AND KENAI
Population Soldotna 4,000, Kenai 7,000, Elevation near sea level

Soldotna has grown because of its convenient location near the junction of the Sterling Highway and Kenai Spur Road. The settlement began to grow in the 1940's. The location along the Kenai River didn't hurt either, today the town really hops when the salmon are running. Soldotna has full services including a large Fred Meyer and a Safeway. Right next to the Kenai River Bridge at Mile 96 is the **Soldotna Visitor's**

Center (Greater Soldotna Chamber of Commerce, 44790 Sterling Highway, Soldotna, Alaska 99669; 907 262-1337). This is an essential stop, they have the huge 97 pound, 4 ounce world record Kenai king salmon on display (it's mounted, of course).

Kenai, by far the older of these towns, is located well west of the Sterling Highway. To get there follow the Kenai Spur Road for 8 miles (13 km) from near Mile 94 of the Sterling Highway. This intersection is in Soldotna across from the Fred Meyer store. Kenai was originally an Indian village and then in 1791 became the second permanent Russian settlement in Alaska. You will still find signs of the Russians in Kenai in the form of the **Holy Assumption Russian Orthodox Church** with its blue onion dome and also **St. Nicholas Chapel**. Kenai has supermarkets, restaurants and other services. The town seems well-clipped and organized compared to upstart Soldotna. Kenai has its own visitor center called the **Kenai Bicentennial Visitors and Cultural Center** (11471 Kenai Spur Highway, Kenai, AK 99611; 907 283-1991).

The Kenai-Soldotna area offers two golf courses. **Kenai Golf Course** (907 283-7500) has 18 holes and a driving range. It is located in Kenai next to Oiler Park on Lawton Drive. The **Birch Ridge Golf Course** (907 262-5270) is a nine-hole course and driving range located on the Sterling Highway east of Soldotna. Both courses have rental equipment.

Both Soldotna and Kenai are well supplied with campgrounds, they're the supply centers for the western Kenai Peninsula.

Soldotna Campgrounds

🚐 Fred Meyer Parking Lot

Location: In Soldotna at Mile 94 of the Sterling Highway

GPS Location: N 60° 29' 17.8", W 151° 03' 03.1"

Fred Meyer is a huge and hugely popular grocery and discount store in Soldotna. To the chagrin of local RV park operators and the delight of frugal RVers it also is one of the more popular campgrounds in town since RVs are allowed to park overnight in the lot. There's no telling how long this situation will last as the commercial and political forces play out.

You can easily find the areas of the parking lot set out for RVers. There are two of them and they are marked with green curbs and separators. There is even a dump station.

The store is impossible to miss, it is located on the east side of the highway near the point where the Sterling Highway enters Soldotna from the north.

🚐 Swiftwater Park (City of Soldotna)

Telephone: (907) 262-5299
Website: www.ci.soldotna.ak.us

GPS Location: N 60° 28' 58.9", W 151° 02' 29.9"

The City of Soldotna maintains two RV parks along the Kenai River. This is the smaller of the two. There are about 40 spaces, many are pull-thrus or parallel-type spaces. Some will take rigs to 40 feet. Many are along the river bank. Picnic tables

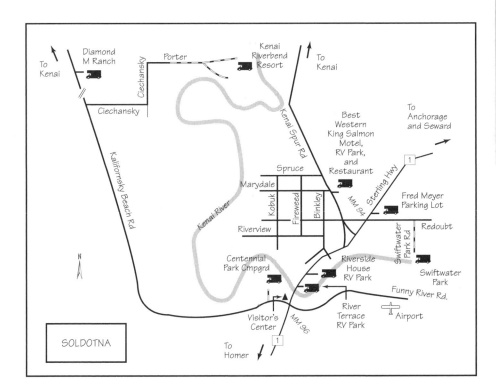

and firepits are provided. There are outhouses, a boat launch, water fill hoses, and a dump station (big extra charge).

To reach the campground leave the Sterling Highway in Soldotna near Mile 94, this is just south of the Fred Meyer store. Drive east on Redoubt for .5 mile (.8 km), then turn right onto Swiftwater Park Road. You'll reach the park in another .3 miles (.5 km).

BEST WESTERN KING SALMON MOTEL, RV PARK AND RESTAURANT

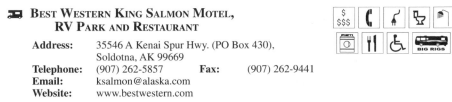

Address:	35546 A Kenai Spur Hwy. (PO Box 430), Soldotna, AK 99669
Telephone:	(907) 262-5857 **Fax:** (907) 262-9441
Email:	ksalmon@alaska.com
Website:	www.bestwestern.com

GPS Location: N 60° 29' 45.7", W 151° 04' 11.9"

This motel has 39 sites located in a large open gravel lot. Most of the sites are pull-thrus suitable for any size rig, they have electric (20 and 30 amp), water, and sewer hookups. Sites have picnic table but not fire pits. A laundromat between the camping area and the motel has restrooms with flush toilets and hot showers, and the motel has a restaurant. To reach the motel just follow the Kenai Spur Road .7 west from its junction with the Sterling Highway at Mile 94. You'll soon see the motel on your right.

RIVER TERRACE RV PARK

Address: PO Box 332, Soldotna, AK 99669
Telephone: (907) 262-5593

GPS Location: N 60° 28' 37.8", W 151° 04' 43.3"

The River Terrace is one of the older and better known campgrounds in Soldotna. You can't miss it as you drive across the bridge over the Kenai. It sits right on the river and has been a popular base for fishermen during June, July, and August every year when the salmon are thick. Unfortunately the campground facilities are old and have seen better days.

The campground occupies a couple of terraces along the river bank. There are about 50 back-in or pull-into sites, many right along the river. Sites are either full-hookup or electric only (20, 30, and 50 amp). Any size rig can find a site here. There is a dump station. Restrooms have flush toilets and hot showers are available. Bank fishing is possible, there's even a fishing platform that is wheel-chair accessible. Fishing is the mainstay of this campground, they can help you arrange charters and fish processing. Reservations are recommended during the summer.

The campground is located on the north bank of the river. As you drive south toward Homer it will be on your left just before you cross the bridge in Soldotna.

RIVERSIDE HOUSE RV PARK

Address: 44611 Sterling Hwy., Soldotna, AK 99669
Telephone: (907) 262-0500 or (877) 262-0500
Fax: (907) 262-0406
Email: bob@riversidehouse.net
Website: www.riversidehouse.net

GPS Location: N 60° 28' 45.2", W 151° 04' 25.2"

The Riverside House is a motel with restaurant on the banks of the Kenai River. They also have a large RV parking area. There are 28 sites, all have 30-amp electric hook-ups. This is a large open field, any size rig can find room. There are two water taps, no dump station, and no dedicated restrooms although campers can use the toilets off the hotel lobby. While dedicated facilities at the campground may be limited you can find anything you need nearby including showers in a laundromat and the price is right. The Riverside House has quite a bit of river bank and fishing is possible.

CENTENNIAL PARK CAMPGROUND (CITY OF SOLDOTNA)

Telephone: (907) 262-5299
Website: www.ci.soldotna.ak.us

GPS Location: N 60° 28' 46.8", W 151° 05' 25.9"

This second campground operated by the City of Soldotna is large. There are about 125 sites set in spruce trees along the Kenai River. Sites have picnic tables and firepits, many are large enough for the larges rigs. There are outhouses and dump stations (big extra charge). The person at the gatehouse kiosk can direct you to the nearby sports center for showers. There is a boat launch at the campground and large areas for parking boat trailers. The campground has lots of riverfront and bank fishing is possible. Reservations are not accepted but there is an overflow camping area where you can stay while waiting for a campsite.

To reach the campground turn onto the Kalifornsky Beach Road from the Sterling Highway at Mile 96. Turn right in just .1 mile into the campground entrance road.

🚐 KENAI RIVERBEND RESORT

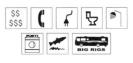

Address:	PO Box 1270, Soldotna, AK 99669
Telephone:	(907) 283-9489, (800) 625-2324
Website:	www.KenaiRiverbend.com

GPS Location: N 60° 30' 50.6", W 151° 06' 06.7"

This large riverside campground is located right on the bank of the Kenai River. It also is totally dedicated to those interested in fishing the Kenai. During the July high season for fishing it's almost impossible to get in here unless you have reservations.

The Riverbend is a big campground. There are about 110 spaces, about half with hook-ups, both full and partial. There are just a few pull-thrus. The spaces are located in large gravel lots and there's lots of room for big rigs. There are flush toilets, hot showers, a laundromat, a small grocery store, a tackle shop, boat rentals, and guide service.

From the junction of the Sterling Highway and the Kalifornsky Beach Road at Mile 96 of the Sterling Highway just south of Soldotna drive 4.7 miles (7.6 km) west on the Kalifornsky Beach Road and turn right on the Ciechansky Loop Road. Follow the road to a T at .8 miles (1.3 km), turn left and then right on Porter Road. Finally at 2.4 miles (3.9 km) take the left at the Y to reach the Kenai Riverbed.

🚐 DIAMOND M RANCH

Address:	PO Box 1776, Soldotna, AK 99669
Telephone:	(907) 283-9424
Email:	martin@diamondmranch.com
Website:	www.diamondmranch.com

GPS Location: N 60° 31' 02.0", W 151° 11' 26.2"

This is a large and fairly new campground. It's a popular place when the fish are running but it's not located next to the river.

The campground has about 35 sites Most of these are large sites with full hookups and 20, 30 and 50-amp power. They're suitable for any size rig. Restrooms have flush toilets and hot showers. There's also a dump station and a laundry.

The Diamond M Ranch is located off Kalifornsky Beach Road at Mile 16.5. From its intersection with the Sterling Highway just south of Soldotna drive 5.7 miles (9.2 km) west on the Kalifornsky Beach Road. You'll see the campground entrance on your right.

Kenai Campgrounds

🚐 BELUGA LOOKOUT RV PARK

Address:	929 Mission Ave., Kenai, AK 99611
Telephone:	(907) 283-5999 or (800) 745-5999
Fax:	(907) 283-4939
Email:	belugarv@ptialaska.net
Website:	www.belugalookout.com

GPS Location: N 60° 33' 03.8", W 151° 15' 55.5"

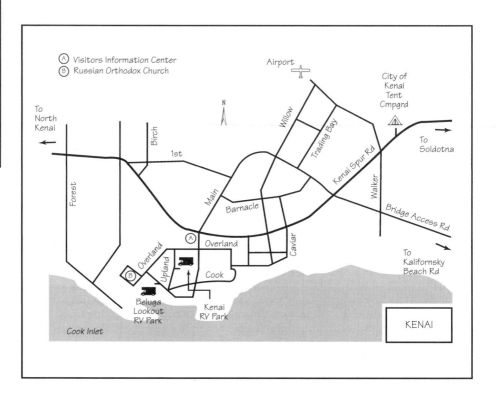

For a campground that takes full advantage of Kenai's view across Cook Inlet of the volcanoes of the Alaska Range you can do no better than the Beluga Lookout. High on a bluff overlooking the outlet of the Kenai River this is also a good place to watch for white beluga whales feeding off the mouth of the Kenai.

The campground has 75 full-hookup spaces (20, 30, and 50 amp) occupying a large open lot at the top of a bluff overlooking Cook Inlet. Some 45 of the sites are large pull-thrus. All sites have picnic tables and many are suitable for rigs to 45 feet. Cable-TV hook-ups are available. There are token-operated showers and flush toilets and a coin-op laundry. The restaurants, sights, and shopping of central Kenai are within walking distance.

To find the campground follow Main Street south from the visitor information center and turn right on Cook Drive. The campground is hard to miss on the lip of the bluff.

🚐 KENAI RV PARK

Address:	507 Upland Street (PO Box 2027), Kenai, AK 99611
Telephone:	(907) 398-3382
Email:	diamondjim@kenai.net
Website:	www.kenairvpark.com

GPS Location: N 60° 33' 10.9", W 151° 15' 45.9"

This small campground near the information center in Kenai is one of the homiest and friendliest around. The owners live onsite and love to introduce visitors to the joys of the Kenai Peninsula.

There are 12 full-service RV sites with 30-amp outlets on a small grassy lot and some additional tent and electric-only camping sites. A few sites are pull-thrus and will take rigs to about 35 feet. Restrooms have flush toilets and hot showers. There is also a fish-cleaning station. The city of Kenai's attractions are within walking distance.

To reach the campground drive south of Main for one block next to the visitors center and turn right on Overland Street. You'll see the campground one block down Overland on the left but you must turn left on Upland Street to enter it.

⛺ CITY OF KENAI TENT CAMPGROUND

Location: Mile 10 Kenai Spur Road in Kenai

GPS Location: N 60° 33' 42.9", W 151° 13' 31.3"

This small campground next to the ball field is run by the city for tent campers. There are 12 sites, they are actually small gravel back-in sites but only tents are allowed here. Sites have picnic tables and firepits, an outhouse is available near the ball field out front.

The campground is located on the north side of the Kenai Spur Highway as it comes into Kenai from the direction of Soldotna near the Mile 10 marker.

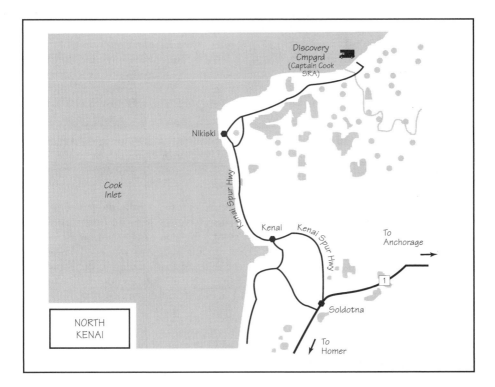

THE KENAI PENINSULA

North Kenai Campgrounds

DISCOVERY CAMPGROUND
– CAPTAIN COOK STATE RECREATION AREA

Location: Near Mile 39 of the Kenai Spur Highway

GPS Location: N 60° 48' 19.8", W 151° 00' 54.0"

Discovery Campground is a large and very nice government campground located a little off the beaten path. The fishing crowds found throughout the rest of the Kenai seldom venture out to the end of the Kenai Spur Highway although fishing can be good in the nearby river. On the other hand, this makes a good place to stay if you are assigned pick-up duties for someone canoeing the Swanson River.

The campground has 53 back-in spaces off a circular access road. Rigs to about 35 feet should fit in some of the larger sites. Sites have picnic tables and firepits, there are outhouses. The campground sits near the bluff overlooking Cook Inlet and there are hiking paths down to the beach. Stays here are limited to 15 days.

From Kenai drive north 27 miles (43.5 km) on the Kenai Spur Road past the refineries at Nikiski to the end of the road. Turn left and you'll soon see the campground.

FROM SOLDOTNA TO HOMER
85 Miles (137 Kilometers)

From Soldotna the Sterling Highway leads directly south toward Homer. At Mile 109 the road crosses the **Kasilof River** and from Mile 115 near Clam Gulch it never strays far from the bluffs overlooking Cook Inlet. The road can't really run along the water because high tides and storms eat away at the foot of the bluffs and they move to the east a few feet each year. Nonetheless there are access roads to the beach at many places and often there are views across the inlet to the snowcapped volcanoes (from left to right): **Augustine** (4,025 ft.), last eruption 1986; **Illiamna** (10,016 ft.); **Redoubt** (10,197 ft.), last eruption 1990; and **Spur** (11,070 ft), last eruption 1992.

At Mile 117 an access road leads west to **Clam Gulch State Recreation Area**. This is the first of several beaches along Cook Inlet where razor clams can be found. Tides here can range 35 feet from low to high water so be careful if you take your rig onto the beach. If you get stuck you may lose it.

As the road continues south it crosses several rivers: the **Ninilchik River** at Mile 135, **Deep Creek** at Mile 137, and the **Anchor River** at Mile 157. Each of these rivers is a popular fishing stream with runs of king and silver salmon as well as Dolly Varden, rainbows, and steelhead. There are lots of campgrounds allowing easy access to the fishing. You might want to note that the road out along the south side of the Anchor River to the beach past the Anchor River state campgrounds and the Kyllonen RV Park is the **westernmost road in North America** that is connected to the road system.

Finally, at Mile 170 the highway crests the bluff overlooking **Kachemak Bay**. Pull off the highway at the developed overlook for one of the most scenic vistas in Alaska. Spread out before you are the Homer Spit, Kachemak Bay, and the snow-covered

MANY CAMPGROUNDS BETWEEN SOLDOTNA AND HOMER HAVE MAGNIFICENT VIEWS

Kenai Mountains forming a magnificent backdrop.

Soldotna to Homer Campgrounds

DECANTER INN

Address: PO Box 1089, Kasilof, AK 99610
Telephone: (907) 262-5917 or (907) 262-5933
Website: www.decanterinn.com

GPS Location: N 60° 20' 26.8", W 151° 13' 38.3"

The Decanter Inn has been in this location for a long time, now they have an RV camping area between the highway and the restaurant, bar, and hotel.

The campground has 28 sites. Most are back-in sites suitable for rigs to about 30 feet. Two are pull-thrus which will take 40-footers. The sites have only electrical hookups (30 amp) but there is a dump site and water fill station.

The Inn is located along the Sterling Highway between Soldotna and the Kasilof River, it's on the east side of the road near Mile 107.

JOHNSON LAKE STATE RECREATION AREA

Location: Near Mile 110.5 of the Sterling Highway

GPS Location: N 60° 17' 34.5", W 151° 16' 05.9"

Johnson Lake is a larger state campground with a nice lake next to the campground and the Clam Gulch beaches not far away. You can catch small rainbows in the lake.

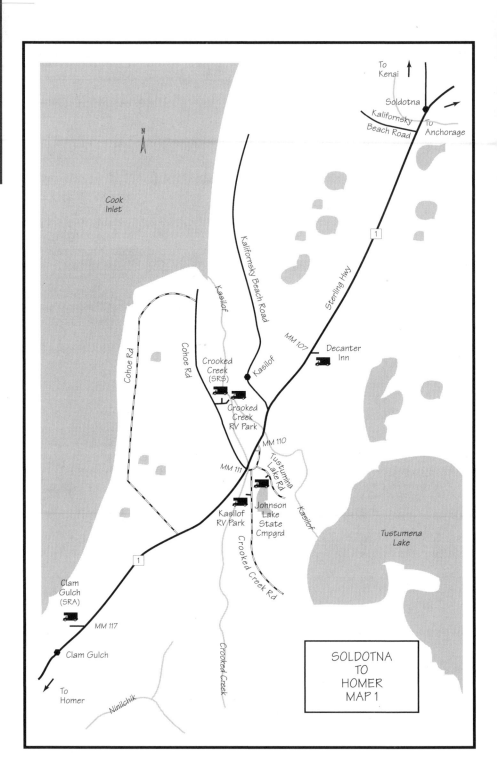

It makes a good base for those planning to spend some time on the Kenai with visits to both the Homer and Kenai areas.

There are about 40 back-in sites off two loops and additional tenting sites. As you enter the campground the older and smaller sites are to the right. Newer and much larger sites, some suitable for rigs to 40 feet, are to the left. A few sites are along the lake, these go first. There's also a tent-camping area. Each campsite has a picnic table and firepit and there are outhouses and water pumps. This campground often has a host and stays are limited to 15 days.

To reach this campground turn east from the Sterling Highway near Mile 110.5 on Ptarmigan Road. In .1 mile (.2 km) turn right at the first road you come to. In .3 mile (.5 km) you'll see the Tustamina Lake Road on your left, marked with a large T. Turn left here and in .2 mile (.3 km) you'll see the Johnson Lake campground entrance on your right.

⊐ KASILOF RV PARK

Address:	PO Box 1333, Soldotna, AK 99669
Telephone:	(907) 262-0418 or (800) 264-0418
Email:	kasilofrv@ak.net
Website:	www.kasilofrvpark.com

GPS Location: N 60° 17' 26.1", W 151° 16' 16.6"

Near the Johnson Lake State Rec. Area is an excellent little commercial RV park. It's not on the main road so many people don't know it's there. This place has a location central to many western Kenai Peninsula attractions with the added advantages of hookups and showers. Johnson Lake is just across the road.

There are 33 sites on a wooded ridge between Crooked Creek and Johnson Lake. These are wooded and separated sites much like a government campground. Twelve of these are full-hookup pull-thru sites, some suitable for rigs to 40 feet. Some sites are full-hookup, others have water and electricity, electricity only, or no hookups. Restrooms are very clean and have hot showers. There is also a dump station and a laundry. Clamming equipment can be rented here too.

The route to this campground is from Mile 110.5 of the Sterling Highway. Turn east on Ptarmigan road. In .1 mile (.2 km) turn right at the first road you come to. In .9 mile (1.5 km) turn left on Crooked Creek Road and you'll see the campground on your right in .5 mile (.8 km).

⊐ CROOKED CREEK STATE RECREATION SITE

Location: 1.8 Miles on Cohoe Loop Road

GPS Location: N 60° 19' 18.2", W 151° 17' 17.4"

This has been a popular campground with fishermen because it is located near a good hole at the confluence of the Kasilof River and Crooked Creek. The Kasilof River is glacial and cloudy during the summer, fishing is best where clear-water streams empty into the river.

There are about 80 camping spaces at the campground. These are side-by-side back-in parking spaces in a gravel parking lot. There's room for any size rig. Fishing is the attraction here, not peaceful enjoyment of an unspoiled setting. Outhouses are provided and a few sites have picnic tables and firepits. Stays here are limited to 7 days.

To reach the campground turn west on the Cohoe Loop Road from Mile 111 of the Sterling Highway. The campground access road is on the right at 1.8 miles (1.8 km).

CROOKED CREEK RV PARK

Address: PO Box 601, Kasilof, AK 99610
Telephone: (907) 262-1299

GPS Location: N 60° 19' 15.6", W 151° 17' 02.4"

This commercial campground is right next to the Crooked Creek State Recreation Area. Access to the banks of clear Crooked Creek is through this RV park and a fee is charged for fishing there. Fishing charters are available here for the Kenai, the Kasilof, and Cook Inlet.

The campground has about 5 full and partial-hookup back-in sites. Many are suitable for rigs to 40 feet. These are separated sites with trees but laid out in a grid-like pattern. There are flush toilets, hot showers, laundry facilities, and a dump station. Many sites are occupied by permanently-located rigs, some of which are available as rentals.

To reach the campground follow the directions given for the Crooked Creek State Recreation Site but continue on past the state site entrance for just a short distance.

CLAM GULCH STATE RECREATION AREA

Location: Mile 117 Sterling Highway

GPS Location: N 60° 14' 19.2", W 151° 23' 47.6"

The beaches along the west shore of the Kenai Peninsula along Cook Inlet provide some the best razor clam digging in the United States. Clam digging can be really fun and easy if you know how, virtually impossible if you don't. You can find information in many places including at the information offices in Kenai and Soldotna. The Clam Gulch State Recreation Area is probably the best place to come for your introduction to this activity.

There are over 100 back-in side-by-side parking lot type camping spaces on the bluff above the beach. Rigs over 25 feet will find maneuvering and parking difficult here if the campground is anywhere near full. This campground is likely to be full on spring and summer weekends with big negative tides, virtually empty otherwise. There is also a tent camping area. Picnic tables, firepits, outhouses and sometimes water are provided. From the campground a steep sand road leads down to the beach. Four-wheel drive vehicles can be used on the beach, no permit is required. Keep in mind, however, that sea salt isn't very good for your rig. Most people just walk the beach or use quads, you can find clams directly in front of the campground. That can still be a healthy walk since Cook Inlet tides have a range of over 20 feet and the beach here is practically flat. Stays here are limited to 15 days.

You'll find the quarter-mile road out to the Clam Gulch Recreation Area leaving the Sterling Highway at about Mile 117.

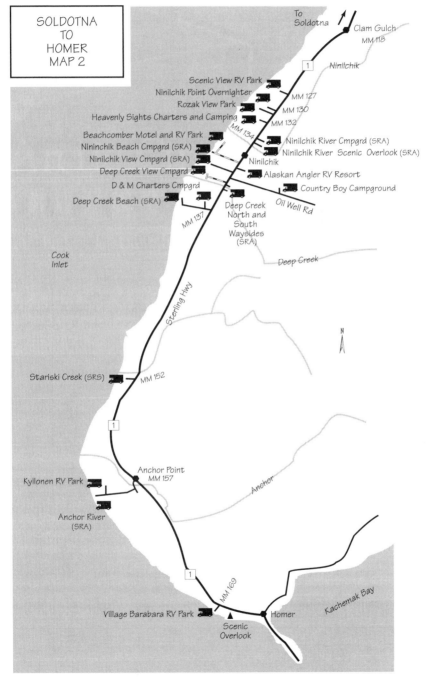

SOLDOTNA
TO
HOMER
MAP 2

To
Soldotna

Clam Gulch
MM 118

1   Ninilchik

Scenic View RV Park
Ninilchik Point Overnighter   MM 127
Rozak View Park   MM 130
Heavenly Sights Charters and Camping   MM 132
MM 134
Beachcomber Motel and RV Park   Ninilchik River Cmpgrd (SRA)
Nininchik Beach Cmpgrd (SRA)   Ninilchik River Scenic Overlook (SRA)
Ninilchik View Cmpgrd (SRA)   Ninilchik
Deep Creek View Cmpgrd   Alaskan Angler RV Resort
D & M Charters Cmpgrd   Country Boy Campground
Deep Creek Beach (SRA)   Oil Well Rd
MM 137   Deep Creek
North and
South
Waysides
(SRA)

Cook
Inlet   Deep Creek

Sterling Hwy

N

Stariski Creek (SRS)   MM 152

1

Anchor Point
MM 157
Kyllonen RV Park   Anchor

Anchor River
(SRA)

1

MM 169
Village Barabara RV Park   Homer   Kachemak Bay
Scenic
Overlook

THE KENAI PENINSULA

SCENIC VIEW RV PARK

Address:	PO Box 39253, Ninilchik, Alaska 99639
Telephone:	(907) 567-3909
Email:	scenicrv@yahoo.com
Website:	www.scenicviewrv.com

GPS Location: N 60° 07' 52.2", W 151° 32' 08.1"

This is another bluff-side RV park along the road north of Ninilchik offering fishing charters. True to its name, this one is very scenic as it perches next to the bluff. There are 27 back-in sites, most will take rigs to 30 feet. A couple will take rigs to 40 feet. Many sites have electric and water and about half with sewer too. They are separated by short hedges. The campground has restrooms with flush toilets and hot showers, a laundry, and a dump station.

The campground is located on the west side of the Sterling highway at Mile 127.

NINILCHIK POINT OVERNIGHTER

Address:	28635 Reflection Lake Rd,		
	Soldotna, AK 99669 (mail only)		
Telephone:	(907) 567-3423	**Fax:**	(907) 262-7087
Website:	www.ptialaska.net/~kathyj		

GPS Location: N 60° 05' 57.6", W 151° 35' 44.2"

This is a small RV park located next to the highway with views to the west of the mountains on the far side of Cook Inlet. The facilities at this time are minimal but being improved. There are 6 back-in sites with full hookups and a restroom building with flush toilets and hot showers.

The campground is located on the west side of the Sterling Highway near Mile 130.5.

ROZAK VIEW PARK

Location:	Near Mile 131 of the Sterling Highway

GPS Location: N 60° 05' 37.8", W 151° 37' 03.0"

Rozak View Park is a very simple campsite. If you drive down a wide gravel road toward the beach you'll find that a large bluff overlooking the water has been cleared and is offered as a camping location. There's lots of room and access is easy, tent campers or any size RV will find this a suitable place to set up camp. There are no hookups but there are scattered picnic tables and fire pits made of concrete blocks. Other amenities are limited to a port-a-potty and dumpster. There's also an access road to the beach.

The campground access road is near Mile 131 of the Sterling Highway, just north of Ninilchik.

HEAVENLY SIGHTS CHARTERS AND CAMPING

Address:	13295 Sterling Highway, Ninilchik, AK 99639
Telephone:	(907) 567-7371 or (800) 479-7371
Email:	martind@ptialaska.net
Website:	www.heavenlysights.com

GPS Location: N 60° 04' 48.6", W 151° 37' 31.4"

This is a campground run in conjunction with a fishing charter operation. There are about 15 back-in sites with 30-amp outlets and another ten or so with no hookups. The sites are in two locations, some by the entrance buildings and the rest in an area down a small hill near the shower and laundry building. Some sites will take larger rigs to 40 feet.

The campground is accessed directly off the Sterling Highway near Mile 132.2. It's on the west side of the road. This is about four miles (6.5 km) north of Ninilchik.

NINILCHIK RIVER CAMPGROUND
(NINILCHIK STATE RECREATION AREA)

Location: Near Mile 134 of the Sterling Highway

GPS Location: N 60° 03' 07.8", W 151° 39' 01.4"

The Ninilchik River Campground is one of four camping areas on the lower Ninilchik River. It is the largest and we think has the most pleasant setting, particularly when the fish are running and this area becomes a madhouse. There's a short trail from the campground down to the river.

There are 43 back-in separated sites off two loop roads in a treed area near the highway north of the Ninilchik River. Spaces have picnic tables and firepits. The campground has a host, outhouses and a hand water pump. A few sites on the upper loop, to the left as you enter, will take rigs to 45 feet. Stays here are limited to 15 days.

Watch for the campground on the east side of the highway near Mile 134 north of the Ninilchik River bridge.

NINILCHIK RIVER SCENIC OVERLOOK CAMPGROUND
(NINILCHIK STATE RECREATION AREA)

Location: Near Mile 134 of the Sterling Highway

GPS Location: N 60° 02' 55.3", W 151° 39' 11.8"

The Ninilchik River area needs lots of camping slots when the fish are running and this parking area provides 25 of them. These are long back-in side-by-side spaces in a parking lot, they're suitable for any size rig. There are some picnic tables, firepits, vault toilets, and a water pump. Stays here are limited to 15 days. The overlook is just north of the Ninilchik River.

NINILCHIK BEACH CAMPGROUND
(NINILCHIK STATE RECREATION AREA)

Location: At the beach on the Ninilchik Beach Road

GPS Location: N 60° 02' 55.2", W 151° 40' 20.8"

Ninilchik is a popular fishing stream and also a good place to chase razor clams. This little campground has 20 back-in slots in an open parking lot next to the beach. Some sites will take any size rig. Winter storms beat this camping area up so bad that it has to be rebuilt each year. There are picnic tables and firepits as well as a pair of outhouses located up out of the way of those winter storms. The campground usually has a host. Stays here are limited to 15 days. Reach the campground by driving down the gravel Ninilchik Beach Access Road from near Mile 135 of the Sterling Highway. The distance from the highway is .5 mile (.8 km).

⊞ BEACHCOMBER MOTEL & RV PARK

Address: Box 367 Ninilchik, AK 99639
Telephone: (907) 567-3417 or (907) 345-1720
Website: www.beachcombermotel-rv.net

GPS Location: N 60° 03' 03.4", W 151° 40' 09.7"

This little motel has an enviable location across a small access road from the Ninilchik Beach. Behind the hotel and its 16 back-in sites is the Ninilchik River where you can moor your small boat. Camping sites have full hookups with 30-amp power but there are no restroom or shower facilities for campers. The campground will take rigs to 40 feet. A word of warning, this is a popular place and you are unlikely to find an empty space when the fish are running. Early reservations are recommended.

The Ninilchik Beach Access Road leaves the Sterling Highway near Mile 135. The road goes down the hill for .5 mile (.8 km) to the beach and turns right. The motel is on the right a short distance along the beach road.

⊞ ALASKAN ANGLER RV RESORT

Address: Box 39388, Ninilchik, AK 99639
Telephone: (800) 347-4114 or (907) 567-3393
Email: info@afishunt.com
Website: www.afishunt.com

GPS Location: N 60° 02' 42.9", W 151° 39' 58.8"

If you like the Ninilchik area but don't want to stay in a government campground there is a good alternative. It's the largest of the fishing-oriented private campgrounds in NInilchik and has the nicest and most complete facilities. This is a full-service campground and also offers guided fishing trips at Deep Creek and in Seward.

The Alaskan Angler has about 70 sites. Most of these are large back-ins in a large open lot with either full (20, 30 or 50-amp) or partial hookups. They are suitable for any size rig. TV hookups are available, so are temporary telephone hookups. There are also wooded tent and dry sites. The campground has good restroom facilities with hot showers, a laundromat, a dump station and a fish and clam cleaning area.

The campground is located near Mile 135.4 of the Sterling Highway.

⊞ NINILCHIK VIEW CAMPGROUND
(NINILCHIK STATE RECREATION AREA)

Location: Near Mile 135.4 of the Sterling Highway

GPS Location: N 60° 02' 46.8", W 151° 40' 05.6"

Ninilchik View is a nice wooded state campground located at the top of the bluffs over the Ninilchik beaches. There are 15 large separated sites with picnic tables and fire rings as well as outhouses. A few sites will take rigs to 40 feet but access roads are narrow and turns tight. A trail leads down to the beach. Stays here are limited to 15 days. There is also a dump and water-fill station off the entrance road to the campground which serves this entire busy area. Watch for the sign marking the campground access road at Mile 135.4 of the Sterling Highway.

Country Boy Campground

Address:	PO Box 39697, Ninilchik, AK 99639
Telephone:	(907) 567-3396
Email:	countryboycamp@woldnet.att.net
Website:	www.countryboy-campground.com

GPS Location: N 60° 01' 26.8", W 151° 35' 36.6"

Country Boy is a bit off the main road but is a large campground with full services.

The campground has about 50 sites with water and electric, some 20 of these are pull-thrus. There are additional sites without hookups. Any size rig can find room to park here. There are restrooms with flush toilets and showers as well as a laundry. A number of other rough buildings are scattered around the campground to give it a bit of a wild-west look.

The campground is located at approximately Mile 3.3 on paved Oil Well Road which leaves the Sterling Highway toward the east in Ninilchik near Mile 136.

Deep Creek View Campground

Address:	PO Box 23, Ninilchik, AK 99639
Telephone:	(907) 567-3320 or (888) 425-4288
Email:	smart@alaska.net
Website:	www.smartcharters.com

GPS Location: N 60° 02' 13.4", W 151° 41' 25.3"

Run in conjunction with a fishing charter operation, this campground sits on the bluff looking out across a beach that is far below.

There are about 30 sites in this commercial campground. They're back-in sites, some large, with 20 or 30-amp service. The large sites can take rigs to 40 feet but access isn't great due to a steep access road and narrow campground roads. They have picnic tables and firepits. There is a dump station and restrooms with hot showers.

To reach the campground leave the highway in Ninilchik near Mile 136 of the Sterling highway opposite the fairgrounds on Gielo Road. Follow the gravel road west for .3 mile (.5 km) to a T, turn right and you'll reach the campground in another .1 (.2 km) mile.

**Deep Creek North and South Waysides
(Deep Creek State Recreation Area)**

Location:	Near Mile 137 of the Sterling Highway

GPS Location: N 60° 01' 47.4", W 151° 40' 57.1"

Deep Creek, like the Ninilchik River just four miles (6.5 km) north, is a popular fishing stream. On both sides of the creek where the Sterling Highway crosses there are open parking lot-style campgrounds. The north wayside has 25 spaces and will take rigs to 40 feet. There are some picnic tables and fire rigs as well as a vault toilet and water pump. The south wayside has 18 sites suitable for rigs to about 35 feet as well as a vault toilet. There are interesting information exhibits at both of these waysides.

THE KENAI PENINSULA

D&M CHARTERS CAMPGROUND

Location:	Along the Deep Creek Beach access road
Telephone:	(800) 479-7357
Website:	www.dnmcharters.com

GPS Location: N 60° 01' 39.9", W 151° 42' 01.5"

This is another campground associated with a fishing charter operation. It's located on a shelf overlooking Deep Creek and Cook Inlet, the views are spectacular.

The camping sites are arranged along the bluff. There are about 24 sites with water and electric hookups as well as dry sites. Sites have fire pits and there are showers and a laundry. There's lots of maneuvering and parking room here, any size rig is fine.

You'll see the entrance on the right as you drive down the Deep Creek Beach access road from Mile 137 of the Sterling Highway.

DEEP CREEK BEACH
(DEEP CREEK STATE RECREATION AREA)

| Location: | At the beach at the end of Deep Creek |
| | Access Road near Mile 137 of the Sterling Highway. |

GPS Location: N 60° 01' 43.9", W 151° 42' 14.7"

Deep creek is a very popular fishing stream but there is another attraction here. Sports fishing guides use the beach next to the creek mouth as a launching ramp for their halibut and salmon boats. These guides go after the same fish as those based in Homer, but the fishing grounds are much closer to Deep Creek.

The state campground at the mouth of Deep Creek is very well used. There are at least 200 back-in parking-lot style sites at this campground. The open gravel sites will take any size rig. It is so popular that there is a manned kiosk guarding the entrance. The campground has picnic tables, firepits, outhouses and a boat-launching ramp into the protected river mouth. Stays are limited to 15 days.

To reach the campground drive down the Deep Creek Access Road from Mile 137 of the Sterling Highway. The road is paved to the beach, then turns to gravel. Turn right when you reach the beach, pass the commercial boat-launching area, and you'll find yourself at the entrance kiosk.

STARISKI CREEK STATE RECREATION SITE

| Location: | Near Mile 152 of the Sterling Highway |

GPS Location: N 59° 50' 32.6", W 151° 48' 45.1"

Stariski is a small state campground in a pleasant location at the top of the bluff above Cook Inlet. Since this isn't a good fishing base (at least not without a drive) it tends to have a different atmosphere than the busy fishing sites near Ninilchik and Deep Creek some 15 miles to the north. Although right above the beach there is no access to it from the campground.

There are 16 sites at Stariski. These are smaller sites by today's standards, they'll take rigs to about 30 feet. They are separated and located in spruce trees. Picnic tables and firepits are at each site and there are outhouses. Stays are limited to 15 days.

The campground is on the west side of the Sterling Highway at about Mile 152.

ANCHOR RIVER STATE RECREATION AREA
    Location: Near Mouth of Anchor River

GPS Location: N 59° 46' 16.0", W 151° 50' 15.2"

The Anchor River is another well-known Kenai Peninsula fishing destination. There are runs of king, silver and pink salmon but the river is probably most famous as a steelhead stream. Near the mouth of the river is an excellent state campground. Nearby are several good fishing holes with names like Slide Hole, Dudas Hole, Campground Hole and Picnic Hole.

Anchor River State Recreation Area has over 100 sites in five different areas called Silverking, Coho, Steelhead, Slide Hole and Halibut. Many are just side-by-side parking-lot spaces but at the Slide Hole area there are about 30 nice back-in separated sites, some of these will take rigs to 40 feet. Picnic tables and firepits are at the sites and there are outhouses near all of the campsites. There are also 26 nice back-in sites for RVs and tents at Halibut which is near the beach and away from the river. Some of these will also take 40 foot rigs. Many of the sites in all of the areas are modern large sites and can take big rigs. Stays are limited to 15 days.

The access road to the campground, the Old Sterling Highway, goes west from today's Sterling Highway in the town of Anchor Point near Mile 157. Drive down the hill and across a bridge for .3 miles (.5 km). Take the first right after the bridge onto Beach Road, you will immediately start seeing the campground entrance roads on your right. Slide Hole is the third one and Halibut is at the beach beyond Kyllonen RV Park, discussed below.

KYLLONEN RV PARK
    Address: PO Box 805, Anchor Point, AK 99556
    Telephone: (907) 235-7762 or (888) 848-2589
    Email: susank@xyz.com
    Website: www.kyllonenrvpark.com

GPS Location: N 59° 46' 15.6", W 151° 51' 36.1"

Right in the middle of the state campgrounds near the mouth of the Anchor River is a commercial one. Kyllonen's has 26 back-in or pull-in sites, all with full hookups with 20 and 30-amp outlets. Maneuvering room is tight but rigs to 40 feet use some of the sites. Sites are partially separated and there are flush toilets, hot showers, and a laundry. Firepits and free firewood are available. There's also espresso and a gift shop.

From Mile 157 of the Sterling Highway follow the old Sterling Highway west down the hill and across the bridge. Turn right onto Beach Access Road at .3 miles (.5 km), you'll find Kyllonen's on your right at 1.2 miles (1.9 km).

VILLAGE BARABARA RV PARK
    Address: Mile 169.3 (42745 Sterling Hwy.), Homer, AK 99603
    Telephone: (907) 235-6404
    Email: villagebarabara@phalaska.net
    Website: www.villagebarabara.com

GPS Location: N 59° 39' 26.1", W 151° 38' 25.9"

The Village Barabara undoubtedly has the most spectacular view of any campground in Alaska. Rigs park at the lip of a bluff that must be 500 feet high overlooking the mouth of Kachemak Bay and the mountains on the far side of the bay.

There are 47 back-in (or pull-in) sites here with picnic tables and lots of maneuvering room. Most are suitable for any size rig. All have 30-amp electrical hookups and water and sewer. There are restrooms with flush toilets, token-operated hot showers, a laundry room and a playground. Out front is a Shell gas station with a small store and an A&W.

The campground is at the top of the long hill that descends into Homer near Mile 169 of the Sterling Highway, watch for the Shell station.

HOMER
Population 4,500, Elevation near sea level

Alaskans often think of Homer as something of an art colony. A combination of a beautiful setting, mild weather, and an isolated end-of-the-road location have combined to make Homer an attractive place to live. The largest part of the economy here, however, is tied to fishing. It's an interesting mix.

Homer spreads over a pretty large area. The central business district occupies a location overlooking Kachemak Bay. Here you'll find the schools, many stores, restaurants, and some RV parks. A 1.5 mile (2.4 km) road runs from town, along Beluga

THE HOMER SPIT AND KACHEMAK BAY

Lake, past many roadside service establishments, to the base of the Spit. Four and one-half miles out on the Spit is another center, this one with a small boat harbor, fish-packing plants, and lots of tourist facilities. The windswept Spit is the scene of lots of action during the summer with hundreds of RVs camped here and there, fishing charter boats heading out to catch halibut, and ferries crossing to the far side of the bay. The **Visitor Center** (Box 541, Homer, AK 99603; 907 235-7740) is located on the Homer Bypass at Main Street.

Homer is one of the best places in the state to take a trip out to catch a **halibut**. The limit is two fish, usually these are "chicken" halibut weighing less than 20 pounds, but halibut over 100 pounds are often caught. Its easy to set up a charter at one of the offices on the Spit or at the reception desk of your RV park. There's a halibut derby from May 1 to Labor Day.

The **Pratt Museum** (3779 Bartlett St., 907 235-8635) has a wide range of exhibits focusing on the natural and cultural history of the Kenai Peninsula. In addition, the Pratt is also an art museum.

Homer is home to the headquarters for the **Alaska Maritime National Wildlife Refuge.** There's a great new facility, finished in late 2003, the **Alaska Islands and Ocean Visitor Center.** Located overlooking the bay near the western entrance to Homer it's actually a joint facility which includes information about the **Kachemak Bay Research Reserve**. Interactive exhibits cover the huge refuge which includes rugged islands all along the Alaska coast all the way from the tip of the panhandle near Ketchikan to Barrow. The visitor center has displays and programs including guided bird and beach walks. Naturalists from the facility also are on board the state ferry to Seldovia, Kodiak and down the Alaska Peninsula.

An early season event in Homer that is becoming more and more popular is the **Kachemak Bay Shorebird festival**, in early May. That's when thousands of migrating shorebirds arrive at the flats around Kachemak Bay for a brief stop before heading farther north. At the same time Homer celebrates **Kachemak Bay Wooden Boat Festival**.

Kachemak Bay and the islands and fjords on the south side across from Homer are a huge attraction. The **Kachemak Bay State Park** covers 350,000 acres with islands, bays, glaciers, and lots of outdoor attractions, see Chapter 14 - *Camping Away From the Road System* for more information. **Gull Island** is home to large numbers of marine birds, a small ferry that runs over to **Halibut Cove** is an excellent way to see them. **Seldovia**, a small town of 300 people, makes a great place to visit if you want to get away from the crowds. The Alaska State Ferry stops there on the route between Homer and Kodiak but most people travel across the bay on smaller commercial passenger ferries or by airplane.

Homer Campgrounds

🚐 **HOMER SPIT CAMPGROUND**

Address:	PO Box 1196, Homer, AK 99603
Telephone:	(907) 235-8206
Email:	chapple@xyz.net

GPS Location: N 59° 36' 02.4", W 151° 25' 01.0"

THE KENAI PENINSULA

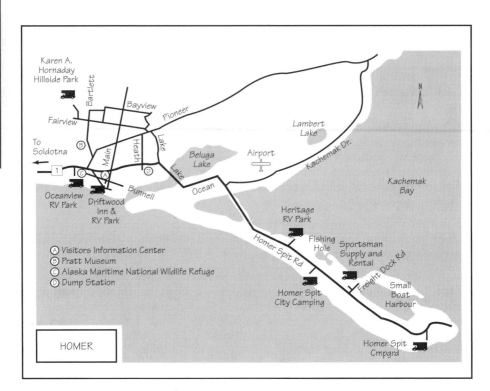

The Homer Spit Campground occupies a waterfront site at the end of the Homer Spit. There are some 120 spaces at this campground, most with 30-amp electrical hook-ups. Some are dry sites along the beach. Flush toilets and hot showers are available, there is a laundromat and a dump station.

The campground is located near the end of the Homer Spit past the fishing hole and the Salty Dog Saloon. It's 3.9 miles (6.3 km) from the base of the Spit. Watch for the sign, the campground is on the right.

🚐 HOMER SPIT CITY CAMPING

Location: Several of the Spit parking
areas and beaches

GPS Location: N 59° 36' 30.4", W 151° 26' 21.3"

The City of Homer lets RVers (any size rig) and tent campers dry camp on much of the Spit. Watch for signs designating camping and no-camping areas. A fee is charged, the registration office is located on the west side of the highway opposite the fishing hole, that's 3 miles from the base of the Spit. There's another pay station right next to the fishing hole, as well as a dump station and handicap-accessible restrooms. Several of the private campgrounds on the Spit will provide showers for a fee.

🚐 SPORTSMAN SUPPLY AND RENTAL

Address: 1114 Freight Dock Rd, Homer, AK 99603
Telephone: (907) 235-2617

GPS Location: N 59° 36' 25.0", W 151° 25' 58.9"

This is a small full-service campground on the Spit. It has 10 large back-in spaces with full hookups including 30-amp power. There are restrooms with nice showers and a laundry room.

The campground fronts on Freight Dock Road. This road goes east of the main Spit road about 3 miles from the base of the Spit, after turning you will see the campground on your left almost immediately.

🚐 HERITAGE RV PARK

Address: 3550 Homer Spit Road (147
                 East Pioneer Ave), Homer, AK 99603
Telephone: (907) 226-4500 or (800) 380-7787
Email: heritagehotelandrv@alaska.net
Website: www.AlaskaHeritageRVPark.com

GPS Location: N 59° 36' 36.7", W 151° 26' 27.8"

This new campground on the Homer Spit has some of the nicest facilities we've seen in any campground, it also has one of the highest prices.

The campground has 81 back-in or pull-in sites. Some are big sites suitable for any rig. Each site has 20, 30 and 50-amp power, water, sewer, satellite TV, instant-on telephone, voice mail, and modem hookups. Some sites are on the beach which is on the east side of the Spit looking up the bay. Campfires are allowed on the beach in front of the beach sites but not in the park. There are also nice restrooms, laundromat, gift shop and coffee shop. Those prices?. During the summer of 2004 they were $50 for a beach site, $45 for the others. Plus 5.5% tax.

The campground is located east of the Spit road at about 3 miles (4.8 km) from the base of the spit. You can't miss it.

🚐 KAREN A. HORNADAY HILLSIDE PARK

Location: Off Fairview Avenue

GPS Location: N 59° 39' 05.6", W 151° 33' 19.2"

The City of Homer operates a campground that is located uphill from the central business area. The Karen A. Hornaday Hillside Park has 31 separated sites set in alders. These are back-in sites and most are pretty small although there are a couple large enough for rigs to 35 feet in an open area near the entrance. Otherwise the campground is best for rigs to 30 feet because maneuvering room is limited. Sites have picnic tables and firepits. The restrooms in the campground are new vault-style types with handicap access, a great improvement over the ones here before and there are flush toilets at the ballpark below the campground.

To reach this campground drive north on Bartlett from central Homer for .1 mile (.2 km). Turn left on Fairview and then right in another .1 mile (.2 km) on Campground Road. The route is fairly well signed.

🚐 DRIFTWOOD INN & RV PARK

Address:	135 West Bunnell Ave., Homer, AK 99603
Telephone:	(907) 235-8019 or (800) 478-8019
Email:	driftwoodinn@alaska.com
Website:	www.thedriftwoodinn.com

GPS Location: N 59° 38' 23.1", W 151° 32' 43.3"

The Driftwood Inn is a hotel with a small RV park that is conveniently located near central Homer. It overlooks the beach which is a good place to walk and, like much of Homer, has a spectacular view of mountains and water. The campground has 22 back-in or drive-in spaces with electricity (30 amps), water, sewer and TV hookups. The campground is best for rigs to 35 feet. There are also tent spaces on grass. The inn has restrooms with showers and a laundry.

Easiest access is from the Homer Bypass. Turn south on Main Street and then west on Bunnell to the campground entrance.

🚐 OCEANVIEW RV PARK

Address:	455 Sterling Hwy., (PO Box 891), Homer, AK 99603
Telephone:	(907) 235-3951
Fax:	(907) 235-1065
Email:	camp4fun@oceanview-rv.com
Website:	www.oceanview-RV.com

GPS Location: N 59° 38' 30.2", W 151° 33' 13.6"

The first campground you will see when you enter Homer (on the right) is the Ocean-view. This is a large and well organized campground, an excellent place to stay since it has convenient access to downtown, access to a good walking beach, and beautiful views of the water and mountains on the far side of Kachemak Bay.

The Oceanview has about 100 spaces. Most have full hookups with 30 or 50-amp power and TV hookups. Tent sites are available. There are a some large pull-thrus and large back-ins suitable for rigs to 45 feet. The campground has flush toilets and hot showers as well as a gift shop and laundromat. They will help you arrange fishing charters or tours at the office.

KENAI PENINSULA DUMP STATIONS

Because the Kenai Peninsula is such a popular RVing destination it has a better selection of dump stations than anywhere else in the state. Many of the campgrounds described in this chapter have their own dump stations, even some of the government campgrounds. Here are some other possibilities.

In **Girdwood** the dump station at the municipal treatment facility is no longer open but there is a dump station at the **Tesoro** station on the corner of the Seward Highway and the Alyeska Highway near Mile 90 of the Seward Highway.

Seward has a nice modern city dump station with easy access. It is located across the street and just north of the new restrooms and hookup sites of the city waterfront camping area on Ballaine Boulevard.

Near the **Quartz Creek Campground** on Kenai Lake, near Mile 95 of the Sterling Highway, there's a dump station. It's outside the campground and easy to access since it's only a quarter-mile off the main highway.

On Skilak Road in the **Kenai National Wildlife Refuge** there is a first-class dump station at Mile 11.5 about half way between Upper and Lower Skilak Campgrounds. It's hard to imagine anyone but users of one of the local campgrounds using it since the Skilak Road is gravel and often very rough.

Soldotna has lots of dump stations to take care of all of you salmon fishing fanatics, here are some of them. The Soldotna Petro Express at 44152 Sterling Highway has a dump station with easy access for large rigs. Thompson's Corner at 44224 Sterling Highway also has one but access is not as good. Across the street the Tesoro 2 Go at 44279 Sterling Highway has a dump station. And don't forget the dump station in the parking lot of the Fred Meyer at 43843 Sterling Highway.

In **Kenai** both the Tesoro and the Petro Express at the junction of Willow and the Kenai Spur Highway have dump stations. So does the Williams Express at the junction of the Kenai Spur Highway and the Kenai Bridge Access Road.

Lots of people frequent the salmon streams near **Ninilchik**. There's a state-operated dump station near the Ninilchik View State Campground at Mile 135.4 to serve them.

Finally, in **Homer** the city has a dump station located next to the Homer Bypass near the junction with Lake Street where traffic heading for the Spit turns right to head across the Beluga Lake dam. There's also a city dump station on the Spit, it's on the left about 3 miles from the base of the Spit just past the fishing hole and next to the city restrooms.

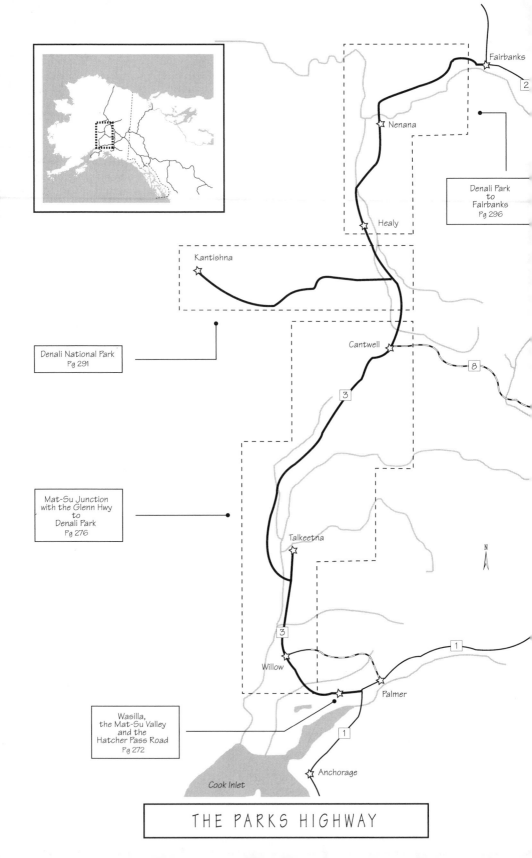

Fairbanks

2

Nenana

Denali Park
to
Fairbanks
Pg 296

Healy

Kantishna

Denali National Park
Pg 291

Cantwell

8

3

Mat-Su Junction
with the Glenn Hwy
to
Denali Park
Pg 276

Talkeetna

N

1

Willow

3

Palmer

Wasilla,
the Mat-Su Valley
and the
Hatcher Pass Road
Pg 272

1

Anchorage

Cook Inlet

THE PARKS HIGHWAY

Chapter 9

The Parks Highway

INTRODUCTION

The Parks Highway runs north from a junction on the Glenn Highway about 35 miles (56 km) from Anchorage to the interior city of Fairbanks. This is the state's newest major road. Until 1971 Fairbanks-bound travelers had to travel the Glenn north to Glennallen and then the Richardson through Delta Junction. The Alaska Railroad follows almost the same route, but the railroad is seldom within sight of the road.

We'll cover the Parks Highway from south to north. This is convenient for folks who are based in Anchorage or who rent rigs there, probably the larger part of the people who will be using this book.

Highlights

Anchorage's northern suburb, **Wasilla**, is growing rapidly in the Mat-Su Valley. You'll find lots of recreation activities near what has become a weekend playground for many people. They include boating, hiking, fishing, and golf.

The **Hatcher Pass Road** runs for 49 miles (79 km) from near Wasilla through the Talkeetna Mountains to meet the Parks Highway near Willow. You can stop and visit **Independence Mine State Historical Park** or hike above the timber line.

Denali State Park, not to be confused with Denali National Park, sits astride the Parks Highway south of the Alaska Range. There you'll find some state camp-

ALASKA'S TOP TOURIST DESTINATION - MOUNT MCKINLEY

grounds, high-country hiking trails, and wonderful views of the south face of Mount McKinley.

The most-visited attraction along the Parks Highway must be **Denali National Park**. At Mile 237 the park road leads westward into the park. The most popular activity at Denali is a bus ride into the park interior to see the wildlife. Vehicle access is limited but there are many camping sites in the park and nearby.

Fishermen will find lots of action on the Parks Highway. **Many good fishing streams** cross under the highway between Mile 57 and Mile 97. They include the Little Susitna, Willow Creek, Little Willow Creek, the Kashwitna River, Sheep Creek, and Montana Creek. The heavy fishing in these creeks is primarily for salmon.

The village of **Talkeetna** is located on a spur road from Mile 99 of the Parks Highway. Talkeetna is the base for Mt. McKinley climbing expeditions. It also is the base for riverboat salmon fishing expeditions, one of the most popular charter fishing options in the state.

The Road and Fuel

Building the Parks Highway was no easy project. Work started in 1959 and it wasn't until 1971 that it was completed. One of the toughest sections was across permafrost along a long section south of Nenana, you'll be able to identify this section by the heaves and dips in the road. Another challenge, a different kind, was the section through the Nenana Canyon north of Denali Park. The

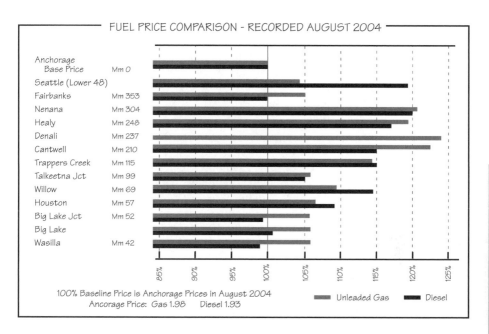

FUEL PRICE COMPARISON - RECORDED AUGUST 2004

Anchorage Base Price — Mm 0
Seattle (Lower 48)
Fairbanks — Mm 353
Nenana — Mm 304
Healy — Mm 248
Denali — Mm 237
Cantwell — Mm 210
Trappers Creek — Mm 115
Talkeetna Jct — Mm 99
Willow — Mm 69
Houston — Mm 57
Big Lake Jct — Mm 52
Big Lake
Wasilla — Mm 42

100% Baseline Price is Anchorage Prices in August 2004
Ancorage Price: Gas 1.98   Diesel 1.93

Unleaded Gas   Diesel

rest of the highway, however, is probably the nicest you'll find in all of Alaska and the Yukon. It was engineered from the beginning for modern traffic and has wide shoulders.

From Anchorage to Fairbanks along a short section of the Glenn Highway and then the entire length of the Parks Highway is 358 miles (577 km), you can easily drive it in one day. It is easy to maintain a constant speed of 60 MPH along virtually the entire distance. Mile markers on the Parks run from south to north. The highway begins at an intersection in the Matanuska Valley 35 miles from Anchorage. Mile markers start at 35 at this point.

Fishing

The Matanuska Valley is full of small lakes, many of them stocked. Once established at a campground in the area you might want to check out **Finger Lake**, the **Kepler-Bradley Lakes State Recreation Area, Meirs Lake, Matanuska Lake, Seymour Lake, Nancy Lake**, or **South Rolly Lake** and the other lakes in the **Nancy Lake Recreation Area**. You'll notice that many of the campgrounds in the Mat-Su are near fishing lakes. Fishing in these lakes is best in the spring or fall. A boat is very helpful.

From Mile 57 at the Little Susitna River to Mile 97 at Montana Creek the highway crosses many small rivers flowing into Cook Inlet or the Susitna River that offer outstanding salmon fishing, much of it can be done from the bank without a boat. As in all salmon fishing timing is important. Kings (Chinook Salmon) peak in June, reds (Sockeye Salmon) peak in July, pinks (Pink Salmon) peak in the last half of July, and the first weeks of August are best for silvers (Coho Salmon). Pinks in this watershed only run in significant numbers in even years (2004, 2006, etc.). Salmon runs can't always be accurately predicted, sometimes the fish are early or late (or don't show up). Since the salmon ascend the rivers from the ocean they reach fishing holes downstream before those that are upstream. Information about the status of the salmon runs in this area is easy to obtain, just ask at sporting goods stores, information offices, campgrounds, or even check the newspapers. Fishing regulations may change during the run based upon the quantity of fish in the streams so make sure you stay abreast of the current rules.

Here are some of the streams and locations in the area: **Little Susitna River** (Mile 57) for kings, reds, silvers, pinks, rainbows, Dollies; **Willow Creek Recreation Area** (Mile 71) for kings, silvers, pinks, rainbows, Dollies, and grayling; **Willow Creek** (Mile 71) for kings, silvers, pinks, rainbows, Dollies and grayling; **Little Willow Creek** (Mile 75) for king salmon, pinks, silvers, grayling and rainbows; **Kashwitna Lake** (Mile 76) for stocked rainbows; **Grey's Creek** (Mile 81) for kings, silvers, pinks, grayling, and rainbows; **Kashwitna River** (Mile 83) for king salmon, silver salmon, grayling and rainbows; **Caswell Creek** (Mile 84) walk in for kings, silvers, grayling and rainbows; **Sheep Creek mouth** (Mile 86) kings, silvers, pinks, grayling and rainbows; **Sheep Creek** (Mile 89) for kings, silvers, pinks, grayling and rainbows; **Montana Creek** (Mile 97) kings, silvers, pinks, grayling, and rainbows. Almost all of these fishing hot spots have campground along the creeks or nearby.

The **Susitna River** is a braided glacial river that is a very popular jet boat river. The Susitna can be dangerous to those who do not know it. You need the right equipment and local knowledge for this river. Charter boat operators offer guided fishing trips on the Susitna from several places including Susitna Landing (Mile 82.5). From Talkeetna jet-boat tours let fishermen access the middle section of the Susitna above Talkeetna and also the **Talkeetna River**. Most fishing from Talkeetna and along the length of the Susitna is in the clear-water rivers that run into the silty Susitna and Talkeetna.

Farther north you might want to try the **Chulitna River** (Mile 133) for grayling, **Troublesome Creek** (Mile 137) for grayling, rainbows and salmon (king fishing not allowed), or **Byers Lake** at Mile 147 for lake trout.

Boating, Rafting, Canoeing, and Kayaking

Big Lake, located in the Mat-Su Valley is probably Anchorage's favorite water-sports destination. It's a large shallow lake that gets plenty warm enough for swimming. Several other nearby lakes are also popular but access isn't as easy for folks who do not have cabins and the lakes aren't as large.

The **Nancy Lake State Recreation Area**, accessible from Mile 67 of the Parks Highway via a 6.6-mile (10.6 km) gravel road is a favorite canoeing area. There's a circular 16 mile (26 km) canoe trail through 14 lakes and a longer one than connects with the Little Susitna River. Lakes offer fishing and there are quite a few black bears and other wildlife in the area. The South Rolly Campground is near the starting point of the canoe trail and makes a good base, there are also designated back-country camping sites along the canoe trail.

The **Little Susitna River** also makes a good canoe route. It is 56 miles (90 km) from the Parks Highway bridge at Mile 57 to a take-out at the end of the Little Susitna Access Road off Knik Road. You can connect into the Nancy Lakes canoe trails using a portage 14 miles (23 km) below the Parks Highway put-in point. The Little Susitna River is a very popular fishing river, there are so many power boats that restrictions on their use have been initiated in the interests of safety.

The **Nenana River** runs right by the entrance to Denali National Park, floating this whitewater river in rafts has become extremely popular as more and more people visit the park. Operators are based near the park entrance and are easy to find. You can make arrangements at your campground if you are staying at one of the commercial ones outside the park. This is a good way to spend a day while waiting for a seat on a bus into the park.

Hiking and Mountain Biking

Hatcher Pass presents some of the best hiking opportunities north of Anchorage. The **Little Susitna Trail** climbs 8 miles (13 km) along the upper Little Susitna River to the foot of the Mint Glacier from about Mile 14 of the Fishhook-Willow Road. The **Reed Lakes Trail** climbs 4 miles (6 km) to Lower and Upper Reed Lakes with branches to the Snowbird Mine and Snowbird Glacier. This trail starts at Mile 2.4 of the Archangel Road which leaves the Fishhook-Willow Road at about Mile 14.5. From the **Independence Mine Historical Park** there are several short day hikes, the park is near Mile 17 of the Fishhook-Willow road. Mountain bikers will find the Fishhook-Willow Road to be a decent ride but automobile traffic can be a problem, particularly on weekends.

The Nancy Lakes Recreation Area is known for its canoe trails but also has a good hiking trail. There is a 3 mile (5 km) **trail to Red Shirt Lake** with an 8-site tent-camping area at the lake. The trail runs along the tops of gravel ridges so it isn't as wet as most of the ground in the area. The trailhead is at the entrance of the South Rolly Lake Campground.

Denali State Park has several hiking possibilities. Most are on the mountain to the east of the highway, it's known as Kesugi Ridge. The **Kesugi Ridge Trail** (also sometimes called the Curry Ridge Trail) starts at the Upper Troublesome Creek Trailhead at Mile 138 of the Parks Highway. It climbs to the top of the ridge and runs 36 miles (58 km) north before descending to the Little Coal Creek Trailhead at Mile 164 of the Parks Highway. An intermediate access points is a 3.5 mile (5.6 km) trail from Byers Lake at Mile 147 of the Parks Highway. For shorter hikes you could do Troublesome Creek to Byers Lake (15 Miles (24 km)) or Byers Lake to Little Coal Creek (27 miles (45 km)). A complicating factor is that during salmon season (middle of July to early September here) the Troublesome Creek portion of the trail is closed because there are too many bears for safety.

At **Byers Lake** there is also a pleasant trail around the lake, a distance of 4.1 miles (6.6 km). There's a walk-in tent campground on the east side of the lake, a distance of 1.8 miles (2.9 km) from the trailhead at Byers Lake Campground.

Also in Denali State Park is the **Lower Troublesome Creek Trail** leading from the road at the Lower Troublesome Creek Recreation Site (Mile 137, Parks Highway) to the Chulitna River, a distance of only half a mile.

Denali National Park really offers three kinds of hiking. First, there's the kind where you climb Mt. McKinley, definitely outside the scope of this book. Second, there's hiking in the high country north of the Alaska Range near the access road, see Chapter 14 - *Camping Away From the Road System* for this. Finally, Denali National Park has several miles of trails near the park entrance. These are easy to access and do not require riding one of the park busses to reach them. The **Horseshoe Lake Trail** is .7 miles (1.1 km) long and starts near the railroad tracks about 1.2 miles (1.9 km) from the park entrance. **Mount Healy Overlook Trail** is 2.5 miles (4 km) long and starts at the Denali Park Hotel which is near the park entrance. The **Rock Creek Trail, Taiga Loop Trail**, and **Morino Loop Trail** are all trails in the entrance area connecting the Denali Park Hotel with nearby facilities.

The 91 mile long (147 km) **Park Road** makes a wonderful mountain-bike ride. Vehicle traffic on the road is restricted largely to tour busses. A bicycle frees you to some degree from reliance on the busses for transportation yet you can use the special camper busses to transport your bicycle so you don't have to ride the whole road. In fact, it is wise to check with rangers about sections of the road that might be dangerous due to concentrations of bears, you can easily bypass these sections on a bus. Bicycles are not allowed off the road but campgrounds have bicycle racks where you can leave yours when you want to hike.

Wildlife Viewing

The **Nancy Lake Recreation Area**, particularly away from the roads on the canoe routes, is an excellent place to see loons (each lake has a pair), beaver, moose, and black bears.

Driving north on the Parks Highway you will pass through **Broad Pass** at about Mile 200. Watch for caribou, stop occasionally and glass the wide-open hillsides on each side of the road.

Denali National Park is definitely the easiest place to see wildlife in Alaska. Grab a window seat on one of the busses that go as far as Eielson Visitor Center, better yet, go all the way to Wonder Lake. No guarantees, but on an average trip you might see a moose or two, caribou, Dall sheep, and probably several grizzly bears. See the *Denali National Park* section of this chapter for more information.

THE ROUTES, TOWNS, AND CAMPGROUNDS

WASILLA, THE MAT-SU VALLEY, AND THE HATCHER PASS ROAD
Wasilla Population 5,000, Elevation 330 feet

The Matanuska-Susitna (Mat-Su) Valley is a huge mostly-flat area north of Anchorage. In the east (the Matanuska portion) the valley is oriented toward farming with Palmer the focal point of settlement (See Chapter 7 - *The Glenn Highway*). To the west is Wasilla which has grown rapidly since the Parks Highway was completed. Even farther west, in the Susitna Valley, there is less settlement with large areas west of the Parks highway and on the far side of the Susitna River having no road access at all.

The **Matanuska-Susitna Valley Visitor's Center** (907 746 5000) is located near the intersection of the Parks and Glenn Highways. Take the Trunk Road Exit at Mile 36 of the Parks Highway and then follow the frontage road north of the highway to the east for about .2 miles (.3 km). This is a good place to educate yourself about the valley's attractions and ask questions.

Wasilla is a spread out town. As real estate prices have increased in the Anchorage area many people have moved to the "valley", and many of them are in or around Wasilla. There are large stores including Wal-Mart, Safeway, and Carrs. All of these stores are strung along several miles of the Parks Highway east of the town center.

Wasilla does have a town center. It is located north of the Parks Highway at about Mile 42. The **Dorothy G. Page Museum** (907 373-9071) includes the **Old Wasilla Town Site Park** with historical buildings. Also interesting is the **Museum of Alaska Transportation and Industry** (907 376-1211) south of the Parks Highway near Mile 47. There's also a **farmers market** on Wednesdays.

From Wasilla at Mile 42.2 of the Parks Highway you can drive south on the **Knik Road** a distance of 29 miles (47 km) to the **Susitna Flats State Game Refuge**. There is a 65-site state campground there as well as a launch ramp for access to the Little Susitna River. You drive on pavement to Mile 17 and then follow the Goose Bay Point Road for another 12 miles (19 km), seven of them paved.

Most visitors to Alaska are very familiar with the Iditarod Sled Dog Race. Held in

THE PARKS HIGHWAY

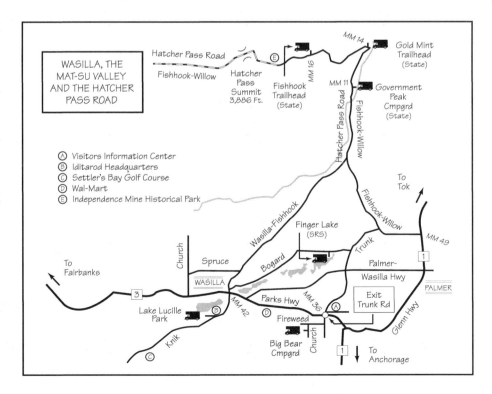

March each year this 1,150 mile (1,856 km) race from Anchorage to Nome attracts entrants from all over the world. The Anchorage to Wasilla portion of the race is ceremonial, the race really starts in Wasilla. You'll find the **Iditarod Trail Sled Dog Race Headquarters** and visitor's center (907 376-5155) near Wasilla at about Mile 2 of the Knik Road. The Lake Lucille Campground is nearby.

The Wasilla area has a good 18-hole course, the **Settler's Bay Golf Course** (907 376-5466 for tee times), located at Mile 8 on Knik Road.

From the intersection in Wasilla at Mile 42.2 of the Parks Highway you can drive north to reach the **Hatcher Pass Road** and **Independence Mine State Historical Park**. There is also access from Mile 49 of the Glenn Highway on the Fishhook-Willow Road. The road from the Glenn Highway and the road from Wasilla meet about 11 miles (18 km) north of Wasilla near Turner's Corner to form the Hatcher Pass Road which runs another 42 miles (68 km) to meet the Parks Highway at Mile 71 near Willow. The highway traverses the very scenic Talkeetna Mountains. At Mile 17 a side road leads to the **Independence Mine State Historical Park**. The park has old mining buildings and a visitors center, you can take guided tours of the buildings and there are hiking trails in the vicinity. Two miles past the park is Hatcher Pass Summit which has an elevation of 3,886 feet. The State of Alaska installed three new camping areas along the Hatcher Pass Road in the section before it reaches Hatcher Pass Historical Park during the late summer of 2004, they had not actually opened when we visited them. They are described in the Wasilla and the Mat-Su Valley Campgrounds section immediately below. The section of the Hatcher Pass Road past the mine is not suitable for large RVs.

Wasilla and the Mat-Su Valley Campgrounds

BIG BEAR CAMPGROUND

Location:	Mile 36 Parks Highway, Wasilla, AK
Telephone:	(907) 745-7445 or (907) 376-7201

GPS Location: N 61° 33' 39.5", W149° 17' 33.9"

New in 2004, this is a full-service big rig campground. It's a welcome addition.

The campground has 22 large full hookup pull-thrus with 30-amp outlets and another 21 back-in sites with electricity and water. Sites and roads are gravel, areas of grass separate the sites. They are large with lots of maneuvering room. Each has a picnic table. There's also a tent-camping area. Other amenities include a laundry, a dump site, and Wi-Fi.

To reach the campground take the Trunk Road exit off the Parks Highway near Mile 36. Go south and turn right on Fireweed which parallels the Parks Highway. In .8 mile (1.3 km) turn left on Church Road and you'll see the campground ahead on the right.

LAKE LUCILLE PARK (MATANUSKA-SUSITNA BOROUGH)

Location:	Mile 2 Knik-Goose Bay Road

GPS Location: N 61° 34' 06.2", W 149° 28' 41.0"

This public campground is separated into two areas. Area #1 is a small loop near the entrance, area #2 is beyond and is a larger loop that is sometimes closed off by a barrier. The Iditarod Sled Dog Race Headquarters located along the entrance road may bring you to the area so take a quick look, you may decide to spend the night.

At area #1 there are 18 small sites on a small loop. Area #2 is 38 sites on a second loop nearby. Both areas have back-in public-campground-type sites set in natural vegetation with pretty good separation. There are picnic tables, firepits, and outhouses. Area #1 has small sites and old outhouses while area #2 (also called Bushnell Campground) has more modern vault toilets and some spaces suitable for large rigs. The campgrounds are not really next to the lake which is just as well since this side of Lake Lucille is very swampy and has plenty of mosquitoes. Fishing for land-locked silver salmon is possible in the lake.

If you follow the Knik-Goose Bay Road south from central Wasilla (near Mile 42 of the Parks Highway) you'll see the Iditarod Sled Dog Race Headquarters at about 2 miles (3 km) on the right. Just beyond turn right on Endeavor Street and drive .6 miles (1 km) to the park entrance.

GOVERNMENT PEAK STATE CAMPGROUND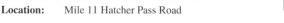
Location: Mile 11 Hatcher Pass Road

GPS Location: N 61° 44' 33.7", W 149° 13' 51.7"

This is a brand new state campground. It's located right alongside the Hatcher Pass Road and Little Susitna River as they climb the valley toward the high country. The campground has 5 paved back-in RV sites, and 3 tent sites. Picnic tables and fire pits are provided. The restrooms are a modern vault toilet. A water well was being dug when we visited but water was uncertain, the daily price will probably be lower if water does not prove to be available.

GOLD MINT TRAILHEAD
Location: Mile 14 Hatcher Pass Road

GPS Location: N 61° 46' 40.5", W 149° 11' 56.1"

This campground is brand new, it's really a large paved lot for people heading up the Gold Mint Trail. In summer it's a popular hiking area, in winter a snow machine area. Overnight camping in vehicles is allowed. There are tables and fire pits and a modern vault toilet. The campground is located at the sharp left turn just past the Motherlode Lodge.

FISHHOOK TRAILHEAD
Location: Mile 16 Hatcher Pass Road

GPS Location: N 61° 46' 01.2", W 149° 15' 59.3"

This is another brand new campground (of sorts). It's a large parking lot with outhouses. Overnight camping in vehicles is allowed. This is primarily a parking lot for snow machine use in the winter but also for summer hiking.

FINGER LAKE STATE RECREATION SITE
(STATE OF ALASKA)
Location: Off Bogard Road

GPS Location: N 61° 36' 37.7", W149° 15' 53.6"

This state recreation site on Finger Lake is a popular fishing destination since the lake has rainbows, grayling, and silver salmon. There's a boat ramp at the campground, only boats without motors are allowed on the lake.

There are about 40 camping sites at this campground, most are smaller back-in wooded sites while the remainder are just back-in slots in a gravel parking lot. All sites have picnic tables and firepits and many are near the lake. Large rigs would probably be limited to the sites in the parking lot due to parking pad size. There are outhouses and a hand-operated water pump. This campground has a host and firewood is on sale. Stays are limited to seven days.

The campground is located off Bogard Road, not exactly a major highway but still a fairly major arterial through the valley. You can reach the campground from many directions and via many routes. The one below is the most scenic. From about Mile 36 of the Parks Highway turn north on Trunk Road. Trunk meanders up past the University of Alaska's experimental farm, it intersects with the Palmer-Wasilla Highway after 3.1 miles (5 km). Drive straight across the intersection and continue to an intersection with Bogard Road after another 1.1 miles (1.8 km). Turn left on Bogard and you will see the campground entrance road on your left in another .8 miles (1.4 km).

FROM THE MAT-SU JUNCTION WITH THE GLENN HIGHWAY TO DENALI PARK
202 Miles (326 Kilometers)

As you head west on the Parks Highway after leaving the Glenn Highway at Mile 35 you'll spot the exit for Trunk Road at Mile 36. If you exit here and then follow the frontage road on the north side of the highway back toward the east you'll soon come to the **Mat-Su Visitor's Center** (HC01 Box 6166 J21, Palmer, AK 99645; 907 746-5000). If you are planning to spend any time in the valley you will probably find a quick visit quite useful.

Continuing westward, the highway soon enters the outskirts of Wasilla. At Mile 42 the Knik Road goes south. Follow it for 2 miles (3.2 km) and you'll see the **Iditarod Museum** on the right.

After passing through Wasilla watch for the **Big Lake** road at Mile 52. This large lake and many smaller surrounding ones attract large numbers of visitors. Because they're shallow they get warm enough for swimming and water sports in the summer. Many people have cabins here, there are also two state campgrounds on the lake and another on a small lake nearby.

From Mile 57 to Mile 97 the Parks Highway crosses many **streams that are popular destinations for Alaskan fishermen**. These streams include: the Little Susitna at Mile 57, Lower Willow Creek at Mile 71, Little Willow Creek at Mile 75, the Kashwitna River at Mile 83, Caswell Creek at Mile 84, Sheep Creek at Mile 89, and Montana Creek at Mile 97. There are many camping areas along this stretch of road, expect them to be very full on weekends during the salmon runs.

At Mile 67 you'll find an access road to another popular lake area, the **Nancy Lake State Recreation Area**. Nancy Lake and many nearby lakes form a popular canoe-

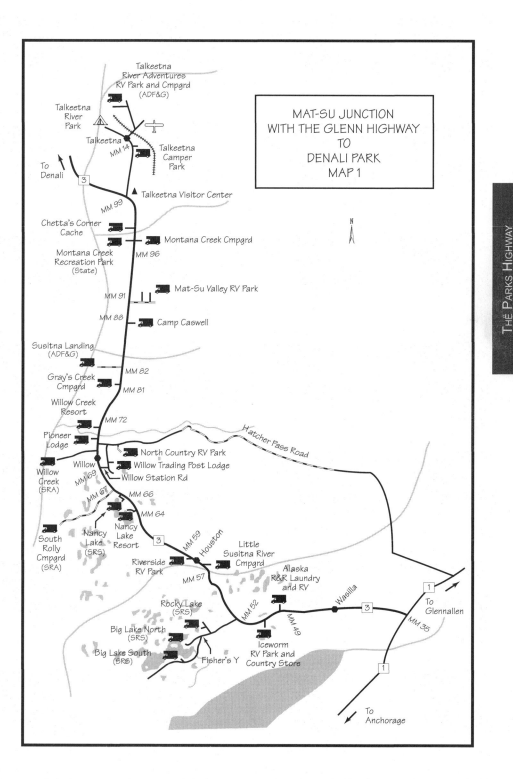

Talkeetna
River Adventures
RV Park and Cmpgrd
(ADF&G)

Talkeetna
River
Park

Talkeetna
MM 14

Talkeetna
Camper
Park

To
Denali

3

▲ Talkeetna Visitor Center

MM 99

Chetta's Corner
Cache

Montana Creek Cmpgrd

Montana Creek
Recreation Park
(State)

MM 96

Mat-Su Valley RV Park

MM 91

MM 88

Camp Caswell

Susitna Landing
(ADF&G)

MM 82

Gray's Creek
Cmpgrd

MM 81

Willow Creek
Resort

MM 72

Hatcher Pass Road

Pioneer
Lodge

North Country RV Park

Willow

Willow Trading Post Lodge

MM 69

Willow Station Rd

Willow
Creek
(SRA)

MM 67

MM 66

MM 64

South
Rolly
Cmpgrd
(SRA)

Nancy
Lake
(SRS)

Nancy
Lake
Resort

3

MM 59

Houston

Little
Susitna River
Cmpgrd

Riverside
RV Park

MM 57

Alaska
R&R Laundry
and RV

Wasilla

3

To
Glennallen

MM 35

Rocky Lake
(SRS)

MM 52

MM 49

1

Big Lake North
(SRS)

Big Lake South
(SRS)

Fisher's Y

Iceworm
RV Park and
Country Store

1

To
Anchorage

MAT-SU JUNCTION
WITH THE GLENN HIGHWAY
TO
DENALI PARK
MAP 1

N

THE PARKS HIGHWAY

ing area complete with a 16 mile (26 km) canoe trail. There's also a large state campground here.

The small town of **Willow**, not long ago an unsuccessful candidate to be Alaska's capital, appears at Mile 69. Almost in the middle of the somewhat spread-out area known as Willow, at Mile 71, is the junction for the gravel **Hatcher Pass Road**. This 42 mile (68 km) road climbs into a scenic mountainous region before dropping into the Matanuska Valley near Wasilla. It is not suitable for large vehicles in the middle section.

At Mile 99 a paved road leads north from the Parks Highway for 14 miles (23 km) to **Talkeetna**. Talkeetna is a friendly little country town that is accustomed to lots of visitors. There are two big reasons for this. Talkeetna serves as the base for air taxi operators specializing in flying Mt. McKinley climbers up to the Kahiltna Glacier. Most of this activity takes place during the summer, the town is a beehive of activity during the climbing season. You can also book a sightseeing flight with one of these air-taxi operators.

Talkeetna also serves as the base for charter riverboats taking fishermen and sightseers up the Susitna, Chulitna, and Talkeetna Rivers. This is one of the most popular fishing charters in the state. Before driving in to Talkeetna you can stop and visit the **Talkeetna Visitor Center** located right at the junction with the Parks Highway.

After passing the Talkeetna junction the highway curves west and crosses the Susitna River. Then it heads north again, up the Chulitna River and into high country at the foothills of the Alaska Range. You enter **Denali State Park** at Mile 133. It is largely undeveloped but offers great views of the Alaska Range. At Mile 135 there is an excellent viewpoint for looking at the south face of Mt. McKinley. Also visible are Mt. Foraker (17,400 ft.) and Mt. Hunter (14,573 ft.). There are trails along the ridges to the east of the highway, they are accessible at Troublesome Creek at Mile 137, Byers Lake at Mile 147, and at Little Coal Creek at Mile 164.

The highway soon enters **Broad Pass**. The name is accurate. You can often see caribou on the hillsides visible from the highway.

The junction with the **Denali Highway**, connecting with the Richardson Highway, is at Mile 210. The Denali Highway is unpaved but quite scenic. There are 113 miles (182 km) of gravel and 21 miles (34 km) of paved road before you reach Paxson on the Richardson Highway. Before the construction of the Parks Highway this was the access road for Denali National Park. See Chapter 6 for more about this highway.

After passing the junction with the Denali Highway the Parks enters a much narrower pass, Windy Pass, and follows the Nenana River north to the Denali National Park access road at Mile 237.

Mat-Su Junction with the Glenn Highway to Denali Park Campgrounds

ALASKA R&R LAUNDRY AND RV

    Address: PO Box 940366, Houston, AK 99694
    Telephone: (907) 373-7286

     GPS Location: N 61° 34' 44.7", W 149° 38' 44.0"

This laundromat has a small campground set behind and off to the side. There are about 20 sites. Fifteen have full hookups with 30-amp power, the others have water and electricity. There's also a dump station. Restrooms and showers are available in the laundromat out front.

The campground is at Mile 49.4 of the Parks Highway on the north side.

🚐 ICEWORM RV PARK AND COUNTRY STORE

Address:	Mile 50 Parks Highway (HC34 Box 2148), Wasilla, AK 99654
Telephone:	(888) 484-9088
Email:	iceworm@icewormrvp.com
Website:	www.icewormrvp.com

GPS Location: N 61° 34' 16.1", W 149° 40' 07.3"

This is a modern campground with plenty of room for big rigs.

There are 15 large pull-thru sites and another 5 back-ins. These are gravel sites with logs between them for separation. Seven have 50-amp power and the remainder have 30, they also have water and sewer. Each site has a picnic table and umbrella and there are firepits. There are also four tent spaces. The campground has a restroom with a shower and a small store and gift shop.

The campground is on the south side of the Parks highway near Mile 50.

🚐 ROCKY LAKE STATE RECREATION SITE (STATE OF ALASKA)

Location:	Near Mile 3 of the Big Lake Road

GPS Location: N 61° 33' 25.0", W 149° 49' 18.3"

Rocky Lake is a small but pleasant state campground, a good place to stop during the week when the area isn't full of Anchorage residents. The lake is stocked and offers small landlocked salmon and a few rainbows.

There are 11 sites, most are right next to the lake. These are back-in sites set in a grove of trees, the 1996 Big Lake forest fire didn't touch this immediate area. Sites are short, this campground is suitable for rigs to about 30 feet. The campground has picnic tables, firepits, outhouses, a hand-operated water pump, a boat ramp, and an overflow parking area. The camping limit here is 7 days.

To find the campground drive south on Big Lake Road from the intersection at about Mile 52 of the Parks Highway. Turn right on Beaver Lake Road at about 3 miles (5 km) and then left on Rocky Lake Road after another half-mile (.8 km), the campground entrance will be on your left.

🚐 BIG LAKE NORTH STATE RECREATION SITE (STATE OF ALASKA)

Location:	End of North Shore Drive off Big Lake Road

GPS Location: N 61° 32' 42.0", W 149° 51' 17.0"

Big Lake is a very popular summer and winter destination for Anchorage residents. The lake is large and shallow with many coves and islands, many cabins line the shore and even occupy some of the islands. The lake is plenty warm enough for swimming and is very popular with owners of recreational vehicles of all kinds, including those that float in the summer and snow machines in the winter.

If you don't own a cabin here then you can use two state recreation sites for access to the lake. The largest of the two is Big Lake North. Camping at Big Lake North means parking in a large paved lot, about 30 of the sites in the lot are set aside for campers. These offers picnic tables, firepits, outhouses, a boat ramp, a designated swimming area, and a covered picnic area. There is a walk-in area for tent campers. The campground has a 7 day limit. There is also sometimes a host. Fishing in Big Lake is for rainbows, arctic char, and burbot.

To reach Big Lake North follow the Big Lake Road from Mile 52 of the Parks Highway. At 3.5 miles (5.6 km) you will come to a fork in the road known as Fisher's Y. Take the right fork (North Shore Drive) and in another 1.5 miles (2.4 km) you will come to the end of the road and the campground. The entire route is paved.

⛺ BIG LAKE SOUTH STATE RECREATION SITE (STATE OF ALASKA)

Location: Near Mile 5 of the Big Lake Road

GPS Location: N 61° 31' 57.5", W 149° 49' 57.0"

Big Lake South is much smaller than Big Lake North but offers much the same features. There is room for about 20 campers here. This campground also has picnic tables, firepits, outhouses, and a paved boat launch. There's also a sandy beach area. Stays are limited to seven days.

To reach the campground just follow the Big Lake Road from about Mile 52 of the Parks Highway. Take the left fork at Fisher's Y at Mile 3.5. The campground is on the right in another 1.5 miles (2.4 km).

⛺ LITTLE SUSITNA RIVER CAMPGROUND (CITY OF HOUSTON)

Location: Mile 57 of the Parks Highway

GPS Location: N 61° 37' 49.5", W 149° 47' 56.4"

This campground is a popular place when the salmon are running in the "Little Su". The river gets runs of kings, silvers, chums, reds, and pinks during May through August. The runs aren't totally predictable but you can tell when the fish are in, just watch for large numbers of fishermen. If there are no fish the campground will probably be almost deserted. This is also a put-in point for boating on the Little Susitna River.

The Little Susitna River Campground is much like other government campgrounds in Alaska. This one might be considered just a little more rustic, the location isn't very scenic. The river and fishing are the draw here, the campground sits in the middle of a fairly unattractive stand of small bedraggled spruce trees. There are over 80 camping sites arranged off a maze of gravel roads, most sites are fairly short but some will take rigs to 40 feet. Picnic tables and firepits are provided. Toilets are outhouses. There is a hand-operated water pump, a playground, and a covered picnic pavilion. There's a 10- day limit.

This campground is located north of the Parks Highway just west of the Little Susitna bridge at about Mile 57. There is also a large parking area and river access on the other side of the highway.

RIVERSIDE RV PARK

Address: PO Box 940087,
                  Houston, AK 99694
Telephone: (907) 892-9020
Email: aksalmon@mtaonline.net

GPS Location: N 61° 37' 47.5", W 149° 48' 47.1"

Just a short distance down the road from the Little Susitna Campground is a good commercial alternative. The Riverside offers a good selection of amenities and also access to the Little Susitna River.

The Riverside RV Park has 56 sites including a few pull-thrus arranged in an open field next to the Little Susitna River. Each site has 20 or 30-amp electricity, sewer, water and a picnic table. Some sites are large enough for 45-foot rigs. There are also several dry camp or tent sites on grass with firepits. The campground offers restrooms with hot showers and a coin-op laundromat. There is also a boat ramp, a covered picnic area, and an RV wash area. Next door is Miller Landing which also offers dry camping, as well as a small store with supplies.

The Riverside is on the south side of the Parks Highway near Mile 59. This is in the commercial center of the "city" of Houston.

NANCY LAKE RESORT

Address: PO Box 114, Willow, AK 99688
Telephone: (907) 495-6284   **Fax:** (907) 495-6285

GPS Location: N 61° 41' 09.2", W 149° 58' 31.7"

This long-time resort on the north shore of Nancy Lake is well-known to float aircraft operators as a handy place to stop and get Avgas. It also has a few small sites for traveling RVers. This place may remind you of a lakeside family resort in Wisconsin or the Northeast.

There are two sites in the upper parking area for rigs to about 30 feet. They have electrical hookups. Below are a few more sites for rigs to about 25 feet with no hookups but with picnic tables and fire rings. There are many resident campers at this resort, most of their rigs have been here for many years. Restrooms have flush toilets and showers and there is a small grocery store. Boat rentals are available for fishing.

The entrance to the resort is at Mile 64.5 of the Parks Highway.

NANCY LAKE STATE RECREATION SITE
(STATE OF ALASKA)

Location: Near Mile 67 of the Parks Highway

GPS Location: N 61° 42' 09.4", W 150° 00' 16.5"

This state campground has a pleasant location atop a small ridge next to Nancy Lake. It is close to the highway and often almost empty, a good place to spend the night. The lake has rainbows, Dollies, burbot, and northern pike.

The campground has 30 back-in sites arranged around three circles. These are decently-separated sites surrounded by natural vegetation and trees, they have picnic tables and firepits and are suitable for rigs to about 30 feet. There is a host at this campground and firewood is available for purchase. Interior roads are gravel as are parking pads. The campground has outhouses and a hand-operated water pump. There is also a boat ramp. Stays are limited to 15 days.

The campground is near Mile 66.7 of the Parks Highway on the south side of the highway. The highway has recently been straightened in this area and the mileage location may change slightly. Turn south on a short access road to the old highway which parallels the new highway at this point. Turn left on the old highway (now called Buckinghorse Road) and follow it for .2 miles, the campground entrance is on the right.

SOUTH ROLLY CAMPGROUND (STATE OF ALASKA)

Location: Nancy Lake Recreation Area, 6.6 miles (10.6 km) south from Mile 67 of the Parks Highway

GPS Location: N 61° 40' 01.4", W 150° 08' 27.0"

The Nancy Lakes Recreation Area is a huge area of popular lakes, most accessible only by canoe trail. The largest formal campground for vehicle campers in the recreation area is the South Rolly Lake Campground.

This is a large and fairly new campground, there are about 100 sites overlooking the lake. Many of these camp sites are pull-thrus. The sites have the traditional picnic tables and outhouses. Interior roads and parking pads are gravel. These campsites are widely spaced and surrounded by trees, some are along the lake. They are suitable for rigs to about 30 feet. The campground has a host so firewood is available for purchase, there are outhouses and a hand-operated water pump. Canoes are sometimes available for rent and there is a boat launch (electric motors only). Stays are limited to 15 days.

The disadvantage to this campground is that it is located well off the highway. An extremely wide gravel access road, 6.6 miles (10.6 km) in length, provides access. Unfortunately the surface is usually like a washboard. The road leaves the Parks Highway at about Mile 67, the campground is at its end.

WILLOW TRADING POST LODGE

Address: PO Box 870, Willow, Alaska 99688
Telephone: (907) 495-1695

GPS Location: N 61° 44' 50.6", W 150° 02' 23.9"

The Willow Trading Post Lodge is located in Willow but off the main highway. Many people whiz by and don't even know it's there.

The lodge has 7 back-in spaces with electricity and water in a secluded area behind the main lodge. The campground is good for rigs to about 30 feet. There are clean restrooms, hot showers, a restaurant and a bar. The lodge also has a liquor store and gift shop.

To find the lodge turn east at Mile 69.5 of the Parks Highway. Turn left at .2 miles (.3 km) after crossing the RR tracks. The lodge will be on your right in another .2 miles (.3 km).

WILLOW CREEK STATE RECREATION AREA (STATE OF ALASKA)

Location: At the end of access road from Mile 71 of Parks Highway

GPS Location: N 61° 46' 27.5", W 150° 09' 40.6"

The Willow Creek campground is another popular fishing destination. It offers access to the Susitna River at the mouth of Willow Creek. Willow Creek gets runs of kings, silvers, and pinks and also rainbows, Dollies, and grayling.

The campground is relatively new, it is one of the big parking-lot type with back-in parking for about 140 rigs. Picnic tables, firepits, and vault toilets are provided. Walking trails lead to the river and bank fishing. Rafters from upstream use this facility as a take-out point. Stays are limited to 7 days.

Access to this campground is via a wide paved 4 mile (6 km) road heading west from near Mile 71 of the Parks Highway.

NORTH COUNTRY RV PARK

Address: Mile 71 Parks Highway, ½ Mile Hatcher Pass Road, Willow, AK 99688
Telephone: (707) 495-8747

GPS Location: N 61° 45' 39.4", W 150° 02' 50.3"

This is a new 49-space RV park located off the Hatcher Pass Road near its intersection with the Parks Highway. Our guess is that the developer of this site must have good access to heavy equipment and lots of gravel, the sites are huge double pull-thrus. They have 50 and 30-amp power and there is a dump and water-fill station. There are no sanitary facilities, the campground is suitable only for self-contained units. Signing in is self-service, there is no on-site host.

To reach the campground head east on the Hatcher Pass Road from Mile 71 of the Parks Highway. In a half-mile you'll see a wide gravel road climbing to the right. You'll pass the dump station and then turn left into the campground.

PIONEER LODGE

Address: Mile 71.4 Parks Highway
          (PO Box 1028), Willow, AK 99688
Telephone: (907) 495-1000   **Fax:** (907) 495-6884
Email: pioneerlodge@gci.net

GPS Location: N 61° 45' 59.2", W 150° 04' 04.3"

The old Pioneer Lodge is one of two campgrounds facing each other across Willow Creek. This is one of the most popular and easily-accessible streams in the state for fishermen after kings, chums, pinks, and silvers. From early June until well into August you can expect this place to be hopping on weekends and active during the week. You can fish from the bank in front of your rig or book a guided trip from the lodge.

There are some 25 camping slots with electric and water hookups at this campground, many along the banks of the river. Large rigs will fit in most of these sites. Many additional campsites are available for tenters and self-contained rigs. The lodge has a dump station although you must back into it. The restrooms require coins for hot showers and there is a coin-op laundry. The lodge also offers a restaurant, bar, and liquor store. Fishing tackle and camping supplies are available.

The lodge is on the west side of the highway near Mile 71 of the Parks Highway. Just watch for the bridge over Willow Creek.

₪ WILLOW CREEK RESORT

Address:	Mile 71.5 Parks Highway (PO Box 85), Willow, AK 99688
Telephone:	(907) 495-6343
Website:	www.willowcreekresort.com

GPS Location: N 61° 46' 05.2", W 150° 04' 05.9"

Just like the Pioneer Lodge across the creek this campground caters to salmon fishermen. This place, however, has a modern camping area and modern lodge building with no bar or restaurant.

The campground has about 40 spaces with utility hookups. The 12 located right on the bank of the creek have electricity and water only, most of the remaining 27 are pull-thrus with 30-amp electricity, sewer, and water. There are also many dry sites extending down the river. There is plenty of maneuvering room for big rigs in this open gravel-surfaced lot. There is also an easy-to-access dump station. The modern lodge building has restrooms, free hot showers, and a coin-op laundry. A small store offers supplies, fishing tackle and a coffee bar with limited food items. Guided fishing trips are available or you can fish from the bank in front of the campground.

The Willow Creek Resort is located near Mile 71 of the Parks Highway, on the west side of the road and the north bank of Willow Creek.

₪ GREY'S CREEK CAMPGROUND

Address:	PO Box 872719, Willow, AK 99687
Telephone:	(907) 373-3679 or (907) 354-0403
Email:	info@evendonsexcursons.com
Website:	www.greyscreekcampground.com

GPS Location: N 61° 53' 43.1", W 150° 04' 47.8"

This small campground overlooks Grey's Creek where it crosses the Parks Highway. It's near the other fishing rivers in the area too. There's a rental cabin as well as a 16-site campground. Eight sites have water and electric hookups and are suitable for rigs to about 25 feet. There are also many sites for tents. The owner plans to offer larger full-hookup sites within the coming year. Restrooms are outhouses at this time but they too are to be upgraded.

The campground is located just west of the Parks Highway at Mile 81.1.

₪ SUSITNA LANDING (ADF&G)

Address:	PO Box 871706, Wasilla, AK 99687
Telephone:	(907) 495-7700 or (907) 373-6700
Website:	www.matnet.com/ron

GPS Location: N 61° 54' 47.5", W 150° 05' 52.0"

If you have a jet boat you probably know about Susitna Landing. If not you will probably enjoy watching the action as fishermen use this launch site at the mouth of the Kashwitna River on the Susitna River to embark and return from successful fishing trips.

The landing has 35 camping sites downstream from the launch site. Five have 30-amp electricity hook-ups. There is plenty of room for big rigs. Most camp sites have firepits and there is a covered picnic area. Sanitary facilities are new handicapped-accessible vault toilets and the office houses an espresso bar. Fishing tackle is available, as are guided fishing trips, float trips, scenic river boat tours, and rental cabins.

To reach Susitna Landing follow the good gravel road west 1 mile (1.6 km) from about Mile 82.5 of the Parks Highway.

🚐 CAMP CASWELL

Location:	Mile 88 of the Parks Highway
	(PO Box 333), Willow, AK 99688)
Telephone:	(907) 495-7829
Email:	campcaswell@webtv.net

GPS Location: N 61° 58' 57.0", W 150° 03' 08.4"

Camp Caswell will remind you of the old-style Alaska roadhouses except that the main building is five stories high. There is a small store in the main building as well as a laundry. Five large formal back-in or pull-thru sites with parking on gravel have electricity (15 and 30 amp) and water hookups and there are many other sites for dry camping. The sanitary facilities are an outhouse but flush toilets and showers are in the main building. There's also a dump station and water is available.

Camp Caswell is on the east side of the highway near Mile 88.

🚐 MAT-SU VALLEY RV PARK

Address:	Mile 90.8 Parks Highway (HC 89, Box 432),
	Willow, AK 99688
Telephone:	(907) 495-6300
Fax:	(907) 495-6300
Website:	www.matsurvpark.com

GPS Location: N 62° 01' 33.8", W 150° 04' 15.0"

This is an older campground that has been substantially upgraded. It has large sites and offers full hookups in a popular fishing region where they are sometimes difficult to find.

The campground has 52 sites. Most have full hookups with 20 or 30-amp outlets, 12 large pull-thrus are available if the campground is not full (they are used as two sites if it is). Parking is on gravel with some grass, there are no trees in the camping area. One building houses the office, groceries and fishing tackle, restrooms, hot showers, and a coin-op laundromat. There is also a dump station. While not right next to a fishing stream they offer guided fishing charters.

To find the campground take the gravel road east from Mile 90.8 of the Parks Highway. The campground is the second driveway on the left.

THE PARKS HIGHWAY

CHETTA'S CORNER CACHE

Location: Mile 97 of the Parks Highway next to Montana Creek

GPS Location: N 62° 06' 20.9", W 150° 03' 37.0"

Montana Creek is one of the popular salmon fishing streams that cross the Parks Highway in this area. Montana Creek actually has three different campgrounds occupying quadrants formed by the crossing of the highway and the stream. Bank fishing for salmon is extremely popular on this river and this and the other nearby campgrounds are very crowded when the fish are running and practically empty when they are not.

Located on the north bank of the river on the west side of the highway is a very basic campground called Chetta's Corner Cache with about 45 smaller back-in sites suitable for tents and rigs to 25 feet and surrounded by natural vegetation. There are picnic tables, firepits, and vault toilets.

MONTANA CREEK CAMPGROUND

Location: Mile 96.5 of the Parks Highway next to Montana Creek
Telephone: (907) 566-camp

GPS Location: N 62° 06' 11.7", W 150° 03' 33.8"

The most sophisticated of the Montana Creek campgrounds is this one. It is the only one with electrical hookups. It is located on the south bank on the east side of the highway.

There are two types of campsites here. Toward the highway are a number of open back-in sites suitable for large rigs and surrounded by clipped grass. Thirty of these have 50-amp and 30-amp electrical outlets. Farther back from the road are many smaller well-separated back-in campsites surrounded by natural vegetation. Most of the sites at this campground have picnic tables and firepits. There is no dump station here but water is available. Chemical toilets are provided and there is also a small store out front selling fishing tackle.

MONTANA CREEK RECREATION PARK

Location: Mile 97 of the Parks Highway next to Montana Creek

GPS Location: N 62° 06' 09.8", W 150° 03' 45.1"

On the south side of Montana Creek on the west side of the highway is the Montana Creek Recreation Park. It is actually managed by the same folks who operate the campground located across the highway. This campground is a big gravel parking lot where camping is allowed with some picnic tables and firepits. There are outhouses and a hand-operated water pump.

TALKEETNA CAMPER PARK

Address: Box 221, Talkeetna, AK 99676
**Telephone
and Fax:**   (907) 733-2693
Email: talkeetnacamper@hotmail.com
Website: www.talkeetnacamper.com

GPS Location: N 62° 19' 03.8", W 150° 06' 14.5"

Talkeetna has long needed a full-service RV park. The wonder is that it has taken so long for one to open. The campground is located just outside the town along the main entrance road, it couldn't be more convenient.

There are 37 sites. Some are full hookup, others offer just electricity and water. Power is 50 or 30 amp. Parking is on gravel. Sites come in a variety of sizes but some are large enough for rigs to 40 feet. Restrooms have flush toilets and hot showers and there is a laundromat, a small store, and a dump station. Day parking is available for RVs, it's easy to walk the half-mile into town.

You can't miss the campground, it's on the right just before you enter Talkeetna at Mile 13.7 of the Talkeetna Spur Road.

TALKEETNA RIVER ADVENTURES RV PARK AND CAMPGROUND (ADF&G)

Address: PO Box 473, Talkeetna, AK 99676
Telephone: (907) 733-2604
Email: riveradv@alaska.net
Website: www.karo-ent.com/riveradv.htm

GPS Location: N 62° 19' 32.1", W 150° 06' 28.6"

North of Talkeetna at the boat launch there is a large area operated as a campground by Talkeetna River Adventures for the Alaska Department of Fish and Game.

There are about 60 camping sites arranged in a wooded area with gravel interior roads. There are no hook-ups but campsites have picnic tables and fire rings and there are outhouses. At the entrance gate is a small store and tackle shop which offers showers. There's also a dump station. Next door is the Swiss-Alaska Inn which has a restaurant and there is a short trail leading to central Talkeetna.

As you enter Talkeetna watch for signs marking a road to the right leading to the airport. Take this road, cross the RR tracks, and turn left just on the far side of the tracks. Drive .7 mile (1.1 km), the campground entrance will be on your left.

TALKEETNA RIVER PARK

Location: Just south of central Talkeetna

GPS Location: N 62° 19' 23.3", W 150° 07' 03.7"

If you drive right through downtown Talkeetna on Main Street you'll spot this little city campground at the far side. There are 11 sites for tents only. The restrooms are port-a-potties. There is a food storage locker. Although there is a host it is not really possible to control access to this campground since the sites actually front on city streets.

HIS & HERS LAKEVIEW CAMPER PARK

Address: HC 89 Box 616, Willow, AK 99688
Telephone: (907) 733-2415

GPS Location: N 62° 08' 27.2", W 150° 03' 20.1"

The H & H is a traditional-style roadhouse offering gas, a good restaurant, rooms and an RV park out back along the shores of a pleasant little lake.

The campground has 10 sites with 30-amp electricity on a gravel surface with plenty of room to maneuver big rigs. There is also lots of room for dry campers and a tent-camping area. There is a wash house with showers and a coin-op laundry. Use of a dump station and water fill-up are available for an extra charge.

The H & H is located near Mile 100 of the Parks Highway.

TRAPPER CREEK INN AND GENERAL STORE

Address:	PO Box 13209, Trapper Creek, AK 99683
Telephone:	(907) 733-2302
Fax:	(907) 733-1002
Email:	innmaster@matnet.com

GPS Location: N 62° 18' 51.9", W 150° 13' 59.1"

The Trapper Creek Inn is a roadhouse-style facility. Watch for the Tesoro station with the red-roofed building. They offer gas, groceries, gifts, rooms, a delicatessen, a laundromat, a cash machine and an RV campground. There's even an airstrip out back and scenic flights are available.

The campground here has about 35 spaces, some are pull-thrus. Eighteen of the spaces have full-hookups with 20-amp electricity. Some sites are long enough for big rigs. There is a covered gazebo at the center of the campground and the sites are separated by trees and natural vegetation and have limited maneuvering room. The inn offers hot showers and a laundromat. There's also a dump station.

The Trapper Creek Inn is located in Trapper Creek at about Mile 115 of the Parks Highway.

LOWER TROUBLESOME CREEK CAMPGROUND (DENALI STATE PARK)

Location: Mile 137 of the Parks Highway

GPS Location: N 62° 37' 30.8", W 150° 13' 40.5"

The Troublesome Creek Campsite is little more than a large paved pull-off next to the highway as far as vehicle campers are concerned but overnight camping in RVs is allowed. There are also several good walk-in tent sites with picnic tables and firepits so it is a decent stopping place for tenters too. The facility has outhouses and a hand-operated water pump and there is a good trail to the Chulitna River. Fishing is for grayling. Stays are limited to 15 days.

BYERS LAKE CAMPGROUND (DENALI STATE PARK)

Location: Mile 147 of the Parks Highway

GPS Location: N 62° 44' 37.6", W 150° 07' 31.0"

One of our favorite state campgrounds for big rigs is Byers Lake. It is well-wooded, has some pull-thrus, and is seldom crowded. There are boats for rent to explore the lake (only electric motors are allowed) and several good hiking trails.

The campground has about 65 campsites. The access road to the campground is paved, interior roads are gravel as are parking pads. The sites are well-separated and surrounded by trees and natural vegetation. Some pull-thrus will take rigs to 40 feet as will a few of the back-ins. There are picnic tables and fire-pits at the sites, a hand-operated water pump, and outhouses. This campground has a host on site and

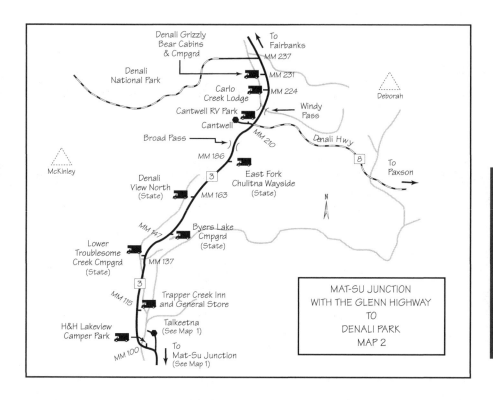

Denali Grizzly
Bear Cabins
& Cmpgrd

To
Fairbanks
MM 237

Denali
National Park

MM 231

Carlo
Creek Lodge

MM 224

Windy
Pass

Cantwell RV Park

Deborah

Cantwell

Broad Pass

Denali Hwy

MM 210

MM 186

8

To
Paxson

McKinley

Denali
View North
(State)

3

MM 163

East Fork
Chulitna Wayside
(State)

N

MM 147

Byers Lake
Cmpgrd
(State)

Lower
Troublesome
Creek Cmpgrd
(State)

MM 137

3

MM 115

Trapper Creek Inn
and General Store

H&H Lakeview
Camper Park

Talkeetna
(See Map 1)

MM 100

To
Mat-Su Junction
(See Map 1)

MAT-SU JUNCTION
WITH THE GLENN HIGHWAY
TO
DENALI PARK
MAP 2

firewood can be purchased. It also has a dump site, one of the few in the area. Stays are limited to 15 days. There are good hiking trails from the campground around the lake and onto Kesugi ridge beyond. Overflow camping is available at nearby Alaska Veterans Memorial/POW-MIA Rest Area which is accessible from the highway, the entrances are north of the campground entrance and there is a walking trail between the two facilities.

The campground is located about a half-mile off the highway, far enough so that there is no highway noise but still easily accessible. The entrance road is on the east side of the highway at about Mile 147 of the Parks Highway.

🚐 DENALI VIEW NORTH (DENALI STATE PARK) $$ 🔥 ♿
Location: Mile 163 of the Parks Highway

GPS Location: N 62° 53' 23.9", W 149° 46' 47.1"

The outstanding feature of this campground is the fantastic view of Denali and the southern side of the Alaska Range. The camping area itself is not much more than a large paved parking lot shared with tour busses and other highway travelers. There are about 20 back-in sites available for camping with picnic tables and firepits as well as some walk-in tent sites. The wayside has vault toilets, a hand-operated water pump, and a telescope. There is also a park host. Stays are limited to 15 days. A paved nature trail loop runs off the south side of the campground and a reader board tells the fantastic story of the first ascent of Denali in 1910 by miners after a bet in a Fairbanks bar.

East Fork Chulitna Wayside (Denali State Park)

Location: Mile 186 of the Parks Highway

GPS Location: N 63° 09' 04.9", W 149° 24' 38.3"

This is a rest area that has formal camping sites. It has been recently redone and has large paved parking areas with adjoining picnic tables and firepits. There are about 20 sites, some are long parallel sites that will take any size rig, others are back-ins that will take only short rigs. There are also four tent-camping sites. Toilets are the modern vault type and there is also a water pump.

The campground is on the east side of the highway near Mile 186.

Cantwell RV Park

Address: PO Box 210, Cantwell, AK 99279
Telephone: (800) 940-2210 or (800) 940-2210
Fax: (907) 768-2210
Email: CantwellRVpark@ak.net
Website: www.alaskaone.com/cantwellrv

GPS Location: N 63° 23' 33.3", W 148° 54' 33.9"

Since it is located some 27 miles (44 km) south of Denali Park you might think that this RV park wouldn't get much business. Nothing could be farther from the truth. Apparently the friendly management and squeaky-clean restrooms and showers provide an adequate tradeoff for the half-hour drive north to the park.

The Cantwell is a large campground with 79 spaces, 68 of them are large pull-thrus. Each site has 30-amp electricity. This campground is basically a very large leveled gravel field so big rigs can easily maneuver. There is a tent-camping area at one end in a grove of trees. The campground has a dump station and water fill hose. The services building houses the office, a small gift shop with a few supplies, hot showers costing $2, clean restrooms, and a laundromat. There is one community fire ring. Tours to the park can be arranged here.

This campground is located on the spur road to Cantwell. Turn west at the junction of the Denali and Parks Highways (about Mile 210 of the Parks), the campground is on the right after a short distance.

Carlo Creek Lodge

Address: HC2 Box 1530, Healy, AK 99743
Telephone: (907) 683-2576 (Summer) or (907) 683-2573 (Winter)
Email: carlocreek@hotmail.com
Website: www.carlocreek.com

GPS Location: N 63° 33' 49.9", W 148° 49' 12.2"

The Carlo Creek Lodge campground is nice. The sites are unique, complete with covered picnic table areas and moveable fire grills that actually work, and they are well separated by trees. There are 25 sites at this small campground/lodge. Seventeen of them have 20-amp electric hookups. Some sites are situated along Carlo Creek near the Nenana River. Most of the sites at this campground are fairly small and maneuvering room is limited, rigs are limited to 32 feet in size by the management. The campground also has a shower house with restrooms with flush toilets, some very cute outhouses, a dump station, a water fill station, and a gift shop and general store. There's a restaurant within walking distance.

The campground is located at about Mile 224 of the Parks Highway, 12 miles (19 km) south of the Denali Park entrance.

DENALI GRIZZLY BEAR CABINS & CAMPGROUND

Address:	Mile 231 Parks Highway (PO Box 7), Denali National Park, AK 99755
Telephone:	(907) 683-2696 (Summer) or (866) 583-2696
Email:	info@denaligrizzlybear.com
Website:	www.denaligrizzlybear.com

GPS Location: N 63° 39' 16.0", W 148° 50' 02.8"

For a campground that can handle big rigs (and small ones, and tents) near Denali Park our choice would have to be the Denali Grizzly. It is located just south of the park, just across the Nenana River.

This campground has about 80 sites, many of them are dry camping sites but some 40 have water and electricity hookups. Many of these are back-in sites long enough for larger rigs in an open area, others for smaller rigs are in a wooded area. Each site has a picnic table and some have firepits. Restrooms have flush toilets and coin-operated hot showers. There is a dump station and also a store with supplies, gifts, and a liquor store. Reservations are recommended.

The campground is located about 6 miles (10 km) south of the Denali Park entrance near Mile 231 of the Parks Highway.

DENALI NATIONAL PARK

Denali Park is one of Alaska's prime attractions and is not to be missed. If you have come north to see wildlife, this is the place. The 6 million plus acre park encompasses the highest portion of the Alaska Range including Mt. McKinley, at 20,320 feet the highest peak in the northern hemisphere. It also includes a huge, mostly treeless alpine region of foothills to the north of the range that is prime habitat for grizzlies, caribou, wolves, and other wildlife.

The park does contain several campgrounds. These are Riley Creek, Savage River, Sanctuary River (tents only), Teklanika River, and Wonder Lake (tents only). These campgrounds are popular, especially the one at Teklanika because it allows you to drive quite a distance into the park to get to your campsite.

One of the reasons for the abundant wildlife in the park is that the Park Service severely limits access. Very few vehicles travel the one road that leads far into the park. Most visitors entering must do so in busses. The difficult access is the price you pay to see wildlife. Don't let the restrictions frustrate you. Instead plan ahead and relax, the park is well worth the effort you will expend to visit it. Shuttle busses run from about the first of June through about the middle of September.

When you arrive at the park your first priority is a visit to the visitor center near the park entrance. You can drive to the center in your RV if it is not too large, it has a

THE CAMPGROUND AND SHUTTLE BUS RESERVATIONS DESK AT DENALI PARK

large parking lot with RV slots. If you're towing you'll want to use the tow car, the lot doesn't have enough room for RVs with tow cars attached. There's also parking near the entrance of the Riley Creek Campground if the visitor center lot doesn't have room. At the visitor center you can find out about the park, arrange reservations, pick up shuttle tickets and sign in for campgrounds in the park. The park has an entrance fee of $5 per person or $10 per vehicle (up to 8 persons) in addition to charges for shuttle busses and campgrounds, you can visit the visitor center without paying this fee.

A reservation system is used to ensure that most visitors are able to enjoy Denali. The procedures seem to change slightly each year but these are the rules for 2004. A similar system is used for bus and campground reservations. Sixty-five percent of shuttle bus seats and 100% of campground spaces in Riley, Savage River, Teklanika and Wonder Lake campsites can be reserved in advance. This can be done by mail, fax, or phone. Mail reservations must be received at least 30 days prior to the planned visit. Fax reservations are accepted up to two days in advance of the planned visit and telephone and internet reservations the day before the planned visit but should be made as far in advance as possible since the available slots are likely to have been claimed by the time you call if you delay. The remaining 35% of bus and available unreserved camping slots are parceled out on a first-come, first-served basis at the park. Your best plan is to reserve far in advance for both bus and campground slots. Failing that, arrive early in the day and hope for the best. Keep in mind that June and July are the most popular months for visiting the park. The crowds begin to taper off by the middle of August. You can stay in a campground just outside the park entrance if you are not able to get a site in the park. Those with large RVs will probably prefer one of the campgrounds outside the park because sites are larger and facilities better.

Phone numbers for reservations are (800) 622-7275 in the U.S. except Alaska, and (907) 272-7275 for international and Alaska calls, the internet reservation site is www.reservedenali.com. The lines are open from the February 15 through about September 15, from 7 a.m. to 5 p.m. Alaska time. Internet reservations can be made from February 15 through September 15 also. Fax and mail reservation service begins December 1 and continues until August 31. The address is Doyon/ARAMARK, 241 West Ship Creek Ave., Anchorage, AK 99501. The fax number is (907) 264-4684. It is easiest to pay by credit card; Visa, Master Card, and Discover Card are accepted. To insure that you enclose all the necessary information you can download a form from the Internet at www.nps.gov/dena. This Website is also a good source of other information about the park.

There is a private tour operator, Kantishna Wilderness Trails (800 230-7275) offering bus trips along the park road to Kantishna. The price is higher than taking a government bus but the tour goes all the way to Kantishna (95 miles (153 km) into the park) and includes lunch.

In addition to the campgrounds inside the park there are also many private camp-

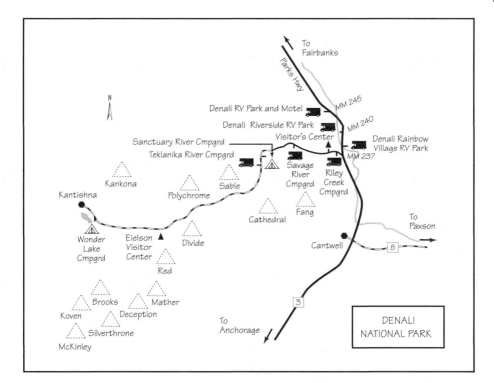

grounds near the park entrance. Most RV visitors to the park will find that these are much more convenient than facilities inside the park.

Denali National Park Campgrounds

**RILEY CREEK CAMPGROUND
(DENALI NATIONAL PARK)**

Location: Inside the park near the entrance

GPS Location: N 63° 43' 51.7", W 148° 53' 37.8"

Riley Creek is the largest of the park's campgrounds and one of the easiest to actually get into. For 2002 there was a new loop of campsites, also newly constructed was a spiffy new building with a store, some prepared food items, laundry, and showers. This is the only campground in the park open all year long, facilities are limited in the winter.

The campground has 146 campsites off large loops, a few are pull-thrus. These sites aren't large, most are suitable only for rigs to about 30 feet although one or two of the back-ins will take any size rig. Each site has a picnic table and firepit. A maximum of 8 people (2 tents) is allowed at each site. Interior roads are paved, parking pads are gravel. There is a central food locker area where you can store food that might attract bears. The restrooms in the campground itself have no showers but they do have flush toilets. A new facility housing a store, a deli, and showers is near the campground. Next to it is a large dump station area. This campground has a host and there is a campfire circle. Reservations are recommended, sign-in at the visitor center is required, see reservation information above.

SAVAGE RIVER CAMPGROUND

Location: Mile 13 of park road

Savage River is a 33-site vehicle campground. Both RVs and tents are allowed. There are flush toilets but not showers. Vehicles are allowed to Mile 15 of the park road so it is possible to drive to this campground without restriction. A maximum of 8 campers (2 tents) are allowed in each space, rig length is limited to 20 feet. Reservations are recommended, sign-in at the visitor center is required, see information about reservations above.

SANCTUARY RIVER CAMPGROUND

Location: Mile 23 of the park road

Sanctuary River is a very small 7-site tent campground. There is a chemical toilet and bear-proof food storage lockers. No campfires are allowed, only stoves. No reservations are taken for this campground, sign-in at the visitor center is required, see information about reservations above.

TEKLANIKA RIVER CAMPGROUND

Location: Mile 29 of the park road

Teklanika River Campground is a large vehicle campground with 53 sites. Each has a firepit and picnic table. The campground is set on a gravel riverbed and many sites can accommodate larger rigs. There are flush toilets but no showers. Only campers in hard-sided vehicles are allowed. The location of this campground inside the park on limited access road beyond the 15 mile (24 km) checkpoint makes it popular but imposes restrictions. Campers are given special permits to drive in and return, vehicles can not be used otherwise. In addition, campers must stay 3 days at the campground to limit road traffic. Campers can board the park shuttle busses to continue on into the park on day trips. Reservations are recommended, sign-in at the visitor center is required, see information about reservations above.

🚐 WONDER LAKE CAMPGROUND

Location: Mile 85 of the park road

The 28-site tent-only campground at Wonder Lake has a choice location with great views of the mountain, when it's out. Food is stored in lockers. No campfires are allowed, only stoves. A maximum of 4 campers (1 tent) are allowed in each site. There are chemical toilets. Reservations are recommended, sign-in at the visitor center is required, see information about reservations above. There are lake trout in Wonder Lake.

🚐 DENALI RAINBOW VILLAGE RV PARK

Address: Mile 238.6 Parks Highway (PO Box 35),
                 Denali National Park, AK 99755
Telephone: (907) 683-7777   **Fax:**   (907) 683-7275
Email: stayatdenalirainbowrvpark@gci.net
Website: www.denalirvrvpark.com

GPS Location: N 63° 44' 48.1", W 148° 53' 53.4"

The Denali Rainbow Village is the closest RV park to Denali Park. It is new, but there is so much building going on around it and the land apparently so valuable that there is some question in our minds about how long it will last. As long as it does, however, this is the most convenient campground outside the park.

For the present there are about 80 sites. Forty-five are pull-thrus with electric and water. Another 20 are back-ins with full hookups. The sites are located on a flat gravel bench. A line of log buildings has been built between the road and the park, they serve to isolate it from the road and house various business establishments. Electricity is via 30 or 50-amp outlets and there is a dump station and water fill station. Rigs to 40 feet will fit in this park. There are restrooms with hot showers, and a coin-op laundry. Restaurants, a gas station, and a small store are conveniently located in the immediate vicinity.

The Denali Rainbow Village RV Park is located on the east side of the Parks Highway at Mile 238.6, about 1.3 miles (2.1 km) north of the Denali Park entrance.

🚐 DENALI RIVERSIDE RV PARK

Address: Milepost 240, Parks Highway (P.O. Box 7),
                 Denali National Park, AK, 99755
Telephone: (866) 583-2696 or (907) 388-1748
Email: info@denaliriversiderv.com
Website: www.denaliriversiderv.com

GPS Location: N 63° 46' 07.0" , W 148' 54' 48.7"

This large newer campground not far north of the Denali Park entrance road sits right where dozens of free-campers parked in years past. It overlooks the Nenana River.

The Riverside has about 100 campsites. Some 70 of them offer electricity (20, 30, and 50 amps) and water hookups. Each site has a picnic table and some are pull-thrus. There's room for rigs to 45 feet. There is a dump station and water fill station. Restrooms have flush toilets and coin-op hot showers, there's also a coin-op laundry and gift shop. A shuttle bus to the park is available.

The campground is located near Mile 240 of the Parks Highway. It is about 3 miles (5 km) north of the park entrance road.

🚐 DENALI RV PARK AND MOTEL

Address:	245.1 George Parks Highway (PO Box 155), Denali National Park, AK 99755
Telephone:	(907) 683-1500 or (800) 478-1501
Email:	stay@denaliRVpark.com
Website:	www.denaliRVpark.com

GPS Location: N 63° 49' 17.0", W 148° 59' 13.2"

Not far north of the Denali Park entrance is a large well-established RV park and motel, the Denali.

This campground has some 90 sites, 30 have full hookups with 30-amp electricity, about 50 more have water and electricity. A few are long pull-thrus and cable TV is available. Sites have picnic tables and are separated by grass. The campground also has a dump station. The restrooms have flush toilets and coin-op showers, they are individual rooms with both toilet and shower. There's also a gift shop, laundromat and a modem outlet for email.

The campground is on the west side of the Parks Highway near Mile 245. It is 7.8 miles (12.6 km) north of the Denali entrance road.

FROM DENALI PARK TO FAIRBANKS
121 Miles (195 Kilometers)

After passing the Denali Park Entrance the Parks Highway continues through the Nenana Canyon and soon passes Healy. **Healy** is the location of Alaska's largest open-pit coal mine, you can sometimes see the giant crane stripping overburden on the hilltop to the east of the highway. Without the crane you wouldn't know that it was there.

As the road descends out of the mountains you will begin to notice the dips and heaves that show that it was built on permafrost. This section of road from the mountains to Nenana on the Tanana River was one of the most difficult sections of the entire highway to build, even though the terrain is flat. At Mile 283 you pass the access road to **Clear**, a large radar site that is part of the ballistic missile early warning system.

At Mile 304 you will enter **Nenana** (population 400). Today this small village of 400 people serves largely as a transfer point for fuel and other goods from the railroad to river barges headed for villages on the Tanana and Yukon Rivers. It is best known as the site of the **Nenana Ice Classic**, an annual betting pool where hundreds of thousands of dollars are wagered by people trying to guess the exact time in the spring when the river ice will go out. The **Nenana Visitor Center** (907 832-9953) is at the corner at Mile 304 where A Street goes into Nenana. When the Alaska Railroad was completed in 1923 President Harding drove a golden spike in Nenana, today the **Alaska Railroad Museum** is in the renovated original **Nenana Railroad Depot** which is on the National Register of Historic Places.

After leaving Nenana the highway crosses the Tanana River and makes its way across rolling hills for 54 miles (87 km) before descending into Fairbanks.

Denali Park to Fairbanks Campgrounds

McKINLEY RV AND CAMPGROUND

Address:	PO Box 340, Healy, AK 99743
Telephone:	(907) 683-2379 or (800) 478-2562
Fax:	(907) 683-2281
Email:	rvcampak@mtaonline.net

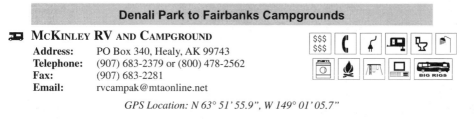

GPS Location: N 63° 51' 55.9", W 149° 01' 05.7"

After (or before, if you're heading south) the high-country gravel campgrounds to the south you'll appreciate the grass at this campground.

There are 89 sites at the McKinley. Full-hookup and pull-thrus are offered as well as sites with only water and electric, electric only, and dry. Sites are big, suitable for any

THE PARKS HIGHWAY

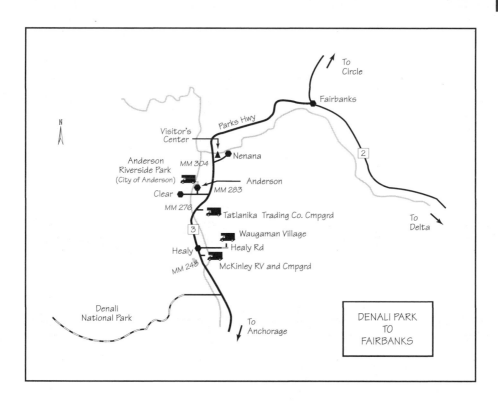

DENALI PARK
TO
FAIRBANKS

large rigs. There's also a tent-camping area. The campground has flush toilets, hot showers, a coin-op laundromat, a gift and supplies shop, gas sales, an ATM, propane sales and a playground.

The campground is located in Healy, on the east side of the Parks Highway at Mile 248.5. This is 11 miles (18 km) north of the Denali Park entrance road.

🚐 Waugaman Village

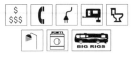

Address:	3.8 Mile Healy Spur Road
	(PO Box 78), Healy, AK 99743
Telephone:	(907) 683-2317

GPS Location: N 63° 51' 17.0", W 148° 56' 31.3"

Well off the beaten path in the community of Healy this campground has 15 large back-in sites with 20-amp outlets and water. Little effort has been devoted to esthetics here, we seldom find any campers using the facility. There is a restroom building with hot showers, some laundry equipment outside the bathrooms, and a dump station.

To find the campground take the Healy Road from Mile 248.8 of the Parks Highway. Drive east past the power plant and at 3.8 miles (6.1 km) turn left into the campground.

🚐 Tatlanika Trading Co. Campground

Address:	Mile 276 Parks Highway
	(PO Box 40179), Clear, AK 99704
Telephone:	(907) 582-2341

GPS Location: N 64° 13' 04.1", W 149° 16' 29.6"

One of the nicer places to stop along the Parks Highway and one of the best deals is the Tatlanika Trading Post.

The place is best known for its great gift shop but the Tatlanika also has 21 camping sites, some are suitable for large rigs. Many of them are situated along the Nenana River. The sites have 20-amp outlets and water with picnic tables. They are well separated with natural vegetation. The campground has a dump station and flush toilets, showers are also available for $2.

The Tatlanika Trading Post is located at Mile 276 of the Parks Highway, just north of a bridge over the Nenana River.

🚐 Anderson Riverside Park (City of Anderson)

Address:	PO Box 3100, Anderson, AK 99744
Telephone:	(907) 582-2500
Fax:	(907) 582-2496

GPS Location: N 64° 20' 36.4", W 149° 12' 07.6"

This park, known as the home of the Anderson Bluegrass Festival on the last weekend of July each year, offers both hookup and boondocking facilities.

Campsites are located in two places. Along the banks of the Nenana River there are 10 back-in dry sites surrounded by trees, some have picnic tables and firepits. Some distance away, on the far side of a large grassy field and next to a bandstand, are 18 sites with either 20 or 30-amp outlets. Nearby is a restroom building with hot showers and a telephone. Near the entrance of the park is a dump station and water fill station.

The road to Clear and Anderson leaves the Parks Highway at Mile 282.5. Drive westward on the paved highway for 1.2 miles (1.9 km) and then turn right following the sign for Anderson. You'll drive through Anderson and on the far side, at 6.3 miles (10.2 km) from the Parks Highway, enter the park. The hookup sites are to the left, the dry sites straight ahead. Watch for a pay station with payment envelopes as you enter the campground.

PARKS HIGHWAY DUMP STATIONS

Many of the campgrounds in this chapter have dump stations or sewer hookups, see the individual entries for these. There is generally a fee charged for using them, particularly if you are not staying at the campground. Here are some additional possibilities:

In **Wasilla** the Williams Express in town at the intersection of the Parks Highway and Boundary has a dump station. There is also one at the Chevron station across the street from Wendy's on Weber. Access to both of these is difficult for larger rigs, however, because there's lots of traffic.

At **Denali National Park** there is a dump station inside the park near the Riley Creek Campground service building which is not far from the highway. It's can be used by folks not staying in the park. The fee is $5.00, free if you're camping in the park.

On the outskirts of **Fairbanks**, at the Parks Highway Chevron at Mile 352.5 there is a dump station.

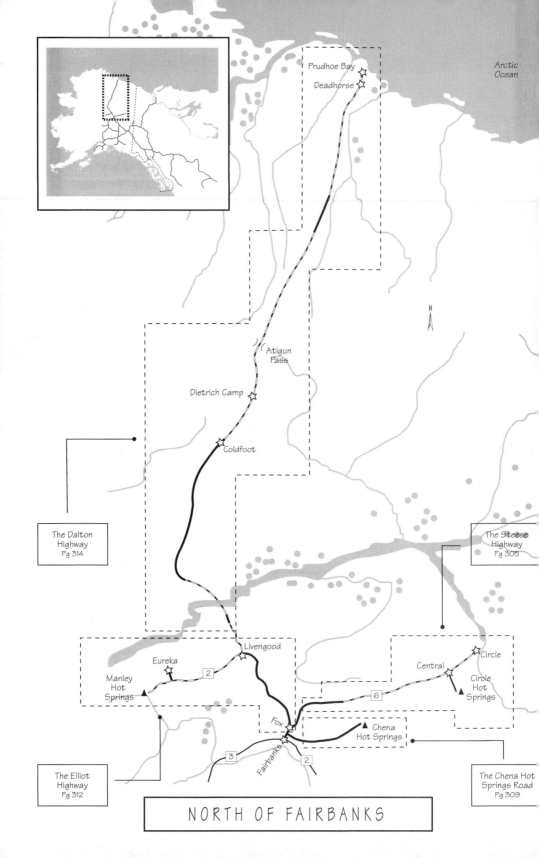

Arctic
Ocean

Prudhoe Bay
Deadhorse

N

Atigun
Pass

Dietrich Camp

Coldfoot

The Dalton
Highway
Pg 314

The Steese
Highway
Pg 305

Eureka

Livengood

2

Circle

Central

Circle
Hot
Springs

Manley
Hot
Springs

Fox

6

Chena
Hot Springs

The Elliot
Highway
Pg 312

3

Fairbanks

2

The Chena Hot
Springs Road
Pg 309

NORTH OF FAIRBANKS

Chapter 10

North of Fairbanks

INTRODUCTION

There are a surprising number of roads giving access to the country north of Fairbanks. Both RVers and tent campers will find much to interest them in this region.

Fairbanks and the area north to the Brooks Range have some of the best summer weather in the state. On many summer days you can expect blue skies with cumulous clouds building in the afternoon to produce a few showers that disperse in the evening. Daytime temperatures approaching 70° are not uncommon. During the middle of the summer you can also expect long days, in fact it will never get really dark during June and July.

The region is definitely not crowded. For a short time before the growth of Dawson City, Circle City was the largest city in the interior. The city served the Birch Creek mining district in the hills to the south. There were also many other mining areas along these roads. When the mining pretty much shut down in the 1940's most people left the area leaving interesting ghost towns and mining relics, and the roads to reach them.

 Highlights

There are several developed and easy to reach hot springs north of Fairbanks. Closest and easiest with a paved road all the way, is **Chena Hot Springs** on the Chena Hot Springs Road. There is also a hot springs at **Manley Hot**

Springs at the end of the Elliott Highway.

The entire region was a mining area. Important strikes or mining areas include **Pedro Creek** on the Circle Hot Springs Road; **Upper Goldstream Creek** near Fox, **Cleary Creek, Chatanika, Nome Creek, Birch Creek** and **Circle-Mastodon Creek** on the Steese Highway; **Tolovana** (Livengood), **Eureka** and **Tofty** on the Elliott Highway; and **Ruby** (Wiseman) and **Coldfoot** on the Dalton Highway. Many relics of these gold rushes remain within easy walking distance of the highways.

The 420 mile (677 km) long **Dalton Highway**, also long known as the Pipeline Haul Road, is a major destination in its own right. You'll find an entire section about this formidable but rewarding route below.

 Fuel

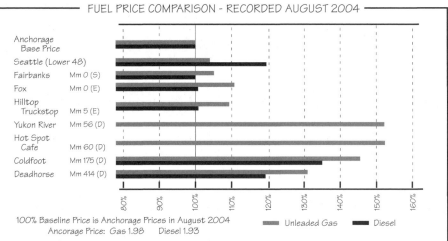

FUEL PRICE COMPARISON - RECORDED AUGUST 2004

Anchorage Base Price		
Seattle (Lower 48)		
Fairbanks	Mm 0 (S)	
Fox	Mm 0 (E)	
Hilltop Truckstop	Mm 5 (E)	
Yukon River	Mm 56 (D)	
Hot Spot Cafe	Mm 60 (D)	
Coldfoot	Mm 175 (D)	
Deadhorse	Mm 414 (D)	

80%   90%   100%   110%   120%   130%   140%   150%   160%

100% Baseline Price is Anchorage Prices in August 2004
Ancorage Price: Gas 1.98   Diesel 1.93

▨ Unleaded Gas   ■ Diesel

Fishing

Fishing in the interior is primarily for grayling, whitefish, and northern pike. King, silver, and chum (also known as calico or dog) salmon do get far into the interior, but by the time they get this far up the river they are quite red and often no good for eating. Local fishermen do enjoy catching and releasing them, however.

The **Chena River**, which runs through Fairbanks, was a very good grayling stream at one time but the fish population crashed in the 80's. The upper reaches in the Chena River State Recreation Area are clear and fun to fish. The grayling are coming back, all grayling fishing in the Chena is catch-and-release. You might want to give it a try. There's easy access off the Chena Hot Springs Road in many places.

The **Chatanika River** is another clear-water river that has seen heavy fishing pressure for grayling. From April 1 to May 31 the Chatanika is catch-and-release for grayling, the rest of the year only fish at least 12 inches long can be kept. Access to the Chatanika is from the Steese Highway at Mile 35 and 39 and from the Elliott Highway at Mile 11. The best access is by canoe, see below.

On the Steese Highway there are several **small lakes in the tailing piles at Chatanika** that are stocked with grayling. They're between Mile 29 and Mile 40 and are marked with signs on the road.

Beaver and Birch Creeks run north into the Yukon River, both have good grayling fishing. Access to Beaver Creek is very limited and along most of the river requires either a hike or airplane ride. The headwaters are road-accessible from Mile 57 of the Steese Highway on the Nome Creek Road. Access to Birch Creek is at Mile 94 and Mile 147 of the Steese Highway. Both of these rivers are popular canoe routes, they're designated Wild and Scenic Rivers, see below.

The **Tolovana River** joins the Chatanika River near Minto. The upper reaches of the river provide good grayling fishing, access is from bridges on the Elliott Highway at Mile 57 and Mile 75. Other creeks to try on the Elliott Highway are **Tatalina Creek** (Mile 45), **Hutlinana Creek** (Mile 129), and **Baker Creek** (Mile 137).

The **Dalton Highway** remains a wilderness road and fishing in the creeks it crosses can be good. These are mostly grayling streams but swampy areas with slow-moving water have northern pike. Try **Hess Creek** (Mile 24), the **Ray River** (Mile 70), **No Name Creek** (Mile 79), the **Kanuti River** (Mile 106), **Fish Creek** (Mile 114), **South Fork of Bonanza Creek** (Mile 125), the **North Fork of Bonanza Creek** (Mile 126), **Prospect Creek** (Mile 135), the **Jim River** (Mile 140, 141), **Grayling Lake** (Mile 151), the **South Fork of the Koyukuk River** (Mile 156), **Minnie Creek** (Mile 187), and the **Dietrich River** (Mile 207).

Boating, Rafting, Canoeing, and Kayaking

There are four popular canoe routes north of Fairbanks and accessible from the road. These are the Chena River, the Chatanika River, Beaver Creek, and Birch Creek.

The **Chena River** has excellent road access. The upper river is in the Chena River State Recreation Area. Short or long floats are available, from a few hours to almost 80 hours (all the way to Fairbanks) of float time. Tent camping on gravel bars along the river is allowed within the Recreation Area. Access points along the Chena Hot Springs Road are at Mile 48.9, Mile 44.0, Mile 39.5, Mile 37.8, Mile 31.6, Mile 28.6, Mile 28, Mile 27, and off the Grange Hill Road at Mile 20.8. There's also access from Nordale Road and at several places in Fairbanks. The river is rated as Class II and has sweepers and log jams so exercise caution. Lower sections of the river are slower and easier to negotiate.

The **Chatanika River** is navigable a distance of about 130 miles (210 km) but most canoeists float no more than the 60 river miles (97 km) between Sourdough Creek and the Elliott Highway which takes three to four days. This is a Class I and Class II river with log jams and sweepers so exercise caution. Access points are from the Steese Highway at Sourdough Creek (Mile 60), Cripple Creek (Mile 53), Long Creek (Mile 45), the Chatanika River Bridge (Mile 39), and on the Elliott Highway at Mile 11.

Birch Creek is a National Wild and Scenic River with road-accessible put-in and take-out points. The put-in is at Twelve Mile Creek on the Steese Highway (Mile 94), the take-out is at the Birch Creek Bridge at Mile 147 of the Steese Highway. Between the two are 126 river miles (203 km) for a 7 to 10 day float. Birch Creek does not run along the road, this is a wilderness float. The water is rated Class I and II with some Class III rapids so exercise caution. Much of the river is within the Steese National Conservation Area.

Beaver Creek is the most remote of these rivers. There is road access to the put-in point but it is necessary to arrange for an aircraft for take-out. This river is a National Wild and Scenic River. The put-in point is on Nome Creek which is accessible via the U.S. Creek Road from Mile 57 of the Steese Highway. From the put-in to take-out at a gravel bar at Victoria Creek is 127 river miles (205 km) and takes 7 or 8 days. The first two days are likely to be slow going as you line your canoe or raft for six miles (10 km) through shallow water as far as Beaver Creek. This is a Class I river in remote country with log jams and sweepers, exercise caution.

Hiking and Mountain Biking

The high country north of Fairbanks is excellent hiking terrain with many designated trails. Most trails are within the Chena River State Recreation Area, the White Mountains National Recreation Area, the Steese National Conservation Area, or the Trans-Alaska Pipeline Utility Corridor.

The **Chena River State Recreation Area** has a good selection of trails. The **Granite Tors Trail** is a 15-mile (24-km) loop trail up a ridge on one side of Rock Creek to a region of rocky pillars in high treeless country, and then back to the starting point along the other side of Rock Creek. The trail has an elevation gain of 2,500 feet and takes from 4 to 8 hours. Access is from the Tors Trail Campground at Mile 39 of the Chena Hot Spring Road. An easier trail is the **Angel Rocks Trail,** a 3.5-mile (5.6-km) (round trip) hike to rock outcroppings above the river. Access is from a parking lot at Mile 48.9 of the Chena Hot Springs Road. Finally, the challenging **Chena Dome Trail** is a 30-mile (40-km) loop through high country following a chain of rock cairns that mark the trail. Altitude gain is over 3,000 feet. Plan on 2 to 4 days to make the loop. Access is from Mile 50.5 of the Chena Hot Springs Road. Of these three trails only the last is open to mountain bikes.

The White Mountains National Recreation Area has lots of trails, unfortunately almost all of them are designed for winter use, they are too wet to make good summer hiking trails. The **Summit Trail** is an exception. This ridge trail from Mile 28 of the Elliot Highway is a one-way day hike of 3.5 miles (5.6-km) to the north side of Wickersham Dome, a climb of 900 feet. It is also possible to follow this trail much farther to Birch Creek. The one-way distance to the creek is 20 miles (32.3 km).

A popular trail along the Steese Highway is the **Pinnell Mountain Trail**. It connects Eagle Summit at Mile 107 and Twelvemile Summit at Mile 85. The trail is 27 miles (44 km) long and follows mountain ridges with wonderful views in all directions. There are basic shelters at Mile 10 and Mile 17.5 as measured from the Eagle Summit trailhead, the BLM recommends walking the trail from Eagle Summit to Twelvemile Summit because it is slightly easier in that direction. Plan on two to four days to finish this hike. Water can be a problem, don't pass up a source. You may have to descend from the ridgeline to find it. Some sections of the trail are marked with cairns. Visiting the summits and walking the trail at the summer solstice has become very popular. From June 18 to June 24 the sun doesn't dip below the horizon at all from higher points on the trail, the solstice is June 20 or 21.

On the Elliott Highway near Manley Hot Springs is the trail to **Hutlinana Warm Springs**. The 8-mile (12.9-km) trail follows Hutlinana Creek north from near the bridge at Mile 139.

Along the **Dalton Highway** hiking options are limited except in the high country. Check at the Coldfoot Interagency Visitor Center at Mile 175 for information. Try the trail up Gold Creek from Mile 197 to **Bob Johnson Lake**. The distance is 13 miles (21 km) and the lake is known for its fishing (grayling, lake trout, and northern pike). Really ambitious hikers can also climb Sukakpak Mountain near Mile 204 for great views.

 Wildlife Viewing

You are likely to run into a moose almost anywhere along the roads north of Fairbanks and there are often grouse and ptarmigan feeding along the shoulders. The **Dalton Highway** is in another class entirely. From Atigun Pass (Mile 245) to Galbraith Lake (Mile 275) you are almost sure to see Dall sheep. Also watch for caribou, arctic fox, muskoxen, and a long list of birds. The BLM even prints a booklet that serves as a checklist titled *Birds Along the Dalton Highway.*

THE ROUTES, TOWNS, AND CAMPGROUNDS

STEESE HIGHWAY
162 Miles (261 Kilometers)

The Steese Highway was the first of the roads north of Fairbanks. Today it is not the busiest, the Dalton Highway claims that honor, but it is the only one of the roads that begins in Fairbanks. The others all branch off the Steese.

For the first 44 miles (71 km) the Steese Highway is paved. Then for another 83 miles (144 km) to Central the road is wide and generally in good shape but not paved. The remaining 35 miles (56 km) to Circle City on the banks of the Yukon River are not as wide or well-maintained but still easily good enough for even the largest RVs.

The Steese Highway starts as the Steese Expressway running just east of downtown Fairbanks. At Mile 5 the Chena Hot Springs Road cuts off to the east. There's a **pipeline viewing area** at Mile 7 and at Mile 11 the expressway reaches the Fox junction.

Fox is in the middle of an area of tailing piles from gold dredges that worked the region until WW II. There is a dredge located near Fox (**Gold Dredge #8**) that is open to the public and another on private land at Mile 29 in Chatanika.

At Fox junction the Steese Highway goes right while the Elliott Highway continues straight. After turning right you'll soon see the **Pedro Monument** on the left at Mile 16. Felix Pedro discovered gold near here, this was the strike that caused the founding of the city of Fairbanks.

The road climbs over the first of three summits, 2,233-foot **Cleary Summit**, at Mile 21 and descends into the **Chatanika River Valley**. This valley was another gold mining area, there are lots more tailing piles. The second Steese Highway dredge is near the road at Mile 29. The Chatanika Valley had two gold mining towns, Cleary and Chatanika. It also has the beautifully clear Chatanika River.

As the road continues northwest up the Chatanika Valley you may notice a large pipeline to the left. This is the **Davidson Ditch**, a system of ditches on the mountaintops and inverted siphons in the valleys that delivered water to the mining operations downstream. It is no longer in use but was only closed down after the 1967 Fairbanks flood.

The road eventually climbs up out of the trees to 2,982 foot **Twelvemile Summit**. The Pinnell Mountain National Recreation Trail, leading 24 miles (39 km) to Eagle Summit, leaves the road here. Note the scattered shiny pieces of airplanes that didn't quite make it over the summit.

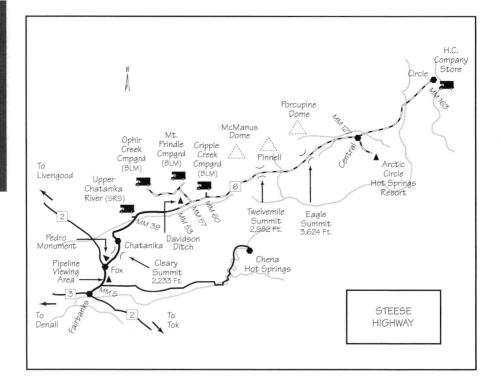

The road takes a slightly lower route than the Pinnell trail to **Eagle Summit** at Mile 108. From there it descends to Central at Mile 127.

Central is a small town with a population of about 400 dating from the days of the Birch Creek strike in the early 1890's. Today there's a post office, an airstrip, a museum, and a couple of roadhouses. Gas is available.

In the middle of town is the junction with a gravel road that leads 8 miles (13 km) to Circle Hot Springs Resort. Unfortunately the resort has been closed recently, hopefully it will reopen soon.

From Central the Steese Highway is narrower and not as straight. It continues another 35 miles (58 km) to **Circle City** on the Yukon River. Circle also dates from the Birch Creek Strike. It was known as the Paris of the north in the few short years before gold was found at Dawson City. Once that happened the miners abandoned Circle and headed upstream. Today you'll find a town with a population of about 100 people. Despite the name Circle is well south of the Arctic Circle, to cross it you'll have to drive up the Dalton Highway. Services in Circle include a small store, gas, a laundromat, and a camping area on the south bank of the Yukon River.

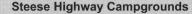

Steese Highway Campgrounds

🚐 **UPPER CHATANIKA RIVER STATE RECREATION SITE (STATE OF ALASKA)**

Location: Mile 39 Steese Highway

GPS Location: N 65° 11' 31.1", W 147° 15' 23.2"

The Upper Chatanika campground is one of the nicest in this area. It offers some sites right on this beautifully clear wilderness river. This is a popular put-in point for canoeing the river.

There are 24 vehicle camping sites at this campground. They are well-separated by trees and natural vegetation and have picnic tables and firepits. There are vault toilets and a hand-operated water pump. The campground is an access point for the Chatanika River Float Trail, a 19-mile (31-km) float to Mile 11 of the Elliott Highway at Whitefish Campground.

The campground is on the Steese Highway to Circle at Mile 39.

🚐 **MT. PRINDLE CAMPGROUND (WHITE MOUNTAINS RECREATION AREA – BLM)**

Location: U.S. Creek Road from Mile 57of the Steese Highway

GPS Location: N 65° 22' 01.2", W 146° 35' 41.3"

This is one of two new campgrounds located off Nome Creek Road (also known as the White Mountains Gateway) in the White Mountains National Recreation Area. It is located in high country with few trees. The Quartz Creek Trail begins nearby and Nome Creek is just to the east.

The campground has 13 rather small sites, probably appropriately so since the access road is not suitable for large rigs. Six are parallel parking sites so larger rigs could park if they successfully braved the road. There are outhouses, hand-pump water, and firewood was being provided when we visited.

The dirt and gravel U.S. Creek road goes north from Mile 57 of the Steese Highway. It is usually suitable for rigs up to about 25 feet. Just after leaving the Steese the road passes the Davidson Ditch Historical Site and then climbs across a pass to the Nome Creek watershed. After 7 miles (11 km) the road crosses Nome Creek and then forks, go right for Mt. Prindle Campground. You will reach the campground in another 4.2 miles (6.8 km).

◼ OPHIR CREEK CAMPGROUND (WHITE MOUNTAINS RECREATION AREA – BLM)

Location: U.S. Creek Road from Mile 57of the Steese Highway

GPS Location: N 65° 22' 07.9", W 147° 05' 03.2"

This is the second of two new campgrounds located off Nome Creek Road (also known as the White Mountains Gateway) in the White Mountains National Recreation Area. It is located in an area forested by small spruce trees. Ophir Creek meets Nome Creek here and they flow into the Beaver Creek National Wild River three miles (4.8 km) downstream. The campground provides the starting point for extended wilderness floats.

Ophir Creek Campground has nineteen campsites off two loops. These are mostly separated back-in sites with some parallel parking of larger rigs possible. Sites have picnic tables and firepits. There are outhouses and hand-operated water pumps, fire-

MOOSE ARE COMMON NEAR THE HIGHWAYS NORTH OF FAIRBANKS

NORTH OF FAIRBANKS

wood was being provided when we visited.

The dirt and gravel U.S. Creek road goes north from Mile 57 of the Steese Highway. It is usually suitable for rigs up to about 25 feet. Just after leaving the Steese the road passes the Davidson Ditch Historical Site and then climbs across a pass to the Nome Creek watershed. After 7 miles (11 km) the road crosses Nome Creek and then forks, go left for Ophir Creek Campground. You will reach the campground in another 12.1 miles (19.5 km).

⛟ CRIPPLE CREEK CAMPGROUND (BLM)

Location: Mile 60 of Steese Highway

GPS Location: N 65° 16' 34.1", W 146° 39' 13.4"

There are 12 back-in vehicle sites in a grove of mixed spruce and birch. Picnic tables and firepits are provided. There is also a tent-camping area. Unfortunately none of the sites are located along the river. There are outhouses and a hand-operated water pump. The BLM also operates a recreational rental cabin at this campground. You must pre-register to use it, see our section about rental recreational cabins in Chapter 14 - *Camping Away From the Road System*.

You will find this campground on the north side of the road near Mile 60.

⛟ H.C. COMPANY STORE

Telephone: (907) 773-1222

GPS Location: N 65° 49' 32.7", W 144° 03' 46.7"

The town of Circle provides parking for RVs at the boat ramp which forms the very end of the Steese Highway. There are back-in spaces for about 10 rigs with some picnic tables and barbecues. An outhouse is nearby and just across the road is the H.C. Company Store with groceries, gifts, and a cafe. Behind the trading post is a laundry which has hot showers.

To find this campground just follow the Steese Highway right to its end at the Yukon River, about Mile 163.

CHENA HOT SPRINGS ROAD
57 Miles (92 Kilometers)

The Chena Hot Springs Road is the most civilized of the routes north of Fairbanks. The road leads almost directly east from a junction at Mile 5 of the Steese Highway. The Chena Hot Springs Road is 57 miles (92 km) long and paved for its entire length. It generally leads up the valley of the Chena River. Along the way there are several campgrounds and access points for fishing or floating the Chena and also access to several good hiking trails into the surrounding hills.

Chena Hot Springs Road Campgrounds

⛟ ROSEHIP CAMPGROUND
(CHENA RIVER STATE RECREATION AREA)
Location: Mile 27 Chena Hot Springs Road

GPS Location: N 64° 52' 39.4", W 146° 45' 56.1"

NORTH OF FAIRBANKS

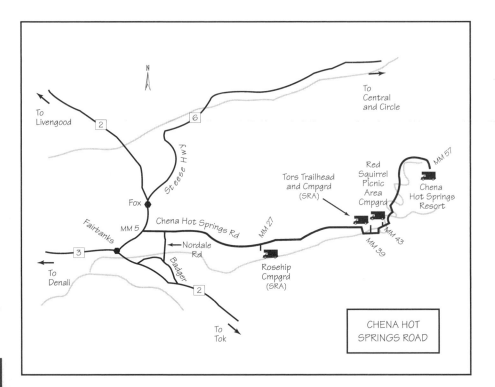

This pleasant riverside campground has 36 camping sites. Many are long back-in sites suitable for any size rig. Trees and natural vegetation separate them. There are also some walk-in tent sites. The campground has picnic tables, firepits, vault toilets, and a hand-operated water pump. Sites are off a circular drive so if you're towing you can drive in and take a look. The Rosehip Campground is a popular access point for Chena River canoeists.

The campground is located on the south side of the Chena Hot Springs Road at about Mile 27.

◼ TORS TRAILHEAD AND CAMPGROUND (CHENA RIVER STATE RECREATION AREA)

| Location: | Mile 39 Chena Hot Springs Road |

GPS Location: N 64° 54' 10.5", W 146° 21' 38.8"

One of the most popular hikes in the Fairbanks area is to the Granite Tors, large granite rocks projecting from rounded hilltops. This campground makes a good base camp since it is where the trail starts.

The campground is located near the North Fork of the Chena River. There are 24 long back-in sites. They are well separated with spruces and other natural vegetation and have picnic tables and firepits. This campground has vault toilets, a hand-operated water pump, a canoe launching area, and a host. Some sites are long enough for 40-foot rigs.

You can't miss this campground since it sits on the north side of the highway near Mile 39 of the Chena Hot Springs Road. A bridge over the North Fork of the Chena helps mark the location.

RED SQUIRREL PICNIC AREA CAMPGROUND
(CHENA RIVER STATE RECREATION AREA)

Location: Mile 43 Chena Hot Springs Road

GPS Location: N 64° 56' 04.8", W 146° 17' 10.8"

This is really just a picnic area with two covered picnic kiosks but camping is allowed in open parking areas. The campground is suitable for rigs to 35 feet. The place is attractive and is next to a small lake. There are picnic tables, fire rings, vault toilets, and a hand-operated water pump.

The campground is located on the north side of the Chena Hot Springs Road at about Mile 43.

CHENA HOT SPRINGS RESORT

Address: PO Box 58740, Fairbanks, AK 99711
Telephone: (907) 451-8104 or (800) 478-4681
Email: chenahotsprings@polarnet.com
Website: www.chenahotsprings.com

GPS Location: N 65° 03' 13.6", W 146° 03' 31.7"

At the end of a 57-mile paved highway Chena Hot Springs is the easiest to reach of the hot springs north of Fairbanks. The springs here were discovered in 1904, the

THE OUTDOOR POOL AT CHENA HOT SPRINGS RESORT

water comes out of the ground at 165° F. The new outdoor pool is a must-see (actually a must-swim).

Chena Hot Springs is a small resort offering campsites, hotel rooms, a restaurant and bar, and an aircraft landing strip. The swimming area includes an indoor pool and hot tubs, outdoor hot tub, and an extremely impressive outdoor pool surrounded by rocks with a smooth gravel bottom and hot water. This pool itself is worth the trip out to the resort.

There are three camping areas. A new area is designed for very large rigs. It sits just north of the entrance road and has four large pull-thru parking sites and eight more back-ins. There are no utility hookups.

A second area, called the Upper Campground, has 13 sites suitable for RVs to about 25 feet. There are no hookups but the sites are separated by trees and natural vegetation and they have fire pits, There are conveniently located outhouses.

The lower campground is really suitable only for very small rigs and tent campers. There are 16 sites here including a grassy tent area and nearby outhouses. Walk the roads of this area before trying it in a rig.

The resort also has a dump station and a laundromat. Nearby cross-country skiing trails can be used as hiking trails in the summer.

Chena Hot Springs Resort is located at the very end of the Chena Hot Spring Road near Mile 57.

ELLIOT HIGHWAY
152 Miles (245 Kilometers)

If the Chena Hot Springs road is the most civilized of these routes north of Fairbanks the Elliot Highway is the quietest, at least once you pass the Dalton Highway Junction. The Elliot Highway leaves the Steese Highway at Mile 11 at the Fox junction. From there it leads northeast to Livengood. Just past Livengood the Dalton Highway turns north to the Arctic Ocean while the Elliot Highway heads westward to Manley Hot Springs.

The Elliot Highway is paved as far as the Dalton Highway Junction at Mile 73. After the Dalton junction the road is much narrower and often rough but still suitable for all rigs. The Elliott follows ridge tops west with vistas to the south across the extensive Minto Flats. Many people camp at an unofficial campground at Mile 75 at the Tolovana River Bridge. A side road at Mile 110 leads 10 miles south to **Minto**, an Athabaskan Indian village. Another side road at Mile 131 leads north to the gold-mining district of **Eureka**.

Finally at Mile 152 the highway reaches **Manley Hot Springs**. The hot springs and town were developed in the early 1900's to service nearby gold fields at Tofty and Eureka. Access to the Tanana River made the town a supply center. Today there are some 100 residents. Dry camping is allowed at the small city park in town just west of the slough bridge. There are firepits, picnic tables, and an outhouse. The Manley Roadhouse has tent and RV camping, a restaurant and bar, showers, and a liquor

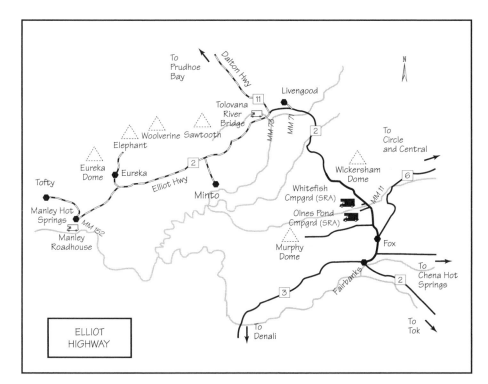

ELLIOT
HIGHWAY

store. The resort at Manly is closed but it is still possible to have a hot soak. Check at the greenhouse run by Chuck and Gladys Dart, it has some spring-fed concrete baths.

From Manley Hot Springs an access road leads 16 miles into the **Tofty** mining area. Mining continues in the district.

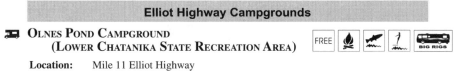

Elliot Highway Campgrounds

OLNES POND CAMPGROUND
(LOWER CHATANIKA STATE RECREATION AREA)   FREE

Location: Mile 11 Elliot Highway

GPS Location: N 65° 04' 36.4", W 147° 44' 47.6"

Olnes Pond is one of the Alaska state campgrounds that has been put on "passive management" status. That means it's not maintained at all so there is no charge. Don't depend upon any services and be prepared for vandalized toilets and other facilities.

This large gravel pit filled with a small lake is a good campground for folks with swimming-age children. Gravel pits are often popular central Alaska destinations since the good interior weather makes them warm enough for swimming by about the first of July. Make sure you take precautions against swimmers itch, however, there is a sign board explaining the phenomena and how to deal with it at the campground.

This is a popular day trip destination as well as a campground so there are large parking lots that can also be used for camping. There are dedicated campsites dotted around the lake along the surrounding tree line, we counted 15 of them. There's quite a bit of room here, big rigs should have no problem finding a good spot to park. The outhouse were usable but grim last time we visited, they probably won't be usable much longer.

To reach the campground follow the road south from the Elliot Highway at about Mile 11. The good entry road is about 1.1 miles (1.8 km) long.

 **WHITEFISH CAMPGROUND**
(LOWER CHATANIKA STATE RECREATION AREA)

Location: Mile 11 Elliot Highway

GPS Location: N 65° 05' 10.2", W 147° 43' 53.0"

This campground along the Chatanika River is a popular place to spearfish for whitefish in the fall, it is also the take-out point for canoeists on the Chatanika River. It, like nearby Olnes Pond which is described above, is "passively managed" so it's free and no longer has useable outhouses or picnic tables.

The campground has about 27 camping spots. Sites are suitable for rigs to about 30 feet. Eleven were formal sites, the remainder are just slots in the parking lot near the boat launch area.

The campground is located about a half-mile past the turnoff to Olnes Pond on the Elliott Highway at Mile 11. If you are coming from Fairbanks turn left just after crossing the bridge.

DALTON HIGHWAY
420 Miles (677 Kilometers)

The North Slope Haul Road, now called the Dalton Highway, is one of the few remaining highways in the U.S. through really remote country. It is now open to tourist traffic all the way to Deadhorse. Along the highway you will find spectacular scenery as well as lots of opportunities for fishing, hiking, wildlife viewing, and just plain experiencing really empty country. Often you'll have nothing but the road and the pipeline to keep you company.

You should check road conditions before heading north. Call the Alaska Department of Transportation at (907) 456-7623 for recorded information or the Alaska Public Lands Information Center at (907) 456-0527.

The Dalton Highway demands preparation. The road surface is gravel and often in poor condition. Travelers should carry at least two mounted spare tires of each size required and any equipment necessary to change them. Your vehicle must be in excellent mechanical condition. Gasoline stops are few and far between, as are service facilities. If you do break down be prepared to pay a hefty price for tow service. Heavy trucks commonly travel the highway so tourists should exercise caution.

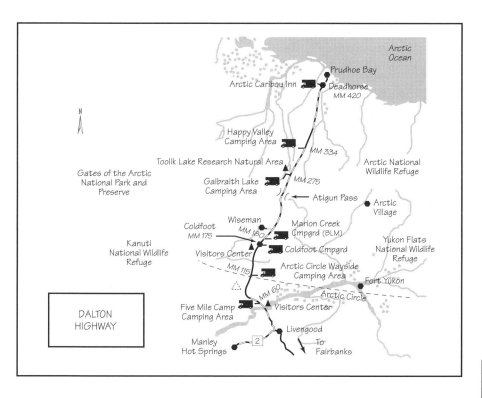

Drive with your lights on at all times. In the event of a breakdown the truckers can relay messages, the commonly used CB channel is 19.

Mileages on the Dalton start at the southern end where the highway leaves the Elliott Highway at Mile 73. Gasoline and services are available at three locations: the **Yukon Crossing** at Mile 56, **Coldfoot** at Mile 175, and **Deadhorse** at Mile 420. Note the 245-mile gap between Coldfoot and Deadhorse.

While not widely known a few sections of the road are paved and more is being completed each year. As you head north gravel starts at the junction with the Elliott Highway at Mile 1 which is 73 miles north of Fairbanks. There's a paved section from Mile 19 to Mile 24 before you reach the Yukon River. Then there's a long section from about Mile 90 to Mile 175 which is just beyond Coldfoot. There are a few other short sections of seal-coated road, some badly worn, including a long section from Mile 334 near Happy Valley to Mile 362 just past Pump Station 2.

Much of the land that the Dalton Highway crosses is public lands. From the Yukon River crossing north to Mile 301 there is a 24-mile-wide utility corridor that is administered by the BLM. To the east along the Yukon River is the **Yukon Flats National Wildlife Refuge**. West of the highway at about Mile 115 is the **Kanuti National Wildlife Refuge**. West of the highway, this time in the Brooks Range, is the **Gates of the Arctic National Park and Preserve**. Finally, east of the highway through the Brooks Range and north to the ocean is the **Arctic National Wildlife**

THE PIPELINE FOLLOWS THE DALTON SOUTH FROM DEADHORSE

Refuge. Information and administrative offices are at the Yukon River Crossing Visitor Contact Station at Mile 56 and the Coldfoot Interagency Visitor Center at Mile 175. Both can provide lots of information about the road, the surrounding country, and recreational opportunities.

There is a historic gold mining area on the Dalton too. The strike at Coldfoot was in 1900, everyone later moved to a new strike at Wiseman. You'll still find some mining activity there as well as a few tourist oriented businesses but no campground.

Once you get to Prudhoe Bay you will find that you can not enter the oil fields and can not drive to the Arctic Ocean. The only access is through an authorized tour company. Check with the Arctic Caribou Inn or the Prudhoe Bay Hotel for tours. You can call the tour companies direct: Tour Arctic/NANA (907 659-2368) or Prudhoe Bay Hotel Tours (907 659-2449).

Dalton Highway Campgrounds

Formal camping facilities along the Dalton Highway are extremely limited. The only commercial campground is in Coldfoot at Mile 175. **Coldfoot Camp** has electrical hookups, water and showers as well as a dump station. At Mile 60.7, five miles north of the Yukon River, there is an old pipeline-camp gravel pad where camping is allowed, facilities include an artesian spring for water, and a dump station. There is also a BLM camping area near **Arctic Circle Wayside** in a revegetated gravel pit at Mile 115 with outhouses but no water. The BLM has a formal campground near

Coldfoot at Mile 179.5. This is called **Marion Creek Campground** and has pull-thru and back-in sites with picnic tables, firepits, a well, and vault toilets. **Galbraith Lake** at Mile 275 is another old pipeline-camp gravel pad, there is an outhouse but no water. There's also a large gravel area suitable for camping at **Happy Valley** at Mile 334.5 with no facilities or water. RVers tend to camp pretty much anywhere that looks good, make sure not to block the pipeline maintenance access roads and do not camp in the Toolik Lake Research Natural Area between Mile 278 and Mile 293. At Deadhorse, the end of the road for tourists, RV parking with electric hookups is available at the **Caribou Inn**, there's a water fill and dump station nearby.

FIVE MILE CAMP CAMPING AREA (BLM)

Location: Mile 60.7 of the Dalton Highway

GPS Location: N 65° 55' 07.2", W 149° 49' 42.6"

Located 5 miles north of the bridge over the Yukon, this camping area was the location of Five Mile Camp when the pipeline was under construction. Reader boards at the camping area describe the camps along the highway during the pipeline construction and their operation.

The camping area is a large gravel area, not completely flat but with lots of flat areas to park any size rig. There is a dump station just north of the parking area along the access road, one of only two available along the Dalton Highway. There is also an artesian well and hose for water nearby. Just .3 mile south of the campground is a commercial roadhouse called the Hotspot Café with restaurant, gift shop, restrooms, and gas sales.

The access road to the campground goes east from the Dalton Highway 5 miles north of the Yukon bridge near mile 60.7. It's .2 mile from the highway to the camping area.

ARCTIC CIRCLE WAYSIDE CAMPING AREA (BLM)

Location: Mile 115 of the Dalton Highway

GPS Location: N 66° 33' 29.7", W 150° 47' 35.3"

Where the highway crosses the Arctic Circle there is a formal rest stop with parking, vault toilets, and some nice picnic areas with tables. From the north end of the rest stop a gravel road goes east for a half mile to a camping area. Gravel roads loop through an area of willows and young cottonwoods, the only formal facility is an outhouse. Any size rig can access the camping area and park.

COLDFOOT CAMP

Address: PO Box 81512, Fairbanks, AK 99708
Telephone: (907) 474-3500
Website: www.coldfootcamp

GPS Location: N 67° 15' 04.6", W 150° 10' 24.5"

Coldfoot Camp is the only hookup campground along the highway. There is a restaurant and gas station here, a small motel called the Slate Creek Inn, and the camping area. At the café there is a telephone a laundromat, showers, and a very small store. Across the highway is the new Arctic Interagency Visitor's Center which has exhibits, a book store, and staff to answer your questions about the area.

The camping area has about ten sites with 20 amp electrical outlets and water. It is located in an open gravel area about a hundred yards northeast of the restaurant and motel. The camping fee includes two showers. There is also a dump station.

The campground is on the east side of the highway at Mile 175.

▣ MARION CREEK CAMPGROUND (BLM)

Location: Mile 179.5 of the Dalton Highway

GPS Location: N 67° 18' 57.9", W 150° 09' 34.0"

This is a modern BLM campground designed for big rigs. There are 27 sites. Many are pull-thrus suitable for any size rig. A few of the smaller back-in sites have tent platforms and all have picnic tables and fire pits. Restrooms are vault toilets and there's a water pump. This campground has a host and a bear-proof storage bin. It is locate on the east side of the highway at Mile 179.5.

▣ GALBRAITH LAKE CAMPING AREA (BLM)

Location: Mile 274.7 of the Dalton Highway

GPS Location: N 68° 27' 13.8", W 149° 28' 55.0"

This camping areas is the former site of the Galbraith Camp. It's a large flat gravel area with outhouses and bear-proof food lockers. Any size rig can park here. The campground is about four miles off the highway to the west with an access road leading past the Galbraith airstrip.

MUSKOXEN AT FRANKLIN BLUFFS NEAR DEADHORSE

HAPPY VALLEY CAMPING AREA (BLM)

Location: Mile 334.5 of the Dalton Highway

GPS Location: N 69° 09' 02.4", W 148° 49' 30.6"

This is another former pipeline camp. On the east side of the highway is the airstrip and a number of cabins. To the west is an open gravel area where it is possible to get some distance from the highway with lots of room to park overnight. There are no facilities and this isn't a formal campground.

ARCTIC CARIBOU INN

Address: P.O. Box 340111, Prudhoe Bay, Alaska 99734
Telephone: (877) 659-2368 or (907) 659-2368
Email: info@arcticcaribouinn.com
Website: www.arcticcaribouinn.com

GPS Location: N 70° 12' 07.0", W 148° 27' 55.2"

This Atco-building style hotel caters to tour groups and other tourists during the summer. They serve as the headquarters for most Prudhoe Bay tourists. In addition to a camping area they have pipeline-camp style buffet food and rental rooms. If you want to book a tour to visit the Arctic Ocean you can do it here.

The camping area here consists of parallel parking along a "rack". Racks are pipe structures designed to mount the electrical connectors used to power heaters that keep engines warm when not running during the Arctic winter. There's room for about ten good size rigs along the rack. There are electrical hookups. Showers cost an additional $10 per person. Water fill and dump facilities (grey water only) are available at Nana Services nearby but the price is $15 per dump. Tent camping is not an option here, there are too many wandering bears.

As you come into Deadhorse you'll find that you've entered an area of huge storage yards filled with oil exploration and production equipment. Follow signs to the Arctic Caribou Inn. It's near the airport.

NORTH OF FAIRBANKS DUMP STATIONS

There's a definite shortage of dump stations north of Fairbanks with the possible exception of the Dalton Highway. There is a dump station at the camping area at Mile 60.7, one at the commercial campground in Coldfoot (sometimes not working), and one in Deadhorse (grey water only, pricey). Be sure to empty your tanks in Fairbanks before you head north.

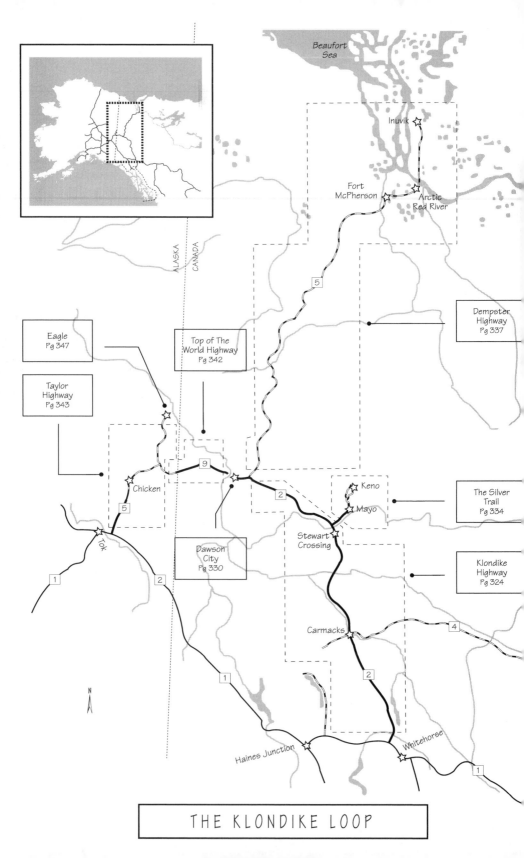

THE KLONDIKE LOOP

Chapter 11

The Klondike Loop

INTRODUCTION

A series of three different highways form a half-loop north of the Alaska Highway from Whitehorse to Tok. They are a not-to-be-missed alternate to the Alaska Highway. We recommend that travelers from the Lower 48 plan to drive the Klondike Loop one way and the Alaska Highway between Whitehorse and Tok the other. However, a warning is in order. When it's wet the 45 miles (73 km) of gravel road between the Alaska border and the beginning of the pavement near Chicken can be difficult, perhaps even downright dangerous for large coaches and trailers. If the weather is wet and you're driving a big rig you should consider driving to Dawson City and then backtracking rather than making the loop. See the Taylor Highway section for more about this.

The Klondike Loop is really three highways. From Whitehorse north to Dawson City in the Yukon you follow the Klondike Highway, the distance is 527 km (327 miles). Then, from Dawson City west for 127 km (78 miles) and across the Alaska-Canada border there is the Top of the World Highway. Finally, in Alaska, the route follows a portion of the Taylor Highway 155 kilometers (96 miles) south. The Taylor really runs from the Alaska Highway near Tok north to Eagle, in this chapter we'll cover that entire highway since Eagle in an interesting destination in its own right.

The Klondike Loop visits true gold rush country. The 1896 Klondike strike was made in the creeks near Dawson City. Many of the Klondike Argonauts traveled on the Yukon River from Whitehorse to Dawson City. The Klondike Highway from

Whitehorse to Dawson City follows this general route, although it follows the much straighter path that was historically a winter trail and gets you there much faster.

Highlights

Gold and the gold rushes are a big part of Alaska and the Yukon, past and present. There was no bigger or more famous rush than Dawson's Klondike rush. Even though the town is really in Canada no visit to Alaska would be complete without a visit to **Dawson City**.

A short but pleasant side trip is the **Silver Trail**. The big mines in the area are shuttered but a few of the people and the history are still there. It's a great chance to visit some small friendly towns off the main highway.

The 742 km (460-mile) **Dempster Highway** heads north from a junction near Dawson City. This is one of only two opportunities in the Yukon and Alaska to drive north of the Arctic Circle and approach the coast of the Arctic Ocean. The Dempster ends at **Inuvik**, from there you can easily fly to other arctic destinations in the area.

A trip along the **Top of the World Highway** isn't to be missed. It comes complete with a ferry crossing of the Yukon River.

Eagle, Alaska is like no other small town in the state. Eagle is truly at the end of the road, but at one time it was in the center of the action. There's lots of history to see and friendly folks to show it to you.

 Fuel

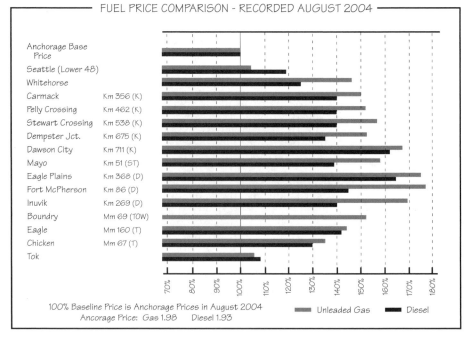

FUEL PRICE COMPARISON - RECORDED AUGUST 2004

Anchorage Base Price		
Seattle (Lower 48)		
Whitehorse		
Carmack	Km 356 (K)	
Pelly Crossing	Km 462 (K)	
Stewart Crossing	Km 538 (K)	
Dempster Jct.	Km 675 (K)	
Dawson City	Km 711 (K)	
Mayo	Km 51 (ST)	
Eagle Plains	Km 368 (D)	
Fort McPherson	Km 86 (D)	
Inuvik	Km 269 (D)	
Boundry	Mm 69 (TOW)	
Eagle	Mm 160 (T)	
Chicken	Mm 67 (T)	
Tok		

70% 80% 90% 100% 110% 120% 130% 140% 150% 160% 170% 180%

100% Baseline Price is Anchorage Prices in August 2004   ▬ Unleaded Gas   ▬ Diesel
Ancorage Price: Gas 1.98   Diesel 1.93

Fishing

Along the Klondike Highway between Whitehorse and Dawson give these waters a try: **Lake Leberge** (Km 225) for lake trout, grayling, and northern pike; **Fox Creek** (Km 228) for grayling; **Fox Lake** (Km 248) for lake trout, grayling and northern pike; **Little Fox Lake** (Km 259) for lake trout, grayling, and northern pike; **Braeburn Lake** (Km 282) for lake trout, grayling, and northern pike; **Twin Lakes** (Km 308) for lake trout, grayling, northern pike; **Nordenskiold River** (Km 354) for grayling; **Tatchun Creek** (Km 382) for grayling; **Tatchun Lake** (take 6 km road at Km 382) for northern pike; **Crooked Creek** (Km 523) for grayling; **Moose Creek** (Km 560) for grayling; **McQuesten River** (Km 582) for grayling; **Klondike River** (Km 698) for grayling; and finally, the **Klondike River mouth** at Dawson City for grayling.

In Alaska the **Fortymile River** has grayling, try Mile 43, Mile 64, Mile 75, and Mile 81 of the Taylor Highway. Also try **Four Mile Lake** at Mile 4 of the Taylor Highway for rainbows, it is reached along a 1-mile (1.6-km) trail.

Boating, Rafting, Canoeing, and Kayaking

The **Yukon River** was the original highway in this country and it continues to be an excellent float trip. It is actually possible to travel the river from the upper end of the Chilkoot Trail at Lake Bennett downstream all the way to the mouth of the river in far western Alaska. Most people limit their trip to the section from Marsh Lake or Whitehorse to Dawson City or Eagle. Access to the river and the logistics of the drop-off and pick-up are easiest on this route. The Whitehorse to Dawson City section is easily done in a canoe, they can be rented in Whitehorse and arrangements made for a pick-up in Dawson City. Plan on about 2 weeks to make the trip to allow plenty of time to explore old gold rush settlements and relics along the way. The river has little in the way of challenges other than a 51-kilometer (32-mile) crossing of Lake Laberge where it is best to stay near the west shore for safety in the event of sudden winds. See chapter 14 for more about this.

The **Fortymile River** is a designated National Wild and Scenic River. It is rated Class II to Class III with rapids to Class IV. Experienced paddlers can float this river in canoes but inflatables are probably best. Put-in points include the four bridges along the Taylor Highway with the take-out near Clinton which is near the Yukon at the end of a 25-mile (40-km) road from Km 59 of the Top Of The World Highway. For information including current river conditions contact: BLM, Tok Field Office, PO Box 309, Tok, Alaska 99780; (907) 883-5121.

Hiking and Mountain Biking

There is a hiking trail from the south end of the Yukon River bridge at Km 357 of the Klondike Highway near Carmacks. It follows the river to **Coal Mine Lake**. Across the river is **Tantalus Butte**, known for its coal seams that were mined for riverboat fuel.

From an overlook at Km 379 there is a good trail down the bluff to the **Five-Finger Rapids** of the Yukon River. Two-hundred and twenty stairs from the highway down to the floor of the valley make this a short but challenging hike, particularly on the way back.

THE KLONDIKE LOOP

Around Dawson City there are several interesting walks. The **sternwheeler grave-yard** is on the west bank of the Yukon River. The trail begins at the Yukon River Campground. Follow the campground loop road as far downstream as possible, then the riverbank. You'll find three abandoned and deteriorated riverboats pulled up on the bank.

There's a trail to the top of **Midnight Dome** where you will find excellent views over Dawson City and the Yukon River. The trail is on the left just after you start up the Old Dome Road at the east end of King Street. It is also possible to drive to the top of Midnight Dome, the New Dome Road cuts off the main highway just outside Dawson.

The "creeks" make an interesting place to explore on foot or mountain bike. Two long gravel loop roads (one off the other) and several access roads leading off them let you explore **Eldorado Creek, Sulphur Creek, Dominion Creek, and Hunker Creek**; all very historic ground although much of it has been dredged in the years since the original 98 rush. A hiking route called the **Ridge Road Trail** runs through the area.

THE ROUTES, TOWNS, AND CAMPGROUNDS

KLONDIKE HIGHWAY
520 Kilometers (322 Miles)

About 13 km (8 miles) north of Whitehorse Alaska-bound travelers have a choice. They can continue north on the Alaska Highway or turn right and head for Dawson City along what is called the Klondike Loop. If the road beyond Dawson City has been cleared of snow and is open you should consider visiting Dawson City on your way north, early fall snows could make a trip on the Top of the World Highway a real trial in September. On the other hand, if you plan to return south before September you can wait until then to visit Dawson.

The Klondike Highway (Yukon Highway 2) is an excellent paved highway. It is not difficult to drive the entire distance from Whitehorse to Dawson in one day in any rig. Don't be in a hurry, however, this is a historic route and there are some good places to do some exploring.

Because the Klondike Highway is in Canada it is marked in kilometers. The highway really starts in Skagway, so the kilometer marker at the beginning of this route near Whitehorse is the 192 km marker.

The first junction, at Km 198, will take you west to **Takhini Hot Springs**. The campground at the hot springs is listed in this book under Whitehorse campgrounds because it is not far from that city. The hot springs are worth a stop even if you decide not to camp there.

After passing the Takhini Hot Springs Cutoff the highway passes along the west side of **Lake Laberge**. You will probably recognize this lake as Lake Lebarge from Robert Service's poem "The Cremation of Sam McGee". Unfortunately the big lake

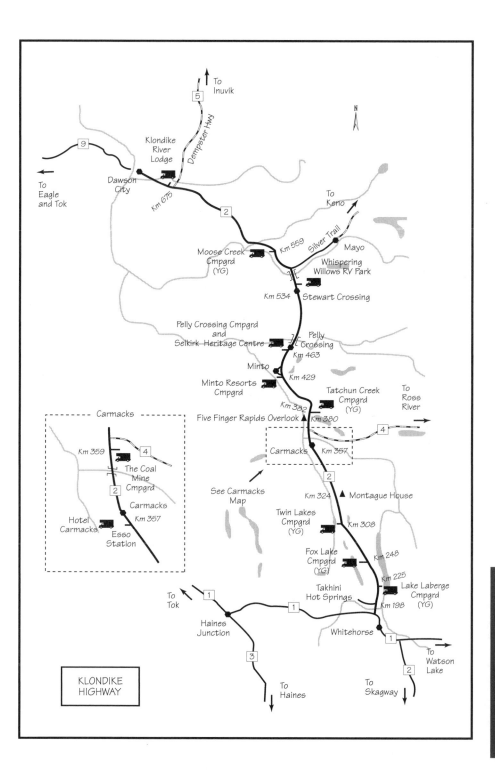

isn't really visible from the road. You can drive down to the lake and take a look at Lake Laberge Campground at Km 225. Lake Laberge was well-known to Klondike travelers since the big lake was the last part of the water route from Whitehorse to Dawson to thaw in the spring.

Like the Richardson Highway in Alaska the Klondike Highway had a series of road-houses to serve travelers in early days. The **Montague House** at Km 324 was one of these.

Carmacks at Km 357 was the location of a trading post founded by one of the three men who made the first gold discovery on the Klondike. George Carmack settled in Carmacks in 1892. Now there's a campground at Carmacks, not to mention other services. It is possible to take a boat tour from there through Five Finger Rapids.

A large pull-off at Km 380 gives a great view of **Five Finger Rapids** far below. These rapids were run by huge sternwheelers. The riverboats didn't have enough power to pass through going upstream so they were winched up on a cable. There is a long stairway and a trail leading from the overlook down to the rapids.

Fort Selkirk was an important trading post along the Yukon. It was originally founded for the Hudson's Bay Company in 1848. Now abandoned, the fort can only be reached by water. Boat tours are available from both Minto (Km 429) and Pelly Crossing (Km 463).

Silver was also mined in this part of the world. Follow the **Silver Trail** east from Km 535 at Stewart Crossing. It will take you to Mayo, Elsa and Keno City, a distance of 111 km (69 miles) one way. The first 58 km (36 miles), to just beyond Mayo, are paved. There are several campgrounds on this routes, see the Silver Trail section in this chapter for information about them.

At Km 675 you'll reach the junction with the **Dempster Highway**. The Highway and its campgrounds are described in the Dempster Highway section in this chapter. Then, in just 37 more kilometers (23 miles) you'll reach the outskirts of Dawson City.

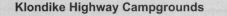

Klondike Highway Campgrounds

🚐 **LAKE LABERGE CAMPGROUND (YUKON GOV.)**
    Location: Km 225 Northern Klondike Highway

GPS Location: N 61° 04' 30.3", W 135° 11' 53.4"

The campground has 16 vehicle sites and additional tent sites. Some are back-ins and others are pull-thru parallel parking type sites around a gravel area near the lake adjoining a boat launch. The campground is good for rigs to about 30 feet due to restricted maneuvering room. Sites have picnic tables and firepits. The campground also offers outhouses, a kitchen/picnic shelter, drinking water, and free firewood.

🚐 **FOX LAKE CAMPGROUND (YUKON GOV.)**
    Location: Km 248 of the Northern Klondike Highway

GPS Location: N 61° 14' 45.4", W 135° 27' 39.0"

THE KLONDIKE LOOP

This popular campground has 33 sites, 3 are tent sites and the rest are separated vehicle sites. These are mostly back-ins, some are along the lakeshore, and many will take rigs of any size. Sites are off a circular drive so even if you're towing you can go in and check for empty sites without fear of finding a dead end. All sites have picnic tables and firepits. The campground also offers outhouses, a playground, a kitchen/picnic shelter, a boat ramp, and a water faucet.

TWIN LAKES CAMPGROUND (YUKON GOV.)

Location: Km 308 Northern Klondike Highway

GPS Location: N 61° 42' 16.9", W 135° 56' 15.7"

Twin Lake Campground offers two different camping areas. The first has 10 back-in sites. They are well-separated by trees and vegetation. Another 8 sites are arranged around a gravel parking lot near one of the lakes. Some sites will take big rigs. All have picnic tables and firepits. The campground also offers a kitchen/picnic shelter, a hand-operated water pump, free firewood, a boat ramp, and a small dock.

HOTEL CARMACKS

Address: PO Box 160, Carmacks, Y.T. Y0B 1G0
Telephone: (867) 863-5221
Email: hotelcarmacks@yt.sympatico.ca

GPS Location: N 62° 05' 25.6", W 136° 16' 58.1"

This is the newest campground along this section of highway. It sits behind the hotel and Esso station but across a small road from the river. It's a relatively quiet location and a pleasant place to stay.

The campground has 25 sites. They're full-hookup sites, several are pull-thrus suitable for rigs to 40 feet. Each site has a patch of grass and a picnic table, some of the back-ins have trees too. The campground has a dump station. The restrooms are in the hotel building, there's also a restaurant.

The hotel is located near Km 357 of the Northern Klondike Highway. This is in the community of Carmacks.

THE COAL MINE CAMPGROUND

Address: PO Box 110, Carmacks, Y.T. Y0B 1C0
Telephone: (867) 863-6363

GPS Location: N 62° 06' 39.3", W 136° 16' 04.3"

This small campground along the shore of the Yukon River provides tent-camping sites that are very popular with folks floating the Yukon. The sites are scattered in the trees along the river. There are also three back-in parking slots for rigs to about 30 feet. There is a floating dock to ease the loading and unloading process for canoeists but RVers will probably be more interested in the small building with flush toilets, hot showers, and laundry. There is a dump station and also a snack bar.

Watch for the campground on the east side of the highway near Km 359. This is north of the bridge over the Yukon and just south of the cutoff to Ross River on the Robert Campbell Highway, about 3 km (2 miles) north of Carmacks.

THE KLONDIKE LOOP

◻ TATCHUN CREEK CAMPGROUND (YUKON GOV.)

Location: Km 382 of the North Klondike Highway

GPS Location: N 62° 17' 00.4", W 136° 18' 22.8"

The campground has 12 spaces, four are pull-thrus and there are several tent sites near the river. Trees and natural vegetation separate the spaces. Each space has a picnic table and firepit, there are outhouses, a hand-operated water pump, a kitchen/picnic shelter, and free firewood. Some sites will take a 40 foot rig and there is a turnaround so even if you're towing you can go in and check for empty sites without fear of finding a dead end.

◻ MINTO RESORT CAMPGROUND

Address: PO Box 9211, Whitehorse, Y.T.
                    Y1A 4A2, (res.)
Telephone: (867) 633-5537 (res.)

GPS Location: N 62° 35' 01.7", W 136° 51' 06.4"

Minto Resorts Campground has a very pleasant location along the bank of the Yukon River. You can relax on benches in a grassy area overlooking the river. There are also hot showers and flush toilets. The resort also caters to tour busses.

Minto is a popular spot to take an excellent river tour to Fort Selkirk, about 40 km (25 miles) downstream. The fort is abandoned but in reasonably good shape. It was founded by the Hudson's Bay Company in 1848 and finally abandoned in the 1950s at which time it was one of the oldest communities in the Yukon. Tours are also available from Pelly Crossing.

Camping sites are located away from the river overlook in a tree-covered area. There are 27 sites with no hookups, most are large pull-thrus suitable for any size rig. Picnic tables and half-barrel-type firepits are provided. The campground has coin-op hot showers, a laundry room, a dump station and potable water fill.

Look for the paved 1 km (.6 mile) driveway near Km 429 of the North Klondike Highway.

◻ PELLY CROSSING CAMPGROUND AND SELKIRK HERITAGE CENTRE

Address: Pelly Crossing, Y.T. Y0B 1PO
Telephone: (867) 537-3031

GPS Location: N 62° 49' 32.6", W 136° 34' 45.5"

If you don't feel the need for hookups but do like having other amenities handy Pelly Crossing Campground is a decent choice. The campground is along the river south of the bridge, you can't miss it. It's just about halfway between Whitehorse and Dawson City. Across the street is Selkirk Center with gas and groceries. Next to it is the Selkirk Heritage Centre, a replica of Big Jonathan House at Fort Selkirk, exhibits explain the First Nation history of the area. Many of the residents moved here from Fort Selkirk which is located downstream where the Pelly runs into the Yukon River. Boat tours to the fort are available from Pelly Crossing and also from Minto as mentioned above.

The campground has about 20 sites with picnic tables and fire pits. Some are suitable for any size rig. Across the highway at Selkirk Centre is a gas station and store, it serves as a commercial center for the community. In addition to the small store there is a laundromat, showers, motel, and public telephone. You'll even find a dump station, free if you fill up on fuel.

The campground is near Km 463 on the south end of the bridge over the Pelly River.

WHISPERING WILLOWS RV PARK

Address:	PO Box 36, Mayo, Y.T. Y0B 1M0
Telephone:	(867) 996-2284
Fax:	(867) 996-2422

GPS Location: N 63° 22' 39.0", W 136° 40' 45.8"

This is one of the few campgrounds with hookups between Whitehorse and the Dawson City.

The Whispering Willows has 32 sites with water and electric hookups on a gravel lot with some grass. There is plenty of room for rigs to 40 feet. There are also dry sites. Picnic tables, fire pits, and firewood are provided. The campground has flush toilets, hot showers (extra fee), a coin-op laundry, and a dump station. There's also a restaurant.

The campground is located at Km 534 of the North Klondike Highway.

MOOSE CREEK CAMPGROUND (YUKON GOV.)

| **Location:** | Km 559 of the North Klondike Highway |

GPS Location: N 63° 30' 36.0", W 137° 01' 41.1"

The campground has 36 spaces, most are large sites suitable for big rigs. Six are tent sites, 4 are pull-thrus, and the remainder are back-in spaces. Aspens and natural vegetation separate the spaces. Each space has a picnic table and firepit, there are outhouses, a hand-operated water pump, a children's playground, and free firewood. A trail leads to fishing at Moose Creek.

KLONDIKE RIVER LODGE

| **Address:** | Box 69, Dawson City, Y.T. Y0B 1G0 |
| **Telephone:** | (867) 993-6892 |

GPS Location: N 63° 59' 27.9", W 138° 45' 00.7"

The Klondike River Lodge is a roadhouse with a cafe, motel, and gas sales. They also have about 28 RV sites. There are both full-hookup and partial hookup sites, they're suitable for any size rig. The sites are located in a gravel lot next to the main building. There are also coin-op hot showers, a coin-op laundromat, a dump station, and a coin-op pressure vehicle wash. For travelers on the Dempster this is often the last stop to get fuel before heading east and the first stop after traveling the Dempster to blast off the thick coating of dirt accumulated on all those miles of gravel road.

The Lodge is located at the junction of the North Klondike Highway and the Dempster Highway. This is at Km 675 of the Klondike Highway, about 40 km (25 miles) from Dawson City.

THE KLONDIKE LOOP

Dawson City
Population 2,000, Elevation 1,050 feet

There's lots to see and do in Dawson. You could reasonably say that the whole place is devoted to providing entertainment for visitors. This wasn't always the case, of course. When Skookum Jim, Tagish Charlie and George Carmack discovered gold on nearby Rabbit Creek in 1896 the Klondike River was best known as a good place to catch salmon. Two years later there was a population of 30,000 people in Dawson City and the surrounding creeks. A year later many of these prospectors had gone home or moved on to new strikes like Nome and the town settled into a long decline. When the Alaska Highway was built through Whitehorse, Dawson eventually became a virtual ghost town.

Today the population of Dawson City explodes in the summer when the tourists arrive and the Top of the World Highway opens.

While you're in Dawson there will be lots to keep you busy. The **Gaslight Follies** are performed in the reconstructed **Palace Grand Theater**. At **Diamond Tooth Gertie's** you can gamble in a saloon much like those of 1898. There are also many interesting historical sites to visit. You can get full information at the **Dawson Visitor Reception Centre** (PO Box 389, Dawson City, Yukon Y0B 1G0, Canada; 867 993-5566) on Front Street, they also have walking tours. Places you'll probably want to visit are

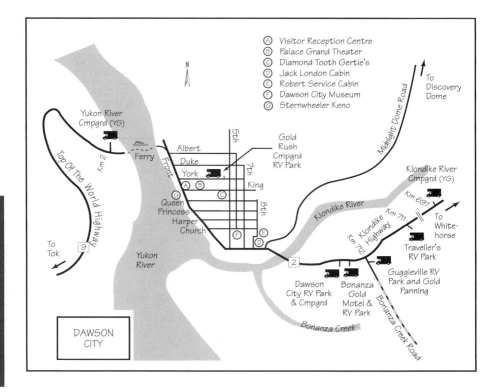

the **cabins of both Jack London and Robert Service**, the **Dawson City Museum** in the old Territorial Administration Building and the old **sternwheeler Keno** down by the waterfront.

If you find the Keno interesting you might want to visit Dawson's **sternwheeler graveyard**, it's on the far side of the river just downstream from the campground. You can walk along the river to get there. If you really get intrigued by Yukon river travel there's also a tour boat operated by Westours (not a sternwheeler) that runs all the way to **Eagle.**

The gold didn't really come from Dawson, it came from the "creeks" located to the southeast. You can drive through the mining area by taking the **Bonanza Creek Road** at Km 712 of the Klondike Highway, just a kilometer or two from town. Twelve kilometers (8 miles) out this road is **Dredge #4** and at Km 15 is the **Original Discovery Claim** on Rabbit (now Eldorado) Creek. There's an area open to gold-panning here that is run by the visitor's association. Smaller vehicles or mountain bikers can make a 96-kilometer (60-mile) loop that takes them along Upper Bonanza Creek Road past **King Solomon Dome** and back down Hunker Creek to the Klondike Highway. There's also an additional loop for the truly adventurous who want to see Sulphur and Dominion Creeks. The total of the two loops is 164 kilometers (102 miles). While you're out exploring the creeks you might want to stop and see **Bear Creek Historical Site** at Km 705 of the Klondike Highway. The Canadian park service operates this Klondike National Historical Site that shows the way of life during the industrial era of the gold fields from 1905 to 1966 when the dredges replaced the original drift-mining techniques.

Also just outside town is the 8-kilometer (5-mile) road up to **Discovery Dome** for a view over the town.

Dawson City Campgrounds

🚐 **YUKON RIVER CAMPGROUND (YUKON GOV.)** $$$ 🔥 ⛺ 🥾

    Location: Directly across Yukon River from Dawson City

GPS Location: N 64° 04' 20.2", W 139° 26' 17.5"

This is a nice Dawson City campground with only one problem, it is a ferry ride away from the town. If you don't mind a short stroll there's no real problem. The ferry runs very frequently, it's free, and there should be no wait for walk-on passengers. From the campground you can easily walk downriver a short distance along the bank to the sternwheeler graveyard. You'll find three sternwheelers pulled up on the bank although they've deteriorated to the point that they're almost unrecognizable as boats.

The campground has almost 95 spaces, about 75 vehicle spaces and the remainder tent sites. Many of the spaces are pull-thrus and some spaces are right along the river. Trees and natural vegetation separate the spaces. Each one has a picnic table and firepit, there are outhouses, hand-operated water pumps, a children's playground, a boat launch, and free firewood. Since this is a busy place it often has an attendant to collect fees, unlike most Yukon Government campgrounds.

The campground is located about .3 kilometers (.2 miles) up the hill from the ferry landing area on the north side of the road.

🚐 Gold Rush Campground RV Park

Address: PO Box 198, Dawson City, Y.T. Y0B 1G0
Telephone: (867) 993-5247 **Fax:** (867) 993-6047
Email: goldrush@cityofdawson.ca
Website: www.goldrushcampground.com

GPS Location: N 64° 03' 46.7", W 139° 25' 36.9"

The Gold Rush is the only campground located conveniently right in Dawson City.

There are about 80 sites, mostly back-ins and a few pull-thrus, any size rig can find a site that will work. Thirty-amp and 15-amp power are available as is water but not sewer hookups, there is also a dump station. For a fee the dump station is available to those not staying at the campground. There are hot showers (token required), a laundromat, and a telephone.

The campground is located at the corner of Fifth Ave. and York, about two blocks from Diamond Tooth Gertie's and near most other popular city destinations.

🚐 Dawson City RV Park and Campground

Address: Box 750, Dawson City, Y.T. Y0B 1G0
**Telephone
and Fax:** (867) 993-5142
Email: dawsonrvpark@netscape.net
Website: www.dawsoncityrvpark.com

GPS Location: N 64° 02' 29.2", W 139° 24' 26.2"

The second closest campground to town is this one (not counting the one on the far side of the river). It is located with two others on the dredge tailing piles just outside town. You can tell this is the place because there's a mammoth out front near the highway.

The campground has over 50 sites with electricity (15 or 30 amp) and water, some have sewer, and many more dry vehicle sites and tent sites. Some sites will take large rigs. The tent sites are in a tree-shaded area and one of the best places to stay in town for tent camping. There's a modern washroom building with individual shower rooms (extra fee). Other services include dump station, laundromat, coin-operated vehicle wash, a service station, and a small grocery store. The pay phone here also offers a modem port.

Dawson City RV Park is located near Km 712 of the North Klondike Highway, about 2.3 kilometers (1.4 miles) outside the city.

🚐 Bonanza Gold Motel and RV Park

Address: Bag 5000, Dawson City, Y.T. Y0B 1G0
Telephone: (867) 993-6789 or (888) 993-6789
Email: bonanzagold@dawson.net
Website: www.bonanzagold.ca

GPS Location: N 64° 02' 29.2", W 139° 24' 11.4"

This newest of Dawson City campgrounds is very popular, many caravans stay here and individual campers like it too. With 50-amp power and big sites it's a favorite of those with big rigs.

The campground is a large one with some 120 sites. They are set on a large gravel lot, really flattened tailing piles from the dredges that thoroughly scoured the area in their search for gold. Hookups vary with 50, 30, and 20-amp power available. Sites will take the largest rigs. Water hookups go to most sites and sewer is available if you want it. Some sites also have TV and telephone hookups. The central building houses handicapped accessible restrooms with coin-op showers. A computer with an internet connection is in the office, Wi-Fi is available, and the pay phones have modem jacks. This facility also has motel rooms, a restaurant, and a vehicle wash.

The campground is located near Km 712 of the North Klondike Highway, about 2.4 kilometers (1.5 miles) outside the city.

🚐 GUGGIEVILLE RV PARK AND GOLD PANNING

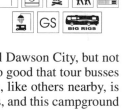

Address: Box 311, Dawson City, Y.T. Y0B 1G0
Telephone: (867) 993-5008 or (866) 860-6535
Fax: (867) 993-5006
Email: guggieville@dawson.net

GPS Location: N 64° 02' 28.0", W 139° 23' 46.0"

Sure, this is the farthest commercial campground from central Dawson City, but not by much. It's also one of the most pleasant. The gift shop is so good that tour busses stop here, and they'll show you how to pan for gold. The site, like others nearby, is located on tailing piles (gravel mounds) from the gold dredges, and this campground has a mining artifact display.

The campground has about 100 sites, 70 or so have water and either 15 or 30-amp electricity hookups, the remainder are unserviced. Some sites are pull-thrus. Many of the sites have landscaping to separate them and there are picnic tables. There's a washhouse with individual shower rooms (extra fee), a laundromat, a coin-op pressure vehicle wash, bike rentals, gold panning, free firewood, a grocery and gift store, and a dump station.

The campground is located near Km 712 of the North Klondike Highway, about 2.7 kilometers (1.7 miles) outside the city. That's right next to the intersection with the Bonanza Creek Road.

🚐 TRAVELLER'S RV PARK

Address: Bag 4000, Dawson City, Yukon
Telephone: (867) 993-2400
Email: callison@cityofdawson.ca

This large gravel lot is the simplest campground near Dawson, and among the least expensive. It's great for big rigs since nothing is in the way. There are no hookups or restrooms but water is available and there is a dump station.

Watch for the camping sign on the south side of the road near Km 711 of the North Klondike Highway.

🚐 KLONDIKE RIVER CAMPGROUND (YUKON GOV.)

Location: Km 697 of the North Klondike Highway,
                    about 18 km (11 miles) from Dawson City

GPS Location: N 64° 03' 03.5", W 139° 06' 45.3"

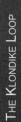

This government campground is close enough to Dawson City to use as a base for visiting the city and there is no ferry to worry about like there is for the other nearby government campground, the Yukon River Campground.

The campground has 38 spaces, a couple are pull-thrus. Some sites are long enough for large rigs. Trees and natural vegetation separate the spaces. Each space has a picnic table and firepit, there are outhouses, a hand-operated water pump, a children's playground, and free firewood. A 1 km (half-mile) interpretive trail will take you to the Rock Creek, which runs into the Klondike River.

From Dawson City drive to Km 697 of the North Klondike Highway, a distance of 19 km (12 miles).

THE SILVER TRAIL
111 Kilometers (69 Miles)

From Stewart Crossing a highway heads east on the north side of the Stewart River. This is the highway leading to the old mining towns of Mayo, Elsa, and Keno City. It's officially called The Silver Trail, Yukon Hwy. 11.

The highway begins at the north end of the Stewart Crossing bridge near Km 535 of the Klondike Highway. This is 343 km (213 miles) north of the Klondike Highway intersection with the Alaska Highway and 306 km (180 miles) south of Dawson City. The Silver Trail leads eastward for 32 miles (52 km) to a junction. If you turn right at that junction you'll reach Mayo in about 2 kilometers (1.2 mile). If you turn left the road continues on another 59 km (37 miles) to Keno City. The road is paved to a point about 6 km (4 miles) beyond the Mayo junction. Beyond that it's usually a well-maintained gravel road. Because this has been an active mining area there's a web of small roads throughout the region, many leading past small lakes offering decent fishing.

From the time of the gold rush until completion of the Silver Highway in 1955 made water transportation unnecessary Mayo was the port town for the mining district. It is the largest town in the area with a population of about 500. The riverboat Keno, now located on the dike on the waterfront in Dawson City, was one of the boats designed and built for this trade.

During the industrial production years of the silver mines in the area Elsa was the place most of the miners lived. Silver was discovered near Elsa in 1924 and large-scale production was closed down in 1989. Elsa is located 50 km (28.6 miles) beyond the junction at Mayo. It is private property and is now being watched by caretakers, visitors are not allowed.

Keno, the town at the end of the road, is also a mining town. Unlike Elsa this somewhat funky little town welcomes visitors and has quite a bit to see and do. There's an excellent museum documenting the history of the area as well as some restaurants and tourist shops, a community campground, and good hiking trails.

THE KLONDIKE LOOP

The Silver Trail Campgrounds

McINTYRE PARK
Location: Just outside Mayo

$$ \qquad \text{\$\$} \qquad \text{🔥}$$

GPS Location: N 63° 36' 15.3", W 135° 54' 04.1"

This is a small local campground located along the Mayo River just outside the town of Mayo. The sign for this campground is the first one you'll see along the Silver Trail. Locals tell us that this campground is a popular hangout for the local teenagers so it might be a little noisy some evenings.

The campground has 8 sites. Two are pull-thrus. The campground is suitable for rigs to 30 feet. Sites have picnic tables and fire rings, firewood is provided. There is also a picnic shelter and outhouses.

To reach the campground start at the intersection of Hwy. 11 with the Klondike Loop. Follow Hwy. 11 for 49.2 km (30.5 miles). The short entrance road to the campground is on the right.

BEAGLE PARK
Location: At the edge of the town of Mayo

GPS Location: N 63° 35' 43.7", W 135° 54' 03.9"

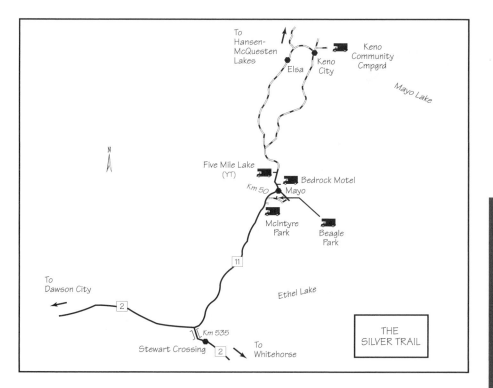

This is another small local campground. It's actually located at the edge of the town of Mayo although the entrance described below is from the road outside town. Another entrance road leads from the waterfront in Mayo.

The campground has 10 back-in sites with picnic tables and fire pits. Some sites are suitable for rigs to 40 feet although maneuvering room for that size rig is limited and this campground is best for rigs to 30 feet. There are outhouses and firewood is provided. The campground is in a grove of dense spruce so it tends to be a little dark.

To reach the campground start at the intersection of Hwy. 11 with the Klondike Loop. Follow Hwy. 11 for 49.5 km (30.6 miles). The entrance road to the campground goes right at this point. It's a long gravel road, you'll reach the first campground entrance at 1.3 km (.8 mile). The road continues another .6 km (.4 mile) to the waterfront in Mayo.

▣ BEDROCK MOTEL

Address:	PO Box 69, Mayo, Y.T. Y0B 1M0
Telephone:	(403) 996-2290
Email:	bedrock@yknet.yk.ca
Website:	www.silvertrail.net/bedrock

GPS Location: N 63° 36' 37.4", W 135° 52' 47.0"

The Bedrock Motel is the only campground with hookups on the Silver Trail. It's also the best campground for big rigs. You can easily use it as a base and explore the area with a tow car.

The Motel has a large grassy area ahead and to the right as you enter the driveway. There are three sites with full hookups and another five back-in sites offering electricity located next to one of the back buildings. All electrical outlets are 20 amp. In addition to the hookup sites there's lots of room for dry camping. The hookup sites are good for rigs to about 35 feet, all of the others will take any size rig. There is a laundry room in the motel building as well as a bathroom with a shower. There is also a restaurant here.

To reach the hotel start at the intersection of Hwy. 11 with the Klondike Loop. Follow Hwy. 11 for 50 km (31 miles) to a T junction. Mayo is to the right, you should turn left. The campground is on your right 1 km (.6 mile) from this turn.

▣ FIVE MILE LAKE (YUKON GOV.)

Location:	Between Mayo and Elsa

GPS Location: N 63° 39' 12.5", W 135° 52' 37.0"

This is a nice territorial campground that is conveniently located for exploring the Silver Trail. There are 20 sites here, most are back-ins but two are pull-thrus. Some sites are suitable for the largest rigs. The campground has picnic tables and fire rings, outhouses, a cooking shelter, and even a dock and swimming beach. Firewood is provided.

The campground is located 8 km (5 miles) from Mayo. Start at the intersection of Hwy. 11 with the Klondike Loop. Follow Hwy. 11 for 50 km (31 miles) to a T. Mayo is to the right, you should turn left. The campground is on your left 6.6 km (4.1 miles) from this turn.

Keno Community Campground
Location: In Keno

GPS Location: N 63° 54' 27.8", W 135° 18' 00.6"

This community campground is pleasantly located on the far side of Keno but within a few minute walk of the center of the little town. Lightning Creek runs alongside. There are 16 spaces here, 2 are pull-thrus. Sites are suitable for rigs to 30 feet. Sites have picnic tables and fire pits, the campground has outhouses and water, and firewood is provided.

Entering Keno you'll come to a T, turn left and then immediately right and proceed .5 km (.3 mile) to the campground entrance on your right.

DEMPSTER HIGHWAY
734 Kilometers (455 Miles)

The Dempster is Canada's road to the arctic north of the Arctic Circle. Designated as Hwy. 5 it leaves the Klondike Loop at Km 675, about 26 km from Dawson City. In length it is similar to Alaska's Dalton Highway. It is gravel and has a reputation for being especially hard on tires. You can get lots of information about the Dempster at the **Dempster Highway and Northwest Territories Information Center** (867 993-6167) in Dawson City, it is just across Front Street from the Dawson Visitor Center. No one should attempt the Dempster without a visit there for first-hand information about road conditions and ferry schedules (there are two of them along the route).

Kilometer markers start at the junction with the Klondike Highway, but they restart at 0 at the Northwest Territories border at Km 465. To try and avoid confusion most of our references below are from the intersection with the Klondike Highway, to get the real Kilometer post number just subtract 465. Gas is available at Eagle Plains (Km 369), Fort McPherson (Km 551), and at Inuvik (Km 734). Your vehicle should be in good condition with good tires and at least one spare of each size needed, two would be much better. Flying rocks can be hard on windshields so slow way down and pull over when you meet someone or when someone comes up behind you. RVers, especially those pulling trailers, should take precautions to protect their rigs from flying gravel. See Chapter 2 - *Details, Details, Details* about doing this.

There are 8 government campgrounds along the highway: **Tombstone Mountain Campground** at Km 72, **Engineer Creek Campground** at Km 193, **Rock River Campground** at Km 446, **Nitainilaii Campground** at Km 541, **Vadzaih Van Tshik Territorial Campground** at Km 685, **Gwich'n Territorial Campground** at Km 699, **Chuk Territorial Park** at Km 731 (with electrical hookups), and the **Happy Valley Territorial Campground** in Inuvik which has electrical hookups and a dump station. Additionally, there is a commercial RV campground at the **Eagle Plains Hotel** at Km 369 with electrical hookups and a dump station. All of these campgrounds are described in more detail below.

There's no question that driving the Dempster is something you'll never forget. Even more than on the Alaska Highway there are "miles and miles of miles and miles". The highway crosses true wilderness, also the Arctic Circle, the Yukon – NW Territories border, two mountain ranges, and two rivers on ferries. You'll find lots of

THE KLONDIKE LOOP

INUVIK'S IGLOO CHURCH

opportunities to see wildlife, particularly birds, and spectacular scenery but more than anything you'll probably be impressed by the sheer size of the country and the solitude.

Once you reach Inuvik (population 3,000) you might expect little to do in this isolated rainbow-colored but modern town but you just might be surprised. Inuvik was built only in 1955 when Aklavik, then the administrative center of the region, was flooded out. Inuvik's **Visitor Center** (Box 1160, Inuvik, N.T. X0E 0T0; 867 777-4321) doubles as a museum for the Inuvialuit (Eskimo) and Gwich'n (Indian) cultures that share this region. Interesting places to visit include the **Igloo Church** and the **huge new Inuvik Community Greenhouse**. The thing to do in Inuvik is to take an air-taxi trip to one of several possible destinations on the Mackenzie Delta or the Arctic coast. Check at the Northwest Territories Information Center in Dawson or the Inuvik Visitor Center for details about fly-out trips to **Hershel Island Yukon Territorial Park**, **Tuktoyaktuk**, and **Aklavik**.

An increasingly popular event in Inuvik is the 10-day **Great Northern Arts and Music Festival** held sometime during the latter half of July each year. It features artists and performers from across the Arctic. If you time your visit to catch this festival (and many RVers do) plan on lots of enthusiastic company.

Dempster Highway Campgrounds

TOMBSTONE MOUNTAIN CAMPGROUND
    Location: Km 71.5 Dempster Highway, Yukon

       GPS Location: N 64° 30' 22.1", W 138° 13' 15.4"

This campground is situated inside the Tombstone Yukon Territorial Park next to the confluence of Black Shale Creek and the North Klondike River. The highway is inside this mountain park from Km 54 to Km 100. The manned Dempster Highway Interpretive Centre is located at the entrance to the campground.

The campground has 31 sites for RVs and an additional 5 tent sites. They're back-in sites suitable for any size rigs and are located off a circular drive. Picnic tables and fire rigs are provided, there's also a shelter that is handy for tent campers. Firewood is provided. There is a good short hiking trail along the river nearby, ask at the interpretive center about other routes.

The campground is located on the north side of the highway at Km 71.5.

 **ENGINEER CREEK CAMPGROUND**
    Location: Km 193 Dempster Highway, Yukon

GPS Location: N 65° 21' 09.5", W 138° 16' 16.8"

This campground is located below Sapper Hill along Engineer Creek. The water in the creek has a lot of iron in it and as a result the rocks are colored red by the growth of mineral-loving algae.

The campground has 15 back-in sites, some are long enough for any size rig. A few of the sites are along Engineer Creek. Picnic tables and fire rings are provided. Firewood is available and there is a cooking shelter. The rock face of Sapper Hill

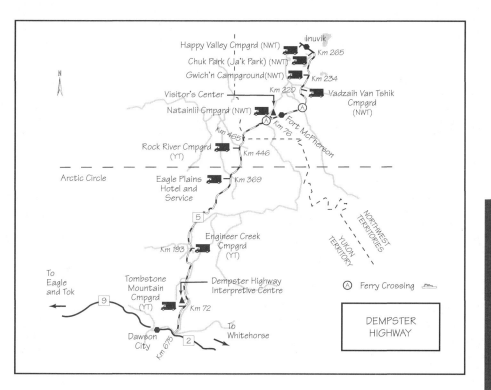

THE KLONDIKE LOOP

visible across the river from the this campground is well known as a good place to spot Peregrine falcons.

Engineer Creek Campground is on the north side of the highway near Km 193.

EAGLE PLAINS HOTEL AND SERVICE

Address:	Bag Service 2735, Whitehorse, Y.T. Y1R 3V5
Telephone:	(867) 993-2453
Email:	eagleplains@yknet.ca

GPS Location: N 66° 22' 20.6", W 136° 43' 10.2"

Despite its name this hotel, gas station, and campground is located on a ridge at 2,360 feet with good views to the north and south. It's the only hookup campground along the highway other than those in Inuvik. The facility also has a restaurant and a gift shop. Lots of people find the garage near the gas pumps to be a good place to get flats fixed.

The campsites are located at the east end of the motel building. Hookups consist of 20-amp electrical outlets mounted on a fence in a gravel lot with room for about 12 RVs. Rigs back up to the fence to plug in. There's room for any size rig and there are picnic tables. There are also a few tent-camping sites at the edge of the brush nearby. Picnic tables and fire rings are provided in these no-hookup sites. The ridge-top location can make this a pretty exposed place for tent camping but the frequent breeze is handy for keeping the bugs down. Restrooms are located at the end of the motel building opposite the camping area, they have hot coin-op showers. There's a dump station behind the motel building.

The campground is located at Km 369 of the Dempster Highway.

ROCK RIVER CAMPGROUND

Location:	Km 446 Dempster Highway, Yukon

GPS Location: N 66° 54' 42.7", W 136° 21' 21.0"

The Rock River Campground has an isolated location on the west side of the Richardson Mountains. The campground is set in a grove of white spruce next to the river. The campground is in an area protected from the wind, it's known for its bugs.

There are 18 RV sites here, three are pull-thrus. Any size rig will fit in some of the sites. There are picnic tables and fire pits, firewood is provided. There's also a picnic shelter and outhouses. The campsites are set off a loop drive so you can easily pull in and take a look.

NITAINILAII CAMPGROUND (NWT CAMPGROUND)

Location:	Km 76 Dempster Highway, Northwest Territory (Km 541 from Hwy. 2)

GPS Location: N 67° 21' 01.0", W 134° 51' 33.0"

Just a kilometer or so after leaving the ferry over the Peel River you'll see the sign for Natainlii Territorial Park Campground on the left. There is also a visitor center located at the entrance to the campground, similar to the one at Tombstone Mountain Campground. You'll notice that the facilities here and at the Northwest Territorial campgrounds farther along are painted a cheerful bright blue trim.

There are 24 sites in this campground. These are back-in sites with some suitable for rigs to 35 feet. Sites have picnic tables and fire pits, firewood is provided. There's a picnic shelter with a stove and outhouses.

VADZAIH VAN TSHIK CAMPGROUND (NWT CAMPGROUND)

Location: Km 220 Dempster Highway, NWT (Km 685 from Hwy. 2)

GPS Location: N 68° 05' 16.1", W 133° 29' 30.0"

This campground is also known as Caribou Creek Campground, it is located in Gwich'n Territorial Park.

This small campground along the creek has 9 sites, two are pull-thrus. There are picnic tables and fire pits, firewood is provided.

GWICH'N TERRITORIAL CAMPGROUND (NWT CAMPGROUND)

Location: Km 234 Dempster Highway, NWT (Km 699 from Hwy. 2)

GPS Location: N 68° 12' 10.7", W 133° 25' 27.3"

This is a newer campground set in a gravel pit near a large lake. There are about 15 vehicle sites here, some are very large pull-thrus suitable for any size rig. There are picnic tables and fire pits. Firewood is provided and there is a cooking shelter and vault toilets.

CHUK TERRITORIAL PARK (JA'K PARK)

Location: Km 265 Dempster Highway, NWT
(Km 730 from Hwy. 2)

GPS Location: N 68° 19' 51.0", W 133° 38' 48.8"

Set in an area of white birches on a ridge top this is a nice campground with hookups within easy driving distance of Inuvik. It's about 5 km from the center of town.

The campground has 34 sites. Many are pull-thrus suitable for 40 foot rigs. There are 20-amp electrical outlets. The campground has no dump station but there is one at the Happy Valley Campground in town. Restrooms have flush toilets and hot showers. There's a tower that you can climb for the view.

The campground road is on the west side of the highway near Km 265, this is about 6 kilometers after the pavement begins if you are coming from the south.

HAPPY VALLEY TERRITORIAL CAMPGROUND

Location: In Inuvik

GPS Location: N 68° 21' 37.8", W 133° 44' 13.1"

Inuvik's in-town campground is a popular place. It has decent facilities and is within walking distance of town so it is often full. Still, unless you arrive during the Great Northern Arts Festival you'll probably find a place if you arrive in the early afternoon.

The campground has 27 sites. Some are pull-thrus, some back-ins. A few will take rigs to 40 feet. They have electrical hookups and there is a dump and water fill station. Sites have picnic tables and fire pits and firewood is available. The restrooms have flush toilets, free hot showers, and good coin-op washers and dryers.

THE KLONDIKE LOOP

The campground is on the north side of town. As you arrive from the south you'll pass the Visitor's Center, zero your odometer here. You'll be coming in to town on McKenzie, .7 km (.4 mile) after leaving the visitor center you'll see the domed church on your right. At 1.4 km (.9 mile) after passing through the center of town turn left on Reliance. Drive a block to a T, turn right and you'll soon see the campground entrance on your left.

TOP OF THE WORLD HIGHWAY
126 Kilometers (78 Miles)

The 126 kilometer (78 mile) Top of the World Highway connects Dawson City with the Taylor Highway. The section from Dawson to the border customs stations, 105 km (65 miles), is seal-coated but beginning to deteriorate. The remaining 13 miles (29 km) to the Taylor Highway and the first part of the Taylor itself are unpaved and the condition can vary dramatically from year to year or day to day depending upon the weather. Kilometer markings start at the Yukon River and run to the border at Boundary. They then turn to mile markers and count up from 0 at the border. Fuel is usually available in Boundary, 111 km (69 miles) from Dawson City, but the best plan is to buy it before leaving either Dawson or Tok because the prices in Boundary are very steep. This highway is only open when the Yukon Ferry operates and snow allows, from May to October.

Virtually all of the Top of the World Highway runs above the timber line with great

VIEW FROM THE TOP OF THE WORLD HIGHWAY

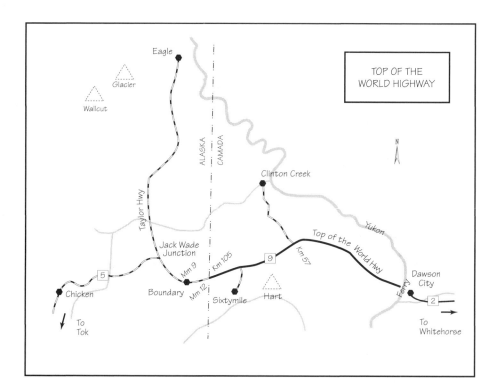

views in all directions. The only civilization is at the border stations and at nearby Boundary where there is a historic roadhouse. At Km 57 a small unpaved side road runs 40 kilometers (25 miles) to **Clinton Creek**, an abandoned trading post and mining town near the mouth of the Fortymile River. Floaters on the Fortymile often use this as a take-out point.

Travelers on the highway should be aware that the customs stations are only open from 9 a.m. to 9 p.m. Yukon time (8 a.m. to 8 p.m. Alaska time). At the very beginning and end of the season the station may not be open at all, check in Dawson City or Tok before taking this route if you are very early or late in the season. You won't be able to pass if they aren't open. The ferry crossing the Yukon at Dawson City runs 24 hours each day except on Wednesdays when it is down for two hours from five to seven a.m. for maintenance. Lines to cross on the ferry can get long at the height of the season.

TAYLOR HIGHWAY
160 Miles (258 Kilometers)

If you are traveling the Klondike Loop you'll find that when you reach the Taylor Highway the kilometer posts become mileposts and they start counting down. The section below starts at the beginning of the Taylor Highway at the Tetlin Junction and proceeds north.

THE KLONDIKE LOOP

The Taylor Highway, also called Alaska Route 5, runs 160 miles (258 km) through high rolling hills to Eagle, Alaska on the Yukon River. En route the gravel highway passes through the Fortymile mining district and also provides a connection to the Top of the World Highway to Dawson City in the Yukon. Mileposts along the Taylor start at the Tetlin Junction at the southern end of the highway. The Tetlin Junction is on the Alaska Highway 10 miles east of Tok. Much of the Taylor Highway is gravel although the southern-most 64 miles (103 km) have now been paved. The section from the end of the pavement to the Jack Wade Junction at Mile 96 has been upgraded in recent years and is fine when dry. The section from Jack Wade Junction to Eagle, a distance of 65 miles (105 km), is often narrow and not as well maintained. Large vehicles (RVs) should drive cautiously along the entire Taylor and Top of the World Highway. Road conditions deteriorate badly in rainy weather and can make the trip miserable and even dangerous for big rigs as the surface becomes slippery and the shoulders soft. Use extreme caution when passing other vehicles, large coaches have toppled over along here due to soft shoulders. The Taylor Highway is closed during the winter by snow.

Services are very limited along the Taylor so start with a full tank and watch your gas gauge. You can get gas at Chicken near Mile 67 and also in Eagle at Mile 160.

For much of its length the highway passes near the **Fortymile National Wild, Scenic, and Recreational River**. For information including current river conditions contact: BLM, Tok Field Office, PO Box 309, Tok, Alaska 99780; (907) 883-5121. There are many popular floats along this river, also lots of gold rush history. This was one of the interior's first large gold rush areas. Miners already working the Fortymile were the first to reach the Klondike near Dawson when word of the strike there got out. Float trips on the Fortymile can be challenging and depend upon having adequate water. Check ahead if you plan to do one.

The town of Eagle and large portions of the Yukon River valley to the east and west are inside the **Yukon–Charley Rivers National Preserve**. The preserve headquarters are in Eagle and can be reached by telephone at (907) 547-2233.

As you head up the Taylor Highway the first point of interest is a trail leading in to Four Mile Lake at Mile 4. The lake offers good rainbow fishing, the trail is a little less than a mile long. The road soon begins climbing to its first summit on Mt. Fairplay at Mile 33.

The first campground is the BLM's West Fork Campground at Mile 49, it is in the valley of the West Fork of the Fortymile River. The nearby bridge is a popular put-in point for floating the river. Another popular access point is the bridge at Mile 64.

Historic **Chicken** is near Mile 67. It seems that everyone traveling the Taylor Highway is anxious to visit Chicken, you might as well stop too. The uninitiated find the whole place a little confusing. Chicken was one of the Fortymile-area gold camps. It is well-known because it was featured in the novel **Tisha** by Ann Purdy. This is a pretty good book, make sure you pick up a copy when you visit Chicken, paperback copies are readily available. The town is also known for it's name. The original settlers apparently planned to call the place Ptarmigan, but none of them could spell the word. They settled for Chicken instead. The original town site is abandoned, it is located along the west bank of Chicken Creek on the north side of the highway.

Unfortunately, it is on private property and access is controlled. Across the highway is the Goldpanner which offers tours of the site. Beyond the Goldpanner the Airport Road cuts southeast and a short distance down it is "Beautiful Downtown Chicken Alaska", really a relatively modern saloon, café, and gift shop gussied up to look old. Many of the folk who visit Chicken actually think this is the old town site. It's not, but it's still worth a visit. There are two places to camp in Chicken, both are listed below. A dredge that was formerly located near Fairbanks and then later on the creeks nearby (the Pedro dredge) has been moved to a location in Chicken and is being restored.

Another Fortymile River access point is the bridge over the South Fork at Mile 75. The BLM has another campground, the Walker Fork Campground, at Mile 82. Nearby, at Mile 86 you'll see the **Jack Wade Dredge** (actually the Butte Creek Dredge) next to the road.

At Mile 96 is the **Jack Wade Junction**. The Top of the World Highway swings east from here to Dawson City. The Taylor Highway goes left and continues to Eagle.

Continuing north the highway crosses Polly Summit and then descends to cross the Fortymile at Mile 113. This is a good put-in for floating the lower river out to where it meets the Yukon near Clinton Creek. The road continues, following O'Brien Creek and then ascends to cross American Summit. You'll get excellent views across the

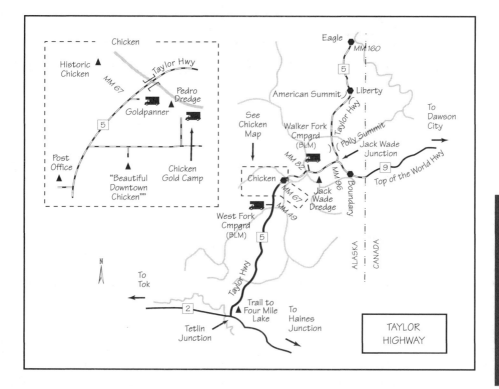

high country before the road descends along American Creek into Eagle.

Taylor Highway Campgrounds

WEST FORK CAMPGROUND (BLM)
Location: Mile 49 of the Taylor Highway

GPS Location: N 63° 53' 12.9", W 142° 14' 06.3"

There are few campgrounds in the Fortymile Country but this and the other BLM site (Walker Fork) are excellent. There are 25 camping sites at West Fork. They are off two loops, one loop has seven pull-thrus and the other 18 are back-ins, some very long. All sites are separated by natural vegetation and trees. There are picnic tables, firepits, handicapped-accessible outhouses, and water is hauled in and available at a large plastic tank. This campground also has a host.

Watch for the West Fork Campground on the west side of the road near Mile 49 of the Taylor Highway.

CHICKEN GOLD CAMP
Location: ¼ Mile Airport Road, Mile 66.4
                  Taylor Hwy., Chicken Alaska
Email: chickengold@yukonalaska.com
Website: www.chickengold.com

GPS Location: N 64° 04' 08.4", W 141° 56' 26.9"

This is a new camping location in Chicken. It's not the first place you'll see, but being off the main road is an advantage, less dust. It's a well-groomed very large gravel lot with lots of room to park and scattered picnic tables. There are also a few pull-thru sites separated by trees with electrical hookups, they're suitable for any size rig. Restrooms are outhouses but there is a dump station. The modern main building here serves as gift shop, restaurant, and expresso bar. Gold panning is available. The Pedro gold dredge was relocated a few years ago and sits at the back of the campground, restoration efforts are underway. Grayling fishing is possible nearby.

This campground is a short distance off the main road. To reach it follow the gravel road south from about Mile 66.4 of the Taylor Highway on the airport road. In .1 mile you'll see "Beautiful Downtown Chicken" on your right with its café, gift shop, and bar. Just beyond is a left turn for the Chicken Gold Camp.

GOLDPANNER (ALSO CALLED CHICKEN CENTER)
Address: Mile 66.6 Taylor Highway (PO Box 41),
                 Chicken, AK 99732
Email: george@impulsedata.net
Website: www.chickenak.com

GPS Location: N 64° 04' 20.1", W 141° 56' 04.7"

The Goldpanner is located on the main road and is the second place to camp overnight in Chicken. The Goldpanner also has a large gravel lot suitable for any size rig, here too there are some electrical hookups and a dump station. There are outhouses, a souvenir store that also has some groceries, gold panning, and gas and propane sales. The Goldpanner offers tours of Historic Chicken, ask at the store for details. Grayling fishing is possible nearby.

THE KLONDIKE LOOP

CHICKEN IS EVERYTHING YOU EXPECT IT TO BE

The Goldpanner is located at Mile 66.6 of the Taylor Highway right next to the bridge over Chicken Creek.

WALKER FORK CAMPGROUND (BLM)

Location: Mile 82 of the Taylor Highway

GPS Location: N 64° 04' 36.9", W 141° 37' 41.8"

This is another excellent BLM campground. It offers 20 campsites, some 12 are pull-thrus. Sites are separated by trees and shrubs. A few of the pull-thrus will take long rigs. There are picnic tables, firepits, and handicapped-accessible vault toilets. Water is available. There is also a host at this campground.

The campground is on the west side of the Taylor Highway near Mile 82 (Km 132).

EAGLE
Population 200, Elevation 850 feet

During the gold rush period Eagle was, for a short time, an important little place. Founded in about 1880 as Belle Isle, Eagle had a population of only thirty or so in 1897 but after the big influx of miners to Dawson City in 1898 some 1,700 people lived there. The first push toward growth was reaction against the control and tax-collection activities of the Mounties on the other side of the border. Eagle soon became the American trading center for the gold-seekers. This activity inevitably attracted the U.S. government and the government activity definitely helped the town grow.

As the first river town west of the border Eagle was a great place to collect customs duties and was the port of entry into Alaska for many miners as they abandoned Dawson City and headed for Nome and Fairbanks. Fort Egbert was established in 1889. A telegraph line, known as the WAMCATS line, running from Valdez to Eagle was finished in 1902. The Third Judicial District and Judge Wickersham set up shop in Eagle in 1900 although he soon threw it over for Fairbanks.

Interesting structures from those days survive. The **Eagle Historical Society** serves as the town visitor information source (PO Box 23, Eagle City, Alaska 99738; 907 547-2325) and runs daily tours. They meet at **Judge Wickersham's courthouse** at 9 a.m. each morning during the summer. The courthouse serves as a museum and gift/book store. There are several other interesting sights in Eagle visited by the tour. These include the **Customs House** down by the river which is also a museum and **Ft. Egbert**, the northern terminus of the WAMCATS telegraph line. Several buildings of the fort have been restored and house many interesting exhibits.

Eagle also is home for the headquarters for the **Yukon-Charley Rivers National Preserve** (PO Box 167, Eagle, Alaska 99738; 907 547-2233). The 2,260,000-acre preserve borders much of the Yukon River downstream almost as far as Circle. It also includes the waters of the remote Charley River which flows into the Yukon from the south about halfway between Eagle and Circle. Many people float the Yukon from Dawson City or from Eagle to Circle City. Canoes are available for rent in Dawson and sometimes in Eagle.

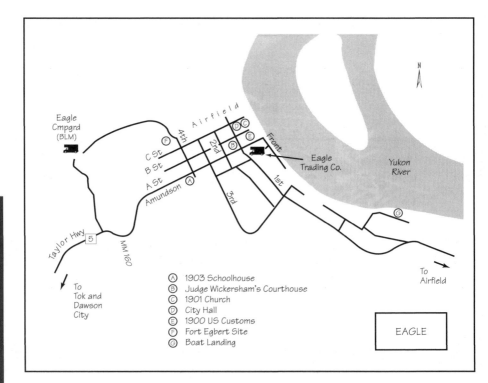

Eagle Campgrounds

🚐 EAGLE TRADING CO.

Address: Box 36, Eagle, AK 99738
Telephone: (907) 547-2220
Website: www.eagletrading.com

GPS Location: N 64° 47' 17.4", W 141° 11' 59.3"

The Eagle Trading Co. is a multi-faceted concern located right across Front Street from the south bank of the Yukon. They have groceries, a laundromat and four full-hookup RV sites (20 amp) that will take rigs to 40 feet. These sites are nothing fancy and they are located right on the corner of Amundson and Front Streets, seemingly right in the center of all activities in town. However, when we've stayed there things have been quiet enough. The view through the front window is great and several locals spend the evening sitting and watching the river go by from the bench across the street. Hot showers are included in the price.

As you come into Eagle just stay on the main road until you reach the river, turn right and you'll find the sites and Trading Co. on your right at the corner.

🚐 EAGLE CAMPGROUND (BLM)

Location: Just northwest of the Eagle town site

GPS Location: N 64° 47' 32.3", W 141° 13' 36.6"

The government alternative while camping in Eagle is very nice. You're a ways from town but in a very pleasant woodland location. Town is an easy hike along the road or the old water pipeline trail.

The campground has 16 sites. They're set in spruce and are well-separated. Some will take rigs to 35 feet. Sites have picnic tables and firepits and there are outhouses. There's also an interesting old cemetery near the entrance. This campground sometimes has a host.

As you enter Eagle turn left on 4th. After .2 miles (.3 km) you'll pass Fort Egbert and the town's grass landing strip. Forge ahead and in another .5 mile (.7 km) you'll come to the campground entrance.

KLONDIKE LOOP DUMP STATIONS

There are a very limited number of dump stations along this route, most located in campgrounds. See the individual campground entries for information. There is a dump station as you enter Dawson City across the highway from the Bonanza Gold RV Park and next to the auto parts store. It is also possible to empty tanks at the local garbage dumps in Carcross, Carmacks, and Pelly Crossing. It is best to make sure you empty your tanks before leaving Whitehorse, Dawson City and Tok.

The Dempster Highway to Inuvik has dump stations in two places: Eagle Plains (Km 369) and at the Happy Valley Campground in Inuvik. There's also one at the Klondike River Lodge on the corner at the junction of the Klondike and Dempster Highways.

THE KLONDIKE LOOP

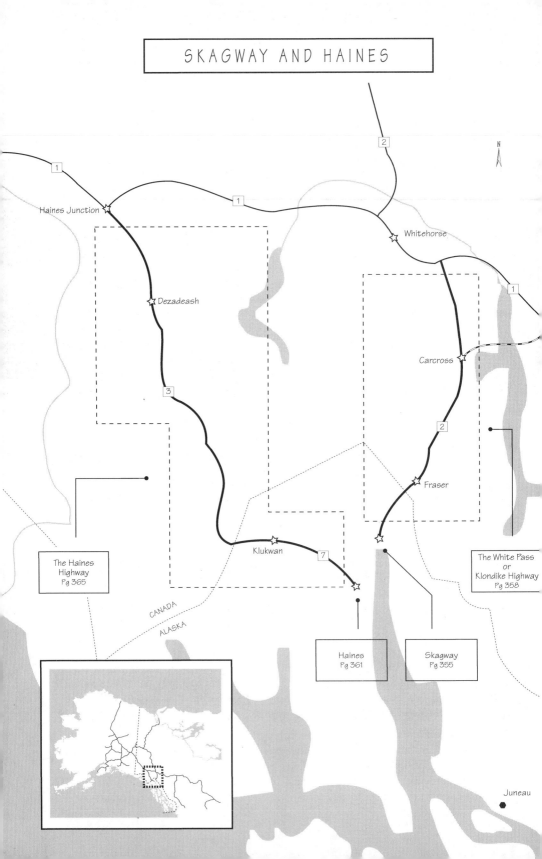

SKAGWAY AND HAINES

Haines Junction

Whitehorse

Dezadeash

Carcross

The Haines
Highway
Pg 365

Fraser

The White Pass
or
Klondike Highway
Pg 358

Klukwan

CANADA
ALASKA

Haines
Pg 361

Skagway
Pg 355

Juneau

Chapter 12

Skagway and Haines

INTRODUCTION

Skagway and Haines, located at the far north end of Southeast Alaska and the Inside Passage, have always been gateways to the interior. In the early days the passes leading up and over the coastal mountains behind these two towns were used as trading routes between the coastal Tlingits and the Indians of the interior. Explorers and prospectors also used Skagway's White and Chilkoot Passes and Haines' Chilkat Pass. Today there are paved highways leading into the interior from both towns, they are now gateways to the Yukon and Alaska for ferry travelers and cruise ship passengers. There's also another little-known attraction to these towns, they receive far less rain than most of Southeast Alaska.

Highlights

When the prospectors headed for the Klondike most of them traveled through **Skagway** or nearby Dyea and then passed over either the **White Pass** or the **Chilkoot Pass**. Today Skagway attracts huge numbers of tourists, most arrive on cruise ships. From there you can ride the historic **White Pass and Yukon Route Railroad** over the White Pass or hike the famous **Chilkoot Trail**.

Many Alaska Highway travelers, those who do not plan to travel on the ferries, will appreciate the opportunity to see part of **Southeast Alaska.** In Skagway and Haines you will see steep mountains dropping into deep fiords with glaciers hanging above. You can easily get out on the water, there are tours, fishing charters, and even a walk-on ferry between the two towns. You can also use Haines as a base for an air-taxi flight over nearby **Glacier Bay**.

Many RVers take their rigs on the **Alaska State Ferry** between Haines and Skagway (or the reverse). That way they can visit both towns without driving many extra miles, and they get a ride on the ferry to boot. It's usually easy to get a reservation since most large rigs get off in Haines leaving lots of room on the car deck, and the rate can be cheaper than the cost of gas to make the loop from Haines to Skagway. Although they are usually not hard to get for this short run it is still wise to get reservations several weeks in advance.

If you are visiting Haines or Skagway with a vehicle you might also consider leaving the rig in a campground and making a walk-on ferry trip to Juneau or other ports in Southeast. Walk-on reservations are easy to get and the cost is reasonable.

Fuel

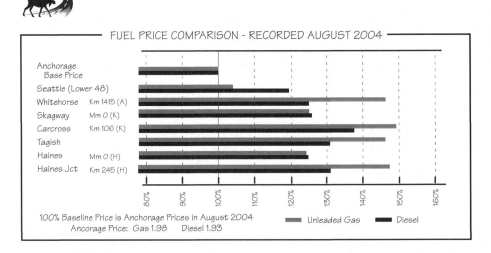

FUEL PRICE COMPARISON - RECORDED AUGUST 2004

Anchorage Base Price
Seattle (Lower 48)
Whitehorse   Km 1415 (A)
Skagway   Mm 0 (K)
Carcross   Km 106 (K)
Tagish
Haines   Mm 0 (H)
Haines Jct   Km 245 (H)

80% 90% 100% 110% 120% 130% 140% 150% 160%

100% Baseline Price is Anchorage Prices in August 2004
Ancorage Price: Gas 1.98   Diesel 1.93

Unleaded Gas   Diesel

Fishing

Skagway and Highway 2 to the north offer a few fishing opportunities. In Skagway there is a salmon hatchery, you can fish **Pullen Creek** or **the harbor** for kings in June, pinks in July and August, and silvers in September. Near Dyea the **Taiya River** has Dolly Varden in the spring and fall, also silvers and chum salmon in the fall. The **Dewey Lakes** (see hiking section), both upper and lower, have brook trout. The upper lake has smaller fish but they are easier to catch. In the salt water try **Taiya Inlet** for kings, silvers, pinks, dogs, Dollies and halibut. Charters are available.

Along Highway 2 the large lakes–**Tutshi, Tagish and Bennett**–all have lake trout and grayling, be aware that all or parts of some of these lakes are in British Columbia, not the Yukon, and a British Columbia fishing license is required. Farther north **Lewes Lake** (on a one-mile road from Km 136) has lake trout, grayling and northern pike.

Haines and the Haines Highway have more to offer. The salt water of **Chilkat Inlet**, **Chilkoot Inlet** and **Lutak Inlet** have all species of salmon as well as sea-run Dollies and halibut. It is possible to catch Dollies and pinks from the shore in many places. The top fresh-water fishing spot has got to be the short (about a mile long) section of the **Chilkoot River** between Chilkoot Lake and Lutak Inlet. It is known for Dolly Varden in April and May, two runs of reds (June/July and August), pinks during the second half of August, and silvers in early October. Fishing is also possible in the lake, particularly for Dollies. On the other side of town the **Chilkat River** also has fish, but silty conditions in the summer limit fishing to clear-water tributary lakes and streams. In the fall it is possible to catch chum and silvers in this river near the airport. **Mosquito Lake** (Mile 27 Haines Highway) is known for both cutthroat trout and Dolly Varden.

Heading north on the Haines Highway try the **Takhanne River** (Km 159) for grayling, Dollies, rainbows, and salmon below the falls; **Dezadeash Lake** (Km 196) for lake trout, grayling, and northern pike; **Kathleen Lake** (Km 220) for lake trout, grayling, and rainbows; and **Kathleen River** (Km 221) for catch-and-release rainbows, lake trout, and grayling. Be aware of where you are fishing, separate licenses are required for Alaska, British Columbia, the Yukon Territory, and Kluane National Park.

Boating, Rafting, Canoeing, and Kayaking

In Skagway the local float trip is down the **Taiya River** near Dyea and the Chilkoot Trail. Kayaks can be rented in Skagway for saltwater exploration.

In Haines commercial float trips and jet boat tours are offered on the **Chilkat River**. It is also possible to book trips here for extended trips to float the famous **Tatshenshini and Alsek Rivers**. Haines is also a good place to go ocean kayaking, guided trips and kayak rentals are available.

Hiking and Mountain Biking

In Skagway the top hiking route has to be the **Chilkoot Trail**. See Chapter 14 - *Camping Away From the Road System* for information about this hike.

Much closer to town and less strenuous are the **Yakutania Point and Smuggler's Cove** waterfront trails. Just walk to the west end of 1st Avenue south of the end of the airport and cross the footbridge over the Skagway River.

From the east end of Third Avenue in Skagway cross the railroad tracks and you'll find the steep trail to the **Dewey Lake Trail System**. Destinations along the trails are Lower Dewey Lake (.7 mile, 1.1 km), Icy Lake (2.5 miles, 4.0 km), Upper Reid Falls (3.5 miles, 5.6 km), Sturgill's Landing (4.5 miles, 7.3 km), Upper Dewey Lake (3.5 miles, 5.6 km) and the Devil's Punch Bowl (4.2 miles, 6.8 km). There are some developed tent-camping sites along the trails as well as solitude and excellent views.

Another worthwhile hike in the Skagway area is really much more of a climb. The **Skyline Trail to AB Mountain** begins at Mile 3 of the Dyea Road. The climb and return should take four to five hours.

Haines also has a selection of trails. The **Seduction Point** trail starts at a trailhead parking lot at Chilkat State Park near the campground there. The trail leads 7 miles (11 km) south to the point at the end of the Chilkat Peninsula called Seduction Point. In several places the trail actually runs along the beach and is not passable at high tide so plan accordingly. There are several tent-camping sites along the way and near the point. Some do not have drinking water including the one at the point.

Another hike not far away is the trail to the top of **Mt. Riley**. This is a good place to head for on clear days for views of Haines, the Lynn Canal, and the surrounding glaciers. There are actually two routes to the top of Mt. Riley. From Mile 3 of the Mud Bay Road (the road out to Chilkat State Park) there is a 2.8 mile (4.5 km) trail that gains 1,500 feet to get to the top. From the end of Beach Road (the road that passes Portage Cove Campground) a four-mile (6.5 km) trail climbs 1,600 feet to the same summit. Of course you can treat this as a traverse if you can arrange for a pick-up at the end.

A tougher trail in the Haines area is the **Mt. Ripinsky** trail. The mountain is an especially good place for views on a clear day, it tops out at 3,560 feet! You don't have to climb all the way to the summit for good views, however. This is fortunate since there is likely to be snow on the trail well into the summer. There are actually a north and south peak, the round-trip hike to the farther north peak is 8 miles (12.9 km), expect a hike that far to take a good six hours. To find the trail, head north on 2nd Ave. or Lutak Road. When Lutak goes right continue on Young Street. Follow Young up the hill and then follow the road along a buried water pipeline for another mile to the trailhead.

THE WHITE PASS AND YUKON TRAIN

Wildlife Viewing

Haines is home to the **Alaska Chilkat Bald Eagle Preserve**. The area is unique in southeast Alaska because the Chilkat River here stays ice-free and affords bald eagles from far and wide the best place to find a meal during the late fall and winter. At the time of their peak numbers in November there can be 4,000 bald eagles in the area. A few eagles can be seen year-round but the real viewing season is October to February. The preserve encompasses 49,000 acres, but the viewing area is between Mile 18 and Mile 22 of the Haines Highway. This area is known as the "Council Grounds". The only facilities are some newly completed restrooms, some parking slots, and limited walking paths. Observers and photographers can conflict with the traffic along the highway, both drivers and those on foot should exercise caution. For information call (907) 465-4563.

In Haines, the Chilkoot River is a great place to watch brown bears when the salmon are running. The best time is the evening, if the bears are around you'll have lots of company trying to get pictures. Don't stray far from your car!

THE ROUTES, TOWNS, AND CAMPGROUNDS

SKAGWAY
Population 900, Elevation sea level

Today's Skagway is something of a shock to someone who hasn't seen it for a few years. Visits by over 300 cruise ships each year have turned a picturesque but sleepy historic gold rush town into a true tourist destination. Much of downtown Skagway is now part of the **Klondike Gold Rush National Historical Park** and the streets are lined with restored buildings housing restaurants, souvenir stores, and hotels. Today's Skagway has become a fascinating place to visit and it's especially convenient since there are several RV parks within just blocks of the center of town.

The large number of cruise boat tourists have given rise to an active tourism infrastructure. A good place to start is the **Klondike Gold Rush Historical Park Visitor Center** (PO Box 517, Skagway, Alaska 99840; 907 983-2921). It is located near the waterfront end of central Broadway Street in the old White Pass Railroad Depot. They have exhibits, films, and information about the Chilkoot Trail, Skagway, and the gold rush. They also have guided walking tours of Skagway. The **Skagway Visitor Center** (PO Box 1025, Skagway, Alaska 99840; 907 983-2854) is in the old Arctic Brotherhood Hall at Second and Broadway. That's the building with the driftwood-covered facade. Also worth a visit is the city's **Skagway Museum** (907 983-3420) in the McCabe College Building at 7th and Spring and the unusual **Corrington Museum of Alaskan History** at 5th and Broadway. You'll probably also want to visit the **Gold Rush Cemetery** where both Frank Reid and Soapy Smith are buried.

The historic **White Pass and Yukon Route** narrow-gauge railroad was finished in 1902. It was considered an engineering marvel as it climbed the precipitous White Pass and then continued on to Whitehorse. After the Klondike Highway to Whitehorse was opened in 1982 the railroad eventually shut down. Today it is running

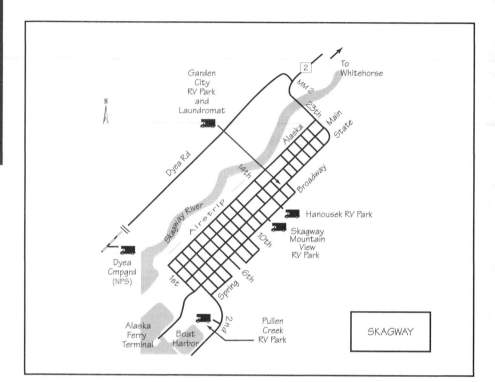

again, but only along the first section up through the pass. On tour-ship-visit days you can ride from Skagway up to Fraser, there are also some runs up to Lake Bennett to pick up hikers who have hiked the Chilkoot Trail. Busses connect with the train to take some cruise ship passengers on to Whitehorse.

The **Chilkoot Trail** is once again very popular, although not quite as heavily traveled as during the gold rush. It is now part of the Klondike Gold Rush National Historical Park. So many people want to hike the 33 mile (53 km) trail over 3,739 foot Chilkoot Pass that access has been limited because there are not enough camping sites. See the information in our Chapter 14 - *Camping Away From the Road System.*

Skagway Campgrounds

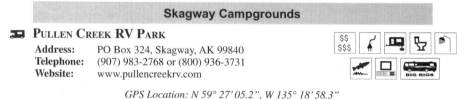

PULLEN CREEK RV PARK

Address:	PO Box 324, Skagway, AK 99840
Telephone:	(907) 983-2768 or (800) 936-3731
Website:	www.pullencreekrv.com

GPS Location: N 59° 27' 05.2", W 135° 18' 58.3"

This is a city-owned campground managed by a subcontractor. It has an excellent location near the boat harbor and within easy walking distance of town.

There are 32 back-in vehicle spaces with electricity (15 and 30 amp) and water. There are also a few tent sites. Spaces are surrounded by grass and a few trees. The restroom buildings are adequate, they have coin-op showers and flush toilets. There is a dump station. There are also 12 large back-in sites on a paved parking area on the ocean side of the campground. These are probably the best-kept secret of the campground, the sites are nothing more than parking slots with 30-amp electric hookups but they offer fantastic views of the many cruise ships that dock in Skagway, the small boat harbor, and the surrounding mountains. A few of the sites in the main campground will take rigs to 40 feet, the ones in front will take any size rig.

To find the park follow 2nd Ave. east from State Street. It crosses the RR tracks and curves right, you will see the campground on your right. Just past the campground entrance there's a right turn into the paved parking area. It's marked no RVs but that apparently means no boondocking, the campground sites are on the right.

☎ SKAGWAY MOUNTAIN VIEW RV PARK

Address:	12th and Broadway (PO Box 375), Skagway, AK 99840
Telephone:	(907) 983-3333 or (888) 778-7700 (res.)
Email:	alaskarv@aol.com
Website:	www.alaskarv.com

GPS Location: N 59° 27' 33.2", W 135° 18' 28.2"

This campground is located within easy walking distance of the central area of town yet is away from all of the noise except the railroad running right along the border of the campground. This doesn't get any use at night so it's no problem, you'll probably enjoy watching the tourist trains pass, especially the steam engines that are occasionally used.

The campground has about 100 spaces, most are back-in sites with both 20 and 30-amp electricity, water, and cable-TV hookups. Some also have sewer. Most are suitable for large rigs with careful maneuvering. There are also two areas with more trees that have back-in dry vehicle spaces for smaller rigs or tent sites. Most sites have picnic tables. The main building houses the office, restrooms, individual shower rooms (coin-op), and a laundromat. There is an RV wash and a dump station.

From State Street, the main north-south arterial in Skagway, head east on 12th. You'll find the campground at the end of the avenue off Broadway.

☎ HANOUSEK RV PARK
Location: 14th and Broadway, Skagway, AK

GPS Location: N 59° 27' 38.7", W 135° 18' 22.9"

Hanousek RV Park is a city-owned operation managed by the Skagway Mountan View RV Park above.

Currently the campground seems to be used more by semi-permanent summer residents than by travelers. There are about 40 back-in sites with electricity and water, a few have sewer hookups. Some will take rigs to 40 feet. There are also quite a few tent sites. Restrooms are in decent shape with individual shower rooms (coin-op).

From State Street, the main north-south arterial in Skagway, head east on 14th. You'll find the campground at the end of the avenue. It is just north of the Skagway Mountain View RV Park.

⛟ GARDEN CITY RV PARK AND LAUNDROMAT

Address:	PO Box 228, Skagway, AK 99840
Telephone:	(907) 983-237 or (866) 983-2378
Fax:	(907) 983-3378
Email:	gcrv@aptalaska.net
Website:	www.gardencityrv.com

GPS Location: N 59° 27' 42.8", W 135° 18' 19.4"

The Garden City RV Park will undoubtedly be the first campground you see as you drive into town, that is probably why it is often difficult to get into this campground during the height of the summer season.

The park has about 100 spaces, all have full-hookups (30 amp). Some pull-thrus are available. Most sites are suitable for any size rig. Parking is on good gravel and larger rigs have room to park. New modern restrooms have hot showers (extra cost) and there is a laundromat that get lots of use by folks from outside the park. There is an internet access point in the laundromat, it's a network, not a telephone hookup.

The campground is located at the corner of State Street and 15th, right on your way in to or out of town. The walk to central Skagway takes only a few minutes.

⛟ DYEA CAMPGROUND (NATIONAL PARK SERVICE)

Location:	Mile 6.8 of Dyea Road

GPS Location: N 59° 30' 19.8", W 135° 20' 50.0"

The Dyea Campground is some distance from Skagway on a minor dirt road so larger rigs must exercise caution. It is located close to the beginning of the Chilkoot Trail and hikers like to use it as a base camp. There is a parking area for the trail located at the campground.

This campground has 22 sites. They are set in an area of alders and cottonwoods near the Taiya River. Most are back-ins and they are well separated, a few are large enough for the largest rigs. Each site has a picnic table and a firepit. There are outhouses and the campground does have a host.

To get to the campground follow the Dyea Road. It leaves the Klondike Highway just outside Skagway at Mile 2. The first 1.8 miles (2.9 km) are paved, then the road narrows. Near the campground is another short section of paved road. The campground is at 6.8 miles (11.0 km).

WHITE PASS OR KLONDIKE HIGHWAY
99 Miles (160 Kilometers)

The South Klondike Highway, Yukon Highway 2, is the southern portion of the same Klondike Highway that runs from Whitehorse to Dawson City. This portion of the highway was completed in 1982 and runs from Skagway up the famous White Pass and then north along several long lakes to Whitehorse. The excellent highway is paved for the entire distance, mile markers run north from Skagway to the border, then they change to kilometer markers and continue north. This short road actually passes through parts of Alaska, British Columbia, and the Yukon. We'll cover the road from south to north.

After leaving Skagway the road passes the junction for the 8 mile (13 km) gravel road to **Dyea** at Mile 1.6 and begins climbing almost immediately. There are several places to pull off and look across the valley at the old gold rush trails and the railroad. The top of the pass is at Mile 14, the altitude is 3,292 feet. U.S. Customs is at Mile 6.7, the border at Mile 15, but Canadian Customs is located at Km 36 (Mile 22) at **Fraser**. It is manned from 8 a.m. to midnight, check at 907 983-3144 if you want to cross from midnight to 8 a.m. Fraser is the turn-around for most White Pass railroad excursions from Skagway. A few miles farther along is **Log Cabin** where the Chilkoot Hiking Trail connects with the road. A few trains also continue on to the south end of Lake Bennett to pick up Chilkoot Trail hikers. The countryside around Fraser and Log Cabin is glacier-scrubbed rock, very forbidding but beautiful.

Continuing north, the highway passes along the shores of Tutshi and Tagish Lake to **Carcross** at Km 105. The name Carcross is a shortened form of Caribou Crossing. The town is located at a point long used by Indians for caribou hunting. During the gold rush, especially after the railroad was built, the town grew. It became a supply center for riverboat accessible destinations on the surrounding lakes. A fleet of sternwheelers serviced these lakes for many years. There's a **Visitor Reception Centre** (867 821-4431) located in the old railway station. The town's cemetery has the graves of two of the men who made the original Klondike strike and the wife of the third: Tagish Charlie, Skookum Jim and Kate Carmack.

Just north of Carcross at Km 107 is another junction, this one for the Tagish Road

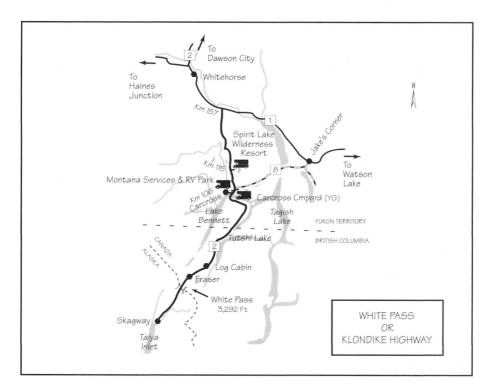

(Yukon Highway 8) which leads east to the Alaska Highway at Jake's Corner. See Chapter 4 of this book for more information about this road and its campgrounds. Just north of the intersection is a pull-off for the **Carcross Desert**. Here a small region of sand dunes will make you do a double-take and probably stop for a photo.

As the highway runs north it passes several lakes including Spirit, Emerald, Rat, Bear and Kookatsoon until meeting the Alaska Highway at Km 157. From there the Klondike and Alaska highways are the same road as they pass through Whitehorse and then split north of town as the Klondike Highway heads for Dawson City.

White Pass or Klondike Highway Campgrounds

MONTANA SERVICES & RV PARK

Address: Box 75, Carcross, Y.T. Y0B 1B0
Telephone: (867) 821-3708 **Fax:** (867) 821-3503

GPS Location: N 60° 10' 11.4", W 134° 42' 18.7"

This is a gas station and grocery store with 40 large pull-thru and back-in camping slots with electricity in a gravel lot behind the main structure. You can have either 30 or 50-amp hookups. There's lots of maneuvering room. There is also a tent camping area with picnic tables and fire rings. Also available are flush toilets, showers, a laundromat, a grocery store, a dump station, a snack bar, and a car wash facility. We found the staff to be very friendly and the facilities much expanded since our last visit. Montana Services is located on the west side of the highway near Km 106.

CARCROSS CAMPGROUND (YUKON GOV.)

Location: Km 106 Klondike Highway

GPS Location: N 60° 10' 25.0", W 134° 42' 08.0"

This is a typical government campground with one exception, the location has very little charm (other than a nearby airstrip). There are 14 long back-in camping sites. They are well-separated with trees and natural vegetation and have picnic tables and firepits. The campground has outhouses and water is available.

Head east from the Klondike Highway at Km 106 just north of Carcross next to the airstrip, you'll soon see the campground entrance on your left.

SPIRIT LAKE WILDERNESS RESORT

Address: Km 115 Klondike Highway, Carcross, Y.T.
Telephone and Fax: (867) 821-4337
Email: spiritlake@excite.com
Website: www.travel.to/spiritlake

GPS Location: N 60° 14' 59.9", W 134° 44' 47.5"

This small campground make a convenient overnight stop. It also makes a good base for canoe trips on the Wheaton River to Lake Bennett, they provide drop-off and pick-up services.

The campground has 6 back-in spaces with 30-amp electric hookups in an open gravel lot behind the main buildings. Big rigs can fit in these sites, they have picnic table and fire pits. Farther back are about 15 more dry spaces in pine trees near the lake for small rigs and tenters that also have picnic tables and firepits. A restroom

SKAGWAY AND HAINES

building provides flush toilets and hot showers. Other services include a dump station and water fill point, hiking trails, canoe rentals, and a restaurant and bar. The campground is located at Km 115 of the Klondike Highway.

HAINES
Population 2,600, Elevation sea level

Haines is the "other" southeast town with a connection to the road system. In fact, Haines has had such a connection for many years. The Haines Road, now called the Haines Highway, was built in 1943 to connect with the Alaska Highway. The pass through the Coastal Mountains at Haines has been in use for centuries, first as a native trading route into the interior, then by Jack Dalton who pioneered a route here just before the Gold Rush and operated a toll road that was used to drive cattle into the Klondike.

Haines gets a few cruise ships so there are some tourist-oriented attractions in town. The helpful **Visitor Information Center** (Second Avenue and Willard Street; (907 766-2234 or 800 458-3579) is just down the hill from Main St. Many of the attractions in town are related to old **Fort William Henry Seward**. It was active from 1904 to 1946 and is now privately owned. The structures are in use as hotels, bed and breakfasts, restaurants, and shops. There is also a traditional Chilkat plank house and totem poles on the old parade grounds. The **Chilkat Dancers** often perform at

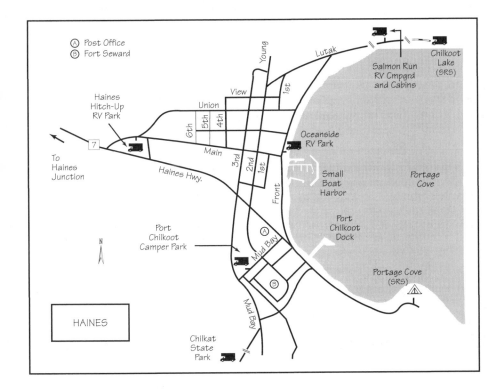

Chilkat Indian Arts (907 766-2540). A salmon bake is sometimes held at the Fort.

Haines is home to the **Alaska Chilkat Bald Eagle Preserve** which is discussed in detail under *Wildlife Viewing* at the beginning of this chapter. A related destination is the **American Bald Eagle Foundation** at the intersection of Second Avenue and the Haines Highway. They have a diorama showing local wildlife and also an eagle display as well as a gift shop.

Haines has an outstanding museum, the **Sheldon Museum** (907 766-2366). It is located just above the small boat harbor in the old Presbyterian mission location. There you'll find displays about the local Chilkat Indian culture and local transportation including the ferry system and highway.

There are two excellent state parks near Haines. **Chilkat State Park** is south of town a few miles, take Mud Bay Road. This shoreline park offers hiking trails and beach walking. North of town on Chilkoot Lake is **Chilkoot Lake State Recreation Site** with a campground located on the shore of Chilkoot Lake. A short river runs from the lake to tidewater.

Haines Campgrounds

CHILKOOT LAKE STATE RECREATION SITE (STATE OF ALASKA)

Location:	9.6 miles (15.5 km) from Haines on the Lutak Rd.

GPS Location: N 59° 20' 08.2", W 135° 33' 42.7"

This is a beautiful state campground sitting in huge evergreens trees at the end of Chilkoot Lake. The short Chilkoot River runs nearby and may be open for salmon fishing during your stay. The river is also a great place to see grizzlies during the fish runs.

There are 32 sites, a few are large pull-thrus. Sites are well separated by giant trees and vegetation, the most popular ones are near the lake. All sites have picnic tables and firepits. The campground has vault toilets, a hand-operated water pump, and a boat ramp. There is also a host.

From downtown Haines follow 2nd Ave. north and zero your odometer at the Y where Young Road goes straight and the paved Lutak Road goes right. Follow Lutak Rd. (and ferry signs). At 3.9 miles (6.3 km) you'll pass the Alaska State Ferries terminal, and at 8.7 miles (14.0 km) come to the Chilkoot River Bridge. Just before the bridge the unpaved campground access road goes left, follow it for .9 miles (1.5 km) along the Chilkoot River to the campground.

SALMON RUN RV CAMPGROUND AND CABINS

Address:	6.5 Miles Lutak Rd. (PO Box 1582), Haines, AK 99827
Telephone:	(907) 766-3240
Email:	salmonrun@wytbear.com
Website:	www.SalmonRunAdventures.com

GPS Location: N 59° 17' 55.1", W 135° 30' 54.2"

This unusual commercial campground sits on a steep heavily wooded hillside overlooking Chilkoot Inlet. The property extends down across the highway to the salt water, fishing is possible from the beach. Fishing charters are also offered.

There are 30 back-in spaces set under huge trees. Sites are in two areas. Twelve of them are in a large gravel area suitable for any size rig overlooking the water. The remainder are well-separated flat spaces off a steep but fairly wide circular access road. There are no hookups, sites have picnic tables, firepits, and free firewood. There are flush toilets and hot showers (extra cost). There is no dump station but water for fill-ups is available.

Head out from central Haines on 2nd Ave. to the north and zero your odometer at the Y where Young road goes straight and Lutak goes right. Follow Lutak. The ferry terminal will be at 3.9 miles (6.3 km) and you'll see Salmon Run Adventures on the left at 6.2 miles (10.0 km) .

CHILKAT STATE PARK (STATE OF ALASKA)

Location: Mile 6.8 of Mud Bay Road
                  southwest of Haines

GPS Location: N 59° 08' 19.7", W 135° 22' 09.7"

This campground is out of the way and usually not too crowded. An excellent hiking route, the Seduction Point beach trail (12 to 14 miles (19 to 23 km) round trip) leaves from this campground. Big rigs need to be aware that the entrance road, while it is a good wide gravel road, is also very steep, it's posted as 14 percent. If your rig lacks climbing power you might want to avoid it.

The campground has 32 vehicle camping sites, 17 are large pull-thrus. Each site has a picnic table and firepit. There are also tent sites down by the beach. The campground has handicapped-accessible vault toilets, a hand-operated water pump, and, downhill from the camp, a boat ramp and a dock on a pretty beach.

To reach the campground start at the Post Office near the end of the Haines Highway (see map). Drive southeast on the Haines Highway and take the first road to the right heading up the hill. This is Mud Bay Road. From there follow frequent signs for both Mud Bay Road and Chilkat State Park approximately 6.7 miles (10.8 km) to the park entrance. The road is paved this entire distance. Turn right into the park and drive about .5 mile (.8 km) down a wide but steeply winding entrance road to the campground.

HAINES HITCH-UP RV PARK

Address: 851 Main Street (PO Box 383), Haines, AK 99827
Telephone
and Fax: (907) 766-2882
Email: HitchupRV@aol.com
Website: www.hitchuprv.com

GPS Location: N 59° 14' 07.7", W 135° 27' 39.1"

The Hitch-Up is the largest and most polished campground in town. It will probably be the first you see when you arrive and it will look so nice that you'll probably turn right into the entrance.

There are 92 large sites with full hookups (30 or 50-amp outlets). Twenty are pull-thrus. Cable TV is available, also Wi-Fi. All parking is on well-clipped very green grass. The modern central services building houses the office with gift shop and tour booking assistance, restrooms with free hot showers, and a laundromat. Central Haines is within easy walking distance on city sidewalks. The physical address is 851 Main Street.

▣ OCEANSIDE RV PARK

Address:	10 Front St. (PO Box 1569), Haines, AK 99827
Telephone:	(907) 766-2437

GPS Location: N 59° 14' 09.7", W 135° 26' 27.9"

Centrally located at the foot of Main Street and right on the water the Oceanside has a lot going for it–a central location and a water view. There are 23 long back-in RV slots with full-hookups. Picnic tables sit out front above the beach. Unfortunately there are no restrooms or showers so only self-contained rigs tend to stay here. The office is at Canal Marine next door. There's a nearby laundromat where you can get a shower if needed. Stores and restaurants are also close.

To reach the campground take the left fork at the Welcome to Haines sign as you enter town. Take a right at the next Y and you'll drive right into central Haines on Main Street. Drive all the way to the waterfront, take a jog to the left, and you're at the Oceanside RV Park.

▣ PORT CHILKOOT CAMPER PARK

Address:	13 Ft. Seward Dr. (PO Box 1649), Haines, Alaska 99827
Telephone:	(907) 766-2000 or (800) 542-6363 (U.S)
	(800) 478-2525 Yukon
Email:	reservations@hotelhalsingland.com
Website:	www.hotelhalsingland.com

GPS Location: N 59° 13' 42.9", W 135° 26' 44.5"

The Port Chilkoot offers something a little different. This campground sits under towering Sitka Spruces on the hillside near Fort Seward. Even so it's within walking distance of town.

The campground has about 40 spaces. Most are partial or dry spaces under the spruces but there are also a few large full-hookup spaces out front with plenty of maneuvering room. Most spaces have picnic tables. There is also lots of room to tent camp. Restrooms are OK but not great, they have flush toilets and coin-op showers. There's also a laundromat and dump station.

To reach the campground head uphill on Mud Bay Road from the Haines Highway near the post office. You'll see the campground almost immediately on your right.

▣ PORTAGE COVE STATE STATE RECREATION SITE

Location:	On Beach Rd. just past Port Chilkoot Dock

GPS Location: N 59° 13' 33.0", W 135° 25' 29.9"

Conveniently located about a mile from downtown Haines is a grass-covered campground only for tenters. It is located right along the shore of Portage Cove just southwest of town on the road to Battery Point. The campground has unmarked tent sites on a grass lawn with firepits and picnic tables and there are water and handicapped accessible vault toilets.

HAINES HIGHWAY
152 Miles (245 Kilometers)

The Haines Highway has as long a history as any highway in this part of the world. Originally this pass through the Coastal Range was an Indian "kleena" or "grease trail" trading route. Coastal Indians carried trading goods, including fish oil from candlefish (also called eulachon, smelt, or hooligan), inland to trade for products of that area. Later, when the Russians arrived it was a fur-trade route. Anticipating an interior gold rush Jack Dalton scouted a route from Haines to Stewart Landing on the Yukon River. This route, which became a toll road, wasn't popular with gold seekers but was used during the Klondike Gold Rush to drive cattle inland. Gradually updated, the route became a gravel road during World War II and was connected to the new Alaska Highway. For many years this road was the only northern access to the Inside Passage and Alaskan ferry system in Southeast Alaska. It was heavily used by Alaskans who didn't want to drive the entire Alaska Highway when traveling to and from Alaska, not to mention state legislators moving to Juneau for the legislative session.

The Haines Highway is now paved for its entire 152 miles (245 km) from Haines to Haines Junction at Km 1,635 of the Alaska Highway. The road is marked with mileposts starting in Haines and running to the border. There they change to kilometer posts for the Canadian section of the road.

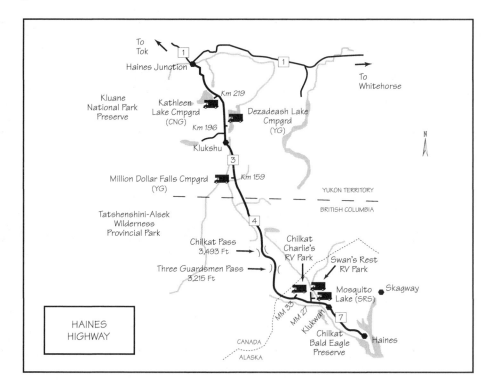

The Haines Highway starts in Haines and follows the Chilkat River north. Border stations are at Mile 40. They are open from 7 a.m. to 11 p.m. Alaska Time, 8 a.m. to midnight Pacific (Canadian) time, you lose an hour as you travel north. The highway then climbs to cross Three Guardsmen Pass (3,215 feet) and Chilkat Pass (3,493 feet). It then descends to follow the Tatshenshini River into the lower lake country and finally hooks up with the Alaska Highway. As the road travels north it passes through or alongside several park areas: the **Alaska Chilkat Bald Eagle Preserve**, the **Tatshenshini-Alsek Wilderness Provincial Park,** and **Kluane National Park Preserve.**

Haines Highway Campgrounds

MOSQUITO LAKE STATE RECREATION SITE (STATE OF ALASKA)

Location: Mile 2.4 of Mosquito Lake Rd, Junction
at Mile 27 of Haines Highway

GPS Location: N 59° 27' 16.0", W 136° 01' 43.6"

This is a very small state campground sitting next to little Mosquito Lake. Despite the name we find few mosquitoes when we visit. There are perhaps 7 poorly-defined small sites sitting under large trees at the lakeshore. The campground is not really suitable for large rigs. Picnic tables, firepits, water, outhouses, a boat launch, and a small dock are provided.

Access is via a paved road leaving the Haines Highway at Mile 27. The campground is at 2.4 miles (3.9 km).

SWAN'S REST RV PARK

Address: HCR 60, Box 2860, Haines, AK 99827
Telephone: (907) 767-5662

GPS Location: N 59° 27' 36.4", W 136° 01' 27.8"

The Swan's Rest is a small RV park in a very pleasant setting well outside Haines but within easy driving distance. It is also near the Chilkat Bald Eagle Preserve and overlooks a quiet lake. The operators of the campground report that this lake is the southern-most nesting area for trumpeter swans in Alaska.

The campground has 11 back-in RV sites, most have full hookups. The parking surface is mowed grass and all of the sites overlook the lake and have picnic tables. There is a restroom with hot shower and a coin-op laundry room.

Access is via a paved road leaving the Haines Highway at Mile 27. The campground is at 2.9 miles (4.7 km), past the Mosquito Lake state campground.

CHILKAT CHARLIE'S RV PARK

Address: HCR 60, Box 3294, Haines, AK 99827
Telephone: (907) 767-5555

GPS Location: N 59° 25' 51.8", W 136° 10' 36.1"

Near Mile 33 of the Haines Highway you may notice a few RV sites in a lawn in front of a small house. This is Chilkat Charlie's. There are 6 sites with parking on grass, only one has full hookups but several others offer electricity. There's also plenty of room for tents. There is a restroom with a shower and flush toilet and next door is a gas station with a small store.

🚐 MILLION DOLLAR FALLS CAMPGROUND (YUKON GOV.)

Location: Km 159 of the Haines Highway

GPS Location: N 60° 06' 29.1", W 136° 56' 42.1"

This nice government campground has lots of room for big rigs although all 28 vehicle spaces are back-ins. There are also 6 tent sites. Spaces are well separated with trees and natural vegetation, there are picnic tables and firepits at each space. The campground also has outhouses, two picnic and cooking shelters, a hand-operated water pump, and a playground. There's an interesting half-mile trail into a rocky ravine to an overlook above Million Dollar Falls.

🚐 DEZADEASH LAKE CAMPGROUND (YUKON GOV.)

Location: Km 196 of the Haines Highway, 32 miles from the Haines Junction

GPS Location: N 60° 23' 50.7", W 137° 02' 32.5"

This Yukon government campground occupies a small gravel point projecting into Dezadeash Lake. It is very pleasant if the wind isn't blowing. Several of the 20 back-in sites are along the shore. This campground is most suitable for rigs to 30 feet although a couple of the sites will take 40 footers and there is plenty of maneuvering room. The area is wooded but the sites tend to be closer together than in some government campgrounds since space is limited on the point. There are picnic tables and firepits and the campground has a cooking and picnic shelter and boat-launching ramp.

🚐 KATHLEEN LAKE CAMPGROUND (CANADIAN NATIONAL GOV.)

Location: Km 220 of the Haines Highway, 27 km (17 miles) from Haines Junction

GPS Location: N 60° 34' 33.3", W 137° 12' 33.7"

Kathleen Lake Campground is located in Kluane National Park so you will notice some differences from the Yukon Government campgrounds you've been staying in, but the differences are small. The largest difference is that only cash is accepted for payment. This campground has 39 very large sites (good for RVs although all are back-ins) arranged on a small knoll in cottonwood and spruce. Sites have picnic tables and firepits and, since this is Canada, free firewood. There are outhouses and a hand-operated water pump. Near the campground in a day-use area on the lake are a dock, a boat launch and a big fully enclosed cooking and picnic area. Fishing in the lake is said to be good and there is even a beach for a short stroll.

SKAGWAY AND HAINES DUMP STATIONS

Most dump stations in the area covered by this chapter are at campgrounds. There are also stations in **Haines** at Haines Tesoro at 900 Main St, Charlie's Repair on Second Ave. (the road leading from downtown toward the ferry) and at Petro Express (Mile 0 Haines Highway).

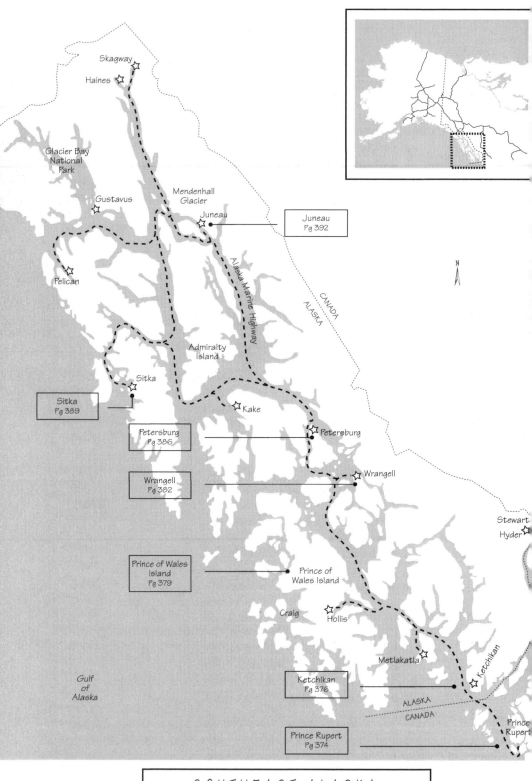

Skagway

Haines

Glacier Bay
National
Park

Gustavus

Mendenhall
Glacier

Juneau

Juneau
Pg 392

Pelican

Alaska Marine Highway

CANADA
ALASKA

N

Admiralty
Island

Sitka

Sitka
Pg 389

Kake

Petersburg
Pg 386

Petersburg

Wrangell
Pg 382

Wrangell

Stewart
Hyder

Prince of Wales
Island
Pg 379

Prince of
Wales Island

Gulf
of
Alaska

Craig

Hollis

Metlakatla

Ketchikan
Pg 376

Ketchikan

ALASKA
CANADA

Prince
Rupert

Prince Rupert
Pg 374

SOUTHEAST ALASKA

Chapter 13

Southeast Alaska

INTRODUCTION

Southeast Alaska, also called the Panhandle, is a different world from the other regions covered in this book. It's a land of water: deep fjords, green shorelines, glaciers, and rain. Travel in Southeast is almost entirely by boat or by air, there are very few roads.

Fortunately, there is a perfect answer to Southeast's transportation difficulties. The Alaska State Ferry System turns the water barriers into highways. The state's seven ferries dedicated to Southeast run frequently, and they can carry any RV. With proper planning you can travel through the Panhandle conveniently and comfortably, stopping occasionally to see the sights.

The Alaska Panhandle is famous for its weather, more specifically, its rain. However, it doesn't really rain in Southeast every day. The monthly rainfall statistics show an interesting pattern. First, it rains much more in the southern Panhandle than in the northern part. Ketchikan in the far south averages about 7¾ inches in June while Juneau averages under 4 inches. Second, the summer is much drier than the winter. The best month is June, followed by July and then May. Be aware–Juneau averages twice as much rain in August as it does in June! In truth, there are many summer days when there is no rain, but luck will have a lot to do with your personal experience when you visit.

Southeast, like the rest of the state, is sparsely populated. There are just seven towns of any size. These are Juneau, the largest and the state's capital, Ketchikan, Petersburg, Wrangell, Sitka, Skagway, and Haines. We've already talked about Skagway and Haines in Chapter 12. Another town, Prince Rupert in British Columbia, is also an important part of most visits to Southeastern Alaska. There are also some smaller towns and islands that are not on the mainline ferry route that make interesting stopping points, many are connected by smaller ferries. The most attractive of these to RVers is Prince of Wales Island.

Highlights

The real highlight of Southeast Alaska is the scenery. As your ferry glides along the shorelines and through the passages you'll probably find yourself spending a lot of time either on deck or in the observation lounge watching both the wildlife and the traffic along the "Inside Passage" marine highway. You're sure to see many bald eagles, as well as the occasional whale, porpoise, and even a bear.

Southeast Alaska has become cruise ship country. Some towns receive over 300 visits by the huge ships during the five-month-long May to September season. The **cruise ships** are themselves an interesting spectacle as they ghost through the fjords and pause to disgorge thousands of passengers for brief middle of the day visits to each port. A side benefit to the cruise industry is that most cities in Southeast offer a large number of tourist-oriented diversions and services. These include day tours, stage shows, scenic flights, museums, shops, and restaurants. A good place to explore each town's offerings is the ubiquitous visitor's center sure to be located near the cruise ship docks. The most popular cruise ship destinations are **Ketchikan, Sitka, Juneau, Skagway**, and of course **Glacier Bay**. Some of the most popular sights include Juneau's **Mendenhall Glacier**, **Ketchikan's totem poles**, and **Sitka's Russian buildings and heritage**.

Those wanting to get away from civilization will find large areas of Southeast easily accessible. Kayakers, hikers, and assorted tent campers will enjoy **Misty Fiords National Monument Wilderness** near Ketchikan and **Glacier Bay National Park** near Juneau. For a place that is easier to access, even with a car or RV, try **Prince of Wales Island**. A ferry runs daily from Ketchikan to Hollis on the island.

The Marine Highway

Since 1962 the State of Alaska has maintained a fleet of large ferries in lieu of a highway system in Southeastern Alaska. There are now ten ships in the fleet. Not all operate in Southeast, there are also routes in South Central and Southwest Alaska. The following information is from the 2004 schedule. It applies to the summer schedule, winter sailings are similar but reduced.

The ferry system is very popular and reservations must be made far ahead for the summer season. Don't cast your plans in concrete until you have your reservations, you might be disappointed. You will need reservations for both your vehicle and each passenger. Staterooms are optional, many people travel the entire passage without one and sleep in airline-style recliners or on deck in tents. If you want a stateroom make sure to reserve one. You can save approximately 50% on a ticket through Southeast by beginning or ending your voyage in Prince Rupert instead of Bellingham. Many people do this, note the high frequency of sailings from Prince Rupert discussed below.

A word here about the cost of traveling on the ferry. For two people and a 21-foot RV to travel between Bellingham and Haines costs approximately $1,600. Between Prince Rupert and Haines the cost would be approximately $800. A stateroom would add about $250 between Bellingham and Haines or $125 between Prince Rupert and Haines. These costs would vary with the type of stateroom and stopovers cost extra. Larger rigs pay much more. You can see that driving the highway is the cheaper way to go even in a small RV, if you only consider gas. On the other hand, if you factor in wear and tear, not to mention the scenery, the ferry may not be such a bad deal.

The ferries usually run pretty much a regular schedule on fixed routes during the height of the summer, the routes from the 2004 schedule are detailed below. During the early summer season and during the spring, fall, and winter the schedules are slightly different and ferries are substituted for each other as ships are taken out of service for a time for maintenance work.

The *Columbia*, at 418 feet long the largest and most luxurious ship in the fleet, runs between Bellingham, Washington and Skagway with stops in Ketchikan, Wrangell, Petersburg, Juneau, Haines and Skagway. Southbound only the ferry also stops in Sitka. The Columbia leaves Bellingham each Friday evening and returns each Friday morning having turned around in Skagway Monday evening.

The *Malaspina*, 408 feet long, also makes the Bellingham to Skagway run also each week. She leaves Bellingham Tuesday evening and makes stops in Ketchikan, Wrangell, Petersburg, Sitka, Juneau, Haines and Skagway. The turnaround in Skagway is about 9 a.m. on Saturday. Southbound the Malaspina does not stop at Sitka.

The *Matanuska*, 408 feet long, or the *Taku*, 352 feet, make two round trips each week between Prince Rupert and Skagway with stops in Ketchikan, Wrangell, Petersburg, Juneau, and Haines. Every second trip they stop in Sitka, but only southbound.

The *Kennicott* joined the fleet in 1999. She is 380 feet long and is designed with open-water capabilities that will allow her to run across the Gulf of Alaska. She usually joins the Malaspina and Taku providing service between Prince Rupert and Skagway. About twice each month in the summer the *Kennicott* makes a trip between Juneau and Seward with a stop in Valdez in each direction.

The new fast ferry, the *Fairweather*, shuttles between Juneau and Haines, Skagway, and Sitka. On Monday, Tuesday, Thursday, Friday, and Saturday she leaves Juneau at 7 a.m. and arrives in Haines at 9:15 a.m., then returns to Juneau by noon. On Tuesday, Thursday, Friday, and Saturday she leaves Juneau at 12:30 p.m. and arrives in Skagway at 3 p.m. and arrives back in Juneau by 6 p.m. On Wednesday and Sunday she leaves Juneau at 7 a.m. and arrives in Sitka at 11:30 a.m., then returns to Juneau by 5:30 p.m.

Two other small state ferries serve mostly smaller ports. The *Le Conte*, 235 feet, services a route from Petersburg to Juneau which includes smaller ports including Kake, Sitka, Angoon, Tenakee and Hoonah with an occasional run up to Haines and Skagway. The *Lituya* services Metlakatla out of Ketchikan.

The new *M/V Prince of Wales*, operated by the **Inter-Island Ferry Authority** has replaced the State of Alaska service between Ketchikan and Hollis on Prince of Wales Island. The *Prince of Wales* makes two round trips daily in the summer from June

1 to September 6 leaving Hollis at 7:00 a.m. and 2:30 p.m. and leaving Ketchikan at 10:45 a.m. and 6:15 p.m. In the winter there is one trip per day. In Ketchikan the ferries run from a dock next to the State of Alaska ferry terminal, the company has a desk in the State terminal. For information and reservations on the Prince of Wales run call (866) 308-4848. For information and fares see the link from our website at www.rollinghomes.com.

The ferries are nice but they aren't cruise ships. They have lounge areas, cafeterias, bars, and shower rooms. During the summer many ferries have a U.S. Forest Service interpreter on board to provide information about the area and the wildlife. This makes sense because most of Southeast is inside the Tongass National Forest. Most of the ferries, the larger ones, have staterooms, but many people do not use them. You can save a lot of money by sleeping either in reclining seats or spreading a sleeping bag in the solarium. The solariums are partially glassed-in areas on upper decks. They have overhead heat lamps but are open to the weather at the aft end. Many people actually pitch tents on the upper decks. Passengers are not allowed to stay on the auto decks while the ferries are underway so sleeping in your rig is not an option. Our advice is to book a stateroom on overnight runs if possible, but don't panic if there isn't one available. Occasionally while underway and also while in port you will be allowed to visit your vehicle. Pets must stay on the vehicle deck, you are allowed to walk them during the visits to the vehicle deck. Propane must be turned off and sealed while on the ferry so you will not be able to keep your refrigerator and freezer running in your RV. Most runs are short enough that things in the refrigerator or freezer of your rig will be fine if they are plenty cold before the propane is turned off and if the door is not opened during the voyage. If you're concerned you can place a block of ice in the refrigerator to keep thing cool longer.

When the ferries dock it is often possible to get off and take a walk. Sometimes the stop will be for several hours. Layover time will be announced before docking and if the time of day is right there might be a bus into town or a tour available so that you can look around. Unfortunately it is not really possible to plan ahead for these layovers, if the ferry is running late the layover is likely to be shorter than expected.

It is possible to make reservations including stops at each port. There is a small extra cost for these stopovers and they must be planned and reserved in advance. It is well worth your time to sit down with a ferry schedule (see below for ordering address) and work out a schedule that will let you see and do all of the things you want.

For information about schedules and rates you can contact the Alaska Marine Highway, 6858 Glacier Highway, Juneau, AK 99801-7909. Their toll free telephone number is (800) 642-0066 or fax (907) 277-4829. They have an excellent website, you'll find a link to it on our website: www.rollinghomes.com.

British Columbia has its own system with a ferry that runs between Port Hardy on Vancouver Island and Prince Rupert. You might want to drive the length of Vancouver Island from Victoria or Nanaimo to Port Hardy, catch the *Queen of the North* to Prince Rupert, and then use the Alaska Marine Highway to travel the rest of the way north. The ferry only runs during daylight hours, north one day and south the next. The route is very scenic and this is the best way to see it since the Alaska state ferries run much of it after dark. For information about schedules and rates contact BC Ferries, 1112 Fort St., Victoria, BC V8V 4V2, Canada. Their telephone number is (250) 386-3431, their fax number is (250) 381-5452, and there is a link to their site on ours – www.rollinghomes.com.

Fishing

Southeast Alaska offers some of the best saltwater fishing in the world. All of the towns with campgrounds have excellent fishing nearby but two locations stand out. Many RVers spend the summer in either Ketchikan or on Prince of Wales Island because they offer access to great fishing on a daily basis yet can be reached with fairly short (and less expensive) ferry trips.

Wildlife Viewing

The ferries offer a wonderful opportunity to see marine mammals and bald eagles. Whales, porpoises, and sea otters are common in Southeast and so are bald eagles. One nice thing about the ferries is that there are many eyes watching for wildlife, if you pay attention you'll know when something is spotted. You'll quickly find that there are two great places to position yourself for the best spotting. The first is the viewing lounge at the front of the superstructure on each ferry, big windows and comfortable chairs make it easy to spend hours watching the view go by. Even better, but less comfortable, is outside on the upper deck, if you stand just behind the open solarium you're sheltered from the wind, pretty comfortable unless it's raining.

THE ROUTES, TOWNS, AND CAMPGROUNDS

BELLINGHAM, WASHINGTON
Population 130,000, Elevation sea level

It may seem strange to include information about a town in Washington in a book about Alaska. You might consider Bellingham an honorary Alaskan town. After all, Bellingham is closer to Ketchikan than Anchorage is. Many people start their Alaska trip in Bellingham.

At one time the southern terminal of the ferry system was in Seattle, 90 miles (145 km) south of Bellingham. Moving to Bellingham cut several hours from the run north, a significant savings. Bellingham is also a lot less intimidating for RVers driving big rigs.

Bellingham has lots of good stores and is an excellent place to stock up on everything except perishables. Ferry rules require that you turn off the propane in your rig so if you depend upon a propane refrigerator you will want to make sure your freezer is empty for the long voyage to Ketchikan. You may be able to keep the refrigerator cool by putting a block of ice in it.

Bellingham to Ketchikan (37 hours)

The ferry usually leaves Bellingham about 6 p.m. so you won't have much of an opportunity to sightsee until first thing the following morning. By then the ship will probably be passing through Johnstone Strait well up the east side of Vancouver Island. Most of the route north is in protected waters, the ferry is usually rock steady. There are a few places where the inside passage is open to the Pacific waves, and the run across Smith Sound to the north of Vancouver Island is one of the longest. You should get there in the early afternoon, the open passage shouldn't take more than two hours.

Once across Smith Sound you'll be in true inside passage country. The passages narrow and you'll see little civilization. Two towns, Namu and Bella Bella will pass by but you will probably see little other than perhaps some lights in the distance. During the night (your second on the ferry) you may notice a little rolling and pitching, that is your signal that the ferry is crossing Dixon Entrance near Prince Rupert and entering Alaska. You must set your watch back an hour to Alaska Time and get ready to dock in Ketchikan in the morning.

PRINCE RUPERT
Population 15,000, Elevation sea level

The northwest British Columbian city of Prince Rupert is the real gateway to Southeast Alaska. Prince Rupert is at the end of a good paved road and is much closer to Alaska than Bellingham. Even Alaskans living in Southeast use the city as a gateway, many think it well worth the effort to drive 900 or so miles (1,450 km) through Canada to reach the Lower 48. Incidentally, you can't get to Prince Rupert on the ferry from Bellingham, that boat doesn't stop here.

Prince Rupert is a very clean and well-organized little town with full services. It is the western terminus for one of Canada's few rail lines to the Pacific Ocean and dates from the early 1900's. Today the town continues to be an important port.

The town's **Visitor Info Centre** is located at 215 Cow Bay Road, Suite 100 (250 624-5637 and 800 667-1994). Probably the most interesting area of Prince Rupert for visitors is **Cow Bay**. This small waterfront area has historical buildings now housing restaurants, pubs, and gift shops. Also interesting is the **Museum of Northern British Columbia** at First and McBride overlooking the water. Other sights include the **Kwinitsa Railway Museum**, and our favorite, the **North Pacific Historic Fishing Village** in nearby Port Edward with displays about the salmon canning industry that was the lifeblood of Southeast for many years.

Prince Rupert Campgrounds

PARK AVENUE CAMPGROUND

Address:	Box 612, Prince Rupert, B.C. V8J 3R5
Telephone:	(250) 624-5861 or (800) 667-1994
Fax:	(250) 622-2619
Email:	campgrd@citytel.net
Website:	tourismprince-rupert.com

GPS Location: N 54° 17' 58.5", W 130° 20' 27.7"

This is the place to stay in Prince Rupert. It couldn't be more convenient for ferry passengers since it is just a kilometer (half-mile) or so up the road from the docks for both the B.C. and Alaska ferries. It can get full on ferry days since almost everyone

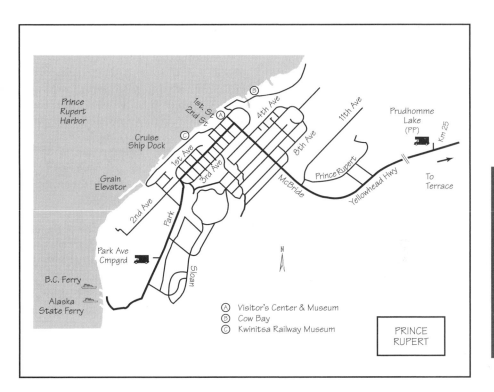

uses it. They have a somewhat remote overflow area for those who arrive after it fills. The office also serves as a local information office.

The campground has spacious paved drives with almost 75 camping sites spread down a gentle slope below the office. All sites are back-ins, most are full hookup sites with 20 and 30-amp power. Most sites have firepits and picnic tables and are separated by grassy areas. There are additional tent sites, some with wooden platforms. Rigs of any size find room to park here. Restrooms are modern frame buildings and have hot showers. There are also a coin-op laundry and a dump station. Reservations are recommended.

To find the campground just follow the signs toward the ferry. You'll find yourself on a wide highway called Park Avenue. The campground is well signed on the right, if you find yourself reaching the ferry parking area you've gone too far. The physical address is 1750 Park Avenue. The campground office stays open late for the convenience of ferry travelers.

🚐 PRUDHOMME LAKE PROVINCIAL PARK

Location: 20 km (12 miles) east of Prince Rupert on Highway 16

GPS Location: N 54° 14' 27.4", W 130° 08' 05.4"

If you prefer a government campground for your visit to Prince Rupert the closest one is at Prudhomme Lake, about 20 km (12 miles) from town but just off the main highway. There are 24 medium-length spaces with the normal British Columbia government campground amenities: picnic tables, firepits, free firewood, and outhouses. The adjacent Prudhomme Lake is said to have decent fishing for Dolly Varden and rainbows.

Prince Rupert to Ketchikan (6 hours)

The ferries leave Prince Rupert at widely varying times. The run up to Ketchikan is relatively short. It runs across Dixon Entrance so a couple of hours of somewhat rough water are possible.

KETCHIKAN
Population 8,000, Elevation sea level

The ferry doesn't usually stop long in Ketchikan. Since the ferry dock is 2.5 miles (4 km) north of town you aren't likely to have enough time to see much of the city except from the deck as you pass by.

Since Ketchikan is Alaska's fourth largest city it is a good place to pause for a while and look around. The town stretches for several miles along the waterfront, it's long and skinny because there isn't much flat building space. Some of the central down-town area is actually built on pilings. The airport for Ketchikan is located on the far side of the Tongass Narrows, you have to take a short ferry ride to get there. The Tongass Narrows are also used as a landing strip by the local floatplane operators and there are several small boat harbors. All of this makes the waterfront an interesting

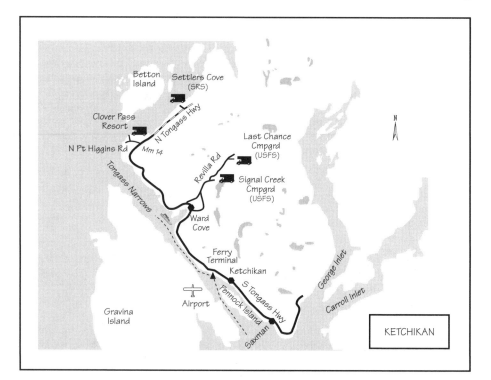

SOUTHEAST ALASKA

and active place to explore. A new addition to town is a Wal-Mart, located about 1.7 miles (2.7 km) north of the ferry docks.

Ketchikan's history is long and varied. The site was first an Indian fishing village, then a cannery town, a mining town, a cannery town for a second time, a timber town, and now something of a tourist town. As the largest town in the southern Panhandle Ketchikan is also a transportation hub and a supply center. If you plan to visit either **Misty Fiords National Monument** or Prince of Wales Island (see below) you'll be passing through Ketchikan or using it as a base.

Ketchikan has one of the four **Alaska Public Lands Information Centers (APLIC)** that have been placed in gateways to Alaska. This one, the **Southeast Alaska Discovery Center**, (50 Main Street; 907 228-6220) is near the cruise ship docks. Others are in Tok, Fairbanks, and Anchorage. This is the first place to go for information about any government-owned lands you are interested in, including state parks, national forests, national monuments, and national parks.

There's another visitor center in Ketchikan, the **Ketchikan Visitors Bureau** (131 Front St.; 907 225-6166 or 800 770-3300) very near the Southeast Alaska Visitor Center. This one specializes in information about Ketchikan itself. **Creek Street**, the town's former red light district seems to be the top attraction for cruise ship passengers. There are shops and a museum with wooden walkways built over a salmon spawning stream. Nearby is a tramway up to a hotel, the **Cape Fox Westmark**. Go on up to see the view and to take a look at some modern totem poles.

Ketchikan is known for its totem poles. The **Totem Heritage Center** is near the downtown area and has 33 of them. The **Saxman Totem Park**, located 2.5 miles (4 km) south of town has another 28 of them and the **Totem Bight State Historical Park** 9.9 miles (16 km) north of town has 14 totems and a model of a Tlingit community house. Along with all those totem poles you'll want to see the **Tongass Historical Museum** (629 Dock Street; 907 225-5600) to gain some perspective and see displays of Tlingit baskets and blankets.

Ketchikan Campgrounds

Ketchikan is pretty well equipped for campers. There are four campgrounds: one is private, two are USFS campgrounds, and one is a state campground. All of the campgrounds are north of town on either the North Tongass Highway or the Ward Lake Road which branches off this highway about 6.5 miles (10.5 km) north of central Ketchikan. There is a **dump station** in town at the Ketchikan Public Works Office (3291 Tongass Ave.) two blocks north of the ferry terminal. The dump station is in the front parking lot of the building, access is difficult except after business hours.

CLOVER PASS RESORT

Address:	PO Box 7322, Ketchikan, AK 99901
Telephone:	(907) 247-2234
Email:	info@cloverpassresort.com

GPS Location: N 55° 28' 17.8", W 131° 48' 46.7"

This campground is the only commercial campground in Ketchikan and is very popular. Not only does it have hookups but it has a very active dock area and is a popular destination for folks from outside Alaska who want to spend the summer fishing the very productive salt water of Southeast. Reservations are definitely recommended.

The campground has about 40 back-in sites. Most are full hookup sites with 20 or 30-amp power. Space is limited and maneuvering room can be scarce but large rigs do use this campground. This facility also has some motel rooms and there is a restaurant overlooking the docks. Other amenities include restrooms with hot showers, a laundromat, a dump station, a dock with boat rentals, fishing charters, a tackle store and a liquor store.

To reach the campground drive north from the ferry terminal on the Tongass Highway for 11.9 miles (19.2 km) and turn left on N. Pt. Higgins Road. The entrance to the campground is on the right in another .6 mile (1.0 km).

SETTLER'S COVE STATE RECREATION SITE

Location: Near Mile 18 of the Tongass Highway

GPS Location: N 55° 30' 28.0", W 131° 43' 41.4"

This is a small state campground located next to a rocky beach in a quiet area quite a distance north of Ketchikan. There are 14 back-in sites arranged off a circular drive, three sites are large enough for rigs to 35 feet, the others are smaller. Sites have no hookups but do have picnic tables and firepits. The restrooms are handicapped-accessible vault toilets and there is a hand water pump.

To reach the campground turn left from the ferry terminal and drive north on the Tongass Highway. After 12.9 miles (20.8 km) the road turns to gravel and at 15.8 miles (25.5 km) you'll see the entrance road to the campground on your left. Automobile access to the campground is closed in the evening from 10 p.m. to 6 a.m.

SIGNAL CREEK CAMPGROUND (U.S. FOREST SERVICE)

Location: At Mile 1.3 of Revilla Road
Res.:   (877) 444-6777
Website
For Res.:   www.reserveusa.com

GPS Location: N 55° 24' 34.3", W 131° 42' 02.3"

The Signal Creek Campground next to Ward Lake is a modern Forest Service campground. The Ward Lake day use area is nearby and the Ward Lake nature trail runs for 1.3 miles around the lake.

There are 24 back-in sites arranged off a circular drive. A few are large enough for rigs to 35 feet. Each site has a picnic table and firepit, there is a hand-operated water pump and handicapped-accessible vault toilets. There's another campground, the Three C's, very close by and really part of the same facility. It is off the Ward Lake access road to this campground and has very similar facilities but only four sites, it's only used for overflow.

To reach the campground turn left from the ferry dock and drive north on the Tongass Highway. After 4.8 miles (7.7 km) turn right on Revilla Road and drive another 1.3 miles (2.1 km). Turn right on the Ward Lake access road, you'll pass the entrance to the Ward Lake day use area on the right, the Three C's campground on the left, and then reach the Signal Creek Campground.

🚐 **LAST CHANCE CAMPGROUND (U.S. FOREST SERVICE)**
    Location: At Mile 2.2 of Revilla Road
    Res.:   (877) 444-6777
    Website
      For Res.:   www.reserveusa.com

GPS Location: N 55° 25' 57.3", W 131° 41' 09.8"

This is another modern Forest Service campground. There are 19 spaces off a paved circular drive. Many of these are long spaces with room for rigs to 35 feet. Sites have picnic tables and firepits and there is a hand-operated water pump as well as handicapped-accessible vault toilets. There is a 14-day limit at this campground.

To reach the campground turn left from the ferry dock and drive north on the Tongass Highway. After 4.8 miles (7.7 km) turn right on Revilla Road and drive another 2.2 miles (3.5 km), you'll see the campground entrance on your right.

> ### Side Trip to Prince of Wales Island from Ketchikan
> ### (2 hours, 45 minutes)

The short run over to Hollis from Ketchikan on the Inter-Island Ferry Authority's *M/V Prince of Wales* has become quite popular. Make sure to secure reservations in advance if you plan to visit Prince of Wales Island.

PRINCE OF WALES ISLAND

Prince of Wales Island offers the best opportunity to explore an undeveloped region of Southeast in your rig. The island has been logged, most of the roads were built for that purpose. Now there are some 2,000 miles of roads, mostly unpaved logging roads but also some paved miles between Hollis and Craig. This is a good place to go to see black bears, there are also many excellent fishing opportunities.

Hollis is near the ferry landing, there is little else there. **Klawock** (population 900), is 24 miles west of Hollis on a paved road and has a good totem pole collection as well as a supermarket. **Craig**, 5 paved miles south of Klawock, is a fishing port and probably would be considered the main service center of the island. The town (population 1,500) has supermarkets, gas, laundromat, and restaurants (including a Burger King). Hollis, Klawock, and Craig are in the central portion of the island.

South of the Klawock/Craig/Hollis axis is **Hydaburg** (population 500). This town of mostly Haida Indians has many totem poles and is an excellent departure point for kayaking the protected west coast of Prince of Wales Island.

To the north of the Klawock/Craig/Hollis axis are most of the logging roads and several smaller communities. **Coffman Cove**, north of Thorne Bay, has a campground and offers services to visitors to the north end of the island. While formal campgrounds are scarce there are many places to park your rig and camp and also a few interesting sights including **El Capitan**, a limestone cave which can be toured with a Forest Service guide.

For information about Prince of Wales Island contact the Craig Ranger District, PO Box 500, Craig, AK 99921 (907) 826-3271 or the Prince of Wales Chamber of Commerce (PO Box 497, Craig, AK 99921 (907) 826-3870).

SOUTHEAST ALASKA

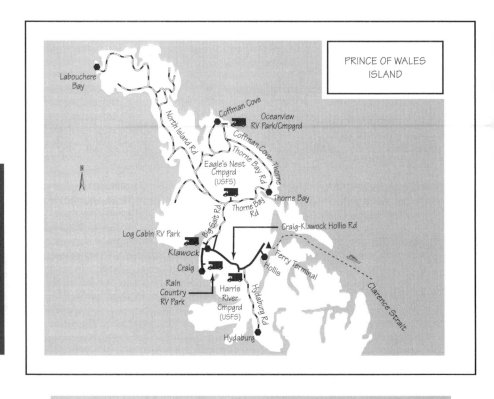

Prince of Wales Island Campgrounds

Camping facilities on Prince of Wales include a few commercial campgrounds and two modern developed USFS campgrounds. There are many spots on the miles of National Forest logging roads where you can free camp without services. Respect private land ownership.

There are two **dump stations** on Prince of Wales Island in addition to the drains at the commercial campgrounds. The first is in Craig next to the Craig City Shop on Cold Storage Road. It is kept locked, during work hours Monday through Friday the key is available next door at the shop, the rest of the time you can get it at the police station. There is no fee.

The second dump station is in Thorne Bay. You'll spot it on the left as you enter town from the west. It too is kept locked, the key is available at City Hall and there is a fee.

▥ HARRIS RIVER CAMPGROUND (U. S. FOREST SERVICE)

Location: Between Mileposts 19 and 20 between Hollis and Klawock

GPS Location: N 55° 28' 03.3", W 132° 51' 22.6"

This is the first campground you'll reach when you leave the ferry. It is a modern forest service campground with 14 camping sites. All are back-in and most are very large. The sites have picnic tables and firepits, there are two hand-operated water pumps, and there are handicapped-accessible vault toilets.

Coming from the ferry landing in Hollis zero your odometer as you leave the parking lot. You'll see the campground on the left in 11 miles (17.7 km). From Klawock if you zero your odometer at the Klawock IGA supermarket you'll reach the campground at 12 miles (19.4).

🚐 LOG CABIN RV PARK

Address:	PO Box 54, Klawock, AK 99925
Telephone:	(907) 755-2205 or (800) 544-2205

GPS Location: N 55° 33' 26.6", W 133° 05' 04.5"

The Log Cabin is a popular destination for fishermen. The waters off the west side of Prince of Wales Island offer excellent fishing, several of the campers here spend the whole summer, every summer. The resort is on the beach and has its own dock facility, charters are offered as well as boat rentals. There are also rental cabins.

There are 14 full-hookup spaces in the camping area. These vary widely because they are located under and between old-growth hemlock and spruce. Some sites are large and others aren't. Definitely walk down the narrow entrance road and look around before entering. Reservations are recommended. The campground has restrooms with hot showers and a laundromat. The office is in the main house at the top of the hill to the right of the entrance drive.

As you enter Klawock from the direction of Hollis zero you odometer at the IGA supermarket. At .1 mile (.2 km) you'll see the road to Thorne Bay go right. Don't turn. At .2 miles you'll see the Big Salt Lake Road go right, turn right and you'll soon see the campground on the left.

🚐 RAIN COUNTRY RV PARK

Address:	510 JS Drive (PO Box 79), Craig, AK 99921
Telephone:	(907) 826-3632
Fax:	(907) 826-2988
Website:	www.raincountryrv.com

GPS Location: N 55° 28' 31.0", W 133° 08' 03.4"

The Rain Country is a new RV park in the town of Craig. It has eleven large back-in sites suitable for the largest rigs, they offer 30 and 50-amp power and full hookups. There are also restrooms with hot showers and a laundry.

To reach the campground zero your odometer in Klawock as you pass over the Klawock River. In 2.6 miles (4.2 km) you'll see the sign for the Craig city limits and at 5.6 miles (9 km) you'll see a sign for the campground and spot the RVs up the hill to the left. When you reach the Burger King you've gone too far. Check-in is at the JS TrueValue hardware store that is off to your right after you enter the park.

🚐 EAGLE'S NEST CAMPGROUND (U.S. FOREST SERVICE)

Location:	19 miles from Klawock on the Thorne Bay Road
Res.:	(877) 444-6777
Website	
For Res.:	www.reserveusa.com

GPS Location: N 55° 42' 07.0", W 132° 50' 11.6"

The second Forest Service campground on Prince of Wales Island is a little smaller than the one at Harris River and also more remote. It has eleven back-in spaces if you count the one occupied by the campground host. These are long spaces suitable for large rigs and they have the usual picnic tables and firepits. The campground has handicapped-accessible vault toilets and also a hand-operated water pump. This campground is adjacent to Ball's Lake and there is a boardwalk trail through the marsh along the lake that is great for watching the lake's wildlife.

To reach the campground you'll have to drive some gravel. From the IGA store in Klawock drive west just .1 mile (.2 km) and you'll spot the road to Thorne Bay on the right. Zero your odometer and head north. In just 2.1 miles (3.4 km) the pavement ends and, for the most part, you won't see any more until you return this way. At 16.6 miles (26.8 km) you'll reach an intersection, turn right toward Thorne Bay, and in another 1.9 miles (3.1 km) you'll see the campground entrance on the left.

OCEANVIEW RV PARK/CAMPGROUND

Address:	PO Box 18035, Coffman Cove, AK 99918
Telephone:	(907) 329-2226
Email:	djeffrey@coveconnect.com
Website:	www.coffmancove.org/rvpark.html

GPS Location: N 56° 00' 56.5", W 132° 49' 33.0"

Little Coffman Cove is well off the beaten path, a distance of 55 miles from Klawock. Amazingly, there's a waterfront campground here with full hookups.

The Oceanview has 14 back-in sites fronting on a rocky beach. All have full hookups with 30-amp power. Restrooms have flush toilets, hot showers, even a laundry.

Coffman cove isn't a large place so finding the campground isn't hard. Approaching town from the south you'll spot a Welcome to Coffman Cove sign, immediately beyond the entrance road to the campground goes right.

Ketchikan to Wrangell (6 hours)

The relatively short run up Clarence Straight to Wrangell offers views of Prince of Wales Island, third largest island in the U.S., to the west along much of the route. The ferry docks right in Wrangell. The layover is generally short but occasionally there are delays due to tide conditions in the Wrangell Narrows to the north which give time for a look around town.

WRANGELL
Population 2,500, Elevation sea level

Wrangell is strategically located near the mouth of the Stikine River. The mouth is on the mainland some 5 miles (8 km) distant. The Stikine has long been a highway into the interior of British Columbia, at one time the swift-flowing river was home to several steamboats. The Russians and British used the town as a fur-trading base and later Wrangell was a supply base for the Stikine (1861), Cassiar, and even the Klondike gold rushes. Today the economy is based on fishing, timber, and tourism, but the Stikine still provides access to mines in the interior.

Wrangell doesn't get nearly as many cruise ships as Ketchikan, Juneau or Skagway so the tourism here is oriented more toward ferry travelers. Sights are open when the ferry is in town, especially if the stopover is going to be long enough for passengers to spend some time ashore. There's a **Visitor's Information Center** (907 874-3901 or 800 367-9745) near the ferry terminal. In town you'll want to visit **Shakes Island** which has totem poles and a tribal house built by the CCC. There are interesting **petroglyphs** along the beach north of town. Wrangell also has a 9-hole golf course known as **Muskeg Meadows**.

If you decide to stay for a while you'll find that **Wrangell Island**, like Prince of Wales Island, has lots of logging roads giving access to some interesting country. The U.S. Forest Service office at 525 Bennett St. (907 874-2323) has information about attractions, campgrounds, trails, and roads.

The **Stikine-LeConte Wilderness** Area is easily reached by boat from Wrangell. The Stikine is a popular float river, particularly the upper reaches near Telegraph Creek. The LeConte tidewater glacier to the north of the Stikine is probably more easily reached from Petersburg which is slightly closer. There are many Forest Service rental cabins along the Stikine as well as two hot springs. For information contact the Tongass National Forest Wrangell Ranger District at PO Box 51, Wrangell, AK 99929; (907) 874-2323.

Wrangell Campgrounds

Surprisingly, Wrangell is one of the better destinations for RVers in Southeast Alas-

WRANGELL

Ferry Terminal
Wrangell
Alaska Waters RV Park — Berger St
City Park
Eastern Passage
Zimovia Hwy
Shoemaker Bay Recreation Area
Stikine Strait
Woronkofski Island
Pat Creek Rd
Chichagof Pass
Zimovia Strait
Etolin Island
McCormack Creek Rd
Nemo Pt Rd
Nemo Campsites (NFS)
Anita Bay Overlook Campsite
Three Sisters Overlook Campsite
The Yunshookuh Loop Campsite

ka. There are two campgrounds offering hookups and many forest service camp-grounds and recreation sites suitable for RVs. Rigs to 30 feet can easily reach the Nemo campsites listed below and rigs to about 25 feet can travel the logging roads and reach many other remote National Forest recreation sites with parking areas that make excellent RV sites, many complete with picnic tables, firepits, and outhouses. Tent campers with an automobile for transportation have an even wider selection because there are many hike-in locations. There is an easily-accessible **dump station** at the Shoemaker Bay campground.

⛟ ALASKA WATERS RV PARK

Address:	241 Berger Street (PO Box 1978), Wrangell, AK 99929
Telephone:	(907) 874-2378 or (800) 347-4462
Email:	info@alaskawaters.com
Website:	www.alaskawaters.com

GPS Location: N 56° 27' 36.8", W 132° 22' 50.2"

This is the commercial campground in Wrangell. It offers 7 back-in spaces with full hookups including 30-amp power. The spaces are large enough for the longest rigs. The building on the site serves as storage and a part-time office for the tour and fish-ing-charter company operated by the same owners, a restroom with shower is avail-able inside the building but you will need a key for access. You may need to visit the main office and gift shop at 109 Lynch Street in town to check in and get a key.

To reach the campground head south on the Zimovia Highway. At Mile 1.1 turn right on Berger Street, the campground is on the right after the turn.

⛟ SHOEMAKER BAY RECREATION AREA

Location:	Mile 4.5 Zimovia Hwy.
Telephone:	(907) 874-2444 for Res.

GPS Location: N 56° 25' 08.4", W 132° 21' 05.8"

For self-contained rigs Shoemaker Bay makes an excellent place to stay while you are in Wrangell. This is a boat harbor, but there are nice RV sites overlooking the harbor, RV parking is allowed in the harbor parking lot, and there is also a tent-camp-ing area. It is possible to make telephone reservations for the RV spaces that have power.

The 16 back-in (or pull-in) spaces overlooking the boat harbor are just off the high-way before you reach the harbor parking lot. Many of these spaces will take the largest rig, 30-amp power is available. A little farther along is the harbor parking lot. RV parking is allowed on the far left along the trees but there are no hookups. There is a tent camping area here too, and restrooms without showers are located across a small footbridge beyond the tent sites. Water is available next to the tennis courts nearby and there is a dump station next to the parking lot entrance. If you are staying at Shoemaker Bay you also may use the city swimming pool facilities on Church Street in town including weight room and showers for no additional charge. You are allowed to stay in this campground for 10 days and this can be extended with permission.

To reach the campground head south on the Zimovia Highway. You'll see the electric sites on the right at Mile 4.4 and the entrance to the harbor parking lot at Mile 4.5.

NEMO CAMPSITES (U.S. FOREST SERVICE)
   Location: Mile 13.7 Zimovia Hwy.

   GPS Location: N 56° 18' 09.2", W 132° 20' 38.2"

The Nemo Campsites are really designed for tent campers but some are suitable for RVs too. There are three different camping areas. All sit high on a mountainside and offer great views. Bald eagles like to perch on snags just below the campsites to enjoy the same views.

The Anita Bay Overlook Campsite has a parking area that could take several RVs to about 30 feet but the parking lot doesn't offer much in the way of amenities or views. There are two tent sites a short distance away with spectacular views, picnic tables, firepits and a handicapped-accessible outhouse.

Three Sisters Overlook Campsite has a parking area right on the main road that will accept several rigs to about 30 feet, there are no amenities at the parking area but the view is pretty good. The one tent-camping site is down a short path and has picnic table, firepit, handicapped-accessible outhouse, and great views.

The Yunshookuh Loop Campsite is the best for RVs. It has three places suitable for parking an RV, all with great views. One has a picnic table and fire ring. The others have tables and fire rings a short distance away. There is also an outhouse at this camping area.

To reach the Nemo Campsites head south on the Zimovia Highway to Mile 13.7. Turn right at the sign for the Nemo Point Recreation Area, zero your odometer, and follow the one-lane gravel road. In .6 mile (1 km) you'll pass a host, the entrance to Yunshookun Loop goes right at .8 mile (1.3 km), the parking for Three Sisters Overlook is on the right at 1.6 miles (2.6 km), and Anita Bay Overlook is at 2.5 miles (4.0 km).

CITY PARK   FREE
   Location: Mile 1.3 Zimovia Hwy.

   GPS Location: N 56° 27' 14.3", W 132° 22' 56.6"

The city park has picnic shelters and allows tent camping for one night only. There are restrooms at the park with flush toilets but they were in very poor condition when we visited. RV camping is not allowed.

To reach the City Park head south on the Zimovia Highway, the City Park is on the right at Mile 1.3.

Wrangell to Petersburg (3 hours)

The ferry trip from Wrangell to Petersburg is one of the most interesting of the entire Inside Passage. Much of the route is through the **Wrangell Narrows** between Kuprenof and Mitkof Islands. This 21-mile passage is often as narrow as 300 feet and quite shallow, there is a string of range markers showing the crew where to steer. The passage through the narrows is very impressive, you'll like the lights at night and the chance to see the intricate passage better during daylight passages. The ferries can only pass through at high tide and this is a big factor in scheduling the ferries. Most cruise ships don't get to go through the narrows because they're too big.

PETERSBURG
Population 3,500, Elevation sea level

Petersburg may be only a few miles from Wrangell but the atmosphere is entirely different. Petersburg is scrubbed and neat and shows its Norwegian heritage. Petersburg is a fishing town with just a little logging thrown in. Like Wrangell, few cruise ships stop in Petersburg.

Also like Wrangell, Petersburg has a local **Visitor Information Office** (907 772-3646) and a **U.S. Forest Service Office** (907 772-3871). Both are located near 1St and Fram and have information and maps of roads, trails, and campgrounds on **Mitkof Island** and other islands nearby.

Sights in Petersburg are limited and show off the town's Norwegian heritage. Wander around town and admire the trim lawns and decorated buildings including the **Sons of Norway Hall**. A Viking boat, the **Valhalla**, sits next to the hall. There's also the **Clausen Memorial Museum** with exhibits on Petersburg's history.

Petersburg, like Wrangell, is used as an access point for the nearby **Stikine-LeConte Wilderness**. There are tours out to see the **Le Conte Glacier** about 25 miles (40 km) east. You can also take jet boat tours up the Stikine River.

Petersburg Campgrounds

Petersburg is well supplied with campgrounds. The town has three commercial ones with hookups, a city tent campground, and a USFS campground. Like Wrangell, Petersburg (Mitkof Island) has a surprisingly large road system in the form of logging roads. Particularly rewarding is the drive to the southern end of the island where you'll find several waterfront locations that are perfect for boondocking, even in large rigs.

In addition to those at the campgrounds there is a **dump station** at Stikine Service Inc, a car wash that is .2 mile (.3 km) north of the ferry dock across from the Petro Express gas station.

⛟ RV STAGING AREA
$$ | BIG RIGS

Location:　Corner of Haugen and Second Street
Telephone:　(907) 772-4430

GPS Location: N 56° 48' 40.4", W 132° 57' 18.0"

Since ferries often arrive in Petersburg in the middle of the night the city has set aside a large parking area that you can drive to when you arrive to spend the time until daylight arrives. Parking is limited to 12 hours or less and the fee is $6 (or $1 per hour). There are no hookups or facilities of any kind, but there is lots of room. Envelopes and a slot are provided for your payment.

When you leave the ferry zero your odometer as you turn left on the highway out front, this is the Mitkof Highway which becomes Nordic Drive as you enter Petersburg. At .9 miles (1.5 km) you'll come to an intersection in downtown Petersburg, turn right on Haugen and drive up the hill for two blocks to 2nd. Turn right here and you'll see the parking area on your right ahead.

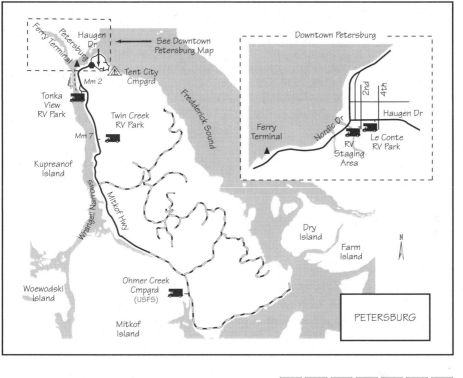

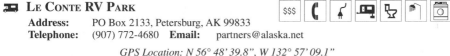 LE CONTE RV PARK

$$$

Address: PO Box 2133, Petersburg, AK 99833
Telephone: (907) 772-4680 **Email:** partners@alaska.net

GPS Location: N 56° 48' 39.8", W 132° 57' 09.1"

This campground is right in Petersburg and very handy. It's primarily a residential trailer park but at least four back-in sites suitable for rigs to 32 feet are kept open for visitors. They are large full-hookup sites with 30-amp power. There is also a tent-camping area. The campground has a laundromat that is also used by folks not staying at the campground and restrooms with hot showers. The owners of this campground do not live on-site. You'll find a phone number posted at the laundromat, give them a call and they'll stop by to check you in.

The campground is located on the corner of 4th and Haugen. Just follow Haugen up the hill from Nordic Drive, the main street through town. This is the same street you follow to reach the RV Staging area above.

TENT CITY CAMPGROUND

$

Location: About 1.5 Miles out Haugen Drive beyond the airport
Telephone: (907) 772-4224

GPS Location: N 56° 48' 13.8", W 132° 55' 23.8"

The tent city campground serves primarily as housing for seasonal cannery workers in Petersburg but is also open to visitors for tent camping but not for RV parking. It is open from May 1 through September 30 each year. There are about fifty wooden platforms for setting up tents or stretching plastic tarps for shelter. A covered area has picnic tables and limited cooking and dish-washing facilities. There are restrooms with flush toilets and coin-operated showers. The campground is operated by the city's Parks and Recreation Department, to stay there you must have a permit. These can be obtained at the Parks and Recreation Department office at City Hall, at the Community Gym, or from the campground manager who is generally at the campground during the afternoon.

To reach the campground just head out Haugen Drive, you'll see the campground on the right in about 1.5 miles (2.4 km).

▥ TONKA VIEW RV PARK

Address: 126 Scow Bay Loop Road (Box 989),
                  Petersburg, AK 99833
Telephone: (907) 772-4814

GPS Location: N 56° 46' 42.1", W 132° 58' 02.8"

This campground is built on gravel fill near the water south of town. While the setting is a little industrial there are fine marine views to the south.

The campground has about 25 sites, both back-in and pull-thru. There's lots of room for big rigs. While many sites are occupied by long-term residents there are quite a few available for overnighters. Sites are full-hookup with 30 and 50-amp power. A large metal building houses both the laundromat and restrooms with showers. This is an adult park and dogs over 30 pounds are not allowed.

From the ferry dock head south. At .1 miles (.2 km) you'll pass the Mile 1 marker, at 2 miles you'll pass the north junction for Sugar Bay Loop Road, and at 2.2 miles (3.5 km) you'll reach the South junction with the Sugar Bay Loop Road. Turn right here and you'll soon see the Tonka View RV Park on the left.

▥ TWIN CREEK RV PARK

Address: PO Box 90, Petersburg, AK 99833
Telephone: (907) 772-3244

GPS Location: N 56° 43' 10.0", W 132° 55' 43.7"

Twin Creek RV Park is located next to the highway south of town. Like the other commercial campgrounds in Petersburg it has a number of permanent residents but there are quite a few spaces for overnighters.

The campground has 15 back-in sites along the front, most with full hookups (30 amp), for overnighters. These are long sites with lots of room to maneuver, big rigs will have no problem. There is a small grocery store here as well as restrooms with showers and a laundry room.

From the ferry dock head south. In 6.1 miles (9.8 km) you'll pass the Mile 7 marker and at 6.6 miles (10.6 km) you'll see the Twin Creek RV Park on the left.

▥ OHMER CREEK CAMPGROUND (U.S. FOREST SERVICE)

Location: Mile 21.5 Mitkoff Highway

GPS Location: N 56° 34' 38.4", W 132° 44' 23.2"

This is a forest service campground with some sites suitable for rigs to 35 feet. There are ten back-in RV sites as well as additional tent sites. Sites have picnic tables and firepits, there is a host, and outhouses are handicapped-accessible. A large turnaround at the back end of the campground lets RVs turn around. A handicapped-accessible trail leads to the nearby creek for fishing.

From the ferry landing head south. After 16.3 miles (26.3 km) the road turns to gravel and you'll see the campground entrance at 20.5 miles (33.1 km).

Petersburg to Sitka (10 hours)

If you look at your map you'll see that unlike other Southeast towns Sitka isn't really located along the Inside Passage. The town sits on the west side of Baranof Island and is quite remote from the normal protected shipping routes. To get to Sitka the ferry must negotiate the narrow and aptly named **Peril Strait**. This must be done at slack water so the ferry is often delayed in Sitka giving visitors a chance to look around. Peril Strait is probably the best place along the entire ferry route to watch for wildlife, particularly bald eagles.

Not all ferries stop at Sitka when passing between Petersburg and Juneau. Those that don't go directly up Stephens Passage on the east side of Admiralty Island. This more direct route to Juneau takes about 8 hours. You'll probably want to make sure yours is a Sitka ferry, even if you don't plan to stop over in Sitka the cost is the same and you have the opportunity to see Peril Strait and perhaps take a quick tour of Sitka while the ferry is in port.

SITKA
Population 9,100, Elevation sea level

Sitka was the capital of Russian America. Long an Indian settlement, the Russians moved in in 1799, were kicked out by the Indians a few years later, and then re-established themselves after a major battle. Sitka is a popular cruise ship port so there are quite a few things to see. The **Visitor's Information Center** (907 747-5940) is located downtown near the Pioneer's Home.

The **Centennial Building**, located at the harbor's edge, is the center of cruise ship activities. Since there is no dock for them in Sitka tourists come ashore in small boats. The **New Archangel Dancers** perform traditional Russian dances and various tours leave from the Centennial Building. Nearby is the **Isabel Miller Museum**, the town's historical museum.

Many of the sights in Sitka are Russian and are located near each other. They include the reconstructed **St. Michael's Cathedral**. The original burned down in 1966 but the irreplaceable icons were saved and are in the new church. There's also the painstakingly restored **Russian Bishop's House**, a reconstructed **Russian blockhouse**, **Castle Hill** where Baranov's Castle was located before it burned in 1894, and a **Russian Orthodox cemetery** with graves dating from long before the U.S. purchase of Alaska.

The Russian and Indian cultures come together forcefully at the **Sitka National Historical Park**. It is located just southeast of town at the mouth of the Indian River.

This is the site of the 1804 Tlingit-Russian battle. There is a Tlingit cultural museum and workshop and several totem poles along pleasant trails. Nearby **Sheldon Jackson Museum** has an excellent museum with artifacts representing many of Alaska's native cultures. Another popular site nearby is the **Alaska Raptor Rehabilitation Center**.

Sitka Campgrounds

Sitka has four campgrounds, one is commercial, one is a city campground with electric and water hookups, and the other two are USFS campgrounds. **Dump stations** are available at the wastewater treatment plant on Japonski Island (see the write-up below about Sealing Cove Boat Harbor Campground for more information), and at the City Maintenance Shop 2.5 miles north of town on Halibut Point Road.

☰ Starrigavan Campground (U.S. Forest Service)

| Location: | North End of Halibut Point Road, just north of ferry dock |
| Res.: | (877) 444-6777 |
| Website |
| For Res.: | www.reserveusa.com |

GPS Location: N 57° 07' 56.2", W 135° 22' 07.6"

This Forest Service campground is convenient to the ferry. From the landing just turn left and you'll be at the entrance gate in just .7 mile (1.1 km). This is about seven miles (11.3 km) from downtown Sitka.

When you enter this campground you have a choice. To the right is the Estuary Loop with 18 RV sites, one is a pull-thru. To the left is the Bayside Loop, it has 7 back-in sites and another seven walk-in tent sites. Some sites will take rigs to 35 feet, they have picnic tables and firepits and there are pit toilets.

☰ Sitka Sportsman's Association RV Park

| Address: | PO Box 3030, Sitka, AK 99835 |
| Telephone: | (907) 747-6033 or (907) 747-8791 |

GPS Location: N 57° 07' 37.7", W 135° 22' 58.3"

This little commercial campground is located right next to the ferry dock so it's an easy place to pull into if you are getting in late. It's a good idea to call and make a reservation if you plan to do that.

The campground has about 16 back-in spaces on a paved surface, the sites have electricity (30 amp) and water. A small handicapped-accessible restroom building has showers and flush toilets.

When you leave the ferry dock turn right. You'll see the campground entrance on the right in just a tenth of a mile.

☰ Sealing Cove Boat Harbor Campground

| Location: | Japonski Island |

GPS Location: N 57° 02' 57.3", W 135° 20' 57.4"

The sites at this campground are essentially long slots in a parking lot overlooking the Sealing Cove Boat Harbor. There are 26 of them, and they offer 30-amp electricity and water hookups. Next door at the marina there is a bathroom with a flush toilet

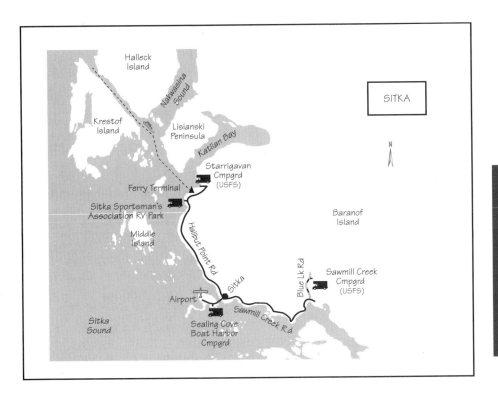

but no showers. There is a 15-day limit for stays here.There is a city dump station nearby. To reach it continue past the camping area toward the airport and take the first left onto Kruzov Ave. The dump station is next to the large gray building on the right ahead.

To drive to Sealing Cove Boat Harbor turn right when you leave the ferry dock. Drive 6.8 miles (11 km) to a major intersection with Lake Street. Turn right here and in .4 miles (.6 km) you'll drive up and over the bridge onto Japonski Island. Immediately after descending on the far side of the bridge you'll see the RV parking area ahead and on the left.

SAWMILL CREEK CAMPGROUND (U.S. FOREST SERVICE)

FREE

Location: 3.6 miles (5.8 km) south of town off Sawmill Creek Road

GPS Location: N 57° 03' 40.8", W 135° 12' 32.9"

This Forest Service campground has about seven RV sites and a additional three walk-in tent sites. Several of the RV sites are arranged around a very large gravel opening in the trees so any size rig has plenty of room to park and maneuver. Camp sites have picnic tables and firepits and there are older outhouses.

To reach the campground drive south from town on Sawmill Creek Road. If you zero your odometer as you pass the post office at Mile 1 you'll come to the intersection with Blue Lake Road at 4.2 miles (6.8 km). Turn left here and follow Blue Lake Road for 1.4 miles (2.3 km), the campground entrance is on your right.

Sitka to Juneau (8 hours, 45 minutes)

The ferries leave Sitka the way they arrive, through Peril Straight. They then travel up Chatham Straight with Admiralty Island to the east and Chichagof Island to the west. At the north end of Admiralty Island the ferry rounds the Mansfield Peninsula and docks at Auke Bay, 13 miles north of downtown Juneau. If the stop is long enough (it often is) you can take a quick bus tour of Juneau even if you don't schedule a stopover.

Juneau
Population 32,000, Elevation sea level

Alaska's capital city is one of the most popular tourist destinations in Southeast, almost all of the cruise ships stop here. There are quite a few things to see and do in Juneau. Government and tourism are the mainstays of the economy here.

Juneau actually spreads over quite a large area for a Panhandle city. The downtown area is cramped, the buildings climb up the side of Mt. Juneau and Gastineau Peak. The population is spread out over neighboring Douglas Island which is connected by a bridge and north into the Mendenhall Valley where there is lots more room.

The **Visitor Information Center** (907 586-2201) in Juneau is in Centennial Hall at 101 Eagan Drive. There's also a small one at the ferry dock. There is a Forest Service information office in Centennial Hall. Juneau is the usual jumping-off point for both Glacier Bay National Park and Admiralty Island's Pack Creek Bear Observatory, see Chapter 14 for more about both of these destinations.

Visitor-oriented sights and activities in Juneau include the **Alaska State Museum** and the **Juneau-Douglas City Museum** downtown. State buildings including the **Governor's Mansion**, **State Office Building** (SOB), **State Capitol Building**, and **House of Wickersham** are worth a look. The downtown area is interesting to explore, you can get walking tour maps at the visitor information center. A new attraction in Juneau is the **Mt. Roberts Tramway and Observatory**, the lower station is near the cruise ship dock. If you have come to appreciate the products of the **Alaskan Brewing Company** you might want to tour the brewery at 5429 Shaune Dr which is in Lemon Creek between Juneau and the Mendenhall Valley. Tours start every 30 minutes.

Probably the most-visited sight in Juneau is the **Mendenhall Glacier**. The glacier is actually inside the city limits, you can drive to the Mendenhall Visitor Center which offers excellent views. There are also hiking trails in the area.

Juneau Campgrounds

Juneau gets a lot of camping visitors and has the facilities to handle them. There are six campgrounds in town: two are commercial RV parks, two are USFS campgrounds, one is a state park, and there is a city-operated parking area. Downtown Juneau is quite cramped and parking is difficult. Try leaving your RV outside town and using the Capital Transit Bus System.

The ferry terminal is located off the Glacier Highway at Mile 13 north of downtown

Juneau. All of the directions to campgrounds below are given from the ferry docks.

In addition to the drains and dump stations at the campgrounds Juneau has several other **dump stations**. There is one near the campsites at Savikko Park on Douglas Island, directions for finding it are found in the write-up for that camping area. Another is at Jackie Renninger Park (2400 Mendenhall Loop Road). There is also a dump station at the Valley Tesoro station near the Mendenhall Center Mall at about Mile 7.5 of the Glacier Highway. It is located behind the station and is difficult to access with large rigs.

▄▄ SPRUCE MEADOW RV PARK

    Address: 10200 Mendenhall Loop Rd., Juneau, AK 99801
    Telephone: (907) 789-1990   **Fax:** (907) 790-7231
    Email: juneaurv@gci.net
    Website: JuneauRV.com

       GPS Location: N 58° 24' 11.8", W 134° 36' 14.9"

This is Juneau's newest commercial RV park. There are about sixty full-hookup back-in sites and they are suitable for rigs to 40 feet. Full hookups include 30-amp power and cable TV. Parking is on gravel and there are wide spaces of natural vegetation between most of the sites. Facilities include handicapped-accessible restrooms (individual rooms) with showers, a laundromat, and a dump station. While the park is located in a country setting it is on the bus line and not far from the Mendenhall Glacier. Reservations are a good idea.

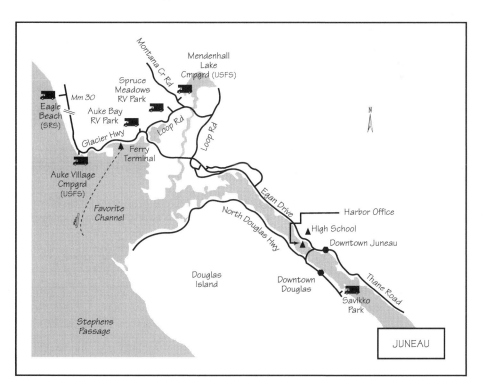

SOUTHEAST ALASKA

To drive to the park from the ferry landing turn right onto the Glacier Highway toward downtown Juneau. After 1.6 miles (2.6 km) turn left onto Mendenhall Loop Road. Drive another 2.1 miles (3.4 km) and you will see the campground sign and entrance on the left side of the highway.

⊞ Mendenhall Lake Campground (U.S. Forest Service)

Location:	Off Montana Creek Road near Mendenhall Glacier
Res.:	(877) 444-6777
Website	
For Res.:	www.reserveusa.com

GPS Location: N 58° 24' 47.1", W 134° 35' 27.0"

The Mendenhall Lake Campground has recently been upgraded and in many ways it is now the nicest campground in Juneau. Would you believe a Forest Service campground with 50-amp hookups and hot showers?

The campground has 96 sites, a few are full-hookup (20, 30, and 50 amp), others have electricity and water or electricity only hookups. Three hookup sites are pull-thrus. Many sites, even those without hookups, are large and are suitable for rigs to 40 feet. There is a dump station and modern handicapped-accessible restrooms with flush toilets and showers. Some of the sites at this campground are on the waterfront with views of the Mendenhall Glacier, but not any of the sites with hookups.

To drive to the park from the ferry landing turn right onto the Glacier Highway toward downtown Juneau. After 1.6 miles (2.6 km) turn left onto Loop Road. Drive another 2.6 miles (4.2 km) and you will see a road to the left marked Montana Creek Road and Mendenhall Lake. Turn left here and you'll reach the entrance to the campground in .6 miles (1 km), it's on the right.

⊞ Auke Bay RV Park

Location:	11930 Glacier Highway, Auke Bay, AK 99801
Telephone:	(907) 789-9467

GPS Location: N 58° 23' 15.9", W 134° 39' 02.4"

This RV park is conveniently located along the Glacier Highway not far from the ferry terminal. While it does have a number of semi-permanent residents there are also a number of spaces for overnighters.

Most of the 30 or so back-in slots for overnighters have full hookups with 30-amp power. They are suitable for large rigs. A small modern building houses restrooms with flush toilets and showers and there is a laundry room.

From the ferry dock turn right and proceed for 1.4 miles (2.3 km), you'll see the campground on the left.

⊞ Auke Village Campground (U.S. Forest Service)

Location:	Glacier Highway Mile 15

GPS Location: N 58° 22' 33.2", W 134° 43' 42.3"

This is an older small U.S. Forest Service Campground located near the beach. It has 12 back-in sites. Most are small, the few largest ones would take RVs to about

25 feet. Sites have firepits and picnic tables and there are outhouses. Short trails lead down to the rocky beach. There is a two-week limit here.

From the ferry dock turn left on the Glacier Highway. In .9 mile (1.5 km) turn left on a small road labeled Auke Village Rec Area and then in another .9 miles (1.4 km) turn left into the campground.

⊞ EAGLE BEACH STATE RECREATION SITE

Location: Glacier Highway Mile 28.5

GPS Location: N 58° 31' 35.7", W 134° 48' 58.3"

This campground is far out of town near the mouth of the Eagle River and seldom used by RV visitors to Juneau. If you prefer this kind of location you'll find a large gravel lot with about 30 parking sites arranged in small cleared back-in areas around the perimeter as well as more parking on gravel in the center of the cleared area. There are some firepits but no picnic tables. Any size rig will find plenty of room. The only facilities are port-a-potties.

From the ferry terminal turn left and proceed 13.8 miles (22.3 km), you'll see the campground on the left.

⊞ SAVIKKO PARK (CITY AND BUROUGH OF JUNEAU)

Location: Douglas Island

GPS Location: N 58° 16' 31.8", W 134° 23' 28.6"

Savikko Park offers 4 back-in RV spaces. They're just paved parking spaces. Camping here is best for self-contained rigs because restrooms are quite a distance away and are really provided for users of the sports fields in the park. There is a dump station nearby across the park access road.

To camp at this park you must register at the harbor office over in Juneau. The following instructions describe the location of both the harbor office and the camping area. From the ferry terminal turn right and head for downtown Juneau. At 10.9 miles (17.6 km) you will see the large high school building to the left, the turn toward the boat harbor and harbor office is to the right. Turn in and register. When you return to the main highway after signing in turn right and proceed another .2 miles (.3 km) to the Douglas Bridge. Turn right and pass over the bridge and then on the far side at the Y turn to the left. In 2 miles (3.2 km) the road to the park and camping goes left, you'll see the dump station on the left almost immediately after this left turn, the campsites are on the right. This road continues to a boat harbor and sports fields.

Juneau to Haines (4 hours, 30 minutes) and Skagway (1 hour more)

From Juneau ferries travel north up the Lynn Canal to Haines and then Skagway. Almost all of the ferries make both stops. Both towns provide access to the Alaska Highway in Canada and eventually to Alaska.

SOUTHEAST ALASKA

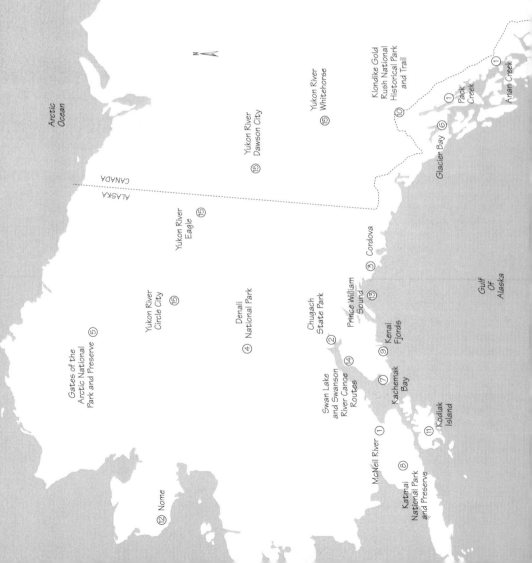

CAMPING AWAY FROM THE ROAD SYSTEM

Arctic Ocean

CANADA
ALASKA

Yukon River
Dawson City ⑮

Yukon River
Whitehorse ⑮

Klondike Gold
Rush National
Historical Park
and Trail ⑩

Pack
Creek ①

Anan Creek ①

Glacier Bay ⑥

Yukon River
Eagle ⑮

Yukon River
Circle City ⑮

Denali
National Park ④

Chugach
State Park ②

Cordova ③

Prince William
Sound ⑬

Gates of the
Arctic National
Park and Preserve ⑤

Gulf
Of
Alaska

Swan Lake
and Swanson
River Canoe
Routes ⑭

Kenai
Fjords ⑨

Kachemak
Bay ⑦

Kodiak
Island

McNeil River ①

Katmai
National Park
and Preserve ⑧

Kodiak Island ⑪

Nome ⑫

Chapter 14

Camping Away From The Road System

INTRODUCTION

A quick look at a map of Alaska will show you that highways reach only a small portion of the huge land area. In the west, the north, the southwest, and even in the central part of the state where the few roads are located there are thousands of square miles with tiny populations only assessable using air or water transportation. No visit to Alaska can really be considered complete if you don't make at least one trip into the true wilderness. It's the only way you can appreciate one of Alaska's truly outstanding features: miles and miles of country with no people.

There are several ways to get away from the highways. The least expensive is no doubt hiking. Several areas have excellent trail systems. But for quick access to really remote country there is no substitute for an aircraft. Alaska has an air transportation system like nowhere else, don't hesitate to use it. In a few areas boats provide the best access whether they are the state ferries of Southeast, Southcentral, and Southwest or a riverboat, kayak, raft or canoe.

Preparation for an Off-Highway Trip

Your first step should be thorough **research** of the planned trip. You need to know all about the destination, how to get there, what kind of weather to expect, and much more. The more information you have the more enjoyable and safer your trip will be. You can find a lot of information in books, magazines, and on the Internet. Alaska's Public Lands Information Centers are also a great place to find information. Contact the one in Anchorage at: Alaska Public Lands Information Center, 605 W. 4th Ave., Suite 105, Anchorage, AK 99501; (907) 271-2737.

Many Alaska off-road camping destinations will be on government lands with a managing agency. Most of these agencies specialize in providing information to interested visitors. A letter and follow-up phone call can net you a lot of information including the names of some possible guides and transportation options.

It is important to have good maps of the area you will visit. These should be USGS maps with good detail including terrain data. They're a great planning tool and will be a big help once you are in the woods. Never go into the wilderness without good maps.

Gear for an Off-Highway Trip

We'll assume that you are an experienced wilderness camper. If not, you should not consider venturing far into the wilderness without an experienced guide. You should outfit yourself for an Alaska trip much like you would elsewhere. The following information and ideas cover areas that may be unfamiliar to you because they are specific to Alaska.

You should, of course, carry good maps and a compass. Alaska is unusual, however, in that some areas have few useful features to allow you to place yourself on a map. Huge flat regions have no mountains for triangulation, and from the ground it is difficult to see the bodies of water that are the only real way of placing yourself. On some river floats it is very difficult to tell how far you have come and therefore to adjust the schedule of your trip. One oxbow bend looks much like another on the map. You may arrive days before your scheduled pickup or days late. Consider carrying a **GPS** (global positioning satellite) receiver. It will give you a lot of peace of mind.

Alaska camping requires a good **tent**. It must be waterproof and bug proof. It must also be very durable. High winds can tear a cheap tent apart and leave you with no protection from the weather and the bugs. Many people like to have a dark-colored tent in Alaska, it helps them to sleep when the sun continues to shine all night. Finally, a tent that can stand without stakes is very useful, particularly when you are camping on gravel bars or moss tussocks where pegs just don't hold well.

Even in the middle of the summer it is a good idea to have a **sleeping bag** that will keep you warm down into the low 30's (Fahrenheit). If it gets colder you can wear clothes in the bag to stay warm. The bag should be a synthetic so that it will be warm when wet and so that you can get it dry if it does get wet. You will need a **foam pad**, the ground can be cold when permafrost is just a few inches beneath the surface.

A **stove** of some kind is essential for camping in Alaska. Many areas do not even have firewood available since they are beyond the timber line. Others have only very wet wood. Many parks do not allow campfires at all. We like the kind that will burn on a wide variety of fuels since it may be hard to find exactly what you need in a remote location. You can almost always find gasoline.

You will need some means of **water purification**. Giardia lamblia (the protozoan that causes beaver fever) is widespread throughout the state. Boiling water for 5 minutes will kill it, but boiling uses fuel and leaves hot water—OK for cooking but not great when you are thirsty. We like a backpacker's water filter. If you start with water that isn't stagnant and smelly you don't need a really expensive one designed for removing viruses and bacteria, in fact a filter with a really small pore size will quickly become unusable when used to filter silty water. A pore size of 2 microns (yes 2, not .2) is small enough to filter out giardia and other protozoans. When you must use silty water you should let it sit in a pan until the suspended material has had a chance to settle, that will extend the life of your filter.

Normal **hiking boots** often don't work well in Alaska. They're fine in high well-drained terrain, but many Alaskan trails are very wet. If you think that your hiking area might be wet make sure to have some kind of rubber boots that will provide enough support to let you hike comfortably. Many hikes require repeated river crossings. These rivers can be cold, many come directly from glaciers. You will need some kind of easy-drying shoe to wear across them, many people bring canvas tennis shoes along. Another alternative is neoprene booties like scuba divers wear. They keep your feet warmer than tennis shoes but aren't very good for wearing around camp.

When around the water in Alaska the footwear of choice is often **hip boots**. When you wear them in a boat never tie them to your belt, if you fall overboard they can kill you. Make sure you can kick out of them in an emergency. Chest waders are a real no-no in a boat unless they are the neoprene type that actually help you float.

When crossing rivers you will need a **hiking stick** or pole. Since such a stick can be hard to find above the tree line you may want to carry poles. The new collapsible walking poles can also be a big help when crossing moss tussocks and other unstable ground with a pack on your back.

Clothing must be warm and capable of keeping you warm when wet. This means wool or synthetics. Cotton is useless unless it is a dry sunny day. Why carry it along? Clothing that can be layered so that you are always comfortably dressed is best. Bring three changes of clothes: one that you will probably have gotten wet, one to wear, and a backup. You'll want synthetic long underwear, even in the summer bring at least one light pair for top and bottom. For rain gear forget ponchos, you want a durable coat and pant combination that will keep you dry. A waterproof hat with a brim will really be appreciated if the rain keeps coming and coming. A wool stocking cap is also very useful, it is light and will keep you warm in cooler temperatures and when sleeping. Finally, bring a mosquito head net that will fit over that wide-brimmed hat. You may not need it but when you do you will love it. Also bring gloves, they'll protect you from the weather and from the bugs.

Insect repellant is essential. See Chapter 2 for a discussion of this.

Many Alaska wilderness trips are float trips on rivers or remote kayak expeditions. Some of those require that you use a small aircraft for transportation. That means you can't use a hard-shell canoe or kayak since it is not legal to fly an aircraft with such a load tied to the float struts when passengers are being carried. Even with no passengers a special permit is required. Folding kayaks and canoes and inflatable rafts are very popular in Alaska. If you plan to do a lot of this type of travel and you want to purchase an expensive piece of gear for Alaska, these are just the ticket. On the other hand, rafts are often available for rent from air-taxi operators. Before allowing yourself to be dropped in the wilderness with a rental raft make sure that you know it is in excellent condition. Also make sure you have a repair kit in your gear.

Safety

There are some safety issues that are unique to Alaska. Even if you have extensive camping experience elsewhere you should be aware of them.

When traveling in the wilderness it is essential that a **reliable person** back home knows where you are. That person should know your exact planned route and schedule and the name of the charter operator responsible for picking you up, if there is one. If you don't show up at the expected time your reliable friend can raise the alarm. We do not feel that having an air taxi or charter boat operator know your plans is enough. Better to have someone who knows you well and who will not drop the ball. Actually, better to have two such people.

Never travel alone in the wilderness. If something happens–you break a leg, an axe slips–you will need help. Also never travel on an isolated river in only one raft or boat. You don't want to be stuck if your only boat is damaged beyond repair.

Almost all Alaskan wilderness areas are home to lots of **bears**. There are very few bear attacks, but there are some. Both black and brown bears are dangerous. It is absolutely essential that you use proper camping techniques in bear country. Pamphlets are distributed from many sources in the state with information about how to camp in bear country and how to react if you meet a bear. There is also a lot of information available about bear habits. The best way to stay safe is to know a lot about the subject.

Here are some of the essentials. Do not set your tent up on a game trail or in an area with bear sign like tracks and droppings. If a bear is attracted to your campsite and then leaves you should pack up and leave immediately, it may return. Bears are attracted by food odors and also by the smell of cosmetics and perfume. Cook well away from your tent. Store food well away from your tent (300 feet minimum) and suspend it high in a tree if there is one. You can throw a rope over a limb to do this. Wrap food in double plastic and seal it. Never cook or eat in your tent. If you ever have cooked in the tent it must be washed thoroughly or replaced. Garbage will attract bears. Double bag garbage in sealed plastic and keep it far from your tent. Clean fish well away from camp, preferably in the water and downstream. Don't wear your cooking or fish-cleaning clothes to bed, store them in a sealed double plastic bag away from your tent. Wash yourself before going to bed to remove food and fish odors.

It is now possible to buy or rent bear-proof containers for trips into bear country. These provide a place to store food that will not attract bears, or failing that, they will not allow the bear to get to the food. Denali and many other parks require their use by off-road campers.

When hiking it is important not to surprise a bear. This is easy to do, particularly when traveling up wind. Make noise, perhaps by talking or even the use of bells attached to your equipment or tin cans filled with pebbles. Most bears will get out of your way if they hear you coming. Mountain bikers should be particularly cautious, they travel quickly and can easily come up on a bear with little warning. Hikers must be alert and watch the trail ahead at all times. Be particularly cautious if your view is obstructed by underbrush or a turn in the trail.

If you do happen to meet a bear on the trail do not approach for a better look. Do not run. Any bear can outrun you over any terrain. Stay calm. Bears seldom attack unless threatened or provoked. Sows with cubs are particularly dangerous because they tend to be very protective. Slowly back away and leave the area. If the bear follows try dropping an item of clothing or even your pack to distract it. Again, do not run. If it continues to come talk in a calm but firm voice. You may try climbing a tree but be aware that bears are quick and can also climb trees, a tree-climbing strategy is not always successful.

If you are attacked try to protect your vital organs. Drop to the ground with your face down, knees drawn up to your chest and hand clasped tightly over the back of your neck. In most cases you want to keep still and not present a threat to the bear, hopefully he will soon leave.

Some experts, including the Yukon Government's bear pamphlet, advise fighting back if the attacking bear is a black bear without cubs. The pamphlet says to yell and fight back as hard as you can, with a rock, a tree branch, or your bare hands. Remember, this is for black bears only, not grizzlies.

Many Alaskans carry weapons in the wilderness. This is not allowed in some park areas but it is allowed in many others. Experts say that nothing less than a 30-06 rifle or shotgun is really useful and these are inconvenient and heavy. An alternative is pepper spray–the big bottles of it designed specifically for bears. The judge is still out on these. They are sometimes ineffective and even if driven off with spray bears often return. Definitely do not spray pepper spray on something as a repellent, bears may actually be attracted. A favorite story in the North is the one about the cheechako who sprayed himself with bear spray as he would have done with insect repellent. There have been cases of airplanes, rafts, and tents that have been chewed by bears attracted by the taste of the pepper.

Many people do not carry any bear protection, they rely on the statistics that show actual bear attacks are unusual.

Hypothermia can be a real danger in Alaska because temperatures are often in a range that is dangerous. Long days of even 40° to 50° temperatures can cause hypothermia, especially if there is moisture involved. Be aware and don't let yourself get chilled. Most rivers and lakes in the north are very cold, immersion even for minutes is life-threatening. Stay near shore and always wear a life preserver when you're in a boat.

There may be lots of wildlife in Alaska but it is foolish to think that you will be able to feed yourself with it during a camping trip. Most game is protected unless it is hunting season. The fish probably won't bite if you are depending upon them. Always **bring enough food** for your planned trip, plus several days extra rations for if you get lost or injured. If you are expecting pickup by a boat or airplane it is not at all unusual for weather to cause delays of up to a week in some areas. Plan accordingly.

Low Impact Camping

Responsible camping in the wilderness means low-impact camping. Try to leave as little sign of your passing as possible.

While you are on the move try to stay on existing trails. Wear boots with shallow treads. Hike single file to keep from widening the trail. When there is no trail try to stay on rocks and creek beds, stay off loose or wet terrain. If you must walk over delicate terrain like a meadow spread out and do not walk single file.

When camping find a place that won't be damaged by your campsite. Gravel is best. Don't cut trees and brush. Wear light shoes instead of heavy boots in camp and avoid making paths. Avoid campfires if there is not a suitable site, use a stove instead. Gravel bars along rivers are good campfire sites since high water in the spring generally scours them. Carry out all garbage. Drain dishwater into a small hole well away from streams and lakes and cover with earth. Use only biodegradable soap and wash well away from lakes and streams. Dispose of human waste by digging a shallow hole well away from streams and lakes and then covering it with earth when you are done, burn or carry out toilet paper.

Air Transportation

Small aircraft are often used for transportation in Alaska. Even small villages usually have an airport and at least weekly-scheduled service. It is usually less expensive to travel on a scheduled carrier than to charter your own aircraft so check into this if you are heading into the bush. Travel to a transportation hub that is close to your final destination before you charter.

The final leg of your trip may require the actual charter of an aircraft. Most transportation hubs have several different outfits so rates are usually competitive. Before shopping you need to know exactly how much your gear weighs. The cost to you will depend upon several factors: the size aircraft required, type of aircraft required (floats or wheels), the flight time, and how busy the air taxi operator is. Check with several outfits and make sure that the one you choose is familiar with your destination. Many off-runway landing sites are not easy to use, actual experience in flying to the place you want to go is important.

Weather can greatly restrict a small aircraft. Depend upon your pilot to make weather decisions. Do not pressure a pilot to fly in questionable weather, that is the cause of many accidents. Weather may delay your departure or pickup. Always have enough food with you on a trip to allow you to comfortably wait out an extended period of bad weather.

Waiting for a pickup can be a stressful experience. Sometimes weather en route is impassable even though the weather you can see seems just fine for flying. You will feel much better about it if you know that someone other than the air taxi operator knows you are out there. Make sure a reliable friend knows when you are to return and who you have contracted for your pickup. There have been a few cases where parties have been dropped off and not picked up as scheduled. There have even been fatal cases where people chartered into the wilderness and didn't set up any pick-up at all. Make sure your pickup arrangements are clear and unambiguous. You and the charter operator must know the exact location. It must be easy to identify from the ground and also from the air.

The Public-Use Cabins

One of the best ways to get out into the wilderness in Alaska is to rent a cabin from the government. Several different management agencies, both Federal and State, have a considerable number of cabins scattered around the state. These cabins are a good deal, most are available for under $50 per night and most are in very desirable locations.

Unfortunately each of the organizations has its own reservation system. Here's a quick rundown of what is available. The first place to go for further information is one of the four public lands information centers, they can tell you what is available and where to go to make reservations. The Anchorage Alaska Public Lands Information Center is at 605 W. 4th, Suite 105, Anchorage, Alaska 99501. The telephone number is (907) 271-2737.

US Forest Service in Tongass National Forest - There are about 150 cabins, almost all require boat, aircraft, or hiking access. All have wood or oil stove, table, chairs, beds without mattresses and outhouses. Some cabins have boats.

US Forest Service in Chugach National Forest - About 45 cabins in the Kenai Mountains and Prince William Sound. All except one require boat, aircraft, or hiking access. All have wood or oil stove, table, chairs, beds without mattresses and outhouses. Some cabins have boats.

Alaska Dept. of Natural Resources - They have 35 cabins in the Interior, Southcentral, and Southeast Alaska. A few are accessible by road, most require a boat, aircraft, or hiking. Cabins are similar to Forest Service cabins.

Bureau of Land Management - The BLM has several cabins near Fairbanks.

Fish and Wildlife Service - The USF&W Service has several cabins on Kodiak Island.

The cabins are nothing luxurious, really just a glorified form of camping. They do provide a roof over your head for protection from the weather, heat, and some protection from bears. Most require that you bring everything you will need: bedding, kitchen utensils, lanterns, and so on. You also must arrange your own transportation, most air and boat charter operators in the region will be familiar with the cabins and how best to access them.

A SELECTION OF OFF-HIGHWAY DESTINATIONS

In this section you'll find a quick summary of just some of the smorgasbord of off-the-road offerings available around the state. Each summary has information about location, attractions, and how best to get there. Since there is no room in this book for the many maps that would be necessary to show all of these places you should read them with a supplementary map in hand. The best would probably be the Alaska Atlas & Gazetteer, see the *Travel Library* in Chapter 2 for more information.

BEAR-VIEWING HOT SPOTS
McNeil River, Pack Creek, Anan Creek, and Others

When the salmon start running the bears soon appear. Coastal brown bears are the same animal as the smaller inland grizzlies, they just eat better. Several places in Alaska have become known as the best places to see bears, lots of bears.

McNeil River is the best of the bunch, and the hardest to get into. The river is located on the west side of Cook Inlet and flows into Kamishak Bay. Literally dozens (often over 50 at one time) of brown bears fish for salmon in the falls near viewing platforms. The presence of observers seems to make little difference to the bears, they just go ahead and mind their own business. Very few people are allowed to be there at one time. The season is from June through the middle of August. The best access is by floatplane from Anchorage, Homer or Kenai. Tent sites are designated and are located away from the river. Access is limited, visitors are selected by lottery, applications must be in by March 1. For more information and lottery applications contact the Alaska Department of Fish and Game, Attn: McNeil River, 333 Raspberry Road, Anchorage, AK 99518; (907) 267-2180.

The McNeil River is not the only river with bears in that same area. Access to some of the others is less restricted. Floatplane operators in Homer specialize in bear-watching flights, check with them about the possibilities. There are also multi-day boat tours to the southern side of the Alaska Peninsula to watch bears. Homer is the place to check on that too.

Pack Creek is located on the east side of Admiralty Island, about 25 miles (40 km) from Juneau. Admiralty Island is known for its brown bears, there are thought to be some 1,700 of them on the island. Pack Creek is the easiest place to see them, there is a viewing platform but no overnight camping is allowed. Usually viewers see only a few bears at a time. The season lasts from the middle of July to the last part of August. Access is by boat or floatplane from Juneau. Eight persons at a time are allowed in the viewing tower, viewing time is limited to three hours, and viewing is allowed from 9 a.m. to 9 p.m. Permits are handed out on a first-come, first-served basis. For information contact the Admiralty Island National Monument, 8461 Old Dairy Road, Juneau, AK 99801; (907) 586-8800 or Tongass National Forest, Regional Office, 709 W. 9th Street (PO Box 21628), Juneau, AK 99802; (907) 586-8806. They can give you a list of approved air-taxi guide services and then you make your own arrangements.

Anan Creek Bear Observatory is another Southeast location. This is primarily a viewing spot for black bears although a few browns do show up. The observatory is located about 30 miles (48 km) southeast of Wrangell near the mouth of Bradfield Canal. There is a viewing platform here also, usually several bears are visible. No camping is permitted in the area although there is a Forest Service rental cabin about a mile away. The season at Anan Creek runs from the first part of July through the first part of September while the pink salmon are running. For information contact the U.S. Forest Service, Wrangell Ranger District, PO Box 51, Wrangell, AK 99929; (907) 874-2323.

CAMPING AWAY FROM THE ROAD

Several good bear-viewing areas are mentioned in other places in this book: Fish Creek near Hyder, Alaska is covered in Chapter 5 and the Brooks River in Katmai National Park is discussed below. Kodiak Island also offers good bear-viewing opportunities, particularly at fly-out locations. And don't forget Denali National Park.

CHUGACH STATE PARK

The 490,000-acre Chugach State Park is a mountainous area that directly adjoins Anchorage to the east. Most of the park, in fact, is technically within the boundaries of the Municipality of Anchorage. Anchorage residents can literally be in the wilderness within minutes of leaving their homes. The park is popular with almost everyone interested in the outdoors and offers opportunities to hike, camp, climb rocks or mountains, mountain bike, kayak, fish, hunt, snow-machine, ski, float rivers, and even hang-glide. Accommodating all these uses means that the park has zones and restricted areas to keep incompatible uses separated. There is wildlife in this park even though it is part of the largest city in the state; you may see black and brown bears, mountain goats, Dall sheep, moose, wolves, bald eagles, and even beluga whales.

There are about 50 miles (81 km) of maintained trails within the park, and many more miles of excellent alpine hiking although alder thickets can be a problem. Popular hikes include **Flattop Mountain** (1.5 miles (2.4 km) one way), **Williwaw Lakes** (5 miles (8 km) one way), **Wolverine Peak** (6 miles (9.7 km) one way), **McHugh and Rabbit Lakes Trail** (7 miles (11.3 km) one way) and **Crow Pass** (26 miles (42 km) one way). There are also good trails from the Eklutna Lake Campground.

Camping in the park is mostly unrestricted. The park has a formal campground, Eklutna Lake, which is covered in Chapter 7 of this book. Fires are not allowed in the park except in the firepits at the few formal campsites. Use camp stoves instead.

Access to the park is from many points including the Seward Highway along Turnagain Arm, the upper hillside area of Anchorage, the Arctic Valley Road (from Mile 6 of the Glenn Highway), the Eagle River Road (from Mile 13 of the Glenn Highway) and the Eklutna Road (from Mile 26 of the Glenn Highway). Visitor centers are located at the end of the Eagle River Road and at the Potter Section House at Mile 115 of the Seward Highway near Potter Marsh and Turnagain Arm. For information contact Chugach State Park, Potter Section House, HC 52, Box 8999, Indian, AK 99540; (907) 345-5014. The Eagle River Visitor Center phone is (907) 694-2108.

CORDOVA AND THE COPPER RIVER DELTA

Cordova is one of two destinations in this chapter that is perfectly suitable for RVs. The other is Kodiak, see below. Access to this small south-central Alaska town is quite easy. The Alaska Marine Highway system connects Cordova frequently with both Whittier and Valdez. Cordova is a pleasant little town, but the town isn't the only attraction here. The **Copper River Highway** leads out of town to the east, crossing the **Copper River Delta**, one of Alaska's premier bird migration and nesting areas, and then turns northeast to dead-end after 48 miles (77 km) at the collapsed **Million**

Dollar Bridge and **Child's Glacier**.

Cordova (population 3,200) today is primarily a fishing town but has good tourist facilities. It was originally the salt-water terminus of the Copper River and Northwestern Railway, which was built to transport copper ore from the Kennicott Mine and operated until 1938. For visitor information go to the **Chamber of Commerce** on first street (907 424-7260). The **Cordova Museum and Library** at 622 1ˢᵗ Street is an excellent place to start your tour of the area, it has historical and art exhibits. Another important information site is the **USFS Cordova Area District Office** at 612 2ⁿᵈ St. (907 424-7661) which has an interpretive center and information about local hikes, attractions, and wildlife viewing areas. Cordova hosts the **Copper River Shorebird Festival** during May and a **silver salmon derby** in August.

An important attraction is the Copper River Highway and its sights. Wildlife often seen along the road includes trumpeter swans, dusky geese, ducks, moose, bears and beavers. There are also several good fishing holes and viewpoints to watch spawning salmon. The road is paved as far as the airport at Mile 12, then turns to gravel. There is a bird-viewing boardwalk and picnic area at the end of a 3 mile (4.8 km) road from Mile 17 known as **Alaganik Slough**. There is also a formal viewing area for **Childs Glacier** at Mile 48 just before you reach the **Million Dollar Bridge**. Be careful here, we know a woman who ended up in the hospital after a huge wave caused by ice falling from the nearby glacier swept over her–keep your eyes open! The bridge at the end of the road is open to traffic although it was severely damaged in the Good

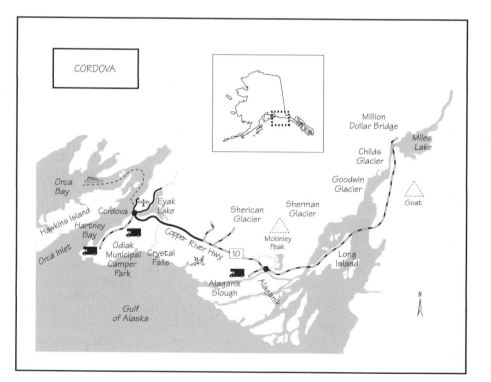

Friday Earthquake in 1964, crossing it is not recommended. The road beyond only goes a short distance.

Cordova has a municipal campground, the **Odiak Municipal Camper Park** with 24 sites, electrical hookups, a dump station, and showers. Reservations are recommended, call (907) 424-6200. It is located at Mile .5 of the Whitshed Road to Hartney Bay which leaves the Copper River Highway at Mile 1.5. Sign in at City Hall. RVers also camp at **Alaganik Slough** at Mile 17 of the Copper River Highway and at **Hartney Bay**, 5 miles (8 km) south of town on Whitshed Road.

DENALI NATIONAL PARK - ON FOOT

Denali National Park is one of the most popular destinations in Alaska. We've described the basics of a visit in Chapter 9–the way most people do it. Denali National Park is also an excellent place to wander around the backcountry. The alpine terrain along both sides of the park access road is relatively easy to hike, even without trails.

Backcountry camping in the park is closely regulated. The park is divided into 43 units. Overnight camping in each is limited, you have to have a permit for the unit in order to overnight there. Permits are only available at the Visitor's Center in the park, it is not unusual to wait for 2 to 4 days before you can get a permit. The permits are issued in person one day in advance and reservations are not accepted. The most popular zones are 8, 9, 10, 11, 12, 13, 15, 18, and 27; largely because they are easily accessible and have good terrain for hiking.

To get your permit go to the Visitor Center. There you watch a video about backcountry traveling in the park including information about bear safety. You then can see what is available in the way of backcountry openings and apply for your permit. Some zones are occasionally closed due to problems with curious or aggressive bears. Once you have your permit you will be issued a bear-proof food container for stays in most zones. Once you have your permit you can reserve space on a bus into the park.

GATES OF THE ARCTIC NATIONAL PARK AND PRESERVE

This park covers 8,090,000 acres of the Brooks Range to the west of the Dalton Highway and north of the Arctic Circle. The area encompassed is largely tundra-covered foothills and mountains to over 7,000 feet and including the **Frigid Crags** and **Boreal Mountain** for which the park is named. There are six national wild and scenic rivers in the park: the **Alatna, John, Kobuk, Noatak, North Fork Koyukuk and Tinayguk**. This is completely undeveloped wild and empty country with wildlife including caribou, moose, grizzly and black bears, wolves, Dall sheep and a host of smaller animals and many birds.

Access to the park is usually by small float aircraft charter from Bettles which gets scheduled air service from Fairbanks. Pick up supplies in Fairbanks since Bettles has little to offer. There is also some access for hikers and river travelers from the Dalton Highway near Wiseman and to the north.

Unrestricted camping is allowed throughout the park although there are no formal campsites. Firewood can be hard to find in treeless areas so bring along a camp stove. Fishing and guns are both allowed. Mosquitoes can be bad. Hiking in the park can be very slow and tedious, even areas free of trees have hard-to-penetrate alder thickets. One of the most popular activities is floating the many rivers in the park with occasional hikes away from the river.

The park is managed by the National Park Service. The Arctic Interagency Visitor Center at Mile 175 of the Dalton Highway has information for travelers using that access route. For information contact Superintendent, Gates of the Arctic National Park and Preserve, 201 First Avenue, Fairbanks, AK 99701-4848; (907) 678-2004.

GLACIER BAY NATIONAL PARK AND PRESERVE

This 3,234,000-acre national park is located at the far north end of the inside passage and extends out along the open Gulf Coast as far as Dry Bay. Most visitor interest is in the southern portion of the park, the huge glacial inlets. These inlets–**Glacier Bay**, **Muir Inlet**, **Reid Inlet**, **Tarr Inlet** and others–have to be the best place in the world to see the effects of glaciation and the re-vegetation process. That is because this entire region was covered by glaciers in 1794 when visited by Captain Vancouver, today the glaciers have retreated as far as 65 miles (105 km). There are 12 tidewater glaciers in the park. The park is also an excellent place to view whales: there are

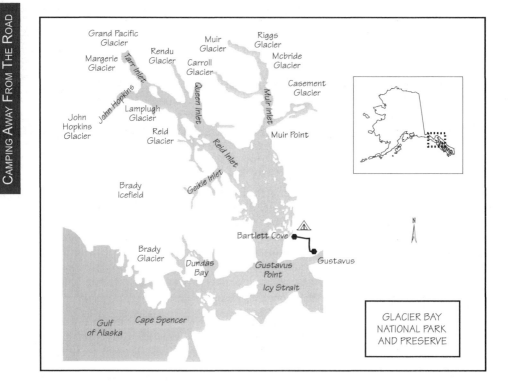

GLACIER BAY
NATIONAL PARK
AND PRESERVE

minkes, humpbacks, and orcas. There are also black and brown bears, moose, mountain goats, harbor seals, sea lions and wolves. Whale watching is also very good in Icy Strait, just outside the entrance to Icy Bay.

There are no roads to the park. Access, however, is not difficult. **Gustavus** (pop. 400) is a gateway to the park. It has a good airport, stores, restaurants, and scheduled jet service. From Gustavus a 10 mile (16 km) road leads into the park terminating at **Bartlett Cove** where park headquarters are located as well as a lodge, a tent campground, and a dock for boats making excursions into the park. Taxis and busses run between Gustavus and Bartlett Cover. From Bartlett Cove an excursion boat runs into the park and up Muir Inlet, they will drop kayakers and hiking parties and pick them up at an agreed time. Charter boats from Gustavus will do the same thing. Kayak rentals are available. Glacier Bay is also heavily visited by cruise ships, they tour the fjords but do not dock.

Campers are offered an orientation at the park headquarters at Bartlett Cove. There is a nearby tent 25-site **campground** that is free but has a 14-day limit. Firewood is available. At Bartlett Cove there are several miles of nature trails. Away from Bartlett Cove camping is not restricted. It is recommended that you fill out a backcountry use permit at Bartlett Cove before heading out. In the park expect lots of rain and be prepared with wet weather gear. Campfires are only allowed below the high tide line, bring a stove. There are no formal trails but hiking is good along beaches and in open areas where the glaciers have recently retreated. Kayaking is very popular. Firearms are not allowed in the park, fishing is permitted.

There is a visitor's center located at the lodge at Bartlett Cove (907 697-2230). Glacier Bay National Park is managed by the National Park Service. For more information contact the park headquarters at: Glacier Bay National Park Headquarters, PO Box 140, Bartlett Cove, Gustavus, AK 99826-0140.

KACHEMAK BAY STATE PARK AND WILDERNESS PARK

A large part of the view that you see across Kachemak Bay from Homer is part of the 300,000-acre Kachemak Bay State Park. Encompassing much of the south side of Kachemak Bay, the park also stretches across the peninsula to take in the fjord country to the west of Kenai Fjords National Park. Across from Homer **Halibut Cove** is the center of activities. There is a ranger station there as well as trailheads giving access to about 30 miles (48 km) of trails to mountain overlooks, glaciers, and lakes. There are also several campsites. Camping is unrestricted, campfires are permitted, as are hunting and fishing. The remote Gulf of Alaska side of the park is much less developed but is popular with kayakers and other boat-oriented visitors.

There is no road access to the park, most visitors catch a daily ferry to Halibut Cove. It swings by **Gull Island**, one of he best places in Southcentral Alaska for viewing seabirds including puffins. Floatplanes from Homer are also used to access the park, particularly the southern Gulf Coast portion.

For information about the park contact Alaska State Parks, PO Box 3248, Homer, AK 99603; (907) 262-5581.

KATMAI NATIONAL PARK AND PRESERVE

One of the oldest federal park areas in Alaska is 3,955,000-acre Katmai National Park and Preserve. It is also one of the most expensive to access since the location is fairly remote. There are many attractions in the park. **Brooks Camp** and the **Brooks River** are the most popular, many tourists visit on day trips to view brown bears fishing for red salmon from viewing platforms constructed for the purpose. The **Valley of Ten Thousand Smokes** is a ash-covered volcanic landscape with good hiking possibilities accessible along a 24 mile (39 km) road by daily van from Brooks Camp. Fishing is also extremely popular in the park, Brooks Camp was originally a fishing camp, today fishing there is limited but there are many other destinations in the park for fishermen. A national wild and scenic river, the **Alagnak**, and also the **Nonvianuk River**, are popular floats for fishermen. Kayakers and canoers will find many routes on the huge lakes of the park including a 40 mile (65 km) round

WESTERN ALASKA KING SALMON

trip paddle from Brooks Camp to the **Bay of Islands** on Naknek Lake and a longer 75 mile (121 km) **circular trip on Naknek Lake, Lake Grosvenor, the Savonoski River and Iliuk Arm**.

The access gateway to the park is King Salmon which gets jet service from Anchorage. From King Salmon access into the park is usually by amphibian or float aircraft.

There is a 30-site tent campground at Brooks Camp with cooking shelters and bear-proof food-storage caches, reservations are required. For reservation call the national park reservation service at (800) 365-2267. Brooks Camp also has other facilities including a ranger station, lodge, dining room, convenience store, and canoe rentals. Camping throughout the rest of the park is allowed although permits are required. Campfires are discouraged since wood is scarce and wet, bring a stove. Weather can be very wet. Grizzly bears can be thick and caution is required. Firearms are not allowed within the park although hunting is allowed in the preserve section in the far north at Kukaklek and Nonvianuk Lakes.

The park is managed by the National Parks Service, for information contact Katmai National Park and Preserve, PO Box 7, King Salmon, AK 99613; (907) 246-3305.

KENAI FJORDS NATIONAL PARK

Kenai Fjords National Park covers 588,000 acres of the southern coast and the ice-covered interior of the Kenai Peninsula near Seward. The **Harding Icefield** overlooks four major fjords and several offshore rookery islands in the park. The rough coastal waters at the mouth of the fjords and the hostile weather has kept development in the fjords to a minimum. This is great place to see glaciers, marine mammals, and seabirds. Visitors often see orcas, minke whales, humpback whales, gray whales, Dall porpoises, harbor seals, sea lions, sea otters, and seabirds including horned and tufted puffins, rhinoceros auklets, common murres, and marbled murrelets. Land mammals include black bears, mountain goats, and moose. Grizzly (brown) bears are uncommon except in Resurrection Bay near Seward.

One of the best features of the park is that access is not difficult. The town of Seward is near, there is actually road access to **Exit Glacier** just outside town. Access to the fjords is by charter boat or floatplane from Seward or floatplane from Homer. Most park visitors are day trippers on tour boats from Seward. Kayakers sometimes paddle into the park from Seward but it is a long paddle, it is easier to arrange for drop-off and pick-up by a charter boat.

There is a small tent-only **campground** at the Exit Glacier (see Chapter 8 of this book). Otherwise camping in the park is mostly unrestricted but there are no formal campsites. Hiking along the glacial fjords is very difficult and even for kayakers camping sites can be hard to find. Kayaking is popular, but only the experienced should venture into the park because the waters are open and often rough. Come prepared for wet weather. Campfires are allowed but bring a stove, wood is often wet. Fishing and firearms are allowed. Much of the shoreline of the park is owned by Native corporations. Check at the Seward visitor center before venturing into the park on a wilderness trip to see how this will affect your visit.

CAMPING AWAY FROM THE ROAD

The park visitor's center is located in Seward near the small boat harbor. The park is managed by the National Park Service. For information contact the park headquarters at PO Box 1727, Seward, Alaska 99664; (907) 224-3175 or (907) 224-2132.

Klondike Gold Rush National Historical Park and Trail

The Klondike Gold Rush National Historical Park celebrates the 1897-1898 gold rush to Dawson City. Park units include the Chilkoot Trail, the White Pass Trail, much of downtown Skagway, Dyea, and even a visitor center in Seattle. The Chilkoot Trail is a 33-mile-long (53 km) hiking trail that starts at Dyea and ends at Lake Bennett in the Yukon Territory. It is jointly administered by Parks Canada and the National Park Service. The trail is extremely interesting to anyone with an interest in the gold rush, it is a sort of museum with ruins and hardware cast aside by the stampeders.

Some parts of the trail are difficult and the weather can turn on you so it is important to be prepared for cold weather, particularly along the alpine section between Sheep Camp and Deep Lake (about 10 miles, (16 km)). Snow in the pass means that it is not usually possible to do the hike except between late June and early September. The Chilkoot is a three to five day hike with designated camping areas. Most people walk it from south to north but it is perfectly acceptable to do it in the opposite direction. The trail starts near the Taiya River bridge near the Dyea town site about 8 miles (12.9 km) outside Skagway. Campgrounds are **Finnigan's Point** at Mile 4.9, **Canyon City** at Mile 7.8, **Pleasant Camp** at Mile 10.5, **Sheep Camp** at Mile 13, **Happy**

ENTRANCE OF CHILKOOT TRAIL NEAR DYEA

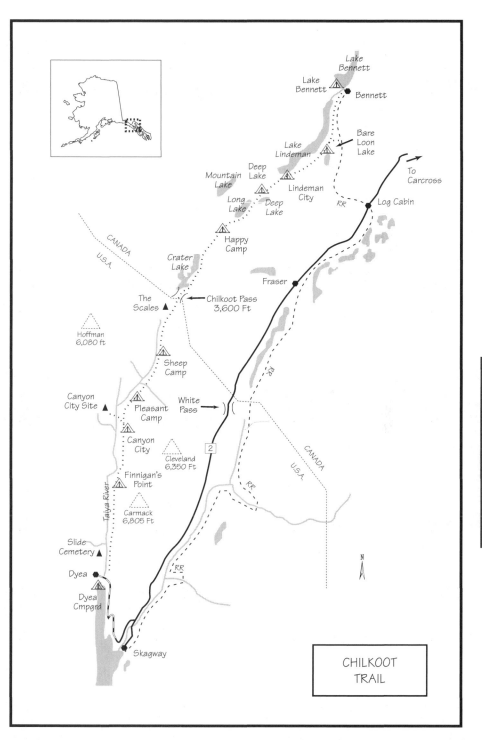

CHILKOOT
TRAIL

Camp at Mile 20.5, **Deep Lake** at Mile 23, **Lindeman City** at Mile 26, **Bare Loon Lake** at Mile 29, and **Lake Bennett** at Mile 33. From the Taiya River bridge the trail follows the Taiya River valley and then a canyon to Sheep Camp. From there the trail climbs across boulders (the golden stairs) to the top of the pass and the Canadian border. From the border the trail gradually descends to Lake Bennett. Once at Bennett hikers can catch a train back to Skagway or a previously arranged boat to Carcross. It is also possible to walk out to Log Cabin which is at about Km 44 of the Klondike Highway from Skagway. A daily shuttle bus returns to Skagway from Log Cabin.

The trail has become very popular so rules are in effect to limit the number of hikers. Only fifty hikers are now allowed to cross into Canada each day and this is administered through a reservation and Canadian hiking permit system. Reservations are highly recommended since 42 of the 50 slots are reserved leaving space for only 8 walk-ins each day. Call (867) 667-3910 or (800) 661-0486 for reservations. When you call be prepared with a credit card number, mailing address, number of people and names, preferred starting date and two alternates, and your itinerary including the camps you intend to use each night. There is a $10 reservation fee per hiker. Detailed information will be mailed to you when you apply for your reservation. A different permit is required for hiking only the U.S. portion of the trial. You pick up permits, both Canadian and U.S., at the Trail Center in Skagway on Broadway near 2nd Avenue. There is a $35 per hiker fee ($17.50 for people younger than 16) for the Canadian permit, the U.S. permit is free. These rules were in effect for 2004, they may change.

KODIAK ISLAND

Kodiak Island is a very interesting destination for RV campers. It is connected to the road system by the Alaska Marine Highway. Service is from both Homer and Seward by the ferry *Tustumena*. This ferry cannot take vehicles over 40 feet long. Kodiak is a very active fishing and fish processing port, but also has good tourist facilities. The island is probably best known for its huge population of very large brown bears.

The town of Kodiak (population 7,000) has a visitor center at 100 Marine Way; (907) 486-4782). Sights in town are limited, you may want to visit the **Baranov Museum** near the visitor center which is located in a Russian-built structure and is a designated National Historic Landmark. It covers the Russian period of Alaska's history. Another museum in town is the **Alutiiq Museum Archaeological Repository Center** which has articles from sites all around the island. You'll also want to visit the **Kodiak National Wildlife Refuge Visitor's Center** at Mile 4 of the Chiniak Road near the Bushkin River Campground (1390 Buskin River Road, Kodiak, AK 99615; (907) 487-2600).

The Kodiak Area has several roads leading to quiet beaches and scenic outlooks. There are also many hiking trails in the area and fishing holes. Rezanof-Monashka Bay Road runs north from town for 11 miles (18 km) to Monashka Bay. En route it passes **Fort Abercrombie State Park**. Chiniak Road goes south for 43 miles (69 km).

The road system really only reaches a small part of the island, many area attractions

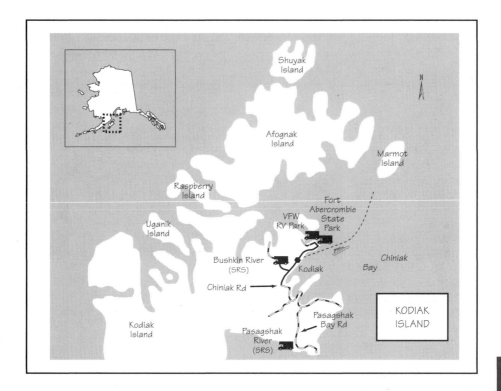

are accessible only by boat or aircraft. Shuyak Island is about 50 miles (81 km) to the north, it is a State Park known for its kayaking waters, there are several rental cabins in the park. **The Kodiak National Wildlife Refuge** covers almost all of Kodiak Island itself. If you want to see bears it is best to get out into it. The air-taxi and tour operators in Kodiak know the places to go, many maintain cabins or campsites for bear-viewing trips.

Campgrounds are not difficult to find in Kodiak. **Fort Abercrombie State Park** at Mile 4 of the Rezanof-Monashka Bay Road has a 13-site campground with the normal state campground facilities. Farther out on the same road is the **VFW RV Park** (Mile 7) which has electricity, water, and sewer hookups.

At Mile 4 of Chiniak Road near the National Wildlife Refuge Headquarters is the **Bushkin River State Recreation Site** which has 15 sites, normal state campground facilities, and also a dump station.

Finally, there is the **Pasagshak River State Recreation Site** with 7 sites. This campground is located at Mile 9 of the Pasagshak Bay Road which leaves the Chiniak Road at Mile 30.

NOME

Nome is the access point for another extensive Alaska road system that in not con-

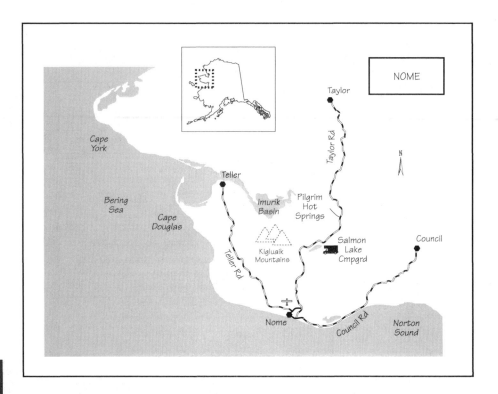

nected to the main highway system. You can't bring your RV here, there is no ferry connection, but it is possible to fly in to Nome and then rent a car or bicycle.

Nome (population 4,000) is a very important town in Alaska's history. The Nome gold rush of 1899 was the state's largest (Dawson City, of course, is in Canada). Mining in Nome during the gold rush was largely on the beaches, but later the area around Nome was heavily dredged, over 40 dredges remain near Nome, some occasionally active, and there are said to be about 100 of them on the Seward Peninsula. Nome is nationally known as the destination for the **Iditarod Sled Dog Race** and is also the center for an unusual industry, growing reindeer.

Despite its remote location Nome does get a lot of tourists. Most are traveling as part of a package tour included as part of their cruise, bus, train, and air tour of the state. The Visitor Center is on Front Street (Nome Convention & Visitors Bureau, Box 240, Nome, AK 99762; 907 443-5535). Nome has lots of gift shops courtesy of the many tourists, ivory carvings are the hot item. Be sure to visit the **Carrie McLain Museum** in the library basement to see the gold rush exhibits.

Three different gravel roads lead out of Nome like the forks of a trident. They make excellent bike or driving trips. It is probably best to bring your own mountain bike to Nome because you can cover a lot of miles here and will appreciate a good bike. Temperatures can be cool and there is often wind so come prepared.

The **Teller Road** is the left hand fork, it leads 73 miles (118 km) north to Teller. Along the way it passes King Island fish camp and through an area that is home to a 25,000-animal reindeer herd. The coast is often within view. Teller is a village with a population of about 300 people, you can stay at the school if you don't want to camp. Teller was the place where the dirigible Norge landed after the first crossing of the North Pole.

The center fork leading out of Nome is the **Kougarok** or **Taylor Road** which leads 86 miles (139 km) northeast past the eastern edge of the **Kigluaikj Mountains**. The Kigluaik Mountains are managed by the Bureau of Land Management and are in interesting hiking area. There is a BLM campground, the **Salmon Lake Campground**, at Mile 38. Hike-in destinations in the area include the Wild Goose Pipeline, Crater Lake, and the Mosquito Pass area. For information contact the BLM, Northern Field Office, 1150 University Avenue, Fairbanks, AK 99709; (907) 474-2332 or the BLM Nome Field Office, PO Box 952, Nome, AK 99762; (907) 443-2177. Another point of interest is **Pilgrim Hot Springs**, located on an eight mile (12.9 km) road leaving the Kougarok Road 13 miles (21 km) north of Salmon Lake Campground. This place was a resort of sorts during the gold rush, later is was a Catholic orphanage. Today it is on the National Register of Historic Places.

The third fork is the **Council Road** which leads 72 miles (116 km) east. Much of the road is along the coast. Sights along the way are Safety Sound at Mile 25 with a bird-watching boardwalk and the Last Train to Nowhere at Mile 33. You have to ford the Bear River to reach Council, it is not recommended unless you have local knowledge.

PRINCE WILLIAM SOUND

Prince William Sound (PWS) has become a well-known Alaskan place name. Bruised but not beaten by the Exxon Valdez oil spill PWS remains a jewel. A huge jewel, but a jewel. The Sound covers some 25,000 square miles and has an estimated 2,500 miles of shoreline. This shoreline is almost all wilderness, the only towns are Whittier, Valdez, Cordova, and Tatitlik. The entire sound with the exception of Port Valdez is within the boundaries of the Chugach National Forest which is administered by the U.S. Forest Service. For information contact USFS, Chugach National Forest, 3301 C Street, Suite 300, Anchorage, AK 99503-3998; (907) 271-2500.

Wildlife viewing opportunities in the Sound are very good. Marine mammals include orcas, gray whales, humpback whales, sea lions, sea otters, and harbor seals. On shore you'll find black and brown bears, mountain sheep, moose, and Sitka black-tailed deer. Over 3,000 bald eagles are said to frequent the Sound, as well as marine seabirds and shorebirds.

Many of the visitors to the Sound travel on cruise ships, ferries, or excursion boats. Many cruise ship schedules now include a visit to **College Fiord**, an excellent place to see a lot of glaciers all in one place. Many excursion cruises also visit College Fjord, usually from Whittier. Excursions from Valdez generally visit **Columbia Glacier** instead, this largest of Alaskan glaciers was the source of the ice that caused the Exxon Valdez to shift course and go aground. State of Alaska Marine Highway fer-

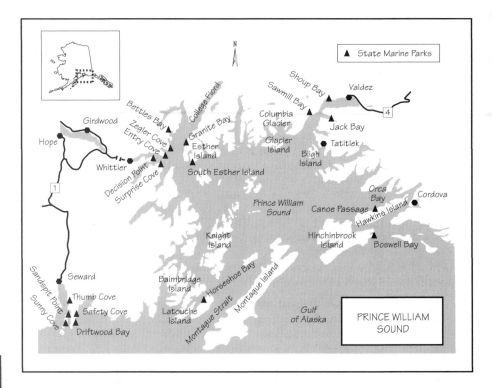

ries also run across the Sound; from Seward to Valdez, from Valdez to Cordova, from Whittier to Cordova, and from Whittier to Valdez. The ferries don't get really close to the glaciers but there are plenty of great views from their decks anyway.

A sailboat, power boat, or a kayak gives you the freedom to really explore Prince William Sound. Access is from Whittier, Valdez, Cordova, or Seward. It is also perfectly feasible to charter a boat or aircraft to deliver you pretty much anywhere in PWS. The State of Alaska has 14 marine parks in the Sound and 5 more near Seward with scenic anchorages, camping sites on shore, and recreational opportunities. Most are clustered around Whittier, Valdez, or Cordova. For more information including individual maps contact Alaska State Marine Parks, Kenai Area Office, PO Box 1247, Soldotna, AK 99669; (907) 262-5581. There are also many rental cabins located around the sound, managed by the USFS. Camping in Chugach National Forest is mostly unrestricted, campfires are allowed but dry firewood can be difficult to find. There are private lands throughout the Sound, particularly the eastern Sound, respect private property.

SWAN LAKE AND SWANSON RIVER CANOE ROUTES

The Kenai National Wildlife Refuge has two excellent canoe routes. They are both accessed off the same road. Follow the Swanson River Road which becomes the Swan Lake Road at Mile 17—it leaves the Sterling Highway at Mile 83, just west of

Sterling. Mileages given here are from the Sterling Highway. There are three small USF&W campgrounds along this road in addition to the canoe routes: **Dolly Varden Lake Campground** (Mile 14), **Rainbow Lake Campground** (Mile 16), and **Fish Lake Campground** (Mile 20). None are good for big rigs. The canoe routes run through an area that has many moose, beavers, loons, bald eagles, and swans. There are also a few black and brown bears, otters, and wolves. Fishing can be good for Dolly Varden, silver and red salmon, and rainbows. Registration at trailheads is required, parties are limited to 15 people. Camping is unrestricted but you should use established campsites if you find them. Fires are usually allowed but it can be difficult to find mineral soil to build one, bring a stove. The area is managed by the USF&W Service. For information contact Refuge Manager, Kenai National Wildlife Refuge, PO Box 2139, Soldotna, AK 99669; (907) 262-7021.

The shortest and easiest of the two routes is the **Swan Lake Route**. It starts from either of two trailheads: the West Entrance at Canoe Lake (Mile 21), and the East Entrance at Portage Lake (Mile 27). From either entrance the routes pass through several lakes connected by portages and then reach the Moose River which flows into the Kenai near Sterling. These routes take about a week to complete and cover a distance of about 60 miles (97 km). Many additional lakes are accessible by making side trips from the main routes.

The **Swanson River Route** begins at Paddle Lake (Mile 30). You travel north through a series of lakes until reaching the Swanson River. You then travel down the Swanson with no portages to either a take-out at the Swanson River Landing (19 river miles, 31 km) near Mile 17 or to a take-out at Captain Cook State Recreation Area (43 river miles, 69 km) off the North Kenai Spur Highway. This trip also takes about a week.

YUKON RIVER

The Yukon River is one of the longest navigable waterways on the North American Continent. It is actually possible to canoe or kayak from the headwaters near the head of the Chilkoot Pass all the way to the Bering Sea. En route you would have to make a portage at Whitehorse around a dam, run rapids at the outlet of Lake Lindeman and below Carmacks, and paddle across 5 rather large lakes, but otherwise your trip would be very uncomplicated.

As a practical matter most people travel the upper river from near Whitehorse to Circle City in Alaska. Distance and approximate time to complete are as follows: Whitehorse to Dawson City, 460 miles (742 km), 2 weeks; Dawson City to Eagle, 100 miles (161 km), 4 days; Eagle to Circle City, 150 miles (242 km), 1 week.

Canoes can be rented in Whitehorse, Dawson City, and Eagle. The rental companies can help you work out the logistics. Many people do this so some of the support structure is in place.

Below Eagle the river runs through the Yukon-Charlie Rivers National Preserve. For information contact: National Park Service, Yukon-Charlie Rivers National Preserve, PO Box 167, Eagle, AK 99738; (907) 547-2233.

TEXT INDEX

MAP INDEX

CAMPGROUND INDEX

Dot Lake Lodge	Tok to Delta Junction	Commercial	115
Downtown RV Park	Watson Lake	Commercial	86
Driftwood Inn and RV Park	Homer	Commercial	264
Dry Creek State Recreation Site	Delta Jct. to S. Glenn Jct.	State of Ak.	162
Dyea Campground	Skagway	NPS	358
Eagle Beach State Park	Juneau	State of Ak.	395
Eagle Campground	Eagle	BLM	349
Eagle Crest RV Park and Cabins	Soldotna to Homer	Commercial	240
Eagle Plains Hotel	Dempster Highway	Commercial	340
Eagle Rising Resort	Anchorage to Tern Lk. Jct.	Commercial	221
Eagle River Campground	Anchorage to Palmer	Chugach St. Park	189
Eagle Trading Co.	Eagle	Commercial	349
Eagle Trail State Recreation Site	Glennallen to Tok	State of Ak.	207
Eagle's Nest Campground	POW Island	USFS	381
Eagle's Rest RV Park	Valdez	Commercial	173
East Fork Chulitna Wayside	Mat-Su Jct. to Denali Park	State of Ak.	290
Eielson Famcamp	Fairbanks to Delta Jct.	Military	158
Eklutna Lake Recreation Area	Anchorage to Palmer	Chugach St. Park	190
Electronic Solutions Midtown Camper Park	Anchorage	Commercial	186
Elmendorf Famcamp	Anchorage	Military	188
Engineer Creek Campground	Dempster Highway	Yukon Ter.	339
Ester Gold Camp	Fairbanks	Commercial	154
Exit Glacier Tent Campground	Seward	NPS	227
Fairway RV Park	Taylor and Ft. St. John	Commercial	68
Farmington Fairways RV Park	Dawson Creek to Ft. St. John	Commercial	65
Fas Gas	From Whitehorse to Tok	Commercial	104
Fielding Lake State Recreation Site	Delta Jct. to S. Glenn Jct.	State of Ak.	160
Finger Lake State Recreation Site	Wasilla and Mat-Su Valley	State of Ak.	275
Finnigan's Point	Klondike Trail NP	NPS	412
Fireside Motel and RV Park	Ft. Nelson to Watson Lake	Commercial	83
Fish Lake Campground	Swanson River Road	USF&W	419
Fishhook Trailhead	Wasilla and Mat-Su Valley	State of Ak.	275
Five Mile Camp Camping Area	Dalton Highway	BLM	317
Five Mile Lake	Silver Trail	Yukon Ter.	336
Fjords RV Park and Campground	Seward	Commercial	212
Fort Abercrombie State Park	Kodiak	State of Ak.	415
Fort Nelson 5th Wheel Truck Stop	Fort Nelson	Commercial	75
Fox Lake Campground	Klondike Highway	Yukon Ter.	326
Fox Run RV Campground	Palmer	Commercial	194
Fred Meyer Parking Lot	Soldotna	Commercial	242
French Creek Forest Service Campsite	Meziadin Jct to Ak. Hwy.	B.C. For. Ser.	139
Gakona Alaska RV Park	Glennallen to Tok	Commercial	205
Galbraith Lake Camping Area	Dalton Highway	BLM	318
Garden City RV Park	Skagway	Commercial	358
Gerstle River Wayside	Tok to Delta Junction	Ak. DOT	116
Glacier Park	Palmer to Glennallen	Commercial	199
Glacier View Campground	Copper Center and McCarthy	Commercial	168

440

Northern Lights RV Park	Dawson Creek	Commercial	62
Northern Nights RV Campground	Glennallen	Commercial	204
Northern Rockies Lodge	Ft. Nelson to Watson Lake	Commercial	81
Oceanside RV Park	Haines	Commercial	364
Oceanview RV Park	Homer	Commercial	264
Oceanview RV Park/Campground	POW Island	Commercial	382
Odiak Municipal Camper Park	Cordova	Local Government	407
Ohmer Creek Campground	Petersburg	USFS	388
Olnes Pond Campground	Elliot Highway	State of Ak.	313
Ophir Creek Campground	Steese Highway	BLM	308
Otter Falls Cutoff	From Whitehorse to Tok	Commercial	102
Park Avenue Campground	Prince Rupert	Local Government	374
Pasagshak River State Recreation Site	Kodiak	State of Ak.	415
Paxson Lake BLM Campground	Delta Jct. to S. Glenn Jct.	BLM	161
Peace Island Park Campground	Taylor and Ft. St. John	Local Government	67
Pelly Crossing Campground	Klondike Highway	Commercial	328
Peters Creek Petite RV Park	Anchorage to Palmer	Commercial	191
Pinacle Mountain RV Park	Palmer to Glennallen	Commercial	197
Pine Creek Campground	Tagish Road and Atlin	Local Government	96
Pine Lake Campground	From Whitehorse to Tok	Yukon Ter.	104
Pine Valley Motel and Café	From Whitehorse to Tok	Commercial	108
Pink Mountain Campsite and RV Park	Ft. St. John to Ft. Nelson	Commercial	72
Pink Mountain Motor Inn	Ft. St. John to Ft. Nelson	Commercial	70
Pioneer Lodge	Mat-Su Jct. to Denali Park	Commercial	283
Pioneer Park	Fairbanks	Local Government	153
Pioneer RV Park	Whitehorse	Commercial	99
Pleasant Camp	Klondike Trail NP	NPS	412
Porcupine Campground	Anchorage to Tern Lk. Jct.	USFS	222
Porcupine Creek State Recreation Site	Glennallen to Tok	State of Ak.	207
Port Chilkoot Camper Park	Haines	Commercial	364
Portage Cove State Campground	Haines	State of Ak.	364
Portage Valley Camping and RV Park	Anchorage to Tern Lk. Jct.	Commercial	219
Primrose Landing Campground	Tern Lk. Jct. to Seward	USFS	225
Prophet River Provincial Park Picnic Ground	Ft. St. John to Ft. Nelson	B.C. Provincial	73
Prudhomme Lake Provincial Park	Prince Rupert	B.C. Provincial	375
Ptarmigan Creek Campground	Tern Lk. Jct. to Seward	USFS	225
Pullen Creek RV Park	Skagway	Local Government	356
Quartz Creek Campground	Tern Lk. Jct. To Soldotna	USFS	233
Quartz Lake Campground	Delta Junction	State of Ak.	120
Rain Country RV Park	POW Island	Commercial	381
Rainbow Lake Campground	Swanson River Road	USF&W	419
Rainey Creek Municipal Campground	Stewart and Hyder	Local Government	130
Rancheria Hotel-Motel and RV Park	Watson Lake to Whitehorse	Commercial	90
Raven RV Park	From Whitehorse to Tok	Commercial	104
Real Alaskan Cabins and RV Park	Tern Lk. Jct. To Soldotna	Commercial	239
Red Goat Lodge	Meziadin Jct to Ak. Hwy.	Commercial	135

Tok River State Recreation Site	From Whitehorse to Tok	State of Ak.	111
Tok RV Village	Tok	Commercial	113
Tolsona Wilderness Campground	Palmer to Glennallen	Commercial	202
Tombstone Campground	Dempster Highway	Yukon Ter.	338
Tonka View RV Park	Petersburg	Commercial	388
Tors Trailhead and Campground	Chena Hot Springs Road	State of Ak.	310
Town and Country RV	Palmer	Commercial	193
Trail River Campground	Tern Lk. Jct. to Seward	USFS	224
Trapper Creek Inn and General Store	Mat-Su Jct. to Denali Park	Commercial	288
Traveller's RV	Dawson City	Commericial	333
Tubby's RV Park	Dawson Creek	Commercial	63
Tundra Lodge and RV Park	Tok	Commercial	115
Twin Creek Campground	Petersburg	Commercial	388
Twin Lakes Campground	Klondike Highway	Yukon Ter.	327
Upper Chatanika River State Recreation Site	Steese Highway	State of Ak.	307
Upper Skilak Lake Campground	Tern Lk. Jct. To Soldotna	USF&W	237
Vadzaih Van Tshik Campground	Dempster Highway	N.W. Ter	341
Valdez Glacier Campground	Edgerton Hwy. to Valdez	Local Government	171
VFW RV Park	Kodiak	Commercial	415
Village Barabara RV Park	Soldotna to Homer	Commercial	259
Walker Fork Campground	Taylor Highway	BLM	347
Walker's Continental Divide	Watson Lake to Whitehorse	Commercial	90
Water's Edge Campground	Meziadin Jct to Ak. Hwy.	Commercial	138
Watson Lake Campground	Watson Lake to Whitehorse	Yukon Ter.	87
Waugaman Village	Denali NP to Fairbanks	Commercial	298
West Fork Campground	Taylor Highway	BLM	346
West McCarthy Wayside Park	Copper Center and McCarthy	Commercial	169
Westend Campground and RV Park	Fort Nelson	Commercial	76
Westmark Inn RV Park	From Whitehorse to Tok	Commercial	109
Whirlpool Canyon Rest Area	Ft. Nelson to Watson Lake	NA	83
Whispering Willows RV Park	Klondike Highway	Commercial	329
White River Crossing Trading Post	From Whitehorse to Tok	Commercial	108
Whitefish Campground	Elliot Highway	State of Ak.	314
Whittier Parking and Camping	Anchorage to Tern Lk. Jct.	Commercial	220
Williwaw Campground	Anchorage to Tern Lk. Jct.	USFS	220
Willow Creek Resort	Mat-Su Jct. to Denali Park	Commercial	284
Willow Creek State Recreation Area	Mat-Su Jct. to Denali Park	State of Ak.	283
Willow Ridge Resort	Meziadin Jct to Ak. Hwy.	Commercial	133
Willow Trading Post Lodge	Mat-Su Jct. to Denali Park	Commercial	282
Wolf Creek Campground	Watson Lake to Whitehorse	Yukon Ter.	93
Wonder Lake Campground	Denali National Park	NPS	295
Young's Chevron Service	Tok	Commercial	113
Yukon Motel and Lakeshore RV Park	Watson Lake to Whitehorse	Commercial	91
Yukon River Campground	Dawson City	Yukon Ter.	331

TERRI AND MIKE AT THE ARCTIC CIRCLE ON THE DALTON HIGHWAY

ABOUT THE AUTHORS

For the last thirteen years Terri and Mike Church have traveled in Mexico, Alaska, Europe, Canada, and the western U.S. Most of this travel has been in RVs, a form of travel they love. It's affordable and comfortable; the perfect way to see interesting places.

Over the years they discovered that few guidebooks were available with the essential day-to-day information that camping travelers need when they are in unfamiliar surroundings. *Traveler's Guide to Alaskan Camping, Traveler's Guide to Camping Mexico's Baja, Traveler's Guide to Mexican Camping, Traveler's Guide to European Camping, RV and Car Camping Vacations in Europe,* and *RV Adventures in the Pacific Northwest* are designed to be the guidebooks that the authors tried to find when they first traveled to these places.

Terri and Mike now live full-time in an RV: traveling, writing new books, and working to keep these guidebooks as up-to-date as possible. The books are written and prepared for printing using laptop computers while on the road.

RV and Car Camping Vacations in Europe
6" x 9" Paperback, 320 Pages, Over 140 Maps
ISBN 0-9652968-9-X

People from North America love to visit Europe on their vacations. One great way to travel in Europe is by RV or car, spending the night in convenient and inexpensive campgrounds. It's a way to travel inexpensively and get off the beaten tourist trail. It's also a great way to meet Europeans. Many of them travel the same way!

Most of us lead busy lives with little time to spend on planning an unusual vacation trip. With this book a camping vacation in Europe is easy. It tells how to arrange a rental RV or car from home, when to go and what to take with you. It explains the process of picking up the rental vehicle and turning it back in when you're ready to head for home. There's also information about shopping, driving, roads, and other things that you should know before you arrive. Then it describes a series of tours, each taking from a week to two weeks. The ten tours cover much of Western Europe and even the capitals of the Central European countries. The book has details about the routes and roads, the campgrounds to use while visiting each destination, and what what to do and see while you are there.

Traveler's Guide To European Camping
6" x 9" Paperback, 640 Pages, Over 400 Maps
ISBN 0-9652968-8-1

Over 350 campgrounds including at least one in virtually every important European city are described in detail, directions are given for finding them, and in many cases information about convenient shopping, entertainment and sports opportunities is included.

This guide will tell you how to rent, lease, or buy a rig in Europe or ship your own from home. It contains the answers to questions about the myriad details of living, driving, and camping in Europe. In addition to camping and campground information *Traveler's Guide To European Camping* gives you invaluable details about the history and sights you will encounter. This information will help you plan your itinerary and enjoy yourself more when you are on the road. Use the information in this book to travel Europe like a native. Enjoy the food, sights, and people of Europe. Go for a week, a month, a year. Europe can fill your RV or camping vacation seasons for many years to come!

RV Adventures in the Pacific Northwest
6" x 9" Paperback, 224 Pages, Over 75 Maps
ISBN 0-9652968-4-9

There are many reasons why the Pacific Northwest is considered an RVers paradise. It offers everything an RV vacationer could desire: seashores, snow-topped mountains, old-growth forests, visitor-friendly cities, and national parks. In fact, the Pacific Northwest is one of the most popular RVing destinations in North America.

RV Adventures in the Pacific Northwest provides eight exciting and interesting 1-week itineraries from the Northwest gateway cities of Seattle, Portland, and Vancouver. Maps and written descriptions guide you along scenic easy-to-negotiate tours. Each day's drive leads to an interesting destination. The book includes descriptions of the local attractions and activities as well as maps showing good local RV campgrounds.

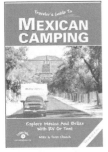

Traveler's Guide To Mexican Camping
6" x 9" Paperback, 480 Pages, Over 250 Maps
ISBN 0-9749471-2-1

Mexico, one of the world's most interesting and least expensive travel destinations, is just across the southern U.S. border. It offers warm sunny weather all winter long, beautiful beaches, colonial cities, and excellent food. Best of all, you can easily and economically visit Mexico in your own car or RV.

The second edition of *Traveler's Guide To Mexican Camping* is now even better! It has become the bible for Mexican campers. With this book you will cross the border and travel Mexico like a veteran. It is designed to make your trip as simple and trouble-free as possible. In additon to camping and campground information the guide also includes information about important cities, tourist destinations, roads and driving, trip preparation, vehicle care, shopping, entertainment and sports opportunities. It will help you plan your itinerary and enjoy yourself more while you are on the road. Some of the features the second edition offers are:

❑ Instructions for crossing the border. New in this edition is detailed information about every important crossing and recommendations for the best places to cross with large RVs.

❑ There are now detailed descriptions of over three hundred Mexican campgrounds, over sixty of them not in the previous edition.

❑ The new edition has information about camping in Belize including border-crossing details and campground descriptions.

❑ A new index map and formatting makes this edition very user friendly.

Traveler's Guide To Camping Mexico's Baja
6" x 9" Paperback, 256 Pages, Over 65 Maps
ISBN 0-9749471-0-5

Sun, sand, and clear blue water are just three of the many reasons

more and more RVers are choosing Mexico's Baja as a winter destination. The Baja is fun, easy, and the perfect RVing getaway.

With the right information crossing the border onto the Baja is a snap. Only a few miles south you'll find many camping opportunities–some on beaches where you'll park your vehicle just feet from the water.

Traveler's Guide To Camping Mexico's Baja starts by giving you the Baja-related infromation from our popular book Traveler's Guide To Mexican Camping. It also covers nearby Puerto Peñasco. We've added more campgrounds, expanded the border-crossing section, and given even more information about towns, roads, and recreational opportunities. Like all our books, this one features easy-to-follow maps showing exactly how to find every campground listed.

To order complete the following and send to:

Rolling Homes Press
161 Rainbow Dr., #6157
Livingston, TX 77399-1061

Name_____

Address_____

City_____State_____Zip_____

Telephone_____

Description	Qty	Price	Subtotal
Traveler's Guide To Alaskan Camping	_____	$21.95	_____
Traveler's Guide To Mexican Camping	_____	$21.95	_____
Traveler's Guide To Camping Mexico's Baja	_____	$14.95	_____
Traveler's Guide To European Camping	_____	$24.95	_____
RV and Car Camping Vacations in Europe	_____	$16.95	_____
RV Adventures in the Pacific Northwest	_____	$14.95	_____

Subtract - Multiple Title Discounts

3 Book Set (3 Different Titles Shown Above)	**-10.00**	_____
4 Book Set (4 Different Titles Shown Above)	**-15.00**	_____
5 Book Set (5 Different Titles Shown Above)	**-20.00**	_____
6 Book Set (All 6 Titles)	**-25.00**	_____

Method of Payment		
❑ Check	Order total	_____
❑ Visa	Shipping:	5.00 *
❑ Mastercard	Total:	_____

Credit Card # _____ Exp. date _____

Signature _____

To order by phone call (425) 822-7846
Have your VISA or MC ready
U.S. Dollars or MC/VISA only for non-U.S. orders
Rolling Homes Press is not responsible for taxes or duty on books shipped
outside the U.S.

*$5 shipping regardless of quantity ordered for all orders sent to the same address in
the U.S. or Canada. Actual cost for multiple books shipped to other destnations.

Visit our web site at **www.rollinghomes.com**

For mail orders allow approximately 1 month for delivery